Contents

INTRODUCTION

What to see	6	When to go	8
Itineraries	7	Things not to miss	10

BASICS   18

Getting there	19	The media	27
Arrival	21	Living in Paris	28
Getting around	23	Travel essentials	30

THE GUIDE   40

1 The Islands	40	10 The Eiffel Tower quarter	145
2 The Louvre	47	11 Montparnasse and southern Paris	158
3 The Champs-Elysées and around	60	12 Montmartre and northern Paris	178
4 The Grands Boulevards and *passages*	70	13 Eastern Paris	195
5 Beaubourg and Les Halles	83	14 Western Paris	211
6 The Marais	91	15 The suburbs	219
7 Bastille and around	106	16 Day-trips from Paris	234
8 The Quartier Latin	117	17 Disneyland Paris	244
9 St-Germain	131		

LISTINGS   252

18 Accommodation	252	23 Festivals and events	318
19 Cafés and restaurants	265	24 Shops and markets	321
20 Bars, clubs and live music	295	25 Activities and sports	339
21 Film, theatre and dance	307	26 Paris for children	348
22 Classical music and opera	315	27 Gay and lesbian Paris	357

CONTEXTS   360

History	361	French	381
Books	378		

SMALL PRINT & INDEX   389

CITY PLAN   403

OPPOSITE GALERIES LAFAYETTE **PREVIOUS PAGE** THE TUILERIES GARDENS

Introduction to
PARIS

Paris has an awesome emotional gravity: Parisians rarely want to escape, while most visitors find themselves yearning to return. Its power derives from the city's rare beauty, of course, and its celebrated style and romanticism, but also from its unique history as the beating cultural heart of Europe over much of the last thousand years. For all the passions the city arouses, its actual fabric can feel inhumanly magnificent, its monuments encompassing the grandeur of the Panthéon, the industrial chic of the Eiffel Tower and the almost spiritual glasswork of the Louvre pyramid. Yet the real Paris operates on a very human scale, with exquisite, secretive little nooks and defined communities revolving around the local boulangerie and café. And even as Paris's culture is transformed by its large immigrant and gay populations, even as extravagant new buildings are commissioned and erected, many of the city's streets, cafés and restaurants remain defiantly unchanged.

In the great local tradition of the *flâneur*, or thoughtful boulevard-stroller, Paris is a wonderful city for aimless wandering. Relaxed quarters such as the vibrant Marais, elegant St-Germain and romantic Montmartre are ideal for strolling, browsing the shops and relaxing in cafés, and the city's lack of open space is redeemed by some beautiful formal gardens and the pathways that run beside the River Seine.

There are nearly 150 **art galleries** and **museums** on offer, and few are duds. **Cafés**, **brasseries** and **restaurants** line the streets and boulevards, ranging from chic temples of gastronomy and grandly mirrored brasseries down to tiny chef-owned *bistrots* and bustling Vietnamese diners. After dark, the city's theatres, concert halls and churches host world-leading productions of **theatre, dance and classical music**, and there is no better place in the world for **cinema**. The live music and clubbing scene is impassioned, and this is a great place to explore jazz, world music and the home-grown singer-songwriter genre of *chanson*.

ABOVE LOUIS VUITTON, CHAMPS-ELYSEES; STALL AT THE MARCHE BIO; LE BARON ROUGE WINE BAR

THE ROUGH GUIDE TO

Paris

written and researched by

Ruth Blackmore and James McConnachie

ROUGH
GUIDES

roughguides.com

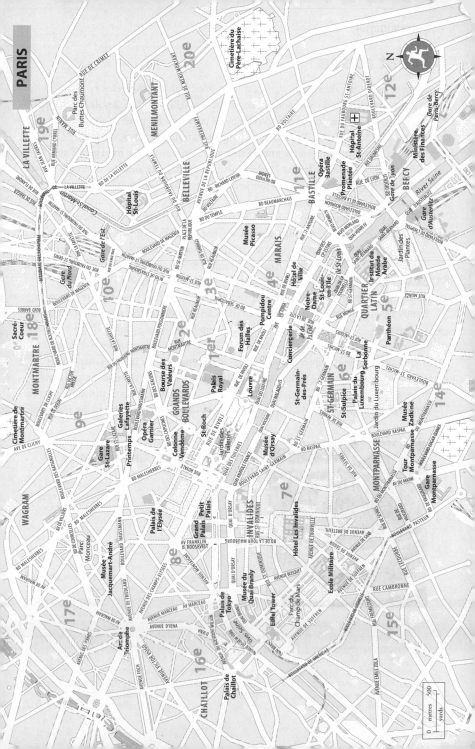

What to see

Lying in its shallow river basin, Paris is still confined within its historic city limits. At its widest point, the city is only about 12km across – roughly two hours' walk. At the hub of the circle, in the middle of the **River Seine**, is the island from which all the rest grew: the **Ile de la Cité** (Chapter 1), defined by its Gothic cathedral of **Notre-Dame**.

The city is divided into twenty **arrondissements**. Centred on the royal palace and museum of the **Louvre** (Chapter 2), they spiral outwards in a clockwise direction. On the north or **Right Bank** (*rive droite*) of the Seine, which is the more bustling and urban of the city's two halves, the longest and grandest vista of the city runs west from the Louvre: this is **La Voie Triomphale** (covered in Chapter 3) – comprising the Tuileries gardens, the glamorous avenue of the **Champs-Elysées** and the Arc de Triomphe. North of the Louvre is the commercial and financial quarter, where you can shop in the department stores on the broad **Grands Boulevards** (Chapter 4), in the little boutiques of the glass-roofed **passages**, or in the giant, underground mall of **Les Halles** (Chapter 5). East of the Louvre, the elegant **Marais** (Chapter 6) and **Bastille** (Chapter 7) quarters are alive with trendy shops, cafés and bars. Further east, the **Canal St-Martin** and **Ménilmontant** (both Chapter 13) are good places to go for cutting-edge bars and nightlife.

The south bank of the river, or **Left Bank** (*rive gauche*), is quieter and less commercial. The **Quartier Latin** (Chapter 8) is the traditional domain of the intelligentsia – from artists to students – along with **St-Germain** (Chapter 9), which becomes progressively more chi-chi until it hits the grand district of ministries and museums that surrounds the **Eiffel Tower** (Chapter 10). As you move south towards **Montparnasse** and the southern

BISTROTS, BRASSERIES AND BARS: DINING IN PARIS

While Paris's gastronomic restaurants may attract the most media attention, for most visitors the best dining experiences are to be had in the city's *bistrots*, brasseries and wine bars.

Bistrots are generally down-to-earth places with wooden chairs crammed in around a zinc bar, and a blackboard list of specials such as *blanquette de veau* or *boeuf bourguignon*. This is the unshowy *cuisine bourgeoise* of meaty classics in deglazed sauces; it's all about doing simple things well and creating a homely atmosphere. There's nothing humble, however, about the decor of the city's big, old-world **brasseries**, many of which retain their splendid original globe lamps, glass cupolas and brass coat racks; the food is also comfortingly traditional, consisting of *steak tartare*, *magret de canard*, seafood and *choucroute* (sauerkraut with sausages and ham). Alongside these classic establishments, an exciting new wave of *néo-bistrots* has emerged, run by talented young chefs keen to experiment with more exotic ingredients – some of the city's most innovative cuisine is to be found in these places, often in casual surroundings and at competitive prices. Meanwhile, even the humble **wine bars** are getting in on the act, with many now offering satisfying, good-value dishes, with an emphasis on carefully sourced, fresh ingredients, accompanied by organic wines.

ITINERARIES

DAY 1

Ile de la Cité Begin at the beginning, on the island where Paris was founded by early Celtic tribes (p.41).

Notre-Dame cathedral Visit the magnifcent Gothic cathedral of Notre-Dame, rising up in the centre of Paris (p.44).

Pont-Neuf Walk across the oldest bridge in the city (p.41) to the Left Bank, and the fashionable St-Germain quarter.

Lunch Head for *Atlas* (p.283), an unpretentious market brasserie set amid the Left Bank bustle.

Jardin du Luxembourg Walk through elegant place St-Sulpice to the Jardin du Luxembourg, the green heart of the Left Bank (p.138).

Musée d'Orsay The world-beating Impressionist collection is housed in a dramatically converted railway station (p.142).

The Eiffel Tower Unmissable, especially at sunset (p.146).

Dinner St-Germain is packed with classy little *bistrots* but few are smaller, or more enjoyable, than *Le Timbre* (p.286).

DAY 2

Pompidou Centre This radical building houses one of the world's best collections of modern art (p.84).

The Marais Explore the elegant Marais *quartier*, with its charming streets lined with handsome Renaissance mansions (p.91).

Lunch Set in Paris's oldest market, *L'Estaminet* (p.277) makes an atmospheric lunch spot.

Musée Carnavalet This fascinating museum is full of glorious interiors, paintings and *objets* illustrating the history of Paris (p.94).

Place des Vosges Arguably the city's most beautiful square, with art galleries and cafés under the arches, and buskers playing jazz and classical favourites (p.92).

Canal St-Martin Take a stroll along the tree-lined canal, with its attractive iron-work bridges, arty shops and cafés (p.198).

Dinner and drinks Soak up the canalside atmosphere on the *terrasse* of locals' favourite *Chez Prune* (p.292).

FROM TOP ILE DE LA CITE; MUSEE CARNAVALET; POMPIDOU CENTRE >

THE SEINE

Referred to by some as Paris's main avenue or the city's 21st arrondissement – and by others as a murky, polluted waterway – the **Seine** is integral to Paris, sashaying through its centre in a broad arc, taking in the capital's grandest monuments. It even makes its way into the city's coat of arms, which depicts a ship sailing on choppy waters accompanied by the words *fluctuat nec mergitur* – "it is tossed about but does not sink", a singularly apt motto for a city that has weathered events as turbulent as the French Revolution and the Commune.

The Seine brought the city into being and was for centuries its lifeblood, a major conduit of **trade** and **commerce**. Floods, however, have always been a regular hazard, sometimes sweeping away bridges, houses and lives. One of the worst recorded was in 1176, when the city was almost completely engulfed. The construction of the **quais** in the nineteenth century helped to alleviate the problem, and these tree-lined walkways have today become one of Paris's major assets – attractive and leafy havens away from the city's bustle. Traffic is banned from a large section of the Right Bank *quai* on Sundays, making way for cyclists, rollerbladers and strollers, and in summer, tonnes of sand are imported to create a kind of Paris-sur-Mer here, complete with palm trees and deck chairs.

swathe of the Left Bank (Chapter 11), however, high-rise flats start to alternate with charming bourgeois neighbourhoods.

Back on the Right Bank, many of the outer arrondissements were once outlying villages. Hilly **Montmartre** (Chapter 12), with its rich artistic associations and bohemian population, is the most picturesque, but **Belleville** (Chapter 13) and **Passy** (Chapter 14), have also retained village-like identities – working-class in the east, wealthy in the west.

Central Paris has lots of wonderful gardens, notably the **Jardin du Luxembourg**, but the best big parks are the **Bois de Vincennes** (Chapter 7) and the **Bois de Boulogne** (Chapter 14), at the eastern and western edges of the city, respectively. The region surrounding the capital, beyond the **boulevard périphérique ring road**, is known as the **Ile-de-France**. It's dotted with cathedrals and châteaux. Nearby sights, such as the Gothic cathedral at **St-Denis** and the royal palace at **Versailles**, are covered in Chapter 15, while full day-trip destinations, including the stunning cathedral town of **Chartres** and Monet's lovely garden at **Giverny**, are described in Chapter 16. An equally accessible outing from the capital is that most un-French of attractions, **Disneyland Paris** (Chapter 17).

When to go

Paris's **climate** (p.31) is fairly stable, with longish stretches of sun (or rain) year round. Summers are generally hot and quite humid, winters cold and sometimes icily windy, and spring and autumn mild. Spring is deservedly the classic time to visit, with bright days balanced by rain showers. In autumn and winter Paris can be pleasingly uncrowded (except during the autumn fashion show and trade-fair season, when hotels fill up early), but overcast days can make the city feel melancholy. Paris in high summer is usually hot and can be uncomfortably humid, especially between mid-July and the end of August, when large numbers of Parisians flee south, leaving the city to the tourists.

CLOCKWISE FROM TOP LEFT CHEESE STALL, MARCHE BIO (P.338); THE KISS, MUSEE RODIN (P.152); ALONG THE CHAMPS-ELYSEES (P.60) >

20

things not to miss

It's not possible to see everything Paris has to offer on a short trip – and we don't suggest you try. What follows is a subjective selection of the city's highlights, in no particular order, ranging from the Sainte-Chapelle to *chanson* concerts, which will help you find the very best things to see, do and experience. All entries have a page reference to take you straight into the guide, where you can find out more.

1

1 JARDIN DU LUXEMBOURG
Page 138
The oasis of the Left Bank: students hang out on the lawns, old men play chess under the trees and children sail toy yachts around the pond.

2 MUSEE RODIN
Page 152
Elegance matched with passion: Rodin's powerful works are shown off to their best advantage in the sculptor's beautiful eighteenth-century mansion.

3 PUCES DE ST-OUEN
Page 228
It's easy to lose track of an entire weekend morning browsing the acres of fine antiques, covetable curios and general bric-a-brac at St-Ouen, the mother of Paris's flea markets.

4 THE EIFFEL TOWER
Page 146

The closer you get to it, the more exhilarating and less familiar the Eiffel Tower feels.

5 MUSEE D'ORSAY
Page 142

A converted railway station makes a stunning setting for France's great collection of Impressionist (and pre- and post-Impressionist) art.

6 MALMAISON
Page 227

Paris is ringed by splendid châteaux. Versailles may be the grandest, but Malmaison, home of Napoleon's Empress Joséphine, is the most intimate.

7 NOTRE-DAME
Page 44

The Gothic cathedral of Notre-Dame is an awe-inspiring sight.

8 BRASSERIES
Page 275

Belle époque interiors, perfect steaks and white-aproned waiters: the city's brasseries offer an authentic slice of Parisian life.

9 PERE-LACHAISE
Page 207

Pay homage to Edith Piaf, Oscar Wilde or Jim Morrison – just some of the notables buried in one of the world's most famous cemeteries.

4

5

10 BISTROTS
Page 274

Forget the Michelin-starred gastronomic temples: the really exciting cooking in Paris takes place in the little chef-owned *bistrots*.

11 PLACE DES VOSGES
Page 92

A superb architectural ensemble, lined with arcaded seventeenth-century buildings.

12 LEFT BANK CAFÉS
Page 163, 273 & from 279

The cafés of St-Germain and Montparnasse remain gloriously Parisian institutions.

13 MUSEE JACQUEMART-ANDRE
Page 66

This sumptuous Second Empire residence is preserved more or less intact, complete with its fabulous art collection.

14 CHANSON
Page 296 & 306

For something utterly Parisian, seek out a concert of *chanson*, the singer-songwriter genre which ranges from rock-ish to art-house in flavour.

15 POMPIDOU CENTRE
Page 84

The Pompidou's radical "inside-out" architecture still draws the crowds, but don't miss its fine modern art museum inside.

16 PARIS BARS
Page 299–302
The SoPi (South Pigalle) and Oberkampf quarters currently offer the city's coolest nightlife and best bars.

17 SAINTE-CHAPELLE
Page 42
The Sainte-Chapelle's glorious interior ranks among the finest achievements of French High Gothic.

18 VELIB' BIKES
Page 26
The city's pay-as-you-go bicycle-hire scheme is roaringly successful, and surely the best way to get around.

19 PALAIS DE TOKYO
Page 155
This Modernist building harbours two superb modern art galleries, both off the usual tourist track.

20 SUNDAYS IN THE MARAIS
Page 91
The twin attractions of "le brunch" and the chance to do some designer shopping make a relaxed Sunday visit to the Marais a must in every trendy Parisian's week.

18

19

20

VELIB' BIKES

Basics

19 Getting there
21 Arrival
23 Getting around
27 The media
28 Living in Paris
30 Travel essentials

Getting there

Paris has direct connections with airports all over the world, and ultra-high-speed rail links to much of Western Europe – London is now just two hours and fifteen minutes away by the Eurostar train link. Air fares usually depend on the season, with the highest being around early June to the end of August; the lowest prices are available from November to March (excluding Christmas and New Year).

By Eurostar from the UK and Ireland

The most enjoyable way to reach Paris from Britain is probably the **Eurostar** train service (☎08432 186186, ⓦeurostar.com). It's competitively priced, and can be quicker than the plane if you live in the southeast: flying time from London is around one hour ten minutes, but you have to add on travel to and from airports, extended check-in times and ever more frequent delays. The train is far less carbon-intensive, too. The Eurostar takes two hours and fifteen minutes from London St Pancras to **Paris Gare du Nord**. A number of services stop at Ashford International and Ebbsfleet International stations, in Kent.

Prices of Eurostar tickets depend on how far in advance you book, and how much flexibility you need. The lowest fares are almost always for early-morning trains, especially those departing midweek. You'll usually pay more if you don't stay over a Saturday night. It's possible to find tickets for as little as £69, but you'll often pay double that. There are also "night clubber" fares from £60, which allow you to travel on Saturday or Sunday after 4pm and return the next day before noon. A number of **discounted seats** are set aside on each train for young people aged 12–25 and for the over-60s; the longer in advance that you book, the better your chances are of securing one of these. Fares for children aged 4–11 start at £49.

Eurostar tickets can be bought from travel agents or by phone or online directly from Eurostar. If you're coming from outside London, it usually pays to buy a through ticket – available from any main-line station.

Eurostar's **monopoly** came to an end in 2010 and "open access" laws on the route came into effect. At the time of research, a number of companies, including Deutsche Bahn and Air France, were thought to be interested in running services, which may result in lower fares in the future.

Flights from the UK and Ireland

The most competitive air fares from the UK and Ireland tend to be with **no-frills airlines** such as **easyJet** and **Ryanair**, as well as a number of other operators on regional routes – **bmibaby**, for instance, currently flies from East Midlands Airport, while **Flybe** serves Paris from Belfast, Birmingham, Cardiff, Edinburgh, Exeter, Glasgow, Manchester and Southampton. Once you've added airport tax, **fares** typically work out at around £70–100 return, though you can often pick up tickets for less if you book well in advance and travel off-peak. The national carriers, **British Airways**, **Air France** and **Aer Lingus**, are usually only slightly more expensive than the low-cost airlines, and they often have special offers; students and those under 26 should enquire about discounts on scheduled flights. The airports they serve may be more convenient too. **Charles de Gaulle** (CDG) and **Orly** (ORY) are both handy airports at which to arrive; Paris **Beauvais** (BVA), however, served by Ryanair, stands a good 65km northwest of the city.

Flights from the US and Canada

The widest choice of flights to Paris is offered by Air France, with regular nonstop scheduled services to Paris CDG from across the **US**. From New York, there are up to seven departures a day. American Airlines, Continental and Delta are usually slightly cheaper, though you may have to stop off en route from smaller cities. The least expensive deals of all may be found with non-French European carriers, though you'll probably have to change flights in their hub city within Europe. Virgin Atlantic, for instance, has frequent flights to London. While you can get deals from around US$410 return from New York or Washington DC, typical midweek fares range from around US$700 in low season to US$1000 in high season; expect to add US$50–250 to the price the further west you go.

Air France and Air Canada both fly nonstop to Paris from all the major cities in **Canada**. It is possible to find fares from as little as Can$750, but it's more realistic to count on Can$1000/1400 (low/high season) from Montréal, Québec and Toronto, and Can$1200/1500 from Vancouver. Air Transat offers good-value charter flights from a number of bases.

Flights from Australia, New Zealand and South Africa

There are scheduled flights to Paris from **Auckland**, **Brisbane**, **Cairns**, **Melbourne**, **Perth** and **Sydney**, but you can find a wider range of options by flying to another European capital – usually **London** – and making a connection from there. The best deals from Australia or New Zealand to Europe are routed **via Asia**, often with a transfer or overnight stop in the airline's home city. Flights **via the US** are usually slightly more expensive. From Australia, you should be able to find scheduled **fares** to Paris for around Aus$1800–2000 in low season (roughly Nov–March, excluding Christmas and New Year), but you'll pay more like AUS$2500 in high season. **From New Zealand** you might pay from NZ$2000 right up to NZ$3000-plus in peak season. **Flight times** vary considerably depending on the route, but it's roughly thirty hours from Sydney or Auckland to Paris.

From **South Africa**, Johannesburg is the best place to start, with Air France flying direct to Paris from around R7500 return. BA, flying via London, is pricier, with fares from around R10,000 from Cape Town and R9000 from Johannesburg. Flight times are around ten hours from Johannesburg to Paris, and fourteen hours from Cape Town including a stopover in Amsterdam (Air France code-shares with KLM).

By car, coach and ferry from the UK and Ireland

The most convenient way of taking a **car** across to France is to drive down to the Channel Tunnel, load it on **Eurotunnel**'s frequent train shuttle service, and be whisked under the Channel in 35 minutes to Sangatte on the French side, just outside Calais. The British tunnel entrance is off the M20 at junction 11A, just outside Folkestone. You can just buy a ticket at one of the booths and drive straight on, as there are departures roughly every fifteen minutes (though only every hour from midnight to 6am), but it's cheaper to book in advance. Expect to pay in the region of £50–150 per car each way, depending on the time of year and how far ahead you book. In summer and around Easter you should definitely book in advance to avoid queues and higher tariffs – don't worry if you miss your departure, as you can usually just roll onto the next available train. Once on the French side, it's little more than three hours' drive to Paris on the fast autoroutes A26 and A1 (tolls payable).

The car **ferries** from Dover to Calais (1hr 30min) or Dunkerque (2hr) are slower but less expensive than Eurotunnel. P&O and SeaFrance run regular services on the former, DFDS on the latter. **Fares** vary according to season (school and bank holidays being the most expensive) and, on certain routes, depending on how many passengers there are. Lower fares are usually available if you can avoid travelling out on Fridays and Saturdays. While you can find deals for as little as £40 return on a ferry, you should normally expect to pay £75–150. The P&O services from Hull to Rotterdam and Zeebrugge can cut driving time if you're travelling from the north.

Eurolines runs four daily **bus-and-ferry** services from London's Victoria coach station to Paris. Off-peak return fares can be as low as £30, but it's usually more like £40–45, and the journey takes a tedious eight to ten hours. Tickets are available from the company direct (see opposite), from National Express agents and most high-street travel agents. As for the classic **ferry–train** route, sadly the few remaining services usually work out more expensive than the Eurostar, and the journey takes roughly nine hours from London Victoria to Paris. For those intent on making the trip, excellent and detailed advice can be found at ⓦseat61.com.

FERRY, EUROTUNNEL AND RAIL CONTACTS

DFDS Seaways UK ☎ 0871 574 7235, ⓦnorfolkline-ferries .co.uk. Dover to Dunkerque ferries.
Eurodrive UK ☎ 0844 371 8021, ⓦ eurodrive.co.uk. Discount agent for ferry and Eurotunnel tickets.

A BETTER KIND OF TRAVEL

At Rough Guides we are passionately committed to travel. We feel that travelling is the best way to understand the world we live in and the people we share it with – plus tourism has brought a great deal of benefit to developing economies around the world over the last few decades. But the growth in tourism has also damaged some places irreparably, and climate change is exacerbated by most forms of transport, especially flying. All Rough Guides' trips are carbon-offset, and every year we donate money to a variety of charities devoted to combating the effects of climate change.

Eurolines UK ☎ 0871 781 8181, ⓦ eurolines.co.uk. International coach company.

Eurotunnel UK ☎ 0844 335 3535, ⓦ eurotunnel.com. Folkestone to Calais car-loading train service through the Channel Tunnel.

Ferrysavers UK ☎ 0844 371 8021, ⓦ ferrysavers.com. Discount agent for the major ferry companies.

P&O Ferries UK ☎ 0871 664 2121, ⓦ poferries.com. Dover to Calais; Hull to Rotterdam and Zeebrugge.

Rail Europe UK ☎ 0844 848 4064, ⓦ raileurope.co.uk. The main UK agent for European trains.

Sea France UK ☎ 0871 423 7119, ⓦ seafrance.com. Ferries from Dover to Calais.

SNCF France ☎ 08 36 35 35 35, ⓦ sncf.fr. The French national rail company.

AIRLINES

Aer Lingus ⓦ aerlingus.com.
Air Canada ⓦ aircanada.com.
Air France ⓦ airfrance.com.
Air Transat ⓦ airtransat.com.
American Airlines ⓦ aa.com.
bmibaby ⓦ bmibaby.com.
British Airways ⓦ britishairways.com.
Cathay Pacific ⓦ cathaypacific.com.
Continental Airlines ⓦ continental.com.
Delta ⓦ delta.com.
easyJet ⓦ easyjet.com.
flybe ⓦ flybe.com.
KLM ⓦ klm.com.
Malaysia Airlines ⓦ malaysiaairlines.com.
Qantas ⓦ qantas.com.
Singapore Airlines ⓦ singaporeair.com.
South African Airways ⓦ flysaa.com.
United Airlines ⓦ united.com.
Virgin Atlantic ⓦ virgin-atlantic.com.

AGENTS AND OPERATORS

Even if you're not interested in a package tour, it's worth considering booking a **hotel-and-flight package** ahead, as these can save you considerable sums, especially if you're aiming to stay in three- or four-star hotels. The drawback is that the hotels on offer tend to be larger or less characterful, and of course you're more restricted in your choice than if you book independently. The Maison de la France, the government tourist office (ⓦ franceguide.com), can provide a list of package operators.

Abercrombie & Kent US ☎ 1 800 554 7016 or 630 954 2944, ⓦ abercrombiekent.com. An upmarket travel agency, which runs a variety of guided tours to France, many including a number of days in Paris. An eight-day tour of Paris and Normandy, for example, starts at US$6300.

Co-op Travel Care UK ☎ 0845 600 3063, ⓦ co-operativetravel .co.uk. Flights and holidays around the world, including economical flight/accommodation packages in Paris.

Discover France US ☎ 1 800 960 2221, ⓦ discoverfrance.com. Offers self-guided tours to France, with a dedicated offshoot putting together flights, hotel reservations and tickets and passes for Paris itself, ⓦ gotoparis.net. Prices are moderate. Carbon neutral since 2007.

Eurostar UK ☎ 0843 218 6186, from France ☎ +44 1233 617575; ⓦ eurostar.com. The website puts together rail-and-hotel packages which can represent significant savings on doing it yourself – though its choice of hotels is relatively limited.

French Travel Connection Australia ☎ 02 9966 1177, ⓦ www .frenchtravel.com.au. Award-winning specialists in French travel, offering everything from cooking classes and barge holidays to Paris accommodation and museum passes.

Martin Randall Travel UK ☎ 020 8742 3355, ⓦ martinrandall .com. High-quality, small-group cultural and wine/gastronomic tours, led by serious experts in their field. Some tours, such as "French Gothic" or "Opera in Paris", take in Paris; these include tickets, hotels, travel and the attentions of an architectural historian and a musicologist respectively.

North South Travel UK ☎ 01245 608291, ⓦ northsouthtravel .co.uk. Friendly travel agency, offering discounted fares – profits are used to support projects in the developing world, especially the promotion of sustainable tourism.

STA Travel UK ☎ 0871 2300 0040, ⓦ statravel.co.uk; US ☎ 1 800 781 4040, ⓦ sta-travel.com; Australia ☎ 134 782, ⓦ statravel .com.au; South Africa ☎ 0861 781 781, ⓦ statravel.co.za. Worldwide specialists in low-cost flights and tours for students and under-26s, though also welcomes other customers.

Trailfinders UK ☎ 0845 0505 945, ⓦ trailfinders.co.uk. One of the best-informed and most efficient agents for independent travellers.

Travelzest UK ☎ 0800 171 2160, ⓦ travelzest.com. Their VFB Holidays brand specializes in cottages and villas in France, but also offers flights from Irish and regional airports as well as London (and Eurostar) as part of travel/hotel packages. The hotels are mostly good, central three- and four-stars, and packages include city travel and museum passes.

Arrival

Many British travellers to Paris arrive by Eurostar at the central Gare du Nord train station, while more far-flung visitors are likely to land at one of Paris's two main airports: Charles de Gaulle and Orly. Trains from other parts of France or continental Europe draw in at one of the six central main-line stations.

By train

Paris has six main-line train stations. **Eurostar** (☎ 08 92 35 35 39, ⓦ eurostar.com) terminates at the **Gare du Nord**, rue Dunkerque, in the northeast of the city – a bustling convergence of international, long-distance and suburban trains, the métro, RER and several bus routes. Coming off the train, turn left for the métro and the RER, right for taxis (a sample price would be €10–15 to a hotel in the 4e) and the secure left-luggage facilities (daily 6.15am–11.15pm; around €7.50 for 24 hours, depending on locker size), both down the escalators opposite the Avis car rental desk. You can get a shower (€6 for 20min) in the public toilets (daily 6am–midnight; €0.70) at the bottom of the métro escalators, and change money at two bureaux de change at the station (daily 8am–10pm). The Gare du Nord is also the arrival point for trains from Calais and other north-European countries. Watch out for scammers offering to "help" with tickets or taxis.

Nearby, the **Gare de l'Est** (place du 11-novembre-1918, 10e) serves eastern France and central and eastern Europe. The **Gare St-Lazare** (place du Havre, 8e), serving the Normandy coast and Dieppe, is the most central, close to the Madeleine and the Opéra Garnier. Still on the Right Bank but towards the southeast corner is the **Gare de Lyon** (place Louis-Armand, 12e), with trains from Italy and Switzerland and TGV lines from southeast France. South of the river, the **Gare Montparnasse** on boulevard de Vaugirard, 15e, is the terminus for Chartres, Brittany, the Atlantic coast and TGV lines from southwest France. **Gare d'Austerlitz**, on boulevard de l'Hôpital, 13e, serves the Loire Valley and the Dordogne. The motorail station, **Gare de Paris-Bercy**, is down the tracks from the Gare de Lyon on boulevard de Bercy, 12e.

All the stations are equipped with cafés, restaurants, *tabacs*, ATMs and bureaux de change (long waits in season), and all are connected with the métro system; most also offer free wi-fi access. The tourist offices at the Gare du Nord, Gare de l'Est and Gare de Lyon can also book same-day accommodation (see p.38). Left-luggage facilities are available at all train stations under heavy security, but are limited in number.

For **information** on national train services and reservations phone ☏ 36 35 (within France only), or consult the website Ⓦ sncf.fr. For information on suburban lines call ☏ 36 58 (within France only) or look up Ⓦ transilien.com.

By air

The two main Paris **airports** that deal with international flights are Roissy-Charles de Gaulle and Orly, both well connected to the centre. Detailed information on both can be found on

Ⓦ aeroportsdeparis.fr. A third airport, Beauvais, is used by some low-cost airlines.

Roissy-Charles de Gaulle airport

Roissy-Charles de Gaulle airport (24hr information in English ☏ 01 48 62 22 80), usually referred to as **Charles de Gaulle** and abbreviated to CDG or Paris CDG, is 23km northeast of the city. The airport has three terminals: CDG 1, CDG 2 and CDG 3. A TGV station links the airport (CDG 2) with Bordeaux, Brussels, Lille, Lyon, Nantes, Marseille and Rennes.

The cheapest and usually the quickest way to get to the centre of Paris is the **Roissyrail** train link which runs on RER line B (every 10–15min from 5am until 11pm; 35 to 50min to Châtelet-Les Halles; €8.70 one way). You can pick it up direct from CDG 3 and most parts of CDG 2; from CDG 1 and CDG 2A and 2B a shuttle bus (*navette*) runs to the RER station. The train stops at Gare du Nord, Châtelet-Les Halles, St-Michel and Denfert-Rochereau, all of which have métro stations for onward travel. On the way back to the airport, if you're picking up the RER from the Gare du Nord, note that all but the first train of the day depart from platform 43, where there's an English-speaking information desk indicated by a large question mark (daily 8am–6pm); confirm here which of the two RER stations you should get off at by checking the airline code on your ticket against the information board, or ask the staff to help you. A number of regular **RER stopping trains** also serve the airports; these only take about five minutes more than the Roissyrail to get to the centre, though they aren't designed to accommodate luggage.

Various bus companies provide services from the airport direct to a number of city-centre locations, but they're slightly more expensive than Roissyrail and may take longer. The **Roissybus**, for instance, connects CDG 1, 2 and 3 with the Opéra Garnier (corner of rues Auber and Scribe; Ⓜ Opéra/RER Auber); it runs every fifteen minutes from 6am to 11pm, costs €9.40 one way and takes around 60 minutes. There are also two **Air France buses**: the green-coded line 2 stops outside Charles-de-Gaulle-Etoile RER/métro while the yellow-coded line 4 stops at the Gare de Lyon before terminating near the Gare Montparnasse. The timings are similar to the Roissybus, but tickets are more expensive at €15–17 single; for detailed information on routes and prices see Ⓦ videocdn.airfrance.com/cars-airfrance.

Taxis into central Paris from CDG cost around €50, and should take about an hour. Slightly less expensive is the **minibus door-to-door service**,

Paris Blue, which costs from €36 for two people, with no extra charge for luggage. It operates round-the-clock but bookings must be made at least 24 hours in advance on ☎01 30 11 13 00 or via Ⓦ paris-blue-airport-shuttle.fr.

If your flight gets in after midnight, the options are a taxi, the minibus, or the Noctilien bus #N143, which links all three terminals to the Gare du Nord and Gare de l'Est every 30 minutes until 4.30am; for timetable and pick-up points see Ⓦ ratp.fr.

Orly airport

Orly airport (information in English daily 6am–11.30pm ☎01 49 75 15 15), 14km south of Paris, has two terminals, Orly Sud (south, for international flights) and Orly Ouest (west, for domestic flights), linked by shuttle bus but easily walkable. One of the easiest ways into the centre is the fast **Orlyval train shuttle** link to RER line B station Antony, followed by métro connection stops at Denfert-Rochereau, St-Michel and Châtelet-Les Halles; it runs every four to seven minutes every day from 6am to 11pm (35min to Châtelet; €9.30 one way). Alternatively, you can take a **Paris par le train shuttle bus** (*navette*) to RER line C station Pont de Rungis, from where trains leave every twenty minutes from 5am to 11.30pm for the Gare d'Austerlitz and other métro connection stops on the Left Bank (train 25min, total journey around 45min; €6.10 one way). Leaving Paris, the trains run from Gare d'Austerlitz from 5.40am to 10.40pm.

Two bus services are also worth considering: the **Orlybus**, which runs to Denfert-Rochereau RER/métro station in the 14ᵉ (every 15–20min, 6am–11.30pm; around 30min; €6.10 one way); and **bus #285**, which runs to métro Villejuif-Louis-Aragon (métro line 7) every ten to twenty minutes (every 30min on Sun) between 5.05am and 1am (15min; €1.60). Finally, the red-coded **Air France bus** on line 2 runs to the Invalides Air France Terminal on rue Esnault Pelterie, close to Les Invalides itself, via Montparnasse (stopping at Porte d'Orléans and Duroc if requested in advance) every fifteen minutes from 6.15am to 11.15pm (about 35min; €18 return). Leaving Paris, the bus can be caught from the Invalides Air France Terminal at 2 rue Esnault Pelterie, and from Montparnasse on rue du Commandant Mouchotte in front of the *Méridien* hotel.

LOST BAGGAGE

Orly ☎01 49 75 04 53; Charles de Gaulle ☎01 48 62 10 86; Beauvais ⓔ bagages @aeroportbeauvais.com.

Taxis take about 35 minutes to reach the centre of Paris and cost around €35.

Beauvais airport

Beauvais airport (☎08 92 68 20 66, Ⓦ aeroport beauvais.com), 65km northwest of Paris, is served by Ryanair from Dublin, Shannon, East Midlands and Glasgow. It's sometimes called Paris Beauvais-Tillé airport. **Coaches** (€13 one way) shuttle between the airport and Porte Maillot in the 17ᵉ arrondissement, where you can pick up métro line 1 to the centre. The journey takes about an hour in all. The coach leaves around twenty minutes after the flight has arrived and three hours and fifteen minutes before the flight departs on the way back. Tickets can be bought at Arrivals or from the Beauvais shop at 1 boulevard Pershing, near the Porte Maillot terminal.

By bus and car

Almost all the **buses** coming into Paris – whether international or domestic – arrive at the main **gare routière** at 28 avenue du Général de Gaulle, Bagnolet, at the eastern edge of the city; métro Gallieni (line 3) links it to the centre. If you're **driving** into Paris yourself, don't try to go straight across the city to your destination unless you know what you're doing. Use the ring road – the **boulevard périphérique** – to get around to the nearest "porte"; apart from during rush hour, it's very quick – sometimes frighteningly so – and relatively easy to navigate.

Getting around

A combination of walking, cycling and public transport is undoubtedly the best way to discover Paris. The amazing bike rental service, Vélib', is hugely useful to the visitor (see p.26), and the city's integrated public transport system of bus, métro and RER trains – the RATP (Régie Autonome des Transports Parisiens) – is cheap, fast and meticulously signposted. There are various tickets and passes available (see p.25).

By métro and RER

The **métro**, combined with the **RER** (Réseau Express Régional) suburban express lines, is the simplest way of moving around the city and also one of the cheapest – €1.70 for a single journey anywhere in the centre. It also has a culture and etiquette of its own (see box, p.182). Many of the métro lines follow the streets above; line 1 for example shadows the Champs-Elysées and rue de Rivoli. The métro runs from 5.30am to around 1am (2.15am on Fridays and Saturdays), RER trains generally from 5am to 1am. **Stations** (abbreviated: ⓂConcorde, RER Luxembourg, etc) are evenly spaced and you'll rarely find yourself more than 500m from one in the centre, though the interchanges at big stations can involve a lot of legwork. You'll find a métro map in the colour section at the back of this book; alternatively, free **maps** of varying sizes and detail are available at most stations: the largest and most useful is the *Grand Plan de Paris numéro 2*, which overlays the métro, RER and bus routes on a map of the city so you can see exactly how transport lines and streets match up. If you just want a handy pocket-sized métro/bus map ask for the *Petit Plan de Paris* or the smaller *Paris Plan de Poche*. Métro lines are colour-coded and designated by numbers for the métro and by letters for the RER. You also need to know the **direction of travel** – signposted using the names of the terminus: for example, travelling from Montparnasse to Châtelet, you follow the sign "Direction Porte-de-Clignancourt"; from Gare d'Austerlitz to Grenelle on line 10 you follow "Direction Boulogne–Pont-de-St-Cloud". The numerous interchanges (*correspondances*) make it possible to cover most of the city in a more or less straight line. For RER journeys beyond the city, make sure that the station you want is illuminated on the platform display board.

By bus and tram

Buses are often rather neglected in favour of the métro, but can be very useful where the métro journey doesn't quite work. They aren't difficult to use and naturally you see much more, plus journeys are getting quicker with the introduction of bus lanes. Free **route maps** are available at métro stations, bus terminals and the tourist office; the best, showing the métro and RER as well, is the *Grand Plan de Paris*. Every bus stop displays the numbers of the buses that stop there, a map showing all the stops on the route, and the times of the first and last buses. Generally speaking, buses run from 7am to 8.30pm with some services continuing to 1.30am. Around half the lines don't operate on Sundays and holidays – the *Grand Plan de Paris* lists those that do. You can buy a single **ticket** (€1.80) from the driver, or use a pre-purchased *carnet* ticket or pass (see opposite). Press the red button to request a stop. All 63 Paris bus lines are now easily accessible for wheelchairs and prams.

From mid-April to mid-September, a special orange-and-white **Balabus** service, not to be confused with Batobus (see p.26), passes all the major tourist sights between the Grande Arche de la Défense and the Gare de Lyon. They run on Sundays and holidays every fifteen to twenty minutes from noon to 9pm. Bus stops are marked "Balabus", and you'll need one to three bus tickets, depending on the length of your journey: check the information at the bus stop or ask the driver. The Paris Visite, Mobilis and Navigo passes (see opposite) are all valid too. **Night buses** (*Noctilien*) run on 47 routes every hour (with extra services on Friday and Saturday) from 12.30am to 5.30am between place du Châtelet, west of the Hôtel de Ville, and the suburbs, and between major train stations such as Gare de Lyon and the suburbs. Details of the routes are available on the website and *Grand Plan de Paris*.

TOURING PARIS BY PUBLIC TRANSPORT

A good way to take in the city sights is to hop on a **bus**. Bus #20 from the Gare de Lyon follows the Grands Boulevards and does a loop through the 1er and 2e arrondissements. Bus #24 between Porte de Bercy and Gare St-Lazare follows the left bank of the Seine. Bus #29 is one of the best routes for taking in the city: it ventures from the Gare St-Lazare past the Opéra Garnier, the Bourse and the Centre Pompidou, through the heart of the Marais and past the Bastille to the Gare de Lyon. For the Champs-Elysées, take a trip on bus #73 between La Défense and the Musée d'Orsay, while bus #63 drives a scenic route along the Seine on the Rive Gauche, then crosses the river and heads up to Trocadéro, where there are some wonderful views of the Eiffel Tower. Many more bus journeys – outside rush hours – are worthwhile trips in themselves: get hold of the *Grand Plan de Paris* from a métro station and check out the routes of buses #38, #48, #64, #67, #68, #69, #82, #87 and #95.

The **métro**, surprisingly, can also provide some scenery: the overground line on the southern route between Charles-de-Gaulle/Etoile and Nation (line 6) gives you views of the Eiffel Tower, the Ile des Cygnes, the Invalides, the new Bibliothèque Nationale and the Finance Ministry.

BEST RIDES

Paris is very compact and walkable and you're never far from a métro station, but it would be a shame to miss out on some of the fun rides that the city has to offer.

A Bateau-Mouche *The* classic boat trip down the Seine. See p.340.

The Pompidou Centre's outdoor escalator Take in the views as you slowly ascend the building. See p.84.

Hire a Vélib' bike Particularly pleasant on Sundays and public holidays when some roads are closed to traffic. See box, p.26.

Donkey rides on the Champ de Mars Children will love them. See p.147.

The Montmartre funicular Head up to the Sacré-Coeur on this quirky driverless tram/lift. See p.179.

Rollerblade round the city En masse rollerblade rides: Friday night is frenetic; Sunday afternoon more tranquil for families. See p.344.

See Paris by balloon The tethered balloon in the Parc André-Citroën gives great views over the city. See p.169.

There are a handful of **tram** lines in the suburbs, running between La Défense and Bezon; Asnières-Gennevilliers-Les Courtilles and St-Denis; and Porte d'Ivry and Pont du Garigliano (currently being extended to Porte de la Chapelle). A new line linking St-Denis and Garges-Sarcelles should be in operation by the end of 2012, and three more new lines are also planned for 2014–15 (see W ratp.fr for updates).

Tickets and passes

For a short stay in the city, it's worth buying a **carnet** of ten tickets, available from any station or *tabac* (€12, as opposed to €1.70 for an individual ticket). Greater Paris's integrated transport system is divided into five **zones**; the métro system more or less fits into zones 1 and 2. The same **tickets** are valid for bus, métro and, within the city limits and immediate suburbs (zones 1 and 2), the RER express rail lines, which also extend far out into the Ile de France. Only one ticket is ever needed on the métro system, and within zones 1 and 2 for any RER or bus journey, but you can't switch between bus and métro/RER on the same ticket. For **RER journeys** beyond zones 1 and 2 you must buy an RER ticket; visitors often get caught out, for instance, when they take the RER to La Défense instead of the métro. **Children** under 4 travel free, and those from ages 4 to 10 travel at half-price. Be sure to keep your ticket until the end of the journey as you'll be fined on the spot if you can't produce one; you'll also need it to exit the RER. If you're doing a number of journeys in one day, it might be worth getting a **Mobilis day-pass** (from €6.10 for zones 1 and 2 to €17.30 for zones 1 to 6, though not the airports), which offers unlimited access to the métro, buses and, depending on which zones you choose, the RER.

If you've arrived early in the week and are staying more than three days, it's more economical to buy a **Navigo** weekly pass (sometimes referred to as a *carte orange*). It costs €18.35 for zones 1 and 2, and is valid for an unlimited number of journeys from Monday morning to Sunday evening. You can only buy a ticket for the current week until Wednesday; from Thursday you can buy a ticket to begin the following Monday. A monthly pass costs €60.40 for zones 1 and 2. You need to factor in the initial one-off purchase of the Navigo swipe card itself (€5; you'll also need a passport photo).

Paris Visites, one-, two-, three- and five-day visitors' passes, (from €9.30 for adults/€4.65 for children) are not as good value as the Navigo and Mobilis passes, but they do give reductions on certain tourist attractions. If you're going to Paris by Eurostar, you could save yourself time by buying the passes from the information point at the St Pancras International Eurostar terminal.

Both the Navigo and the Paris Visites entitle you to unlimited travel (in the zones you have chosen) on bus, métro, RER, SNCF, trams and the Montmartre funicular.

For 24-hour **recorded information** in English on all RATP services call ☎08 92 68 41 14 (premium rate), or see W ratp.fr.

By taxi

The best place to get a **taxi** is at a taxi rank (*arrêt taxi* – there are around 470 of them) – which is usually more effective than hailing from the street. Currently, the white light on top of the vehicle signals the taxi is free and the orange light means it's in use. However, by July 2012 all taxis will follow a new system: a green light will mean the taxi is free and a red light will indicate that it is in use. If there are no taxis waiting at the rank you can call for one using the number displayed at the taxi rank (☎01 45 30 30 30). You can also call a taxi company such as Taxis Bleus (☎08 91 70 10 10, ⓦ taxis-bleus .com), Alpha Taxis (☎01 45 85 85 85, ⓦ alphataxis .fr) or Taxis G7 (☎01 47 39 47 39, ⓦ taxisg7.fr). That said, finding a taxi at lunchtime and after 7pm can be almost impossible: the powerfully unionized and heavily regulated system is stacked against the user, and there simply aren't enough cabs, or drivers willing to work the graveyard shifts.

Taxis are metered and **charges** are fairly reasonable: between €6.20 and €15 for a central daytime journey, though considerably more if you call one out. Before you get in, you can tell which of the three rates is operating from the three small indicator lights on its roof: "A" (passenger side; white) indicates the daytime rate (Mon–Sat 10am–5pm) for Paris within the *boulevard périphérique* (€0.92 per km); "B" (orange) is the rate for Paris at night (Mon–Sat 5pm–10am), on Sunday and on public holidays, and for the suburbs during the day (€1.17 per km); "C" (blue) is the night rate for the suburbs (€1.42 per km). There's a minimum charge of €6.20, a pick-up charge of €2.30, and a charge of €1 per item if more than one piece of (bulky) luggage is carried. Taxi drivers do not have to take more than three passengers (they don't like people sitting in the front); if a fourth passenger is accepted, an extra

€3 will be added. A **tip** of 10 percent, while optional, is generally expected.

By boat

There remains one final mode of public transport, **Batobus** (ⓦ batobus.com), which operates all year round, stopping at eight points along the Seine between Port de la Bourdonnais (Ⓜ Eiffel Tower/Trocadéro) and Port des Champs-Elysées (Ⓜ Champs-Elysées). Boats run every fifteen to thirty minutes from 10am to 9.30pm June to August; 10.30am to 4.30pm November to March; and 10am to 7pm March to May and September to November. The total journey time is around thirty minutes, and a day-pass costs €14. You can buy tickets at Batobus stops and at the tourist office (see p.38).

By car

Travelling around **by car** – in the daytime at least – is hardly worth it because of the difficulty of finding parking spaces. You're better off finding a motel-style place on the edge of the city and using public transport. But if you're determined to use the pay-and-display parking system you currently need to buy a **Paris Carte** (like a phonecard) worth €15–40 from a *tabac*, then look for the blue "P" signs alongside grey parking meters. Introduce the card into the meter and it automatically deducts from the value on the card – it costs €1.20–3.60 an hour depending on location, for a maximum of two

---

PARIS BY BIKE

Paris has 250km of **cycle lanes**, mostly along the busier roads; the volume of traffic means you need to keep your wits about you. The smaller, quieter roads have no cycle lanes and many are one-way. You can pick up a free leaflet, *Paris à Vélo*, outlining the routes, from town halls, the tourist office or bike rental outlets, or download it from ⓦ paris.fr – click on the "Paris Pratique" link, then "Déplacements" and "Vélos".

The easiest way to **rent a bike** is to get hold of one of the town hall's sixteen thousand **Vélib'** machines. These three-gear municipal bikes can be picked up from any one of the 1450 stations (found every 300m or so across Paris), and can be deposited at any other. You have to first buy a subscription card from one of the bigger bike stations (or alternatively online at ⓦ velib.paris.fr, at any arrondissement's *mairie*, or at any of the small shops and boulangeries, etc that display the Vélib' logo). This **carte Vélib'** can be valid for one day (€1.70), seven days (€8) or one year (€29). Once you've got a card, you put it into the *borne*, the pillar-shaped automatic vending machine at every bike station, then type in how long you want to rent a bike for and pay the total amount displayed. The first half-hour of any bike rental in that period is free; after that you have to pay a €1 supplement for the second half-hour, €2 for the third, and €4 per half-hour thereafter. Once your card is paid up, you simply press it against the reader by the bike you want – which is then released automatically.

It's worth researching other bike rental outlets and suggested **routes** (see p.345).

hours. The parking meters are gradually being replaced, however, and by the end of 2012 all meters will also accept bank cards, making the purchase of a Paris Carte unnecessary.

Alternatively, make for one of the many underground **car parks**, which cost up to €2.50 per hour, or from around €15 for 24 hours. Whatever you do, don't park in a bus lane or the Axe Rouge express routes (marked with a red square). Should you be towed away, you'll find your car in the pound (*fourrière*) belonging to that particular arrondissement – check with the local *mairie* for the address. If you'll be using your car for a while, you might want to pick up *Parkings de Paris*, a guide to locating over two hundred public car parks in the city. It's available in most large bookstores and you can even pre-book your parking space on their website (Ⓦparkingsde paris.com).

The French **drive on the right**, and, if your car is right-hand drive, you must have your headlight dip adjusted to the right before you go – it's a legal requirement – and as a courtesy, change or paint them to yellow or stick on black glare deflectors. Remember also that you have to be 18 to drive in France, regardless of whether you hold a licence in your own country.

In the event of a **breakdown**, call Dan Dépann (Ⓣ08 00 25 10 00, Ⓦdandepann.fr) or Action Auto Assistance (Ⓣ08 00 00 80 00) for round-the-clock assistance. Alternatively, ask the police for advice. For **traffic conditions** in Paris tune in to 105.1 FM (FIP); for the *boulevard périphérique* and main routes in and out of the city, ring Ⓣ08 26 02 20 22, or log onto Ⓦwww.securiteroutiere.gouv.fr.

Car rental

If you're intending to rent a car in Paris your cheapest option is the city's pioneering electric car rental scheme, Autolib' (Ⓦautolib-paris.fr), which will operate on the same model as the successful bike rental scheme Velib' and is due to launch in October 2011. Some three thousand cars will be available to rent from around a thousand stands (700 in central Paris itself) dotted all over the greater Paris region. Cars can be picked up at one station and deposited at another. As with Velib', users will need to buy a subscription card first from one of the 75 Espaces Autolib' that are being built in the city. You can buy a card valid for a day (€10), a week (€15) or a year (€12 a month). The first half-hour costs €7, the second €6 and subsequent ones €8 (a bit less for annual subscriptions). You can reserve a car up

---

PEDESTRIAN CROSSINGS
Pedestrian/zebra crossings, marked with horizontal white stripes on the road, have a different meaning from those back home: they're there to suggest a good place to cross, and certainly won't give you priority over cars. It's very dangerous to step out onto one and assume drivers will stop. Take just as much care as you would crossing at any other point, even at traffic lights.

---

to twenty minutes beforehand by phone, online or directly from one of the car rental points. The scheme is open to anyone with a driving licence over the age of 18, and, unlike with most car rental companies, you don't have to have been driving for a couple of years before you're eligible to rent a vehicle.

The big international **car rental** companies have offices at the airports and at several locations in the city. **Avis** (Ⓣ01 53 32 79 10, Ⓦavis.com), located at the Gare du Nord, does good weekend rates: their "Parisien weekend" car rental extends from noon on Thursday to noon on Tuesday, with two days working out at around €50 per day, to five days at about €45 per day. Other big names are listed below; look up "Location d'automobiles" in the *Yellow Pages* for others. North Americans and Australians in particular should be aware that it's difficult to rent a car with automatic transmission in France; if you can't drive a manual/stickshift, try and book an automatic (*voiture à transmission automatique*) well in advance, and be prepared to pay a much higher price for it.

CAR RENTAL AGENCIES

Budget Ⓣ 08 25 00 35 64, Ⓦ budget.fr.
Europcar Ⓣ 08 25 35 83 58, Ⓦ europcar.com.
Hertz Ⓣ 01 55 31 93 21, Ⓦ hertz.com.
Locabest 3 rue Abel, 12ᵉ Ⓣ 01 43 46 05 05; Ⓜ Gare-de-Lyon; also at 104 bd Magenta, 10ᵉ (Ⓣ 01 44 72 08 05; Ⓜ Gare-du-Nord); Ⓦ locabest.fr.

The media

The French press is currently in something of a financial crisis – circulation is low, prices high and print costs some of the highest in Europe. Things are slightly healthier in TV, where the choice of stations has widened in recent years,

though the quality of programmes isn't generally very high, with lots of light entertainment and dubbed foreign soaps. Some serious programmes, such as political and philosophical debates do exist, though, and make no attempt to dumb down for their audience.

Newspapers and magazines

British **newspapers**, as well as the *Washington Post*, *New York Times* and the *International Herald Tribune* are widely on sale in the city on the day of publication. The free monthly *Paris Voice* magazine (W paris-voice.com), produced by the American Church at 65 quai d'Orsay, 7e, has good listings, ads for flats and courses, and interesting articles on current events. It's available from the church and from English-language bookshops (see p.330). *FUSAC* (France USA Contacts; W fusac.fr), a free American fortnightly available in various cafés, restaurants, shops and colleges, is also useful for flats, jobs and travel.

Of the quality **French daily papers**, the centre-left *Le Monde* is the most intellectual; it is widely respected, though somewhat austere. Left-leaning *Libération*, founded by Jean-Paul Sartre in the 1960s, is slightly more colloquial and choosy in its coverage, but its survival is currently in question as circulation dwindles. *Le Figaro* is the most respected right-wing national. The best-selling tabloid is *Le Parisien* (known as *Aujourd'hui* outside Paris), good on local news and events.

Weeklies of the *Newsweek/Time* model include the wide-ranging and socialist-inclined *Le Nouvel Observateur*, the centrist *L'Express* and staunchly republican *Marianne*. The best investigative journalism is to be found in the weekly satirical paper *Le Canard Enchaîné*. *Charlie Hebdo* is a sort of *Private Eye* or *Spy Magazine* equivalent.

TV and radio

Viewers in France can access fourteen free French **TV channels**, providing they have a decoder or are hooked up to satellite or cable. The main public channels are **France 2** (W france2.fr), which puts out variety acts, chat shows and crime series, and slightly more highbrow **France 3** (W france3.fr), which serves up drama, debates and arts programmes; **Arte/France 5** (W arte-tv.com) is a Franco-German cultural channel, with lots of documentaries and subtitled films. The two main commercial channels are distinctly lowbrow **TF1** (W tf1.fr), with dubbed soaps and reality shows, and **M6** (W m6.fr), which does mostly low-budget shows

such as cookery and home improvement programmes, and kids' TV. The main French **news broadcasts** are at 8pm on F2 and TF1. The main subscription channel is **Canal Plus**, good for films and sports. In addition, there are numerous cable networks. France also has its own rolling news station, **France 24** (W france24.com), to rival CNN and BBC World and put across a French outlook on world affairs. It broadcasts in both English and French, and has an Arabic service. As well as politics, it covers arts and culture.

With a **radio**, you can tune into various English-language broadcasts. BBC (W bbc.co.uk/worldservice), Radio Canada (W rcinet.ca) and Voice of America (W voa.gov) list all the world service frequencies around the globe. You can also listen to the news in English on Radio France International (RFI; W rfi.fr) at 7am, 2.30pm and 4.30pm on 738kHz AM. For radio news in French, there's the state-run France Inter (87.8FM), Europe 1 (104.7FM), or round-the-clock news on France Info (105.5FM).

Living in Paris

Work

EU nationals can legally **work in France**, while most North Americans and Australasians (specialists aside) who manage to work and live in Paris do so on luck, brazenness and willingness to live in pretty grotty conditions. The days when Hemingway could live for months on his wife's dollars are definitely over. Unless you've got a serious trust fund, an exhausting combination of bar and club work, freelance translating, data processing, typing, busking, providing novel services like home-delivery fish'n'chips, teaching English or computer programming, dancing or modelling are some of the ways you'll need to get by. Great if you're into self-promotion and living hand-to-mouth, but, if you're not, it might be wise to think twice – and remember that unemployment in France is high.

Anyone staying in France for more than three months must have a **Carte de Séjour**, or residency permit – citizens of the EU are entitled to one automatically. You must apply for your *carte* within three months of your arrival in France at the *préfecture* in the arrondissement you reside in. For other, non-EU citizens, it is more complicated and generally involves applying for a long-stay visa before leaving your home country; contact the French embassy in your country for your specific situation. France has a **minimum wage** (the SMIC – *Salaire Minimum Inter-*

professionnel de Croissance); indexed to the cost of living, it's currently around €9 an hour (for a maximum 152-hour month). By law, all EU nationals are entitled to exactly the same pay, conditions and trade union rights as French nationals. Employers, however, are likely to pay lower wages to temporary foreign workers who don't have easy legal resources, and make them work longer hours. It's also worth noting that if you're a full-time non-EU student in France (see p.30), you can get a **non-EU work permit** for the following summer as long as your visa is still valid.

If you're looking for secure employment, it's important to begin planning before you leave home. A couple of **books** that might be worth consulting are *Work Your Way Around the World* by Susan Griffith, *Live and Work in France* by Victoria Pybus and Jack Sims, and *Summer Jobs Abroad*, all published by Vacation Work, an imprint of Crimson Publishing (**W** crimsonpublishing.co.uk). Another, slightly more irreverent, treatise is *Vagabonding* written by Rolf Potts and published by Villard.

Finding a job in a **French-language school** is best done in advance. In Britain, jobs are often advertised in the *Guardian*'s "Education" section (every Tues) and in the weekly *Times Educational Supplement*. Late summer is usually the best time. You don't need fluent French to get a post, but a degree and a TFFL (Teaching English as a Foreign Language) qualification are usually required. A useful resource is *Teaching English Abroad* published by Vacation Work (see above), while the British Council's website, **W** britishcouncil.org, has a list of English-teaching vacancies. If you apply for jobs from home, most schools will fix up the necessary papers for you. EU nationals don't need a work permit, but getting a *Carte de Séjour* and social security can still be tricky should employers refuse to help. It's quite feasible to find a teaching job once you're already in France, but you may have to accept semi-official status and no job security. For addresses of schools, look under "Cours de langues" in the *Yellow Pages* (**W** pagesjaunes.fr). If you offer **private lessons** (via university notice-boards or classified ads), you'll have lots of competition.

For **temporary work** check the ads in *Paris Voice* and *FUSAC* (see opposite) and keep an eye on the notice boards at the Anglophone churches: the American Church in Paris (65 quai d'Orsay, 7e; **M** Invalides); St George's English Church (7 rue Auguste-Vacquerie, 16e; **M** Charles-de-Gaulle/Étoile); St Michael's Anglican Church (5 rue d'Aguesseau, 8e; **M** Madeleine); and the American Cathedral (23 av George V, 8e; **M** Alma-Marceau). You could also try the notice boards located in the offices of CIDJ at 101 quai Branly, 15e (Mon–Sat 10am–6pm; **M** Bir-Hakeim), and CROUS, 39 av Georges-Bernanos, 5^e (RER Port-Royal), both youth information agencies which advertise a number of temporary jobs for foreigners.

The **national employment agency**, ANPE (Agence Nationale pour l'Emploi; **W** anpe.fr), advertises temporary jobs in all fields and, in theory, offers a whole range of services to job-seekers; though it's open to all EU citizens, it is not renowned for its helpfulness to foreigners. If your French is up to par, France 5 (**W** keljob.com) hosts an informative site that can help with your CV, interview questions and other job-seeking issues.

Other possible sources include the "Offres d'Emploi" (Job Offers) in *Le Monde*, *Le Figaro* and the *International Herald Tribune*, and notice boards at English bookshops. Some people have found jobs **selling magazines** on the street and **leafleting** just by asking people already doing it for the agency address. The American/Irish/British **bars and restaurants** sometimes have vacancies. You'll need to speak French, look smart and be prepared to work very long hours. Obviously, the better your French, the better your chances are of finding work.

FRENCH BUREAUCRACY: A WARNING

French officialdom and bureaucracy can damage your health. That Gallic shrug and "*C'est pas possible*" is not the result of training programmes in making life difficult for foreigners: they drive most French citizens mad as well. Sorting out social security, long-stay visas, job contracts, bank accounts, tenancy agreements, university enrolment or any other financial, legal or state matter requires serious commitment. Your reserves of patience, diligence, energy (both physical and mental) and equanimity in the face of bloody-mindedness and Catch 22s will be tested to the full. Expect to spend days repeatedly visiting the same office, plus considerable sums of money for official translations of every imaginable document. Before you throw yourself into the Seine in despair, remember that others are going through it, too, and sharing the frustration may well help: the American Church (see p.28) is the place for such contacts.

Although **working as an au pair** is easily set up through any number of agencies (lists are available from French embassies or consulates, and there are lots of ads in *The Lady* in the UK), this sort of work can be total misery if you end up with an unpleasant employer. If you're determined to try – and it can be a very good way of learning the language – it's better to apply once in France, where you can at least meet the family first and check things out. If you want to arrange it first through an agency try Avalon Au Pairs in Britain (☎0800 298 8807, ⊚aupairsbyavalon.com), or in the US the American Institute for Foreign Study (☎866 906 2437, ⊚aifs.com). These have positions for female au pairs only and will fill you in on the general terms and conditions (never very generous); pocket money is usually around €80 a week (on top of board and lodging, and some sort of travel pass). Working hours are officially capped at thirty hours a week, plus two or three evenings' babysitting.

Claiming benefit

Any EU citizen who has been signing on for **unemployment benefit** for a minimum period of four to six weeks at home, and intends to continue doing so in Paris, needs a letter of introduction from their own social security office, plus an E303 certificate of authorization (be sure to give them plenty of warning to prepare this). You must register within seven days with the Agence Nationale pour l'Emploi (ANPE), whose offices are listed under "Administration du Travail et de l'Emploi" in the *Yellow Pages* or "ANPE" in the *White Pages*.

It's possible to claim benefit for up to three months while you look for work, but it can often take that amount of time for the paperwork to be processed (see box, p.29). Pensioners can arrange for their **pensions** to be paid in France, but cannot receive French state pensions.

Study

It's relatively easy to be a **student** in Paris. Foreigners pay no more than French nationals to enrol on a course, and the only problem then is to support yourself. Your *Carte de Séjour* and – for EU nationals – social security will be assured, and you'll be eligible for subsidized accommodation, meals and all the student reductions. Few people want to do undergraduate degrees abroad, but for higher degrees or other diplomas, the range of options is enormous. Strict entry requirements, including an exam in French, apply only for undergraduate degrees.

Generally, French universities are much less formal than British ones, and many people perfect their fluency in the language while studying. For full details and prospectuses, go to the Cultural Service of any French embassy or consulate (see p.33).

Embassies and consulates can also give details of **language courses**, which often combine with lectures on French "civilization" and are usually very costly. In Britain, the **French Institute**, 17 Queensbury Place, London SW7 2DT (☎020 7073 1350, ⊚institut-francais.org.uk), can provide a list of language courses in France. Courses at the non-profit-making **Alliance Française** (101 bd Raspail, 6ᵉ; ☎01 42 84 90 00, ⊚alliancefr.org; Ⓜ St-Placide) are fairly reasonably priced (from €93 per week for nine hours of classes) and well regarded, while the **Sorbonne** (47 rue des Ecoles, 5ᵉ; ☎01 40 46 22 11, ⊚ccfs-sorbonne.fr) has special short courses aimed at foreigners. Saying you studied French at the latter may impress your friends, but there are no entry requirements and the courses are very old-fashioned and grammar-based. US students could also get in touch with the **CIEE** (Council on International Educational Exchange; ⊚ciee.org), which can arrange gap-year and study programmes in Paris.

STUDENT/YOUTH ORGANIZATIONS

Student information (CROUS) 39 av Georges-Bernanos, 5ᵉ ☎01 40 51 36 00, ⊚crous-paris.fr; RER Port-Royal. The University of Paris student organization, providing help with student accommodation and other services.

Youth information (CIDJ) (Centre d'Information et de Documentation de la Jeunesse) 101 quai Branly, 15ᵉ ☎01 43 06 15 38, ⊚cidj.com; Ⓜ Bir-Hakeim. Mon–Fri 10am–6pm, Sat 9.30am–1pm. Provides all sorts of information for young people and students, for example on studying in France and finding somewhere to live.

Travel essentials

Addresses

Paris is divided into twenty districts, or **arrondissements**. The first arrondissement, or "1ᵉʳ" is centred on the Louvre, in the heart of the city. The rest wind outward in a clockwise direction like a snail's shell: the 2ᵉ, 3ᵉ and 4ᵉ are central; the 5ᵉ, 6ᵉ and 7ᵉ lie on the inner part of the left (south) bank; while the 8ᵉ–20ᵉ make up the outer districts.

PARIS CLIMATE

	Jan	Feb	Mar	Apr	May	Jun	Jul	Aug	Sep	Oct	Nov	Dec
AVERAGE DAILY TEMPERATURE												
Max/min (°F)	43/34	45/34	54/40	61/43	68/50	72/55	77/59	75/57	70/54	61/46	50/41	45/36
Max/min (°C)	6/1	7/1	12/4	16/6	20/10	23/13	25/15	24/14	21/12	16/8	10/5	7/2
AVERAGE RAINFALL												
mm	56	46	35	42	57	54	59	64	55	50	51	50

Parisian addresses generally quote the arrondissement, along with the nearest métro station, or stations, too. The **postcode** in Parisian addresses consists of the generic 750 plus the number of the arrondissement: so, for example, the 14ᵉ becomes 75014 Paris. *Bis* and *ter* (as in 4bis rue de la Fontaine) are the equivalent of "a" and "b".

Climate

Paris's **climate** is fairly stable, with longish stretches of sun (or rain) year round. Summers are generally hot and quite humid, winters cold and windy, and spring and autumn mild. It can rain at any time of year, however: summer sees fewer heavy showers, while at other times of the year there's a tendency to drizzle. Spring is deservedly the classic time to visit, with bright days balanced by rain showers. Autumn and winter can be very rewarding, but on overcast days – all too common – the city can feel very melancholy, and icy winds cut down the boulevards. Winter sun, on the other hand, is the city's most flattering light.

Costs

Paris has the potential to be very expensive, certainly more so than the rest of France, particularly for visitors from outside the eurozone. Transport and accommodation prices, however, compare favourably with other north-European capitals, and if you are one of two people sharing a comfortable central hotel room, you can get by happily on around €120 per person per day (around £105/US$175). At the bottom line, by watching the pennies, staying at a hostel and visiting monuments and museums on free entry days (see box, p.32), you could survive on as little as €60 (around £53/US$85) a day, including a cheap restaurant meal.

In budget **hotels**, simple doubles can be had from as little as €45, but for reasonable comfort,

prices start at around €90. Single rooms are often available, starting at around €40 in a cheap hotel. At most hotels breakfast is an extra €6–12.

Eating out is expensive. Typically, a three-course evening set menu costs around €30 and upwards. The lunchtime *menu* is nearly always cheaper (from around €14) and you can get a filling midday *plat du jour* (dish of the day) of hot food for around €10. **Drinks** in cafés and bars can easily mount up; remember that it's cheaper to stand at the bar than sit at a table in cafés, and most expensive to sit outside on the terrace. A black espresso coffee (*un café*) is the cheapest drink (around €2.30); a *café crème* ranges from around €2.60 at the bar to anything up to €9 on the terrace. Glasses of wine cost from around €2.60, but draught lager tends to be a bit more expensive. Mixed drinks or cocktails cost €6.50–16.

Transport within the city is inexpensive. A *carnet* of ten tickets, valid on buses and métro/RER in central Paris, for example, costs €12.

Discounts

Institutions have different policies, but at the time of writing, national museums are free to all under-18s, plus all EU nationals (as well as students studying in the EU who can prove it) under the age of 26. All monuments are free for under-12s. Under-4s usually go free everywhere, less often under-8s. Privately owned sights usually offer half-price or reduced admission to 5- to 18-year-olds, though more commercial places charge adult rates at age 12.

If you are a full-time **student**, it's worth carrying the **ISIC Card** (International Student Identity Card; Ⓦisic.org) to gain entrance reductions (usually about a third off). The card is universally accepted as ID, while the student card from your home institution is not. You have to be 26 or younger to qualify for the **International Youth Travel Card**. For those over 60 or 65 (depending on the institution), reductions are only patchily available; carry your passport with you as proof of age.

PARIS ON A BUDGET

The permanent collections at all **municipal museums** are **free** all year round. These museums are: Musée d'Art Moderne de la Ville de Paris; Maison de Balzac; Musée Carnavalet; Musée Cognac-Jay; Musée de la Vie Romantique; Musée Zadkine; and Maison de Victor Hugo. All **national museums** are free the first Sunday of the month, including the Louvre, Pompidou Centre, and the Picasso and Rodin museums; see ⓦrmn.fr for a full list.

Churches, **cemeteries** and, of course, **markets** are free (except for some specialist annual antique and book markets). Most **parks** are free but some gardens within have small entry charges, usually around €1.50. **Libraries** and the cultural centres of different countries put on films, shows and exhibitions for next to nothing – details in the listings mags (see p.38). Other **free cultural offerings** appear regularly, from bands in the streets to firework shows, courtesy of the Mairie de Paris (publicized on the electronic billboards around Paris).

Whatever your age, if you are going to visit a lot of museums, it's worth considering the **Carte Musées et Monuments** (€35 two-day, €50 four-day, €65 six-day; ⓦparismuseumpass.com). Available from the tourist office, Fnac stores and museums, as well as the Eurostar terminal at London St Pancras, the pass is valid for more than sixty museums and monuments, including all the main ones (though not special exhibitions) in and around Paris, and allows you to bypass ticket queues (though not the security checkpoints).

Crime and personal safety

Petty **theft** is as common in the crowded hangouts of the capital as in most major cities; the métro, train stations and Les Halles are notorious pickpocketing grounds. It makes sense to take the normal precautions. If you need to report a theft, go to the commissariat de police of the arrondissement in which the theft took place, where they will fill out a *constat de vol*. The first thing they'll ask for is your passport, and vehicle documents if relevant. Although the police are not always as cooperative as they might be, it is their duty to assist you if you've lost your passport or all your money. If you've lost something less serious, you could try the **lost-and-found office** at 36 rue des Morillons, 7ᵉ ☏08 21 00 25 25.

Should you be **arrested**, you have the right to contact your consulate (see opposite). **Drug use** is as risky and as severely punished in France as anywhere else in Europe. If you're discreet, you're probably not likely to get caught, but if you do get caught don't expect the authorities – or your consulate – to be sympathetic just because you're on holiday.

Travellers of North African or Arab appearance may occasionally encounter excessive police interest, or sometimes outright hostility. Carrying your passport at all times is a good idea (everyone is legally required to have some identification on them in any case). There are occasional reports of hotels or restaurants claiming to be fully booked, or clubs refusing entry, but racist incidents involving tourists are fairly rare.

French **police** (in popular slang, *les flics*) are barely polite at the best of times, and can be extremely unpleasant if you get on the wrong side of them. You can be stopped at any time and asked to **produce ID**. If that does happen to you, it's highly inadvisable to be difficult or facetious. The two main types of police – the Police Nationale and the Gendarmerie Nationale – are for all practical purposes indistinguishable. The CRS (Compagnies Républicaines de Sécurité), on the other hand, are an entirely different proposition. They are a mobile force of paramilitary heavies, used to guard sensitive embassies, "control" demonstrations and generally intimidate the populace on those occasions when the public authorities judge it to be stepping out of line.

Free legal advice over the phone (in French) is available from SOS Avocats (☏08 03 39 33 00; Mon–Fri 7–11.30pm; closed July & Aug).

Electricity

220V out of double, round-pin wall sockets. If you haven't bought the appropriate adaptor (*adapteur*) or transformer (*transformateur* – for US appliances) before leaving home, try the electrical section of a large department store like BHV (see p.322).

EMERGENCY NUMBERS

Police ☏17 (or ☏112 from a mobile)
Medical emergencies/ambulance ☏15
Fire brigade/paramedics ☏18
Rape crisis (SOS Viol) ☏08 00 05 95 95
SOS Help (crisis line/any problem: daily 3–11pm) in English ☏01 46 21 46 46, ⓦsoshelpline.org

Entry requirements

Citizens of EU (European Union) countries, and 31 other countries, including Canada, the United States, Australia, New Zealand and Norway, do not need any sort of visa to enter France, and can stay for up to ninety days. Citizens of all other countries must obtain a visa before arrival. A complete list of all French government websites, including **embassies** and **consulates**, can be found at Ⓦ gksoft.com/govt/en/fr.html.

Three types of tourist **visa** are currently issued: a transit visa (*visa de circulation*), valid for multiple stays of up to ninety days in a three-year period; a short-stay (*court séjour*) visa, valid for multiple stays of up to ninety days in a six-month period; and a long-stay (*long séjour*) visa, which allows for multiple stays of more than ninety days over three years, but which is issued only after an examination of an individual's circumstances. Note that it's very hard to get a long-stay visa if you've already arrived in France on a short-stay visa.

EU citizens and non-visa citizens who stay longer than ninety days are officially supposed to apply for a **Carte de Séjour**, for which you'll have to show a passport, birth certificate, proof of residence (eg, an electricity bill or copy of a lease), details of a French bank account, evidence of health insurance (if you're not an EU citizen), and proof of adequate funds to support a long stay in France; you'll also need two stamped SAEs and three passport-size photos. Make your application at the Préfecture de Police, 9 boulevard du Palais, on the Ile de la Cité, where there's a special counter. However, EU passports are rarely stamped, so there may be no evidence of how long you've been in the country. For further information on visa regulations consult the Ministry of Foreign Affairs website Ⓦ diplomatie .gouv.fr.

FOREIGN EMBASSIES AND CONSULATES IN PARIS

Australia 4 rue Jean-Rey, 15ᵉ; Ⓜ Bir-Hakeim ☎ 01 40 59 33 00, Ⓦ www.france.embassy.gov.au.
Canada 35 av Montaigne, 8ᵉ; Ⓜ Franklin-D-Roosevelt ☎ 01 44 43 29 00, Ⓦ amb-canada.fr.
Ireland 4 rue Rude, 16ᵉ; Ⓜ Charles-de-Gaulle-Etoile ☎ 01 44 17 67 00, Ⓦ embassyofireland.fr.
New Zealand 7 rue Léonard-de-Vinci, 16ᵉ; Ⓜ Victor-Hugo ☎ 01 45 01 43 43, Ⓦ nzembassy.com/france.
South Africa 59 quai d'Orsay, 7ᵉ, Ⓜ Invalides ☎ 01 53 59 23 23, Ⓦ afriquesud.net.
UK 35 rue du Faubourg-St-Honoré, 8ᵉ; Ⓜ Concorde ☎ 01 44 51 31 00, Ⓦ ukinfrance.fco.gov.uk.
US 2 av Gabriel, 1ᵉʳ; Ⓜ Concorde ☎ 01 43 12 22 22, Ⓦ france .usembassy.gov.

Health

Citizens of all EU countries are entitled to take advantage of French health services under the same terms as residents, provided they have the correct documentation. For British citizens, this means the European Health Insurance Card (**EHIC**), which can be applied for, free of charge, at UK post offices or online at Ⓦ nhs.uk. Non-EU citizens have to pay for most medical attention and are strongly advised to take out some form of travel insurance.

Under the French Social Security system, every hospital visit, doctor's consultation and prescribed medicine incurs a charge, which you have to pay upfront. Although all EU citizens with the correct documents are entitled to a refund of 70–75 percent of the standard fee for medical and dental expenses, providing the doctor is government-registered (a *médecin conventionné*), this can still leave a hefty shortfall, especially after a stay in hospital.

In **emergencies** you will always be admitted to the nearest hospital (*hôpital*), either under your own power or by ambulance, which even French citizens must pay for. Many people call the fire brigade (*pompiers*) instead; they are equipped to deal with medical emergencies and are the fastest and most reliable emergency service. There are two English-speaking private hospitals: the American Hospital in Paris at 63 bd Victor-Hugo, Neuilly-sur-Seine (Ⓜ Porte-Maillot, then bus #82 to terminus; ☎ 01 46 41 25 25, Ⓦ american-hospital .org), and the Hertford British Hospital at 3 rue Barbès, Levallois-Perret (Ⓜ Anatole-France; ☎ 01 46 39 22 22, Ⓦ british-hospital.org).

To find a **doctor**, ask at any *pharmacie*, local police station, tourist office or your hotel. Alternatively, look under "Médecins" in the *Yellow Pages*. An average consultation fee should be between €20

MEDICAL EMERGENCY NUMBERS
Fire brigade/paramedics ☎ 18
Medical emergencies/ambulance ☎ 15
SOS Médecins ☎ 01 47 07 77 77. Doctor call-out
SOS Dentaire ☎ 01 43 37 51 00. Emergency dental care

and €25. You will be given a *Feuille de Soins* (statement of treatment) for later insurance claims. Prescriptions (*ordonnances*) should be taken to a *pharmacie* and must be paid for; the medicines will have little stickers (*vignettes*) attached to them, which you should remove and stick to your *Feuille de Soins*, together with the prescription itself.

Pharmacies, signalled by an illuminated green cross, can give advice on minor complaints and are also equipped to provide first aid on request (for a fee). Most are open roughly 8am to 8pm; details of the nearest one open at night are posted in all pharmacies. You can find a good English-speaking chemist at Swann, 6 rue Castiglione, 1er (☎01 42 60 72 96). For a list of pharmacies that open at night, check Ⓦ pharmaciesdegarde.fr or try Dérhy/Pharmacie des Champs-Elysées, 84 avenue des Champs-Elysées, 8e (☎01 45 62 02 41; 24hr; ⓂGeorge-V), or Pharmacie des Halles, 10 bd Sébastopol, 4e (☎01 42 72 03 23; Mon–Sat 9am–midnight, Sun 9am–10pm; ⓂChâtelet).

Paris has the highest incidence of **AIDS** of any city in Europe; condoms (*préservatifs*) are readily available in supermarkets, and from dispensers in clubs, on the street – often outside pharmacies – and in the métro.

Insurance

Even though EU health-care privileges apply in France, you'd do well to take out an **insurance policy** before travelling to cover against theft, loss and illness or injury. Many policies can be chopped and changed to exclude coverage you don't need – for example, sickness and accident benefits can often be excluded or included at will. If you do take **medical coverage**, check whether benefits will be paid as treatment proceeds or only after you return home, and whether there is a 24-hour medical emergency number. When securing **baggage cover**, make sure that the per-article limit – typically under £500 – will cover your most valuable possession. If you need to make a claim, you should keep **receipts** for medicines and medical treatment (p.33), and in the event you have anything stolen you must obtain an official statement from the police (called a *constat de vol*).

Internet

Many hotels have **internet** access, and internet cafés are all over Paris; expect to pay anything between €2.50 and €8 per hour. Free **wi-fi** access is widespread and offered by many hotels, cafés, bars, train stations and sites such as the Pompidou Centre. You can also connect to the Paris wi-fi network from over 250 parks and libraries; the municipal website, Ⓦ paris.fr/wifi, tells you how to connect and has a downloadable pdf listing all the hotspots.

Laundry

You shouldn't have any trouble finding a **laundry** in Paris. If you can't spot one near your hotel, look in the phone book under "Laveries Automatiques". They're often unattended, so come with small change. Generally, self-service laundries open at 7am and close between 7pm and 10pm. The alternative *blanchisserie*, or pressing services, are likely to be expensive, and hotels in particular charge high rates. If you're doing your own washing in hotels, keep quantities small, as most forbid doing any laundry in your room.

Lost property

The **lost property office** (Bureau des Objets Trouvés) is located at the Préfecture de Police, 36 rue des Morillons, 15e; ☎08 21 00 25 25 (Mon–Thurs 8.30am–5pm, Fri 8.30am–4.30pm; ⓂConvention). For property lost on public transport, phone the RATP on ☎3246. If you lose your passport, report it to a police station and then your embassy (see p.33).

ROUGH GUIDES TRAVEL INSURANCE

Rough Guides has teamed up with WorldNomads.com to offer great travel insurance deals. Policies are available to residents of over 150 countries, with cover for a wide range of adventure sports, 24hr emergency assistance, high levels of medical and evacuation cover and a stream of travel safety information. Roughguides.com users can take advantage of their policies online 24/7, from anywhere in the world – even if you're already travelling. And since plans often change when you're on the road, you can extend your policy and even claim online. Roughguides.com users who buy travel insurance with WorldNomads.com can also leave a positive footprint and donate to a community development project. For more information go to Ⓦ roughguides.com/shop.

Mail

French **post offices** (*bureaux de poste* or *PTTs*) – look for bright yellow-and-blue La Poste signs – are generally open from 8am to 7pm Monday to Friday, and 8am to noon on Saturday. However, **Paris's main office**, at 52 rue du Louvre, 1er ($\textcircled{M}$ Etienne-Marcel), is open 24 hours (for all postal services, but not banking and money changing).

Standard letters (20g or less) and postcards within France and to European Union countries cost €0.75 and to North America, Australia and New Zealand €0.87. For sending letters, remember that you can also buy **stamps** from *tabacs*. For further information on postal rates, among other things, log on to the post office website $\textcircled{W}$ laposte.fr.

You can send **faxes** from post offices: the official French word is *télécopie*, but "fax" is commonplace. You can also use the Internet at post offices, change money, and make photocopies and phone calls. To post your letter on the street, look for the bright-yellow **post boxes**.

Maps

The **maps** in this guide and the free *Paris Map* available from the tourist office (see p.38) should be adequate for a short sightseeing stay, but for a more detailed map your best bet is the pocket-sized *L'Indispensable Plan de Paris* 1:15,000, published by Atlas Indispensable; it comes in a robust plastic cover, and gives full A–Z street listings. Also very detailed, but rather more unwieldy, is the large fold-out Michelin no. 10, the 1:10,000 *Plan de Paris*.

Money

France's currency is the euro (€), which is split into 100 cents. There are seven euro notes – in denominations of 500, 200, 100, 50, 20, 10 and 5 (though many vendors are reluctant to accept the 500 and 200 euro notes) – and eight different coin denomi-nations, from 2 euros down to 1 cent. For the most up-to-date exchange rates, consult the currency converter website $\textcircled{W}$ oanda.com.

The easiest way to access your funds while away is with a **debit or credit card** – but it's not necessarily the cheapest option, with many UK banks levying charges totalling around 5 percent on foreign withdrawals. Most foreign cards will work in a French ATM/cash machine (called a *distributeur* or *point argent*). Credit cards are widely accepted but it's always worth checking first that restaurants and hotels will accept your card; some smaller ones won't, despite the sign. And note that some machines don't recognize foreign cards – transport vending machines and automatic petrol pumps are particularly problematic. North American credit cards, for example, are not accepted at RATP/SNCF machines. French cards use the **chip-and-pin system**.

To cancel **lost or stolen cards**, call the following 24-hr numbers: American Express $\textcircled{T}$ 01 47 77 72 00; Diners' Club $\textcircled{T}$ 08 10 31 41 59; MasterCard $\textcircled{T}$ 0800 90 13 87; Visa $\textcircled{T}$ 0800 90 11 79.

Changing money and banking hours

Exchange rates and **commission fees** charged by banks and bureaux de change vary considerably. On the whole, the best exchange rates are offered by **banks**, though there's always a commission charge on top (1–2 percent commission on travellers' cheques, and a 2–4 percent commission on cash). **Bureaux de change** can give terrible rates, though the ones at the airports and those on the Champs-Elysées, near *McDonald's*, are usually pretty reputable.

Standard **banking hours** are Monday to Friday from 9am to 4 or 5pm. Some banks close at midday (noon/12.30pm–2/2.30pm); some are open on Saturday 9am to noon. All are closed on Sunday and public holidays. Money-exchange bureaux stay open longer (until 6 or 7pm), tend not to close for lunch and may even open on Sundays in the more touristy areas.

THE BEST SMALLER ART GALLERIES AND MUSEUMS

Although the Louvre, Musée d'Orsay and the Pompidou Centre's museum have unrivalled collections of art that could easily fill an entire trip, it's well worth making time for at least one of the city's smaller, more intimate art galleries and museums. Here are some of our favourites:

Musée Rodin See p.152
Musée Jacquemart-André See p.66
Musée d'Art Moderne
  de la Ville de Paris See p.156
Musée Picasso See p.100

Musée Marmottan See p.214
Orangerie See p.69
Musée Carnavalet See p.94
Château de Chantilly See p.235

There are **automatic exchange machines** at the airports and train stations and outside many money-exchange bureaux. They accept £10 and £20 notes as well as dollars, but offer a very poor rate of exchange.

Opening hours and public holidays

Most shops, businesses, information services, museums and banks in Paris stay open all day. The exceptions are the smaller shops and enterprises, which may close for lunch sometime between 12.30pm and 2pm. Basic **hours of business** are from 8 or 9am to 6.30 or 7.30pm Monday to Saturday for the big shops and Tuesday to Saturday for smaller shops, though some may also open on Monday afternoons. You can always find boulang-eries and food shops that stay open on days when others close – on Sunday normally until noon. The French government is currently considering easing Sunday trading restrictions, and there are some areas of the city where shops are allowed to open on a Sunday (see p.322). See above for standard **banking hours**.

Restaurants, **bars** and **cafés** often close on Sunday or Monday, and quite a few restaurants also close on Saturdays, especially at midday. It's common for bars and cafés to stay open to 2am, and even extend hours on a Friday and Saturday night, closing earlier on Sunday. Restau-rants won't usually serve after 10pm, though some brasseries cater for night owls and serve meals till the early hours. Many restaurants and shops take a **holiday** between the middle of July and the end of August, and over Easter and Christmas.

Museums generally open at 9/10am and close at 5/6pm. Summer hours may differ from winter hours; if they do, both are indicated in the listings of this guide. Don't be caught out by museum **closing days** – usually Monday or Tuesday and sometimes both. **Churches** and **cathedrals** are almost always open all day.

France celebrates eleven **national holidays** (*jours fériés* or *j.f.*) – not counting the two that fall on a Sunday anyway. Throughout the guide, opening hours given for Sundays also apply to public holidays. With three, and sometimes four, holidays, **May** is a particularly festive month. It makes a peaceful time to visit, as people clear out of town over several weekends, but many businesses will have erratic opening hours.

Just about everything, including museums, is closed on May 1. July 14 heralds the beginning of the French holiday season and people leave town en masse between then and the end of August.

Note that if a public holiday falls on a Tuesday or a Thursday, many people *faire le pont* ("bridge it") by taking an unofficial day off on the adjacent Monday or Friday.

NATIONAL HOLIDAY DATES

January 1 le Jour de l'an
Easter Sunday Pâques
Easter Monday Lundi de Pâques
May 1 la Fête du travail/May Day
May 8 la Fête de la Victoire 1945/VE Day
Ascension Day (40 days after Easter: mid-May to early June) l'Ascension
Whitsun (7th Sunday after Easter: mid-May to early June) la Pentecôte
Whit Monday (7th Monday after Easter: mid-May to early June) Lundi de Pentecôte
July 14 la Fête nationale/Bastille Day
August 15 l'Assomption/Feast of the Assumption
November 1 la Toussaint/All Saints' Day
November 11 l'Armistice 1918/Armistice Day
December 25 Noël

Phones

For **calls within France** – local or long-distance – dial all ten digits of the number. Paris and Ile-de-France numbers start with ☎01. Numbers beginning with ☎08 00 are free numbers; ☎08 10 is charged at local rates, no matter where you're calling from; all other ☎08 numbers are premium rate (from €0.34 per minute) and can't be accessed from outside France. Numbers beginning with ☎06 are **mobile** and therefore expensive to call (usually around €0.40 per minute). Local calls are timed in France.

Off-peak times (30 percent less than the peak rate, for local, long-distance and interna-tional calls) are weekdays between 7pm and 8am, and all day Saturday and Sunday, as well as holidays.

France operates on the European GSM standard, so US **cellphones** won't work in France unless you've got a tri-band phone. If you're making a lot of calls, consider buying a local SIM card or a pre-pay (*mobicarte*) package once in Paris. These are sold in mobile phone shops, Fnac stores (see p.330) and some supermarkets. Expect to pay around €30 for a SIM card.

INTERNATIONAL CALLS

To **call France from abroad**, use the IDD code for your country (00 or 011 in most cases) followed by the French country code (33), then the local number minus the initial "0". So to call Paris from the UK, Ireland, New Zealand and Netherlands dial ☎00 33 1 then the eight-digit number; from the US, Canada and Australia, dial ☎011 33 1.

CALLING HOME FROM PARIS

International off-peak hours are the same as for domestic phone calls (see opposite). At peak rates, €1 gets you about five minutes to EU countries and the US, or two minutes to Australia and New Zealand. Note that the initial zero is omitted from the area code when dialling the UK, Ireland, Australia and New Zealand from abroad.

UK international access code + 44
US & **Canada** international access code + 1
Ireland international access code + 353
Australia international access code + 61
New Zealand international access code + 64
South Africa international access code + 27

USEFUL NUMBERS

French directory enquiries ☎12
International directory enquiries ☎32 12 + country code (around €3 per call)
Collect/reverse charge calls (*téléphoner en PCV*) to the UK ☎0800 99 00 44; to North America ☎0800 99 00 11; to other countries ☎30 06

Sales tax

VAT (Value Added Tax) is referred to as **TVA** in France (*taxe sur la valeur ajoutée*). The standard rate in France is currently 19.6 percent; it's higher for luxury items and lower for essentials, but there are no exemptions. However, non-EU residents who have been in the country for less than six months are entitled to a refund (*détaxe*) of some or all of this amount (but usually around fourteen percent) if you spend at least €175 in a single trip to one shop. Not all stores participate in this scheme, though, so ask first. The procedure is rather complicated: present your passport to the shop when you pay and ask for the three-page *bordereau de vente à l'exportation* form. They should help you fill it in and provide you with a self-addressed envelope. When you leave the EU, get customs to stamp the filled-in form (look for the *douane de détaxe* counter); you will then need to send two of the pages back to the shop in the envelope within six months; the shop will then transfer the refund through your credit card or bank. Some shops deduct the VAT there and then, but you still have to go through the procedure described above. The Centre de Renseignements des Douanes (☎08 25 30 82 63, ⓦdouane.gouv.fr) can answer any customs-related questions.

Smoking

Smoking is banned in public places in France. Restaurants, bars, cafés and nightclubs are still allowed to have smoking rooms, but these are strictly supervised and staff are not obliged to enter or serve them.

Time

Paris, and all of France, is in the **Central European Time Zone** (GMT+1): one hour ahead of the UK, six hours ahead of Eastern Standard Time and nine hours ahead of Pacific Standard Time. France is eight hours behind all of eastern Australia and ten hours behind New Zealand from April to October (but ten hours behind southeastern Australia and twelve hours behind New Zealand from November to March).

Toilets

Paris has around four hundred automatic public toilets, known as "*sanisettes*", which are free. Elsewhere, ask for *les toilettes* or look for signs for the WC (pronounced "vay say"); when reading the details of facilities outside hotels, don't confuse *lavabo*, which means washbasin, with lavatory. French toilets in bars are still occasionally of the hole-in-the-ground variety, and often lack toilet paper. Standards of cleanliness aren't always high. Toilets in railway stations and department stores are commonly staffed by attendants who will expect a bit of spare change.

Tourist information

The main **Paris tourist office** is at 25 rue des Pyramides, 1er (Mon–Sat 10am–7pm, Sun 11am–7pm; ☎08 92 68 30 00, ⓦparis-info.com; Ⓜ Pyramides/RER Auber). There are **branch offices** at the Gare du Nord (daily 8am–6pm); at the Gare de Lyon (Mon–Sat 8am–6pm) by the Grandes Lignes arrivals; at the Gare de l'Est (Mon–Sat 8am–7pm); opposite 72 boulevard Rochechouart (daily 10am–6pm; Ⓜ Anvers); and 21 place du Tertre, 18e (daily 10am–7pm; Ⓜ Abbesses). The tourist offices give out information on Paris and the suburbs, and all but the place du Tertre branch can book hotel accommodation and also sell the Carte Musées et Monuments (see p.32) and Paris Visite travel passes (see p.25).

While you're there, pick up the free *Paris Map* – this might be behind the counter, so you'll need to ask. The tourist office's website has a hotel booking service, with many hotels offering discounted stays, and it also allows you to buy advance tickets online for some of the most popular sights, such as the Arc de Triomphe and the Sainte-Chapelle, enabling you to bypass long queues. Within the Carrousel du Louvre, underground, below the triumphal arch at the east end of the Tuileries, is the **Espace du Tourisme d'Ile de France** (daily 10am–6pm; ☎08 92 68 30 00, ⓦnouveau-paris-ile-de-france.fr), which has information on attractions and activities in Paris and the surrounding area.

An alternative source of information is the **Hôtel de Ville information office** – Bureau d'Accueil – at 29 rue de Rivoli, 4^e (Mon–Sat 9.30am–6pm; ☎01 42 76 43 43, ⓦparis.fr; Ⓜ Hôtel-de-Ville). For detailed **what's-on information** you'll need to buy one of Paris's **listings magazines**, *Pariscope* (€0.40) or *L'Officiel des Spectacles* (ⓦoffi.fr; €0.35), available from all newsagents and kiosks. *Pariscope*, in particular, has a huge section on films and a small English section with weekly entertainment highlights, restaurant reviews and a special-interest page put together by *Time Out*. On a Wednesday, both *Le Monde* and *Le Figaro* have free listings supplements, offering a more discerning selection of the week's events. You could also keep a lookout for the free weekly listings paper, *A nous Paris*, which comes out

on Mondays and is available from métro stations. In addition, a number of free pocket independent nightlife guides (*Lylo* is a good one) can be picked up in stores and cafés all over the city.

Travellers with disabilities

Paris has never had a particularly good reputation for **access facilities**, though there have been significant improvements, especially to the bus network, while the city's four hundred public toilets (*sanisettes*) are now fully accessible to wheelchair users.

Many museums, such as the Cité des Sciences et de l'Industrie, the Louvre, Musée d'Orsay and Pompidou Centre, offer **guided visits and activities** for disabled people; and in a number of theatres the text is displayed for the deaf and hard-of-hearing during some performances. Note that admission to museums is free for blue badge holders and one companion.

Up-to-date **information** is best obtained from organizations at home before you leave, as well as from the French tourist board (ⓦfranceguide.com) or from the French disability organizations (see opposite). One of the best sources of information for travellers with disabilities in France (with a large section on Paris) is *Handitourisme*, published in 2011 in France by Petit Futé (ⓦpetitfute.fr; €15.95). Written in French, the book lists hundreds of sites, museums, hotels and restaurants with full accessibility to handicapped travellers. Another useful resource, in English, is *Access in Paris* by Gordon Couch and Ben Roberts, published in Britain by Quiller Press, a thorough guide to accommodation, monuments, museums, restaurants and travel to the city, updated in 2008. Holiday Care (☎0845 124 9971, ⓦholidaycare.org.uk) also has an information sheet on accessible accommodation in France. In the US, try the Society for the Advancement of Travel for the Handicapped (☎212 447 7284, ⓦsath.org).

Eurostar offers an excellent deal for wheelchair-users. There are two spaces in the first-class carriages for wheelchairs, each with an accompanying seat for a companion. Fares are a flat rate of £69 return for both passengers from Paris and London (with semi-flexible conditions), and though it's not absolutely guaranteed, you will normally get the first-class meal as well. No advance bookings are necessary, though it's wise to reserve ahead and arrange the special assistance which Eurostar offers at either end.

The French Government Tourist Office in London distributes a booklet on hotels, called *Paris, Ile de France: Hôtels et Residences de Tourisme* which details those with disabled access. For more information contact the specialist organizations (see below).

Getting around

If you are physically handicapped, **taxis** are obliged by law to carry you and to help you into the vehicle, and also to carry your guide dog if you are blind. The PAM network (☎08 10 08 10 75, ⓦpam.paris.fr) has taxicabs and minibuses fully adapted for wheelchairs; 24-hour advance notice is needed. Two taxi companies, G7 Horizon (☎01 47 39 00 91, ⓦtaxis-g7.fr) and PMR (☎06 14 67 75 02, ⓦtaxipmr.onlc.fr), make journeys to and from the airports; they offer fully adapted vehicles and trained drivers. Fares are the same as for classic taxis; you just need to reserve four hours in advance.

Since 2009, all 63 Paris **bus** lines have been made easily accessible for wheelchairs. They have mechanical platforms for getting on and off and a designated wheelchair space in the bus. Only around twenty **RER** stations are accessible, and most require an official to work the lift for you. The Météor **métro** line (14), opened in 1998, and the RER line E, however, are designed to be easily accessible by all. You can download a transport map of Paris from ⓦratp.fr showing exactly which RER stops are wheelchair accessible.

For travel on the buses, métro or RER, the RATP offers **accompanied journeys** for disabled people not in wheelchairs – *Les compagnons du voyage* (ⓦwww.compagnons.com) – which costs €27 an hour on weekdays (twice as much on weekends) and is available daily 6.30am to 8pm. You have to book on ☎01 58 76 08 33 (Mon–Fri 6am–7pm, Sat & Sun 9am–6pm) at least a day in advance. As long as they are registered with the organization, **blind passengers** can request a free companion from the volunteer organization Auxiliaires des Aveugles (☎01 43 06 39 68, ⓦlesauxiliairesdesaveugles.asso.fr).

Another useful source of **information** on getting around Paris (in French only) is ⓦinfomobi.com, which among other things, offers real-time information on network accessibility.

A **Braille métro map** and a separate bus map are obtainable from L'Association Valentin Haüy (AVH), 5 rue Duroc, 7ᵉ (☎01 44 49 27 27, ⓦavh.asso.fr). **Cars with hand controls** (category O) can be rented from Hertz, usually with 48 hours' advance notice (in France call ☎01 39 38 38 38).

PARIS CONTACTS

APF (Association des Paralysés de France) 17 bd Auguste-Blanqui, 13ᵉ ☎01 40 78 69 00, ⓦapf.asso.fr. A national organization providing guides on Paris (in French only) for disabled visitors. *Paris comme sur des roulettes*, detailing how to get about on wheels (not cars) in Paris, is available at Fnac, Virgin Megastore, Gilbert Jeune and other large bookstores.

ⓦ**jaccede.com** A handy website (in French only) giving a list of museums, monuments and other public places in Paris that are wheelchair accessible.

PONT-NEUF

The Islands

There's no better place to start a tour of Paris than the two river islands at its centre, the Ile de la Cité and the Ile St-Louis. The former is the core from which the rest of Paris grew and harbours the cathedral of Notre-Dame, a superb example of Gothic grandeur and harmony, and the stunning Sainte-Chapelle, preserved within the precincts of the Palais de Justice. Linked to the Ile de la Cité by a footbridge, the smaller Ile St-Louis has no heavyweight sights, but possesses a beguiling charm all of its own, with its tall, austerely beautiful houses on single-lane streets, tree-lined *quais*, a church and assorted restaurants, cafés and shops. The island feels removed from the rest of Paris, an oasis little touched by the city's turbulent years of revolution and upheaval. Inhabitants of the island even have their own name: "Louisiens".

Ile de la Cité

1

The Ile de la Cité is where Paris began. It was settled in around 300 BC by a Celtic tribe, the Parisii, and in 52 BC was overrun by the Romans, who built a palace-fortress at the western end of the island. In the tenth century, the Frankish kings transformed this into a splendid palace, of which the **Sainte-Chapelle** and the **Conciergerie** prison survive today. At the other end of the island they erected the great cathedral of **Notre-Dame**. By the twelfth century the small Ile de la Cité teemed with life, somehow managing to accommodate twelve parishes, plus numerous chapels and monasteries. It was all too much for the monks at St-Magloire, who moved out in 1138 to quieter premises on the Right Bank.

It takes some imagination today to picture what the medieval city must have looked like, as most of it was erased in the nineteenth century by Baron Haussmann, Napoléon III's Préfet de la Seine (equivalent to mayor of Paris), displacing 25,000 people and destroying ninety streets – which had, admittedly, become squalid and notoriously dangerous at night. In their place were raised four imposing Neoclassical edifices, largely given over to housing the law and police.

The few corners of the island untouched by Haussmann include the tranquil **square du Vert-Galant**, **place Dauphine** and the medieval streets **rues Chanoinesse, des Ursins** and **de la Colombe**, to the north of the cathedral.

Pont-Neuf

Ⓜ Pont-Neuf

A popular approach to the Ile de la Cité is via the graceful, twelve-arched **Pont-Neuf**, which, despite its name, is Paris's oldest surviving bridge, built by Henri IV, who is commemorated with a statue halfway across. Made of stone and free of the usual medieval complement of houses, it was a radical departure from previous structures, hence its name, "New Bridge". Henri IV, one of the capital's first great town-planners, took much interest in the Pont-Neuf's progress and would sometimes come to inspect it, delighting the workmen on one occasion by taking a flying leap over an incomplete arch.

So impressive was the bridge in scale and length that it soon became symbolic of the city itself, drawing large crowds; pedlars, secondhand book and flower sellers, dog-barbers and tooth-pullers set up stalls, while acrobats and actors entertained passers-by.

The square du Vert-Galant

Ⓜ Pont-Neuf

The **square du Vert-Galant** is enclosed within the triangular stern of the island, and reached via steps leading down behind the statue of Henri IV on the Pont-Neuf. "Vert-Galant", meaning a "green" or "lusty" gentleman, is a reference to the king's legendary amorous exploits, and he would no doubt have approved of this tranquil, tree-lined garden, a popular haunt of lovers – the prime spot to occupy is the knoll dotted with trees at the extreme point of the island. From here you can also hop onto one of the river boats that dock on the north side of the *square* (see p.26).

Place Dauphine

Ⓜ Pont-Neuf

On the eastern side of the Pont-Neuf, across the street from the Henri IV statue, red-brick seventeenth-century houses flank the entrance to **place Dauphine**, one of the city's most secluded and attractive squares. The traffic noise recedes, often replaced by nothing more intrusive than the gentle tap of boules being played in the shade of the chestnuts. At the eastern end is the hulking facade of the **Palais de Justice**, which swallowed up the palace that was home to the French kings until Etienne Marcel's bloody revolt in 1358 frightened them off to the greater security of the Louvre.

1

Sainte-Chapelle

Palais de Justice, bd du Palais, 1er • Daily: March–Oct 9.30am–6pm; mid-May to mid-Sept also Wed till 9pm; Nov–Feb 9am–5pm • €8, combined admission to the Conciergerie €11 • ☎ 01 53 40 60 80 • ⓜCité

The only part of the Ile de la Cité's old palace that remains in its entirety is the **Sainte-Chapelle**, its fragile-looking spire soaring above the Palais buildings and its excessive height in relation to its length giving it the appearance of a lopped-off cathedral choir. Though damaged in the Revolution, during which it was used as a flour warehouse, it was sensitively restored in the mid-nineteenth century, and remains one of the finest achievements of French High Gothic, renowned for its exquisite stained-glass windows. It was built by Louis IX in 1242–48 to house a collection of holy relics bought at an extortionate price – far more than it cost to build the Sainte-Chapelle – from the bankrupt Byzantium Empire. The relics, supposedly Christ's crown of thorns and fragments of the True Cross, are now in Notre-Dame's treasury, displayed only on certain days, including Good Friday.

The upper and lower chapels

The Sainte-Chapelle actually consists of two chapels: the simple **lower chapel** was intended for the servants, and the **upper chapel**, reached via a spiral staircase, was reserved for the court. The latter is dazzling, its walls made almost entirely of stained glass held up by powerful supports, which the medieval builders cleverly crafted to appear delicate and fragile by dividing them into clusters of pencil-thin columns. When the sun streams through, the glowing blues and reds of the stained glass dapple the interior and you feel like you're surrounded by myriad brilliant butterflies. There are 1113 glass panels, two-thirds of which are original (the others date from the nineteenth-century restoration); they tell virtually the entire story of the Bible, beginning on the north side with Genesis, continuing with the Passion of Christ (east end) and the history of the Sainte-Chapelle relics (on the south side), and ending with the Apocalypse in the rose window. The chapel is frequently used for classical **concerts** – buy tickets a day or so in advance to avoid long queues.

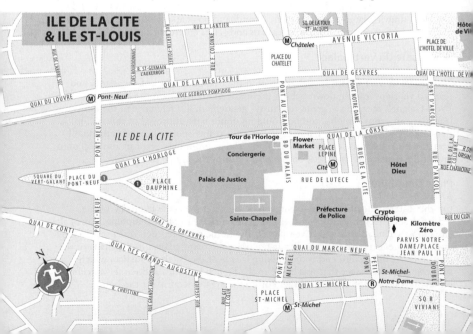

The Conciergerie

Palais de Justice, 2 bd du Palais, 1er • Daily 9.30am–6pm • €7, combined ticket with Sainte-Chapelle €11 • Ⓜ Cité

The **Conciergerie** is one of the few remaining vestiges of the old medieval Palais de Justice and is Paris's oldest prison, where Marie-Antoinette and the leading figures of the Revolution were incarcerated before execution. Inside are several splendid, vaulted Gothic halls, including the Salle des Gens d'Armes, built in 1301–15. The far end is separated off by an iron grille; during the Revolution this area was reserved for the *pailleux*, prisoners who couldn't afford to bribe a guard for their own cell and had to sleep on straw (*paille*).

Beyond is a corridor where prisoners were allowed to wander freely. There are a number of reconstructed rooms here, such as the "salle de toilette", where the condemned had their hair cropped and shirt collars ripped in preparation for the guillotine. On the upper storey is a mock-up of **Marie-Antoinette's cell** in which the condemned queen's crucifix hangs forlornly against peeling fleur-de-lys wallpaper.

The Tour de l'Horloge

Ⓜ Cité

Outside the Conciergerie is the recently restored **Tour de l'Horloge**, a tower built around 1350, and so called because it displayed Paris's first public clock. The ornate face, set against a background of fleur-de-lys, is flanked with statues representing Law and Justice, added in 1585. The clock tower's bell, which would once have rung out to mark special royal occasions, sounding during the St Bartholomew's Day massacre (see p.365), was melted down during the Commune (see p.370).

Place Lépine

Ⓜ Cité

East from the Conciergerie is **place Lépine**, named after the police boss who gave Paris's coppers their white truncheons and whistles. The police headquarters, known popularly as the Quai des Orfèvres (as any readers of Georges Simenon's Maigret novels will

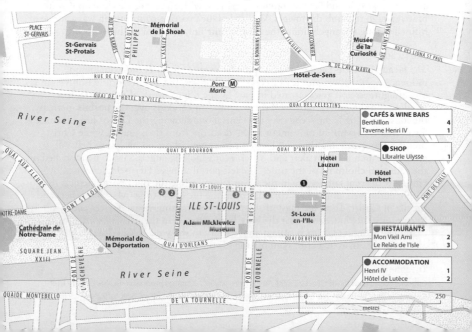

1

know), stands on one side of the square, though the police are set to move to new modern offices before long. Livening up the square on the other side is an exuberant daily **flower market**, augmented by a chirruping bird market on Sundays.

Cathédrale de Notre-Dame

Place du Parvis Notre-Dame, 4ᵉ • Mon–Fri 8am–6.45pm, Sat & Sun 8am–7.15pm • Free • Ⓦ cathedraledeparis.com • Ⓜ St-Michel/Cité

A Gothic masterpiece, the **Cathédrale de Notre-Dame** rears up from the Ile de la Cité like a great ship moored by huge flying buttresses. Built on the site of the Merovingian cathedral of St-Etienne, itself sited on the old Roman temple to Jupiter, Notre-Dame was begun in 1160 under the auspices of Bishop de Sully and completed around 1345. The cathedral's seminaries became an ecclesiastical powerhouse, churning out six popes during the thirteenth and fourteenth centuries, though it subsequently lost some of its pre-eminence to other sees, such as Rheims and St-Denis. The building later fell into decline, and during the Revolution the frieze of Old Testament kings on the facade was damaged by enthusiasts who mistook them for the kings of France. Napoleon restored some of the cathedral's prestige, crowning himself emperor here in 1804, though the walls were so dilapidated they had to be covered with drapes to provide a sufficiently grand backdrop.

Viollet-le-Duc's restoration and the towers

Towers April & Sept daily 10am–6.30pm; May–Aug Mon–Fri 10am–6.30pm, Sat & Sun 10am–11pm; Oct–March daily 10am–5.30pm • Last entry 45min before closing • €8

In the 1820s the cathedral was given a much-needed **restoration**, largely thanks to a petition drawn up by Victor Hugo. Hugo had stirred public interest through his novel *Notre-Dame de Paris*, in which he lamented the building's sorry state (Gothic architecture was particularly favoured by Romantic novelists, who deemed the soaring naves of the great cathedrals singularly suited to sheltering "tormented souls"). The task was given to architect Viollet-le-Duc, who carried out an extensive and thorough renovation, some would say too thorough, remaking much of the statuary on the facade – the originals can be seen in the Musée National du Moyen Age (see p.123) – and adding the steeple and baleful-looking gargoyles, which you can see close up if you're brave enough to climb the **towers**. Viollet-le-Duc's parting contribution was a statue of himself among the angels lining the roof: it's the only one looking heavenwards.

The facade

The **facade** is Notre-Dame's most impressive exterior feature; the Romanesque influence is still visible, not least in its solid H-shape, but the overriding impression is one of lightness and grace, created in part by the filigree work of the central rose window and the gallery above. Of the magnificent **carvings over the portals**, perhaps the most arresting is the scene over the central one showing the Day of Judgement: the lower frieze is a whirl of movement as the dead rise from their graves, while Christ presides above, sending those on his right to heaven, those on his left to hell. All around the arch peer out alert and mischievous-looking angels, said to be modelled on the cathedral choirboys of the time. The left portal shows Mary being crowned by Christ, with scenes of her life in the lower friezes, while the right portal depicts the Virgin enthroned and, below, episodes from the life of St Anne (Mary's mother) and the life of Christ. These are masterfully put together, using visual devices and symbols to communicate more than just the bare-bones story – in the nativity scene, for example, the infant Christ is placed above Mary to show his elevated status and lies on an altar rather than in a crib, symbolizing his future sacrifice.

The interior

Cathedral guided tours 1hr–1hr 30min in English (Wed & Thurs 2pm, Sat 2.30pm) and French (Mon–Fri, though not 1st Fri of the month or any Fri during Lent, 2pm & 3pm, Sat & Sun 2.30pm) • Free • **Trésor** Mon–Fri 9.30am–6pm, Sat 9.30am–6.30pm, Sun 1.30–6.30pm • €3

Inside Notre-Dame, you're struck immediately by the dramatic contrast between the darkness of the nave and the light falling on the first great clustered pillars of the choir. It is the end walls of the transepts, nearly two-thirds glass, including two magnificent rose windows coloured in imperial purple, that admit all this light. These, the vaulting and the soaring shafts reaching to the springs of the vaults, are all definite Gothic elements, while there remains a strong influence of Romanesque in the stout round pillars of the nave and the general sense of four-squareness. The **trésor** is unlikely to appeal unless ornate nineteenth-century monstrances and chalices are your thing.

To join the free guided **tours**, meet at the welcome desk near the entrance. Free **organ recitals** are also held every Sunday at around 4 or 5pm; the instrument, crafted by the great nineteenth century organ-maker Aristide Cavaillé-Coll, is one of France's finest, with over six thousand pipes.

The kilomètre zéro
Ⓜ Cité

Notre-Dame, at the heart of Paris, is also the symbolic heart of France: outside on the pavement by the cathedral's west door is a bronze star, known as **kilomètre zéro**, from which all main-road distances in France are calculated. The large windswept square in front of the cathedral, built by Haussmann in the 1860s, is known as the **Parvis** (from "paradise") Notre-Dame. White paving blocks set into it show the outlines of the small streets and buildings that stood here in medieval times.

Crypte archéologique
Place du Parvis Notre-Dame, 4ᵉ • Tues–Sun 10am–6pm • €4 • Ⓜ Cité/St-Michel

At the far end of the Parvis Notre-Dame is the entrance to the atmospherically lit **crypte archéologique**. This large excavated area holds remains of the original cathedral (St-Etienne) plus vestiges of the streets and houses that once clustered around Notre-Dame; most are medieval, but some date as far back as Gallo-Roman times and include parts of a Roman hypocaust (heating system).

Mémorial de la Déportation
Square de l'Ile de France, 4ᵉ • Daily 10am–noon & 2–7pm, closes 5pm in winter • Free • Ⓜ Cité/Pont Marie

At the eastern tip of the Ile de la Cité is the stark and moving symbolic tomb of the 200,000 French who died in Nazi concentration camps – among them Resistance fighters, Jews and forced labourers. The **Mémorial de la Déportation** is barely visible above ground; stairs hardly shoulder-wide descend into a space like a prison yard, and off here is a stifling crypt where thousands of quartz pebbles represent the dead. Floor and ceiling are black, and it ends in a dark, raw hole, with a single naked bulb hanging in the middle. On either side are empty barred cells. Above the exit are the words "Pardonne. N'oublie pas" ("Forgive. Do not forget"). In contrast, the little green park surrounding the memorial is more of a celebration of life and a popular hangout.

SCHOOL FOR SCANDAL
On rue Chanoinesse, the cathedral school of Notre-Dame, forerunner of the Sorbonne, once flourished. Around the year 1200, one of the teachers was **Peter Abélard**. A philosophical whiz kid and cocker of snooks at establishment intellectuals, he was very popular with students but not with the authorities, who thought they caught a distinct whiff of heresy. Forced to leave the school, he set up shop on the Left Bank with his disciples, in effect founding the University of Paris. Less successful was the story of his love life. While living near the rue Chanoinesse, he fell passionately in love with his landlord's niece, Héloïse, and she with him. She had a baby, her uncle had Abélard castrated, and the story ended in convents, lifelong separation and lengthy correspondence. They were reunited in death, however, and lie side by side in Père-Lachaise cemetery (see p.207).

1

Ile St-Louis

The **Ile St-Louis** is arguably the most romantic part of Paris, and prime strolling territory. For centuries the island was nothing but swampy pastureland, a haunt of lovers, duellists and miscreants on the run, until in the seventeenth century real-estate developer Christophe Marie had the bright idea of filling it with elegant mansions; by 1660 the island was transformed. Unlike its larger neighbour, the Ile St-Louis has no sights as such, save for a very small **museum** (☎01 43 54 35 61; ⓂPont Marie) at 6 quai d'Orléans devoted to the Romantic Polish poet Adam Mickiewicz.

Hôtel Lauzun
17 quai d'Anjou, 4ᵉ • ⓂPont Marie/Sully Morland

One of the island's most elegant mansions is the **Hôtel Lauzun**. Built in 1657 by Versailles architect Le Vau, it has an intact interior, complete with splendid trompe l'oeil decorations. Its most famous inhabitant was the poet Baudelaire who lived in a small apartment on the second floor from 1843 to 1845. He wrote much of *Les Fleurs du mal* here and hosted meetings of the Haschischins club, attended by bohemian writers and artists, including Manet, Balzac and Delacroix, and during which, as the name suggests, hashish was handed round – apparently in the form of a green jelly. Flutes of champagne are probably as heady as things get these days, as the mansion is often used for government receptions. It's also sometimes open for guided tours to the public – details are given in the "Visites conférences" section in *Pariscope* (see p.38).

Hôtel Lambert
1 quai d'Anjou, 4ᵉ • ⓂPont Marie/Sully Morland

More splendid still than the Hôtel Lauzun is the **Hôtel Lambert**, also built by Le Vau, at the tip of the island. Decorated by two of seventeenth-century France's greatest artists, Charles Le Brun, who painted Versailles' Galerie des Glaces, and Eustache Le Sueur, it's widely thought to be the most beautiful residence in Paris. Voltaire, a past inhabitant, thought it was fit for a king. The building was bought by the Qatari royal family in 2007 for an estimated €80 million; their controversial refurbishment plan, including the construction of a lift and underground carpark, and described by one French architect as having "the aesthetics of a James Bond villa", had to be scaled back after prominent historians and politicians protested.

Berthillon and the southern *quais*
31 rue St-Louis-en-l'Ile, 4ᵉ • ⓂPont Marie/Sully Morland

A visit to the island wouldn't be complete without a stop at *Berthillon* (see p.268); eating one of its exquisite ice creams while wandering down rue St-Louis-en-l'Ile is something of a tradition. For absolute seclusion, head for the southern *quais*, or climb over the low gate on the right of the garden across boulevard Henri-IV to reach Paris's best sunbathing spot. The island is particularly atmospheric in the evening, and an arm-in-arm stroll along the *quais* is a must in any lovers' itinerary.

THE LOUVRE PYRAMIDES AT NIGHT

The Louvre

The Louvre – catch-all term for the palace and the museum it houses – cuts a grand Classical swathe through the very centre of the city, running west along the right bank of the Seine from the Ile de la Cité towards the Champs-Elysées. Even if you don't venture inside, the sheer bravado of the architectural ensemble is thrilling. If you do, you'll find a truly gigantesque museum. Its paintings, sculptures and decorative arts cover everything from the Middle Ages to the beginnings of Impressionism, while the collection of antiquities from Egypt, the Middle East, Greece and Rome is unrivalled. The hoard of Italian Renaissance paintings is priceless, and the French collection acts as nothing less than the gold standard of the nation's artistic tradition. Separate from the Louvre proper, but still within the palace are three design museums dedicated to fashion and textiles, decorative arts and advertising.

2

INFORMATION

Opening hours Permanent collection: daily except Tues (plus Jan 1 and May 1) 9am–6pm, Wed & Fri till 10pm. Doors shut half an hour before the museum closes. Almost a quarter of the museum's rooms are closed one day a week on a rotating basis, so if you're interested in a less popular section it's worth checking the schedule online.

Admission €10, or €14 with entry to any temporary exhibitions; free to under-18s and under-26s from (or studying in) most European countries; free to under-26s from any country on Friday evenings (after 6pm), and to all on the first Sunday of each month. Tickets can be bought in advance from branches of Fnac (see p.330), Virgin Megastore (there's one right outside the entrance under the Arc du Carrousel) and the big department stores. You can also buy tickets online in France via Ⓦ ticketnet.fr, or in the US (and in US dollars) via Ⓦ ticketweb.com.

Contact details ☎ 01 40 20 50 50, Ⓦ louvre.fr
Métro Ⓜ Palais Royal-Musée du Louvre

Access The main entrance is via the Pyramide, but you'll find shorter queues at the Porte des Lions, just east of the Pont Royal (closes at 5.30pm); and via the entrance directly under the Arc du Carrousel (which can also be accessed from 99 rue de Rivoli and from the line #1 platform of the Palais Royal-Musée du Louvre métro stop). If you've already got a ticket or a museum pass (see p.32) you can also enter from the passage Richelieu (closes at 6pm). Disabled access is via the futuristic sinking column in the middle of the Pyramide; entry is free to registered disabled visitors along with one companion.

Eating The elegantly modern *Café Richelieu* (first floor, Richelieu) has a wonderful summer-only terrace with a view of the Pyramide. *Café Mollien* (first floor, Denon) is the busiest but also has a summer terrace. *Café Denon* (lower ground floor, Denon) is cosy and classy. The various cafés and restaurants under the Pyramide itself are mostly noisy and unpleasant.

The original **Palais du Louvre** was little more than a feudal fortress, begun by Philippe-Auguste in the 1190s, and Charles V was the first French king to make the castle his residence, in the 1360s. The ground plan of his new palace can be seen traced on the pavement of the Cour Carrée. It wasn't until 1546, the year before the death of François I, that the first stones of the Louvre we see today were laid by the architect, Pierre Lescot. Henri II continued François I's plans, building the two graceful wings that now form the southwestern corner of the **Cour Carrée**. It's still possible to imagine how extraordinary the building would have looked, a gleaming example of the new Renaissance style surrounded by the late Gothic of Charles V's day.

When Henri IV took charge in 1594, he set about linking the Louvre with Catherine de Médicis' Palais des Tuileries (see box, p.68), building the long, riverside Grande Galerie. Louis XIII and Louis XIV contented themselves with merely completing the Cour Carrée in a style copied from Lescot's original facade, and the only architectural intrusion of this era was Claude Perrault's Classical colonnade facing rue de l'Amiral de Coligny, which tragically beat Bernini's stunning Baroque design for the same contract. Napoléon III's main contributions – the courtyard facades of the nineteenth-century Richelieu and Denon wings – merely repeated the basic theme of the Cour Carrée, with typical conservatism.

The great 1980s makeover

For all its many additions and alterations, the palace remained a surprisingly harmonious building, its grandeur and symmetry soberly suited to this most historic of Parisian landmarks. Then, in 1989, I.M. Pei's controversial glass **Pyramide** erupted from the centre of the Cour Napoléon like a visitor from another architectural planet. (Just for the record, the pyramid has 673 panes of glass, not the fabled 666.) It was the centrepiece of President Mitterrand's "**Grand Louvre**" makeover, along with the basement Carrousel du Louvre shopping complex and fashion arena, the weird, downward-pointing **Pyramide Inversée** (which later found a starring role in *The Da Vinci Code*) and the dramatic glazing over of the courtyards of the Richelieu wing – out of which the Finance Ministry was ejected. The Pyramide has since found a place for itself in the hearts of even the most conservative Parisians, outstaging even Napoleon's pink marble **Arc du Carrousel**, and new restoration projects are now afoot in the courtyards of the Denon wing.

Brief history of the collections

The **Musée du Louvre** began as the personal art collection of François I, who in 1516 summoned Leonardo da Vinci from Milan. Leonardo brought his greatest works with him across the Alps, and later kings set up "cabinets" of artworks and antiquities in the Louvre, but these were all very much private collections. Artists and academics – as well as prostitutes – lived in the palace under Louis XIV, and a royal arts academy mounted exhibitions here, known as *salons*, as early as 1725. But the plan for a public museum was only conceived in the 1740s, and it wasn't until 1793, the year of Louis XVI's execution, that the gallery actually opened. Within a decade, Napoleon's wagonloads of war booty – not all of which has been returned – transformed the Louvre's art collection into the world's largest. The only major changes since then have been President Mitterrand's makeover in the 1980s, and the recent plan for a controversial "Louvre Abu Dhabi" annexe, due to open in 2012, which will borrow pictures from the main collection.

Orientation, and where to begin

The Louvre has **three named wings**, each accessible from under the great pyramid: Denon (south), Richelieu (north) and Sully (east, around the giant quadrangle of the Cour Carrée). The Louvre is arranged in themed sections: Antiquities (Near Eastern, Egyptian and Greek/Roman); Painting; Sculpture; Decorative Arts; Prints and Drawings (exhibited on a temporary, rotational basis); Islamic Art; and the Medieval Louvre. Some sections spread across two wings, or two floors of the same wing. A map, freely available from information booths under the pyramid, shows exactly what is where.

Most visitors head straight to the **Denon wing**, whose first floor contains the *Mona Lisa* and Italian paintings, plus the great French nineteenth-century canvases and the

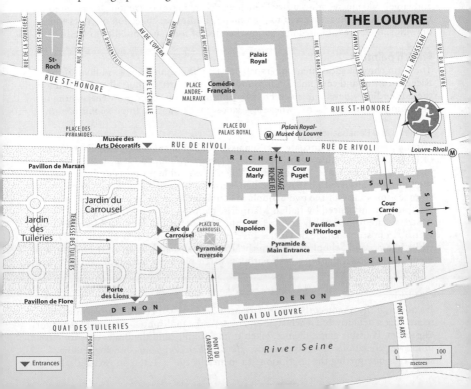

THE LOUVRE

2

HOW TO SURVIVE THE LOUVRE

Tales of queues outside the Pyramide, miles of corridors and paparazzi-style jostles in front of the *Mona Lisa* can leave you feeling somewhat intimidated by the Louvre before you've even set foot in the place. Here are three key **survival tips**.

• Don't attempt to see too much – even if you spend the entire day here you'll only see a fraction of the collection.

• Arrive early or come for the evening openings; Thursdays are also relatively quiet, though more sections than usual tend to close on this day.

• If you want to avoid the crowds, stay away from the busy Denon wing; after all, the Louvre is much more than just the Italian Renaissance and the *Mona Lisa*.

---

stunning, gilded Galerie d'Apollon; its lower floors house the sublime **Classical sculpture collection**. Denon is the busiest part of the museum, however, and a relatively peaceful alternative would be to focus on the grand chronologies of French painting and sculpture in the **Richelieu wing**, starting on the second floor. It's in Richelieu, too, that you'll find the dramatic glazed-over courtyards, and the superb Decorative Arts section (first floor). Few visitors begin with the **Sully wing**, though it's well worth seeing the foundations of Philippe-Auguste's twelfth-century fortress on the lower ground floor, and there are some rooms preserved from the original palace above (see box, p.68).

Painting

The largest section by far is **Painting**. The Richelieu side of the museum houses the main French and Northern European painting collections, while the Italian, Spanish and large-scale nineteenth-century French works are found in Denon. Interspersed throughout are rooms dedicated to the Louvre's impressive collection of **prints and drawings**; these are exhibited in rotation, because of their susceptibility to the light.

French painting

The main chronological circuit of **French painting** begins on the second floor of the Richelieu wing, and continues right round the Cour Carré in the Sully wing. It traces the extraordinary development of French painting from its edgy pre-Renaissance beginnings through to Corot, whose airy landscapes anticipate Impressionism.

Medieval and Renaissance

Surprisingly few works predate the Renaissance. There are some intriguing portraits of French kings, notably the Sienese-style *Portrait of John the Good*, Jean Fouquet's pinched-looking *Charles VII* and Jean Clouet's two noble portraits of *François I*, the king who attracted numerous Italian artists to his court. Look out for the strange atmosphere of the two **Schools of Fontainebleau** (rooms 9 and 10), which were heavily influenced by Italian Mannerist painting. Two portraits of royal mistresses are provocatively erotic: from the First School of Fontainebleau (1530s), Henri II's mistress, Diane de Poitiers, is depicted semi-nude as the huntress Diana, while in a Second School piece from the 1590s, Gabrielle d'Estrées, the favourite of Henri IV, is shown sharing a bath with her sister, pinching her nipple as if plucking a cherry.

Classicism

It's not until the seventeenth century (rooms 12–16), when Poussin breaks onto the scene, that a definitively French style emerges. As the undisputed master of **French Classicism**, Poussin's grand themes, taken from antiquity and the Bible, were to influence generations of artists to come. *The Arcadian Shepherds*, showing four shepherds interpreting the inscription "Et in arcadia ego" ("I, too, in Arcadia"), has

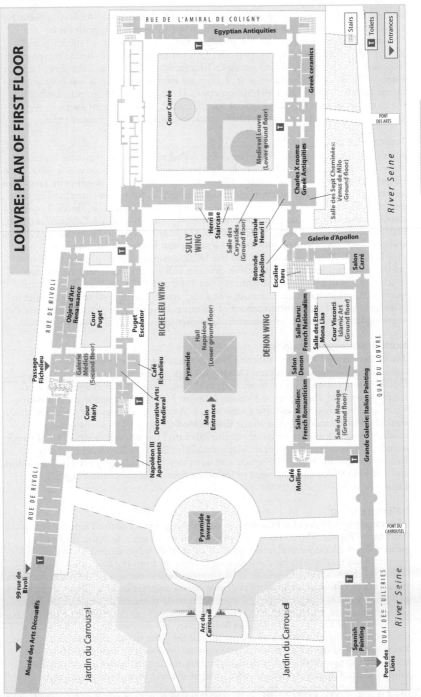

LOUVRE: PLAN OF FIRST FLOOR

RUE DE L'AMIRAL DE COLIGNY

Egyptian Antiquities

Cour Carrée

Greek ceramics

Medieval Louvre (Lower ground floor)

PONT DES ARTS

River Seine

Charles X rooms: **Greek Antiquities**

Salle des Sept Cheminées: Venus de Milo (Ground floor)

Henri II Staircase

SULLY WING

Salle des Caryatides (Ground floor)

Vestibule Henri II

Rotonde d'Apollon

Galerie d'Apollon

Escalier Daru

Salon Carré

Objets d'Art: Renaissance

RUE DE RIVOLI

Cour Puget

Salle Daru: French Nationalism

Salle des Etats: Mona Lisa

RICHELIEU WING

Puget Escalator

Passage Richelieu

Galerie Médicis (Second floor)

Café Richelieu

Hall Napoléon (Lower ground floor)

Pyramide

DENON WING

Salon Denon

Cour Visconti: Islamic Art (Ground floor)

Decorative Arts: Medieval

Cour Marly

Main Entrance

Salle Mollien: French Romanticism

Salle du Manège (Ground floor)

Grande Galerie: Italian Painting

QUAI DU LOUVRE

Napoléon III Apartments

RUE DE RIVOLI

Café Mollien

Pyramide Inversée

PONT DU CARROUSEL

Arc du Carrousel

Jardin du Carrousel

Jardin du Carrousel

QUAI DES TUILERIES

River Seine

99 rue de Rivoli

▶ Musée des Arts Décoratifs

Spanish Painting

▶ Porte des Lions

River Seine

Stairs

T Toilets

▶ Entrances

2

been taken to mean that death exists even in paradise. You'll need a healthy appetite for Classicism in the next suite of rooms, but there are some arresting portraits by Hyacinthe Rigaud, whose *Louis XIV* shows all the terrifying power of the king, and Philippe de Champaigne, whose portrait of his patron Cardinal Richelieu is even more imposing. The paintings of Georges de la Tour (rooms 28 & 29) and the three Le Nain brothers (look out for their *Denial of St Peter*, an intense work which was only acquired by the Louvre in 2010) are more idiosyncratic. De la Tour's *Card Sharp* is compelling for its uneasy poise and strange lack of depth, though his *Christ with Joseph in the Carpenter's Shop* is a more representative work, mystically lit by a single candle.

Rococo to Realist

After the Classical bombast of the likes of Le Sueur and Le Brun, the more intimate or movement-filled eighteenth-century **Rococo** paintings of Watteau come as a relief, as do Chardin's intense still lifes – notably *The Skate* – and the inspired sketches by Fragonard known as the *Figures of Fantasy*, traditionally thought to have been completed in just one hour. From the southern wing of Sully to the end of this section, the chilly wind of **Neoclassicism** blows through the post-Revolution paintings of Gros, Gérard, Prud'hon, David and Ingres, contrasting with the more sentimental style that begins with Greuze, and continues into the **Romanticism** of Géricault and Delacroix, which largely supplanted the Neoclassical style from the 1820s onwards. Ingres' glassily exquisite portraits were understandably much in demand in his day, but modern visitors are much taken with his nudes: the bathers from 1808 and 1828, and the *Turkish Bath* (room 60), a painting at once sensuous and abstracted. The final set of rooms takes in Millet, Corot and the **Barbizon School** of painting, the precursor of Impressionism. For anything later than 1848, you'll have to head over to the Musée d'Orsay (see p.142).

Northern European painting

The western end of Richelieu's second floor is given over to a relatively selective collection of **German**, **Flemish** and **Dutch** paintings, though the seventeenth-century Dutch suite is strong, with no fewer than twelve paintings by Rembrandt – look out for *Bathsheba* and *The Supper at Emmaus* in room 31 – and two serene canvases from Vermeer, *The Astronomer* and *The Lacemaker*, in room 37. An awesome set of two dozen works by Rubens can be found in the **Galerie Médicis** (room 18), a stripped-down modern replica of a room originally in the Palais du Luxembourg (see p.138). The cycle is dedicated to the glory of Queen Marie de Médicis, as commissioned by herself. Rubens painted the entire 300 square metres of canvas himself, and his swirling colours and swathes of flapping cloth were to influence French painters from Fragonard to Delacroix.

Italian painting

The staggering **Italian collection** spreads across the first floor of the Denon wing, at the head of the Escalier Daru. Things begin well with two exquisite Botticelli frescoes painted for the Villa Lemmi near Florence. Next, the high-ceilinged **Salon Carré** (room 3) was used to exhibit contemporary paintings from the first exhibition or "salon" of the Académie Royale in 1725; it now displays the so-called Primitives, with thirteenth- to fifteenth-century works from Italian painters such as Giotto, Cimabue and Fra Angelico, as well as one of Uccello's bizarrely theoretical panels of the Battle of San Romano.

To the west of the Salon, the **Grande Galerie** stretches into the distance, a ribbon of pale, perfect parquet. On its walls, it parades all the great names of the Italian Renaissance, kicking off with Mantegna's opulent *Madonna of Victory* and his meticulous miniature of the Crucifixion, and continuing through Giovanni Bellini, Filippo Lippi, Raphael, Coreggio and Titian, in the first part of the gallery alone.

Leonardo da Vinci's *Virgin of the Rocks*, *St John the Baptist* and *Virgin and Child with St Anne* are on display just after the first set of pillars, untroubled by crowds. The restored **Salle des Etats** (room 6) is the noisy, bustling setting for Leonardo da Vinci's **Mona Lisa** (see box, p.56), as well as Paolo Veronese's vast *Marriage at Cana*, which once hung in the refectory of Venice's island monastery of San Giorgio Maggiore. Sadly, there's little chance to enjoy the other Venetian works nearby in peace, but you can walk through to the twin galleries of French Nationalism and Romanticism.

2

A little further down the Grande Galerie, the Mannerists make their entrance with a wonderfully weird *St Anne with Four Saints* by Pontormo and a Rosso Fiorentino *Pietà*. From here on, the quality falls off.

Spanish painting

The relatively small **Spanish collection** is relegated to the far end of the Grande Galerie. There are a few gems, however, notably Murillo's tender *Beggar Boy*, and the *Marquise de Santa Cruz* among the Goya portraits. Zurbarán's *St Bonaventure Lying in State* splendidly betrays the artist's obsession with cloth, while it's hard not to be beguiled by De Ribera's bittersweet portrait of *The Clubfoot*, or blown away by the overwrought genius of El Greco's *Crucifixion*. From room 32, stairs lead down to the ground floor and the collection of art from Africa, Asia, Oceania and the Americas.

French Nationalism

Running parallel to the Grande Galerie are two giant rooms dedicated to post-Revolution **French Nationalism** and early to mid-nineteenth-century Romanticism. The plan labels this section "large-format French paintings", and it features some of the

---

THE LOUVRE AS PALACE: AN ALTERNATIVE GUIDE

The Louvre is more than an art gallery: it is one of the greatest of France's royal palaces. To tour its historic rooms and galleries, many of which are stunningly decorated, take the entrance marked "Sully" in the Hall Napoléon. On the lowest level of the Sully wing you can continue through to the Louvre's medieval foundations (see p.58), or take the Henri II staircase – with its intertwined monograms H and D, for Henri and his mistress, Diane de Poitiers – up to the Renaissance Salle des Caryatides (see p.57) on the ground floor.

Up again, on the first floor, there's a succession of **finely decorated rooms**: the Vestibule Henri II, where the gilded sixteenth-century ceiling is graced with George Braque's simple but stirring *The Birds* (room 33); the Salle des Sept Cheminées, once the royal bedroom (room 74); and the Rotonde d'Apollon (off room 34), built for Louis XIV by Le Vau, the architect of Versailles. Most stunning of all is the golden Galerie d'Apollon (room 66), its utterly splendid decor conceived by Charles Le Brun in 1661. It represents Louis XIV (the Sun King) as Apollo (the sun god); Eugène Delacroix added his *Apollo Slaying the Serpent Python* to the central medallion of the ceiling in 1851. It's particularly atmospheric at night. From here you can skirt the grand Escalier Daru (see p.57) to enter the Italian painting section, passing through the lofty Salon Carré (see p.52) on your way to the Grande Galerie (rooms 5, 8 and 12), which was originally built to link the Louvre and Tuileries palaces.

For **architectural gems** from the grand Third Empire remodelling, seek out the Salle du Manège on the ground floor of Denon (room A), and the Appartements Napoléon III on the first floor of Richelieu. For the lavish museum established for Charles X in the 1820s, visit the first floor of Sully (rooms 33–44); room 40, the Salle des Colonnes, has a fine mosaic floor and Neoclassical ceiling paintings of French monarchs by Antoine-Jean Gros. The highlights of I.M. Pei's 1980s makeover are the Pyramide and its strange twin, the Pyramide Inversée in the Carrousel du Louvre shopping complex; the two glazed-over courtyards of the Richelieu wing; and the magnificent escalator climbing alongside the Cour Puget. As of 2012, don't miss the Cour Visconti, either: at the time of writing a stunningly sinuous new glass roof was being installed, designed in conscious tribute to a "flying carpet" by the Franco-Milanese architectural team of Mario Bellini and Rudy Ricciotti.

best-known French works. The Salle Daru (room 75) boasts David's epic *Coronation of Napoleon I*, in which Napoleon is shown crowning himself with a rather crestfallen clergy in the background; almost unbelievably, David conceived this work as part of a much larger composition. Nearby are some fine portraits of women, including Prud'hon's Leonardo-like *Josephine in the Park at Malmaison*, and some compellingly perfect canvases by Ingres.

Romanticism

Romanticism is heralded in the Salle Mollien (room 77), by Géricault's dramatic *Raft of the Medusa*, based on a notorious incident off the coast of Senegal in 1816. The survivors are seen despairing as a ship disappears over the horizon – as a survivor described it, "from the delirium of joy we fell into profound despondency and grief". The fifteen shown here were the last of 150 shipwrecked sailors who had escaped on the raft – thirst, murder and cannibalism having carried off the rest. The dead figure lying face down with his arm extended was modelled by Delacroix, whose *Liberty Leading the People* also hangs in this room; Delacroix's work is a famous icon of revolution, though you can tell by the hats that it depicts the 1830 revolution, which brought in the "bourgeois king" Louis-Philippe, rather than that of 1789. On seeing the painting, Louis-Philippe promptly ordered it to be kept out of sight so as not to give anyone dangerous ideas.

2

Sculpture

French sculpture fills the lowest two levels of the Richelieu wing, including the twin, glass-roofed courtyards. Cour Marly shelters the four triumphal Marly Horses, which once stood in the park at Marly-le-Roi: two were done by Coysevox for Louis XIV (the ones at the top of the stairs), and two by Costou for Louis XV. Cour Puget has Pierre Puget's dynamic *Milon de Crotone* as its agonizing centrepiece, the lion's claws tearing into Milon's apparently soft flesh.

The surrounding rooms trace French sculpture from painful Romanesque Crucifixions through to the lofty nineteenth-century works of David d'Angers. Don't miss the Burgundian *Tomb of Philippe Pot*, borne by hooded mourners known as *pleurants,* Michel Colombe's Italianate relief of *St George Slaying the Dragon*, or the distinctively French and strangely liquid bas-reliefs sculpted by Jean Goujon in the 1540s, at around the same time as he was working on Lescot's facade for the Cour Carrée. Towards the end of the course, however, you may find yourself crying out for an end to all the gracefully perfect nudes and grandiose busts of noblemen. François Rude's charming *Neapolitan Fisherboy* provides some respite, but the only real antidote is Rodin – and, unfortunately, his career postdates the Louvre's self-imposed 1848 cut-off, so you'll have to visit the Musée d'Orsay (see p.142) or Musée Rodin (see p.152) to explore his work.

Italian sculpture

The small, intense **Italian sculpture** section fills the long Galerie Michel Ange (room 4), on the ground and basement floors of Denon. Here you'll find such bold masterpieces as two of Michelangelo's torturedly erotic *Slaves*, Giambologna's airy *Flying Mercury*, the anonymous *Veiled Woman* and Canova's irresistible *Cupid and Psyche*. At the gallery's western end, the grand Escalier Mollien leads up towards the main Painting section (see p.50) while, immediately below, in the old stables on the lower ground floor (room 1), you'll find early Italian sculpture, notably Duccio's virtuoso *Virgin and Child Surrounded by Angels*, and the **Tactile Gallery**, where you can run your hands over copies of some of the most important sculptures from the collection. In the small adjacent rooms A to C you can seek out some severe but impressive **Gothic Virgins** from Flanders and Germany.

2

THE MONA LISA

The **Mona Lisa** receives some six million visitors a year. Reason enough to smile, maybe, but how did a small, rather dark sixteenth-century portrait acquire such unparalleled celebrity? It can't be Leonardo da Vinci's sheer excellence, as other virtuoso works of his hang nearby, largely ignored. Nor the painting's famously seductive air – even if Napoleon was so captivated that he had the picture hung in his bedroom in the Tuileries, there are other, far sexier portraits in the Louvre. (Sadly, the nude version Leonardo apparently painted has been lost for centuries, and is known only from early copies.) Instead, the answer lies in the painting's own story.

The English title is a corruption of *Monna* ("milady") Lisa, the title of the painting's (probable) subject, **Lisa Gherardini**. She was the wife of one Francesco del Giocondo. It's from his surname that the Italians get their name for the painting, *La Gioconda*, and the French their *La Joconde*, and it may even explain the *Mona Lisa's* "smile", as *giocondo* means "light-hearted" in Italian. It is said that Lisa smiled because Leonardo employed singers and jesters to keep her happy while he painted.

The *Mona Lisa* probably came to France along with Leonardo himself, when he joined the service of François I. It remained largely neglected, however, until the mid-nineteenth century, when the poet Théophile Gautier described how the painting "mocks the viewer with such sweetness, grace and superiority that we feel timid, like schoolboys in the presence of a duchess". Then the English critic Walter Pater famously gushed that she is "expressive of what in the ways of a thousand years men had come to desire… She is older than the rocks among which she sits; like the vampire, she has been dead many times, and learned the secrets of the grave; and has been a diver in deep seas, and keeps their fallen day about her; and trafficked for strange webs with Eastern merchants … and all this has been to her but as the sound of lyres and flutes, and lives only in the delicacy with which it has moulded the changing lineaments, and tinged the eyelids and hands".

Pater made her famous, but the *Mona Lisa* only really went stellar when she was **stolen** by an Italian chancer and self-professed nationalist in August 1911. By the time the painting was recovered, in December 1913, that face had graced the pages of countless newspapers. Since then, celebrity has fed on itself, despite the complaints of art critics. Bernard Berenson, for example, decided she was "watchful, sly, secure, with a smile of anticipated satisfaction and a pervading air of hostile superiority"; Roberto Longhi called her a "wan fusspot". Still, she now faces more flashguns every day than a well-dressed starlet on Oscar night.

Visitors today are sometimes unimpressed. The painting is surprisingly small (53x76cm, or 21x30 inches, to be exact) and fogged by filth – no art restorer has yet dared to propose actually working on the picture. Eventually, time may force the museum's hand, as the thin poplar panel the image is painted on is reported to be slowly warping. The new, air-conditioned glass frame – designed, appropriately, by a Milanese firm – may help. Meanwhile, if you can struggle past the crowds, the patina of fame and the dirt of centuries, you might just discover a strange and beautiful painting. If not, try the Leonardo portrait known as *La Belle Jardinière*, in the Grande Galerie, adjacent.

Decorative Arts

The vast **Decorative Arts** section, on the first floor of the Richelieu wing, presents the finest tapestries, ceramics, jewellery and furniture commissioned by France's most wealthy and influential patrons, beginning with an exquisite little equestrian sculpture of Charlemagne (or possibly Charles the Bald) and continuing through 81 relentlessly superb rooms to a salon decorated in the style of Louis-Philippe, the last king of France. Walking through the entire chronology gives a powerful sense of the evolution of aesthetic taste at its most refined and opulent, and numerous rooms have been partially re-created in the style of a particular epoch, so it's not hard to imagine yourself strutting through a Renaissance chamber or gracing an eighteenth-century salon, especially as whole suites are often devoid of other visitors. Towards the end, the circuit passes through the breathtaking **apartments** of Napoléon III's Minister of State (room 87), full of plush upholstery, immense chandeliers and dramatic ceiling frescoes, in true Second Empire style.

Antiquities

The enormous **Antiquities** collection offers an embarrassment of riches. The superb Egyptian and Near Eastern collections reflect the long-standing French fascination with both regions, while the outstanding Greek and Roman collections date back to the eager acquisitions of François I, Richelieu and Mazarin.

Near Eastern Antiquities

Near Eastern Antiquities (Richelieu wing, ground floor) covers the Mesopotamian, Sumerian, Babylonian, Assyrian and Phoenician civilizations, plus the art of ancient Persia. The highlight is the boldly sculpted stonework, much of it in relief. Watch out for the statues and busts depicting the young Sumerian prince Gudea, and the black, 2m-high Mesopotamian Code of Hammurabi, which dates from around 1800 BC. Standing erect like a warning finger, a series of royal precepts (the "code") is crowned with a stern depiction of the king meeting the sun god Shamash, dispenser of justice. The Cour Khorsabad, adjacent, is dominated by two giant Assyrian winged bulls (one is a reproduction) that once acted as guardians to the palace of Sargon II, from which many treasures were brought to the Louvre.

Egyptian Antiquities

Jean-François Champollion, who translated the hieroglyphics of the Rosetta Stone, began collecting **Egyptian Antiquities** for France, and the collection is now second only to Cairo's. Starting on the ground floor of the Sully wing, the thematic circuit leads up from the atmospheric crypt of the Sphinx (room 1) to the Nile, source of all life in Egypt, and takes the visitor through the everyday life of pharaonic Egypt by way of cooking utensils, jewellery, the principles of hieroglyphics, musical instruments, sarcophagi and a host of mummified cats. Upstairs, on the first floor, the chronological circuit keeps the masterpieces on the right-hand side, while pots and statuettes of more specialist interest are displayed to the left. Look out for the *Great Sphinx*, carved from a single block of pink granite; the polychrome statue *Seated Scribe*; the striking, life-size wooden statue of Chancellor Nakhti; a bust of Amenophis IV; and a low-relief sculpture of Sethi I and the goddess Hathor.

Greek and Roman Antiquities

The magnificent collection of **Greek and Roman Antiquities** brings together everything from the stylized Cycladic *Woman's Head* of around 2700–2300 BC, to the finest Roman marbles. On the ground floor of Denon, the handsomely vaulted **Salle du Manège** (room A) was built as a riding school for the short-lived son of Napoléon III, but now houses Italian Renaissance copies and restorations of antique sculptures. To the east of the adjoining vestibule, the grand **Galerie Daru** (room B) kicks off with the poised energy of Lysippos's *Borghese Gladiator*. At its eastern end, the imperial **Escalier Daru** rises triumphantly under the billowing feathers of the *Winged Victory of Samothrace*. Skirt this staircase to continue into the **Etruscan and Roman** collections, with their beautiful mosaics and stunning, naturalistic frescoes.

Beyond, in the Sully wing, you enter Pierre Lescot's original sixteenth-century palace. In the **Salle des Caryatides** (room 17), which houses Roman copies of Greek works, the musicians' balcony is supported by four giant caryatids, sculpted in 1550 by Jean Goujon. Beyond, in the main Greek section of Sully, you'll find the graceful marble head known as the *Tête Kaufmann* (room 16) and the delightful *Venus of Arles* – both early copies of the work of the great sculptor Praxiteles. Up on the first floor, the gorgeous marble-and-gilt decor of rooms 32–44 dates from a museum created here for Charles X (see box, p.54). The works are primarily a daunting run of terracotta and ceramics.

Islamic Art

As of 2012, an entirely new section of the museum will be opened. Centred on the refurbished – and dramatically glazed-over (see box, p.54) – Cour Visconti, the Saudi-sponsored **Islamic Art collection** will display some two thousand objects from the Louvre's mighty collection. This section of the museum is particularly strong on ceramics and textiles, of course, but it includes everything from early Islamic inscriptions to intricate Moorish ivories, and from ninth-century Iraqi moulded glass to exquisite miniature paintings from the courts of Mughal India.

2

The Medieval Louvre

For a complete change of scene, you can always descend to the strange **Medieval Louvre** section, on the lower ground floor of Sully. The dramatic stump of Philippe-Auguste's keep soars up towards the enormous concrete ceiling like a pillar holding up the entire modern edifice, while vestiges of Charles V's medieval palace walls buttress the edges of the vast chamber. A similar but more intimate effect can be felt in the adjacent Salle St-Louis, with its carved pillars and vaults cut short by the modern roof.

Les Arts Décoratifs

Entrance at 107 rue de Rivoli, 1ᵉʳ • Tues, Wed & Fri–Sun 11am–6pm, Thurs 11am–9pm • €9 • ☎ 01 44 55 57 50, 🖥 lesartsdecoratifs.fr

The westernmost wing of the Palais du Louvre, on the north side, houses a second, entirely separate museum called, simply, **Les Arts Décoratifs**. It's an umbrella for three separate museums. The revamped **Musée des Arts Décoratifs** focuses on "the art of design" or, more prosaically, the "applied arts". Fashion and advertising are showcased in the **Musée de la Mode et du Textile** and **Musée de la Publicité**.

Musée des Arts Décoratifs

The Musée des Arts Décoratifs centres on its grand "nave" on the first floor – an original feature of the building, which dates from the 1870s. It's used for temporary exhibitions. The second floor of the museum is occupied by a quartet of themed galleries. The **toys gallery** runs from wooden soldiers and china dolls to *Star Wars* figures and (playable) computer games. **Jewellery** focuses on twentieth-century designs, notably from the Art Nouveau jeweller René Lalique. A third gallery contains paintings by the "outsider" artist **Jean Dubuffet** (1901–85), while the **Galerie d'Etudes** houses clever themed exhibitions – recent shows have included the use of animals in everything from tableware to jewellery, and the appearance of the colour red in design.

Medieval to Renaissance

At the museum's heart is the grand chronology of French furnishings, which begins on the third floor, with the rooms dedicated to furnishings and tapestries of the **Middle Ages** and **Renaissance**. The highlight is a reconstruction of a late fifteenth-century bedchamber, complete with original wall panelling, canopied bed, chairs and benches – even the door, fireplace and windows date from the period. The rooms covering the **seventeenth, eighteenth** and **nineteenth centuries** may represent the glory years of French furniture design, but the endless gilt cabinets, commodes and consoles can get a little wearisome. Look, again, for the reconstructed rooms. One shows off panelling installed in the Hôtel de Verrûe in the 1720s, when the fashion for *singeries*, or frescoes themed around monkeys dressed in human clothing, was in full swing. Another, found on the terrace level overlooking the nave, is a reconstruction of the splendid panelling from the aptly named "golden study" of the Hôtel de Rochegude, at Avignon.

Art Nouveau to Philippe Starck

In the first decades of the twentieth century, French designers shaped the tastes of the world, and in this section of the museum (first, third and fourth floors, at the far end of the nave) it's easy to see why. There's a complete 1903 bedroom by Hector Guimard – the Art Nouveau designer behind the original Paris métro stations. Representing the Art Deco era, there's a 1925 study by Pierre Chareau, and an entire apartment created in the early 1920s by Armand-Albert Rateau for the *couturière* Jeanne Lanvin. Down on the first floor, don't miss the **Salon des Boiseries**, which shows off the best in French wood-panelling, and the **Salon du Bois**, a huge drawing room made for the 1900 Universal Exhibition by Georges Hoentschel.

The final part of the chronology takes you through a suite of interlinked rooms stacked inside the lofty **Pavillon Marsan** (with stunning views down the rue de Rivoli and over the Tuileries). You begin on the ninth floor with the 1940s, and end many, many designer chairs later on the fifth floor, with the contemporary collections. On the sixth floor, you'll find the original carriage design for the TGV high-speed train, and various podiums devoted to individual designers of the 1980s and 90s. **Philippe Starck**, for instance, is represented by five hyper-cool chairs, a stool, a mirror and a lampshade.

Musée de la Mode and Musée de la Publicité

The eastern half of the museum, to the left of the main entrance, puts on exhibitions dedicated to fashion and advertising. These can be among the city's most innovative, as most shows are curated by industry professionals rather than state museum administrators. On the first and second floors, the **Musée de la Mode et du Textile** holds high-quality temporary exhibitions drawn from the large permanent collection. Recent shows have included a grand retrospective of the 1990s and a personal "history of fashion" curated by Christian Lacroix. On the third floor, directly above, the **Musée de la Publicité** shows off its collection of advertising posters and video through cleverly themed, temporary exhibitions, such as one on Henri de Toulouse-Lautrec's posters of Montmartre nightlife. The space is appropriately trendy – exposed brickwork and steel panelling meets crumbling Louvre finery – and you can access the digital archive too.

ARC DE TRIOMPHE

The Champs-Elysées and around

Synonymous with glitz and glamour, the Champs-Elysées sweeps through one of the city's most exclusive districts, studded with luxury hotels and top fashion boutiques. The avenue in turn forms part of a grand 9km axis, extending from the Louvre at the heart of the city to the business district of La Défense in the west. With impressive vistas along its length, this axis, sometimes referred to as the Voie Triomphale (Triumphal Way), incorporates some of the city's most famous landmarks – the place de la Concorde, Tuileries gardens and the Arc de Triomphe. The whole ensemble is so regular and geometrical it looks as if it were laid out by a single town-planner rather than successive kings, emperors and presidents, all keen to add their stamp and promote French power and prestige.

Last to join the list was President Mitterrand (whose *grands projets* for the city outdid even Napoleon's) – his glass pyramid entrance to the Louvre (see Chapter 2) and immense marble-clad cubic arch at La Défense (see p.220) effectively mark each end of the historic axis. The two great constructions echo each other in scale and geometry, with both aligned at the same slight angle away from the axis – a detail that, given the distance involved, has to be appreciated conceptually rather than visually.

The Arc de Triomphe

Daily: April–Sept 10am–11pm; Oct–March 10am–10.30pm • €9 • ⓂCharles-de-Gaulle-Etoile

The **Arc de Triomphe** towers up in the middle of place Charles-de-Gaulle, better known as place de l'Etoile, essentially a giant roundabout. The arch is modelled on the ancient Roman triumphal arches and is impressive in scale, memorably likened by Guy de Maupassant in his novel *Bel Ami* to "a shapeless giant on two monstrously large legs, that looks as if it's about to stride off down the Champs-Elysées". The arch was begun by Napoleon in 1806 in homage to his Grande Armée, but only completed in 1836 by Louis Philippe, who dedicated it to the French army in general. Later, victorious German armies would make a point of marching through the arch to compound French humiliation. After the Prussians' triumphal march in 1871, Parisians lit bonfires beneath the arch and down the Champs-Elysées to eradicate the "stain" of German boots. Still a potent symbol of the country's military might, the arch is the starting point for the annual Bastille Day procession, a bombastic march-past of tanks, guns and flags.

The tomb of an unknown soldier

A poignant ceremony is conducted every evening at 6.30pm at the foot of the Arc de Triomphe, when war veterans stoke up the flame at the **tomb of an unknown soldier**, killed in the Great War. Not even the Nazi occupation of Paris on June 14, 1940, could interrupt this sacred act. At 6.30pm that day, German troops gathering around the Arc de Triomphe were astonished to see two elderly French soldiers marching towards them in full dress uniform. The Germans instinctively stood to attention while Edmond Ferrand, the guardian of the Eternal Flame, and André Gaudin, a member of the flame's committee, solemnly saluted it; the Germans, somewhat disconcerted, apparently followed suit.

Visiting the arch

Access to the arch is via underground stairs on the north corner of the Champs-Elysées. The names of 660 generals and numerous French battles are engraved on its inside, while reliefs adorn the exterior; the best is François Rude's extraordinarily dramatic *Marseillaise*, in which an Amazon-type figure personifying the Revolution charges forward with a sword, her face contorted in a fierce rallying cry. If you're up for climbing the 280 steps to the top, you'll be amply rewarded with panoramic views, at their best towards dusk on a sunny day when the marble of the Grande Arche de la Défense sparkles in the setting sun and the Louvre is bathed in warm light.

The mini-museum at the top of the arch has recently undergone a revamp; dusty glass display cases have been replaced by video screens showing the arch's history, including extraordinary images of Victor Hugo's funeral in 1885, when over half the population of Paris turned out to pay their respects to the poet, his coffin mounted on a huge bier beneath the arch, draped in black velvet for the occasion.

The Champs-Elysées

Twelve avenues radiate out from place de l'Etoile (*étoile* meaning "star"), of which the best known is the **Champs-Elysées** ("Elysian Fields"). Tree-lined and broad, it sweeps down from the Arc de Triomphe towards the place de la Concorde. Close up it can be a little disappointing, with its constant stream of traffic, fast-food outlets and chain stores, though over the last decade or so it has begun to regain something of its former cachet. The avenue's renaissance started with a facelift in the mid-1990s, when the rows of trees the Nazis removed during World War II were replanted and pavements were repaved. A number of exclusive designers subsequently moved in, luxury hotels appeared and formerly dowdy shops underwent stylish makeovers. Major fashion brands are now queuing up for a toe-hold on the Champs, with recent arrivals including Banana Republic and H&M (though only after a long battle with Paris city council, who were worried that cheap fashion stores were lowering the tone of the avenue). The southern side of the Champs, where Louis Vuitton, Lanvin and the like flaunt their wares, is more sought after than the northern side.

THE CHAMPS-ELYSEES & AROUND

● SHOPS
Le 66	17
Arturial	19
Les Caves Augé	4
Caviar Kaspia	8
Comme des Garçons	10
Fnac	15
Fromagerie Alléosse	5
Hédiard	6/20
Hermès	12
IGN	14
Lanvin	13
Maison de la Truffe	7
Au Nain Bleu	9
Le Pot à Tabac	2
Séphora	16
Trousselier	1
La Vaissellerie	1
Virgin Megastore	18
YSL	11

● CAFÉS & WINE BARS
Le Café Jacquemart-André	1
Le Dada	2
Le Fouquet's	5

● RESTAURANTS
Al Ajami	8
Lasserre	10
Mini Palais	9
La Maison de l'Aubrac	6
La Maison Blanche	13
Pierre Gagnaire	4
Plaza-Athénée	12
Le Relais de l'Entrecôte	11
Spoon	7
Taillevent	3

● BARS & CLUBS
Flûte L'Etoile	1
Pershing Lounge	4
Showcase	5
Sir Winston	3

● GAY CLUB
Queen	2

Brief history

The Champs-Elysées began life as a leafy promenade, an extension of the Tuileries gardens. It became fashionable during the Second Empire when members of the *haute bourgeoisie* built splendid mansions along its length and high society came to stroll and frequent the cafés and theatres. Most of the mansions finally gave way to office blocks and the beau monde moved elsewhere, but remnants of the avenue's glitzy heyday live on at the *Lido* cabaret, *Fouquet's* café-restaurant (see p.270), the perfumer Guerlain's shop, occupying an exquisite 1913 building, and the former *Claridges* hotel, now a swanky shopping arcade. One of the most opulent of the mid-nineteenth-century mansions also survives: the swanky *La Païva* restaurant and bar at no. 25 was once the residence of the

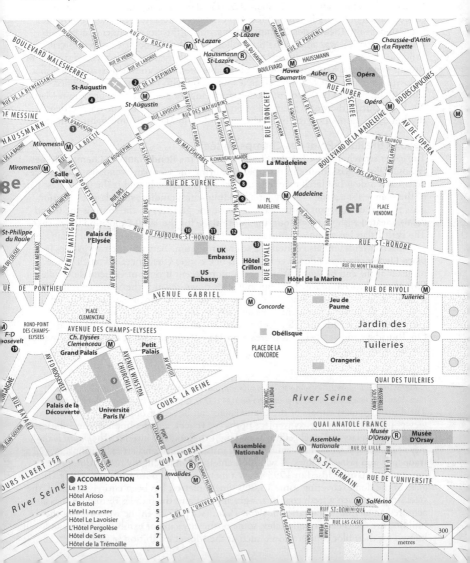

● ACCOMMODATION	
Le 123	4
Hôtel Arioso	1
Le Bristol	3
Hôtel Lancaster	5
Hôtel Le Lavoisier	2
L'Hôtel Pergolèse	6
Hôtel de Sers	7
Hôtel de la Trémoille	8

famous courtesan, La Païva, whose bathroom alone, it is said, was worthy of a Sultana in the *Arabian Nights*.

The Champs-Elysées occupies an important place in the national psyche and is a rallying point at times of crisis and celebration; crowds thronged here to greet Général de Gaulle as he walked down the avenue just after the Liberation in May 1944 and many turned out to support him again in 1968 in the wake of the student riots, while thousands congregated here in 1998 to party after France won the World Cup.

Théâtre des Champs-Elysées

Av Montaigne Ⓜ Alma-Marceau

The area bounded by the Champs-Elysées and, to the south, avenue Montaigne and rue Francois 1er, is nicknamed the **Triangle d'Or** (Golden Triangle) on account of its high concentration of luxury hotels and flagship designer stores. At the bottom of avenue Montaigne is the **Théâtre des Champs-Elysées**, one of the city's premier concert halls. Erected in 1913, it was among the first buildings in Paris to be made of reinforced concrete, its exterior softened with marble reliefs by the sculptor Bourdelle, a student of Rodin. The theatre has seen a number of notable premieres and debuts, including that of Josephine Baker in 1925, who created a sensation with her sensual, abandoned dancing. It's perhaps best known, though, for being the scene of great uproar on May 29, 1913, during the world premiere of Stravinsky's *Rite of Spring*, the unprecedented rhythmic and harmonic ferocity of which provoked loud catcalls and fights in the stalls.

Beyond the Rond-Point des Champs-Elysées

The lower stretch of the Champs-Elysées between the **Rond-Point des Champs-Elysées** (whose Lalique glass fountains disappeared during the German occupation) and place de la Concorde is bordered by chestnut trees and flowerbeds, and is the pleasantest part of the avenue for a stroll. The gigantic building with grandiose Neoclassical exterior, glass roofs and exuberant statuary rising above the greenery to the south is the **Grand Palais**, created with its neighbour, the **Petit Palais**, for the 1900 **Exposition Universelle**. The Petit Palais has a fine arts museum, while the Grand Palais hosts major exhibitions and special events and also contains a science museum. Between the two palaces lies **place Clemenceau**, presided over by statues of Georges Clemenceau, French prime minister at the end of World War I, and a more recent bronze of Général de Gaulle. From here, the **avenue Winston Churchill** leads down towards the Seine, culminating with a statue of the man himself. To the north of place Clemenceau, police guard the high walls around the presidential **Palais de l'Elysée** and the line of ministries and embassies ending with the US in prime position on the corner of place de la Concorde. On Thursdays and at weekends there's a **postage-stamp market** at the corner of avenues Gabriel and Marigny.

The Grand Palais

Av Winston Churchill, 8ᵉ • Galeries Nationales entry at 3 av du Général-Eisenhower • Mon, Thurs, Sat & Sun 10am–8pm, Wed & Fri 10am–10pm • €11, though some exhibitions can cost extra • ☎ 01 44 13 17 17, ⓦ grandpalais.fr • Ⓜ Champs-Elysées-Clemenceau

The 45m-high glass cupola of the **Grand Palais** can be seen from most of the city's viewpoints and forms the centrepiece of the *nef* (nave), a huge, impressive exhibition space, whose glass and steel ceiling allows light to flood the interior. The *palais* is the city's premier special-events venue, hosting music festivals and art exhibitions, as well as trade fairs and fashion shows. It will soon emerge from a lengthy restoration project, having been hastily closed in 1993 when a metal rivet fell 35m from the ceiling. The glass of the dome, covering some 15,000 square metres, has been entirely replaced, the steel supports given a fresh coat of sea-green paint and the facades restored. It has also acquired an elegant restaurant, the *Mini Palais* (see p.272). In the west wing of the building are the **Galeries Nationales**, some of the city's major exhibition spaces and well known for their blockbuster shows, such as the Monet exhibition in 2010/11.

The Palais de la Découverte

Av Franklin D. Roosevelt, 8ᵉ • Tues–Sat 9.30am–6pm, Sun 10am–7pm • €7, combined ticket with planetarium €10.50 • ☎ 01 56 43 20 20, ⓦ palais-decouverte.fr • ⓂChamps-Elysées-Clemenceau/Franklin-D.-Roosevelt

The Grand Palais' eastern wing houses the **Palais de la Découverte**, Paris's original science museum, dating from 1937. It covers physics, biology, chemistry, geography, mathematics and astronomy. The museum's emphasis is, as the name suggests, very much on discovery and experiment; there are plenty of interactive exhibits and working models to help you discover the properties of electro-magnets, for example, or find out how ants and spiders communicate, and around forty live experiments are conducted throughout the day. In addition, there are engaging temporary exhibitions on subjects as diverse as dinosaurs, clay and climate change, as well as an excellent **planetarium**.

The Petit Palais

Av Winston Churchill, 8ᵉ • Tues–Sun 10am–6pm • Free • ☎ 01 53 43 40 00, ⓦ petitpalais.paris.fr • ⓂChamps-Elysées-Clemenceau

The **Petit Palais**, facing the Grand Palais on avenue Winston Churchill, holds the **Musée des Beaux Arts de la Ville de Paris**. It's hardly "petit", but it's certainly palatial, with its highly decorated Neoclassical exterior, interior garden with Tuscan colonnade, beautiful spiral wrought-iron staircases and a grand gallery on the lines of Versailles' Hall of Mirrors. The museum's extensive holdings of paintings, sculpture and decorative artworks are displayed on two floors and range from the ancient Greek and Roman period up to the early twentieth century. At first sight it looks like it's mopped up the leftovers after the city's other galleries have taken their pick, but there are some real gems here, such as Monet's *Soleil couchant sur la Seine à Lavacourt,* Courbet's provocative *Demoiselles du bord de la Seine* and Pissarro's delicate *Le Pont Royal et le Pavillon de Flore,* painted a few months before he died. Decorative arts feature strongly, especially eighteenth-century furniture and porcelain, including a whimsical clock decorated with a monkey orchestra in Meissen china. There's also fantasy Art Nouveau jewellery, an elegant pear-wood dining room designed by Hector Guimard (who also designed the original Paris métro stations), Russian icons and a fine collection of seventeenth-century Dutch landscape painting. Changing exhibitions allow the museum to display works from its vast reserves. If your own reserves are running low you could head for the smart café, which opens out onto the restored interior garden. Popular classical music **concerts** (12.30pm; free; arrive 30min beforehand to pick up a ticket) are held in the gallery on Thursday lunchtimes.

North of the Arc de Triomphe and Champs-Elysées

North of the Arc de Triomphe, the 16ᵉ and 17ᵉ arrondissements are largely cold and soulless, their huge fortified apartments empty much of the time while their owners – royal, exiled royal, ex-royal or just extremely rich – jet between their other residences dotted about the globe. The 8ᵉ arrondissement, north of the Champs-Elysées, however, has more to offer, with some of the *hôtels particuliers* (mansions) housing select museums – the **Musée Cernuschi**, the **Musée Nissim de Camondo**, and, most magnificent of all, the **Musée Jacquemart-André**.

Avenue de Wagram

The best avenue to start wandering down from place de l'Etoile – apart from the Champs-Elysées – is the northerly **avenue de Wagram**. Art Nouveau devotees can stop at no. 34 and contemplate Jules Lavirotte's 1904 facade, which shocked the Académie des Beaux Arts with its swirly lines and brightly painted ceramics (now rather faded). A little further on you come to the flower market and cafés of **place des Ternes**, the first big junction on avenue de Wagram. From here you could make a short detour down avenue des Ternes to savour the sights and aromas of the little **rue Poncelet street market**, the first turning on the right. Alongside the butchers, grocers and fishmongers' stalls are some very fine food shops, such as Alléosse at no. 13 (see p.333), arguably the best cheesemonger in Paris.

Cathédrale Alexandre-Nevsky
12 rue Daru, 8ᵉ • Tues & Fri 3–5pm, Sun 10am–12.30pm & 3–6pm • Free • ⓂCourcelles

From place des Ternes, you can head southeast down rue du Faubourg-St-Honoré and take the second left (rue Daru) to admire the five gold onion domes of the Russian Orthodox **Cathédrale Alexandre-Nevsky**, witness to Picasso's marriage to Olga Khokhlova in 1918 (they lived for a while at 29 rue de la Boétie, a few blocks southeast).

Parc Monceau
ⓂMonceau

Turning right from rue Daru onto rue de Courcelles brings you to the enormous gilded gates of the avenue Hoche entrance to **Parc Monceau**, an informal English-style garden with undulating lawns, rock gardens, moss-grown mock-Classical columns and statues of brooding, romantic French poets.

Musée Cernuschi
7 av Velásquez, 8ᵉ • Tues–Sun 10am–6pm • Free • ☎ 01 53 96 21 50 • ⓂMonceau/Villiers

The **Musée Cernuschi** houses a small collection of Far Eastern art, mainly ancient Chinese, bequeathed to the state by the banker Cernuschi, who nearly lost his life for giving money to the insurrectionary Commune of 1871. Cernuschi's elegant mansion is the setting for the museum. A grand staircase takes you up to the permanent collection on the first floor, where there are some exquisite pieces, including a selection of ceremonial jade objects dating from 3000 BC, highly worked bronzes from the Shang era (1550–1005 BC), and some unique ceramics detailing everyday life in ancient China. On the mezzanine, among a collection of Buddhas and other statuary, a beautiful, sinuous figure playing a lute, dating from the Wei dynasty, stands out.

Musée Nissim de Camondo
63 rue de Monceau, 8ᵉ • Wed–Sun 10am–5.30pm • €7 • ☎ 01 45 63 26 32 • ⓂMonceau/Villiers

Beside the Musée Cernuschi is the **Musée Nissim de Camondo**, with an impressive collection of eighteenth-century decorative art and painting, built up by Count Moïse de Camondo, son of a wealthy Sephardic Jewish banker who emigrated from Istanbul to Paris in the late nineteenth century. To provide a fitting showcase for his treasures, the count commissioned a mansion in eighteenth-century style, modelled on the Petit Trianon at Versailles.

The ground-floor rooms overflow with Gobelin tapestries, paintings of pastoral scenes by Huet and Vigée-Lebrun, gilded furniture and delicate Sèvres porcelain; an excellent free audioguide helps you get the most out of the exhibits. The upper-floor rooms, where the family spent most of their time, are homelier; here and there some of the anachronistic mod-cons of an early twentieth-century aristocratic home surface, such as the count's well-appointed bathroom. These rooms take on a progressively melancholy air, however, as you learn more about the Camondos and their fate: after a few years of marriage Moïse's wife left him for the head groom; his beloved son, Nissim, after whom the museum is named, died on a flying mission in World War I, while his remaining child, Béatrice, perished together with her children in the camps in World War II.

Musée Jacquemart-André
158 bd Haussmann, 8ᵉ • Daily 10am–6pm • €10 • ☎ 01 45 62 11 59, ⓦ musee-jacquemart-andre.com • ⓂMiromesnil/St-Philippe-du-Roule

A few blocks south of the Parc de Monceau stands the lavishly ornamented palace of the nineteenth-century banker and art-lover Edouard André and his wife, society portraitist Nélie Jacquemart. Built in 1870 to grace Baron Haussmann's grand new boulevard, the Hôtel André is now the **Musée Jacquemart-André**, housing the couple's impressive art collection and a fabulous *salon de thé* (see p.270). Bequeathed to the Institut de France by Edouard's widow, the Hôtel André deploys the couple's collection exactly as they ordained. Nélie painted Edouard's portrait in 1872 – on display in what were their private apartments on the ground floor – and nine years later they were married, after which Nélie gave up her painting career and the pair devoted their spare time to collecting art, travelling around Europe for six months of the year searching for pieces. Their preference for **Italian art** is evident in the stunning collection of fifteenth- and sixteenth-century genius, including the works of Tiepolo, Botticelli, Donatello, Mantegna and Uccello, which form the core of the collection. Almost as compelling as the interior and art collection is the insight gleaned into an extraordinary marriage and grand nineteenth-century lifestyle, brought to life by the fascinating narration on the free audioguide.

French and Dutch painting

In Room 1, mostly eighteenth-century French paintings are displayed, including several portraits by **Boucher**, in addition to two lively paintings of Venice by Canaletto. Room 2, the reception area, has specially constructed folding doors which, when opened, transformed the space into a ballroom large enough to contain a thousand guests. Room 3 contains three huge tapestries depicting Russian scenes that capture the fashion for Slav exoticism of the mid-eighteenth century. Room 6, formerly the library, focuses on Dutch and Flemish paintings, including three by **Van Dyck** and two by **Rembrandt**. Room 7 is the Salon de Musique (and the other half of the ballroom), whose dramatic high ceiling is decorated with a mural by Pierre Victor Galant; the musicians would play from the gallery, and you're treated to a mini-concert on the audioguide as you gaze at the ceiling. In Room 8, a huge, animated fresco by **Tiepolo**, depicting the French king Henri III being received by Federico Contarini in Venice, graces the extraordinary marble, bronze and wrought-iron double spiral staircase that leads from an interior garden of palm trees up to the musicians' gallery. Room 9, once the smoking room, where the men would retreat after dinner, is hung with the work of eighteenth-century English portraitists, among them **Joshua Reynolds**.

Italian Renaissance paintings

Leading off the music gallery are the rooms in which the couple displayed their **early Renaissance Italian collection**. The first was intended as Nélie's studio, but she instead decorated it as a sculpture gallery – including three bronzes by **Donatello** – its walls covered in low-relief sculpture. The dimly lit Florentine room next door includes a wonderful, brightly coloured *Saint George Slaying the Dragon* (1440) by **Paolo Uccello**, a **Botticelli** *Virgin and Child* (1470) depicted with touching beauty and fragility, and an exquisite sixteenth-century inlaid choir-stall. Adjacent is the Venetian room, with paintings by **Bellini** and **Mantegna** among others.

Place de la Concorde

ⓂConcorde

At the eastern end of the Champs-Elysées lies the grand, pleasingly harmonious **place de la Concorde**, marred only by its constant stream of traffic. Its centrepiece is a gold-tipped obelisk from the temple of Ramses at Luxor, given by Mohammed Ali to Louis-Philippe in 1831, and flanked by two ornate bronze fountains, modelled on those in St Peter's Square, Rome. The square's history is much less harmonious than its name "Concorde" suggests. The equestrian statue of Louis XV that formerly stood at the centre of the square was toppled in 1792, and between 1793 and 1795, 1300 people died here beneath the Revolutionary guillotine, including Louis XVI, Marie-Antoinette, Danton and Robespierre. When deciding later what to put in place of

Louis XV's statue, Louis-Philippe thought the obelisk would be ideal – having no political message, it wasn't likely ever to be demolished or become the focus of popular discontent. It was erected with much pomp in October 1836 in the presence of 200,000 spectators, while an orchestra played tunes from Bellini's *I Puritani*.

From the centre of the square there are magnificent views of the Champs-Elysées and Tuileries, and you can admire the symmetry of the Assemblée Nationale, on the far side of the Seine, with the church of the Madeleine at the end of rue Royale, to the north. The Neoclassical luxury *Hôtel Crillon* and its twin, the Hôtel de la Marine, housing the Ministry of the Navy, flank the entrance to rue Royale, which, naturally, meets the Champs-Elysées at a precise right angle.

The Tuileries gardens

Extending for around 1km from the place de la Concorde to the Louvre, the **Jardin des Tuileries** is the formal French garden *par excellence*. The grand central alley is lined with clipped chestnuts and manicured lawns, and framed by ornamental ponds. Surrounding these is an impressive gallery of statues (by the likes of Rodin, Coustou and Coysevox), many brought here from Versailles and Marly (Louis XIV's retreat from Versailles, no longer in existence), though a number are copies, with the originals in the Louvre. The much-sought-after chairs strewn around the ponds are good spots from which to admire the surroundings and there are also a number of cafés nestling among the trees.

THE LOST PALAIS DES TUILERIES

For much of its life, the Louvre stood facing a twin sister some 500m to the west, the **Palais des Tuileries**. Built in 1559 for **Catherine de Médicis** shortly after the accidental death of her husband, Henri II, it was a place where she could maintain her political independence while wielding power on behalf of her sickly son, François II. It was apparently Catherine herself who conceived the idea of linking the two palaces with a *grande galerie* running along the right bank of the Seine, but in 1572 she abandoned the entire project. Tradition has it that she was warned by a soothsayer to "beware of St-Germain" if she wanted to live into old age – the Tuileries lay in the parish of St-Germain l'Auxerrois. It's more likely that the palace's situation just outside the protection of the city walls was the problem, as 1572 was a dangerous year: on August 24, the bells of St-Germain l'Auxerrois rang out according to a pre-arranged signal, whereupon radical Catholics set about the murder of some three thousand Parisian Protestants, possibly under the secret orders of Catherine herself.

It wasn't until forty years after the St Bartholomew's Day Massacre that the two palaces were finally linked, in the reign of Henri IV. Louis XIV moved across from the Louvre in 1667, but the court soon departed for Versailles, and the Tuileries remained largely empty until the Revolution, when Louis XVI was kept under virtual house arrest there by the revolutionary mob until the *sans-culottes* finally lost patience on June 20, 1792, breaking in and forcing the king to don the revolutionary red bonnet. The Tuileries was revived under Napoleon, who built the **Arc du Carrousel** facing its central pavilion, and its status grew still greater under his nephew, Napoléon III, who finally enclosed both royal palaces around a single gigantic courtyard, the whole complex being dubbed the Cité Impériale. This glorious perfection didn't last long: the Tuileries was set alight by the revolutionary Communards as they lost control of the city in May 1871 (see p.371).

The ruins of the Tuileries were cleared away for the gardens that now bear the illustrious name. A recent campaign to rebuild the Tuileries palace attracted frenzied press attention, but drew a negative response from the Ministry of Culture in 2008. It wasn't just the estimated €350 million cost that was the problem, nor rebuilding a sixteenth-century palace to a high enough standard, nor how such a building would "traumatize" the architectural setting which has been created in the last hundred years, blocking off the grand axis which extends all the way from the Pyramide to La Défense. The true problem was undoubtedly the political awkwardness of resurrecting such a powerful royalist symbol.

Flanking the garden at the western Concorde end, are two Neoclassical buildings, the **Orangerie** art gallery, by the river, and the **Jeu de Paume**, the city's premier photographic exhibition space, by the rue de Rivoli. At the eastern end of the gardens in front of the Louvre is the **Jardin du Carrousel**, a raised terrace where the Palais des Tuileries, burnt down by the Communards in 1871, was sited. It's now planted with yew hedges, interspersed with oddly static bronzes of buxom female nudes by Maillol.

Brief history

The garden originated in the 1570s when **Catherine de Médicis** had the site cleared of the medieval warren of tile manufacturers (*tuileries*) that stood here to make way for a palace and grounds (see box opposite). The Palais des Tuileries, as it became known, was surrounded by formal vegetable gardens, a labyrinth and a chequerboard of flowerbeds. The present layout, however, is largely the work of the landscape architect Le Nôtre, who was commissioned by Louis XIV a hundred years later to redesign the gardens on a grander scale. Employing techniques he later perfected at Versailles, **Le Nôtre** took the opportunity to indulge his passion for symmetry, straight avenues, formal flowerbeds and splendid vistas. During the eighteenth century, the gardens were where chic Parisians came to preen and party, and in 1783 the Montgolfier brothers, Joseph and Etienne, launched the first successful hot-air balloon here. Serious replanting was carried out after the Revolution, and in the nineteenth century rare species were added to the garden, by now dominated by chestnut trees.

3

The Jeu de Paume

1 place de la Concorde, 1er • Tues noon–9pm, Wed–Fri noon–7pm, Sat & Sun 10am–7pm • €8.50 • ☎ 01 47 03 12 50, Ⓦ jeudepaume .org • Ⓜ Concorde

The **Jeu de Paume** was once a royal tennis court and the place where French Impressionist paintings were displayed before being transferred to the Musée d'Orsay. Since 2004 it's been a major exhibition space dedicated to photography and video art, with a sister site at the Hôtel de Sully (see p.94). It's not as well lit as you might expect from the soaring, light-filled foyer, but it's one of the top venues for major retrospectives of photographers such as Martin Parr and Edward Steichen. There's also a small café and a good bookshop.

The Orangerie

Jardin des Tuileries, 1er • Daily except Tues 9am–6pm • €7.50 • ☎ 01 44 77 80 07, Ⓦ www.musee-orangerie.fr • Ⓜ Concorde

Opposite the Jeu de Paume is the **Orangerie**, an elegant Neoclassical-style building, originally designed to protect the Tuileries' orange trees, and now housing a private art collection including eight of **Monet**'s giant water lily paintings. It reopened in 2006 after a six-year renovation designed to bring Monet's masterpieces "back into the light": once again the natural light illumines the water lilies – exactly how Monet wished them to be seen. Displayed in two oval rooms, these vast canvases were executed in the last years of the artist's life, when he almost obsessively painted the pond in his garden at Giverny, attempting to capture the fleeting light and changing colours.

On the lower floor is a rather fine collection of paintings by Monet's contemporaries. Highlights include some **Cézanne** still lifes, portraits and landscapes, including *Le Rocher Rouge*, in which the intense colours seem to vibrate and shimmer. **Renoir** is represented by some sensuous nudes and touching studies of children, such as *Jeunes filles au piano*, the two girls' rapt concentration on the music wonderfully conveyed. There are fine works by **Picasso** and **Matisse**; the latter's *Les Trois Soeurs* stands out for its striking portrayal of three women, the simplicity of line and colour reminiscent of a Japanese print. Space is also devoted to works by **Derain**, including some iridescent nudes and vibrant landscapes, and **Soutine**'s more expressionistic canvases.

The Grands Boulevards and *passages*

Built on the site of the city's old ramparts, the Grands Boulevards stretch
from the Madeleine in the west to the Bastille in the east. Once fashionable
thoroughfares where "le tout Paris" came to seek entertainment, they're
still a vibrant part of the city, with their brasseries, theatres and cinemas.
The streets off the Grands Boulevards constitute the city's main commercial
and financial district, incorporating the solid institutions of the Banque de
France and the Bourse, while to the northwest is the glittering Opéra Garnier.
Well-heeled shopping is concentrated on rue St-Honoré and around place
Vendôme, and to the south, the Palais Royal gardens provide a retreat from
the traffic. Threading their way throughout the district are the *passages*
– delightful shopping arcades, full of old-fashioned charm.

The Grands Boulevards

The **Grands Boulevards** is the collective name given to the eight streets that form one continuous thoroughfare running from the Madeleine to République, then down to the Bastille. Lined with classic nineteenth-century apartment blocks, imposing banks, cinemas, theatres, brasseries and neon-lit fast-food outlets, the Grands Boulevards are busy and vibrant, if not the most alluring or fashionable parts of Paris – though this was not always so. As recently as the 1950s, a visitor to Paris would, as a matter of course, have gone for a stroll along the Grands Boulevards to see "*Paris vivant*". Something of this tradition still survives in the theatres, cinemas – including the Max Linder and Rex, the latter an extraordinary building inside and out (see p.309) – brasseries and cafés.

Brief history

The **western section** of the Grands Boulevards, from the Madeleine to Porte St-Denis, follows the rampart built by Charles V in the mid-fourteenth century. When its defensive purpose became redundant with the offensive foreign policy of Louis XIV in the seventeenth century, the walls were pulled down and the ditches filled in, leaving a wide promenade. However, it wasn't until the nineteenth century that the boulevards became a fashionable place to be seen; Parisians came in droves to stroll and frequent the numerous cafés. The chic café clientele of the west-end **boulevard des Italiens** set the trends for all of Paris in terms of manners, dress and conversation, and there was much intellectual debate and ferment.

The **eastern section** developed a more colourful reputation, derived from its association with street theatre, mime, juggling, puppets, waxworks and cafés of ill repute, earning itself the nickname the *boulevard du Crime*, immortalized in the film *Les Enfants du Paradis*. Much of this area was swept away in the latter half of the nineteenth century by Baron Haussmann's huge place de la République.

It was at 14 **boulevard des Capucines**, in 1895, that Paris saw its first film, or animated photography, as the Lumière brothers' invention was called. Some years earlier, in 1874, another artistic revolution had taken place at no. 35 in the former studio of photographer Félix Nadar – the first **Impressionist exhibition**, greeted with outrage by the art world; one critic said of Monet's *Impression, soleil levant* ("Impression: sunrise"), "it was worse than anyone had hitherto dared to paint".

Musée Grévin

10 bd Montmartre, 9ᵉ • Mon–Fri 10am–6.30pm, Sat & Sun 10am–7pm; last admission an hour before closing • €21, children €13 • ☎ 01 47 70 85 05, ⓦ grevin.com • Ⓜ Grands Boulevards

A remnant from the fun-loving times on the Grands Boulevards is the waxworks museum, the **Musée Grévin**. You can have your photo taken next to Isabelle Adjani, Zinedine Zidane and many other French and international celebrities, but perhaps the best thing about the museum is its rooms: the recently restored, magical Palais des Mirages (Hall of Mirrors), built for the Exposition Universelle in 1900; the theatre with its sculptures by Bourdelle; and the 1882 Baroque-style Hall of Columns.

The Opéra Garnier

Cnr rues Scribe and Auber, 9ᵉ • ⓦ operadeparis.fr • Ⓜ Opéra

Set back from boulevard des Capucines is the dazzling Opéra de Paris – usually referred to as the **Opéra Garnier** to distinguish it from the newer opera house at the Bastille. Constructed between 1865 and 1872 as part of Napoléon III's vision for Paris, it crowns the avenue de l'Opéra. The architect, Charles Garnier, whose golden bust by Carpeaux can be seen on the rue Auber side, drew on a number of existing styles and succeeded in creating a magnificently ornate building the like of which Paris had never seen before – when the Empress Eugénie asked in bewilderment what style it was,

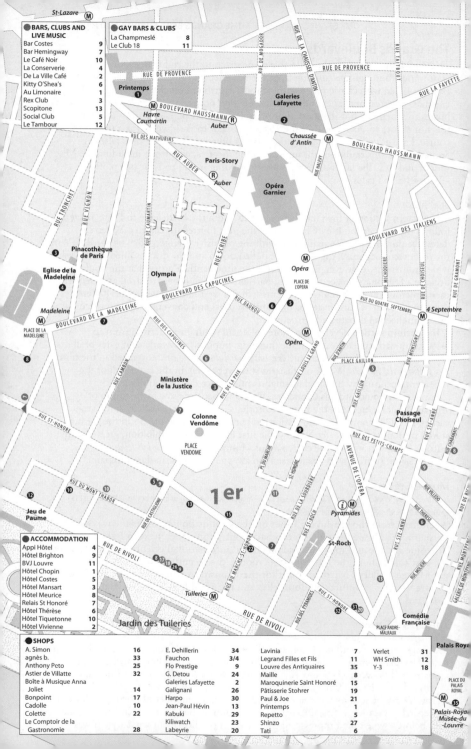

BARS, CLUBS AND LIVE MUSIC

Bar Costes	9
Bar Hemingway	7
Le Café Noir	10
La Conserverie	4
De La Ville Café	2
Kitty O'Shea's	6
Au Limonaire	1
Rex Club	3
Scopitone	13
Social Club	5
Le Tambour	12

GAY BARS & CLUBS

La Champmeslé	8
Le Club 18	11

ACCOMMODATION

Appi Hôtel	4
Hôtel Brighton	9
BVJ Louvre	11
Hôtel Chopin	1
Hôtel Costes	5
Hôtel Mansart	3
Hôtel Meurice	8
Relais St Honoré	7
Hôtel Thérèse	6
Hôtel Tiquetonne	10
Hôtel Vivienne	2

SHOPS

A. Simon	16	E. Dehillerin	34
agnès b.	33	Fauchon	3/4
Anthony Peto	25	Flo Prestige	9
Astier de Villatte	32	G. Detou	24
Boîte à Musique Anna		Galeries Lafayette	2
Joliet	14	Galignani	26
Bonpoint	17	Harpo	30
Cadolle	10	Jean-Paul Hévin	13
Colette	22	Kabuki	29
Le Comptoir de la		Kiliwatch	23
Gastronomie	28	Labeyrie	20

Lavinia	7	Verlet	31
Legrand Filles et Fils	11	WH Smith	12
Louvre des Antiquaires	35	Y-3	18
Maille	8		
Maroquinerie Saint Honoré	15		
Pâtisserie Stohrer	19		
Paul & Joe	21		
Printemps	1		
Repetto	5		
Shinzo	27		
Tati	6		

Garnier replied that it was "Napoléon III style". Certainly, if any building can be said to exemplify the Second Empire, it is this – in its show of wealth and hint of vulgarity. In the event, however, it was only completed in 1875 after the Empire had been swept away by the Third Republic, and even Garnier had to pay for his ticket on the opening night. Part of the reason construction took so long – fourteen years in all – was the discovery of a water table which had to be drained and replaced by a huge concrete well, giving rise to the legend of an underground lake, popularized by Gaston Leroux's *Phantom of the Opera*.

The theatre's **facade** is a fairytale concoction of white, pink and green marble, colonnades, rearing horses, winged angels and gleaming gold busts of composers. The group sculpture on the right of the entrance, Carpeaux's *La Danse*, caused a stir on unveiling for its frank sensuality; one outraged protestor went as far as to throw black ink over the fleshy thigh of the female nude dancer.

The interior
Daily 10am–5pm • €9

The opulent **interior**, with its spacious gilded-marble and mirrored lobbies, was intended to give Second Empire society suitably grand spaces in which to meet and be seen. The auditorium itself is all red velvet and gold leaf, hung with a six-tonne chandelier; the colourful ceiling was painted by Chagall in 1964 and depicts scenes from well-known operas and ballets jumbled up with famous Parisian landmarks. You can **visit** the interior, including the auditorium – as long as there are no rehearsals; your best chance is between 1 and 2pm. The entry ticket includes the **Bibliothèque-Musée de l'Opéra**, containing model sets, dreadful nineteenth-century paintings and rather better temporary exhibitions on operatic themes. Amid the postcards and memorabilia in the **shop** is one of the city's most unusual souvenirs – honey collected from hives kept by former backstage worker Jean Paucton on the vast copper and zinc roof of the opera house; his 125,000 bees seek out nectar from parks, cemeteries and window boxes and produce up to 300kg of honey a year.

Paris-Story
11bis rue Scribe, 9ᵉ • Daily with 50min shows on the hour 10am–6pm • €10, children €6 • ☎ 01 42 66 62 06, Ⓦ paris-story.com • Ⓜ Opéra

On the western side of the Opéra is the **Paris-Story** multimedia show, a partial and highly romanticized history of Paris "narrated" by Victor Hugo, with simultaneous translation in English. The film uses a kaleidoscope of computer-generated images and archive footage, set against a luscious classical-music soundtrack.

Printemps and Galeries Lafayette
Bd Haussmann, 9ᵉ • Ⓜ Chausée d'Antin/Havre Caumartin

Just to the north you'll find two of the city's big department stores, **Printemps** and **Galeries Lafayette** (see p.323). Built at the beginning of the twentieth century, they may have lost their grand central staircases, but they still sport their proud Art Nouveau stained-glass domes. Printemps' dome is particularly splendid, in glowing hues of green and blue, best appreciated from the brasserie beneath.

The Madeleine and around
Place de la Madeleine, 8ᵉ • Ⓜ Madeleine

South of boulevard Haussmann, occupying nearly the whole of the place de la Madeleine, is the imperious-looking **Eglise de la Madeleine**, a favourite venue for society weddings. Modelled on the Parthenon, the building is surrounded by 52 Corinthian columns and fronted by a huge pediment depicting the Last Judgement; its facade is a near mirror image of the Assemblée Nationale, directly opposite, on the far side of the place de la Concorde – a fine vista best appreciated from the top of the

Madeleine steps. Originally intended as a monument to Napoleon's army – a plan abandoned after the French were defeated by the Russians in 1812 – the building narrowly escaped being turned into a railway station before finally being consecrated to Mary Magdalene in 1845.

Inside, a theatrical stone sculpture of the Magdalene being swept up to heaven by two angels draws your eye to the high altar. The half-dome above is decorated with a fresco by Jules-Claude Ziegler (1804–56), a student of Ingres; entitled *The History of Christianity*, it commemorates the concordat signed between the church and state after the end of the Revolution, and shows all the key figures in Christendom, with Napoleon centre stage, naturally. The church's interior is otherwise rather gloomy, heavy with gilt-edged marble. If you're lucky, the sombre atmosphere may be broken by the sound of the organ, reckoned to be one of Paris's best – the church is a regular venue for recitals and choral concerts. Illustrious past organists include Saint-Saëns and Fauré, whose famous *Requiem* was premiered at the Madeleine in 1888 – to be heard here again at the composer's own funeral 36 years later.

Place de la Madeleine

ⓂMadeleine

If the Madeleine caters to spiritual needs, much of the rest of the square is given over to nourishment of a rather earthier kind, for this is where Paris's top **gourmet food stores**, Fauchon and Hédiard (see box, p.332), are located. Their remarkable displays are a feast for the eyes, and both have fine restaurants. East of the church is one of the city's oldest flower markets dating back to 1832, open every day except Monday, while nearby some rather fine Art Nouveau public toilets, built in 1905, are definitely worth inspecting.

The Pinacothèque de Paris

28 place de la Madeleine and 8 rue Vignon, 8ᵉ • Daily 10.30am–7.30pm, Wed till 9.30pm • €10 • ☎ 01 42 68 02 01, Ⓦ www .pinacotheque.com • ⓂMadeleine

The **Pinacothèque de Paris** is the city's newest art museum and the only one that's privately run. When it first opened in 2007 on place de la Madeleine, it staged only temporary art exhibitions, but a new annexe, unveiled in 2011, just around the corner, displays a fine permanent collection of around one hundred paintings on loan from forty private individuals; they include works by Rembrandt, Ghirlandaio, Picasso, Vuillard, Bonnard and Pollock, many rarely or never seen before. What also makes this collection unusual is the way in which the artworks are hung – not by artist or school, but by theme, such as "landscape" or "intimacy", rather in the manner a private collector might display their paintings. The museum's pioneering owner, Marc Restellini, takes the same approach with his temporary exhibitions, some of which, such as the Xi'an Terracotta Warriors in 2008 and Edvard Munch in 2011, have drawn queues round the block.

BEAUTIFUL BANKS

Following in the wake of the Printemps and Galeries Lafayette department stores on boulevard Haussmann, a number of **imposing banks** were built in the area. The Crédit Lyonnais at 19 boulevard des Italiens, south of boulevard Haussmann, is perhaps the most impressive, with its huge gold clock flanked by gigantic caryatids. Across the road at no. 20 the Banque Nationale de Paris occupies another striking building, with gilded wrought-iron balconies and finely sculpted friezes depicting hunting scenes. It used to be the *Maison Dorée*, a restaurant from the 1840s, where you might have bumped into Balzac, Hugo, Flaubert and Nerval, among other literary figures. At no. 16 is the bank's main building – a sleek 1930s Art Deco edifice. As you cross over rue Laffitte to reach it, you get a wonderful view of Notre-Dame de Lorette, with the Sacré Coeur rearing up in the background.

Place Vendôme and around
ⓂPyramides/Opéra

A short walk east of place de la Madeleine lies **place Vendôme**, one of the city's most impressive set-pieces, built by Versailles architect Hardouin-Mansart during the final years of Louis XIV's reign. It's a pleasingly symmetrical, eight-sided *place*, enclosed by a harmonious ensemble of elegant mansions, graced with Corinthian pilasters, mascarons and steeply pitched roofs. Once the grand residences of tax collectors and financiers, they now house such luxury establishments as the *Ritz* hotel (from where Di and Dodi set off on their last journey), Cartier, Bulgari and other top-flight jewellers, lending the square a decidedly exclusive air. The Ministry of Justice is also sited here, on the west side; its facade still has the marble plaque showing a standard metre put here in 1795 in order to familiarize Parisians with the new unit of measure. No. 12, on the opposite side, now occupied by Chaumet jewellers, is where Chopin died, in 1849.

The Colonne Vendôme

Somewhat out of proportion with the rest of place Vendôme, the centrepiece is a towering triumphal **column**, modelled on Trajan's column in Rome, and surmounted by a statue of Napoleon dressed as Caesar. It was raised in 1806 to celebrate the Battle of Austerlitz – bronze reliefs of scenes of the battle, cast from 1200 recycled Austro-Russian cannons, spiral their way up the column. The column that stands here today is actually a replica of the original, brought crashing down during the Commune in 1871 – the main instigator behind this act was the artist Gustave Courbet, who was imprisoned and ordered to pay for the column's restoration; he was financially ruined and lived the rest of his life in exile in Switzerland.

4

Rue St-Honoré

ⓂPyramides/Madeleine/Palais-Royal-Musée-du-Louvre

A healthy bank balance is required if you intend to do more than window-shop in the streets around place Vendôme, especially ancient **rue St-Honoré**, a preserve of top fashion designers and art galleries; all the classic designers such as Hermès, Yves Saint Laurent and Christian Lacroix are here, or for something more up to date, join the style-conscious young Parisians perusing the latest designs at the Colette concept store at no. 213 (see p.326).

East of place Vendôme, on rues **St-Roch** and **Ste-Anne**, in particular, the Japanese community has established a mini-enclave; you'll find some good noodle and sushi bars here, such as *Higuma* (see p.273).

Eglise St-Roch

296 rue St-Honoré, 1ᵉʳ • ⓂPyramides

On the corner of rue St-Roch and rue St-Honoré stands the **Eglise St-Roch**, begun in 1653 but not completed until 1740, as money kept running out. Its handsome honey-coloured classical facade was recently scrubbed clean and shows little sign of the battering it received in 1795 when the young Napoleon dispersed a Royalist uprising with cannon (or a "whiff of grapeshot", as he famously put it), and was rewarded with promotion to the rank of general. The St-Roch *quartier* was much more densely populated than it is now and boasted many illustrious parishioners, some of whom – Corneille, Diderot and Le Nôtre (who landscaped the Versailles and Tuileries gardens) among them – are buried in the church. The nave is very long, almost as long as Notre-Dame's, filled with light and flanked with numerous chapels richly decorated with paintings and sculpture by Coysevox and Coustou, and other leading artists of the day. A free leaflet detailing the works is available from the welcome desk. The church is also a venue for evening concerts, and holds free lunchtime song and chamber music recitals most Tuesdays from 12.15 to 1pm.

The Palais Royal

Place du Palais Royal, 1ᵉʳ • Ⓜ Palais-Royal-Musée-du-Louvre

Following rue St-Honoré east you come to the **Palais Royal**, a complex of handsome buildings and gardens. There are two main parts: the palace itself and, beyond it, galleries surrounding gardens on three sides. The palace, a fine colonnaded building, dates back to 1624, though it has been much modified and renovated since. It was built for Cardinal Richelieu, who left it to the king, Louis XIV, then just a boy; he and his mother lived in the palace for a time. The palace later passed to his brother, the duc d'Orléans, and provided sanctuary to Henrietta Maria, widow of executed English king, Charles I. The palace is now occupied by various government departments and is rarely open to the public; an annexe to the side houses the **Comédie Française**, long-standing venue for the classics of French theatre.

The gardens and arcades

Beyond the palace lie sedate **gardens** lined with stately **arcaded buildings**, put up in the 1780s by Philippe-Egalité, a descendant of the duc d'Orléans. Desperate to pay off his debts, he let out the spaces under the arcades to shops. One of them, Guillaumot, founded in 1785 and selling antiquarian books mostly on genealogy and heraldry (153 Galerie de Valois), is still there today. Many of the other shops also specialize in antiques or quirky collectors' items, such as lead soldiers and Légion d'Honneur medals. At no. 142 Galerie de Valois is an exquisite purple-panelled *parfumerie*, Les Salons du Palais Royal Shiseido, while the bright-red decor at Didier Ludot's La Petite Robe Noire (no. 125) sets off to advantage his wonderful collection of new and vintage little black dresses.

Past residents of the desirable flats above the arcades include Cocteau and Colette – the latter enjoyed looking out over the gardens when she was too crippled with arthritis to walk. It's certainly an attractive and peaceful oasis, with avenues of limes, fountains and flowerbeds. You'd hardly guess that for many years this was a site of gambling dens, funfair attractions and brothels (it was to a prostitute here that Napoleon lost his virginity in 1787). The clearing of Paris's brothels in 1829–31 and the prohibition on public gambling in 1838, however, put an end to the fun; later, the Grands Boulevards took up the baton. Folly, some might say, has returned – in the form of Daniel Buren's black-and-white striped pillars, rather like sticks of Brighton rock, all of varying heights, dotted about the main courtyard in front of the palace. Installed in 1986, they're rather disconcerting, but certainly popular with children and rollerbladers, who treat them as an adventure playground and obstacle course respectively.

The *passages* and around

The 2ᵉ arrondissement is scattered with around twenty **passages**, or shopping arcades, that have survived from the early nineteenth century. In 1840 over a hundred existed, but most were later destroyed to make way for Haussmann's boulevards. After decades of neglect, some have now been restored. Some chic boutiques have moved in, though the overall atmosphere is one of nostalgia, as most of the shops, selling old-fashioned toys, prints, secondhand books, postcards and stamps, hark back to another age. Their entrances are easy to miss and where you emerge at the other end can be quite a surprise. Most are closed at night and on Sundays.

The accounts here explore the best of the *passages*, including the elegant **Galerie Véro-Dodat** and **Galerie Vivienne**, the scruffier, but no less fascinating **passage Choiseul** and **passage des Panoramas**, and the **passages Jouffroy and Verdeau**, with their quirky old-fashioned shops. You could also make detours to the **Bibliothèque Nationale**, the National Library of France, and the **Bourse**, the city's stock exchange.

4

Galerie Véro-Dodat

Between rues Croix-des-Petits-Champs and Jean-Jacques Rousseau, 1er • Ⓜ Palais-Royal-Musée-du-Louvre

The most homogeneous and aristocratic of the *passages*, with painted ceilings and panelled mahogany shop fronts divided by faux marble columns, is **Galerie Véro-Dodat**, named after the two butchers who set it up in 1824. Renovated in 1980, it's been largely colonized by design shops, fashion boutiques (such as Christian Louboutin) and art galleries, though some older businesses, such as R.F. Charle, at no. 17, specializing in the repair and sale of vintage stringed instruments, remain.

The **Banque de France** lies a short way northwest. Rather than negotiating its massive bulk to reach the *passages* further north, it's more pleasant to walk through the garden of the Palais Royal via place de Valois. Rue de Montpensier, running alongside the gardens to the west, is connected to rue de Richelieu by several tiny *passages*, of which Hulot brings you out at the statue of Molière on the junction of rues Richelieu and Molière. A certain charm also lingers about rue de Beaujolais, bordering the northern end of the gardens, with its corner café looking out on the Théâtre du Palais-Royal, and with glimpses into the venerable *Grand Véfour* restaurant (see p.273), plus more short arcades leading up to rue des Petits-Champs.

Galerie Vivienne

Ⓜ Bourse

The flamboyant decor of Grecian and marine motifs in Galerie Vivienne, linking rue Vivienne with rue des Petits-Champs, establishes the perfect ambience in which to buy Jean-Paul Gaultier gear. Alternatively, you could browse in the antiquarian bookshop, Librairie Jousseaume, dating back to the *passage*'s earliest days, or check out the delightful wooden toys at Si Tu Veux toy shop, before taking a tea break in *A Priori Thé* (see p.272).

Place des Victoires

At the eastern end of rue des Petits-Champs rears up a grand equestrian statue of Louis XIV, at the centre of attractive **place des Victoires**, surrounded by elegant seventeenth-century townhouses. Designer fashion boutiques, such as Kenzo and Cacharel, occupy most of the shops here. Adjoining the square to the north is the appealingly asymmetrical place des Petits-Pères, once the courtyard of the monastery of the Petits-Pères, closed during the Revolution. Its church, Notre-Dame des Victoires, survives, notable for its collection of paintings by Carl Van Loo. Across the street at no. 10 is *Au Panetier*, a lovely Art Nouveau boulangerie that's been around since 1896 and is renowned for its chewy baguettes and delicious pastries. The large isolated building on the west side of the square (no. 1) once housed, as a plaque testifies, the notorious French Commissariat for Jewish Affairs (1941–44), which more than willingly collaborated in rounding up the city's Jews for deportation to German concentration camps.

Bibliothèque Nationale

5 rue Vivienne, 2e; Temporary entrance during renovation work • Temporary exhibitions Tues–Sat 10am–7pm, Sun noon–7pm • €7 • ☎ 01 53 79 59 59, Ⓦ bnf.fr • Ⓜ Bourse

Across from the Palais Royal, on the other side of rue des Petits-Champs, looms the forbidding wall of the **Bibliothèque Nationale**, part of whose enormous collection has been transferred to the new François Mitterrand site in the 13e (see p.176). It's currently undergoing major renovation work to improve the conditions in which the library's twenty million documents are kept, and to open up more of the building to the public. Work is due to finish in 2017. Parts of the library will remain open during this period for exhibitions, though it's best to check the website for the latest updates.

The library's origins go back to the 1660s, when Louis XIV's finance minister Colbert deposited a collection of royal manuscripts here, and it was first opened to the public

in 1692. There's no restriction on entering the library, nor on peering into the atmospheric reading rooms, such as the huge Salle Ovale and the Salle Labrouste, with its slender iron columns supporting nine domes, a fine example of the early use of iron frame construction.

Cabinet des Monnaies, Médailles et Antiques
Bibliothèque Nationale • Mon–Fri 1–5.45pm, Sat 1–4.45pm, Sun noon–6pm • Free • ⓂBourse

Installed on the first floor of the Bibliothèque Nationale, the **Cabinet des Monnaies, Médailles et Antiques** is a fine collection of coins and ancient treasures built up by successive kings from Philippe-Auguste onwards. Exhibits include Etruscan bronzes, ancient Greek jewellery and some exquisite medieval cameos. One of the highlights is Charlemagne's ivory chess set, its pieces malevolent-looking characters astride elephants. The cabinet will close in 2014, probably for a couple of years, during which period it will be transferred to grander rooms in the building as part of the library's extensive revamp.

Passage Choiseul
ⓂPyramides/Quatre-Septembre

West of Galerie Vivienne along rue des Petits-Champs lies **passage Choiseul**, alluringly dark and dingy-looking. It was here, in the early 1900s, that the author Louis-Ferdinand Céline lived as a boy, and judging by his account of it in his autobiographical *Death on Credit*, it was none too salubrious: "The gas lamps stank so badly in the stagnant air of the *passage* that towards evening some women would start to feel unwell, added to which there was the stench of dogs' urine to contend with." Nowadays the only aromas likely to assail you come from the takeaway food shops, which keep company with discount clothes and book stores, jewellery shops, galleries and well-known supplier of artists' materials, Lavrut (no. 52). Also here is an entrance to the Théâtre des Bouffes Parisiens, where Offenbach conducted the first performance of *Orpheus in the Underworld*.

The Bourse
Rue Notre-Dame des Victoires, 2ᵉ • Book your visit a week in advance on ☎ 01 49 27 14 70 • Guided tours €8.50 • ⓂBourse

A little to the north of the Bibliothèque Nationale stands the **Bourse**, the Paris stock exchange, an imposing Neoclassical edifice built under Napoleon in 1808 and enlarged in 1903 with the addition of two side wings. Guided tours around the eerily quiet building (most of the action takes place online these days) last about an hour and include a presentation on how the Bourse works. Overshadowing the Bourse from the south is the antennae-topped building of AFP, the French news agency. Rue Réaumur, running east from here, used to be the Fleet Street of Paris, but all the newspapers have now moved elsewhere.

Passage des Panoramas
ⓂGrands Boulevards/Bourse

The grid of arcades north of the Bourse, just off rue Vivienne, is known as the **passage des Panoramas**. It was around here, in 1817, that the first Parisian gas lamps were

---

LE CROISSANT

Just up the road from the Bourse, on the corner of rue du Croissant and rue Montmartre, **Le Croissant**, now a *bistrot* but once a popular drinking den, was the scene of the assassination on July 31, 1914 of **Jean Jaurès**, the Socialist leader. He was shot by young French nationalist Raul Vilain, protesting at Jaurès's pacifism. Even if he had survived it seems unlikely that Jaurès could have held back the slide to war: just three days later Germany declared war on France. The table at which Jaurès was drinking when he was shot can still be seen, preserved by the owners of *Le Croissant*.

tried out. A little shabby and frayed around the edges, the *passage* combines old-fashioned chic and workaday atmosphere. Most of the eateries here – mainly Indian and Chinese restaurants – make no pretence at style, but one café, *L'Arbre à Cannelle*, has beautiful carved wood ornamentation and painted ceiling panels dating from the 1900s. Another place that's kept its original decor is printshop Stern, dating back to 1867. Most of the other outlets are given over to bric-a-brac and secondhand postcard, coin and stamp dealers.

Passages Jouffroy and Verdeau
Ⓜ Grands Boulevards

On the other side of boulevard Montmartre from the passage des Panoramas, **passage Jouffroy** is full of the kind of stores that make shopping an adventure rather than a chore. One of them, M & G Segas, sells eccentric walking canes and theatrical antiques opposite Pain d'Epices, stocking every conceivable fitting and furnishing for a doll's house. Near the romantic *Hôtel Chopin* (see p.255), Paul Vulin's secondhand books spill out into the passageway, and Ciné-Doc appeals to cinephiles with its collection of old film posters. Crossing rue de la Grange-Batelière, you enter equally enchanting **passage Verdeau**, sheltering antiquarian books, old prints, and a photography shop selling and restoring old and new images.

Passage des Princes
Ⓜ Richelieu-Drouot

At the top of rue de Richelieu, the tiny **passage des Princes**, with its beautiful glass ceiling, stained-glass decoration and twirly lamps, has been taken over by the toy emporium JouéClub. Its erstwhile neighbour, the passage de l'Opéra, described in surreal detail by Louis Aragon in *Paris Peasant*, was eaten up with the completion of Haussmann's boulevards.

While in the area, you could also take a look at what's up for sale at auction house **Hôtel Drouot** (9 rue Drouot; Ⓜ Le Peletier/Richelieu-Drouot). You can simply wander round looking at the goods before the action starts (11am–6pm on the eve of the sale, 11am–noon on the day itself). Auctions are announced in the press, under "Ventes aux Enchères"; you'll find details, including photos of pieces, in the widely available weekly *Gazette de l'Hôtel Drouot* or on their website: Ⓦ www.drouot.fr.

Sentier and around

At the heart of the 2e arrondissement lies the **Sentier** *quartier*, largely given over to the rag trade, where the frenetic trading and deliveries of cloth and the general to-ing and fro-ing make a lively change from the office-bound districts further west. On **place du Caire**, beneath an extraordinary pseudo-Egyptian facade of grotesque Pharaonic heads (a celebration of Napoleon's conquest of Egypt), an archway opens onto a series of arcades, the **passage du Caire**. Entirely monopolized by wholesale clothes shops (not open to the public), it is very dilapidated and little frequented these days, though it's actually the oldest of the *passages*, built in 1798. More recently, the area has been dubbed Silicon Sentier on account of the growing number of e-commerce companies setting up here.

Tour Jean Sans Peur
20 rue Etienne Marcel • April–Oct Wed–Sun 1.30–6pm; Nov–March Wed, Sat & Sun 1.30–6pm • €5 • Ⓜ Etienne Marcel

Bordering the Sentier district to the south is rue Etienne Marcel, which is roughly where the old medieval city wall used to run. At no. 20 a rare vestige from this period survives: the **Tour Jean Sans Peur**, a fine Gothic tower, the only remnant of a grand townhouse that used to straddle the old wall. It was built by Jean Sans Peur, the duc de Bourgogne, who had the tower erected as a place of refuge; he feared reprisal after having assassinated Louis d'Orléans, the king's brother – a murder that kicked off a

4

thirty-year war between the Armagnacs and Burgundys. A spiral stone staircase (138 steps) inside the tower ends with a beautiful vaulted roof decorated with stone carvings of oak leaves, hawthorn and hops, symbols of the Burgundy family. The rooms off the staircase contain information on the tower and the period.

Passage du Grand-Cerf

Ⓜ Etienne Marcel

Between rue St-Denis and rue Dussoubs arches the lofty, three-storey **passage du Grand-Cerf**, one of the most attractive of all the arcades. The wrought-iron work, glass roof and plain-wood shop fronts have all been restored, attracting chic arts, craft and design shops. There's always something quirky and original on display in the window of Le Labo (no. 4), specializing in lamps and other lighting fixtures made from recycled objects, while As'Art, opposite, is a treasure-trove of home furnishings and objects from Africa.

Rue St-Denis

Ⓜ Etienne Marcel

The northern stretch of **rue St-Denis**, beyond rue Etienne Marcel, is the city's centuries-old red-light area, where weary women wait in doorways between strip clubs and sex shops. The area is changing, however, and some of the older outlets are closing down, partly because sex megastores have taken some of their business and partly because the 2ᵉ arrondissement *mairie* is attempting to clean up the area by encouraging new businesses to move in.

Rue Montorgueil and around

Ⓜ Etienne Marcel

The emphasis on rues Montmartre, Montorgueil and Turbigo, as they lead south from rue Réaumur, is firmly on food as they approach the Les Halles complex. Worth lingering over in particular is the picturesque, pedestrianized market street **rue Montorgueil**, where grocers, horse butchers and fishmongers ply their trade alongside traditional restaurants, such as *L'Escargot*, serving snails since 1875, and cafés catering to a cool crowd. It's hard to pass by Stohrer's pâtisserie, in business since 1730, without stopping to gaze at its exquisite cakes and beautiful old decor.

Rue Montmartre is characterized by its excellent kitchenware shops, such as A. Simon, MORA and Bovida (see p.336), stocking all the essential utensils for making the perfect *tarte tatin* or *coq au vin*.

THE POMPIDOU CENTRE

Beaubourg and Les Halles

Straddling the third and fourth arrondissements, the Beaubourg *quartier* hums with cafés, shops and galleries, and has the popular Pompidou Centre at its heart. The groundbreaking architecture of this huge arts centre provoked a storm of controversy on its opening in 1977, but has since won over critics and the public alike, and become one of the city's most recognizable landmarks, drawing large numbers to its modern art museum and high-profile exhibitions. By contrast, nearby Les Halles, an underground shopping complex built at around the same time as the Pompidou Centre, has never really endeared itself to the city's inhabitants and is probably the least inspired of all the capital's developments in the last thirty years; it's currently undergoing a major revamp.

5

The Pompidou Centre

Ⓦ centrepompidou.fr • Ⓜ Rambuteau/Hôtel-de-Ville

Attracting over five million visitors a year, the **Pompidou Centre**, known locally as Beaubourg, would seem to have fulfilled its founder Georges Pompidou's vision of a world-class modern art museum and multidisciplinary arts centre. When the centre first opened, however, it met with a very mixed reception, with one critic dubbing it an oil refinery. The design is certainly radical. The architects, Renzo Piano and Richard Rogers, wanted to move away from the idea of galleries as closed treasure-chests to create something more open and accessible, so they stripped the "skin" off the building and made all the "bones" visible. The infrastructure was put on the outside: escalator tubes and utility pipes, colour-coded according to their function, climb around the exterior, giving the building its crazy snakes-and-ladders appearance.

The centre's main draw is its outstanding modern art museum, the **Musée National d'Art Moderne**, the largest in Europe, with some 65,000 works. Only a small fraction of the artworks can be displayed at any one time and are frequently rotated, though with the opening in 2010 of its sister gallery, the Pompidou Metz, many more can now be enjoyed by the public. The collection is displayed on the fourth and fifth floors, with temporary exhibitions on the sixth. One of the added treats of visiting these is that you get to ascend the transparent escalator on the outside of the building, affording superb views over the city. Equally good is the vista from the sleek sixth-floor restaurant *Georges* (see p.274). On the lower floors there are cinemas, a performance space and the BPI, or **Bibliothèque publique d'information** (Mon–Fri noon–10pm, Sat & Sun 11am–10pm; free), which has an impressive collection of 2500 periodicals, including international press, 10,000 CDs and 1500 documentary films.

Musée National d'Art Moderne

Pompidou Centre • Daily except Tues 11am–9pm • Early May to mid-Aug €12, rest of year €1 • Free to under-18s and EU residents aged 18–25, and free to all first Sun of the month • Combined ticket with the Atelier Brancusi • Tickets can be bought online

Thanks to an astute acquisitions policy and some generous gifts, the **Musée National d'Art Moderne** is a near-complete visual essay on the history of twentieth-century art. The fifth floor covers 1905 to 1960, while the fourth floor brings the collection from 1960 to the present day. Your ticket is valid for a single visit only, so you can't, for example, pop out for a break in one of the centre's cafés and re-enter. The collection is densely and efficiently organized, so, unlike many of the more unwieldy museums in Paris, half a day is probably enough for a rewarding visit. The queues to get in can be long; note that tickets can be booked online.

Fauvism

The collection on floor five is organized more or less chronologically and starts in a blaze of colour with the **Fauvists – Braque**, **Derain**, **Vlaminck** and **Matisse**. Their vibrant works reflect the movement's desire to create form rather than imitate nature. Colour becomes a way of composing and structuring a picture, as in Braque's *L'Estaque* (1906), where trees and sky are broken down into blocks of vibrant reds and greens. Matisse's series of *Luxe* paintings also stands out, the colourful nudes recalling the primitive figures of Gauguin.

Cubism

After the Fauvists, shape is broken down even further in Picasso's and Braque's early **Cubist paintings**. Highlights include **Picasso**'s portrait of his lover Fernande (*Femme assise dans un fauteuil*; 1910), in which different angles of the figure are shown all at once, giving rise to complex patterns and creating the effect of movement. Hung alongside Picasso's works, and almost indistinguishable from them, are a number of **Braque**'s works, such as *Nature morte au violon* (1911) and *Femme à la guitare* (1913). The juxtaposition of these paintings illustrates the intellectual and artistic dialogue that went on between the two artists, who lived next door to each other at the Bateau-Lavoir in Montmartre.

Another artist heavily influenced by the new Cubism was **Fernand Léger**. In paintings such as *Femme en rouge et vert* (1914) and *Contraste de formes* (1913) Léger creates his own distinctive form of Cubism based on tubular shapes, inspired by the modern machinery of World War I, in which he fought.

● RESTAURANTS		● CAFÉS & WINE BARS		● BARS, CLUBS & LIVE MUSIC		● GAY BAR	
Georges	9	Café Beaubourg	10	Le Baiser Salé	4	Le Troisième Lieu	1
Le Gros Minet	8	Le Café des Initiés	4	Au Duc des Lombards	5		
Au Pied de Cochon	3	A la Cloche des Halles	1	Le Fumoir	2	● SHOPS	
La Robe et le Palais	12	Le Cochon à l'Oreille	2	Kong	6	Comptoir des Ecritures	1
La Tour de Montlhéry (Chez Denise)	6	Dame Tartine	11	Le Sunset/Le Sunside	3	Free "P" Star	2
Yam'Tcha	5	Le Petit Marcel	7	Au Trappiste	7		

● ACCOMMODATION	
Hôtel du Cygne	1
Relais du Louvre	2
Hôtel Saint-Merry	3

BEAUBOURG & LES HALLES

5

Dadaism

Reaction to the horror of the 1914–18 war gave rise to the nihilistic **Dada movement**, a revolt against petty bourgeois values; leading members included **Marcel Duchamp**, who selected everyday objects ("ready-mades") such as the *Hat Rack* (1917), and elevated them, without modification, to the rank of works of art, simply by taking them out of their ordinary context and putting them on display. As well as the *Hat Rack*, you can inspect Duchamp's most notorious ready-made – a urinal which he called *Fontaine* and first exhibited in New York in 1917.

Abstract art

The museum holds a particularly rich collection of **Kandinsky's abstract paintings**. His series entitled *Impressions, Improvisations and Compositions* consists of non-figurative shapes and swathes of colour, and heralds a move away from an obsession with subject towards a passion for the creative process itself. Fellow pioneering abstract artists **Sonia and Robert Delaunay** set the walls ablaze with their characteristically colourful paintings. In Sonia Delaunay's wonderfully vibrant *Marché de Minho* (1916), the juxtaposition of colours makes some appear to recede and others come forward, creating a shimmering effect.

Surrealism and abstract expressionism

Surrealism, an offshoot of the Dada movement, dominates in later rooms with works by Magritte, Dalí and Ernst. Typical of the movement's exploration of the darker recesses of the mind, **Ernst**'s disturbing *Ubu Imperator* (1923) depicts a figure that is part man, part Tower of Pisa and part spinning top, and would seem to symbolize the perversion of male authority. A more ethereal, floating world of abstract associations is depicted in **Joan Miró**'s and **Jean Arp**'s canvases.

American **abstract expressionists Jackson Pollock** and **Mark Rothko** are also represented. In Pollock's splattery *No. 26A, Black and white* (1948), the two colours seem to struggle for domination; the dark bands of colour in Rothko's large canvas *No. 14 (Browns over Dark)*, in contrast, draw the viewer in.

Matisse's later experiments with form and colour are usually on display. His technique of *découpage* (creating a picture from cut-out coloured pieces of paper) freed colour from drawing and line, and is perfected in his masterpiece *La Tristesse du roi* (1952), in which a woman dances while an elderly king plays a guitar, mourning his lost youth.

Contemporary art

The fourth floor is given over to **contemporary art**, as well as displays of architectural models and contemporary design. Of the more established artists, **Yves Klein** stands out for his series of "body prints", for which he turned female models into human paintbrushes, covering them in paint to create his artworks. Most of the prints are executed in International Klein Blue, a beautiful, deep and luminous blue patented by the artist. Also known for their experiments with new methods and materials, the **Nouveaux Réalistes César** and **Dubuffet** are usually represented, César recognizable for his "compressions", striking sculptures of compressed cars and scrap metal.

Other established French artists you're likely to come across include Annette Messager, Sophie Calle, Christian Boltanski and Daniel Buren. **Christian Boltanski** is known for his large, disturbing *mise-en-scène* installations, often containing veiled allusions to the Holocaust, while **Daniel Buren**'s works are easy to spot: they nearly all bear his trademark stripes, exactly 8.7cm in width. Some space is dedicated to **video art**, with installations by artists such as Francis Alÿs and Rineke Dijkstra.

Atelier Brancusi

Off Pompidou Centre piazza • Daily except Tues 2–6pm • Combined ticket with the Musée National d'Art Moderne • ⓜRambuteau

On the northern edge of the Pompidou Centre, down some steps off the piazza in a small, separate one-storey building, is the **Atelier Brancusi**. Upon his death in 1956, the sculptor **Constantin Brancusi** bequeathed the contents of his 15ᵉ arrondissement studio to the state, on the condition that it be reconstructed exactly as it was found. The artist had become obsessed with the spatial relationship of the sculptures in his studio, going so far as to supplant each sold work with a plaster copy, and the four interconnected rooms of the studio faithfully adhere to his arrangements. Studios one and two are crowded with fluid sculptures of highly polished brass and marble, his trademark abstract bird and column shapes, stylized busts and objects poised as though they're about to take flight. Unfortunately, the rooms are behind glass, adding a feeling of sterility and distance. Perhaps the most satisfying rooms are ateliers three and four, his private quarters, where his tools are displayed on one wall almost like works of art themselves.

Quartier Beaubourg

The lively **quartier Beaubourg** around the Pompidou Centre also offers much in the way of visual art. The colourful moving sculptures and fountains in the pool in front of Eglise St-Merri on **place Igor Stravinsky**, on the south side of the Pompidou Centre, were created by Jean Tinguely and Niki de Saint Phalle; the squirting waterworks pay homage to Stravinsky – each fountain corresponds to one of his compositions (*The Firebird, The Rite of Spring*, etc) – but show scant respect for passers-by. Stravinsky's music in many ways paved the way for the pioneering work of **IRCAM** (Institut de la Recherche et de la Coordination Acoustique/Musique), whose entrance is on the west side of the square. Founded by the composer Pierre Boulez, it's a research centre for contemporary music and a concert venue (see p.316), much of it underground, with an overground extension by Renzo Piano. To the north of the Pompidou Centre numerous commercial art galleries and the odd bookshop and *salon de thé* occupy the attractive *hôtels particuliers* of narrow, pedestrianized **rue Quincampoix**.

Musée de la Poupée

Impasse Berthaud, 3ᵉ • **Museum** Daily except Mon 10am–6pm • €8, children €3 • **Workshops** Wed 11am • €8–13 • Advanced booking necessary • ☎ 01 42 72 73 11, ⓦ museedelapoupeeparis.com • ⓜRambuteau

Off rue Beaubourg is the **Musée de la Poupée**, a doll museum certain to appeal to small children. In addition to the impressive collection of antique dolls, there are displays of finely detailed tiny irons and sewing machines, furniture, pots and pans, and other minuscule accessories. There are fun **workshops** for children on Wednesday mornings.

Hôtel de Ville

Place de l'Hôtel de Ville, 4ᵉ • **Guided tours** Once a week (days and times vary); book ahead on ☎ 01 42 76 50 49 or at the Salon d'Accueil at 29 rue de Rivoli • **Exhibitions** Entrance usually at 5 rue de Lobau • Mon–Sat 10am–7pm • Free • Ice rink Dec–Feb: Mon–Fri noon–10pm, Sat & Sun 9am–10pm • Skate hire €5 • ⓜHôtel de Ville

South of the Pompidou Centre, rue du Renard runs down to the **Hôtel de Ville**, the seat of the city's government and a mansion of gargantuan proportions in florid néo-Renaissance style. It was built in 1882 and modelled pretty much on the previous building burned down in the Commune in 1871. Guided tours, held once a week, allow you to see some of the lavish reception rooms, decorated with murals by the leading artists of the day, such as Puvis de Chavannes and Henri Gervex. The Hôtel de Ville also stages regular free **exhibitions** on Parisian themes, often well worth checking out.

5

An illustrated history of the building is displayed along the platform of ⓜChâtelet on the Neuilly–Vincennes line. Those opposed to the establishments of kings and emperors created their alternative municipal governments in this building: the Revolutionaries installed themselves in 1789, the poet Lamartine proclaimed the Second Republic here in 1848, and Gambetta the Third Republic in 1870. But, with the defeat of the Commune in 1871, the conservatives, in control once again, concluded that the Parisian municipal authority had to go if order was to be maintained and the people kept in their place. Thereafter Paris was ruled directly by the ministry of the interior until eventually, in 1977, the city was allowed to run its own affairs and Jacques Chirac was elected mayor.

The square in front of the Hôtel de Ville, once a notorious execution site, is the location of a popular **ice rink** from December to the end of February.

Les Halles

Located right at the heart of the city is the sprawling underground shopping and leisure complex of **Les Halles**, built in the 1970s and now widely acknowledged as an architectural disaster – so much so, in fact, that it is currently being given a major facelift. Described by Zola as "the belly of Paris", the original Les Halles was Paris's main food market for over eight hundred years until it was moved out to the suburbs in 1969; its departure is still widely mourned today.

Forum des Halles
ⓜLes Halles/Châtelet/RER Châtelet Les Halles

Victor Baltard's elegant nineteenth-century iron pavilions were destroyed (two were saved – one is in Nogent-sur-Marne, the other in Yokohama, Japan) to make way for an ugly, irretrievably Seventies glass-and-steel shopping mall, known as the **Forum des Halles**, and a huge métro station, the biggest in Europe. The working-class quarter, with its night bars and *bistrots* for the market traders, was largely swept away, and though much of the area above ground was landscaped, providing some welcome green space, the gardens have developed an unsavoury reputation as the preferred hangout of drug dealers.

The Forum is spread over four levels. The bottom level is the métro/RER station, where five métro lines and three suburban lines intersect, used by some 800,000 commuters a day. The other levels accommodate numerous shops, housed in aquarium-like arcades around a sunken patio; they're mostly devoted to high-street fashion outlets (H&M, Zara, Gap and Muji, to name a few), though there's also a decent Fnac bookshop and the Forum des Créateurs (level -1), an outlet for young fashion designers. Leisure facilities comprise a swimming pool (see p.343) and a number of cinemas, including the **Forum des Images** (see below).

Future of the Forum

A major renovation scheme for the Forum started in 2010 and is due to be completed in 2014. French architects Patrick Berger and Jacques Anziutti will suspend a vast glass roof, known as **La Canopée**, over the site, allowing light to flood in, while, overground, architect and urban planner David Mangin has been entrusted with redesigning the gardens; he intends to create a wide promenade on the model of Barcelona's Ramblas, as well as ponds and playgrounds. His plan was chosen as the most sensitive to local needs, though it's hard not to feel an opportunity has been missed to go for something really exciting and ambitious. Jean Nouvel, for example, put in a proposal for an enormous hanging garden, complete with a 100m open-air swimming pool.

Forum des Images

Forum des Halles • Tues–Fri 1–10pm, Sat & Sun 2–10pm • ☎ 01 44 76 63 00, ⓦ forumdesimages.fr • ⓜLes Halles/Châtelet/RER Châtelet Les Halles

The **Forum des Images** has five screens and an archive of some 5500 films, all connected with Paris and any of which you can watch in your own private booth (€5 for four hours, free weekdays after 7.30pm). The Forum des Images came out of a multimillion-euro revamp in late 2008 with a fresh look, more space and a new café. Regular lectures, classes and courses on the film-making process are held here, as well as events for children and teenagers.

St-Eustache

2 impasse St-Eustache, 1er • ⓂLes Halles

For an antidote to steel-and-glass troglodytism head for the soaring vaults of the beautiful church of **St-Eustache**, on the north side of the gardens. Built between 1532 and 1637, the church is Gothic in structure, with lofty naves and graceful flying buttresses, and Renaissance in decoration – all Corinthian columns and arcades. Molière, Richelieu and Madame de Pompadour were baptized here, while Rameau and Marivaux were buried here. The side chapels contain some minor works of art, including, in the tenth chapel in the ambulatory, an early Rubens (*The Pilgrims at Emmaus*), and, in the sixth chapel on the north side, Coysevox's marble sculpture over the tomb of Colbert, Louis XIV's finance minister. In the Chapelle St-Joseph there is a naïve relief by British artist Raymond Mason, *The Departure of Fruit and Vegetables from the Heart of Paris, 28 February 1969*, showing a procession of market traders, resembling a funeral cortege, leaving Les Halles for the last time. The church has a long and venerable musical tradition and is a popular venue for concerts and organ recitals; its organ is reputedly the largest in France, with eight thousand pipes.

Fontaine des Innocents

Place Joachim du Bellay, 1er • ⓂLes Halles

On the other side of Les Halles from St-Eustache stands the perfectly proportioned Renaissance **Fontaine des Innocents** (1549), adorned with reliefs of water nymphs. It looks slightly marooned amid the fast-food joints, tattoo parlours and shoe shops of the place Joachim du Bellay; on warm days shoppers sit around its edge, drawn to the coolness of its cascading waters. The fountain takes its name from the cemetery that used to occupy this site, the Cimetière des Innocents. Full to overflowing, the cemetery was closed down in 1786 and its contents transferred to the catacombs in Denfert-Rochereau.

Châtelet and around

The labyrinth of tiny streets heading southeast from Les Halles to **place du Châtelet** teems with jazz bars, nightclubs and restaurants, and is far more crowded at 2am than at 2pm. One of these streets, narrow little rue de la Ferronnerie, was the scene of Henri IV's assassination in 1610. A plaque at no. 11 marks the spot where Henri's carriage came to a standstill, caught in the seventeenth-century equivalent of a traffic jam, giving his assassin, religious fanatic Ravaillac, the chance he was seeking to plunge his dagger into the king's breast.

Théâtre du Châtelet and Théâtre de la Ville

Place du Châtelet, 1er • ⓂChâtelet

Place du Châtelet was once the site of a notorious fortress prison and is now a maelstrom of traffic overlooked by two of the city's most prestigious theatres, the **Théâtre du Châtelet** (see p.313)and the **Théâtre de la Ville** (see p.314), built in the 1860s during Haussmann's *grands travaux*. The latter was formerly known as the Théâtre Sarah Bernhardt (changed to Théâtre des Nations during the German occupation on account of Bernhardt's Jewish origins) after the great actress bought it and regularly performed on stage here until her death in 1923.

5

Tour St-Jacques

Rue de Rivoli, 1er • ⓂChâtelet

One block north of the place du Châtelet stands the **Tour St-Jacques**. Built in Flamboyant Gothic style and dating from the early sixteenth century, it's all that remains of the Eglise St-Jacques-de-la-Boucherie, built by butchers from nearby Les Halles and destroyed in the Revolution. The church used to be an important stopping point for pilgrims on their way to Santiago de Compostela. At the base of the tower a statue commemorates Blaise Pascal, who carried out experiments on atmospheric pressure here in the seventeenth century. The tower, which is closed to the public, is now used as a weather station and monitors pollution and air quality.

59 Rivoli

59 rue de Rivoli, 1er • Tues–Sun 1–8pm, Sat 11am–8pm • Free • Ⓦ 59rivoli.org • ⓂChâtelet

West of the Tour St-Jacques lies busy rue de Rivoli, dominated by high-street clothing stores. No. 59, however, shelters the famous **artists' squat**, Chez Robert, Electron Libre, now better known as **59 Rivoli**. The building, which had been left empty by its owners Crédit Lyonnais, was occupied by artists in 1999 and fast became one of the capital's most important contemporary art spaces. The Paris authorities agreed to buy and renovate it and the building reopened in 2009. Some thirty artists live and work in what is now being styled an "aftersquat". You're free to wander around their studios, spread over six floors, and see the artists at work. Graffiti, slogans and murals cover nearly every surface, canvases and all sorts of *objets* are stacked up higgledy piggedly, and the smell of paint, varnish and coffee permeates everywhere. Most artists work through the medium of paint, but there are also sculptors and photographers; many artworks are on display and regular exhibitions are held.

The Samaritaine and quai de la Mégisserie

Rue de Rivoli, 1er • ⓂPont-Neuf

To the west of the 59 Rivoli squat is the grand **Samaritaine** building, built in 1903 in pure Art Nouveau style. This famous department store was declared a fire risk in 2005 and suddenly closed down, an event that sent ripples of dismay throughout the capital; work is underway however to transform it into a luxury hotel and shopping complex by 2014. The quayside just behind the Samaritaine is known as **quai de la Mégisserie** ("mégisserie" meaning the tanning of hides), a reference to the treatment of animal skins in medieval times when this was an area of abattoirs; nowadays there are plants and pets for sale all along this stretch up to the Pont au Change.

The Marais

The Marais is one of the most seductive areas of central Paris, known for its
sophistication and artsy leanings, and for being the neighbourhood of
choice for gay Parisians. Largely untouched by Baron Haussmann and
modern development, it preserves its enchanting narrow streets and
magnificent Renaissance *hôtels particuliers* (mansions). Some of these
mansions have become chic flats, boutiques and commercial art galleries,
while others provide splendid settings for a number of excellent museums,
not least among them the Musée Picasso, the Musée Carnavalet history
museum and the Musée d'Art et d'Histoire du Judaïsme. As the Marais is one
of the few areas of the city to remain open on a Sunday, many Parisians come
here for brunch and a leisurely afternoon's shopping.

The area was little more than a riverside swamp (*marais*) up until the thirteenth century, when the Knights Templar (see p.102) moved into its northern section and began to drain the land. It became a magnet for the aristocracy in the early 1600s after the construction of the place des Vosges by Henri IV in 1605. This golden age was relatively short-lived, however, for the aristocracy began to move away after the king took his court to Versailles in the latter part of the seventeenth century, leaving their grand houses to the trading classes, who were in turn displaced during the Revolution. From this point on, the mansions became slum tenements and the streets degenerated into squalor. It was only in the 1960s, with its designation as a *secteur sauvegardé* (a conservation area), that efforts were made to smarten up the area and improve living conditions.

The main artery running through the Marais, dividing it roughly north and south, is the busy **rue de Rivoli** and its continuation to the Bastille, rue St-Antoine. South of this line is the **quartier St-Paul**, with its antique shops and atmospheric backstreets. To the north lies the beautiful place des Vosges; the old Jewish quarter centred on rue des Rosiers; and the Marais' other main street, **rue des Francs-Bourgeois**, lined with aristocratic mansions and chic fashion and interior-design boutiques. Other streets worth exploring are rue Vieille du Temple, with its terraced cafés and bars, and the streets further north in the **Haut Marais**, an area on the up, home to young designers and contemporary art galleries.

Place des Vosges and around

Ⓜ Bastille/Chemin-Vert/St-Paul

As you approach via the narrow streets from Bastille or from the north or west, nothing quite prepares you for the size and grandeur of the **place des Vosges**, a magnificent square bordered by arcaded pink-brick and stone mansions, with a formal garden at its centre. A masterpiece of aristocratic elegance and the first example of planned development in the history of Paris, the square was commissioned in 1605 by Henri IV, and was inaugurated in 1612 for the wedding of Louis XIII and Anne of Austria; it is Louis' statue – or, rather, a replica of it – that stands hidden by chestnut trees in the middle of the gardens. Originally called place Royale, it was renamed Vosges in 1800 in honour of the *département*, the first to pay its share of the expenses of the revolutionary wars.

A royal palace, the Hôtel des Tournelles, stood on what is now the north side of the square until 1559, when it was demolished by Catherine de Médicis after her husband Henri II was killed here during a joust. The vacant space became a huge weekly horse market, trading between one and two thousand horses. So it remained until Henri IV decided on the construction of his place Royale.

Through all the vicissitudes of history, the *place* has never lost its cachet as a smart address. Today, the arcades harbour upmarket art, antique and fashion shops, as well as a number of restaurants and cafés. Buskers play classical music and jazz, and in the garden toddlers play in the sandpits and families picnic on the grass; this is one of the few Parisian gardens where the *pelouse* is not *interdite*.

Maison de Victor Hugo

6 place des Vosges, 4ᵉ • Tues–Sun 10am–6pm; closed hols • Free • ☎ 01 42 72 10 16 • Ⓜ Bastille

Among the many celebrities who made their homes in the place des Vosges was Victor Hugo; the second-floor apartment, at no. 6, where he lived from 1832 to 1848 and wrote much of *Les Misérables*, is now a museum, the **Maison de Victor Hugo**. Hugo's life, including his nineteen years of exile in Jersey and Guernsey, is evoked through a somewhat sparse collection of memorabilia, portraits, photographs and first editions of his works. What you do get, though, is an idea of Hugo's prodigious creativity: as well as being a prolific writer, he drew – a number of his ink drawings are exhibited – and designed his own Gothic-style furniture, in which he let his imagination run riot, as

seen in some of the pieces displayed. He even put together the extraordinary Chinese-style dining room, originally designed for the house of his lover, Juliette Drouet, in Guernsey, re-created in its entirety here. Among the family portraits is one by Auguste de Châtillon of Hugo's daughter, Léopoldine, shown holding a Book of Hours open at the Dormition of the Virgin – a poignant detail, given that eight years later at the age of 19 she drowned, along with her husband of just six months. Her loss inspired some of Hugo's most moving poetry, including the well-known *Demain dès l'aube*.

Hôtel de Sully

62 rue St-Antoine, 4ᵉ • Photographic exhibitions Tues noon–9pm, Wed–Fri noon–7pm, Sat & Sun 10am–7pm • €5, combined ticket with Jeu de Paume €8 • Ⓦ jeudepaume.org • Ⓜ St-Paul/Bastille

From the southwest corner of the place des Vosges, a door leads through to the formal château garden, orangerie and exquisite Renaissance facade of the **Hôtel de Sully**. The garden, with its park benches, makes for a peaceful rest stop; it's also a handy shortcut through to rue St-Antoine. Part of the building is used for temporary photographic exhibitions, usually with social, historical or anthropological themes, mounted by the Jeu de Paume, whose main site (see p.69) is in the Tuileries. The *hôtel* is also the headquarters of the Centre des Monuments Nationaux, which manages over a hundred national monuments and publishes numerous books and guides, many of which are on sale in the excellent ground-floor bookshop near the rue St-Antoine entrance; it's also worth a look for its fine seventeenth-century painted beamed ceiling. A branch of the *Angélina* tearoom (see p.271) is due to open in the orangerie by the end of 2011.

A short distance back to the west along rue St-Antoine, almost opposite the sixteenth-century **church of St-Paul-St-Louis**, which was inaugurated by Cardinal Richelieu, you'll find another square. A complete contrast to the imposing formality of the place des Vosges, the tiny **place du Marché-Ste-Catherine**, with its trees and little restaurant terraces, is intimate and irresistibly charming.

Rue des Francs-Bourgeois and around

Running west from the place des Vosges, the main lateral street of the northern part of the Marais is the narrow **rue des Francs-Bourgeois**. Beatnik Jack Kerouac translated it as "the street of the outspoken middle classes", which is a fair description of the contemporary residents, though the name in fact means "people exempt from tax", in reference to the penurious inmates of a medieval almshouse that once stood on the site of no. 34.

Along or just off this street lie some of the Marais' finest mansions, including the superb **Musée Carnavalet**, tracing the history of Paris; the bijou **Musée Cognacq-Jay**, devoted to eighteenth-century art and decorative arts; the engaging **Musée d'Art et d'Histoire du Judaïsme**; and the **Musée de l'Histoire de France**, the state archives museum, housed in one of the grandest mansions of all.

Musée Carnavalet

23 rue de Sévigné, 4ᵉ • Daily except Mon 10am–6pm • Free; entry to special exhibitions varies • ☎ 01 44 59 58 58 • Ⓜ St-Paul

The **Musée Carnavalet** is a fascinating museum that charts the history of Paris from its origins up to the *belle époque* through an extraordinary collection of paintings, sculptures, decorative arts and archeological finds. The museum's setting alone, in two beautiful Renaissance mansions (Hôtel Carnavalet and Hôtel Le Peletier) surrounded by attractive gardens, makes a visit worthwhile. There are 140 rooms in all, probably too much to see in one go, so it's best to pick up a floor plan and decide which areas you'd like to concentrate on.

The ground floor

The **ground floor** displays nineteenth- and early twentieth-century shop and inn signs and engrossing models of Paris through the ages, along with maps and plans, showing how much Haussmann's boulevards changed the face of the city. The renovated **orangerie** houses a significant collection of Neolithic finds, including a number of wooden pirogues (dug-out canoes) unearthed during the redevelopment of the Bercy riverside area in the 1990s.

The post-Revolution and **Napoleonic period** is also covered on the ground floor, in rooms 115–121; look out for Napoleon's favourite canteen, which accompanied him on his military exploits (and also followed him into exile on St Helena), consisting of 110 pieces ingeniously contained within a case no bigger than a picnic hamper. Among the items is a full set of gold cutlery, a gold-handled toothbrush, two candelabras and a dinky geometry set – everything an emperor could possibly need while on campaign.

6

The first floor

On the **first floor**, decorative arts feature strongly, with numerous re-created salons and boudoirs full of richly sculpted wood panelling and tapestries from the time of Louis XII to Louis XVI, rescued from buildings that had to be destroyed for Haussmann's boulevards. Room 21 is devoted to the famous letter-writer **Madame de Sévigné**, who lived in the Carnavalet mansion from 1677 until her death in 1696, and wrote a series of letters to her daughter here which vividly portray her privileged lifestyle under the reign of Louis XIV. You can see her Chinese lacquered writing desk, as well as portraits of her and various contemporaries, such as Molière and Corneille. Rooms 128 to 148 are largely devoted to the **belle époque** (early twentieth century), evoked through numerous paintings of the period and some wonderful **Art Nouveau** interiors, among which is the sumptuous peacock-green interior designed by Alphonse Mucha for Fouquet's jewellery shop in the rue Royale. Also well preserved is José-Maria Sert's **Art Deco** ballroom, dating from the 1920s, with its extravagant gold-leaf decor and grand-scale paintings, including one of the Queen of Sheba with a train of elephants. Nearby is a section on literary life at the beginning of the twentieth century, including a reconstruction of Proust's modestly furnished bedroom (room 147), with its cork-lined walls, designed to muffle external noise and allow the writer to work in peace – he spent most of his last three years closeted away here, penning his great novel, *A la recherche du temps perdu*.

The second floor

The **second floor** has rooms full of mementos of the **French Revolution**: models of the Bastille, original declarations of the Rights of Man and the Citizen, sculpted allegories of Reason, and crockery with revolutionary slogans and glorious models of the guillotine. There are also execution orders to make you shed a tear for the royalists, and one of the rooms of the Temple prison where Louis XVI and his family were locked up has been re-created, complete with the king's chess set and the Dauphin's toy tin soldiers.

Bibliothèque Historique de la Ville de Paris

24 rue Pavée, 4ᵉ • Mon–Sat 10am–6pm • Free • Ⓦ paris-bibliotheques.org • Ⓜ St-Paul

Just across from the Musée Carnavalet on rue des Francs-Bourgeois stands the **Bibliothèque Historique de la Ville de Paris**, housed in the splendid sixteenth-century Hôtel Lamoignon and safeguarding centuries' worth of texts and picture books about the city. The library is open to the public, and exhibitions on the history of Paris are often held here; details can be found on the website. Next to the Lamoignon on rue Pavée – so called because it was among the first of Paris's streets to be paved, in 1450 – was the site of **La Force prison**, where many of the Revolution's victims were incarcerated, including the Princesse de Lamballe, who was lynched in the massacres of September 1792; her head was presented on a stake to her friend Marie-Antoinette.

Musée Cognacq-Jay

8 rue Elzévir, 4ᵉ • Daily except Mon 10am–5.40pm • Free • ☎ 01 40 27 07 21 • Ⓜ St-Paul/Chemin-Vert

One block west of the Musée Carnavalet lies the intimate **Musée Cognacq-Jay**, occupying

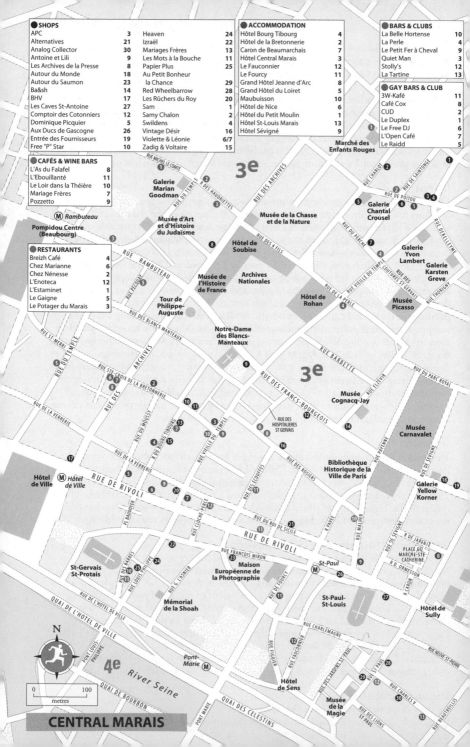

● SHOPS

APC	3	Heaven	24
Alternatives	21	Izraël	22
Analog Collector	30	Mariages Frères	13
Antoine et Lili	9	Les Mots à la Bouche	11
Les Archives de la Presse	8	Papier Plus	25
Autour du Monde	18	Au Petit Bonheur	
Autour du Saumon	23	la Chance	29
Ba&sh	14	Red Wheelbarrow	28
BHV	17	Les Rûchers du Roy	20
Les Caves St-Antoine	27	Sam	1
Comptoir des Cotonniers	12	Samy Chalon	2
Dominique Picquier	5	Swildens	4
Aux Ducs de Gascogne	26	Vintage Désir	16
Entrée des Fournisseurs	19	Violette & Léonie	6/7
Free "P" Star	10	Zadig & Voltaire	15

● CAFÉS & WINE BARS

L'As du Falafel	8
L'Ebouillanté	11
Le Loir dans la Théière	10
Mariage Frères	7
Pozzetto	9

Ⓜ *Rambuteau*

Pompidou Centre (Beaubourg)

● RESTAURANTS

Breizh Café	4
Chez Marianne	6
Chez Nénesse	2
L'Enoteca	12
L'Estaminet	1
Le Gaigne	5
Le Potager du Marais	3

● ACCOMMODATION

Hôtel Bourg Tibourg	4
Hôtel de la Bretonnerie	2
Caron de Beaumarchais	7
Hôtel Central Marais	3
Le Fauconnier	12
Le Fourcy	11
Grand Hôtel Jeanne d'Arc	8
Grand Hôtel du Loiret	5
Maubuisson	10
Hôtel de Nice	6
Hôtel du Petit Moulin	1
Hôtel St-Louis Marais	13
Hôtel Sévigné	9

● BARS & CLUBS

La Belle Hortense	10
La Perle	4
Le Petit Fer à Cheval	9
Quiet Man	3
Stolly's	12
La Tartine	13

● GAY BARS & CLUB

3W-Kafé	11
Café Cox	8
CUD	2
Le Duplex	1
Le Free DJ	6
L'Open Café	7
Le Raidd	5

Marché des Enfants Rouges

RUE MICHEL LE COMTE

3e

RUE DES ARCHIVES

RUE CHARLOT

RUE DE SAINTONGE

RUE DE POITOU

RUE DU TEMPLE

R DES HAUDRIETTES

Galerie Marian Goodman

Galerie Chantal Crousel

RUE DEBELLEYME

Musée de la Chasse et de la Nature

RUE DU PERCHE

Galerie Yvon Lambert

Galerie Karsten Greve

Musée d'Art et d'Histoire du Judaïsme

Hôtel de Soubise

RUE DES 4 FILS

RUE VIEILLE DU TEMPLE

RUE DES COUTURES ST GERVAIS

RUE THORIGNY

RUE RAMBUTEAU

Musée de l'Histoire de France

Archives Nationales

Hôtel de Rohan

RUE DE LA PERLE

Musée Picasso

RUE PASCALE

Tour de Philippe-Auguste

Notre-Dame des Blancs-Manteaux

RUE BARBETTE

RUE DU PARC ROYAL

RUE DES BLANCS MANTEAUX

3e

RUE ELZEVIR

RUE ST-MERRI

RUE DU TEMPLE

RUE STE-CROIX DE LA BRETONNERIE

RUE DES ARCHIVES

RUE DES FRANCS-BOURGEOIS

Musée Cognacq-Jay

RUE PAYENNE

Musée Carnavalet

RUE DE LA VERRERIE

RUE DU MOUSSY

RUE BOURG TIBOURG

RUE VIEILLE DU TEMPLE

RUE DES HOSPITALIERES ST GERVAIS

RUE DES ROSIERS

Bibliothèque Historique de la Ville de Paris

RUE DE SÉVIGNÉ

Hôtel de Ville

Ⓜ Hôtel de Ville

RUE DE RIVOLI

RUE DES ÉCOUFFES

Galerie Yellow Korner

PL. BAUDOYER

RUE CLOCHE-PERCE

R PAVÉE

RUE MALHER

R DE JARENTE

PLACE DU MARCHÉ-STE-CATHERINE

RUE DE RIVOLI

RUE DU ROI DE SICILE

R.D. ORMESSON

RUE FRANCOIS MIRON

St-Paul

Ⓜ

R CARON

St-Gervais St-Protais

RUE DES BARRES

RUE LOUIS PHILIPPE

RUE DE L'AVE MARIA

RUE DE L'HÔTEL DE VILLE

Maison Européenne de la Photographie

RUE DE FOURCY

St-Paul-St-Louis

RUE DE SÉVIGNÉ

Hôtel de Sully

QUAI DE L'HÔTEL DE VILLE

Mémorial de la Shoah

RUE CHARLEMAGNE

Hôtel de Sens

PONT LOUIS-PHILIPPE

N

River Seine

4e

Pont-Marie Ⓜ

RUE DU FIGUIER

RUE FAUCONNIER

RUE NEUVE ST-PIERRE

RUE DES JARDINS ST-PAUL

RUE CHARLES V

RUE DES LIONS ST PAUL

RUE BEAUTREILLIS

0 ——— 100
metres

QUAI DE BOURBON

QUAI DES CÉLESTINS

Pont Marie

Musée de la Magie

CENTRAL MARAIS

the fine Hôtel Donon. The Cognacq-Jay family built the Samaritaine department store, now closed (see p.90), and were noted philanthropists, as well as lovers of eighteenth-century European art. Their small collection of pieces on show includes a handful of works by Canaletto, Fragonard, Rubens and Quentin de la Tour, as well as an early Rembrandt and an exquisite still life by Chardin, displayed in beautifully carved wood-panelled rooms filled with Sèvres porcelain and Louis XV furniture.

Musée de l'Histoire de France

60 rue des Francs-Bourgeois, 4ᵉ • Mon–Fri 10am–12.30pm & 2–5.30pm, Sat & Sun 2–5.30pm • €3 • ⓜRambuteau/St-Paul

At the western end of the rue des Francs-Bourgeois there once stood a magnificent, early eighteenth-century palace complex, filling the entire block from rue des Quatre Fils to rue des Archives, and from rue Vieille-du-Temple to rue des Francs-Bourgeois. Only half remains today, but it is utterly splendid, especially the grand colonnaded courtyard of the **Hôtel de Soubise**, with its fabulous Rococo interiors, paintings by Boucher and vestigial fourteenth-century towers on rue des Quatre Fils. The opening of the site's formal gardens in 2011, after many years of closure to the public, makes it possible to admire the setting all the more.

The **Hôtel de Soubise** houses the city archives and the **Musée de l'Histoire de France**, which mounts changing exhibitions drawn from its extensive holdings; its fascinating haul includes Joan of Arc's trial proceedings, with a doodled impression of her in the margin, and a Revolutionary calendar, where "J" stands for Jean-Jacques Rousseau and "L" for "labourer". The *hôtel's* ground-floor Chambre du Prince is the scene of **chamber music recitals** (€12), held here most Saturdays, usually at 6pm.

Hôtel de Rohan and around

The adjacent **Hôtel de Rohan**, recently renovated, is also part of the archives complex and is sometimes used when there are large exhibitions. It has more fine interiors, including the Chinese-inspired Cabinet des Singes, whose walls are painted with monkeys acting out various aristocratic scenes.

Opposite the Hôtel de Soubise, at the back of a driveway for the Crédit Municipal bank, stands a pepperpot tower that formed part of the **city walls**; these were built by King Philippe-Auguste early in the thirteenth century to link up with his new fortress, the Louvre. Further east, past several more imposing facades, you can admire the delicate filigree ironwork of the balcony above the main entrance to the **Hôtel d'Albret** (no. 31), built in 1740, its stately courtyard a delightful setting in summer for jazz concerts.

Musée de la Chasse et de la Nature

62 rue des Archives, 3ᵉ • Tues–Sun 11am–6pm • €6, under-18s free • ☎ 01 53 01 92 40, ⓦ chassenature.org • ⓜRambuteau

Housed in the beautiful Hôtel Guénégaud and the neighbouring Hôtel Mongelas, the **Musée de la Chasse et de la Nature** is devoted largely to the theme of hunting, especially animals of the hunt. The museum starts with a series of rooms each devoted to a particular animal, such as the wild boar, wolf and dog. A "cabinet of curiosities" invites

---

THE FUTURE OF THE ARCHIVES AND THE MAISON DE L'HISTOIRE

There are plans to transfer archive documents dating from after 1789 from the **Hôtel de Soubise** to a new site being specially built in Pierrefitte-sur-Seine, outside Paris, so that the Marais site can concentrate on better conserving the pre-1789 documents, many of which are currently kept in cramped conditions. More controversially, in 2010 President Sarkozy announced he wanted to site a new national history museum, the **Maison de l'Histoire de France**, in the Hôtel de Soubise in 2015. Staff were up in arms and staged a five-month-long sit-in, while prominent historians argued it was too narrowly nationalistic, serving the president's right-wing, anti-immigration agenda. Debate is ongoing and it's unclear at the time of writing what the outcome will be.

you to pull open drawers and discover miscellaneous bits and bobs, such as paw prints, animal droppings and drawings, and you can look through eyeglasses and watch a video of the animal in its natural habitat – all quite appealing to children in particular. The rest of the museum's collection includes a formidable array of stuffed animals, including a giant polar bear, weapons ranging from prehistoric stone arrowheads to highly decorative crossbows and guns, and paintings by French artists, such as Desportes, romanticizing the chase.

6

Musée d'Art et d'Histoire du Judaïsme

71 rue du Temple, 3ᵉ • Mon–Fri 11am–6pm, Sun 10am–6pm • €6.80 • ☎ 01 53 01 86 53, ⓦ mahj.org • Ⓜ Rambuteau

Two blocks west of the Musée de la Chasse et de la Nature stands the attractively restored Hôtel de St-Aignan, home to the **Musée d'Art et d'Histoire du Judaïsme**. The museum traces the culture, history and artistic endeavours mainly of the **Jews in France**, though there are also many artefacts from the rest of Europe and North Africa. The result is a very comprehensive collection, as educational as it is beautiful. Free audioguides in English are available and worth picking up if you want to get the most out of the museum.

The medieval period to the nineteenth century

Highlights of the museum's holdings from the medieval period to the nineteenth century include a Gothic-style Hanukkah lamp, one of the very few French-Jewish artefacts to

---

THE DREYFUS AFFAIR

The **Dreyfus Affair** was one of the biggest crises to rock the Third Republic. It centred on Alfred Dreyfus, a captain in the French army and a Jew, who was arrested and convicted of spying for the Germans in 1894 on the flimsiest of evidence – his handwriting was said to resemble that on documents detailing French armaments found in the German embassy. In a humiliating public ceremony of "*dégradation*" in the courtyard of the Ecole Militaire his epaulettes were torn from his uniform and his sword broken, while anti-Semitic slogans were chanted by crowds outside. He was then sent to the notorious penal colony of Devil's Island, off Guyana. His family, convinced of his innocence, began campaigning for a retrial. Two newspapers, *L'Eclair* and *Le Matin*, questioned the evidence and in 1897 Colonel Georges Picquart, the new head of the Statistical Section, discovered a document which suggested that the true culprit was Major Ferdinand Walsin-Esterhazy. Esterhazy was perfunctorily tried by the Ministry of War, and let off. The government, keen to uphold the army's authority and reputation, acquiesced to the verdict, and Colonel Picquart was packed off to Tunisia.

However, a storm broke out when shortly afterwards writer **Emile Zola** published his famous open letter, titled *J'accuse…!*, to the President of the Republic in the *Aurore* newspaper on January 13, 1898. In it he denounced the army and authorities and accused them of a cover-up. Zola was convicted for libel and sentenced to a year's imprisonment, which he avoided by fleeing to England. The article triggered a major outcry and suddenly the *affaire* was the chief topic of conversation in every café in France. French society divided into two camps: Dreyfusards and anti-Dreyfusards. The former, convinced the army was guilty of a cover-up, comprised republicans committed to equal rights and the primacy of parliament and included many prominent intellectuals and left-wing figures such as Jean Jaurès, Anatole France, Léon Blum, Georges Clemenceau and Marcel Proust. Ranked among the anti-Dreyfusards were clerics, anti-Semitic newspapers such as *La Libre Parole*, monarchists and conservatives, all suspecting a Jewish conspiracy to tarnish the army's reputation. The former clamoured for justice, while the latter called for respect and order.

In June 1897, the secret dossier that convicted Dreyfus was finally re-examined; there was a retrial and, again, Dreyfus was convicted of treason, but was quickly pardoned by President Loubet, desperate to draw a line under the whole affair. Finally, in 1906, Dreyfus, his health broken by hard labour, was granted a full pardon and awarded the *Légion d'honneur*. The matter was formally closed, but the repercussions of the affair were deep and long-lasting; it had revealed fundamental divisions in French society, and split the country along lines that would determine France's development in the twentieth century.

survive from the period before the expulsion of the Jews from France in 1394; an Italian gilded circumcision chair from the seventeenth century; and a completely intact, late nineteenth-century Austrian *sukkah*, "a temporary dwelling built for the celebration of the Harvest, decorated with paintings of Jerusalem and the Mount of Olives". Other artefacts include Moroccan wedding garments, highly decorated marriage contracts from eighteenth-century Modena and gorgeous, almost whimsical, spice containers.

The Dreyfus archives

The museum also holds the Dreyfus archives, donated as a gift from Dreyfus's grandchildren. The notorious **Dreyfus affair** (see box opposite) is documented with letters, photographs and press clippings; you can read Emile Zola's famous letter "*J'accuse…!*" in which the novelist defends Dreyfus's innocence, and the letters that Dreyfus sent to his wife from prison on Devil's Island in which he talks of *épouvantable* ("terrible") suffering and loneliness.

6

The twentieth century

The museum also hosts a significant collection of paintings and sculpture by **Jewish artists** – Marc Chagall, Samuel Hirszenberg, Chaïm Soutine and Jacques Lipchitz – who came to live in Paris at the beginning of the twentieth century. The Holocaust is only briefly touched on, since it's dealt with in depth by the Musée de la Shoah (see p.104). The main reference is an installation by contemporary artist Christian Boltanski: one of the exterior walls of a small courtyard is covered with black-bordered death announcements printed with the names of the Jewish artisans who once lived in the building, a number of whom were deported.

The Jewish quarter: rue des Rosiers

Ⓜ St-Paul

One block south of the rue des Francs-Bourgeois, the area around narrow, pedestrianized **rue des Rosiers** has traditionally been the **Jewish quarter** of the city ever since the twelfth century. However, soaring property prices and the area's burgeoning popularity with tourists have forced many of the traditional grocers, bakers, bookshops and cafés to close, and the area is in real danger of losing its identity. The hammam (no. 4) now houses a clothing store, as does *Jo Goldenberg* (no. 7), once the city's most famous Jewish restaurant. Despite these changes, the area still retains a Jewish flavour, with a number of kosher food shops and Hebrew bookstores. There's also a distinctly Mediterranean feel in the *quartier*; on Sunday lunchtimes the street fills with people who come to pick up a falafel wrap from one of the handful of Middle Eastern cafés. This development is testimony to the influence of the **North African Sephardim**, who, since the end of World War II, have sought refuge here from the uncertainties of life in the French ex-colonies. They have replenished Paris's Jewish population, depleted when its Ashkenazim, having escaped the pogroms of Eastern Europe, were rounded up by the Nazis and the French police and transported back east to concentration camps.

The Haut Marais

The northern part of the Marais, known as the Haut Marais (the "upper Marais"), encompasses the old **Quartier du Temple**, named after the Knights Templar's stronghold that once stood at its heart, and the city's original **Chinatown**, concentrated on the upper end of rue du Temple and the streets west. Here the aristocratic stone facades of the lower Marais give way to the more humble, though no less attractive, stucco, paint and thick-slatted shutters of seventeenth- and eighteenth-century streets. Some bear the names of old rural French provinces: Beauce, Perche, Saintonge, Picardie. Formerly a quiet backwater, the area now attracts an arty crowd, who come to browse the many contemporary art galleries (see box below), interior design shops and boutiques of young fashion designers concentrated on **rue Charlot**, rue de Poitou, rue Vieille du Temple and around. The area's chief visitor attractions are the excellent Musée Picasso, the absorbing Musée des Arts et Métiers and the new state-of-the-art Gaîté Lyrique digital arts centre.

Musée Picasso

5 rue de Thorigny, 3ᵉ • Closed until early 2012 for renovation, see website for updated opening hours and admission • ☎ 01 42 71 25 21, ⓦ musee-picasso.fr • ⓜ Chemin-Vert/St-Paul

On the northern side of rue des Francs-Bourgeois, rue Payenne leads up to the lovely gardens and houses of **rue du Parc-Royal** and on to **rue de Thorigny**. Here, at no. 5, the magnificent classical facade of the seventeenth-century **Hôtel Salé**, built for a rich salt-tax collector, conceals the **Musée Picasso**, which is closed until early 2012 for renovation. It houses the largest collection of Picassos anywhere, representing almost all the major periods of the artist's life from 1905 onwards. Many of the works were owned by Picasso and on his death in 1973 were seized by the state in lieu of taxes owed. The result is an unedited body of work, which, although not among the most recognizable of Picasso's masterpieces, nevertheless provides a sense of the artist's development and an insight into the person behind the myth.

The collection

The exhibition starts with the Blue Period, studies for the *Demoiselles d'Avignon*, and experiments with Cubism and Surrealism. It then moves on to his larger-scale works on themes of war, peace, love and death. Perhaps some of the most engaging works are his more personal ones. The portraits of the artist's lovers, Dora Maar and Marie-Thérèse, show how the two women inspired Picasso in different ways: Dora Maar is

---

PRIVATE ART GALLERIES

The Marais, and the Haut Marais in particular, is where most of the city's private commercial **art galleries** are concentrated. Many occupy handsome old mansion houses, which are set back from the road and reached via cobbled courtyards. The following are some of the highlights; all are free to visit.

Galerie Chantal Crousel 10 rue Charlot, 3ᵉ ⓦ crousel.com; ⓜ Filles-du-Calvaire; map p.96. Around since 1980, this gallery represents mostly foreign and some French artists, such as Gabriel Orozco and Monica Hatoum, working in a variety of media. It also promotes the work of emerging video artists, such as Melik Ohanian. Tues–Sat 11am–1pm & 2–7pm.

Galerie Emmanuel Perrotin 76 rue de Turenne, 3ᵉ ⓦ galerieperrotin.com; ⓜ St-Sébastien-Froissart; map p.93. One of the most influential galleries on the French contemporary art scene, Perrotin has exhibited French artists like Sophie Calle as well as international names such as Takashi Murakami and Maurizio Cattelan. Tues–Sat 11am–7pm.

Galerie Karsten Greve 5 rue Debelleyme, 3ᵉ ⓦ artnet.com/kgreve.html;

ⓜ St-Sébastien-Froissart; map p.96. Paris branch of the German gallery, showing the work of world-class artists such as Louise Bourgeois and Willem de Kooning. Tues–Sat 11am–7pm.

Galerie Marian Goodman 79 rue du Temple, 3ᵉ ⓦ mariangoodman.com; ⓜ Rambuteau; map p.96. This offshoot of the famed New York gallery recently exhibited Pierre Huyghe and Yang Fudong. Tues–Sat 11am–7pm.

Galerie Yellow Korner 8 rue des Francs-Bourgeois, 3ᵉ ⓦ yellowkorner.com; ⓜ St-Paul; map p.96. Contemporary photography gallery with outposts throughout Europe, showcasing established and up-and-coming talent. Tues–Sat 11.30am–7pm, Sun & Mon 2–7pm.

Galerie Yvon Lambert 108 rue Vieille du Temple, 3ᵉ ⓦ yvon-lambert.com; ⓜ Filles-du-Calvaire; map p.96. A major player for more than thirty years: the likes of Andres Serrano, Giulio Paolini and Andy Warhol have all been exhibited here in recent years. Tues–Fri 10am–1pm & 2.30–7pm, Sat 10am–7pm.

painted with strong lines and vibrant colours, suggesting a vivacious personality, while Marie-Thérèse's muted colours and soft contours convey serenity and peace.

Passage de Retz and around

9 rue Charlot, 3ᵉ · Daily except Mon 10am–7pm · Free · Ⓦ passagederetz.com · Ⓜ Filles-du-Calvaire

Contemporary art galleries abound in the Marais particularly in the streets around the Musée Picasso (see box, p.100); also check the listings in *Pariscope* (see p.38). At the lower end of rue Charlot you could check out what's happening at **Passage de Retz**, a gallery which stages occasional exhibitions of fine art and design from young artists and is attractively set in an old mansion; there's also a bookshop and café.

Opposite, in the dead-end **ruelle de Sourdis**, one section of the street has remained unchanged since its construction in 1626. Further along, on the corner of **rue du Perche**, a little Classical facade on a leafy courtyard hides the **Armenian church of Ste-Croix**, testimony to the many Armenians who sought refuge here from the Turkish pogroms of World War I.

The Marché des Enfants-Rouges

39 rue de Bretagne, 3ᵉ · Tues–Sat 8.30am–2pm & 4–7.30pm, Sun 8.30am–2pm · Ⓜ Filles-du-Calvaire

Just west off rue Charlot, a little short of the vibrant rue de Bretagne, is the easily missed entrance to the **Marché des Enfants-Rouges**, one of the smallest and oldest food markets in Paris, dating back to 1616, its name a reference to the red uniforms once worn by children at the orphanage that stood nearby. It has a very lively atmosphere and outdoor tables where you can eat takeaway soups, couscous, sushi and more standard fare. **Rue de Bretagne** itself is full of traditional food shops such as cheesemongers, bakeries and coffee merchants, as well as some popular cafés such as *Café Charlot* and *Le Progrès* (see p.276).

Quartier du Temple

Ⓜ Temple

The **Quartier du Temple** – bounded by rue de Bretagne, rue du Temple, rue de Béranger and rue de Picardie – designates the area that was once the central stronghold of the **Knights Templar**, a military order established in Jerusalem at the time of the Crusades to protect pilgrims to the Holy Land. Its members were exceedingly rich and powerful, with some nine thousand commands spread across Europe. They came to a sticky end early in the fourteenth century, however, when King Philippe le Bel, alarmed at their growing power, and in alliance with Pope Clement V, had them tried for sacrilege, blasphemy and sodomy. Fifty-four of the order's members were burnt, and the order abolished. The Temple buildings survived until the Revolution, when Louis XVI and the royal family were imprisoned in the keep (see box opposite), but they were demolished in 1808 by Napoleon, and nothing remains beyond the name "Temple", preserved in the **Square du Temple** gardens and the **Carreau du Temple**, a former clothes market. The Carreau is currently being converted into a performing arts and sports centre; the shell of the nineteenth-century brick, glass and iron-frame structure is being preserved, and there are plans to build underground.

Chinatown

Ⓜ Arts-et-Métiers/Temple

A couple of blocks to the west of the Carreau du Temple, on and around the top end of **rue du Temple**, lies Paris's original **Chinatown** district. The area was settled during World War I when Chinese immigrants came over to fill the gap in the workforce left by the departure of French troops for the front. Rue du Temple, lined with many beautiful houses dating back to the seventeenth century (no. 41, for instance, the Hôtel Aigle d'Or, is the last surviving coaching inn of the period), is full of Chinese-run wholesale businesses trading in leather and fashion accessories.

The streets to the west of rue du Temple are narrow, dark and riddled with passages, the houses half-timbered and bulging with age. No. 51 rue Montmorency is Paris's oldest house, built in 1407 for the alchemist Nicolas Flamel, whose name will ring a bell with Harry Potter fans; the building is now a restaurant, *Auberge Nicolas Flamel*.

The Musée des Arts et Métiers

60 rue de Réaumur, 3ᵉ • Daily except Mon 10am–6pm, Thurs until 9.30pm • €6.50 • ⓦ arts-et-metiers.net • ⓂArts-et-Métiers

The **Musée des Arts et Métiers** is a fascinating museum of technological innovation. It's part of the Conservatoire des Arts et Métiers and incorporates the former Benedictine priory of St-Martin-des-Champs, its original chapel dating from the fourth century. The museum's most important exhibit is Foucault's pendulum, which the scientist used to demonstrate the rotation of the earth in 1851, a sensational event held at the Panthéon and attended by a huge crowd eager to "see the earth go round". The orb itself, a hollow brass sphere, is under glass in the chapel and there's a working model set up nearby.

Other exhibits include the laboratory of Lavoisier, the French chemist who first showed that water is a combination of oxygen and hydrogen, and, hanging as if in mid-flight above the grand staircase, the elegant "Avion 3", a flying machine complete with feathered propellers, which was donated to the Conservatoire after several ill-fated attempts to fly it.

La Gaîté Lyrique

3bis rue Papin, 3ᵉ • Tues–Sat 2–8pm, Sun 2–6pm • ☎ 01 53 01 51 51, ⓦ gaite-lyrique.net • ⓂRéaumur-Sébastopol/Arts-et-Métiers

The **Gaîté Lyrique** is a new centre for digital arts and contemporary music, opened in 2011. This venerable Italian-style theatre, built in 1862, was once renowned as a venue for operettas under such illustrious directors as Jacques Offenbach, and hosted the Ballets Russes in the 1920s. After twenty years of closure, it has been given a radical makeover: the architects have preserved and restored the facade, splendid marble foyer and entrance hall, while opening up the interior to accommodate a state-of-the-art concert hall, exhibition spaces and artists' studios, as well as a shop and café. The centre's busy programme of events includes regular concerts, exhibitions, dance and theatre performances, and art installations.

THE TEMPLE AND LOUIS XVII

Louis XVI, Marie-Antoinette, their two children and immediate family were all imprisoned in the keep of the Knights Templar's ancient fortress in August 1792 by the revolutionary government. By the end of 1794, when all the adults had been executed, the two children – the teenage Marie-Thérèse and the 9- or 10-year-old Dauphin, now, in the eyes of royalists, **Louis XVII** – remained there alone, in the charge of a family called Simon. Louis XVII was literally walled up, allowed no communication with other human beings, not even his sister, who was living on the floor above (Marie-Thérèse, incidentally, survived, went into exile in 1775, and returned to France in 1814 with the Bourbon restoration). He died of tuberculosis in 1795, a half-crazed imbecile, and was buried in a public grave.

For many years afterwards, however, **rumours** circulated that Louis XVII was in fact alive. The doctor, for example, who certified the child's death kept a lock of his hair, but it was later found not to correspond with the colour of the young Louis XVII's hair, as remembered by his sister. Furthermore, Mme Simon confessed on her deathbed that she had substituted another child for Louis XVII. One theory is that the real Louis XVII died early in 1794. But since Robespierre needed the heir to the throne as a hostage with which to menace internal and foreign royalist enemies, he had Louis disposed of in secret and substituted another child.

Taking advantage of this atmosphere of uncertainty, 43 different people subsequently claimed to be Louis XVII. After nearly two centuries of speculation, all rumours were put to rest in 2000 when DNA from the child who died of TB was found to match samples obtained from locks of Marie-Antoinette's hair, and also that of several other maternal relatives.

Quartier St-Paul

The southern part of the Marais, the **Quartier St-Paul**, between the rue de Rivoli, rue de St-Antoine and the Seine, is less buzzy than the rest of the district, its quiet, atmospheric streets lined with attractive old houses. The chief sights are the moving **Mémorial de la Shoah**, with its museum documenting the fate of French Jews in World War II; the **Maison Européenne de la Photographie**, which hosts exhibitions by contemporary photographers; and the **Pavillon de l'Arsenal**, a showcase for the city's current architectural projects. The area is also a good hunting ground for antiques, concentrated mostly in the **Village St-Paul** and rue St-Paul.

6

St-Gervais-St-Protais

Place St-Gervais, 4ᵉ • ⓂHôtel-de-Ville

There's been a church on the site of **St-Gervais-St-Protais** since the sixth century; the current building was started in 1494, though not completed until the seventeenth century, which explains the mismatched late-Gothic interior and Classical exterior. There's some lovely stained glass inside, sixteenth-century carved misericords and a seventeenth-century organ; it's one of Paris's oldest and has been played by eight generations of the Couperin family, including the famous François Couperin. The third chapel down on the right commemorates the 88 victims of a German shell that hit the church on Good Friday 1918 and caused part of the nave to collapse.

Exiting the church round the altar at the back, you enter cobbled **rue des Barres**, a picturesque little street, filled with the scent of roses from nearby gardens in summer, and a nice setting for the outdoor terrace of *L'Ebouillanté* café (see p.275).

Mémorial de la Shoah

17 rue Geoffroy l'Asnier, 4ᵉ • Daily except Sat 10am–6pm, Thurs till 10pm • Free • ☎ 01 42 77 44 72, ⓌV memorialdelashoah.org • ⓂSt-Paul/Pont-Marie

The grim fate of French Jews in World War II is commemorated at the **Mémorial de la Shoah**, within the Centre de Documentation Juive Contemporaine, access to which usually involves queuing, as visitors and bags are scanned at the entrance. President Chirac opened a new museum here in 2005 and, alongside the sombre **Mémorial du Martyr Juif Inconnu** (Memorial to the Unknown Jewish Martyr), unveiled a Wall of Names; ten researchers spent two and a half years trawling Gestapo documents and interviewing French families to compile the list of the 76,000 Jews – around a quarter of the wartime population – sent to death camps from 1942 to 1944. In 2006, the **Mur des Justes** was added, a wall listing the names of French people who aided Jews at this time.

Chirac, in 1995, was the first French president to formally acknowledge that France was involved in systematically persecuting Jews during World War II. In most instances, it was the French police, not the Nazi occupiers, who rounded up the Jews for deportation. The most notorious case was in July 1942, when 13,152 Jews (including over 4000 children) were rounded up in the Vel d'Hiv bicycle stadium in Paris and sent to death camps.

The museum

The Vel d'Hiv incident, along with much else, is documented in the excellent **museum**, with plenty of information in English. The main focus is events in France leading up to and during World War II, but there is also lots of background on the history of Jews in France and in Europe as a whole. Individual stories are illustrated with photos, ID cards, letters and other documents. You learn about model citizens such as the Javel family, who were all deported and died in the camps, their long-established residence in France and distinguished record of military service counting for naught in the relentless Nazi drive to exterminate all Jews. Others, such as the Lifchitz family, who fled pogroms in Russia and settled in France in

1909, managed to survive the war – in this case by going into hiding and obtaining false ID as Orthodox Christians. The collection also features some drawings and letters from Drancy, the holding station outside Paris, from which French Jews were sent on to camps in Germany. The museum ends with the **Mémorial des Enfants**, an overwhelming collection of photos, almost unbearable to look at, of 2500 French children, each image marked with the date of their birth and the date of their deportation.

Maison Européenne de la Photographie

6

4 rue de Fourcy, 4ᵉ • Wed–Sun 11am–8pm • €7, free Wed after 5pm • ☎ 01 44 78 75 00, ⓦ mep-fr.org • ⓂSt-Paul/Pont-Marie

Between rues Fourcy and François-Miron, a gorgeous Marais mansion, the early eighteenth-century Hôtel Hénault de Cantobre now houses the **Maison Européenne de la Photographie**, dedicated to the art of contemporary photography. Temporary shows combine with a revolving exhibition of the permanent collection; young photographers and photo journalists get a look-in, as well as artists using photography in multimedia creations or installation art. There's also a library, *vidéothèque* and stylish café.

Village St-Paul and around

ⓂSt-Paul/Pont-Marie

East of the Maison Européenne de la Photographie is the **Village St-Paul**, a network of courtyards and streets housing around a hundred antique, interior-design and art shops. This part of the Marais suffered a postwar hatchet job, and, although seventeenth- and eighteenth-century magnificence is still in evidence (there's even a stretch of the city's defensive wall dating from the early thirteenth century in the lycée playground on rue des Jardins St-Paul), it lacks the architectural cohesion of the Marais to the north. The fifteenth-century **Hôtel de Sens**, on the rue du Figuier, looks bizarre in its isolation. The public library it now houses, the **Bibliothèque Forney** (see p.341), filled with volumes on fine and applied arts, gives a good excuse to explore this outstanding medieval building.

Musée de la Magie

11 rue St-Paul, 4ᵉ • Wed, Sat & Sun 2–7pm; live magic show every 30min from 2.30–6pm • €11, children €9 • ☎ 01 42 72 13 26, ⓦ museedelamagie.com • ⓂSt-Paul/Sully-Morland

Set amid the antique shops on rue St-Paul is the **Musée de la Magie**, a delightful museum of magic and illusion. Automata, distorting mirrors and optical illusions, things that float on thin air, a box for sawing people in half – they're all on view, with examples from the eighteenth and nineteenth centuries, as well as contemporary magicians' tools and hands-on exhibits for children. Most fun is a live magician's demonstration. The museum shop sells books on conjuring, plus magic cards, wands, boxes, scarves and the like. Groups of school children tend to visit on Wednesdays, so it's better to visit at weekends.

Pavillon de l'Arsenal

21 bd Morland, 4ᵉ • Tues–Sat 10.30am–6.30pm, Sun 11am–7pm • Free • ☎ 01 42 76 33 97, ⓦ pavillon-arsenal.com • ⓂSully-Morland

The **Pavillon de l'Arsenal** is an exhibition centre that presents the capital's current **architectural projects** to the public, such as the new Les Halles venture. There's also a permanent exhibition on Paris's architectural development, "Paris, visite guidée", including a huge interactive model of the city.

Bastille and around

A symbol of revolution since the toppling of the Bastille prison in 1789, the Bastille quarter used to belong in spirit and style to the working-class districts of eastern Paris. Since the construction of the opera house in the 1980s, however, it has become a magnet for artists, fashion folk and young people, who have brought with them stylish shops and an energetic nightlife. Much of the action takes place around rue de Lappe, where cocktail lounges and theme bars have edged out the old tool shops, cobblers and ironmongers. However, some of the working-class flavour lingers on, especially along rue de la Roquette and in the furniture workshops off rue du Faubourg-St-Antoine, testimony to a long tradition of cabinet-making and woodworking in the district.

South of Bastille, the relatively unsung **twelfth arrondissement** offers an authentic slice of Paris, with its neighbourhood shops and bars, and traditional markets, such as the lively Marché d'Aligre. Among the area's attractions are the **Promenade Plantée**, an ex-railway line turned into an elevated walkway running from Bastille to the green expanse of the **Bois de Vincennes**, and **Bercy Village**'s attractive cafés and shops set in old wine warehouses.

Place de la Bastille

Place de la Bastille, a vast, traffic-choked square, is indissolubly linked with the events of July 14, 1789, when the Bastille prison fortress was stormed, triggering the French Revolution and the end of feudalism in Europe. Bastille Day (July 14) is celebrated throughout France and the square is the scene of dancing and partying on the evening of July 13. The prison itself no longer stands – its only visible remains have been transported to square Henri-Galli at the end of boulevard Henri-IV. A Société Générale bank is situated on the site of the prison and the place de la Bastille is where the fortress's ramparts would have been.

7

Opéra Bastille

Place de la Bastille, 11ᵉ · ⓦ operadeparis.fr · ⓜ Bastille

The Bicentennial of the French Revolution in 1989 was marked by the inauguration of a new opera house on place de la Bastille, the **Opéra Bastille**, one of François Mitterrand's pet projects. It fills almost the entire block between rues de Lyon, Charenton and Moreau. One critic described it as a "hippopotamus in a bathtub", and you can see his point. The architect, Uruguayan Carlos Ott, was concerned that his design should not bring an overbearing monumentalism to place de la Bastille. The different depths and layers of the semicircular facade do give a certain sense of the building stepping back, but self-effacing it is not. With time, use and familiarity, Parisians seem to have become reconciled to it, and people happily sit on its steps, wander into its shops and libraries, and camp out all night for the free performance on July 14.

The Port de l'Arsenal

ⓜ Bastille

Just south of the place de la Bastille is the **Port de l'Arsenal** marina, occupying part of what was once the moat around the Bastille. The Canal St-Martin starts here, flowing underneath the square and emerging much further north, just past place de la République, a route plied by canal pleasure-boats run by Canauxrama (see p.340). Some two hundred boats are moored up in the marina, and the landscaped banks, with children's playgrounds, make it quite a pleasant spot for a wander.

Maison Rouge

10 bd de la Bastille, 11ᵉ · Wed–Sun 11am–7pm, Thurs till 9pm · €7 · ☎ 01 40 01 08 81, ⓦ lamaisonrouge.org · ⓜ Bastille/Quai de la Rapée

One of the former industrial spaces bordering the port de l'Arsenal has been converted into a light and spacious contemporary art gallery, called the **Maison Rouge – Fondation Antoine de Galbert**. Founded in 2004 by collector Antoine de Galbert, the Maison Rouge, which takes its name from the bright-red pavilion at the centre of the building, holds changing exhibitions, either devoted to an individual artist or a private collection, such as the recent exhibition of works by Japanese artist Chiharu Shiota. The recent opening of a branch of *Rose Bakery* here also makes it a nice place for a bite to eat.

BASTILLE & EAST

● **RESTAURANTS**

A la Biche au Bois	19	Jacques-Mélac	1
Bistrot Paul Bert	11	Le Mansouria	12
Le Bistrot du Peintre	9	Paris-Hanoï	8
Bofinger	6	Le Train Bleu	20
Chez Paul	10	Au Vieux Chêne	13
L'Encrier	17	Waly Fay	4
La Gazzetta	14		

● **CAFÉS & WINE BARS**

L'Armagnac	5
Le Baron Rouge	16
Café des Anges	3
Café de l'Industrie	2
Chez Prosper	18
Pause Café	7
La Ruche à Miel	15

● **SHOPS**

Abdon	2
Anne Willi	4
La Bague de Kenza	1
Le Baron Rouge	7
Caves Michel Renaud	8
Cécile et Jeanne	9
Galerie Patrick Séguin	3
Isabel Marant	5
Du Pareil au Même	6

● **ACCOMMODATION**

Auberge Internationale des Jeunes	2
Marais Bastille	1
Maurice Ravel	4
Nouvel Hôtel	3
Hôtel de la Porte Dorée	5
Le Quartier Bercy Square	6

● **BARS, CLUBS & LIVE MUSIC**

L'Atelier Charonne	6
Café de la Danse	4
Café de l'Industrie	2
Le Lèche-Vin	3
Les Marcheurs de Planète	1
SanZSanS	7
La Scène Bastille	5

Cimetière du Père-Lachaise

20e

Philippe Auguste

Alexandre Dumas

Charonne

BD DE MÉNILMONTANT

BOULEVARD DE CHARONNE

AVENUE PHILIPPE-AUGUSTE

RUE DE CHARONNE

SQUARE DE LA ROQUETTE

RUE DE LA ROQUETTE

RUE DE LA FOLIE REGNAULT

RUE MERLIN

RUE SERVAN

RUE GERBIER

RUE LÉON FROT

RUE MERCŒUR

BOULEVARD VOLTAIRE

RUE L. VALLÈS

RUE J. MACÉ

RUE CHANZY

RUE DE NICE

C. BEAUHARNAIS

RUE ALEXANDRE DUMAS

AVENUE PHILIPPE-AUGUSTE

Boulets Montreuil

Avron

RUE PAUL BERT

CITÉ PROST

RUE TITON

RUE DE BOULETS

RUE DE MONTREUIL

BOULEVARD VOLTAIRE

RUE DU FAUBOURG ST-ANTOINE

Faidherbe Chaligny

Reuilly Diderot

Reuilly Diderot

BOULEVARD DIDEROT

RUE DE REUILLY

RUE CLAUDE TILLIER

RUE CHALIGNY

RUE ÉRARD

RUE DE REUILLY

SQUARE SAINT-CHARLES

IMP. MOUSSET

RUE DU SERGENT BAUCHAT

St-Eloi

Montgallet

RUE MONTGALLET

R. DE CHARENTON

Triomphe de la République

PLACE DE LA NATION

Nation

Nation

AV DU TRONE

COURS DE VINCENNES

RUE DE PICPUS

AVENUE DU BEL AIR

R. DES COLONNES DU TRÔNE

BD DE PICPUS

AVENUE DE ST-MANDÉ

N

0	300
	metres

East of place de la Bastille

Northeast of place de la Bastille, off rue de la Roquette, narrow, cobbled **rue de Lappe** is a lively place at night, crammed with bars drawing a largely teenage and out-of-town crowd. At no. 32, *Balajo* is one remnant of a very Parisian tradition: the *bals musettes*, or music halls of 1930s *gai Paris*, established by the area's large Auvergnat population and frequented between the wars by Piaf, Jean Gabin and Rita Hayworth. It was founded by one Jo de France, who introduced glitter and spectacle into what were then seedy gangster dives, enticing Parisians from the other side of the city to drink absinthe and savour the rue de Lappe lowlife. Parisians are still drawn here and to the bars on neighbouring streets, such as **rue Daval** to the north.

Off rue Daval, on the left as you walk up from rue de la Lappe, is charming little pedestrianized **cour Damoye**, a narrow cobbled street formerly lined with furniture workshops and now mostly inhabited by architects' studios, design shops and the fragrant Brûlerie Daval coffee merchant. Other streets worth exploring are the nearby section of **rue de Charonne**, home to fashion boutiques and wacky interior designers, and **rue Keller**, clustered with alternative, hippy outfits, indie record stores and young fashion designers such as Anne Willi (see p.326).

Church of Ste-Marguerite

36 rue St-Bernard, 11e • Mon–Sat 8am–noon & 3–7.30pm, Sun 8.30am–noon & 5–7.30pm • Free • Ⓜ Charonne

South of rue de Charonne, between rue St-Bernard and impasse Charrière, stands the rustic-looking **church of Ste-Marguerite**, with a garden dedicated to the memory of Raoul Nordling, the Swedish consul who persuaded the retreating Germans not to blow up Paris in 1944. The church itself was built in 1624 to accommodate the growing local population, which was about 40,000 in 1710 and 100,000 in 1900. The sculptures on the transept pediments were carved by its first full-blown parish priest. The inside of the church is wide-bodied, low and quiet, with a distinctly rural feel. The stained-glass windows record a very local history: the visit in 1802 of Pope Pius VII, who was in Paris for Napoleon's coronation; the miraculous cure of a Madame Delafosse in the rue de Charonne in 1725; the fatal wounding of Monseigneur Affre, the archbishop of Paris, in the course of a street battle in the faubourg in 1848; the murder of sixteen Carmelite nuns at the Barrière du Trône in 1794; and the *quartier*'s dead of World War I. In the now disused cemetery of Ste-Marguerite lies the body of Louis XVII, the 10-year-old heir of the guillotined Louis XVI, who died in the Temple prison (see box, p.103). The cemetery also received the dead from the Bastille prison.

THE COLONNE DE JUILLET

A gleaming gold statue, a winged figure of Liberty, stands atop the bronze **Colonne de Juillet** at the centre of place de la Bastille. The plinth on which it stands was once intended to hold quite a different monument – **Napoleon** had wanted a giant elephant fountain to stand here, with a spiral staircase inside one leg and viewing platform on top. The project never came to fruition, but the full-scale model that was made became a curiosity in its own right and stood for a while near the Gare de Vincennes (Gavroche in Victor Hugo's *Les Miserables* sought shelter in it). After 35 years it was sold for 3833 francs. The same architect (Jean-Antoine Alavoine) who had worked on the elephant built the present column, which was erected to commemorate the **July Revolution of 1830**, replacing the autocratic Charles X with the "Citizen King" Louis-Philippe. When Louis-Philippe fled in the more significant 1848 Revolution, his throne was burnt beside the column and a new inscription added. Four months later, the workers again took to the streets. All of eastern Paris was barricaded, with the fiercest fighting on rue du Faubourg-St-Antoine, until the rebellion was quelled with the usual massacres and deportation of survivors. The square is still an important rallying point for political protest.

Rue de la Roquette
ⓂBastille/Voltaire

Running parallel to rue de Charonne is rather scruffy **rue de la Roquette**, home to cheap and cheerful shops, Turkish restaurants and local bars. Towards its eastern end is **square de la Roquette**, the site of an old prison, where four thousand members of the Resistance were incarcerated in 1944. The low, forbidding gateway on rue de la Roquette has been preserved in their memory.

The Faubourg-St-Antoine
ⓂBastille/Ledru-Rollin/Faidherbe Chaligny

After Louis XI licensed the establishment of craftsmen in the fifteenth century, the **rue du Faubourg-St-Antoine**, running east from place de la Bastille, became the principal working-class *quartier* of Paris, cradle of revolutions and mother of street-fighters. From its beginnings, the principal trade associated with it has been **furniture-making**, and this was where the classic styles of French furniture – Louis XIV, Louis XV, Second Empire – were developed. There are still quite a few furniture shops on the street, and a number of workshops, as well as related trades such as inlayers, stainers and polishers, still inhabit the maze of interconnecting yards and *passages* that run off the faubourg, especially at the western end. One of the most attractive courtyards is at no. 56, the cour du Bel Air, with its lemon trees, and ivy- and rose-covered buildings.

7

Place de la Nation
ⓂNation

Rue du Faubourg-St-Antoine leads eastwards to **place de la Nation**. The *place* is adorned with the *Triumph of the Republic*, a monumental bronze group topped with a stately female figure personifying the Republic. To the east, framing the avenue du Trône, are two tall Doric columns, surmounted by statues of medieval monarchs, looking very small and insignificant. During the Revolution, when the old name of place du Trône became place du Trône-Renversé ("the overturned throne"), more people were guillotined here than on the more notorious execution site of place de la Concorde.

Marché d'Aligre
ⓂLedru-Rollin

South of rue du Faubourg-St-Antoine is the **Marché d'Aligre**, a lively, raucous market, held every morning except Monday, and particularly animated on Saturdays and Sundays. The square itself is given over to clothes and bric-a-brac stalls, selling anything from old gramophone players to odd bits of crockery. There's also a covered food market with traditional fromageries and charcuteries, plus more unusual stalls such as Sur les Quais, selling numerous varieties of olive oil. It's along the adjoining rue d'Aligre, however, where the market really comes to life, with the vendors, many of Algerian origin, doing a frenetic trade in fruit and veg. As the market winds down, you could follow the locals to the old-fashioned *Le Baron Rouge* wine bar (see p.278) for a glass of wine and some *saucisson*, or drink in the North African atmosphere at the *Ruche à Miel* café (see p.278) at 19 rue d'Aligre and order some mint tea with sticky cakes. Before leaving the area it's also worth taking a look at the old-style boulangerie on the corner of rues Charenton and Emilio-Castelar, with its beautiful painted glass panels, the queue of shoppers outside testifying to the excellence of its bread and pâtisseries.

The Promenade Plantée and around
ⓂBastille/Ledru-Rollin

The **Promenade Plantée**, also known as the Coulée Verte, is an excellent way to see a little-visited part of the city – and from an unusual angle. This disused railway viaduct, part of the old Paris–Cherbourg line, has been ingeniously converted into an elevated walkway and planted with a profusion of trees and flowers – cherry trees, maples, limes, roses and lavender.

The walkway starts near the beginning of **avenue Daumesnil**, just south of the Bastille opera house, and is reached via a flight of stone steps – or lifts – with a number of similar access points further along. It takes you to the Parc de Reuilly, then descends to ground level and continues as far as the *périphérique*, from where you can walk to the Bois de Vincennes. The whole walk is around 4.5km long, but if you don't feel like doing the entire thing you could just walk the first part, along the viaduct – a twenty-minute stroll – which also happens to be the most attractive stretch, running past venerable old mansion blocks and giving you a bird's-eye view of the street below. Small architectural details such as decorative mouldings and elaborate wrought-iron balconies that you wouldn't normally notice at street level come to light – the oddest sight is the series of caryatids adorning the police station at the end of avenue Daumesnil.

Viaduc des Arts

Ⓜ Bastille/Gare de Lyon/Ledru-Rollin

Underneath the Promenade Plantée, the red-brick arches of the viaduct itself have been converted into attractive spaces for artisans' studios and craft shops, collectively known as the **Viaduc des Arts**. The workshops house a wealth of creativity: furniture and tapestry restorers, interior designers, cabinet-makers, violin- and flute-makers, embroiderers, and fashion and jewellery designers.

Jardin de Reuilly

Ⓜ Montgallet/Dugommier

The Viaduc des Arts ends around halfway down avenue Daumesnil, but the Promenade Plantée continues, taking you to the **Jardin de Reuilly**, an old freight station, now an inviting, circular expanse of lawn, popular with picnickers on sunny days, and bordered by terraces and arbours. The open-air café here makes a good refreshment stop if you're walking the length of the *promenade*. You can also choose to bypass the park altogether by taking the gracefully arching wooden footbridge that spans it.

Allée Vivaldi to the *boulevard périphérique*

Ⓜ Dugommier

Towards the eastern end of the Promenade Plantée walkway is the **allée Vivaldi**, a rather nondescript road lined with modern blocks. Next, you enter a tunnel and emerge at the other end in the old railway cutting, a delightful stretch that meanders through a canopy of trees and flowers, below the level of the surrounding streets. At this point the path divides into two – one for pedestrians, the other for cyclists – landscaped all along, taking you through a series of ivy-draped, ex-railway tunnels and shadowing the rue du Sahel for most of the way. The walk comes to an end at the *boulevard périphérique*. From here you're not too far from the Porte Dorée métro station and the Porte Dorée entrance to the **Bois de Vincennes**. A pathway to the right takes you behind a sports stadium (with the *périphérique* on your left). The pathway turns into rue Edouard Lartet, then rue du Général Archinard. At the end of this turn left into avenue du Général Messimy, which leads into the main avenue Daumesnil; the métro station is to the right and entrance to the *bois* to the left.

Bercy

Over the last couple of decades, the former warehouse district of **Bercy**, along the Seine just east of the Gare de Lyon, where for centuries the capital's wine supplies were unloaded from river barges, has been transformed by a series of ambitious, ultra-modern developments designed to complement the grand-scale "Paris Rive Gauche" project (see p.176) on the opposite bank.

Ministère des Finances

139 rue de Bercy, 12ᵉ • Ⓜ Bercy

As you emerge from Bercy métro station, the first thing you notice is the imposing bulk of the **Ministère des Finances**, constructed in 1990 to house the treasury staff after they had finally agreed to move out of the Richelieu wing of the Louvre. Housing some 4700 employees, it stretches like a giant loading bridge from above the river (where higher bureaucrats and ministers arrive by boat) to rue de Bercy, a distance of some 400m.

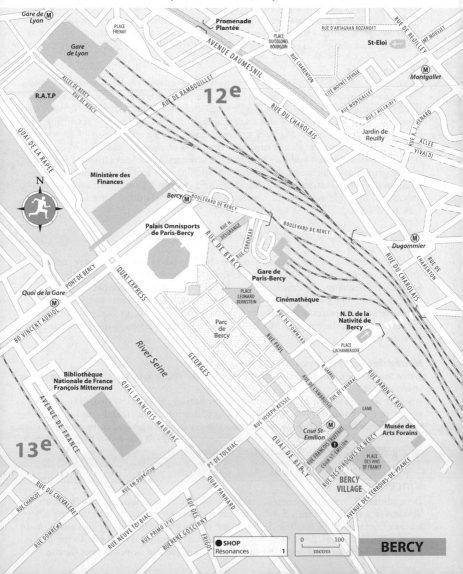

Parc de Bercy

Maison du Jardinage March–Oct Tues–Fri 1–5.30pm, Sat & Sun 1–6.30pm; Nov–Feb Tues–Sat 1–5.30pm • Free • ⓜBercy

Southeast of the Ministère des Finances squats the charmless **Palais Omnisports de Paris Bercy**. Built in 1983, its concrete bunker frame clad with grass covers a vast arena used for sporting and cultural events (see p.347). Beyond it, the area that used to house the old Bercy warehouses, where for centuries the capital's wine supplies were unloaded from river barges, is now the extensive **Parc de Bercy**. Here, the French formal garden has been given a modern twist with geometric lines and grid-like flowerbeds, but it also cleverly incorporates elements of the old warehouse site such as disused railway tracks and cobbled lanes. The western section of the park is a fairly unexciting expanse of grass with a huge stepped fountain (popular with children) set into one of the grassy banks, but the area east has arbours, rose gardens, lily ponds, an orangerie and a **Maison du Jardinage**, a garden exhibition centre, where you can consult gardening books and magazines and visit the adjoining greenhouse and vegetable garden.

Cinémathèque

51 rue de Bercy, 12ᵉ • Museum Mon, Tues & Thurs–Sat noon–7pm, Sun 10am–8pm • €5 • ☎ 01 71 19 33 33, ⓦ cinematheque.fr • ⓜBercy

Of the new buildings surrounding the park, the most striking, on the north side, is the **Cinémathèque**. Designed by Guggenheim architect Frank Gehry, it's constructed from zinc, glass and limestone and resembles a falling pack of cards – according to Gehry, the inspiration was Matisse's collages, done "with a simple pair of scissors". Its huge archive of films dates back to the earliest days of cinema, and regular retrospectives of French and foreign films are screened in its four cinemas. It also has an engaging **museum** tracing the history of cinema, with lots of early cinematic equipment, magic lanterns, silent-film clips and costumes from films, such as the dress worn by Vivienne Leigh in *Gone with the Wind* and outfits from Eisenstein's *Ivan the Terrible*.

Cour St-Emilion

ⓜCour-St-Emilion

A little east of the Cinémathèque, arched footbridges take you over the busy rue Kessel into the eastern extension of the park and the adjoining **Bercy Village**, the hub of which is the **Cour St-Emilion**, a pedestrianized, cobbled street lined with former wine warehouses that have been stylishly converted into shops, restaurants and wine bars. These are popular places to come before or after a film at the giant Bercy multiplex at the eastern end of the street, particularly on Sundays when shops in most other areas of Paris are closed.

Musée des Arts Forains

53 av des Terroirs-de-France, 12ᵉ • Daily tours to be booked in advance by phone • €13, children €5 • ☎ 01 43 40 16 15, ⓦ artsforains.com • ⓜCour-St-Emilion

Another set of old stone wine warehouses now houses the privately owned funfair museum, the **Musée des Arts Forains**, with its collection of nineteenth- and early twentieth-century funfair rides (which you can try out), fairground music and Venetian carnival rooms. It's only open to groups, though individuals can join a tour (in French, lasting 90min) if they book in advance by phone.

Vincennes

Beyond the 12ᵉ arrondissement, across the *boulevard périphérique*, lies the **Bois de Vincennes**, a favourite family Sunday retreat and the largest green space that the city has to offer, aside from the Bois de Boulogne in the west. The Bois de Vincennes' main draw is the **Parc Floral**, an attractive park with an adventure playground. To the east is the **Cartoucherie de Vincennes**, an old ammunitions factory, home to four theatre companies, including the radical Théâtre du Soleil (see p.312), while bordering the Bois to the north stands the **Château de Vincennes**, the country's only surviving medieval royal residence. West of the Bois de Vincennes is the **Cité Nationale de l'Histoire de l'Immigration**, a museum devoted to the history of immigration in France.

Bois de Vincennes

Ⓜ Porte-Dorée/Porte-de-Charenton/Château-de-Vincennes; buses #46 and #86

The extensive **Bois de Vincennes** was once a royal hunting ground roamed by deer; nowadays, unfortunately, it's crisscrossed with roads, but it does have some pleasant corners, such as the Parc Floral and the two lakes. Sights are quite a long distance from each other, so to avoid a lot of footslogging you may want to just target one or two, or you could pick up a Vélib' bike from near the entrance to the Parc Floral.

Parc Floral

Bois de Vincennes • Daily 9.30am–8pm, winter till dusk • Free except Wed, Sat & Sun from June to Sept when entry is €5 • ⓦ parcfloraldeparis.com • Ⓜ Château-de-Vincennes, then bus #112 or a short walk

If you've only got a limited amount of time, you should make for the **Parc Floral**, just behind the Château de Vincennes. This is one of the best gardens in Paris – flowers are always in bloom in the Jardin des Quatre Saisons, and you can picnic beneath pines, then wander through concentrations of camellias, rhododendrons, cacti, ferns, irises and bonsai trees. Between April and September there are art and horticultural

7

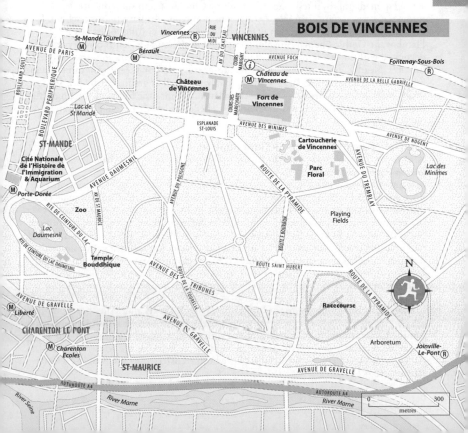

exhibitions in several pavilions, free jazz and classical music concerts, and numerous activities for children including a mini-golf of Parisian monuments.

The lakes and around

If you're after a lazy afternoon in the park, you could go boating on the **Lac Daumesnil**, near the Porte Dorée entrance, or feed the ducks on the **Lac des Minimes** (bus #112 from Vincennes métro), on the other side of the wood. North of the Lac Daumesnil, at 53 avenue de St-Maurice, is the city's largest **zoo**, which closed for a much-needed renovation in late 2008 and is scheduled to reopen in 2014.

The fenced enclave on the southern side of Lac Daumesnil harbours a **Buddhist centre** (information on ☎01 43 41 54 48) with Tibetan temple, Vietnamese chapel and international pagoda, all occasionally visitable. As far as real woods go, the *bois* comes into its own once you're east of avenue de St-Maurice. Boules competitions are popular – there's usually a collection of devotees between route de la Tourelle and avenue du Polygone.

7

Château de Vincennes

Daily 10am–6pm, Sept–April till 5pm • *Chapelle* €8, *donjon* €8, combined admission €12 • ☎ 01 48 08 31 20, ⓦ chateau-vincennes.fr • ⓜChâteau-de-Vincennes

On the northern edge of the *bois* stands the **Château de Vincennes**, enclosed by an impressive defensive wall and surrounded by a (now empty) moat. France's only surviving medieval royal residence was built by Charles V, and subsequently turned into a state prison, porcelain factory, weapons dump and military training school. It presents a rather austere aspect on first sight, but is worth visiting for its beautiful Flamboyant-Gothic **Chapelle Royale**, completed in the mid-sixteenth century and decorated with superb Renaissance stained-glass windows; a restoration was completed in 2009. Nearby, in the renovated fourteenth-century **donjon** (keep), you can see some fine vaulted ceilings and Charles V's bedchamber, as well as graffiti left by prisoners, which included the Marquis de Sade. The château fell into the hands of the English in the fifteenth century and it was in Charles V's bedchamber that Henry V of England died of dysentery.

Cité Nationale de l'Histoire de l'Immigration

293 av Daumesnil, 12ᵉ • Tues–Fri 10am–5.30pm, Sat & Sun 10am–7pm • €5; aquarium €6.50, children €5 • ☎ 01 53 59 58 60, ⓦ histoire-immigration.fr • ⓜPorte-Dorée

Just outside the Bois de Vincennes, across the way from the Porte Dorée entrance, a huge Art Deco building, the Palais de la Porte Dorée, houses the **Cité Nationale de l'Histoire de l'Immigration**, which examines the history of immigration to France over the last two centuries (around 15 million French citizens have foreign roots) through photos, artwork, multimedia displays and audio installations. The museum is located in a building erected for the 1931 Colonial Exhibition and sports a vast, somewhat dubious bas-relief illustrating the former French colonies. Artworks themed around immigrants' struggles to integrate into French society and images of vehicles loaded with possessions arriving at the border are among the thought-provoking exhibits. Perhaps the most poignant items on display, though, are the suitcases brought over by immigrants, containing photos of loved ones, religious texts and teddy bears. There are also regular temporary exhibitions, such as the recent one on Polish immigrants. On the lower ground floor is an **aquarium** with a collection of tropical fish and a crocodile pit, left over from the *palais'* previous incarnation as the Musée des Arts Africains et Océaniens, whose exhibits have been transferred to the Musée du Quai Branly (see p.147).

JARDIN DU LUXEMBOURG

The Quartier Latin

The traditional heartland of the Quartier Latin lies between the river and the Montagne Ste-Geneviève, a hill once crowded with medieval colleges and now proudly crowned by the giant dome of the Panthéon. In medieval times, the name "Latin quarter" was probably a simple description, as this was the area whose inhabitants – clergymen and university scholars for the most part – ordinarily spoke Latin. It's still a scholarly area, home to the famous Sorbonne and Jussieu campuses, plus two of France's most elite lycées and a cluster of stellar academic institutes. Few students can afford the rents these days, but they still maintain the quarter's traditions in the cheaper bars, cafés and *bistrots*, decamping to the Luxembourg gardens, over in the 6e arrondissement (see p.138), on sunny days.

These days, the term Quartier Latin is often used, as here, as shorthand for the entire 5e arrondissement. It's one of the city's more palpably ancient districts, retaining some of the medieval lanes, venerable churches and hidden corners that, elsewhere in Paris, were so often "improved" in later centuries. The romantically antiquated thoroughfare of the **rue Mouffetard** still snakes its way south to the boundary of the 13e arrondissement, while Roman and sixteenth-century buildings house the **Musée National du Moyen Age** – a medieval museum worth visiting for the sublime tapestry series, *The Lady and the Unicorn*, alone. The churches of St-Séverin and St-Etienne-du-Mont are among the most atmospheric in the city, too. The giant domed **Panthéon**, meanwhile, provides a touch of splendour atop the Left Bank's highest point. Out towards the eastern flank of the 5e, beside the Seine, the theme is more Arabic than Latin, what with the brilliantly designed **Institut du Monde Arabe** and **Paris mosque**. Nearby, the verdant **Jardin des Plantes** stretches lazily down to the river, a lovely swathe of lawns and flowerbeds with splendid hothouses and a zoo.

Place St-Michel and the riverside

Ⓜ St-Michel

The pivotal point of the Quartier Latin is **place St-Michel**, where the tree-lined boulevard St-Michel or "boul' Mich" begins. The once-famous student chic has these days given way to commercialization, but the cafés around the square are still jammed with students and backpackers. A favourite meeting place is by the fountain, which spills down magnificently from a statue of the archangel Michael stamping on the devil. Just east of the square, rue de la Huchette and the surrounding huddle of streets – notably the tight-squeezed rue du Chat-qui-Pêche – are rare vestiges of the medieval city's pinched footprint. Sadly, the ubiquitous kebab joints and Greek tavernas rather strip the zone of its atmosphere. There's also a single relic of the era when rue de la Huchette was a hub for postwar Beat poets

8

RIVE GAUCHE

In French, *rive gauche* means much more than just the "left bank" of the Seine. Technically, all Paris south of the river is the Left Bank (imagine you're looking downstream), but to Parisian ears the name conjures up the cerebral, creative, sometimes anarchic spirit that once flourished in the two central arrondissements, the 5^e and 6^e, in vigorous opposition – supposedly – to the more conformist, commercial and conservative *rive droite*. In the **Quartier Latin**, around the 5^e, a distinctively alternative ambience has long been sustained by the powerful and independent-minded university, while for much of the twentieth century any painter, writer or musician with good Bohemian credentials would have lived or worked in or around **St-Germain** and the 6e arrondissement. Between the wars you could find the painters Picasso and Modigliani in the cafés of **Montparnasse**, hobnobbing with writers such as Guillaume Apollinaire, André Breton, Jean Cocteau and Anaïs Nin, and expat wannabes like Henry Miller and Ernest Hemingway. After World War II the glitterati moved on to the cafés and jazz clubs of St-Germain, which became second homes to writers and musicians such as Jacques Prévert, Boris Vian, Sidney Bechet and Juliette Gréco – and, most famously, to the existentialists Jean-Paul Sartre and Simone de Beauvoir.

But what really defined the Rive Gauche's reputation for turbulence and innovation were *les événements*, the political "events" of **May 1968** (see box, p.122). Escalating from leftist student demonstrations to factory occupations and massive national strikes, they culminated in the near-overthrow of De Gaulle's presidency. Since that infamous summer, however, conservatives have certainly had their vengeance on the spirit of the Left Bank. The last three decades have seen rampant **gentrification**, the streets from which such revolution sprang now housing expensive apartments, art galleries and high-end fashion boutiques, while the cafés once frequented by penniless intellectuals and struggling artists are filled with designers, media and political magnates, and scores of well-heeled foreign residents.

and Absurdists, too: the pocket-sized **Théâtre de la Huchette**, at no. 23
(⚭theatrehuchette.com). After almost fifty years, it's still showing two Ionesco plays
nightly – well worth a trip if your French is up to it.

At the end of rue de la Huchette, **rue St-Jacques** follows the line of Roman Paris's
main thoroughfare, though its name comes from the celebrated pilgrimage to the
shrine of Santiago (St James/St-Jacques) de Compostela. The pilgrimage began at Paris's
church of St-Jacques, just across the river, and for countless medieval pilgrims this
gentle slope was the first taste of what lay ahead.

Church of St-Séverin

1 rue des Prêtres St-Séverin, 5ᵉ • Mon–Sat 11am–7.30pm, Sun 9am–8.30pm • Free • Ⓜ St-Michel/Cluny-La Sorbonne

The mainly fifteenth-century **church of St-Séverin** is one of the city's more intense
churches, its interior seemingly focused on the single, twisting, central pillar of the
Flamboyant choir. The effect is heightened by deeply coloured stained-glass designed
by the modern French painter Jean Bazaine. The flame-like carving that gave the
flamboyant ("flaming") style its name flickers in the window arch above the entrance
while, inside, the first three pillars of the nave betray the earlier, thirteenth-century
origins of the church. Outside, on the south side of the building, you can see the
remains of what looks like a cloister enclosing a modest courtyard garden on two sides;
this was in fact a **charnel house** for the mortal remains of fifteenth-century
parishioners. Today, it's the last surviving one anywhere in the city.

One block to the south of the church, **rue de la Parcheminerie** is where medieval
scribes and parchment sellers used to congregate. It's worth cricking your neck to look
at the decorations on the facades, including that of no. 29, where you'll find the
Canadian-run Abbey Bookshop.

8

St-Julien-le-Pauvre

1 rue St-Julien-le-Pauvre, 5ᵉ • Daily 9.30am–1pm & 3–6pm • Free • Ⓜ St-Michel/Maubert-Mutualité

The much-mutilated church of **St-Julien-le-Pauvre** is almost exactly the same age as
Notre-Dame. It used to be the venue for university assemblies until rumbustious
students tore it apart in 1524. For the last hundred years it has belonged to an
Arabic-speaking Greek Catholic sect, the Melchites, hence the unexpected iconostasis
screening the sanctuary, and the liturgy of St John Chrysostom sung in Greek and
Arabic every Sunday at 11pm.

Outside, look for a hefty slab of brownish stone by the well, to the right of the
entrance; it is all that remains of the paving of the Roman thoroughfare now replaced
by rue St-Jacques. The adjacent pocket of worn grass that is **square Viviani** provides a
perfect view of Notre-Dame. The three-quarters-dead tree propped on a couple of
concrete pillars is reputed to be Paris's oldest, a false acacia brought over from Guyana
in 1680.

Shakespeare and Co

37 rue de la Bûcherie, 5ᵉ • Mon–Fri 10am–11pm, Sat & Sun 11am–11pm • ⚭ shakespeareandcompany.com • Ⓜ St-Michel

A few steps from square Viviani is the home of the American-run English-language
bookshop **Shakespeare and Co**. The original Shakespeare and Co, owned by the
American Sylvia Beach, long-suffering publisher of James Joyce's *Ulysses*, was on rue de
l'Odéon, over in St-Germain, but this "new" incarnation has played host to plenty of
literati since it opened in 1951. In 1957, when Allen Ginsberg, William Burroughs and
Gregory Corso were living in the so-called Beat Hotel, over on rue Gît-le-Cœur, they'd
read their poems on the street outside the store. It still has a lively roster of literary
events, and is staffed by "tumbleweeds": young would-be Hemingways who sleep
upstairs, borrow freely from the library and pay their rent by manning the tills. More
books, postcards and prints are on sale from the **bouquinistes**, who display their wares
in green padlocked boxes hooked onto the parapet of the riverside *quais*.

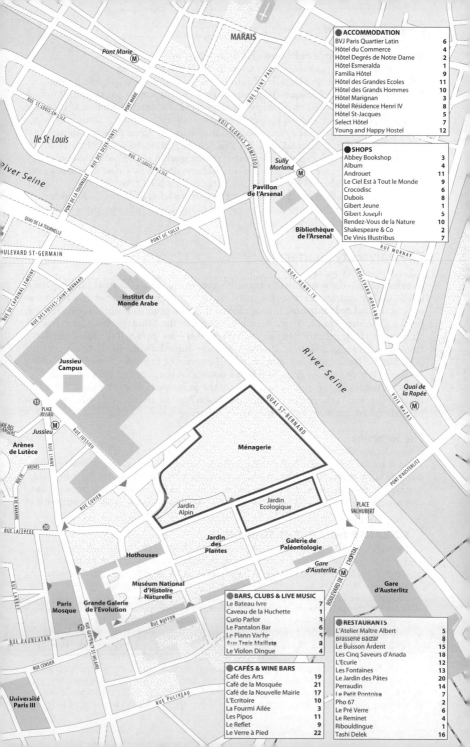

MARAIS

Pont Marie Ⓜ

RUE ST-LOUIS-EN-L'ILE

Ile St Louis

River Seine

QUAI DE LA TOURNELLE

BOULEVARD ST-GERMAIN

RUE DE CARDINAL LEMOINE

RUE DES FOSSÉS-SAINT-BERNARD

Institut du Monde Arabe

Jussieu Campus

15 PLACE JUSSIEU

Jussieu Ⓜ

RUE DES ...ANGERS

Arènes de Lutèce

RUE LINNÉ

ARENES

RUE DE...

RUE NAVARRE

RUE LACEPEDE

20

RUE LARREY

RUE JUSSIEU

RUE CUVIER

Paris Mosque

Grande Galerie de l'Evolution

21

RUE GEOFFROY ST-HILAIRE

RUE DAUBENTON

Université Paris III

RUE CENSIER

RUE FULIVEAU

PONT DE LA TOURNELLE

RUE ST-LOUIS-EN-L'ILE

RUE DES DEUX-PONTS

PONT MARIE

VOIE GEORGES POMPIDOU

Sully Morland Ⓜ

Pavillon de l'Arsenal

PONT DE SULLY

Bibliothèque de l'Arsenal

RUE SAINT PAUL

QUAI HENRI IV

BOULEVARD MORLAND

RUE MORNAY

River Seine

QUAI ST-BERNARD

Ménagerie

Jardin Alpin

Jardin Ecologique

Hothouses

Jardin des Plantes

Galerie de Paléontologie

Muséum National d'Histoire Naturelle

RUE BUFFON

Gare d'Austerlitz Ⓜ

PLACE VALHUBERT

PONT D'AUSTERLITZ

BOULEVARD DE L'HOPITAL

VOIE MAZAS

Quai de la Rapée Ⓜ

Gare d'Austerlitz

● ACCOMMODATION
BVJ Paris Quartier Latin	6
Hôtel du Commerce	4
Hôtel Degrés de Notre Dame	2
Hôtel Esmeralda	1
Familia Hôtel	9
Hôtel des Grandes Ecoles	11
Hôtel des Grands Hommes	10
Hôtel Marignan	3
Hôtel Résidence Henri IV	8
Hôtel St-Jacques	5
Select Hôtel	7
Young and Happy Hostel	12

● SHOPS
Abbey Bookshop	3
Album	4
Androuet	11
Le Ciel Est à Tout le Monde	9
Crocodisc	6
Dubois	8
Gibert Jeune	1
Gibert Joseph	5
Rendez-Vous de la Nature	10
Shakespeare & Co	2
De Vinis Illustribus	7

● BARS, CLUBS & LIVE MUSIC
Le Bateau Ivre	7
Caveau de la Huchette	1
Curio Parlor	3
Le Pantalon Bar	6
Le Piano Vache	5
Aux Trois Maillets	8
Le Violon Dingue	4

● CAFÉS & WINE BARS
Café des Arts	19
Café de la Mosquée	21
Café de la Nouvelle Mairie	17
L'Ecritoire	10
La Fourmi Ailée	3
Les Pipos	11
Le Reflet	9
Le Verre à Pied	22

● RESTAURANTS
L'Atelier Maître Albert	5
Brasserie Balzar	8
Le Buisson Ardent	15
Les Cinq Saveurs d'Anada	18
L'Ecurie	12
Les Fontaines	13
Le Jardin des Pâtes	20
Perraudin	14
Le Petit Pontoise	7
Pho 67	2
Le Pré Verre	6
Le Reminet	4
Ribouldingue	1
Tashi Delek	16

Musée de l'Assistance Publique - Hôpitaux de Paris

47 quai de la Tournelle, 5ᵉ • Tues–Sun 10am–6pm; closed Aug • €4 • ☎ 01 40 27 50 05 • ⓜMaubert-Mutualité

The seventeenth-century Hôtel de Miramion provides an imposing home for the **Musée de l'Assistance Publique - Hôpitaux de Paris**, a museum recounting the history of Paris's hospitals, and their charitable work, especially. The small collection of paintings, sculptures, documents and old surgical instruments doesn't make for a thrilling visit, especially if you don't speak French, though the pharmacy room preserves some fine old ceramic medicine jars, and there are some moving paintings and sculptures of hospital scenes. One desperate little marble representation of the "awakening of the abandoned child" represents the countless children taken in by Paris's hospitals – over seven thousand of them every year, in the hungry, crisis-hit 1770s.

Almost in front of the museum, the **Pont de l'Archevêché**, or archbishop's bridge, crosses the Seine to the delightful park behind Notre-Dame, offering views of the sunlit southern fringe of the Ile-St-Louis.

The University quarter

ⓜCluny-La Sorbonne/RER Luxembourg

Rue des Ecoles – the appropriately named "street of the schools" – marks the beginning of the student quarter. It's here that you'll find a bronze statue of the great Renaissance essayist, **Michel de Montaigne**, his toe rubbed shiny by generations of students seeking good luck in their exams. Above stretch the slopes of the Montagne Ste-Geneviève, clustered with the modern heirs of the colleges that once attracted the finest scholars from all over medieval Europe. Paris doesn't have quite the same world-beating status now, but the Lycée Louis-le-Grand attracts the cream of France's schoolchildren, the Sorbonne remains one of France's top universities for the arts, and the Collège de France is the leading research institution for the humanities. For the visitor, the chief draw of this area is the **Musée National du Moyen Age**, an astoundingly rich storehouse of medieval art, set in an early Renaissance palace.

The Sorbonne

ⓜCluny-La Sorbonne/RER Luxembourg

From rue des Ecoles, rue Champollion, with its huddle of arty cinemas, leads to the **place de la Sorbonne**. It's a peaceful place to sit, in a café or just under the lime trees, listening to the play of the fountains and watching students toting their books about. Overshadowing the graceful ensemble is the **Chapelle Ste-Ursule**, built in the 1640s by

---

SOIXANTE-HUIT AT THE SORBONNE

The Sorbonne is much more to Parisians than just an elite educational institution. It's a living memorial to one of the defining events of the postwar era. On **May 3, 1968**, a riot broke out there after police violently intervened to break up a political meeting. The Sorbonne wasn't actually the first to flare up – the lead was taken by the campus in surburban Nanterre – but it was the university's central, historical location that caught the nation's attention. To send police into the Sorbonne was a flagrant contravention of centuries of tradition separating the university and civic authorities. To see students fighting police down on the boulevard St-Michel – as millions did, on national television – aroused powerful national memories of revolution, and the unions came out on strike in sympathy. The Sorbonne's faculty buildings were occupied by a potent mix of left-wing radicals, poseurs and intellectuals, and the college briefly became the flashpoint of France's student-led rebellion against institutional stagnation, housing a vibrant, anarchic commune before finally being stormed by the police on June 16. The shake-up in the higher education system that followed transformed the Sorbonne into the more prosaic Paris IV (though the old name is still used unofficially), largely attended by arts and social science students.

the great Cardinal Richelieu, whose tomb it contains. It helped establish a trend for Roman Counter-Reformation-style domes, which mushroomed over the city's skyline in the latter part of the century. It is certainly the most architecturally distinctive part of the **Sorbonne**, as the university buildings were entirely (and unfortunately) rebuilt in the 1880s. Sadly, you can't get inside, or even look into the Sorbonne's main **courtyard,** unless you can produce some kind of student ID and bluff convincingly in French.

Collège de France and Lycée Louis-le-Grand
ⓂMaubert-Mutualité

The foundation of the **Collège de France** was first mooted by the Renaissance king François I, in order to establish the study of Greek and Hebrew in France. Its modern incarnation, as a research institution, has attracted intellectual giants such as Michel Foucault and Claude Lévi-Strauss. Behind it, on rue St-Jacques, the **Lycée Louis-le-Grand** numbers Molière, Robespierre, Sartre and Victor Hugo among its former pupils. It's a portal to academic and political success, hothousing some of France's brightest students for their entry exams to the *grandes écoles*, France's elite colleges of higher education.

Musée de la Préfecture de Police
4 rue de la Montagne Ste-Geneviève, 5ᵉ • Mon–Fri 9am–5pm, Sat 10.30am–5.30pm • Free • ☎01 44 41 52 50 • ⓂMaubert-Mutualité

The **Musée de la Préfecture de Police** offers its few visitors a dusty collection of uniforms, arms and documents, thus stitching together a history of the Paris police force. It's dry stuff, for the most part, but the murder weapons used by legendary criminals may titillate, and voluntarily walking into a working Paris police station – even one as brutally ugly as this – has its own frisson. To the north, **place Maubert** provides a spot of colour on an otherwise lifeless stretch of the broad boulevard St-Germain, with its busy food market (Tues, Thurs and Sat mornings) and associated cluster of food and wine shops.

8

The Musée National du Moyen Age
6 place Paul Painlevé, 5ᵉ • Daily except Tues 9.15am–5.45pm • €8 • For concert tickets call ☎01 53 73 78 16, ⓦmusee-moyenage.fr • ⓂCluny-La Sorbonne

The best-preserved Roman remains in all Paris, the third-century **baths**, front onto the busy boulevard St-Michel, and behind, on rue du Sommerard, stands the sixteenth-century **Hôtel de Cluny**. It's a beautiful Renaissance mansion, as befits the Paris pied-à-terre of the abbots of Burgundy's powerful Cluny monastery, and provides a fine setting for the **Musée National du Moyen Age**. This treasure house of medieval art owns one of the great masterpieces of European art: the tapestry series *La Dame à la licorne* ("The Lady and the Unicorn"). It also puts on an excellent programme of medieval music **concerts**; look out especially for the regular "heure musicale", held on Monday lunchtimes (12.30pm) and Sunday afternoons (4pm), with tickets at just €6. There's no charge to enter the gorgeous courtyard or the grounds running along boulevard St-Germain, where you'll find lawns, benches and a children's playground.

Ground floor
Seemingly the backdrop to the artefacts on display, the **tapestries** that hang in most rooms are in fact the highlight of the collection. In room 2, there's an exquisite Resurrection scene, while gloriously naturalistic scenes of manorial life are hung in room 3. Room 3 holds attractively naive wood and alabaster **altarpiece plaques** found in homes and churches all over Europe. In room 6 there are some wonderful backlit fragments of **stained glass** from the Sainte-Chapelle. It's fascinating to see the artistry so close up, and to feel the storytelling urge behind scenes such as one of Samson having his eyes gouged out.

Down the steps, in the modern structure built around the old baths, you'll find the melancholy row of 21 thirteenth-century heads of the **Kings of Judea**. Lopped off the west front of Notre-Dame during the Revolution, they were only discovered in a 1977 excavation. Arching over the *frigidarium*, the cold room of the **Gallo-Roman baths**, the magnificent brick-and-stone vaults are preserved intact. They shelter some beautifully carved pieces of first- and second-century columns, notably the so-called *Seine Boatmen's Pillar*, inscribed with the legend "Boatmen of the city of the Parisii", and the *Pillar of St-Landry*, which has gods and musicians animating three of its faces.

The Lady and the Unicorn

Undisputed star of the collection is the truly exquisite **Lady and the Unicorn tapestry series**, displayed in a specially darkened, chapel-like chamber on the first floor. Dating from the late fifteenth century, the highly allegorical tapestries were probably made in Brussels for the Le Viste family, merchants from Lyon, perhaps to celebrate the family acquiring its own coat of arms – three crescents on a diagonal blue stripe, as shown on the flags floating in various scenes. Each tapestry centres on a richly dressed woman, a lion, a unicorn and a monkey, set against a deep red millefleurs or "thousand-flower" background. Scholarly debate rages over the meaning of the tapestries but, at one level, they are clearly allegories of the five senses: the woman takes a sweetmeat from a goblet (taste); plays the organ (hearing); strings together a necklace of carnations (smell); holds a mirror up to the unicorn (sight); and holds the unicorn's horn (touch). The final panel, entitled *A Mon Seul Désir* ("To My Only Desire") and depicting the woman putting away (or picking up) her necklace, remains ambiguous. Some authorities think it represents the dangerous passions engendered by sensuality – the open tent behind is certainly suggestive – others that it shows the sixth "moral sense" that guards against such sinfulness.

The first floor

The rest of the first floor is an amazing ragbag of carved choir stalls, altarpieces, ivories, stained glass, illuminated Books of Hours, games, brassware and all manner of precious objets d'art, including the stunning **Golden Rose of Basel**, a papal gift dating from 1330. In the main Hôtel de Cluny section, the bright tapestries, beams and carved fireplaces make it possible to forget you're in a museum. The *hôtel*'s original Flamboyant **chapel**, for instance, preserves its remarkable vault splaying out from a central pillar.

The Panthéon

Place du Panthéon, 5e • Daily 10am–6.30pm, Oct–March till 6pm; free guided tours April–Sept 10am–5.15pm • €8 • ⑩ pantheon .monuments-nationaux.fr • RER Luxembourg/⑪ Cardinal-Lemoine

The towering hulk of the **Panthéon** squats atop the Montagne Ste-Geneviève under its vast dome. It was originally built as a church by Louis XV, on the site of the ruined Ste-Geneviève abbey, to thank the saint for curing him of illness and to emphasize the unity of the church and state, troubled at the time by growing divisions between Jesuits and Jansenists. Not only had the original abbey church entombed Geneviève, Paris's patron saint, but it had been founded by Clovis, France's first Christian king. The building was only completed in 1789, whereupon the revolutionary state promptly turned it into a secular mausoleum, adding the words "*Aux grands hommes la patrie reconnaissante*" ("The nation honours its great men") underneath the pediment of the giant portico. The remains of French heroes such as Voltaire, Rousseau, Hugo and Zola are now entombed in the vast crypt below, along with more recent arrivals: Marie Curie (1995 – and still the only woman, not counting the wife of chemist Marcellin Berthelot, who was allowed in on sentimental grounds); writer and landmark culture minister André Malraux (1996); and Alexandre Dumas (2002), who arrived in a coffin covered with a cloth embroidered with the phrase "All for one, one for all", from his novel *The Three Musketeers*. There's also a plaque to Saint-Exupéry, author of the much-loved *Petit Prince*. He'd have a full-scale monument, but because his plane was lost at sea he fell foul of the rule that without a body part to inter, you cannot be *panthéonizé*.

The interior and dome

The Panthéon's **interior** is bleak and chilly, and its muscular frescoes and sculptures do little to lift the spirits. You can, however, see a working model of **Foucault's Pendulum** swinging from the dome. The French physicist Léon Foucault (see p.103) devised the experiment, conducted at the Panthéon in 1851, to demonstrate vividly the rotation of the earth. While the pendulum appeared to rotate over a 24-hour period, it was in fact the earth beneath it turning. The demonstration wowed the scientific establishment and the public alike, with huge crowds turning up to watch the ground move beneath their feet. In summer, you can join regular guided tours, which take small groups up into the vertiginous cupola and out onto the high **balcony** running round the outside of the dome. As you'd expect, the views are spectacular.

St-Etienne-du-Mont

Place Ste-Geneviève, 5ᵉ • Sept–June Tues–Sat 8.45am–noon & 2–7.45pm, Sun 8.45am–12.15pm & 2.30–7.45pm; July & Aug Tues–Sun 10am–noon & 4–7.15pm • Free • ⓦ saintetiennedumont.fr • RER Luxembourg/ⓜCardinal-Lemoine

Sloping downhill from the main portico of the Panthéon, broad rue Soufflot entices you west towards the Luxembourg gardens (see p.138). On the east side of the Panthéon, however, peeping over the walls of the Lycée Henri IV, look out for the lone Gothic tower which is all that remains of the earlier church of Ste-Geneviève. The saint's remains, and those of two seventeenth-century literary greats who didn't make the Panthéon, Pascal and Racine, lie close at hand in the church of **St-Etienne-du-Mont**. The church's facade is a splendidly mad seventeenth-century dog's dinner, its three levels stacking Gothic atop Renaissance atop neo-Grecian. The interior is no less startling, the transition from Flamboyant Gothic choir to sixteenth-century nave smoothed by a strange high-level catwalk which springs from pillar to pillar before transforming itself into a rood screen which arches across the width of the nave. This last feature is highly unusual in itself, as most French rood screens were destroyed by Protestant iconoclasts, reformers or revolutionaries. Exceptionally tall windows flood the church with light, while an elaborately carved organ loft crams itself into the west end of the nave. In the fifth chapel along, on the south side of the nave, there's a finely sculpted, sixteenth-century Entombment scene – done lifesize, as was long the custom in France.

North of the church, the villagey **rue de la Montagne-Ste-Geneviève** descends towards place Maubert (see p.123), passing the pleasant cafés and restaurants around rue de l'Ecole-Polytechnique.

Val-de-Grâce

1 place Alphonse Laveran, 5ᵉ • Tues–Thurs, Sat & Sun noon–6pm; closed Aug • €5 • ⓜCensier-Daubenton/RER Luxembourg

The southern half of the student quarter is lorded over by the elite, scientific Curie Institute and the **Ecole Normale Supérieure**, on rue d'Ulm, which grooms its *normaliens* for the top arts jobs in the country. It's a closed world to outsiders, however, and the only sight as such is the magnificent church of **Val-de-Grâce**, set just back from rue St-Jacques. Built by Anne of Austria as an act of pious gratitude following the birth of her first son in 1638, it's a suitably awesome monument to the young prince who went on to reign as Louis XIV.

You can only enter Val-de-Grâce via the **Musée du Service de Santé des Armées**, a thorough history of military medicine that probably isn't for non-French speakers – though the mock-ups of field hospitals, prosthetic limbs and reconstructive plastic surgery exert a gruesome fascination. The church, properly known as the **Chapelle St-Louis**, is reached via a curved iron grille behind which the Benedictine nuns once attended Mass. Inside, Roman Baroque extravagance is tempered by cool French Classicism. In the dome, Pierre Mignard's trompe l'oeil fresco of Paradise depicts Anne of Austria offering a model of the church up to the Virgin.

If you're quailing before all this piety, bear in mind that it's only a short step from here to the big, brash cafés of Montparnasse (see p.163).

The Mouffetard quarter

Medieval travellers heading south would leave Paris along the narrow, ancient incline of **rue Descartes** and its continuation, **rue Mouffetard**, following the line of the old Roman road to Italy. The quarter still feels distinctively like a border town, its cheap restaurants and watering holes drawing students and tourists alike.

Place de la Contrescarpe

ⓂMonge

Just south of the church of St-Etienne-du-Mont, you pass the medieval city limits – a giant stump of Philippe-Auguste's early thirteenth-century **city wall** still protrudes into rue Clovis, a few steps short of rue Cardinal Lemoine. Rue Descartes climbs briefly from here, past a landmark blue **mural** of a tree by the Belgian artist Pierre Alechinsky, before suddenly arriving at the pleasingly run-down oasis of **place de la Contrescarpe**. The little square has been a dubious watering hole for centuries: the medieval poet-outlaw François Villon drank at taverns here, as did the scurrilous sixteenth-century writer François Rabelais; and the modern-day *Café Delmas*, on the square's sunny side, was once the run-down café *La Chope*, as described by Ernest Hemingway in *A Moveable Feast*. He knew it well, as he lived just round the corner on the fourth floor of 74 rue Cardinal Lemoine, in a miserable flat amply paid for by his wife's trust fund. Just to the east of the square, the curved frontage of a municipal crèche on rue Lacépède was inspired by the shape of a pregnant belly.

Rue Mouffetard market

ⓂMonge

"La Mouffe", as the rue Mouffetard is known to locals, was for generations one of the great **market streets** of Paris. Some traces of the past can be found on the old shop fronts overlooking place de la Contrescarpe, most obviously the two cows adorning a former butcher's at no. 6, and no. 12's hand-painted sign depicting a black man in striped trousers waiting on his mistress, with the unconvincing legend, "*Au Nègre Joyeux*". These days, the top half of rue Mouffetard is given over to tacky eating places, especially around rue du Pot de Fer – which George Orwell described as a "ravine of tall, leprous houses" given over to cheap drunkenness; things haven't changed much since. Mouffetard's market traditions still cling on at the southern end, however, where you'll find fruit and vegetable stalls in the mornings, excellent shops selling fine cheeses and wines, and a couple of old-fashioned market cafés, notably *Le Verre à Pied* (see p.280). There are more old shop signs, too: at no. 69 there's a fine old carved oak tree, while no. 122, labelled "*La Bonne Source*" (the Good Spring), seems to advertise the fresh water or perhaps produce once available there.

St-Médard and around

141 rue Mouffetard, 5ᵉ • Mon 5–7pm, Tues–Sat 8am–12.30pm & 2.30–7.30pm, Sun 8.30am–12.30pm & 4–8.30pm • Free • Ⓦ saintmedard.org • ⓂCensier-Daubenton

Opposite the beautiful painted facade at no. 134 rue Mouffetard, sits **St-Médard**. It's easy to imagine that it was once a country parish church, and only brought within the city walls during the reign of Louis XV. The church twice achieved notoriety: in 1561, when it was sacked by Protestant rioters in the so-called Tumult of St-Médard, and again in 1727, when fanatical supporters of François de Paris – a leading light in the reforming Jansenist movement, which had been condemned by pope and king alike but drew massive popular support in Paris – gathered at his fresh grave. Rumours of

miracles led crowds of "*convulsionnaires*" into collective hysteria, rolling on the ground around their saint's tomb, eating the earth and even wounding or crucifying themselves. These excesses helped split the Jansenist movement, and led the authorities to post armed guards at the church gates in 1732, beside a sign reading "*De par le roi, défense à Dieu/De faire miracle en ce lieu*" (By order of the king, God is forbidden to work miracles in this place). The church today preserves its simple, narrow Gothic nave and more elaborate late sixteenth-century choir. A fine Zurbarán painting of *The Promenade of St Joseph and the Child Jesus* lurks in the right transept, while the outstanding organ loft is topped by statues carved by the great Renaissance sculptor Germain Pilon in the 1640s.

Below St-Médard lay the marshy ground of the now-covered **River Bièvre** (see p.172) where tanners and dyers worked in the Middle Ages – which may explain the origin of the name Mouffetard, from a slang term for "stinking". Today, avenue des Gobelins leads into the 13ᵉ arrondissement, passing the Gobelins tapestry workshops (see p.172) on the way up to busy place d'Italie.

Jardin des Plantes and around

Daily: April–Aug 7.30am–7.30pm; Sept–March 8am–dusk • Free • ⓦ mnhn.fr • Ⓜ Gare d'Austerlitz/Jussieu/Monge

The **Jardin des Plantes**, which stretches east all the way to the Seine, is one of Paris's loveliest green spaces, an oasis of shady woods, lawns, meticulously tended flowerbeds, hothouses and even a zoo. It's more than just a place for jogging, strolling and lolling, however. Founded as a medicinal herb garden in 1626, it has long retained a scientific role. Its great eighteenth-century director, the Comte de Buffon, is rightly regarded as the father of natural history, while Henri Becquerel stumbled upon radioactivity in the physics labs overlooking the gardens, in 1896, and the Curies cooked up radium here two years later. The gardens still house a suite of natural history museums.

The gardens

There are entrances to the Jardin des Plantes on all sides except around the northern corner. The southwesternmost entrance, on the corner of rues Buffon and Geoffroy St-Hilaire, takes you past a sophora tree planted by Buffon in 1747 and straight to the **roseraie**, which contains over three hundred varieties of rose and is at its glorious best in June. If you enter by the rue Cuvier/rue Lacépède gate, at the northwest corner, and climb the little mazy hillock on the right up to an elegant gazebo (it actually predates the Revolution, making it the oldest ironwork structure in Paris), you can then descend along pleasantly shaded, winding paths, past a stately cedar of Lebanon planted in 1734, to the central area of lawns and flowerbeds. If you're here in spring, don't miss the famous flowering of the two Japanese cherries – one white, one pink – two thirds of the way down.

The hothouses

Jardin des Plantes • Daily except Tues 10am–6pm, Oct–March till 5pm • €5 • Ⓜ Jussieu

The recently restored *serres*, or **hothouses**, are one of the glories of the Jardin des Plantes. You enter via the Art Deco *serre tropicale*, with its graceful, vegetal-themed facade. It's hot, humid and splendidly lush, and there's a three-storey grotto which you can climb as far as the canopy level, and a section, on the sunny side, of desert plants. From here you pass into the elegant twin hothouses, built in the 1830s when they were revolutionary structures. The first houses an amazing diversity of plants from Nouvelle Calédonie, in the Pacific; the second is a kind of living exhibition on the evolution of plant life.

Jardin Alpin and Jardin Ecologique

Jardin des Plantes **Jardin Alpin** April–Oct Mon–Fri 8am–4.40pm free, Sat & Sun 1.30–6pm €1 **Jardin Ecologique** Occasional guided tours only, call ☎ 01 40 79 56 01 • Ⓜ Jussieu/Gare d'Austerlitz

The north side of the Jardin des Plantes' central lawns is given over to the **Jardin Alpin**, a sheltered, sunken space filled with mountain plants from all over the world – and a favourite spot among Parisians. You can stroll freely here, but you'll probably have to just peer through the fence at the **Jardin Ecologique**, a hidden gem which was an arboretum before being closed off for forty years. It now shelters the natural flora of the Parisian basin, somehow cramming in miniature wildflower meadows, the typical mixed oak-and-hornbeam woodland of the region and even a small stream. It attracts bees, butterflies and, so far, over 35 species of bird – including a kingfisher.

Muséum National d'Histoire Naturelle

Jardin des Plantes **Galeries de Paléontologie et d'Anatomie Comparée** Daily except Tues 10am–5pm • €7 • ☎ 01 40 79 56 01
Grande Galerie de l'Evolution Daily except Tues 10am–6pm • €9 • ☎ 01 40 79 54 79 • Ⓜ Jussieu/Gare d'Austerlitz

The southern edge of the Jardin des Plantes is lined with the grand buildings of the **Muséum National d'Histoire Naturelle**. The first, the splendid mineralogy gallery, was due to reopen after restoration at the time of writing. At the eastern end of the garden, towards the river, the **Galeries de Paléontologie et d'Anatomie Comparée** (gallery of paleontology and comparative anatomy) isn't as dull as it sounds. On the ground floor of the vast, vaulted hall, serried thousands of animal skeletons seemingly evolve in well-marshalled order. Among them is the skeleton of the rhino that was shipped to Versailles in 1770, and that of Rock-Sand, the horse which won the triple crown in 1903. On the first floor, dinosaurs (some plastercast, some real) are arranged by era. Don't miss – well, you can't miss – the mammoth, the diplodocus and the magisterial megatherium, the giant ancestor of the crocodile.

The splendidly restored **Grande Galerie de l'Evolution** stands beside the Jardin des Plantes' southwestern entrance. It tells the story of evolution using stuffed animals, rescued from the dusty old zoology museum, and given new life with clever lighting effects and ambient sounds, with wooden lecture boards in English. On the lower level, submarine light suffuses the space where the murkiest deep-ocean creatures are displayed. Above, glass lifts rise silently from the savannah, where a closely packed line of huge African animals look as if they're stepping onto Noah's ark. It's great fun for children, and there's a small interactive centre for kids on the first floor (see p.355).

The ménagerie

Jardin des Plantes • Summer Mon–Sat 9am–6pm, Sun 9am–6.30pm; winter daily 9am–5pm • €9, under-26s €7, under-4s free •
☎ 01 40 79 37 94 • Ⓜ Jussieu/Gare d'Austerlitz

The small **ménagerie** in the Jardin des Plantes near rue Cuvier was founded just after the Revolution; it is France's oldest zoo – and feels it. The old-fashioned iron cages of the big cats' *fauverie* and the glazed-in primate house are not exactly uplifting, even if they are historic Art Deco structures. These animals will at least be spared the fate of their predecessors during the starvation months of the 1870 Prussian siege. Thankfully, most of the rest of the zoo is pleasantly park-like and given over to deer, antelope, goats, buffalo and other marvellous beasts that seem happy enough in their outdoor enclosures.

The Paris mosque

2bis place du Puits de l'Ermite, 5ᵉ • Daily except Fri & Muslim holidays 9am–noon & 2–6pm • €3 • ☎ 01 45 35 97 33,
Ⓦ mosquee-de-paris.org • Ⓜ Jussieu

East of rue Mouffetard, beyond place Monge and its busy market (Wed, Fri & Sun mornings) the main **Paris mosque** stands behind its crenellated walls, with its gate on the western side. Built by Moroccan craftsmen in the early 1920s, in a style influenced by Moorish Spain, it feels oddly repro in style, though the artisanship of tiles and wood carvings is very fine, and the cloistered gardens are deliciously peaceful. You can stroll freely, but non-Muslims are asked not to enter the prayer room. Towards the back of the building, on the rue Geoffroy St-Hilaire side, lies a simple monument to the Algerian scholar and national hero Abd el-Kader, who led the resistance against French invasion before finally being forced to surrender in 1847. The gate on the southeast corner of the mosque complex, on rue Daubenton, leads into a lovely courtyard **tearoom** (see p.279), and an atmospheric **hammam** (see p.344).

The Arènes de Lutèce
Ⓜ Jussieu

The surprisingly large – and remarkably well hidden – open space of the **Arènes de Lutèce** lies a few steps to the north of the Paris mosque, with entrances in rue de Navarre, rue des Arènes and another through a *passage* on rue Monge. A few ghostly rows of stone seats are all that's left of the Roman amphitheatre that once amused ten thousand here; the entertainment is now provided by the old men playing boules in the sand below. Benches, gardens and a kids' playground stand behind.

Institut du Monde Arabe
1 rue des Fossés-St-Bernard, 5ᵉ · Tues–Sun 10am–6pm, July & Aug from 1pm · Museum €6 · ☎ 01 40 51 38 38, ⓦ imarabe.org · Ⓜ Jussieu/Cardinal-Lemoine

North of the Jardin des Plantes stands the much-loathed **Jussieu campus**, an uncompromising structure constructed around the brutal skyscraper of the Tour Zamansky. Built to house the baby-boomers coming of university age in the late 1960s – and, they say, to thwart any unseemly outbreaks of student rebellion with its single entrance **gate** – its population has since outgrown it once again, and has partly decamped upstream to a new site (see p.176).

However, the campus hides a more recent and vastly more successful piece of modern metal-and-glass architecture. Created by the Mitterrand government in collaboration with the Arab League, the **Institut du Monde Arabe** is a stunning and radical piece of architectural engineering, designed by a team including the architect of the moment, Jean Nouvel, who subsequently built the Musée du Quai Branly (see p.147). Its broad southern facade comprises thousands of tiny light-sensitive shutters which should modulate the light levels inside while simultaneously mimicking a *moucharabiyah*, the traditional Arab latticework balcony. Unfortunately, the computer system operating the little steel diaphragms has a habit of crashing, so it's rarely in operation. On the riverfront side of the building, a boldly curving curtain wall of glass seems to symbolize the transition from the glass box behind to the flowing water at its feet. To the north, the **Pont de Sully** cuts across to the tip of the Ile-St-Louis, providing a fine view downstream towards Notre-Dame.

Inside the institute
Exhibitions, films and concerts by leading artists from the Arab world pull in the Parisian intelligentsia, while a thoughtful new **museum** traces five themes – Arabs, the sacred, cities, beauty and daily life – using its collection of exquisite ceramics, metalwork and textiles. Scholars have use of a library and multimedia centre, and there's a specialist bookshop with an excellent selection of Arab music. Up on the ninth floor, the terrace offers some of the best **views** in the city, looking downriver towards the apse of Notre-Dame. At the adjacent **café-restaurant** *Le Moucharabieh* you can drink mint tea and eat sweet cakes, but to eat and enjoy the view at the same time you'll have to sit down at the more formal (and more expensive) Lebanese restaurant, *Le Ziryab* (☎ 01 55 42 55 42).

TOY BOATS IN THE JARDIN DU LUXEMBOURG

St-Germain

Encompassing the 6^e arrondissement and the eastern fringe of the 7^e, St-Germain has all the sophistication of the Right Bank, but has a certain easy-going chic that makes it uniquely appealing. The *quartier* has moved ever further upmarket since the postwar era, when it was the natural home of arty mould-breakers and trendsetters, but it still clings to its offbeat charm. Among the designer boutiques and fashionable *bistrots*, you can still find the cafés that made the quarter famous, and left-wing media types and intellectuals still rub shoulders in them along with crowds of well-dressed Parisians and international visitors. The quarter also preserves its two landmark attractions: the lovely Jardin du Luxembourg and the Musee d'Orsay.

9

Historically, St-Germain has stood outside the city proper for most of its life. From the sixth century onwards, its fields and riverine meadows fell under the sway of the giant Benedictine abbey of St-Germain-des-Prés. Marie de Medicis built the Palais du Luxembourg in the early seventeenth century, but the area only became urbanized a hundred years later, as aristocrats migrated across the Seine from the Marais in search of spacious plots of land for their mansions. The Faubourg St-Germain thus became one of Europe's most fashionable districts.

The now-celebrated **boulevard St-Germain** was driven right through the heart of the quarter by Baron Haussmann in the mid-nineteenth century, but it became famous in its own right after the war, when the cafés **Flore** and **Les Deux Magots** attracted the resurgent Parisian avant-garde – Sartre debated existentialism with de Beauvoir and Boris Vian sang in smoky cellar jazz bars. As Guy Béart and, later, Juliette Gréco sang, "*Il n y a plus d'après à Saint-Germain-des-Prés*" – there's no tomorrow in St-Germain.

Of course, there was – even if an older Juliette Gréco tried to fight it with her movement "SOS St-Germain" in the late 1990s. The glitterati may still prefer the Left Bank – apart from Gréco, **Serge Gainsbourg** lived here until his death in 1991 – but high-rolling publishers, designers and politicians have long since shouldered out boho intellectuals and musicians. **Fashion**, now, is king; the streets around the carrefour de la Croix-Rouge and place St-Sulpice, in particular, swarm with internationally known clothing boutiques, while a little further west the historic Bon Marché department store stocks an ever-classier range. Towards the river, antique shops and **art dealers** dominate, with one pricey cluster around rue Jacob and rue Bonaparte, and another in the "Carré Rive Gauche", the three blocks south of quai Voltaire. After shopping, eating and drinking are the main attractions, though, once again, the scene is distinctly chichi these days. Well-heeled foodies now flock to the gastronomic **restaurants** of celebrity chefs like Hélène Darroze and Joël Robuchon, and foreign visitors fill the *bistrots* around Mabillon.

There are excellent markets and cafés to take in as you shop or stroll, as well as some fine buildings – from the domed **Institut de France**, by the river, to the churches of St-Germain-des-Prés and majestic **St-Sulpice**. Two small museums, the **Musée Maillol** and **Musée Delacroix**, make intimate antidotes to the grand Right Bank institutions, while the exhibitions at the **Musée du Luxembourg** are regularly among the city's most exciting. And of course there's the **Musée d'Orsay**, at the western edge of the quarter, loved as much for its stunning railway-station setting as its Impressionist collection. But St-Germain's most beguiling attraction lies in the southeastern corner of the quarter, hard up against the Quartier Latin. Notoriously romantic, and often packed with students, the **Jardin du Luxembourg** is one of the largest green spaces in the city – and surely the loveliest.

The riverside quarter

The riverside slice of St-Germain – north of the bustling, restaurant-lined rue St-André-des-Arts – feels both secretive and aristocratic, its fine seventeenth- and eighteenth-century mansions concealing private gardens and courtyards behind massive *portes cochères* gates. The area is also strewn with artistic and philosophical memories. Picasso painted *Guernica* in rue des Grands-Augustins. In rue Mazarine, Molière opened his first theatre, and Champollion finally deciphered Egyptian hieroglyphics in his attic rooms. In rue Visconti, Racine died, Delacroix painted and Balzac's printing business went bust. In the parallel rue des Beaux-Arts, the Romantic poet Gérard de Nerval went walking with a lobster on a lead and a disgraced Oscar Wilde died "fighting a duel" with his hotel room's wallpaper – "One or the other of us has to go", he remarked. You can still stay in the hotel, now named simply *L'Hôtel* (see p.258), or call in for a drink at its fashionable bar.

Musée des Lettres et Manuscrits

8 rue de Nesle, 6ᵉ • Tues, Wed & Fri–Sun 10am–7pm, Thurs 10am–9.30pm • €7 • ☎ 01 42 22 48 48 , ⓦ museedeslettres.fr • ⓜ Odéon

Some of the famous characters associated with St-Germain are remembered in the **Musée des Lettres et Manuscrits**, where historic letters and documents handwritten by anyone of note, from Catherine de Médicis to Simone de Beauvoir, are permanently exhibited. Churchill, Roosevelt and Eisenhower crop up in a handful of wartime letters, Einstein is represented by some scrawled equations, and there are some delightfully miniature letters sent by balloon during the 1870 siege of Paris, but otherwise you'll need to be able to read French for the entry fee to be worth it.

Pont des Arts

ⓜ St-Germain-des-Prés/Louvre-Rivoli

The pedestrian **Pont des Arts** is arguably the most charming of all the city's bridges and a classic place to loiter. You can watch the touristy bateaux-mouches and the working barges, and soak up the view upstream to the Ile de la Cité and across to the Louvre, screened behind its elegant double row of gentle white poplars and muscular plane trees. An ever-burgeoning collection of padlocks has been left on the bridge's wire fencing by couples seeking to bear witness to the immortality of their love; the town hall seems to be leaving them attached, for the time being.

Institut de France

23 quai de Conti, 6ᵉ • Bibliothèque Mazarine Mon–Fri 10am–6pm • Free • ⓜ Mabillon/Pont-Neuf

The Pont des Arts owes its name not to the artists who have long sold their work here but to the institute that sits under the elegant dome on the St-Germain side. This is the **Collège des Quatre-Nations**, seat of the **Institut de France**. Of the Institut's five academies of arts and sciences, the most famous is the **Académie Française**, an august body of writers and scholars whose mission is to award literary prizes and defend the integrity of the French language against Anglo-Saxon invasion. The chosen few are known as *Immortels* – though ironically, by the time they have accumulated enough prestige to be elected, most are not long for this world. That said, the list has evolved in recent years: among the forty-strong group at the time of writing, four were women.

You'd need an invitation to attend one of the Institut's lectures, but if you ask politely at the gate and present ID and a couple of passport-sized photos for registration, you will be given a visitor's pass for the exquisite **Bibliothèque Mazarine**, where scholars of religious history sit in hushed contemplation of some of the 200,000 sixteenth- and seventeenth-century volumes, surrounded by *rocaille* chandeliers, marble busts and Corinthian columns.

Next door to the Institut, the **Hôtel des Monnaies** was the Mint in the late eighteenth century. It now houses a museum of coinage (ⓦ monnaiedeparis.fr), which is closed for restoration until at least 2013.

Ecole des Beaux-Arts

14 rue Bonaparte, 6ᵉ • Mon–Fri 9.30am–6pm • Free • ⓜ St-Germain-des-Prés

To the west of the Institut lies the **Ecole des Beaux-Arts**, the School of Fine Art, whose glory days gave its name to an entire epoch. It's worth poking your nose into the courtyard. The elaborate, three-storey facade of the chapel on the right actually came from the sixteenth-century château d'Anet, which was built by Henri II for his lover, Diane de Poitiers – you can see their intertwined initials above the doors. On the left is what the French call a *mur renard* – a false or "fox" facade, built to mask a neighbour's blank gable end. But the centrepiece is the grand Italianate building at the end of the courtyard, Félix Duban's Palais des Etudes, which dates to the 1830s. You can enter the serene covered court, with its polychrome decoration and immense conservatory roof – added by the architect in 1863. You're not supposed to explore any further, so you won't see the gardens, Duban's Cour du Mûrier – a lovely cloister set around a

ST-GERMAIN

BARS & CLUBS
Le 10	10
Bar du Marché	5
Bistrot des Augustins	2
Chez Georges	9
Les Etages St-Germain	7
Lutetia Bar	11
La Mezzanine de l'Alcazar	4
Le Montana	6
La Palette	1
Prescription	3
WAGG	4

GAY CLUB
Le Rive Gauche	8

ACCOMMODATION
Hôtel de l'Abbaye	10
La Belle Juliette	11
Hôtel du Danube	3
L'Hôtel	2
Hôtel Louis II	6
Hôtel Michelet-Odéon	9
Hôtel de Nesle	4
Hôtel Odéon Saint-Germain	7
Relais Christine	5
Relais Saint-Sulpice	8
Hôtel Stanislas	12
Hôtel de Verneuil	1

CAFÉS & WINE BARS
L'Assignat	1
L'Avant Comptoir	18
Bar du Marché	9
Bistrot des Augustins	6
Café de la Mairie	20
La Crèmerie	19
Les Etages St-Germain	11
Le Flore	13
Ladurée	7
La Palette	5
Au Petit Suisse	23
Au Vieux Colombier	21

RESTAURANTS
Allard	12
L'Atlas	10
Au Babylone	22
Brasserie Lipp	14
Le Comptoir du Relais	18
L'Epi Dupin	26
L'Epigramme	15
Ferrandaise	24
Gaya Rive Gauche	4
Hélène Darroze	25
Maison de l'Amerique Latine	2
Le Petit St-Benoît	8
La Tourelle	16
Vagenende	17
Ze Kitchen Galerie	3

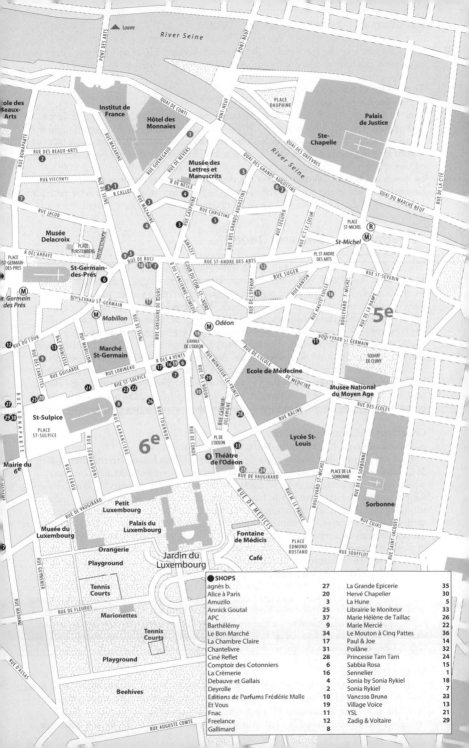

● SHOPS

agnès b.	27		La Grande Epicerie	35
Alice à Paris	20		Hervé Chapelier	30
Amuzilo	3		La Hune	5
Annick Goutal	25		Librairie le Moniteur	33
APC	37		Marie Hélène de Taillac	26
Barthélémy	9		Marie Mercié	22
Le Bon Marché	34		Le Mouton à Cinq Pattes	36
La Chambre Claire	17		Paul & Joe	14
Chantelivre	31		Poilâne	32
Ciné Reflet	28		Princesse Tam Tam	24
Comptoir des Cotonniers	6		Sabbia Rosa	15
La Crèmerie	16		Sennelier	1
Debauve et Gallais	4		Sonia by Sonia Rykiel	18
Deyrolle	2		Sonia Rykiel	7
Editions de Parfums Frédéric Malle	10		Vanessa Bruno	23
Et Vous	19		Village Voice	21
Fnac	11		YSL	21
Freelance	12		Zadig & Voltaire	29
Gallimard	8			

9

mulberry tree – or the remnants of the sixteenth-century Hôtel de Chimay. There are occasional exhibitions of work by students, however; the entrance is on quai Malaquais.

The house of Serge Gainsbourg
5bis rue de Verneuil, 6ᵉ • ⓜSt-Germain-des-Prés

West of the Ecole des Beaux-Arts is the house where iconoclastic pop legend **Serge Gainsbourg** lived until his death in 1991 – it's now owned by his film-star daughter Charlotte. Over the years, the garden wall was steadily covered by layer upon layer of graffiti quoting famous lyrics like "God smokes Havanas" and aerosol-sprayed versions of *Gainsbarre*'s distinctive silhouette. Ever since a catastrophic day in April 2000, however, the **Mur de Gainsbourg** has received regular coats of whitewash. It hasn't deterred the fans in the slightest, but to get the full effect you'll have to hope you don't visit just after the decorators – the official decorators, that is – have visited.

St-Germain-des-Prés and Odéon
ⓜSt-Germain-des-Prés

The **boulevard St-Germain** was bulldozed right through the Left Bank under Baron Haussmann (see p.370), and is a fairly undistinguished thoroughfare for much of its length. One short stretch around **place St-Germain-des-Prés**, however, makes up one of Paris's most celebrated micro-neighbourhoods. The **Deux Magots** café stands on one corner of the square, while the equally celebrated **Flore** (see p.282) lies a few steps further along the boulevard. Both are chiefly renowned for the postwar writers and philosophers who drank and debated there – most famously the philosopher-novelist Simone de Beauvoir and her existentialist lover, Jean-Paul Sartre. Although both cafés charge high prices and attract plenty of tourists, they're still genuine St-Germain institutions – albeit patronized by designers and directors rather than writers these days. The cognoscenti judge *Flore* to have maintained that edge of authenticity. *Brasserie Lipp* (see p.283), across the boulevard, is another long-time haunt of moneyed intellectuals, and maintains its traditions proudly.

Church of St-Germain-des-Prés
Place St-Germain-des-Prés, 6ᵉ • Daily 8am–7.45pm • Free • ⓜSt-Germain-des-Prés

The powerful tower dominating place St-Germain-des-Prés belongs to the **church of St-Germain-des-Prés**, and is all that remains of an enormous Benedictine monastery whose lands once stretched right across the Left Bank. Having survived a post-Revolution stint as a saltpetre factory, the church itself is one of twenty-first-century Paris's oldest surviving buildings, a rare Romanesque structure that dates back to the late tenth and early eleventh centuries. The choir, however, was rebuilt in the fashionable Gothic style in the mid-twelfth century – work that's just about visible under the heavy greens and golds of nineteenth-century paintwork. The marble columns of its middle triforium level date from an even earlier church on this site, erected in the sixth century, which housed the remains of the Merovingian kings. A later tomb, a simple slab engraved with the name René Descartes, can be found in the last chapel on the south side. Outside the church, on the corner of rue de l'Abbaye and rue Bonaparte, there's a pretty little garden with some strange fragments of Gothic stonework. These, along with a single stained-glass window in the apse of the main church, are the melancholy last remains of a thirteenth-century chapel. They make a perfect backdrop to the Picasso statue of a woman's head which also stands here, dedicated to the memory of the poet Apollinaire.

Musée Delacroix
6 rue de Furstenberg, 6ᵉ • Daily except Tues 9.30am–5pm • €5 • ☎ 01 44 41 86 50, ⓦ musee-delacroix.fr • ⓜMabillon/St-Germain-des-Prés

Hidden away round the back of St-Germain-des-Prés, **place de Furstenberg** is one of Paris's most lovable squares, huddling round its quartet of Paulownia trees and candelabra-like street lamp. Tucked into its northwest corner is the **Musée Delacroix**, a charming miniature museum displaying sketches by the artist and various personal effects. Delacroix lived and worked in the house here from 1857 until his death in 1863, watched over by Jenny Le Guillou, who'd been his servant since 1835. You can visit the bedroom where he died, now graced by Jenny's portrait, while the little sitting room houses the museum's only really important work, the intense *Madeleine au désert* (1845). Delacroix had his studio built outside, its large window overlooking a hidden garden. Today, watercolours and a few more substantial works are hung here, alongside temporary exhibitions, but for Delacroix's major work you'll have to visit the Louvre and Musée d'Orsay, or head over to the murals at nearby St-Sulpice (see p.138).

Looming at the southern end of the rue de Furstenberg is the sixteenth-century **Palais Abbatial**, built for Charles de Bourbon, the powerful abbot of St-Germain, in an early version of what became the Louis XIII style. Today, it still belongs to the Catholic Church, housing an institute for Augustinian studies.

Rue de Buci
Ⓜ Mabillon/Odéon

Rue de Buci was once a proper street market, and still preserves a brash and faintly chaotic air. That said, the morning-only greengrocers' stalls are known locally as jewellery shops – for their prices rather than the colour of the fruit. The oyster-seller works for the *Atlas* brasserie (see p.283), and even the *Bar du Marché* (see p.281) has given in to a fashionable clientele, though the waiters still wear natty cloth caps and overalls. The entire street is now ringed by delis, sandwich shops and restaurants – as well as some of the livelier bars on the Left Bank, such as *Les Étages St-Germain* (see p.299).

Cour du Commerce St-André
Ⓜ Odéon

A few steps east of the main rue de Buci crossroads on rue de Seine, the little covered *passage* of the **cour du Commerce St-André** cuts through enticingly from rue St-André-des-Arts to the boulevard St-Germain. Marat had a printing press here, and Dr Guillotin honed his fabled scientific execution device by practising on sheep's heads. Backing onto the street is *Le Procope* – Paris's first coffee house, which opened its doors in 1686. It was the favourite watering hole and talking shop of Voltaire and Rousseau, among others, and the Enlightenment's great project, the *Encyclopédie*, was dreamed up here in a fug of caffeine. The café is still open for business, but sadly commercialized; you'll find laminated menus there now, not philosophers. A couple of smaller courtyards open off the alleyway, revealing another stretch of Philippe-Auguste's twelfth-century city wall.

Marché St-Germain
Ⓜ Mabillon

The **Marché St-Germain** is a 1990s reconstruction of a covered market which was one of the few architectural legacies left to the city by Napoleon. The site is more ancient still, having been the venue for the raucous St-Germain fair, held at the gates of the abbey in medieval times. Sadly, market stalls have been replaced by boutique shops and a swimming pool and gym complex. The area around the Marché, on rues Princesse, Lobineau, Guisarde and des Canettes, is known collectively as *rue de la soif*, or the "street of thirst", and it heaves with diners and drinkers of an evening. There are plenty of passable (and very popular) "pubs", but few really good addresses – though the wine bar *Chez Georges* (see p.299) is a classic.

The Odéon quarter
Ⓜ Odéon

The broad **Odéon** stretch of the boulevard St-Germain is best known for its cinemas and, since 2004, its infamous *Starbucks* – widely regarded as the vanguard of the barbarian invasion. At this eastern edge of St-Germain you start to feel the gravitational

9

pull of the university, and indeed this area is sometimes considered to be part of the Quartier Latin. The ethnic restaurants of **rue Monsieur le Prince** cater for student budgets while, around the **Ecole de Médecine**, university bookshops display skeletons and instruments of medical torture. The defining landmark of the area, however, is the recently restored **Théâtre de l'Odéon**, its proud Doric facade fronting a handsome semicircular plaza. This was one of the learned King Louis XVI's last projects before the Revolution, and had a then-unheard-of capacity of 1900.

St-Sulpice

The fact that the actress Catherine Deneuve has an apartment on **place St-Sulpice** is a good clue to its character. This is a classy yet still faintly arty corner of the city. On the sunny north side of the square, the outside tables at the *Café de la Mairie* (see p.282) hum with chatter on fine days – it's one of the city's finest outdoor *terrasses* – facing the original boutique of **Yves Saint Laurent Rive Gauche**. Architecturally the square is enchanting, with its lion fountain and chestnut trees overlooked by the church's not-quite-twin towers: the south tower has long waited in sculptural limbo – you can see uncut masonry blocks at the top, still awaiting the sculptor's chisel.

Church of St-Sulpice
Place St-Sulpice, 6ᵉ • Daily 7.30am–7.30pm • Free • ⓦ paroisse-saint-sulpice-paris.org • Ⓜ St-Sulpice

The church of St-Sulpice is a muscular Classical edifice erected either side of 1700. For decades, the gloomy **interior** was best known for three **Delacroix murals**, found in the first chapel on the right, and a huge, 101-stop, five-manual, part-eighteenth-century **organ**, which is thought to be among the finest in the world and is used at frequent recitals. Since the publication of *The Da Vinci Code*, however, the chief sight is the remains of the **solar observatory**. A lens in the south transept window, long since removed, once focused the sun's rays on a narrow brass strip, or meridiana, which still runs right across the floor of the nave and up a stone pillar on the north side. At its winter low, the sun would exactly crown the obelisk at noon; at its summer height, it would burn down on the start of the brass line. As a printed notice points out, the device is an "instrument of astronomy" designed in 1727 by an English clock-maker called Henry Sully. The original project was liturgical: to establish the exact time of noon and determine the proper dates for the church's moveable feasts. The instrument as it survives now, however, is the remnant of a 1740s scientific attempt to measure the exact time of the winter and summer solstices. Either way, as the sign tartly observes, "no mystical notion can be derived" from it. And the brass strip does not follow any "Rose Line", nor even the Paris meridian – though it runs close by.

Jardin du Luxembourg
Roughly dawn to dusk • RER Luxembourg/Ⓜ Odéon

Hemingway liked to claim he fed himself in Paris by shooting pigeons in the **Jardin du Luxembourg**. These lovely gardens belong to the **Palais du Luxembourg**, which now houses the French Senate, but was originally built for Marie de Médicis, Henri IV's widow. They are the Left Bank's heart, and quite possibly its lungs as well. They get fantastically crowded on summer days, especially the shady **Fontaine de Médicis** in the northeast corner and the tail of the gardens that points south towards the Paris observatory – the latter being the only place where you're allowed to sit out on the **lawns**. Everywhere else you'll have to settle yourself on the heavy, sage-green metal chairs, which are liberally distributed around the gravel paths. Alternatively, there's a pleasant, tree-shaded (and not exorbitantly priced) **café** a few steps east of the central pond.

9

Exploring the gardens

Children rent toy yachts to sail on the pond, but the western side of the gardens, beside the **tennis courts** (see p.346), is the more active area: there are donkey rides, go-karts, a marionette show (see p.350) and a large playground for children, plus the inevitable sandy area for boules. **Sculptures** are scattered around the park, including an 1890 monument to the painter Delacroix by Jules Dalou and a suitably bizarre homage to the Surrealist poet Paul Eluard by the sculptor Ossip Zadkine (see p.164). In the quieter, wooded, western section of the park you can also find one of Paris's miniature versions of the Statue of Liberty, just bigger than human size, and a cluster of well-tended beehives. The southwest corner ends in a fabulous miniature orchard of elaborately espaliered pear trees whose fruit graces the tables of senators or, if surplus to requirements, are given to organizations for the homeless.

The north–south spine of the gardens extends down into a tail pointing towards the Paris observatory, following the line of the old Paris meridian (see p.165). At the extreme southern end of the gardens, the circular **Fontaine de l'Observatoire** symbolizes Paris's historic self-conception as the very navel of the world, with Jean-Baptiste Carpeaux's fine sculptures of the four continents supporting a mighty iron globe.

Orangerie

Jardin du Luxembourg • Exposition d'Automne hours and prices vary, see Ⓦ senat.fr/evenements • ⓂSt-Sulpice/RER Luxembourg

For two or three weeks in the latter part of September, the half-glazed **Orangerie** is the venue for the annual **Exposition d'Automne**, which shows off the garden's finest fruits and floral decorations. For the rest of the winter, it's closed to visitors, as it shelters the garden's collection of scores of exotic trees – palms, bitter oranges, oleanders and pomegranates, some of them over two hundred years old. All are wheeled back outside, in their giant wooden containers, every spring.

Musée du Luxembourg

19 rue de Vaugirard, 6ᵉ, Jardin du Luxembourg • Hours and prices vary • ☎ 01 40 13 62 00, Ⓦ museeduluxembourg.fr • ⓂSt-Sulpice/RER Luxembourg

Immediately behind the Orangerie, but with its entrance on rue de Vaugirard – Paris's longest street – stands the **Musée du Luxembourg**. Some of Paris's biggest and most exciting art exhibitions are held here, often causing long queues to form alongside the giant railings of the Jardin du Luxembourg. Recent successes have included twentieth-century self-portraits and the works of Lucas Cranach.

The western fringe of St-Germain

The broad, ugly gash of rue de Rennes signals the western boundary of the core St-Germain neighbourhood, but the 6ᵉ arrondissement continues officially as far west as rue des Sts-Pères – and, in feel, this quarter extends well into the 7ᵉ arrondissement, or at least as far as rue du Bac. The whole area, certainly, is stuffed to bursting with chichi shops, and it's here that you'll find the landmark Left Bank department store, Le Bon Marché. On Sunday mornings, meanwhile, the celebrated Raspail organic food market, or **Marché Bio** (see p.338), lines the boulevard Raspail between the Sèvres-Babylone and Rennes métro stations.

Around the carrefour de la Croix Rouge

ⓂSt-Sulpice/Sèvres-Babylone

You might not find the most exclusive Right Bank designers or the more alternative-minded Marais boutiques here, but rues Bonaparte, Madame, de Sèvres, de Grenelle, du Vieux-Colombier, du Dragon, du Four and des Sts-Pères are lined with the big names in Parisian clothes and accessories, from Agnès b. to Zadig et Voltaire. It's hard to imagine now, but smack in the middle of all this, at the **carrefour de la Croix Rouge**, there was a major barricade in 1871, during the Paris Commune (see box, p.185). These days you're more likely to be suffering from till-shock than shell-shock, though César's 4m statue of a **Centaure**, cast in homage to Picasso in 1983, is distinctly alarming. It surveys the crossroads with ferocity, and two sets of genitals.

Le Bon Marché

24 rue de Sèvres, 6ᵉ • Mon–Wed & Sat 10am–8pm, Thurs & Fri 10am–9pm • Ⓦ lebonmarche.com • ⓂSèvres-Babylone

Just over the boundary with the 7ᵉ arrondissement, at the far side of the green square Boucicaut, stands the grand department store, **Le Bon Marché** (see p.323). One of the great institutions of the nineteenth century (and the setting for Zola's novel *Au Bonheur des Dames*), its name means "inexpensive", but these days it's one of Paris's most upmarket shopping spaces. A 1920s annexe on the west side of rue du Bac now houses the luxurious **Grande Epicerie**, or "big grocer's".

Notre-Dame de la Médaille Miraculeuse

140 rue du Bac, 7ᵉ • Daily 7.45am–6pm • Free • Ⓦ chapellenotredamedelamedaillemiraculeuse.com • ⓂSèvres-Babylone

If you stand outside Le Bon Marché, especially on a Sunday, you'll notice that a surprisingly large proportion of people among the crowds isn't here for the shopping. The reason lies down an alley hidden behind 140 rue du Bac, just north of the aerial bridge joining the two wings of the department store. Tucked away at its end is a little chapel with the unwieldy name of **Notre-Dame de la Médaille Miraculeuse**. It was here, in 1830, that a 24-year-old nun called Catherine Laboure had visions of the Virgin Mary dressed in silk, with her feet resting on a globe. A voice told Catherine to "have a medal struck like this – those who wear it will receive great graces". The nuns duly obeyed, and have been quite literally coining it ever since. You can buy a souvenir medal and visit the chapel, which was rebuilt to accommodate huge pilgrim congregations in 1930.

Hôtel Lutetia

45 bd Raspail, 6ᵉ • Ⓦ lutetia-paris.com • ⓂSèvres-Babylone

Facing the Bon Marché department store across square Boucicaut is the monumental **Hôtel Lutetia**, one of the finer Art Deco buildings in the city. Its sinuous (and projecting) sculpted stonework is currently masked by netting for health and safety reasons, but the Art Deco brasserie and bar inside are still gloriously untouched. At the outbreak of World War II, scores of artists fled here, seeking sanctuary of a kind. Among them was James Joyce – peeved, it's said, that the growing conflict of war had overshadowed the publication of his novel, *Finnegans Wake*. After the defeat of Germany, the hotel became a repatriation centre for survivors of the concentration camps.

Musée Maillol

61 rue de Grenelle, 7ᵉ • Daily 10.30am–7pm, Fri till 9.30pm • €11 • ☎ 01 42 22 59 58, Ⓦ museemaillol.com • ⓂRue-du-Bac

This pocket museum is gloriously overstuffed with post-Impressionist sculptor Aristide Maillol's buxom female nudes – copies of which stand in the Louvre's Jardin du Carrousel. The artist's most famous work, the dumpily curvacious *Mediterranean*, sits on the first floor at the top of the stairs. The exhibits belonged to Dina Vierny, Maillol's former model and inspiration, and works by other contemporaries are also collected here, including drawings by Matisse, Dufy and Bonnard, for whom Dina also modelled, and a room full of Pollakoff's Jaggedy abstracts on the second floor. The museum also organizes excellent exhibitions of twentieth-century art, with recent shows including sculptures by Miró.

A few steps east of the museum stands the **Fontaine des Quatre-Saisons**, less a fountain than a piece of early eighteenth-century architectural theatre. At the centre of the curved stone arcade sits the City of Paris herself, flanked by two sinuous figures representing the rivers Seine and Marne.

9

Deyrolle

46 rue du Bac, 7ᵉ • Mon 10am–1pm & 2–7pm, Tues–Sat 10am–7pm • Free • ☎ 01 42 22 30 07, Ⓦ deyrolle.com • Ⓜ Rue-du-Bac

You might not normally go out of your way to visit a taxidermist's, but **Deyrolle** should be an exception. The chichi garden tool shop below is a mere front for the real business upstairs, in a room perfumed with the sharp, coal-tar smell of taxidermy. Giant, antique wooden display cases are stuffed with pinned butterflies and shards of prehistoric trilobites, while above and all around them are scores of stuffed rabbits, ducks, sheep, boar, bears and even big cats. Astonishingly, this isn't a museum: the entire stock (apart from a billy goat and a donkey) was replaced from scratch after a disastrous fire in 2008, and all the pieces on view are for sale. A lion could be yours for around €10,000, or you can pick up a fossil for a couple of euros. Children, in particular, tend to be fascinated by the place.

Musée d'Orsay

62 rue de Lille, 7ᵉ, entrance at 1 rue de la Légion d'Honneur • Tues, Wed & Fri–Sun 9.30am–6pm, Thurs 9.30am–9.45pm • €8; free to under-18s, to under-26s from the EU, and to all on first Sun of the month • ☎ 01 40 49 48 14, Ⓦ musee-orsay.fr • Ⓜ Solférino/RER Musée-d'Orsay

As it comes into the 7ᵉ arrondissement, boulevard St-Germain swings up towards the river, disgorging its traffic across the Pont de la Concorde onto the Right Bank. On the east side of this wedge of the city are the expensive art and antiques shops of the **Carré Rive Gauche**, between rue de l'Université and the quai Voltaire. To the west, facing the Tuileries gardens across the river, is the **Musée d'Orsay**. The museum's collection of the electrifying works of the **Impressionists** and Post-Impressionists has made it one of Paris's most-visited attractions. There's more to it than just Monet and Renoir, however. The collection covers the artistically revolutionary era between 1848 and 1914 – between the end of the Louvre's Classical traditions and the start of the modern era, as represented in the Pompidou Centre.

The building

The building itself was inaugurated as a **railway station** for the 1900 World Fair. It spans the worlds of nineteenth-century Classicism and industrial modernity brilliantly, its elegant, formal stone facade cunningly disguising the steel-and-glass construction of the railway arch within. It continued to serve the stations of southwest France until 1939, but its platforms became too short for postwar trains and it fell into disuse. De Gaulle made it the backdrop for the announcement of his coup d'état of May 19, 1958, but such was the site's degradation by the 1960s that Orson Welles thought it the perfect location for his film of Kafka's nightmarish *The Trial*. Despite this illustrious history, the station was only saved from destruction by the backlash of public opinion

---

VISITING THE MUSEE D'ORSAY

At the time of writing, a **major renovation** was almost complete. The new Pavillon Amont is to provide new hanging space – and much better access to the Impressionist Galleries in the attics – but this does mean that the locations of many paintings is likely to shift around, and the general orientation of the museum may alter too. That said, the basic **layout** isn't changing much, and it'll still be easy to confine your visit to a specific section, each of which has a very distinctive atmosphere. Chronologically, the collection begins on the ground floor, under the huge vault of steel and glass, then continues up to the attics of the upper level, where you'll find the Impressionists. It then continues through to the Post-Impressionists – displayed on the terraces and galleries of the middle level, overlooking the main "nave" chamber. The **café** on the upper level of the museum – with its summer terrace and wonderful view of Montmartre through the giant railway clock – and the resplendently gilded restaurant and tearoom on the middle level are great spots to recuperate. Tea and a dessert will set you back around €12.

that followed the demolition of Les Halles. The job of redesigning the interior as a museum was given, in 1986, to the fashionable Milanese architect Gae Aulenti. Hers is a considered, beautiful design with one major drawback: the Impressionist section is crammed under the roof, putting the biggest crowds in the most cramped area.

Ground floor nave
The **ground floor "nave"**, under the great glass arch, is devoted to pre-1870 work, with a double row of sculptures running down the central aisle like railway tracks, and paintings in the odd little bunkers on either side. Chief among the **mid-nineteenth-century sculptors** in the central aisle is Carpeaux, whose *Ugolin* shows the damned Count Ugolino, from Dante's *Divine Comedy*, gnawing at his fingers in pain and hunger as he contemplates consuming the bodies of his dying children. The original plaster of the *Four Quarters of the World Bearing the Celestial Sphere*, the bronze version of which lies at the foot of the Jardin du Luxembourg, is also his. Nearby stand Charles Cordier's bizarre polychrome busts of black Africans, in bronze and coloured stone.

Ground floor paintings
On the south side of the ground floor level, towards rue de Lille, one set of rooms is dedicated to **Chassériau, Gérôme, Ingres, Delacroix** – the bulk of whose work is in the Louvre – and the serious-minded artworks of the "academic" painters acceptable to the mid-nineteenth-century salons. The adjacent suite displays the relatively wacky works of Bouguereau, Gustave Moreau and the younger Degas.

The influential **Barbizon School** and the **Realists** are represented on the Seine side with canvases by Daumier, Corot and Millet. These were some of the first to break with the established norms of moralism and idealization of the past. The soft-toned landscapes by Millet and Corot, and quickly executed scenes by Daubigny, such as his *La Neige*, were influential on later, avowed Impressionists, as can be seen in two paintings by **Monet** and **Manet** both entitled *Déjeuner sur l'herbe*.

Courbet's *L'Origine du monde* has the power to shock even contemporary audiences – many of whom simply pretend it's not hanging there. The explicit nude female torso was acquired from psychoanalyst Jacques Lacan, who screened it behind a decorative panel in his offices. Adjacent rooms are dedicated to other exercises in realism, as well as early Impressionist landscapes by **Sisley, Monet** and **Pissarro**, among others. Don't miss Monet's lovable *Coquelicots* ("Poppies").

Upper level: Impressionism
To continue chronologically, proceed straight to the **upper level**, whose rooms have a more intimate feel, done almost like a suite of attic studios. After the initial shock of the relatively monochrome, realist portraits by **Eugène Carrière** and **Henri Fantin-Latour** – which prove that not everybody at this time was painting light and colour – you arrive in deep Impressionist territory. In this section of the museum you'll have to fight off the persistent sense of familiarity or recognition – Degas' *L'Absinthe*, Renoir's *Bal du Moulin de la Galette*, Monet's *Femme à l'ombrelle* – in order to appreciate Impressionism's vibrant, experimental vigour.

A host of small-scale landscapes and outdoor scenes by Renoir, Sisley, Pissarro and Monet are owed to the novel practice of setting up easels in the open – often as not, on the banks of the Seine. Less typical works include Degas' ballet dancers, which demonstrate his principal interest in movement and line as opposed to the more common Impressionist concern with light. Monet's obsessive Rouen cathedral series, each painted in different light conditions, fills one entire room, while another is dominated by the pink and green tones of Renoir's fleshy nudes – an obsession quite as intense as Monet's with cathedrals – along with his joyous pairing *Danse à la ville / Danse à la campagne*. Don't miss the dimly lit chamber devoted to more

9

THE SHOCKING SALON OF 1863

Manet's magnificent painting of *Le Déjeuner sur l'herbe*, or *The Picnic*, which hangs in the Musée d'Orsay, caused outrage at the **1863 Salon des Refusés**. This was a deliberately confrontational show of works (a "salon") that had been rejected by the judges of the official Salon of 1863. It has often been said to mark the beginning of the **Impressionist** movement. The problem with Manet's picnic scene wasn't so much the nakedness of its female figure, as female nudity was absolutely standard in French Classical art (just look at the extremely erotic canvases hung nearby, by the likes of Bouguereau and Chabanel). It was rather the fact that Manet had juxtaposed her with male figures in modern dress, making her look not like an idealized representation of womanhood so much as a common harlot. Manet had shifted his interest away from the ideal and towards the everyday, and this was regarded as amoral at best. Manet's provocative *Olympia*, with its brash and sensual surfaces, appeared at the same salon. No less shocking, it portrayed Olympia as a high-class whore who returns the stares of her audience with a look of insolent defiance.

---

pastels, by Redon, Manet, Mondrian and others. Towards the end of the collection, in terms of artistic development, **Van Gogh** contributes his fervid colours and disturbing rhythms, and **Cézanne** attempts to restore his own particular kind of order.

Middle level

On the rue de Lille side of the **middle level**, the flow of the painting section continues with the various offspring of Impressionism. In works such as Rousseau's dreamlike *La Charmeuse de serpent* and **Gauguin**'s ambivalent Tahitian paintings there's an edgier, more modern feel, with a much greater emphasis on psychology. More decorative effects are attempted by **Pointillists** such as Seurat (the famous *Cirque*), Signac and others. There are also some iconic caricatures by **Toulouse-Lautrec**, including the splendidly smoky *Danse Mauresque*, which depicts the celebrated cancan dancer, La Goulue, entertaining an audience of lowlifes including an obese, washed-up Oscar Wilde.

On the **sculpture terraces**, nineteenth-century marbles on the Seine side face early twentieth-century pieces across the divide, but the **Rodin terrace** bridging the two puts almost everything else to shame. Rodin's *Ugolin* is even grimmer than Carpeaux's, immediately below, while his *Fugit amor*, a response to his pupil and lover Camille Claudel's *L'Age mûr*, adjacent, is a powerful image of the end of their liaison. It's a pity, but few visitors will have energy left for the half-dozen rooms of **Art Nouveau** furniture and objets d'art, or the troubling handful of international **Symbolist** paintings, which includes Gustav Klimt's gorgeous *Rosiers sous les arbres*.

The Pavillon Amont

On the ground floor of the newly opened Pavillon Amont, you can see a less familiar side of late nineteenth-century painting, with large-scale, epic works such as Detaille's stirring *Le Rêve* and Cormon's *Caïn*. Orientalist works are displayed in the adjacent Vestibule area. Above, on Level 2, is a superb collection of works by Vuillard and Bonnard, painters who began their careers as part of an Art Nouveau group known as the **Nabis**; strong Japanese influences can be seen in Vuillard's decorative screen, *Jardins publics* and Bonnard's *La Partie de croquet*. Levels 3 and 4 now show works long hidden in storage, chiefly Art Deco pieces by non-French painters, notably from the Vienna and Glasgow schools.

THE EIFFEL TOWER

The Eiffel Tower quarter

Standing sentinel over a great bend in the Seine as it flows southwest out of
Paris is the monumental flagpole that is the Eiffel Tower. It surveys the most
relentlessly splendid of all Paris's districts, embracing the palatial heights of
the Trocadéro, on the Right Bank, and the wealthy, western swathe of the
7e (septième) arrondissement, on the Left. These are street vistas planned for
sheer magnificence: as you look out across the river from the terrace of the
Palais de Chaillot to the Eiffel Tower and the huge Ecole Militaire, or let your
gaze run from the ornate Pont Alexandre III past the parliament building to
the vast Hôtel des Invalides, you are experiencing city design on a truly
monumental scale.

The quarter is home chiefly to diplomats, government officials and aristocrats, both old-school and new. It's here that the Prime Minister has his well-guarded official residence, the **Hôtel Matignon**, with its giant garden stretching south as far as rue de Babylone. Unsurprisingly, it is pretty dead in terms of shops and restaurants, but it is studded with some compelling **museums**, from the stunningly designed new one devoted to "primitive" art at **quai Branly**, down to another dedicated to Paris's sewer system – found, appropriately enough, down in the **sewers**. In the heart of the septième, the imposing **Hôtel des Invalides** houses the French army's vast war museum, centred on the tomb of the still-idolized little general, Napoleon. The **Musée Rodin**, nearby, shows off the sculptor's works in the intimate surroundings of a handsome private *hôtel*, or mansion house. Just across the river, in the **Trocadéro** quarter of the 16e arrondissement, you'll find a pocket of fine museums specializing in Asian Buddhist art, fashion and architecture, along with two of the most exciting art museums in the city: the **Palais de Tokyo**'s galleries of Parisian modern art and contemporary French artworks.

For all the pomp, there are some appealing little neighbourhoods, notably in the wedge of homely streets centred on the **rue Cler** market and in the arrondissement's eastern fringe, towards the 6e. Note, however, that this easternmost end of the 7e – including the Musée d'Orsay and the shopping area around rue du Bac and the Sèvres-Babylone métro – belongs more in feel to the St-Germain quarter, and is therefore covered in Chapter 9.

The Eiffel Tower and around

Daily: mid-June to Aug 9am–12.45am; Sept to mid-June 9.30am–11.45pm; upward-bound lifts stop 45min before closing time, Sept to mid-June access to stairs closes 6pm; ticket sales for the top end at 10.30pm (or 11pm from mid-June to Aug) • Tickets €13.40 (for the top), €8.20 (second level); you can climb the stairs as far as the second level for €4.70, then buy a "supplément ascenseur" ticket to the top for a further €5.20 • Save queueing time by buying tickets online • Ⓦ tour-eiffel.fr • RER Champ de Mars-Tour Eiffel

It's hard to believe that the **Eiffel Tower**, the quintessential symbol both of Paris and the brilliance of industrial engineering, was designed to be a temporary structure for a fair. Late nineteenth-century Europe had a taste for giant-scale, colonialist–capitalist extravaganzas, but Paris's 1889 Exposition Universelle was particularly ambitious: at 300m, its tower was the tallest building ever yet built. Outraged critics protested against this "grimy factory chimney". "Is Paris," they asked, "going to be associated with the grotesque, mercantile imaginings of a constructor of machines?" Eiffel believed it was a piece of perfectly utilitarian architecture. "The basic lines of a structure must correspond precisely to its specified use," he said. "To a certain extent the tower was formed by the wind itself."

Curiously, this most celebrated of landmarks was only saved from demolition by the sudden need for "wireless telegraphy" aerials in the first decade of the twentieth century, and nowadays the original crown is masked by an efflorescence of antennae. The tower's colour scheme has changed too: the early coats of deep red then canary yellow paint have been covered with a sober, dusty brown since the late 1960s. The only structural maintenance it has ever needed was carried out in the 1980s, when one thousand tonnes of metal were removed to make the tower ten percent lighter, and the frame was readjusted to remove a slight warp.

Paris looks surreally microscopic from the top and the views are arguably better from the second level, especially on hazier days. But there's something irresistible about taking the lift all the way up. The view is, of course, the main attraction, but you can also peer through a window into Eiffel's airy little show-off study, at the very top, while at the second level is the gastronomic restaurant, *Jules Verne* (see p.285).

The tower at night

Outside daylight hours, distinctive sodium **lights** illuminate the main structure, while twin xenon arc-lamps, added for the millennium celebrations, have turned the tower into an oversized urban lighthouse. There's also a third lighting system: for the first ten minutes of every hour thousands of lamps scramble about the structure, defining the famous silhouette in luminescent champagne.

The Champ de Mars

Parading back from the Eiffel Tower, the **Champ de Mars** has been an open field ever since it was used as a mustering ground for royal troops – hence the name "Martial Field". After 1789 it became the venue for the great revolutionary fairs, including Robespierre's vast "Fête of the Supreme Being" in 1794, while the Second Empire turned it into a giant industrial exhibition area, which explains the location of the Eiffel Tower. It's now a popular place for sunbathing on hot days. At the far southern end lie the eighteenth-century buildings of the **Ecole Militaire**, originally founded in 1751 by Louis XV for the training of aristocratic army officers – including the "little corporal", Napoleon Bonaparte.

10

The UNESCO building

7 place de Fontenoy, 7ᵉ · Book guided tours three months in advance on 🅔 visits@unesco.org; ID required for visit · Ⓜ Ecole Militaire

The *quartier* surrounding the Ecole Militaire is expensive, elegant and classic, and the Y-shaped **UNESCO building** is the controversial exception. Built in reinforced concrete in 1958 by, appropriately, an international team, it houses artworks by Giacometti, Calder, Le Corbusier, Miró and Picasso, as well as the so-called "Nagasaki angel" – a rare survivor of the atomic atrocities of August 1945. You can join a **guided tour** of the building if you book by email three months in advance and bring ID. Alternatively, come for one of the regular exhibitions or evening concerts, which range from "colours and impressions of Albania" to Tchaikovsky dances.

Behind UNESCO, the avenue de Saxe continues the grand line southeast towards the giant Necker hospital, passing through the **place de Breteuil**, a huge roundabout – even by Parisian standards – centred on a **monument to Louis Pasteur**, the much-loved inventor of pasteurization. His role as the saver of millions of lives is represented by the Grim Reaper cowering beneath him, while healthy lambs and children gambol all around.

Musée du Quai Branly

37 quai Branly, 7ᵉ · Tues, Wed & Fri–Sun 11am–7pm, Thurs 9.30am–9pm · €8.50 · 🕿 01 56 61 70 00, 🅦 quaibranly.fr · Ⓜ Iéna/RER Pont de l'Alma

A short distance upstream of the Eiffel Tower, the brash new **Musée du Quai Branly** cuts a postmodern swathe along the riverbank. It's well worth visiting for Jean Nouvel's exciting architectural design alone, which plays with the divide between structure and outside world. Fronting the riverbank is a tall glass wall, which turns the glorious, half-wild garden into a half-indoor space. Elsewhere, there's a huge, living "green wall". The building itself curls on stilts, its brightly coloured panels revealing sudden cavities or box-like swellings that pop outwards from the skin of the structure.

Parisians have taken to Nouvel's design but the museum is more controversial. It was the pet project of former president Jacques Chirac, who has a passion for non-Western art, or what was once called Arts Premiers – "Primitive Art". Inside the museum, folk artefacts (from every part of the world except Europe and North America) are arranged by their place of origin. As if to emphasize some sort of ethnic spookiness, you follow a trail in semi-darkness on blood-red flooring between curving "mud" walls in brown leather, while screens show film footage collected in the field by anthropologists. The actual artefacts, or artworks, are stunning. Even if their original contexts aren't always made clear, it's hard not to be moved by the potency and craftsmanship of – to cherry-pick a few examples – monstrous Papua New Guinean full-body masks, Aboriginal Australian dot-paintings, exquisite Indonesian gold jewellery, or man-sized wooden statues of the spirits of god-kings from Abomey, in West Africa.

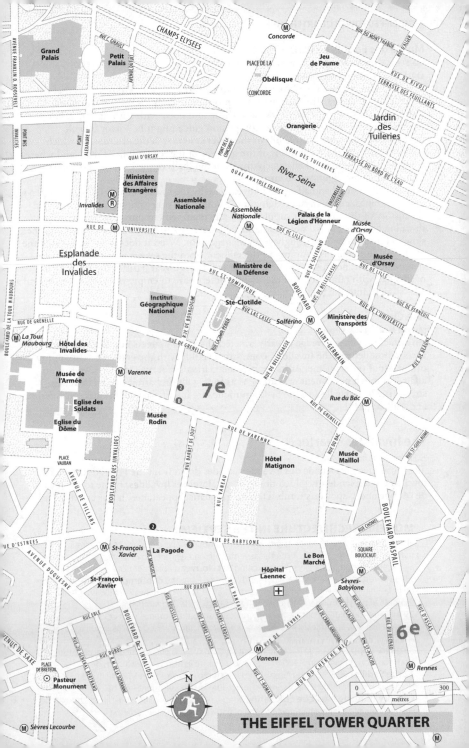

THE EIFFEL TOWER QUARTER

Musée des Egouts de Paris

Quai d'Orsay, 7ᵉ • Entrance on northeast side of place de la Résistance • Sat–Wed 11am–5pm, Oct–April till 4pm • €4.30 •
☏ 01 53 68 27 81 • Ⓜ Alma-Marceau/RER Pont de l'Alma

The chief attraction of the **Musée des Egouts de Paris**, or **Sewers Museum**, is that it's
actually in the sewers. The main part of the visit runs along a gantry walk poised
alarmingly above a main sewer. It's dark, damp and noisy with gushing water, but not
as smelly as you might fear. A good companion guide might be Victor Hugo's
Les Misérables: he turns the history of the sewer system – "a dread sink-hole which
bears the traces of the revolutions of the globe as of the revolutions of man, and where
are to be found vestiges of all cataclysms from the shells of the Deluge to the rag of
Marat" – into a magnificent lecture.

The visit is more than half a publicity exercise by the sewage board. Bilingual displays
of photographs, engravings, dredging tools, lamps and other flotsam and jetsam turn
the history of the city's water supply and waste management into a fascinating topic,
revealing how the natural water cycle was disrupted by the city's dense population, then
slowly controlled by increasingly good management. What it doesn't tell you is that the
work isn't quite finished. Almost all the effluent from the sewers goes to the Achèves
treatment plant, northwest of Paris, but several times a year parts of the system get
overloaded with rainwater, and the sewer workers have to empty the excess – waste and
all – straight into the Seine.

Rue Cler

Ⓜ La Tour-Maubourg/Ecole Militaire

An attractive, villagey wedge of early nineteenth-century streets huddles between
avenue Bosquet and the Invalides, contrasting starkly with the grand austerity of much
of the rest of the septième. At its heart is the market street **rue Cler**. It's a well-to-do
affair – as much permanent delicatessens as fruit stalls on barrows – and the cross-
streets, rue de Grenelle and rue St-Dominique, are full of classy boutiques, posh *bistrots*
and little hotels.

The Invalides quarter

Ⓜ/RER Invalides/La Tour-Maubourg

The broad green **Esplanade des Invalides** parades down from the Pont Alexandre III
towards the resplendently gilded dome of the **Hôtel des Invalides**, home to the **Musée
de l'Armee** and Napoleon's tomb. Despite its palatial appearance, it was actually built

---

MODERN ARCHITECTURE IN THE SEPTIEME

The septième is renowned for its grand state monuments and extravagant aristocratic
mansions, which mostly date from the seventeenth and eighteenth centuries, but you can
also seek out a trio of the city's most exciting **Art Nouveau** apartment buildings, the work of
Jules Lavirotte at the turn of the nineteenth century. From the **contemporary era**, the Musée
du Quai Branly is the most trumpeted representative, but hidden away nearby is a fascinating
example of the postmodernist architecture of Christian de Portzamparc.

29 avenue Rapp (RER Pont de l'Alma). Art Nouveau to the extreme, with colourful, glazed
ceramic tiles and an extravagant doorway representing an inverted phallus inside a vulval
arch. Designed by Jules Lavirotte in 1901.

3 square Rapp Off avenue Rapp (RER Pont de l'Alma). More of Lavirotte's extravagant Art
Nouveau work, dating from 1900. There's also a fine trellis trompe l'oeil alongside.

12 rue Sédillot (RER Pont de l'Alma). From the studio of Lavirotte in 1899, featuring Art
Nouveau and Art Deco elements, with superb dormers and wrought-iron balconies.

Conservatoire de Musique Erik Satie 7 rue Jean-Nicot (Ⓜ Invalides). Architect Christian de
Portzamparc plays with a half-peeled tube of a tower in this building dating from 1988.

for wounded soldiers in the reign of Louis XIV – whose foreign wars gave the building a constant supply of residents and whose equestrian statue lords it over a massive central arch. Architecturally, the building is a kind of barracks version of the awesome spirit of Versailles, stripped of finer flourishes – other than the gilded dome – but crushingly grand nonetheless. Even the cobbles on the esplanade seem made for giants' feet. You'll find muscularity of a more stirring kind in the adjacent **Musée Rodin**, which brings the sculptor's greatest works under the roof of a fine Parisian mansion.

Musée de l'Armée

10

51 bd de La Tour-Maubourg, 7ᵉ • April–Sept daily 10am–6pm, Tues till 9pm; Oct–March daily 10am–5pm; closed first Mon of each month • €9; ticket also valid for Napoleon's tomb (see p.152) • ☎ 01 44 42 38 77, ⓦ invalides.org • Ⓜ La Tour-Maubourg/Varenne

Les Invalides today houses the vast **Musée de l'Armée**, the national war museum. The moat around the whole Invalides complex means you can only approach from the north or south ends of the building; the ticket office is in the southwest wing, where it faces in towards the Eglise du Dôme.

Antique arms to Napoléon III

The northern half of the museum, on either side of the front court, is a relatively traditional display of uniforms and weaponry. In the **west wing**, the lofty old refectory and arsenal have been filled with a staggering array of **medieval** and **Renaissance** weaponry and armour, including the extraordinary mail made for François I, a big man for his time, and a chamber of beautifully worked Oriental arms and armour. The east wing, covering 1643 to 1871, is relatively dreary, apart from the glossy Ingres portrait of **Napoleon** on his throne and the room devoted to the little emperor's personal effects – notably his campaign bed and trademark hat and coat. The collection of super-scale models of French ports and fortified cities in the **Musée des Plans-Reliefs**, on the top floor, is surprisingly engaging, however. Essentially giant three-dimensional maps, they were created to plan defences and plot artillery positions from the late seventeenth century. With the eerie green glow of their landscapes only just illuminating the long, tunnel-like attic, the effect is rather chilling. All that's missing is a few miniature armies.

The World Wars

The "modern" section of the museum pushes the ultra-traditionalist view of modern French history: that, after a seventy-year struggle with the German aggressor, *la Patrie* finally emerged victorious. The area covering 1871 to **World War I** focuses more on maps, uniforms and strategy. The horrors – ten million dead soldiers, 1.37 million of them French – are only really represented by the gas shells, machine guns and grenades that killed them. The section on **World War II** is much more excitingly presented. War, resistance and liberation are reconstructed using clever memorabilia and gripping film reels (most of which have an English-language option). You leave shocked, stirred, and with the distinct impression that Général de Gaulle was personally responsible for the liberation of France – an impression that's reinforced by the hagiographic **Historial de Gaulle** in the basement, an exhibition celebrating the man and his myth using ultra-high-tech audiovisuals and interactive screens.

Eglise des Soldats

Hôtel des Invalides • April–Sept daily 10am–6pm, Tues till 9pm; Oct–March daily 10am–5pm; closed first Mon of each month • Free • Ⓜ La Tour-Maubourg/Varenne

At the core of the Invalides complex is a double church, built by Jules Hardouin-Mansart in the 1670s. The giant **Eglise du Dôme**, to the south, was formerly the Eglise Royale, intended for the private worship of Louis XIV and the royal family, while the relatively spartan northern section is known as the **Eglise des Soldats**. A glass wall divides the two churches, a design innovation which would have allowed worshippers

10

BONAPARTE'S BONES

In 2002 a French historian asked for **Napoleon's ashes** to be exhumed for DNA testing, claiming that the remains had been swapped for those of his *maître d'hôtel* on St Helena, one Jean-Baptiste Cipriani. Apparently, a witness at the original 1821 burial observed that the great man's teeth were "most villainous", whereas at the exhumation it was reported that they were "exceptionally white". There is some reason for suspicion, as the last round of tests – on a lock of the emperor's hair – suggested he had died of arsenic poisoning, not cancer, as the British claimed. Some said the traces were caused by the green – and therefore arsenic-laced – pigment in the imperial wallpaper, others that he was murdered by his captors. In 2008, however, the latter conspiracy theory was rebutted. Italian researchers found hairs from Napoleon's boyhood home and compared them with others taken on Elba and on St Helena. The arsenic levels were found to be consistently high, not just in the final sample; the British, it seems, were not as perfidious as all that.

to share the same high altar without the risk of coming into social contact. The door to the Soldiers' Church (no ticket required) is in the main northern courtyard of Les Invalides. Inside it's bright and airy, the high walls lined with almost a hundred banners captured by the French army over the centuries. The collection once numbered three thousand trophies at its peak, but was largely destroyed in 1817 by a governor of Les Invalides too proud to see them fall back into the hands of Napoleon's triumphant enemies. A commemorative Mass is still said here on May 5, the anniversary of the emperor's death.

Eglise du Dôme

Hôtel des Invalides • April–Sept daily 10am–6pm, Tues till 9pm; Oct–March daily 10am–5pm; closed first Mon of each month • €9; ticket also valid for the Musée de l'Armée (see p.151) • Ⓜ La Tour-Maubourg/Varenne

The **Eglise du Dôme** has a separate entrance on the south side of the complex. Unlike its northern twin, the Soldiers' Church, it's awesomely grand. **Napoleon's tomb**, a mighty sarcophagus of deep red quartzite, is itself entombed in a giant circular pit, overlooked by guardian statues that represent his military victories. Friezes on the surrounding gallery parade the emperor's civic triumphs, along with quotations of gigantic (and occasionally accurate) conceit such as "Wherever the shadow of my rule has fallen, it has left lasting traces of its value". Napoleon's shadow still fell heavily on Paris on December 14, 1840, the day on which his ashes, freshly returned from St Helena, were carried through the streets from the newly completed Arc de Triomphe to Invalides. Even though Louis-Philippe, a Bourbon, was on the throne, and Napoleon's nephew, Louis-Napoléon, had been imprisoned for attempting a coup four months earlier, the Bonapartists came out in force – half a million of them – to watch the emperor's last journey. Victor Hugo commented that "it felt as if the whole of Paris had been poured to one side of the city, like liquid in a vase which has been tilted".

More affecting than Napoleon's tomb is the simple memorial to **Maréchal Foch**, commander-in-chief of the allied forces at the end of World War I, which stands in the side chapel by the stairs leading down to the crypt. The marshal's effigy is borne by a phalanx of bronze infantrymen displaying a soldierly grief, the whole chamber flooded by blue light from the stained-glass windows.

Musée Rodin

77 rue de Varenne, 7ᵉ • Daily except Mon: April–Sept 9.30am–5.45pm, garden closes at 6.45pm; Oct–March 9.30am–4.45pm, garden closes at 5pm • €6, garden only €1 • ☎ 01 44 18 61 10, ⓦ musee-rodin.fr • Ⓜ Varenne

The **Musée Rodin** has surely the loveliest setting of all Paris's museums: a superb, generously gardened eighteenth-century mansion which the sculptor leased from the state in return for the gift of all his work upon his death. Bronze versions of major projects like *The Burghers of Calais*, *The Thinker* and *The Gate of Hell* are set among the grounds – the latter forming the centrepiece of the ornamental pond. There's a pleasant outdoor café at the back and a good collection of roses at the front.

Inside the museum

Inside, the passionate intensity of the sculptures contrasts with the graceful wooden panelling and chandeliers, while the many tarnished mirrors make the perfect foil for Rodin's theory of profiles, in which each sculpture is formed from a collection of views from different standpoints. The museum is usually crowded with visitors eager to see much-loved works like *The Kiss*, which actually portrays Paolo and Francesca da Rimini, from Dante's *Divine Comedy,* in the moment before they were discovered and murdered by Francesca's husband. Contemporaries were scandalized by Francesca's distinctly active engagement; art critics today like to think of it as the last masterwork of figurative sculpture before the whole art form was reinvented – largely by Rodin himself. Paris's *Kiss* is one of only four marble versions of the work. Don't miss Paolo's ecstatically scrunched-up toes.

It's well worth lingering over the museum's vibrant, impressionistic clay works, small studies that Rodin took from life. In fact, most of the works here are in clay or plaster, as these are considered to be Rodin's finest achievements – after completing his apprenticeship, he rarely picked up a chisel, in line with the common nineteenth-century practice of delegating the task of working up stone and bronze versions to assistants. On the ground floor, a room is devoted to Camille Claudel, Rodin's pupil, model and lover. Among her works is *The Age of Maturity*, symbolizing her ultimate rejection by Rodin, and a bust of the artist himself.

La Pagode

57bis rue de Babylone, 7ᵉ • ☎ 01 46 34 82 54, ⓦ etoile-cinemas.com • ⓂSt-François-Xavier

The Chinese-style roofs of **La Pagode**, overlooking the corner of rue Monsieur, were originally built as a fashionable toy for the wife of a director of the Bon Marché department store, and later turned into a historic cinema – in 1959 it premiered Cocteau's *Le Testament d'Orphée*, and, a year later, took part in the first screenings of the Nouvelle Vague. Following a superb renovation, it is now once again one of the most enjoyable art-house cinemas in the city, with its Art Deco-meets-Oriental decor and delightful garden.

Pont Alexandre III

Ⓜ/RER Invalides

North of the Invalides complex, the eastern end of the quai d'Orsay opens out into a grand esplanade. Parading across the river towards the giant conservatories of the Grand and Petit Palais is the Pont Alexandre III. The vista here was so cherished that when this bridge was built it was set as low as possible above the water so as not to get in the way of the view. That said, it's surely the most extravagant bridge in the city, its single-span metal arch stretching 109m across the river. It was unveiled in 1900, just in time for the Exposition Universelle, its name and elaborate decoration symbolizing Franco–Russian friendship – an ever more important alliance in the face of fast-growing German power. The nymph stretching out downstream represents the Seine, matched by St Petersburg's River Neva facing upstream.

The quai d'Orsay

To the west of the Pont Alexandre III, the pale neo-Gothic tower and copper spire of the **American Church** stand out on the **quai d'Orsay**. Together with the American College nearby at 31 avenue Bosquet, it plays a key role in the busy life of Paris's large expat American community. Newspapers reporting on French foreign policy use "the quai d'Orsay" to refer to the Ministère des Affaires Etrangères (Ministry of Foreign Affairs), which sits next to the Esplanade des Invalides and the Palais Bourbon, home of the **Assemblée Nationale**. Napoleon, never a great one for democracy, had the riverfront facade of the Palais Bourbon done to match the pseudo-Greek of the Madeleine. The result is an entrance that sheds little light on what's happening within.

The Trocadéro quarter

On the western side of the Eiffel Tower area, the **Trocadéro quarter** lies on the elevated northern bank of the Seine. The river forms little barrier to a visit, however, as there's a picturesque above-ground métro line (line 6, which crosses the river on the Pont de Bir-Hakeim, offering excellent views of the Eiffel Tower). The entire *quartier* is also connected to the septième by three fine bridges: the businesslike Pont de l'Alma, the graceful Passarelle Debilly and the handsome Pont d'Iéna, which thrusts north as if from under the very legs of the Tower into the embrace of the breathtakingly ugly **Palais de Chaillot**.

The Palais de Chaillot

1 place du Trocadéro et du 11 novembre, 16e **Musée de la Marine** Mon, Wed & Thurs 11am–6pm, Fri 11am–9.30pm, Sat & Sun 11am–7pm • €7 • ☎ 01 53 65 69 69, Ⓦ musee-marine.fr • Ⓜ Trocadéro

The **Palais de Chaillot** stands on a site favoured by imperialist-minded rulers ever since Catherine de Médicis constructed one of her playpens here in the early sixteenth century. Napoleon planned (but never built) a palace here for his short-lived son, and, in 1878, an Oriental-style confection was erected (but soon after demolished). The current Modernist-Neoclassical monster went up in 1937 as part of the globalist-minded Exposition Universelle. Adorned as it is with heroic statues and symmetrical acres of marble paving, it would look less out of place in Fascist Rome than here, though the two curving wings do neatly embrace the shadow of the Eiffel Tower.

Underneath the central terrace lies the **Théâtre National de Chaillot**, which stages diverse and usually radical productions; its entrance is via the northern wing. Also below ground, but accessed from a ramp on the riverfront side of the palace is the **Cinéaqua** aquarium and cinema complex. The southern wing houses the rather specialized **Musée de la Marine**, which traces French naval history using model ships. It's also home to the original Jules Verne trophy, awarded for nonstop round-the-world sailing – a hull-shaped streak of glass invisibly suspended by magnets within its cabinet.

The Cité de l'Architecture

Palais de Chaillot • Mon, Wed & Fri–Sun 11am–7pm, Thurs 11am–9pm • €8 • ☎ 01 58 51 52 00, Ⓦ citechaillot.fr • Ⓜ Trocadéro

The northern wing of the Palais de Chaillot is occupied by the splendid **Cité de l'Architecture et du Patrimoine**, a combined institute, library and **museum of architecture**. The bedrock of the museum, the long and lofty **Galerie des Moulages**, on the ground floor, displays giant plaster casts of sections of great French buildings. There are entire portals from Romanesque cathedrals, Gothic windows, Renaissance tombs and exact reproductions of the finest statuary in France. The casts date from an earlier, nineteenth-century museum, and to see French architecture laid out as a kind of grand historical panorama is as eye-opening now as it was for the original curiosity-seekers.

On the second floor, the **Galerie d'Architecture Moderne et Contemporaine** showcases the nineteenth and twentieth centuries with some stunning original architectural models, and a full-size – and distinctly poky – reconstruction of an "E2 superior" apartment from Le Corbusier's Cité Radieuse, which you can actually walk around in. This gallery offers a fascinating lesson in the evolution of modern design, but more wondrous is the **Galerie des Peintures Murales et des Vitraux**, which occupies the central pavilion on the second and third floors. In the same spirit as the *moulages* gallery, it displays life-size copies of French wall paintings, frescoes and stained glass. Its stunning centrepiece is the lofty, Byzantine-style cupola from Cahors cathedral, but it's well worth penetrating deeper into the maze-like sequence of rooms as far as the claustrophobic reconstruction of the Romanesque crypt of the church of Tavant, in the Loire region, and heading up to the third floor for the terrifying sequence of medieval Passions and Last Judgements. The **library** on the first floor is also well worth visiting for its copy of a Romanesque vault mural from the church of St-Savin-sur-Gartempe.

There's always a **temporary exhibition** or two: shows have included "La Ville Fertile", about greening cities, and a hugely significant presentation of competing architects' visions for "Le Grand Pari'" – the plan for the sustainable, low-carbon conurbation of the future.

10

Musée Guimet
6 place d'Iéna, 16ᵉ • Daily except Tues 10am–6pm • €7.50 • ☎ 01 56 52 53 00, Ⓦ museeguimet.fr • Ⓜ Iéna

The **Musée National des Arts Asiatiques-Guimet** winds round four floors groaning under the weight of statues of Buddhas and gods, some fierce, some meditative, all of them dramatically displayed alongside ceramics, paintings and other objets d'art. Each room is devoted to a different country of origin, stretching from the Greek-influenced Buddhist statues of the **Gandhara civilization**, on the first floor, to fierce demons from Nepal and pot-bellied Chinese Buddhas. The highlight, however, is the breathtaking roofed-in courtyard: it's a perfectly airy space in which to show off the museum's world-renowned collection of **Khmer sculpture** – from the civilization that produced Cambodia's Angkor Wat. On the third floor is a rotunda used by the collection's founder, **Emile Guimet**, for the first Buddhist ceremony ever held in France. A great collector and patron of the arts, Guimet espoused the Christian-socialist-egalitarian theories about society, class and government proposed by Fournier, Saint-Simon and, in Britain, Robert Owen.

Galeries du Panthéon Bouddhique
19 av d'Iéna, 16ᵉ • Daily except Tues 9.45am–5.45pm • Free • ☎ 01 40 73 88 00, Ⓦ guimet.fr/Pantheon-bouddhique • Ⓜ Iéna

Emile Guimet's original collection, which he brought back from his travels in Asia in 1876, is exhibited near the Musée Guimet in the **Galeries du Panthéon Bouddhique**. While far smaller, in some ways it's a more satisfying affair than the larger museum, as the gilded ranks of Buddhas are presented with a Buddhist's eye rather than an art collector's. At the back of the museum is a small Japanese garden, complete with bamboo, pussy willow and watery reflections.

Musée de la Mode de la Ville de Paris
10 av Pierre 1er de Serbie, 16ᵉ • Closed for restoration until spring 2012, normally open for temporary exhibitions only, see website •
☎ 01 56 52 86 00, Ⓦ galliera.paris.fr • Ⓜ Iéna/Alma-Marceau

The rather exquisite and bizarrely Italianate bijoux box of the Palais Galliera was built in the 1880s by the Duchesse de Galliera to house her private art collection. It now belongs to the city, and is the home of the **Musée de la Mode**. The museum's unrivalled collection of historic and modern clothes and fashion accessories is exhibited in two or three shows a year, with themes such as "Under the Empire of Crinolines, 1852–70" and "Creating the Myth of Marlene Dietrich". During changeovers the museum is closed.

The Palais de Tokyo and around
13 av du Président Wilson, 16ᵉ • Ⓜ Iéna/Alma-Marceau

The **Palais de Tokyo** houses two galleries of modern art, both of which are among the most rewarding in Paris, though they see fewer visitors than the Pompidou Centre. The entrance to the palace is on its north side, but most people arrive across the Seine via the pedestrian **Passerelle Debilly**. Rather surprisingly, given its modern looks, this bridge is a contemporary of its near neighbour, the profoundly more ornate Pont

10

Alexandre III – both were opened in 1900, in time for the Exposition Universelle. The Palais de Tokyo dates from a later exhibition, the tension-filled 1937 world fair, at which the German and Russian pavilions faced each other across the Seine in an architectural standoff. **Antoine Bourdelle**'s bronze statue of "Eternal France", which surveys the central terrace of the Tokyo building, is a living reminder of the fervid nationalism of those times. The palace was always intended to be a gallery of modern art, however, and most of its decoration takes a more consciously artistic theme; Alfred Auguste Janniot's vast Art Deco bas-reliefs, which frame the central staircase, represent the nine muses. The colonnaded building itself is simple and beautiful. It's also a perfect suntrap, and much favoured by skateboarders and graffiti artists.

On Wednesday and Saturday mornings a bustling **market** takes over avenue du Président Wilson, from Iéna métro station down to the palace. You'll find organic meats and cheeses and craft jewellery alongside fruit, veg and cheap clothing.

Musée d'Art Moderne de la Ville de Paris

Palais de Tokyo • Tues–Sun 10am–6pm; closed public hols • Free • ☎ 01 53 67 40 00, ⓦ mam.paris.fr • ⓜ Iéna/Alma-Marceau

The east wing of the Palais de Tokyo houses the **Musée d'Art Moderne de la Ville de Paris**. The collection can't rival the Pompidou Centre's, but it's free, relatively empty and the environment is far more contemplative – and architecturally more fitting when it comes to works by early twentieth-century artists. The ground floor, by the entrance, is given over to temporary exhibitions.

The Dufy and Matisse murals

The gallery received unwelcome publicity in May 2010 when a lone thief made off with half a dozen literally priceless canvases by Picasso, Matisse, Modigliani and others, but it still has its two marvellous (and entirely untransportable) centrepieces. Just above the main stairs leading down to the permanent collections, a vast, curving chamber provides wall-space for Raoul Dufy's **mural** *La Fée Electricité* ("The Electricity Fairy"). Originally designed for the Electricity Pavilion in the 1937 Exposition Universelle, its 250 vivid, cartoon-like panels tell the story of electricity from the earliest experimenters to the triumph of industrialization that was the power station. Facing the stairs as you descend, the chapel-like **salle Matisse** is devoted to Matisse's balletic and heart-lifting *La Danse de Paris*, beginning with an incomplete early version and progressing through to the finished work, displayed high on the wall. Daniel Buren's *Mur de Peintures* (1995–2006), in his trademark stripes, is displayed in the same room.

The permanent collection

The main permanent collection is chronologically themed, starting with Fauvism and Cubism, and progressing through to Dada and the Ecole de Paris, and beyond. Most artists working in France – Braque, Chagall, Delaunay, Derain, Duchamp, Dufy, Klein, Léger, Modigliani, Picasso and many others – are represented, and there is a strong Parisian theme to many of the works. The collection is kept up to the minute by an active buying policy, and some bold acquisitions of sculpture, painting and video by contemporary artists are displayed in the final suite of rooms. Look out in particular for the intimate scrapbook works of Annette Messager, Jean-Marc Bustamante's chilly photography, Christian Boltanski's sinister photographs and harrowing installations of old clothing and phone books, and, towards the end, Philippe Parreno's mesmerizing video works.

Palais de Tokyo Site de Création Contemporaine

Palais de Tokyo • Tues–Sun noon–9pm • €3 • ☎ 01 47 23 54 01, ⓦ palaisdetokyo.com • ⓜ Iéna/Alma-Marceau

Set in the western wing of the Palais de Tokyo, the **Palais de Tokyo Site de Création Contemporaine** has staged a number of avant-garde exhibitions, events, talks, installations and projections since it opened in 2002, including a temporary occupation by squatter-artists and a concept show on revolutions by Turner Prize-winning artist, Jeremy Deller. At the time of writing it was undergoing a major renovation, but it hasn't changed the ambience much – the interior was long left deliberately semi-derelict to create a sense of "work in progress", and young French artists continue to hang out in the bar/restaurant, bookshop and library. The hippy-pattern floor painting in the downstairs café, by the Paris-based Taiwanese artist Michael Lin, and the giant, Benetton-like photo-portrait windows in the restaurant, *Tokyo Eat*, by Swiss photographer Beat Streuli, are the gallery's sole permanent exhibits – though the small row of allotment **gardens** alongside the museum on rue de la Manutention apparently counts, too, as it was conceived by the artist Robert Milin.

10

Place de l'Alma
Ⓜ Alma-Marceau

A few steps upstream of the Palais de Tokyo, on **place de l'Alma**, stands a full-scale, golden replica of the flame from the Statue of Liberty. It was given to France in 1987 as a symbol of Franco–American relations but is now an unofficial memorial to **Princess Diana**, whose Mercedes crashed in the underpass beneath. The authorities clean up the site regularly, but you'll often find bunches of withered flowers and graffiti messages left as tributes.

Pont de l'Alma
Ⓜ Alma-Marceau

The **Pont de l'Alma**, which crosses the Seine towards the sewers, is a rather brutal 1970s steel-and-concrete affair. It's worth taking a peek at its celebrated **zouave** statue, however, which hides away by the waterline, on the upstream side. The name comes from the North African soldiers who fought in the French army during the Crimean War, and it was one of four military statues that adorned the previous Alma bridge. It has long served as Parisians' yardstick for describing the Seine's flooding. In 1910, for instance, the water came up to the zouave's shoulders. On the new bridge, he actually stands slightly higher than he used to, so even a knee-high flood is a fairly serious event.

MUSEE BOURDELLE

Montparnasse and southern Paris

The swathe of cafés, brasseries and cinemas that runs through the heart of modern Montparnasse has long been a honeypot for pleasure-seekers, as well as a kind of border town dividing well-heeled St-Germain from the amorphous populations of the three arrondissements of southern Paris, the 13e, 14e and 15e. Overscale developments from the 1950s to the present day have scarred parts of this southern side of the city, but there are three great parks – André-Citroën (with its very own tethered balloon), Georges-Brassens and Montsouris – and some enticing pockets of Paris that have been allowed to evolve in a happily patchy way. Lively areas such as Pernety and Plaisance in the 14e, the quartier du Commerce in the 15e and the Butte-aux-Cailles in the 13^e are pleasant places to explore.

Montparnasse and the 14ᵉ

The story goes that, before it was levelled in the early eighteenth century, students used to drink and declaim poetry from the top of a pile of spoil deposited from the Denfert-Rochereau quarries, calling the mound "Mount Parnassus" after the legendary home of the muses of poetry and song, and of drunken Bacchus. This may or may not be how the area got its name, but the reputation of **Montparnasse** for carousing persists to this day, though its status as a nightspot really stems from the construction of the Mur des Fermiers Généraux in 1784, or "Customs Wall", which split the high-taxed city from the poorer, less regulated township areas beyond. In the nineteenth century, Bohemians, left-leaning intellectuals and poets such as Verlaine and Baudelaire abandoned the city centre for Montparnasse, drawn by the inexpensive cafés and nightlife. The quarter's lasting fame, however, rests on its role as the **birthplace of Modernism**, following the artistic exodus from Montmartre. In the *Années Folles*, or "Mad Years" following World War I, artists such as Picasso, Matisse, Brancusi, Kandinsky, Modigliani, Giacometti and Chagall were all habitués of the celebrated cafés around **place Vavin**. They were soon joined by a self-professed "lost generation" of Bohemia-hunting and Prohibition-fleeing Americans – Hemingway, Pound, Man Ray and Dos Passos among them. Many were buried in **Montparnasse cemetery**, and still more bones lie nearby in the grim **catacombs**.

The area immediately around Montparnasse's Modernist railway station is dominated by the gigantic **Tour Montparnasse**, which you can ascend for a superb view of the city. In the tower's shadow, a handful of **artists' museums** recall Montparnasse's traditions, while the **Fondation Cartier** showcases contemporary art and architecture. South of the station, the **14ᵉ** is one of the most characterful of the outer arrondissements. The old-fashioned networks of streets still exist in the **Pernety** and **Plaisance** *quartiers*, where many artists chose to live in the affordable *villas* (similar to mews) built in the 1920s and 1930s. Down in the southeast corner of the arrondissement you'll find plenty of green space in the **Parc Montsouris** and the giant student campus of the **Cité Universitaire**.

Tour Montparnasse

33 av du Maine, 15ᵉ • Rooftop platform daily: April–Sept 9.30am–11.30pm; Oct–March 9.30am–10.30pm, Fri & Sat till 11pm • €10 • ☎ 01 45 38 52 56, ⓦ tourmontparnasse56.com • ⓂMontparnasse-Bienvenüe

Montparnasse station's arch gives onto a broad concrete esplanade surrounded by traffic, the prospect of the city blocked by the brown glass blade of the **Tour Montparnasse**. At the time of its deeply controversial construction, this was one of Paris's first skyscrapers, defying the problem of the city's quarried-out limestone bedrock with 56 massive piles driven into a chalk layer over 40m below ground. Few Parisians have a good word to say for such a monolithic landmark, but the **view** from the open, often windy **rooftop platform** is arguably better than the one from the Eiffel Tower – it has the Eiffel Tower in it, after all, plus there are no queues. Nervous view-seekers can settle for the 56th-floor café and gallery room. Sunset is the best time to visit.

The Jardin Atlantique

Daily 9am–dusk • Free • ⓂMontparnasse-Bienvenüe

Montparnasse was once the great arrival and departure point for boat travellers across the Atlantic and Bretons seeking work in the capital. Brittany's influence is still evident in the abundance of crêperies near the station, such as *Crêperie Josselin* (see p.286), but the connection is best evoked by the **Jardin Atlantique**, a public park suspended above the tracks behind the station. Completed in 1994, between cliff-like glass walls of high-rise blocks, it's a remarkable piece of engineering – and imagination. Well-hidden ventilation holes reveal sudden glimpses of TGV roofs and rail sleepers, while the lawns some planted with long coastal grasses – rise and fall in symbolic waves. A double line of trees runs south from the station end – the trees on the eastern side are of American origin, those on the West, European – to the central **Ile des Hespérides**

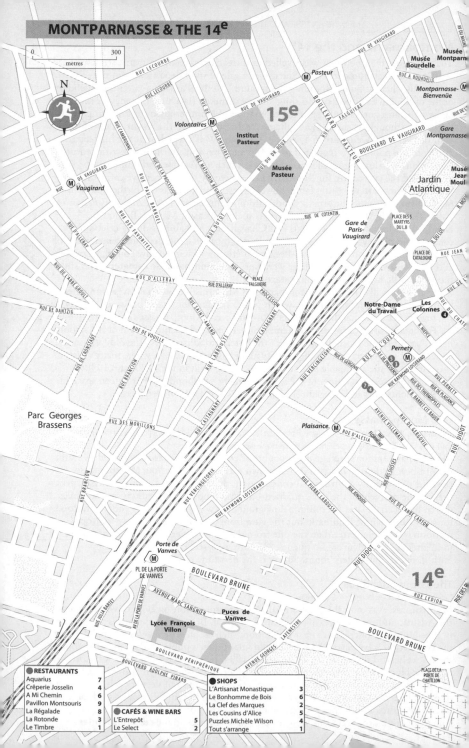

MONTPARNASSE & THE 14ᵉ

0   300
metres

N

RUE LECOURBE

RUE LECOURBE

RUE DE VAUGIRARD

RUE DE VAUGIRARD

Musée
Bourdelle

Musée
Montparn

Pasteur

RUE A. BOURDELLE

Montparnasse-
Bienvenüe

RUE DE VAUGIRARD

BOULEVARD PASTEUR

RUE FALGUIERE

Volontaires

15ᵉ

BOULEVARD DE VAUGIRARD

Gare
Montparnasse

RUE CAMBRONNE

RUE DE LA PROCESSION

RUE MATHURIN RÉGNIER

Institut
Pasteur

RUE DU DR ROUX

RUE DUPLEIX

Musé
Jear
Moul

Jardin
Atlantique

RUE DE VAUGIRARD

Vaugirard

RUE PAUL BARRUEL

Musée
Pasteur

RUE DE COTENTIN

PLACE DES 5
MARTYRS
DU L.B

R. MOU

R. LOLOT

R. N

RUE D'ALLERAY

RUE DES FAVORITES

RUE DE LA QUINTINE

RUE DE L'ARBE GROUE

RUE DUTOT

Gare de
Paris-
Vaugirard

PLACE DE
CATALOGNE

RUE JEAN

RUE D'ALLERAY

RUE DE LA
PROCESSION

PLACE
FALGUIERE

RUE DU CHATE

RUE DE DANTZIG

RUE DE VOUILLE

RUE SAINT AMAND

RUE D'ALLERAY

Notre-Dame
du Travail

Les
Colonnes

4

RUE DE L'OUEST

Pernety

RUE DE CRONSTADT

RUE DE VOUILLE

RUE LARGOUSSE

RUE CASTAGNARY

RUE VERCINGETORIX

RUE DE GERGOVIE

RUE DE LA SABLIERE

RUE PERNETY

RUE DES THERMOPYLES

R. DE RANCE

RUE R. BARRET CH. BAUER

RUE RAYMOND LOSSERAND

RUE BRANCION

RUE DES MORILLONS

RUE CASTAGNARY

AVENUE VILLEMAIN

RUE DE GERGOVIE

RUE DIDOT

Parc Georges
Brassens

Plaisance

RUE D'ALESIA

IMP
FLORIMONT

RUE BRANCION

RUE VERCINGETORIX

RUE RAYMOND LOSSERAND

RUE PIERRE LAROUSSE

RUE JONQUOY

RUE DES SUISSES

RUE DE L'ABBE CARTON

14ᵉ

RUE LEDION

RUE DES

Porte de
Vanves

PL DE LA PORTE
DE VANVES

BOULEVARD BRUNE

RUE DIDOT

AVENUE MARC SANGNIER

RUE JULIA BARTET

AV DE LA PORTE DE VANVES

Lycée François
Villon

Puces de
Vanves

LAFENESTRE

BOULEVARD BRUNE

BOULEVARD PERIPHERIQUE

BOULEVARD ADOLPHE PINARD

AVENUE GEORGES

PLACE DE LA
PORTE DE
CHATILLON

RESTAURANTS
Aquarius	7
Crêperie Josselin	4
A Mi Chemin	6
Pavillon Montsouris	9
La Régalade	8
La Rotonde	3
Le Timbre	1

CAFÉS & WINE BARS
L'Entrepôt	5
Le Select	2

SHOPS
L'Artisanat Monastique	3
Le Bonhomme de Bois	6
La Clef des Marques	2
Les Cousins d'Alice	5
Puzzles Michèle Wilson	4
Tout s'arrange	1

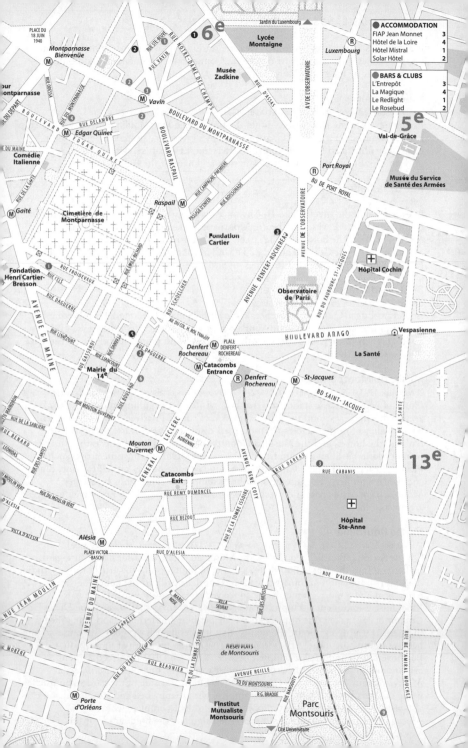

PLACE DU
18 JUIN
1940

Montparnasse
Bienvenüe

Jardin du Luxembourg

6e

Lycée
Montaigne

Luxembourg

5e

● ACCOMMODATION
FIAP Jean Monnet   3
Hôtel de la Loire   4
Hôtel Mistral   1
Solar Hôtel   2

● BARS & CLUBS
L'Entrepôt   3
La Magique   4
Le Redlight   1
Le Rosebud   2

Val-de-Grâce

RUE STE-BEUVE
RUE VAVIN
RUE NOTRE-DAME-DES-CHAMPS

Musée
Zadkine

RUE D'ASSAS

AV DE L'OBSERVATOIRE

Vavin

RUE ODESSA
RUE DU MONTPARNASSE
RUE DELAMBRE
RUE DU DEPART

BOULEVARD DU MONTPARNASSE

Edgar Quinet

EDGAR QUINET

BOULEVARD RASPAIL

Port Royal

BD DE PORT ROYAL

Musée du Service
de Santé des Armées

BOULEVARD

RUE DE LA GAITE

Comédie
Italienne

DU MAINE

Gaité

Cimetière de
Montparnasse

Raspail

RUE CAMPAGNE-PREMIÈRE

PASSAGE D'ENFER

RUE BOISSONADE

Fondation
Cartier

AVENUE DENFERT-ROCHEREAU

AVENUE DE L'OBSERVATOIRE

Observatoire
de Paris

RUE DU FAUBOURG ST-JACQUES

Hôpital Cochin

Fondation
Henri Cartier-
Bresson

RUE FROIDEVAUX

RUE FELS

RUE EMILE RICHARD

RUE SCHOELCHER

AVENUE DU MAINE

RUE DAGUERRE

RUE LIANCOURT

AV. DU COL. H. ROL TANGUY

BOULEVARD ARAGO

Vespasienne

Denfert
Rochereau

PLACE
DENFERT-
ROCHEREAU

La Santé

RUE GASSENDI
RUE BOULARD
RUE LIANCOURT

RUE DAGUERRE

Catacombs
Entrance

Denfert
Rochereau

St-Jacques

BD SAINT- JACQUES

RUE DE LA SANTÉ

Mairie du
14e

RUE MOUTON DUVERNET

LECLERC

VILLA
ADRIENNE

Mouton
Duvernet

GÉNÉRAL

AVENUE RENÉ COTY

RUE DAREAU

13e

RUE DE LA SABLIÈRE

RUE BÉNARD

RUE DES PLANTES

Catacombs
Exit

RUE REMY DUMONCEL

RUE CABANIS

Hôpital
Ste-Anne

RUE SCHANDRIN
LÉONIDAS

RUE DU MOULIN VERT

RUE BEZOUT

D'ALÉSIA
VILLA D'ALÉSIA

Alésia

PLACE VICTOR
BASCH

RUE D'ALÉSIA

RUE D'ALÉSIA

RUE DE LA TOMBE ISSOIRE

RUE JEAN JEAN MOULIN

AVENUE DU MAINE

RUE SARRETTE

R. MARIE
ROSE

VILLA
SEURAT

RUE DES ARTISTES

RUE DE L'AMIRAL MOUCHEZ

MORÈRE

RUE DU PÈRE CORENTIN

RUE BEAUNIER

Réservoirs
de Montsouris

AVENUE REILLE

Porte
d'Orléans

SQ DU MONTSOURIS

R.G. BRAQUE

Parc
Montsouris

RUE NANSOUTY

l'Institut
Mutualiste
Montsouris

Cité Universitaire

fountain. It's a giant-scale disguised weather station, and a favourite spot for children on sunny days. Access is via lifts on rue du Commandant Mouchotte and boulevard Vaugirard, or by the stairs alongside platform #1.

Musée Jean Moulin

Jardin Atlantique • Daily except Mon 10am–6pm • €4 • ☎ 01 40 64 39 44 • ⓂMontparnasse-Bienvenüe

Facing out onto the Jardin Atlantique, the tiny **Musée Jean Moulin** may be worth a stop if you're waiting for a train to Chartres. It gives a rather dry potted history of the Resistance illustrated by a few photos, posters and newspapers, with a special section on Jean Moulin, wartime prefect of Chartres and hero of the Resistance.

Rue de la Gaîté

ⓂEdgar-Quinet/Gaîté

Rue de la Gaîté, the street where Trotsky once lived, is a slice of turn-of-the-twentieth-century theatreland, with the Théâtre Montparnasse facing the Théâtre Gaîté-Montparnasse at the bottom of the street. At the northern end, the **Comédie Italienne** advertises its diet of Goldoni and the like with a wonderfully camp, golden exterior painted with commedia dell'arte scenes – you'd never know it used to be a police station.

Boulevard Edgar-Quinet market

Wed and Sat mornings, Sun roughly 10am–dusk • ⓂEdgar-Quinet

Boulevard Edgar-Quinet is entirely taken over by a lively food **market** on Wednesday and Saturday mornings, while on Sundays over a hundred craftworkers take over; photographers jostle with potters, clothes designers with painters, and it's a great place to browse away the day.

Musée du Montparnasse

21 av du Maine, 15ᵉ • Tues–Sun 12.30–7pm • €6 • ☎ 01 42 22 91 96, ⓦ museedumontparnasse.net • ⓂMontparnasse-Bienvenüe/Falguière

North of Montparnasse station are two little-visited yet beguiling **museums**. At 21 avenue du Maine, beyond the raised slip-road of rue de l'Arrivée, lies a half-hidden, ivy-clad alley of former stables. As motorcars displaced Paris's horse traffic, artists replaced the horses, and the **Musée du Montparnasse** occupies what was the Russian painter Marie Vassilieff's studio from 1912 to 1929. During this time artists such as Picasso, Léger, Modigliani, Chagall and Braque, among others, visited to wine, dine and dance with her. The museum now hosts temporary exhibitions based on Montparnasse artists past and present. Neighbouring studios have now given way to architects' offices.

Musée Bourdelle

18 rue Antoine Bourdelle, 15ᵉ • Tues–Sun 10am–6pm • Free • ☎ 01 49 54 73 73 • ⓂMontparnasse-Bienvenüe/Falguière

On rue Antoine Bourdelle, opposite the Musée du Montparnasse, a sculpture garden invites you into the **Musée Bourdelle**, a museum built around the artist's former studio. As Rodin's pupil and Giacometti's teacher, Bourdelle bridged the period between naturalism and a more geometrically conceived style; he was arguably the first Modernist. Monumental sculptures such as *Heracles Archer* (1910) and *The Dying Centaur* (1914) take pride of place in the chapel-like, Modernist grand hall; asked why the centaur was dying, Bourdelle replied that he dies like all the gods, "because no one believes in him any more". Elsewhere, there's a wonderful series of tumultuous Beethoven busts and masks, sculpted between 1887 and 1929, and a basement extension with studies for the sculptor's great works, the muscular *Monument à Mickiewicz* and *Monument au Général Alvear*. On the far side of the garden Bourdelle's living quarters have been preserved, complete with shabby bed and stove, and you can also visit his atmospheric old **studio**, littered with half-complete works.

Just around the corner to the right, on rue Falguière, the bold facade of the

Ile-de-France urban-planning department veers up and away from the line of the street in the smoothest of curves, like the hull of a fantasy spaceship.

The Montparnasse cafés

Ⓜ Vavin

Most of the life of the Montparnasse *quartier* is concentrated on **boulevard du Montparnasse**. The numerous **cinemas** here – six on the boulevard alone – are almost all of the multi-screen variety, specializing in mass-market French and US films. The liveliest point of the boulevard is around Vavin métro, where you'll find Rodin's **Balzac** ruminating over the crossroads, and a cluster of celebrated cafés: the *Select*, *Coupole*, *Dôme* and *Rotonde*. Their heyday was in the 1910s and 1920s, when artists and poets such as Apollinaire, Chagall, Léger, Modigliani, Picasso and Zadkine rubbed shoulders with exiled revolutionaries, including Lenin and Trotsky, paying a few centimes to occupy tables for hours on end. Even by the 1930s, the fashionable intelligentsia were moving on to St-Germain, but the brasseries remain proudly Parisian classics – if no longer Bohemian haunts – and this stretch of the boulevard still stays up late.

All the cafés except the *Select* have moved steadily upmarket, and the swankiest by far is the **Closerie des Lilas**, with its fabled (and now sadly glazed-in) *terrasse* on the corner of the tree-lined avenue de l'Observatoire. In the days when it was a cheap café, Hemingway wrote most of *The Sun Also Rises* here. The café's most stirring historical association, however, is with Napoleon's Marshal Ney, the "bravest of the brave", as his master called him. His sword-wielding statue – admired by everyone from Auguste Rodin to George Orwell, as well as Hemingway – now marks the spot on the pavement where he died at the hands of a royalist firing squad.

11

MONTPARNASSE ARCHITECTURE

Dominated as it is by the skyscraping blade of its tower, the busy boulevards, and the large-scale developments around the station, Montparnasse can feel a little inhuman and over-modernized. Wandering down the backstreets, however, you can find some kindlier examples of **architecture**, ranging from the playful lines of early **Art Deco** to the diaphanous **contemporary** glasswork of Jean Nouvel's Fondation Cartier.

26 rue Vavin 6ᵉ; Ⓜ Vavin. Decked in white and blue tiles, the terraced balconies of this apartment block are stepped back, allowing gardens to flourish in the light. Built by Henri Sauvage in 1912.

Rue Schoelcher and rue Froidevaux 14ᵉ; Ⓜ Raspail/Denfert-Rochereau. A parade of varied nineteenth- and early twentieth-century styles. Check out 5 rue Schoelcher, especially, for its beautiful Art Deco balconies and windows, dating from 1911 (Picasso had his studio at 5bis for a short time in 1916). The artists' studios at 11 rue Schoelcher are just sixteen years younger, but the transformation to modernity is complete. Also worth seeing are nos. 11 and 23 rue Froidevaux, the latter being a 1929 block of artists' studios, with huge windows for northern light and fabulous ceramic mosaics.

266 bd Raspail 14ᵉ; Ⓜ Raspail/Denfert-Rochereau. A recently completed private architecture and interior design academy with a marked Beaubourg influence, notably the external stairs and blue pipe columns in front. The original Ecole Spéciale d'Architecture building, at no. 254, dates from 1904.

31 rue Campagne-Première 14ᵉ; Ⓜ Raspail. Myriad shell-like, earthenware tiles by Alexandre Bigot encrust the concrete structure of André Arfvidson's utterly desirable 1912 *appartements*, with their huge, iron-framed studio windows. Man Ray had a studio here in the early 1920s.

Fondation Cartier pour l'Art Contemporain 261 bd Raspail, 14ᵉ; Ⓜ Raspail. One of Jean Nouvel's most successful, airy, postmodern steel-and-glass structures. See p.164.

Passage d'Enfer 14ᵉ; Ⓜ Raspail. Parallel to rue Campagne-Première, this narrow cobblestone street – whose name translates as "Hell Alley" – was once a Cité Ouvrière, or cul-de-sac of nineteenth-century workers' housing. The unusually small, terraced buildings are now utterly covetable.

Musée Zadkine

100bis rue d'Assas, 14e • Tues–Sun 10am–6pm • Free • ☎ 01 55 42 77 20 • Ⓜ Vavin/RER Port-Royal

The miniscule **Musée Zadkine** occupies the Russian-born sculptor **Ossip Zadkine**'s studio-house, where he lived and worked from 1928 until his death in 1967. In the garden, enclosed by ivy-covered studios and dwarfed by tall buildings, angular Cubist bronzes such as his compelling *Orphée* seem to struggle for light. Inside is a collection of his gentler wooden torsos, along with smaller-scale bronze and stone works, notably *Femme à l'éventail*. Studies for the renowned *La Ville détruite*, whose twisted, agonized torso was intended to express the horror of aerial bombing, can be seen inside and in the garden.

Fondation Cartier pour l'Art Contemporain

261 bd Raspail, 14e • Tues noon–10pm, Wed–Sun 11am–8pm • €9.50 • ☎ 01 42 18 56 50, Ⓦ fondation.cartier.com • Ⓜ Raspail

The **Fondation Cartier pour l'Art Contemporain** occupies one of the best contemporary buildings in Paris, a stunning glass-and-steel construction designed in 1994 by Jean Nouvel, architect of the Institut du Monde Arabe (see p.130). A glass wall follows the line of the street like a false start to the building proper, leaving space for the Tree of Liberty, planted by Chateaubriand during the Revolution, to grow in the garden behind. The glass of the building itself cleverly suggests a kind of fade-out into the air. Inside, all kinds of contemporary art – installations, videos, multimedia, graffiti – often by foreign artists little known in France, are shown in temporary exhibitions that use the light and generous spaces to maximum advantage.

Montparnasse cemetery

March 16–Nov 5 Mon–Fri 8am–6pm, Sat 8.30am–6pm, Sun 9am–6pm; Nov 6–March 15 closes 5.30pm • Free • Ⓜ Raspail/Gaîté/Edgar-Quinet

Montparnasse cemetery suffers by being second in size to Père-Lachaise (see p.207), and a long way behind it in celebrity. It's an impressive space, nonetheless, sheltering in the lee of the Tour Montparnasse behind high walls. In the southwest corner, the old, sail-less windmill was once one of the taverns whose literary-minded customers are said to have given the Montparnasse district its name.

To track down the cemetery's illustrious residents, pick up a leaflet and map from the guardhouse by each entrance. The joint grave of Jean-Paul Sartre and Simone de Beauvoir lies immediately right of the entrance on boulevard Edgar-Quinet – Sartre lived out the last few decades of his life just a few metres away on boulevard Raspail. Down avenue de l'Ouest, which follows the inside western wall of the cemetery, you'll find the tombs of Baudelaire (who has a more impressive cenotaph by rue Emile-Richard, on the cemetery's avenue Transversale), the sculptor Zadkine and the Fascist Pierre Laval, who was executed for treason. As an antidote, you can pay homage to Proudhon, the anarchist who coined the phrase "Property is theft!"; he lies in Division 2, by the central roundabout, near the great photographer of Paris, Brassaï. In the adjacent Division 1, the tomb of singer Serge Gainsbourg is regularly festooned with métro tickets – the "lilacs" of his ticket-punching song *Le Poinçonneur des lilas* – and packets of Gitanes cigarettes.

Monuments and sculptures

Grave-hunting aside, it's worth seeking out some of the cemetery's finer monuments. Horace Daillion's 1889 winged bronze, *Le Génie du sommeil éternel*, dominates the central roundabout, but far more moving is the tragic sculptural scene *La Séparation du Couple*, which stands a short distance below the windmill (in Division 4, beside the allée des Sergeants de la Rochelle). A giant bird created by the sculptor Niki de Saint Phalle in mirrored mosaic hovers in the northeast corner of Division 18, next to the avenue de l'Est; the title reads "To my friend Jean-Jacques: a bird which has flown too soon". The most poignant monument of all is found in the eastern angle of the cemetery, on the other side of rue Emile-Richard; in the far northern corner of this section is a tomb crowned with a version of Brancusi's sculpture *The Kiss*. Seekers of the bizarre should make for the inside wall of this part of the cemetery, along avenue du Boulevard (parallel to boulevard Raspail), where you can see the inventor of a safe gas lamp, Charles Pigeon, in bed next to his sleeping wife, reading a book by the light of his invention.

The catacombs

1 av du Colonel Henri Rol-Tanguy, 14ᵉ, on place Denfert-Rochereau • Tues–Sun 10am–5pm • €8 • ☎ 01 43 22 47 63, ⓦ catacombes-de-paris .fr • ⓜ Denfert-Rochereau

You won't find any celebrity dead in the nearby **catacombs**, only row on row of anonymous human bones. The entrance is on the square that Parisians have long known as place d'Enfer, or "Hell Square", though the name may derive from nothing more sinister than the Latin Via Inferiora ("The Low Road"). The huge lion in the middle of the square was designed by Bartholdi, better known for the Statue of Liberty. Underneath lies an underground warren of tunnels, originally part of the gigantic quarry network underlying Paris (see box, p.167). From 1785, a use was found for all that empty space, when it was realized that the city's overflowing graveyards and charnel houses were poisoning the water supplies and sparking epidemics. For the next eighty years, the stony corridors were gradually filled with skeletal remains, and it's estimated that the remains of six million Parisians are interred here – more than double the population of the modern city, not counting the suburbs.

The underground passages

There's one claustrophobic passageway to follow. The first turning takes you into the Galerie de Port-Mahon, a chamber dominated by a bas-relief of a fortress in Menorca, where its sculptor was once imprisoned. Beyond, passing a door inscribed "Arrête! C'est ici l'empire de la mort" ("Stop! This is Death's empire"), the catacombs proper begin. Passages are lined with long thigh bones stacked end-on, forming a wall to keep in the smaller ones heaped higgledy-piggledy behind. These macabre walls are inset with skulls and plaques carrying light-hearted quotations such as "Happy is he who always has the hour of his death in front of his eyes, and readies himself every day to die". Older children often love the whole experience, though there are a good couple of kilometres to walk, and if you're unlucky, you might find yourself in a bottlenecked queue of shrieking teenagers. It's fairly cold (a constant 14 degrees) and a touch squidgy underfoot, so flip-flops and a T-shirt aren't the best attire for a visit.

Back up at street level, the area just west of Denfert-Rochereau is also worth exploring. Rue Daguerre is one of Paris's more appealing market streets, almost like a provincial high street, and there's some interesting architecture (see box, p.163) in the area around the cemetery.

Observatoire de Paris and around

Av de l'Observatoire, 14ᵉ • ⓜ Denfert-Rochereau/RER Port Royal

About 500m northeast of the catacombs is the classical **Observatoire de Paris** which sat precisely on 0° longitude from the 1660s, when it was constructed, until 1914, when France finally gave in and agreed to recognize the Greenwich Meridian as the standard. The Observatoire itself is rarely open to visitors, but you can check out a couple of commemorative bronze medallions set in the pavement on either side of the front gate. Similar discs run right through the city, marking the old meridian, now named the **Arago line** after the early nineteenth-century astronomer. The building itself was the work of Claude Perrault, brother of the more famous Charles, the original author of *Sleeping Beauty*. It's a graceful structure, and the telescope cupola perched on the east tower adds an exotic touch.

On the other side of the boulevard de Port-Royal, the green avenue de l'Observatoire stretches due north into the Jardin du Luxembourg (see p.138). Curiosity-seekers might want to stroll down to boulevard Arago where, beside the high wall of the Santé prison, a few steps west of rue de la Santé, stands Paris's last remaining **Vespasienne**: Paris's last open-air, public urinal. It still works – and still stinks.

Fondation Henri Cartier-Bresson

2 impasse Lebouis, 14ᵉ • Tues, Thurs, Fri & Sun 1–6.30pm, Wed 1–8.30pm, Sat 11am–6.45pm; closed around Easter and during Aug • €6 • ☏ 01 56 80 27 00, ⓦ henricartierbresson.org • Ⓜ Gaîté

The slender steel-and-glass **Fondation Henri Cartier-Bresson** houses the archive of the father of photo journalism and arch-documenter of Paris, who died shortly after its opening in August 2004. Fascinating, often intimate shows of the work of Cartier-Bresson and his contemporaries alternate with exhibitions promoting younger photographers, including the winner of the foundation's annual prize.

Notre-Dame du Travail

36 rue Guilleminot, 14ᵉ • Mon–Fri 7.30am–7.45pm, Sat 9am–7.30pm, Sun 8.30am–7.30pm • Free • ⓦ notredamedutravail.net • Ⓜ Gaîté

The name of this distinctly odd church – **Notre-Dame du Travail**, or "Our Lady of Work" – reflects the artisanal and industrial jobs of the men it was built for: the workers who constructed the 1899 Exposition Universelle, including the Eiffel Tower. Its construction is deliberately factory-like too: some of its stone came from the Cloth Pavilion, when it was dismantled after the Exhibition closed, while the exposed metal columns of the interior came from the Palace of Industry. Architecturally, it's a fascinating industrial take on Gothic, which was way ahead of its time.

Les Colonnes and around

Ⓜ Gaîté

Immediately north of the church of Notre-Dame du Travail stand the two great wings – one oval, the other squared off – of Ricardo Bofill's postmodern Classical housing development, **Les Colonnes**. Beyond again, circular **place de Catalogne** is filled with a giant, flat disc of a fountain designed by the Israeli artist Shamaï Haber. Looking northwest, **place des 5 Martyrs du Lycée Buffon** offers a little-known but lovely view down the horse-chestnut-lined slope of boulevard Pasteur towards the Eiffel Tower, apparently floating over the city below.

Pernety

Ⓜ Pernety/Plaisance

The southwestern swathe of the 14ᵉ arrondissement is deeply residential, often village-like in atmosphere, especially around **Pernety** métro station. Wandering around Cité Bauer, rue des Thermopyles and rue Didot reveals adorable houses, secluded courtyards and quiet mews, and on the corner of rue du Moulin Vert and rue Hippolyte-Maindron you'll find **Giacometti**'s ramshackle old studio and home. Cinema has one of its best Parisian venues, meanwhile, at **L'Entrepôt**, 7–9 rue Francis-de-Pressensé (see p.285), with spaces for talks, meals and drinks, an excellent live music programme and even a garden.

Puces de Vanves

Sat & Sun 7am–1pm • ⓦ pucesdevanves.typepad.com • Ⓜ Porte-de-Vanves

At the weekend it's worth heading out to the southern edge of the 14ᵉ arrondissement for one of the city's best **flea markets**, known as the **Puces de Vanves** (see p.337). Starting at daybreak, it spreads along the pavements of avenues Marc Sangnier and Georges Lafenestre (where some stalls open in the afternoon as well), petering out at its western end in place de la Porte-de-Vanves, where the city fortifications stood until the 1920s. It's smaller and less formal than the St-Ouen Clignancourt market (see p.228), with more bric-a-brac and fewer out-and-out antiques.

UNDERGROUND PARIS

In September 2004, while on a training exercise in a group of **tunnels** underneath the Palais de Chaillot, the Parisian police stumbled upon a clandestine underground cell. Nothing to do with terrorism, this one, but an actual **subterranean chamber**, 400 square metres in size, which had been fitted out as a cinema by a dedicated club of *film noir* lovers. As the story hit the press, a band of troglodytes emerged blinking into the full beam of the media spotlight. Since the 1980s, it turned out, hundreds of these *"cataphiles"* had been holding anything from underground parties and art exhibitions to festivals and, it was rumoured, orgies. Experienced tunnel-goers talked of elaborate murals and a huge, pillared party room known as "La Plage", overlooked by a graffiti version of Hokusai's *The Wave*.

In fact, the tunnels underneath Chaillot form only a small part of a vast network that dates back to the **medieval era**, when the stone for building Paris was quarried out from its most obvious source, immediately underfoot – almost as if Paris were matched by a negative image of itself below ground. Today, over 300km of underground galleries lie beneath the city, especially on the Left Bank's 5ᵉ, 6ᵉ, 14ᵉ and 15ᵉ arrondissements, where the Grand Réseau Sud runs for over 100km. Another separate network lurks beneath the 13ᵉ arrondissement, while in the 16ᵉ, it's said that the rock is like Gruyère cheese – full of holes. In 1774, after a cave-in swallowed up whole buildings in what is now avenue Denfert-Rochereau, a royal commission was set up to map the old quarries and shore up the most precarious foundations. Great galleries were cut along the lines of the roads and the material used to infill the worst voids. Today, some of these underground "streets" still exist, while those above have disappeared. Some attribute modern Paris's relative lack of skyscrapers to doubts about the quality of the city's foundations.

In the nineteenth century, many tunnels were used for mushroom cultivation (the everyday supermarket variety is still known in France as the *champignon de Paris*), others for growing endives or brewing, while Carthusian monks even practised distillation under the modern-day Jardin du Luxembourg. The most creative scheme, however, involved the hygienic storage of human remains. From the 1780s, the contents of Paris's unhealthily overcrowded cemeteries were slowly transferred underground. In Montparnasse, one bone-lined section of the **catacombs** can still be visited (see p.165) but, otherwise, "penetrating into or circulating within" the network has been illegal since 1955. You can always get down into the métro, of course, while at the Musée des Egouts de Paris (see p.150) you can descend into a part of the city's 2300km of sewers. But it would be foolish to try anything more adventurous; in 1993, one *cataphile* apparently disappeared into the labyrinth, never to return.

Parc Montsouris and around

Daily 9am–dusk • RER/Tramway Cité Universitaire

With its undulating contours, waterfall cascading into a lake and RER tracks cutting right through the middle, the **Parc Montsouris** is one of Paris's more eccentric parks, but also one of the more charming. Further surprising features include a meteorological office, a marker of the old meridian line, near boulevard Jourdan, and, by the southwest entrance, a kiosk run by the French Astronomy Association. The surrounding area offers plentiful artistic and historic associations. Le Corbusier's first building in Paris was the **Studio Ozenfant**, at 53 avenue Reille – designed for his co-founder of the Purist movement, Amédée Ozenfant. The handsome, 1920s private mews of **Villa Seurat**, off rue de la Tombe-Issoire, was home to the artists Dalí, Chaïm Soutine, André Derain and Jean Lurçat, along with expat writers Henry Miller and Lawrence Durrell – it was here that Miller wrote his notorious *Tropic of Cancer*.

The Cité Universitaire

RER/Tramway Cité Universitaire • ⓦ ciup.fr

Several thousand students from more than a hundred different countries occupy the **Cité Universitaire**, whose buildings follow a kitsch international theme. The central Maison Internationale resembles a traditional French château, while the red brick of the Collège Franco-Britannique all too accurately recalls Britain's institutional buildings. Two of the most remarkable buildings, however, were designed by Le Corbusier: the graceful suspended shoebox of the Pavillon de la Suisse (1931–33) is one of his major works, and still has original mural paintings inside; the more brutal Pavillon du Brésil (1957–59) recalls his famous Cité Radieuse in Marseille. As you'd expect, there's an active programme of film, theatre and other events.

The 15^e

Though it's the largest and most populous of them all, the **quinzième (15e) arrondissement** falls off the agenda for most visitors as it lacks even a single important building or monument. Its most distinctive features, in fact, are an odd island walkway in the middle of the Seine, the **Allée des Cygnes**, and a bristle of miniature skyscrapers on the riverbank, the shabby remainder of a 1960s and 1970s development known as the Front de Seine. There's little reason to penetrate this latter maze unless you're a particular fan of postwar architecture, or perhaps raised pedestrian walkways; even the distinctively slender, skylon-like white tower turns out to be nothing more interesting than a central-heating chimney. The 15e does, however, have a delightfully provincial high street, the rue du Commerce, and two lovely and distinctly offbeat parks in its southern corners, the **Parc André-Citroën** and the **Parc Georges-Brassens**.

Around the Pont de Bir-Hakeim

Ⓜ Bir-Hakeim

Heading south from the Eiffel Tower, the first landmark on the city's southwestern **riverbank** front is the glass **Maison de la Culture du Japon à Paris** (ⓦwww.mcjp.asso.fr), which puts on excellent programmes of Japanese theatre, dance, music and cinema. Immediately south, you can watch the métro trains trundling across to Passy on the top level of the two-decker **Pont de Bir-Hakeim**, a lovable structure dating from 1902. Up on the adjacent raised walkway, at the beginning of boulevard de Grenelle, a bronze sculptural group stands in memorial to the notorious **rafle du Vel d'Hiv**, the mass arrest of 13,152 Parisian Jews in July 1942. Nine thousand people, including four thousand children, were interned for a week at the cycle track which once stood here, before being carted off to the death camps. Only thirty adults survived.

Allée des Cygnes

Ⓜ Bir-Hakeim

One of Paris's most curious walks leads down from the very middle of the Pont de Bir-Hakeim, along the **Allée des Cygnes**, a narrow, midstream island built up on raised concrete embankments. It's a strange place – one of Samuel Beckett's favourites – with just birds, trees and a path to walk along, and, at its furthest point downstream, a smaller-scale version of the **Statue of Liberty**, or *Liberty Lighting the World*, to give it its full title. This was one of the four preliminary models constructed between 1874 and 1884 by sculptor Auguste Bartholdi, with the help of Gustave Eiffel, before the finished article was presented to New York.

Parc André-Citroën

Daily 9am to dusk • Ⓜ Javel-André-Citroën/Balard

The **Parc André-Citroën**, on the banks of the Seine between Pont du Gariglinano and Pont Mirabeau, is not a park for traditionalists. The central grassy area is straightforward enough, but around it you'll find futuristic terraces and concrete-walled gardens with abstract themes. It's as much a sight to visit in its own right as a place to lounge around or throw a frisbee.

At the top end, away from the river, are two large glass **hothouses**, one housing mimosa, fish-tailed palms and other sweet-smelling shrubbery, the other used for temporary exhibitions. On hot days, however, the most tempting feature is the large platform between them, which sprouts a capricious set of automated **fountain** jets, luring children, and occasionally adults, to dodge the sudden spurts of water. On either side of the greenhouses, the White and Black gardens are for plants that show off the two extreme colours, but the most exciting themed gardens lie along the northern side of the park, where high walls surround the **Serial Gardens**. Here, the Green Garden is dedicated to sound, with bubbling water and *Miscanthus sinensis* grasses rustling dryly in the wind; the Blue Garden is for scent, planted with wisteria and strong-smelling herbs; the Orange Garden, for touch, is highly textured; and there are Red, Silver and Gold gardens too. At the foot of this section, towards the river, is the Garden in Movement, whose semi-wild, constantly changing plants are broken up by miniature greenhouses, and a long stone staircase flowing with water.

The Air de Paris tethered balloon

Parc André-Citroën • Daily 9am to 30min before the park closes • Mon–Fri €10, Sat & Sun €12, children aged 3–11 €5/6 • To check weather conditions on the day call ☎ 01 44 26 20 00, ⊛ ballondeparis.com

Perhaps the best feature of all in the Parc André-Citroën is the **tethered balloon**, which rises and sinks regularly on calm days, taking small groups 150m above the ground – higher than the second level of the Eiffel Tower – for great views of the city. In the ten years since it was installed, it has become one of the chief landmarks of the 15ᵉ, but in 2008 it took on a new complexion – quite literally: the balloon now changes colour to reflect levels of air pollution. A strip of LEDs on the south side indicates the air quality near traffic – from green (good) via orange (don't panic) to red (gas masks on). At night, the whole thing lights up – rather charmingly – to reflect the ambient air quality across the entire city.

11

The quartier du Commerce

Ⓜ Avenue Emile Zola/Commerce

The best way to get the flavour of the **quartier du Commerce** is to start walking down **avenue de la Motte-Picquet**, where the Champ de Mars meets the Ecole Militaire. At the corner, the brasseries throng with officers from the Ecole, and the hundred-odd antique shops in the 1960s-built **Village Suisse** (all Thurs–Mon; ⊛ villagesuisse.com) display everything from crystal chandeliers to gilt-framed oils. At the **boulevard de Grenelle**, where the métro trundles above the street on iron piers, things relax a little. **Rue du Commerce**, which stretches to the south, preserves a distinctive and very pleasant village atmosphere, its prettily shuttered houses lined with small shops and cafés. This upscale respectability would have been a surprise to the working-class diners who once filled the three storeys of *Le Café du Commerce* (see p.286), or to George Orwell, who worked on the street as a dishwasher, a gritty experience described in his *Down and Out in Paris and London*. Towards the street's southern end, place du Commerce is distinguished by its bandstand, while, just beyond, the nineteenth-century church of **St-Jean Baptiste de Grenelle** frames the end of the road handsomely.

Parc Georges-Brassens

Entrance on rue des Morillons, 15ᵉ • Daily dawn to dusk • Ⓜ Convention/Porte-de-Vanves

The main entrance of the **Parc Georges-Brassens** is flanked by two bronze bulls. The old Vaugirard abattoir was transformed into this park in the 1980s, and named after the legendary postwar poet-singer-satirist, who lived nearby at 42 villa Santos-Dumont. The abattoir's original clock tower remains, surrounded by a pond, and the park is a delight, especially for children; attractions include puppets, rocks and merry-go-rounds for the kids, a mountain stream with pine and birch trees, beehives and a tiny terraced vineyard, a climbing wall and a garden of scented herbs and shrubs designed principally for the blind (best in late spring). The corrugated pyramid with a helter-skelter-like spiral is a theatre, the Théâtre Silvia Montfort.

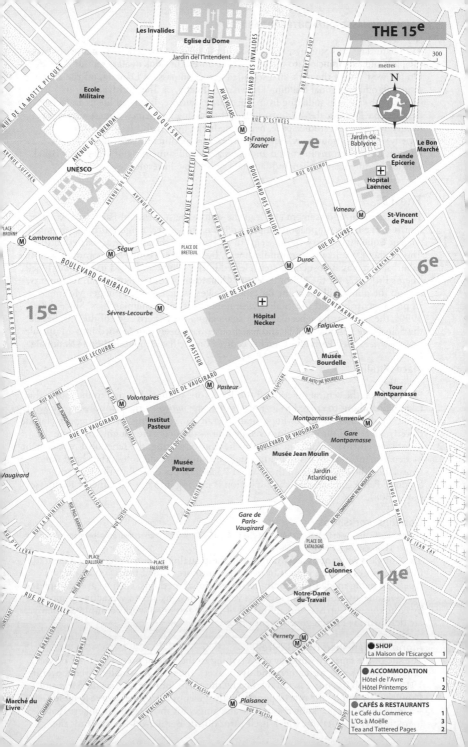

THE 15ᵉ

Les Invalides

Eglise du Dome

Jardin del l'Intendent

BOULEVARD DES INVALIDES

RUE RABELAI DE JOUY

0   300
metres

N

Ecole
Militaire

RUE DE LA MOTTE PICQUET

AV DUQUESNE

RUE D'ESTREES

RUE DE VILLARS

AVENUE DE LOWENDAL

AVENUE DE SAXE

AVENUE DE SÉGUR

AVENUE DE SUFFREN

UNESCO

St-François
Xavier

7ᵉ

Jardin de
Bablyóne

RUE OUDINOT

Le Bon
Marché

Grande
Epicerie

AVENUE DE BRETEUIL

BOULEVARD DES INVALIDES

Hópital
Laennec

PLACE
BRONNE

Cambronne

Ségur

PLACE DE
BRETEUIL

RUE DU GÉNÉRAL BERTRAND

RUE DUROC

RUE DE SEVRES

Vaneau

St-Vincent
de Paul

RUE DU CHERCHE-MIDI

6ᵉ

RUE CAMBRONNE

BOULEVARD GARIBALDI

Sévres-Lecourbe

RUE DE SEVRES

Duroc

RUE MAYET

BD DU MONTPARNASSE

RUE DE SÈVRES

15ᵉ

BLVD PASTEUR

RUE LECOURBE

Hôpital Necker

Falguiere

AVENUE DU MAINE

Musée
Bourdelle

RUE DE VAUGIRARD

Pasteur

RUE ANTO INE BOURDELLE

Tour
Montparnasse

RUE BLOMET

Volontaires

RUE DES VOLONTAIRES

RUE FALGUIERE

RUE DU POCTEUR ROUX

Institut
Pasteur

Montparnasse-Bienvenüe

BOULEVARD DE VAUGIRARD

Gare
Montparnasse

Vaugirard

RUE DE VAUGIRARD

Musée
Pasteur

Musée Jean Moulin

AVENUE DU MAINE

RUE FALGUIERE

RUE DE LA PROCESSION

BOULEVARD PASTEUR

Jardin
Atlantique

RUE DU COMMANDANT RENE MOUCHOTTE

RUE DUTOT

Gare de Paris-
Vaugirard

RUE DE LA QUINTINIE

RUE PAUL BARRUEL

PLACE
D'ALLERAY

PLACE
FALGUIERE

PLACE DE
CATALOGNE

RUE JEAN SAY

RUE D'ALLERAY

RUE BRANCION

RUE BARGUE

Les
Colonnes

14ᵉ

RUE DU CHÂTEAU

RUE DE VOUILLE

Notre-Dame
du-Travail

RUE VERCINGETORIX

RUE ROSENWALD

RUE BLOMET

Marché du
Livre

RUE DE L'OUEST

Pernety

RUE DES GERCOVIE

RUE RAYMOND LOSSERAND

RUE PERNETY

RUE VERCINGETORIX

Plaisance

RUE D'ALESIA

RUE D'ALESIA

RUE DES GERGOVIE

● SHOP	
La Maison de l'Escargot	1

● ACCOMMODATION	
Hôtel de l'Avre	1
Hôtel Printemps	2

● CAFÉS & RESTAURANTS	
Le Café du Commerce	1
L'Os à Moëlle	3
Tea and Tattered Pages	2

On Saturdays and Sundays, take a look in the sheds of the old horse market between the park and **rue Brancion**, to the east, where dozens of **book dealers** set out their stock. On the west side of the park, in a secluded garden in passage Dantzig, off rue Dantzig, stands an odd polygonal building known as **La Ruche**, or The Beehive, after its honeycomb-like cells radiating from the central staircase. It started life as an Eiffel-designed pavilion for the 1900 world fair, showcasing fine wines, after which it was resurrected here as a studio space, becoming home to Fernand Léger, Modigliani (briefly), Chagall, Soutine, Ossip Zadkine and many other artists, mainly Jewish refugees from pogroms in Poland and Russia. It's still something of a Tower of Babel, with Irish, American, Italian and Japanese artists now in residence.

The 13^e

The **treizième arrondissement** (**13e**), in the southeastern corner of Paris, has two faces. North of the mega-roundabout of **place d'Italie**, the genteel neighbourhood around the ancient **Gobelins** tapestry works seems to look towards the adjacent Quartier Latin. The southern swathe of the arrondissement, by contrast, has more in common with the suburbs, as it was almost completely cleared in the 1960s, and filled in by tower blocks. There's little here for the visitor except in **Chinatown**, with its many Asian restaurants, and on the minor hillock of the **Butte-aux-Cailles**, which is like a budget Montmartre, its pretty, gentrified old streets alive with restaurants and bohemian bars. Since the 1990s, the planners have been at work again along the eastern edge of the 13e, beside the Seine. The old quays, mills and warehouses have been transformed into an upscale new *quartier* called **Paris Rive Gauche**, centred on the flagship **Bibliothèque Nationale**.

Place d'Italie
Ⓜ Place d'Italie

Place d'Italie, the central junction of the 13e, is one of those Parisian roundabouts that takes half an hour to cross. On its north side is the *mairie* of the arrondissement, while to the south is Kenzo Tange's huge Grand Ecran Italie building. Its curving glass facade cleverly advertised the giant film screen within – the two were roughly the same size – until the cinema was shut in 2006; at the time of writing, the scheduled replacement by department stores was still being fought by outraged cinephiles. They have some consolation, however: just up the road, at 73 avenue des Gobelins, the Jérôme Seydoux-Pathé cinema research foundation is moving into the old Cinéma Rodin (see box, p.308).

Gobelins workshops
42 av des Gobelins, 13e • Guided tour in French only Tues–Thurs 1.45pm & 2.45pm • €11.50; tickets must be booked in advance through Fnac (see p.330) • ☎ 01 44 08 53 49 • Ⓜ Gobelins

The **Gobelins workshops** are where the highest-quality tapestries have been created for some four hundred years. On the ninety-minute guided tour, you can watch tapestries being made by painfully slow traditional methods; each weaver completes between one and four square metres a year. The designs are now exactingly specified by contemporary artists, and almost all of the dozen or so works completed each year are destined for French government offices.

Along the vanished river Bièvre
The site of the tapestry works owes everything to the hidden presence of the Bièvre. Once a virtual sewer for tanners and dye-makers, the river was finally covered over in 1910, although its course is still marked by the curves of rues Berbier-du-Mets and Croulebarbe, and by the row of poplars in the green space of the **square René-le-Gall** – a former island once known as the Ile aux Singes for the jugglers' monkeys that lived there. Just off rue Geffroy, which itself turns off rue Berbier-du-Mets, stands the

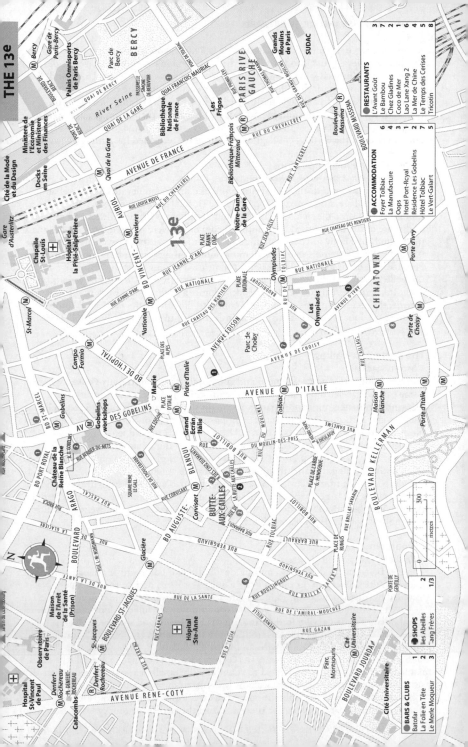

THE 13e

13e

BERCY

PARIS RIVE GAUCHE

CHINATOWN

BUTTE-AUX-CAILLES

River Seine

Gare de Paris-Bercy
Palais Omnisports de Paris Bercy
Parc de Bercy
Ministère de l'Économie et Ministère des Finances
Cité de la Mode et du Design
Docks en Seine
Gare d'Austerlitz
Chapelle St-Louis
Hôpital de la Pitié-Salpêtrière
Bibliothèque Nationale de France
Les Frigos
Grands Moulins de Paris
SUDAC
Bibliothèque-François Mitterand
Notre-Dame de la Gare
Les Olympiades
Parc de Choisy
Gobelins workshops
Château de la Reine Blanche
Grand Écran Italie
Mairie
Maison Blanche
Observatoire de Paris
Maison de l'Arrêt de la Santé (Prison)
Hôpital Ste-Anne
Hospital St-Vincent de Paul
Catacombs
Parc Montsouris
Cité Universitaire

QUAI DE BERCY
QUAI DE LA GARE
AVENUE DE FRANCE
QUAI FRANÇOIS MAURIAC
RUE DU CHEVALERET
RUE LOUISE WEISS
RUE DU CHEVALERET
BD VINCENT-AURIOL
RUE JEANNE-D'ARC
RUE CHATEAU DES RENTIERS
RUE NATIONALE
RUE CANTAGREL
RUE TOLBIAC
RUE DE TOLBIAC
RUE BAUDRICOURT
AVENUE DE CHOISY
AVENUE D'IVRY
AVENUE D'ITALIE
BOULEVARD MASSENA
BOULEVARD KELLERMAN
AVENUE EDISON
PLACE D'ITALIE
PLACE NATIONALE
PLACE JEANNE D'ARC
PLACE DES ALPES
BD DE L'HÔPITAL
AV DES GOBELINS
BD ST-MARCEL
BD ARAGO
RUE PASCAL
RUE CORVISART
RUE VERGNIAUD
RUE BARRAULT
RUE BOBILLOT
RUE TOLBIAC
RUE BRILLAT-SAVARIN
RUE BOUSSINGAULT
RUE DE LA SANTÉ
RUE DE L'AMIRAL-MOUCHET
AVENUE RENE-COTY
BOULEVARD JOURDAN
RUE GAZAN
RUE DE LA GLACIÈRE
BD AUGUSTE BLANQUI
BD PORT ROYAL
RUE BROCA
BD ST-JACQUES
SQUARE RENE LE GALL
RUE DU MOULIN-DES-PRES
PLACE DE RUNGIS
PLACE DE L'ABBÉ G. HENOCQUE
PORTE DE GENTILLY

Métro stations:
Bercy (M), St-Marcel (M), Campo-Formio (M), Nationale (M), Tolbiac (M), Olympiades (M), Porte d'Ivry (M), Porte de Choisy (M), Porte d'Italie (M), Chevaleret (M), Glacière (M), Corvisart (M), Les Gobelins (M), Place d'Italie (M), St-Jacques (M), Denfert-Rochereau (M)(R), Paris Rive Gauche (M)(R), Boulevard Masséna (M)(R)

● ACCOMMODATION
Foyer Tolbiac	6
La Manufacture	4
Oops	3
Hotel Port-Royal	1
Résidence Les Gobelins	2
Hôtel Tolbiac	7
Le Vert-Galant	5

● RESTAURANTS
L'Avant Goût	3
Le Bambou	7
Chez Gladines	2
Coco de Mer	1
Lao Lane Xang 2	6
La Mer de Chine	4
Le Temps des Cerises	5
Tricotin	8

● BARS & CLUBS
Batofar	1
La Folie en Tête	2
Le Merle Moqueur	3

● SHOPS
Les Abeilles	2
Tang Frères	1/3

0   300 metres

N

surprising, fairy-tale rump of the **Château de la Reine Blanche**, which once guarded the main medieval route into Paris from the south – along what is now avenue des Gobelins. The turreted wing (now luxury apartments) was built in the 1520s and 1530s by the aristocratic Gobelins family, but it occupied the site of a much older château torn down after a tragic party in 1393 in which the young Charles VI of France nearly died. Charles and five friends had disguised themselves as tarred-and-feathered savages but one of them brushed against a candle flame; the king was the only survivor of the ensuing conflagration, and never recovered his sanity.

Hôpital de la Pitié-Salpêtrière

Chapelle St-Louis 8.30am–5.30pm • Free • ⓜSt-Marcel/RER Austerlitz

Over to the east, towards the gare d'Austerlitz, the ornate boulevards St-Marcel and Vincent-Auriol are dominated by the immense **Hôpital de la Salpêtrière**, built under Louis XIV to house the sick, the disabled and the poor, to jail prostitutes and generally to dispose of the dispossessed. The imprisoned women were released by a revolutionary mob who broke in by force in September 1792. It later became a psychiatric hospital – Jean Charcot staged his theatrical demonstrations of hysteria and hypnosis here, with Freud as one of his fascinated witnesses. Today, it's a leading teaching hospital, but the **Chapelle St-Louis**, at the northern side of the complex, is open to visitors. It's a bleakly beautiful Baroque structure under a modest dome, a fairly typical work by Libéral Bruant, the architect of Les Invalides. It comes to life during the Festival d'Automne, when it's used for art installations, attracting artists of the calibre of Bill Viola (1996) and Jenny Holzer (2001).

The Butte-aux-Cailles

ⓜCorvisart/Place d'Italie

Between boulevard Auguste-Blanqui and rue Bobillot is the **Butte-aux-Cailles**, whose name can be translated picturesquely as the hill (*butte*) of the quails (*cailles*). It's a pleasantly animated miniature quarter, the main sloping rue de la Butte-aux-Cailles cobbled and furnished with attractive lampposts, as well as one of the classic, green Art Nouveau drinking fountains (see box, p.181). Alongside the old left-wing establishments – the bar *La Folie en Tête* at no. 33 and the restaurant *Le Temps des Cerises* at nos. 18–20 (see p.287) – are plenty of relaxed places to eat and drink till the small hours, making this an attractive area for low-key nightlife.

If you're coming from métro Corvisart, cross the road and head straight through the passageway in the large apartment building opposite, then climb the steps that lead up through the small Brassaï gardens to rue des Cinq Diamants. Alternatively, it's a short walk up rue Bobillot from place d'Italie.

Chinatown

ⓜOlympiades

The area between rue de Tolbiac, avenue de Choisy and boulevard Masséna is what is known as the **Chinatown** (or the *quartier Chinois*) of Paris, despite the fact that it was founded by Vietnamese refugees in the late 1970s, and is now home to several other east-Asian communities. Avenues de Choisy and d'Ivry are full of Vietnamese, Thai, Cambodian, Laotian and indeed Chinese restaurants and food shops. On avenue d'Ivry, you'll find the huge Tang Frères **Chinese supermarket** (see p.334), a former railway warehouse now stocked with an incredible variety of Asian goods. The chief landmark of Chinatown, however, is **Les Olympiades**, a set of giant tower blocks, each named after a city which has hosted the games, with a mall below and a pedestrian area strangely suspended above. One escalator leads up from 66 avenue d'Ivry; alongside this escalator, an easily missable slip road, rue du Disque, leads down to an underground car park; and part of the way down this access road lurks a tiny

Buddhist temple and community centre: the Association des Résidents en France d'Origine Indochinoise. It's advertised by a pair of red Chinese lanterns dimly visible in the gloom. Another Buddhist temple, belonging to a community organization for the Téochew people, the Amicale des Téochew en France, can be reached by heading up the escalator at 66 avenue d'Ivry to the "Stadium" sports centre; from here head for the Tour Anvers tower block – the temple is tucked away behind, on the right. Ceremonies with traditional chants take place every day at around 10am and 3pm.

Paris Rive Gauche

ⓂQuai de la Gare/Bibliothèque François Mitterrand

Stretching from the Gare d'Austerlitz right down to the *boulevard périphérique*, the once-isolated, desolate, industrial strip between rail tracks and river is being transformed into the swanky new **Paris Rive Gauche** district. The railway lines are slowly being roofed over, the old docks have become "Docks en Seine", incorporating a fashion institute, the Austerlitz station is undergoing a major makeover (it's being connected to a new TGV line to Bordeaux) and a fine pedestrian footbridge, the **Passerelle Simone de Beauvoir**, now crosses the Seine in a futuristic double-ribbon strip. The area is finding a new, more leisure-driven purpose, too. Tethered beside the **Bibliothèque Nationale**, the flagship of the quarter, is a floating swimming pool, the **Piscine Josephine Baker** (see p.343), and two unusual **barges** have also made the area a nightlife attraction in its own right, notably the ex-lighthouse boat, *Batofar* (see p.302).

In the south of the quarter, the massive **Grands Moulins de Paris** and Halle aux Farines have been ambitiously rebuilt for the Université Denis Diderot, aka "Paris 7", an annexe of the Jussieu site (see p.130). Finally, just short of the *périphérique*, another early twentieth-century industrial-era site, the handsomely arched **SUDAC** compressed-air building, is now the home of a new school of architecture. If in the area, serious **Le Corbusier** fans might want to slog across to rue Cantagrel, where the architect's colourful Cité de Refuge (1933), or Salvation Army building, stands at no. 12.

Bibliothèque Nationale de France

Quai François-Mauriac, 13ᵉ • Public reading rooms Tues–Sat 10am–8pm, Sun 1–7pm • €3.50 for a day-pass, bring ID • ⓌΘ bnf.fr •
ⓂQuai de la Gare/Bibliothèque François Mitterrand

The star architectural attraction of the **Paris Rive Gauche** development, which Mitterrand managed to inaugurate, though not open, just before his death in 1996, is the **Bibliothèque Nationale de France**. There are regular exhibitions – typically serious, arty and high quality – and the **reading rooms** on the "haut-jardin" level, along with their unrivalled collection of foreign newspapers, are open to everyone over 16. The garden level, below, is reserved for accredited researchers only, while the garden itself is completely out of bounds.

The four enormous L-shaped towers at the corners of the site were intended to look like open books, but attracted widespread derision after shutters had to be added behind the glazing in order to protect the collections from sunlight. Once you mount the dramatic wooden steps surrounding the library, however, the perspective changes utterly. From here you look down into a huge sunken pine wood, with glass walls that filter light into the floors below your feet; it's like standing at the edge of a secret

---

TRAVEL TIP: GO BY VOGUEO

If you're heading down to the Paris Rive Gauche area from the Quartier Latin, and don't want to walk, the little green **Voguéo boat-bus** (Ⓦ voguео.fr) makes a pleasant alternative to bus route 89. Services run roughly every 15 minutes (7am–8.20pm) from the Gare d'Austerlitz via Parc de Bercy (on the Right Bank) to the Bibliothèque Nationale, before heading off south towards Ivry. You can use the Navigo métro pass or buy a single €3 ticket on board.

ravine. The concept is startlingly original, and almost fulfils architect Dominique Perrault's intention to combine "rigour and emotion", to "generate a sense of dignity, a well-tempered soul for the buildings of the French Republic". Cynics might feel that the steel stays added to stop the trees blowing over are rather less than dignified.

Les Frigos and the private galleries

Les Frigos 19 rue des Frigos, 13ᵉ • Ⓦ les-frigos.com **Les Voûtes** Ⓦ lesvoutes.org • Ⓜ Quai de la Gare/Bibliothèque François Mitterrand
Rosenblum Collection 183 rue du Chevaleret, 13ᵉ • Tours Sat 10am & 3pm • €10, online booking only • Ⓦ rosenblumcollection.eu •
Ⓜ Chevaleret

On the south side of rue de Tolbiac, opposite the library, the giant, decaying cold-storage warehouse of **Les Frigos** is occupied by artists and musicians, and has been since the 1980s when it was an infamous/celebrated squat. It's now officially sanctioned, and holds open-door exhibitions once or twice a year. There's often a gig or an event going on in the space known as Les Voûtes ("The Vaults"), plus a couple of galleries, and you can visit the bar/restaurant – though it's officially only for the artists. Just west of the library, near métro Chevaleret, a few small but cutting-edge art galleries are now well settled on **rue Louise Weiss** and round the corner on rue du Chevaleret. You can also take a tour of the private and up-to-the-moment Rosenblum Collection of art.

Docks en Seine

Ⓦ paris-docks-en-seine.fr • Ⓜ Austerlitz/Quai de la Gare

The most recent development, the **Docks en Seine** complex on the quai d'Austerlitz, lies upstream of the Pont de Bercy. The ugly concrete warehouses which once belonged to Paris's central port have been rebuilt as the **Cité de la Mode et du Design**, a fashion institute. The intrusive design of twisting, lime-green tubes, by Dominique Jacob and Brendan MacFarlane, is supposed to recall the sinuous shape of the river. The **Institut Français de la Mode** (Ⓦ ifm-paris.com), a new fashion school, may eventually host exhibitions, and a floating café-restaurant-venue, *Petit Bain*, is already in place. You can stroll along the riverbank here – gardens and a pedestrian promenade were being created at the time of writing, and were due to be complete in 2013 – perhaps admiring the giant Bercy development across the river (see p.112). Those tiring of post-industrial mega-design may want to walk just a little further north, beyond the Gare d'Austerlitz, to the refreshingly historic green space of the Jardin des Plantes (see p.128).

Montmartre and northern Paris

Stacked on its hilltop in the northern 18e arrondissement of Paris, Montmartre sets itself apart from the city at its feet. Its chief landmark, visible from all over the city, is the church of Sacré-Coeur, crowning the Butte as if an overenthusiastic pâtissier had run riot with an icing gun. The slopes below, around Abbesses métro, preserve something of the spirit of the village that once basked here, but unlike most villages Montmartre has a diverse and dynamic population, by turns lefty, trendy and sleazy. Between Montmartre and the Grands Boulevards, which define the edge of the city centre proper, stretch the 9e (neuvième) and 10e (dixième) arrondissements, whose shared nineteenth-century architecture and almost total lack of green space make them look quite similar. Yet where the 9e arrondissement is largely genteel and well groomed, the 10e is mostly boisterous and shabby.

The 9e arrondissement has two beguiling museums devoted to its nineteenth-century artistic heyday, the **Musée Moreau** and **Musée de la Vie Romantique**, and the northern fringe of the arrondissement, around Pigalle, just below the Butte Montmartre, is famous for its cabarets and sex shows. The main interest of the 10e lies in the shops, restaurants and markets of the immigrant population, especially in the poor, largely African **Goutte d'Or** *quartier*, east of Montmartre. Another good area for eating is bourgeois **Batignolles**, just west of Montmartre.

Montmartre

In spite of being one of the city's chief tourist attractions, **Montmartre** retains a surprising whiff of its rural origins. It's an unusually proud and tight-knit neighbourhood, and there are few cars. Incorporated into the city only in the mid-nineteenth century, its heyday was from the last years of the nineteenth century to World War I, when its rustic charms and low rents attracted crowds of artists. Since then, the *quartier's* physical appearance has changed little, thanks largely to the warren of **plaster-of-Paris quarries** that perforate its bowels and render the ground too unstable for new building. Tiny squares still give way to sudden vistas south over the rooftops of central Paris, and the occasional studio window is a tangible reminder of its illustrious artistic past.

In the second half of the twentieth century, the Butte, along with Pigalle at its foot (see p.187), slumped into a sleazy half-life of porn shows and semi-genteel poverty, but both neighbourhoods have undergone radical gentrification in recent years. Fashionable nightspots have displaced the sex shows, and the young and moneyed have largely replaced artists and prostitutes. The heart of the action is around **Abbesses** métro, extending right down to Pigalle, with **rue des Martyrs** as the chief artery of cool. It's a lively area on Sundays but relatively dead on a Monday.

Most visitors make straight for the landmark church of **Sacré-Coeur** via the steps or **funicular** railway (covered by ordinary métro tickets) immediately below. But for a less touristy approach, head up via place des Abbesses, around which you'll find a host of bijou bars and cafés.

12

Abbesses
Ⓜ Abbesses

You could almost be persuaded that pretty, tree-shaded **place des Abbesses** was a village square – if it weren't for its centrepiece, one of Guimard's rare, canopied Art Nouveau métro entrances; there are only two others in the city (see box, p.182). The métro canopy isn't in fact an authentic Abbesses sight, as it was transferred from the Hôtel de Ville, complete with its glass porch, tendril-like railings and lascivious-looking lanterns – but it looks perfectly at home here in the square. At the north end of the square, "Le mur des je t'aime" is a tiled wall inscribed with the words for "I love you", handwritten

---

MONTMARTROBUS

The diminutive size of the **Montmartrobus** is designed to help it negotiate the twisting streets of the Butte, but its eccentric shape and determinedly ecological electric engine also make it fit right in with the *quartier's* spirit. If you don't want to walk, taking this bus is probably the best way of doing a Montmartre tour, and normal métro/bus tickets are valid. Starting at place Pigalle, the route heads up rue des Martyrs and west along rue des Abbesses and rue Durantin, then follows the curve of rue Lepic to rue des Saules and rue Caulaincourt, before jinking up to Jules-Joffrin métro. On the return leg it heads down rues Ramey, Custine and Lamarck, curling round the foot of Sacré-Coeur and the *funiculaire* and heading back up to place du Tertre. It then winds back towards place des Abbesses via rues Cortot, Girardon and Gabrielle, before finally running down rues Chappe, Yvonne Le Tac and Houdon, back to place Pigalle.

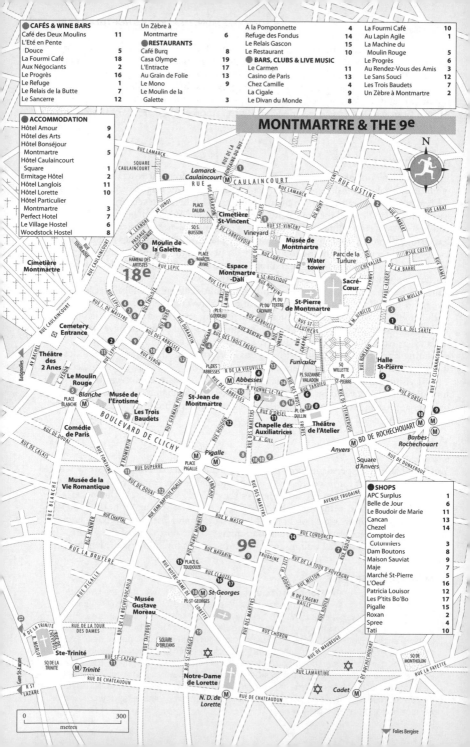

CAFÉS & WINE BARS
Café des Deux Moulins | 11
L'Été en Pente Douce | 5
La Fourmi Café | 18
Aux Négociants | 2
Le Progrès | 16
Le Refuge | 1
Le Relais de la Butte | 7
Le Sancerre | 12

Un Zèbre à Montmartre | 6

RESTAURANTS
Café Burq | 8
Casa Olympe | 19
L'Entracte | 17
Au Grain de Folie | 13
Le Mono | 9
Le Moulin de la Galette | 3

A la Pomponnette | 4
Refuge des Fondus | 14
Le Relais Gascon | 15
Le Restaurant | 10

BARS, CLUBS & LIVE MUSIC
Le Carmen | 11
Casino de Paris | 13
Chez Camille | 4
La Cigale | 9
Le Divan du Monde | 8

La Fourmi Café | 10
Au Lapin Agile | 1
La Machine du Moulin Rouge | 5
Le Progrès | 6
Au Rendez-Vous des Amis | 3
Le Sans Souci | 12
Les Trois Baudets | 7
Un Zèbre à Montmartre | 2

ACCOMMODATION
Hôtel Amour | 9
Hôtel des Arts | 4
Hôtel Bonséjour Montmartre | 5
Hôtel Caulaincourt Square | 1
Ermitage Hôtel | 2
Hôtel Langlois | 11
Hôtel Lorette | 10
Hôtel Particulier Montmartre | 3
Perfect Hotel | 7
Le Village Hostel | 6
Woodstock Hostel | 8

MONTMARTRE & THE 9e

SHOPS
APC Surplus | 1
Belle de Jour | 6
Le Boudoir de Marie | 11
Cancan | 13
Chezel | 14
Comptoir des Cotonniers | 3
Dam Boutons | 8
Maison Sauviat | 9
Maje | 7
Marché St-Pierre | 5
L'Oeuf | 16
Patricia Louisor | 12
Les P'tits Bo'Bo | 17
Pigalle | 15
Roxan | 2
Spree | 4
Tati | 10

0 — 300
metres

in eighty languages; it is something of a rendezvous for courting couples. For aimless wandering and café sitting, the area around Abbesses is particularly satisfying, and the unusual number of high-quality, artisan boulangeries is proof that the quarter has held on to its residential roots – you'll find three on rue des Abbesses alone.

St-Jean de Montmartre

Place des Abbesses, 18ᵉ • Free • ⓂAbbesses

On the downhill side of place des Abbesses, the red-brick church of **St-Jean de Montmartre** is well worth putting your nose inside for its radical construction, dating from the early 1900s. The incredibly slender pillars and broad vaulting were only made possible by the experimental use of reinforced concrete, a material that was, as the church's architect Anatole de Baudot claimed, both the bones and the skin.

Chapelle des Auxiliatrices and around

11 rue Yvonne-Le-Tac, 18ᵉ • Fri 3–6pm • Free • ⓂAbbesses

East of place des Abbesses, the **Chapelle des Auxiliatrices** is where Ignatius Loyola founded the **Jesuit** movement in 1534. This is also supposed to be the spot where **St Denis**, the first Bishop of Paris, was decapitated by the Romans, shortly before he carried his own head to St-Denis (see p.230). One block south, rue d'Orsel makes the transition from chichi Montmartre to cheap Barbès, with trendy clothes shops at its top end, near Abbesses, and cheap fabric shops at the bottom. Towards its western end is the picturesque **place Charles Dullin**, centred on the small Théâtre de l'Atelier, where the great mime Jean-Louis Barrault – the inimitable Baptiste in *Les Enfants du Paradis* – made his debut.

12

The Butte

At 130m, the "Mound", or **Butte Montmartre**, is the highest point in Paris. The various theories as to the origin of its name all have a Roman connection: it could be a corruption of *Mons Martyrum* – "the Martyrs' hill", the martyrs being St Denis and his companions; on the other hand, it might have been named *Mons Mercurii*, in honour of a Roman shrine to Mercury; or possibly *Mons Martis*, after a shrine to Mars.

If you're in any doubt about finding your way **up the Butte**, just keep heading uphill – the area is so charming that there's no such thing as a wrong turn. One of the quietest and most attractive paths begins at place des Abbesses, climbing **rue de la Vieuville** and the stairs in rue Drevet to the minuscule **place du Calvaire**, which has a lovely view back over the city.

Bateau-Lavoir

Place Emile-Goudeau, 18ᵉ • ⓂAbbesses

With its graceful Wallace fountain, its steps and its view, the tiny place Emile-Goudeau is one of the more adorable squares in Paris. It's also overlooked by a building that

---

WALLACE'S FOUNTAINS

After the Prussian siege and the bloody fighting of the Commune (see box, p.185), Paris was physically and emotionally scarred, and badly in need of succour. In 1872, a wealthy British resident of the city called **Richard Wallace** came up with the perfect symbol of renewal. He gave the city fifty cast-iron drinking fountains, each topped with a kind of miniature temple designed by the sculptor Charles-Auguste Lebourg, its roof supported by four caryatids representing Simplicity, Temperance, Charity and Goodness. More fountains were added in later years, and today some 65 still stand in the city. Painted in lustrous green, their usefulness is limited these days by the loss of the cups once permanently attached to them. All the same, *les fontaines Wallace* remain quintessential symbols of Paris. (Curiously, the fountains have an unusual status in the French language, too, being one of the few French words to begin with "w"; like *le whisky*, *le weekend* and *le walkman*, they are a treasured import.)

encapsulates Montmartre's rich artistic history: a former piano factory known as the **Bateau-Lavoir**. In 1904 Picasso took up a studio here, and he stayed for the best part of a decade, painting *Les Demoiselles d'Avignon* and sharing loves, quarrels and opium trips with Braque, Juan Gris, Modigliani, Max Jacob, Apollinaire and others, both famous and obscure. It was on the place Emile-Goudeau that he had his first encounter with the beautiful Fernande Olivier, thrusting a kitten into her hand as she passed by. "I laughed," she said, "and he took me to see his studio." Fernande became his model and lover. Although the original building burnt down some years ago, the modern reconstruction still provides studio space for artists, and you wouldn't notice any change on the square itself.

Moulin de la Galette

Rue Lepic, 18^e • ⓂAbbesses

Perhaps the most historic route up the Butte is via rue Lepic, which owes its winding contours to the requirements of the slow wagons that carried plaster of Paris down from the quarries. The street begins at the seedy place Blanche, which is occupied by a resolutely ordinary food market at its lower end. Above rue des Abbesses, however, it becomes progressively more elegant. Just short of the top the **Moulin de la Galette** looks

12

THE METRO: MIRROR OF PARIS

The **métro** holds up a mirror to Paris. When you descend into its network, Paris's true ethnic and social mix is instantly revealed. The centre of the city may be flush with the white and wealthy, but the *franciliens* who live beyond the *périphérique* ring road – women in Islamic veils, streetwise kids from the housing projects, working men in overalls – mostly travel to and from work underground. And every new immigrant group fleeing the latest conflict zone sends a wave of buskers down the tunnels.

The métro is almost a world in itself. It certainly has its own **culture**. When it gets crowded everyone knows you're not supposed to use the *strapontins*, the folding seats by the doors, and it's tacitly understood that only someone really pushy walks up or down an escalator. And predictably, there's a certain style about the way Parisians travel, notably the casual upward flick of the wrist that turns the door handle just before the train has stopped moving. For tourists, the best things about the métro are its reliability – except when there's a strike – and its cost: roughly two thirds of the ticket price is subsidized by the French taxpayer.

Internationally, however, the métro is best known not for its social niceties but for its beautiful Art Nouveau signs and entrances, designed by **Hector Guimard** in 1900. As with most of their city's cutting-edge design icons, Parisians were, at first, less than impressed, Guimard's sinewy green railings and lantern holders being compared to threatening insects' tentacles. The last three complete Guimard stations, with their glazed roofs intact, can be found at **Abbesses**, below Montmartre; at the **Porte Dauphine**, on the edge of the Bois de Boulogne; and, since 2000, at **Châtelet**'s place St-Opportune entrance. Some stations have distinct characters below ground, too: check out the funky multicoloured lamps at Bonnes Nouvelles station, for example, the hanging globe lights at Cité, the museum cabinets and jewelled entrance at Palais-Royal-Musée-du-Louvre, the sci-fi copper-submarine styling of Arts-et-Métiers, Varennes' massive Rodin sculptures, St-Germain-des-Prés' sleek comic-book projections, the historic cartoons at Bastille and the one-letter-per-tile decor of Concorde – which spells out the Revolutionary Declaration of the Rights of Man.

Technologically, the métro is one of the finest underground systems in the world, though the famous rubber tyres are actually restricted to lines 1, 4, 6, 11 and 14. Line 1 now has the very latest in air-conditioned, articulated, compartmentless carriages, while the new and extremely swanky line 14 goes one better with driverless trains, which offer exciting views down the tunnels. There are more elevated métro pastimes than playing train drivers, too. The writer Jacques Jouet and the avant-garde literary group, Oulipo, invented a system for composing métro poems; you have to write a single line every time the train is still, and think up the next while the train is moving.

down from atop its modest patch of green – the last remnant of Montmartre's *maquis*, the scrub that once covered the Butte. The abandoned dances here were immortalized by Renoir in his *Bal du Moulin de la Galette*, now hanging in the Musée d'Orsay. Today, the windmill is one of just two survivors of the many that once spun atop Montmartre. The other, the Moulin Radet, stands at its feet, above the confusingly named *Moulin de la Galette* restaurant. If you're approaching from place des Abbesses, you can cut straight up to the windmills via rue Durantin and rue Tholozé.

Place Marcel Aymé to place Dalida

Towards the top of rue Lepic, rue Girardon climbs up to **place Marcel Aymé**, a peaceful square with a lovably eccentric statue that celebrates Aymé's best-loved short story: **Le Passe-Muraille** or *The Man Who Could Walk Through Walls*. A few steps higher up, square Suzanne-Buisson provides another quiet haven, with a sunken boules pitch and fountains overlooked by a statue of St Denis clutching his head to his breast. Above that again, **place Dalida** offers fine views of Sacré-Coeur; it once had as its centerpiece a distinctly busty bust of the singer and gay icon Dalida, but the original was stolen, presumably by seekers of the ultimate camp curio. Her empty plinth is overlooked by the elegant Château des Brouillards, or "Fog House", where Renoir once lived. It gets its romantic name not from the fact that Renoir used to sit on the steps smoking, but from the clouds that used to gather around the top of the Butte.

Avenue Junot

From place Marcel Aymé, the gorgeously exclusive avenue Junot sweeps west, giving onto still more exclusive enclaves. Beside no. 11 is a desirable nest of houses and gardens, the **Hameau des Artistes** – its digicoded gate usually firmly shut against the hoi polloi. Behind the (closed) gate of the next private lane, the **passage Lepic–Junot**, lies the weighty "witch's stone" that gives it its local name: the passage de la Sorcière. The secluded cul-de-sac **Villa Léandre**, with its lovingly tended plants and village-like feel, is just round to the left. Don't miss the house of Dadaist poet Tristan Tzara at no. 15 avenue Junot; built by Adolf Loos in 1926, it's a Cubist masterpiece.

Espace Montmartre-Salvador Dalí

9–11 rue Poulbot, 18ᵉ · Daily 10am–6pm, July & Aug till 8pm · €10 · ☎ 01 42 64 40 10, ⓦ daliparis.com · ⓜ Abbesses

Rue Poulbot, at the beginning of rue des Norvins, leads round to the underground **Espace Montmartre-Salvador Dalí**. It mostly shows reproduced engravings and wacky sculptures signed off by the artist. There's a certain interest in seeing this, less familiar side of his work, but it's really more of a giant souvenir shop than a museum, and lives up to the anagram that André Breton made of Dalí's name: Avida Dollars.

Place du Tertre

ⓜ Abbesses/Lamarck-Caulaincourt

If you want to preserve romantic memories of the Butte Montmartre, stop short of the top. What was once a pretty, tree-shaded square at Montmartre's crown, **place du Tertre**, has completely fallen victim to its own fame. Today, it's jammed with tour groups, souvenir stalls and street artists knocking up lurid oils of Paris landmarks from memory. Even the famous trees are mostly modern replacements for the ones planted here in the seventeenth century.

St-Pierre de Montmartre

2 rue du Mont-Cenis, 18ᵉ · Daily 8.30am–7.30pm · Free · ⓦ saintpierredemontmartre.net · ⓜ Abbesses/Lamarck-Caulaincourt

The **church of St-Pierre**, between place du Tertre and the Sacré-Coeur, offers sanctuary from the tourist bustle. It once served a Benedictine convent which occupied the Butte Montmartre from the twelfth century onwards, and now rivals St-Germain-des-Prés for the title of oldest church in Paris. Though much altered, with modern stained glass by

Max Ingrand throughout, it still retains its Romanesque and early Gothic structures. More ancient still are four columns inside the church, two by the west door and two in the choir; they probably date from a Roman shrine that stood on the hill, though their capitals were carved in Merovingian times.

Sacré-Coeur

Church Daily 6.45am–10.30pm • Free **Tower access** Daily 9.30am–6.45pm, June–Aug till 8pm, Nov–March till 5pm • €5 • Ⓜ Abbesses/Anvers

Parisian poet Jacques Roubaud compared the **Sacré-Coeur** to a big baby's bottle for the angels to suck. Certainly, it's a sickly sweet confection of French and Byzantine architecture, yet its pimply tower and white ice-cream dome has somehow become an essential part of the Paris skyline. The site has been sacred since the Romans venerated Mars and Mercury here, but today's temple dates from the 1870s, after the Catholic Church raised a public subscription to atone for the "crimes" of the Commune (see box below). The thwarted opposition, which included Clemenceau, eventually got its revenge by naming the space at the foot of the monumental staircase **square Willette**, after the local artist who turned out on inauguration day to shout "Long live the devil!"

The interior is gloomily neo-Byzantine, and apart from its carillon of bells – the largest bell in France, at 19 tonnes, swings here – and its collection of holy relics from all over France, the only exciting thing about the Sacré-Coeur is the **view from the top**. The gateway to the stairs – with 300 steps, it's a steep and claustrophobic climb – is

---

THE PARIS COMMUNE

12

In March 1871, **Montmartre** saw the first sparks fly in what would become the great conflagration of the **Paris Commune**. After Napoléon III's disastrous campaign against the Prussians in the summer of 1870, and the declaration of the Third Republic in September of the same year, Paris finally fell to the Prussian army on January 28, 1871, after a four-month siege. Peace terms were agreed by the end of February, and the Prussians withdrew, leaving the new Republic in the hands of a shaky conservative administration. Paris's situation was least secure of all, as the city's workers – and their armed representatives in the National Guard – had been disenfranchised by the February settlement, and were not inclined to respect it. The new Prime Minister, **Adolphe Thiers**, dispatched a body of regular troops under General Lecomte to take possession of 170 guns which the National Guard controlled on the high ground of the Butte Montmartre. Although the troops seized the guns easily in the darkness before dawn, they had failed to bring any horses to tow them away. That gave the revolutionary Louise Michel time to raise the alarm.

An angry crowd of workers and National Guard members quickly gathered. They persuaded the troops to take no action and arrested General Lecomte, along with another general, Clément Thomas, who was notorious for the part he had played in the brutal repression of the 1848 republican uprising. The two generals were shot and mutilated in the garden of no. 36 rue du Chevalier-de-la-Barre, behind the Sacré-Coeur. Across the city, soldiers and National Guard members joined the rebellion, and, by the following morning, a panicking government had decamped to Versailles, leaving the Hôtel de Ville and the whole of the city in the hands of the National Guard. The rebels quickly proclaimed a **revolutionary Commune**, decreeing the separation of church and state, the enfranchisement of women and numerous measures to protect workers' rights.

By the beginning of April, the Communards were under attack from Thiers' army, its numbers newly swelled by prisoners of war helpfully released by the Prussians. Isolated and ill equipped, they didn't stand a chance. In the notorious **semaine sanglante**, of May 21–28, something like 25,000 Communards died – no one knows the exact figure – with some 10,000 executed or deported. The cost to Paris was also severe; the Hôtel de Ville and Tuileries palace (see box, p.68) were reduced to smouldering ashes. Today the Communards are commemorated in Père Lachaise cemetery (see p.207), and in the enduringly martial spirit of the French Left; since 1871, not to be revolutionary has somehow seemed a betrayal of the dead.

under the church's west flank; you'll need change for the automatic ticket machine by the turnstile. Once at the top, you're almost as high as the Eiffel Tower, and you can see the layout of the whole city – a wide, flat basin ringed by low hills, with stands of high-rise blocks in the corners.

Montmartre vineyard

Rue des Saules, 18ᵉ • ⓦ fetedesvendangesdemontmartre.com • ⓜ Lamarck-Caulaincourt

Rue des Saules tips steeply down the northern slopes of the Butte past the terraces of the tiny **Montmartre vineyard**, whose annual harvest yields an extraordinary 1500-odd bottles of wine. Sadly, the actual pressing is no longer down on place du Tertre, as it was in the 1940s; it's now done in a basement of the arrondissement's own town hall. The result is pretty rough, yet few wine buffs would be hard-hearted enough to resist having at least one bottle in the cellar. A raucously celebrated festival marks the *vendange*, or wine harvest, on the first weekend of October. It's really a celebration of Montmartre's left-wing, separatist spirit, and now includes the riotously romantic Cérémonie des Non-Demandés en Mariage, at which ardently secular, republican couples publicly state that they "have the honour not to ask your hand in marriage" – as the singer Georges Brassens famously put it.

The picturesque house standing opposite the lowest corner of the vineyard is the cabaret club **Au Lapin Agile**, made famous by the Montmartre artists who drank there in the 1900s – among them Picasso, whose fifty-million-dollar self-portrait as a harlequin is set inside. The "nimble rabbit" is still alive today and still serving up classic French *chanson* (see p.306).

Musée de Montmartre

12 rue Cortot, 18ᵉ • Tues–Sun 11am–6pm • €8 • ☏ 01 49 25 89 37, ⓦ museedemontmartre.fr • ⓜ Lamarck-Caulaincourt

The **Musée de Montmartre** occupies an elegant old house on rue Cortot that is particularly rich in artistic associations: it was home, at various times, to Auguste Renoir, Raoul Dufy, and Suzanne Valadon and her troubled son Maurice Utrillo. Its low-key exhibits attempt to re-create the atmosphere of Montmartre's heyday via a selection of Toulouse-Lautrec posters, mock-ups of period rooms and painted impressions of how the Butte once looked. It's not terribly gripping, but the museum does offer a fine view from the back over the hilly northern reaches of the city and the vineyard, and the shop usually has a few bottles of Montmartre wine.

The street outside the museum is overlooked by a lighthouse-like white water-tower, which is one of the landmarks of the city's skyline. Nearby, Berlioz lived with his English wife in the corner house on the steps of rue du Mont-Cenis, from where there's a breathtaking view northwards to the Stade de France, along the canyon of the steps. This is perfect, sepia-tinged, romantic Montmartre – a double handrail runs down the centre, with the lampposts between – and the streets below are among the quietest and least touristy in Montmartre.

The eastern slopes of the Butte

ⓜ Abbesses/Château-Rouge

To the south and east of the Sacré-Coeur, the slopes of the Butte drop steeply down towards boulevard Barbès and the Goutte d'Or quarter. Directly below are the gardens of square Willette, milling with tourists. To avoid the crowds, make for the quiet gardens to the north of the Sacré-Coeur, the **Parc de la Turlure**, and descend via rue Chevalier de la Barre, a pretty little road whose steep stairs, towards the top, are adorned with an art installation made up of LED lights. Alternatively, make your way down the steps of rue Utrillo, passing the pleasant café, *L'Eté en Pente Douce* (see p.287), which has outdoor tables. From here, more steps lead down along the edge of the gardens to rue Ronsard, where you can see the (sealed) entrances to the quarries where the original plaster of Paris was extracted.

Halle St-Pierre

2 rue Ronsard, 18e • Daily 10am–6pm • €7.50 • ⓦ hallesaintpierre.org • Ⓜ Anvers

Once a workaday market building, the pavillion-like **Halle St-Pierre** is now an exhibition space dedicated to Art Brut, or works by artists – often autodidacts – that mainstream galleries won't touch. The biannual exhibitions range from the visionary to the indigestible; a recent exhibitor was H.R. Giger, the artist behind the film *Alien*. The Halle is energetically run by a charitable association, with evening concerts (mostly classical, mostly on Thursdays), kids' workshops, book readings and a café with good cakes and teas. All around the Halle are bustling shops selling cheap fabrics by the metre. From here it's a short walk to the busy, multi-ethnic crossroads around Barbès-Rochechouart métro station. Contraband cigarettes are sold under the iron viaduct here, among other scams, while the streets around are lined with takeway couscous joints.

Montmartre cemetery

Entrance on avenue Rachel, 18e, underneath the bridge section of rue Caulaincourt • March 16–Nov 5 Mon–Fri 8am–6pm, Sat 8.30am–6pm, Sun 9am–6pm; Nov 6–March 15 closes 5.30pm • Free • Ⓜ Blanche/Place-de-Clichy

West of the Butte, near the beginning of rue Caulaincourt in place Clichy, lies the **Montmartre cemetery**. Tucked down below street level in the hollow of an old quarry, it's a tangle of trees and funerary stone, more intimate and less melancholy than Père-Lachaise or Montparnasse. A few metres inside the gates, watch out for the antique cast-iron poor-box (*Tronc pour les Pauvres*).

The illustrious dead at rest here include Stendhal, Berlioz, Degas, Feydeau, Offenbach, Nijinsky and François Truffaut, as well as La Goulue, the dancer at the Moulin Rouge immortalized by Toulouse-Lautrec. Emile Zola's grave stands beside the roundabout, near the entrance, though his actual remains have been transferred to the Panthéon (see p.124). In division 15, left of the entrance, lies Alphonsine Plessis, the real-life model for the consumptive courtesan Marguerite, the "Dame aux Camélias" of Alexander Dumas' novel and, later, the original "Traviata". Liszt, who became her lover after Dumas, called her "the most absolute incarnation of Woman who has ever existed". Dumas himself lies on the other side of the cemetery, in division 21. Nearby, in division 22, beside avenue Samson, Vaslav Nijinsky's tomb is adorned with a bronze statue of the dancer in his famous role as the Harlequin in Diaghilev's production of *Carnaval*. Tucked away behind him, the tomb of the 1830s ballerina Marie Taglioni is usually strewn with rotting ballet shoes, left there by dancers from the Paris ballet in honour of the first woman to dance on pointe. A large Jewish section lies by the east wall.

12

The 9^e

Immediately south of Montmartre, the **9e (neuvième) arrondissement** isn't much visited by tourists. Yet lurking inside the limits of the broad east–west boulevards that frame it is a handsome, distinctly urban residential district with a powerful nineteenth-century atmosphere, especially around **place St-Georges**. The once-seedy northern fringe has now been rebranded as the trendy SoPi, or "South of Pigalle" district; it still has its gritty elements, though bohemian shops and bars are moving in, especially in the streets around rue des Martyrs. The wealthier, more businesslike, southernmost strip of the arrondissement, next to the Opéra and Grands Boulevards, is covered in Chapter 4.

Blanche and Pigalle

From place de Clichy in the west to Barbès-Rochechouart métro in the east, the hill of Montmartre is underlined by the sleazy **boulevards de Clichy** and **de Rochechouart**. The pedestrianized centre of the boulevards was occupied by dodgem cars and other tacky sideshows for most of the twentieth century, but Montmartre's upward mobility is now dragging its shabby hem along with it. The traffic-choked roads have now been "civilized", as the Paris planners put it, with bus and cycle lanes, and lots more greenery. It remains to be seen whether or not they will be recolonized by the sophisticated strollers, or *flâneurs*, that defined them in the late nineteenth century. At the eastern **Barbès** end, where the métro clatters by on iron trestles, the crowds teem round the Tati department store, the cheapest in the city, while the pavements are thick with Arab and African street vendors hawking watches, trinkets and textiles.

At the **place de Clichy** end, tour buses from all over Europe feed their contents into massive hotels. In the middle, between **place Blanche** and **place Pigalle**, sex shows, sex shops and prostitutes – male and female – vie for the custom of *solitaires* and couples alike. It's an area in which respectability and sleaze rub very close shoulders. In the adjacent streets – rues de Douai, Victor-Massé and Houdon – specialist music and hi-fi shops jostle with exploitative "hostess" clubs, and some of the city's trendiest shops and bars. At the more respectable end of this zone is rue des Martyrs; it's one of Paris's most enjoyable gastro-streets, lined with fancy food and flower shops as it descends from the Butte towards the more respectable districts to the south.

Musée de l'Erotisme

72 bd de Clichy, 18e • Daily 10am–2am • €8 • Ⓦ musee-erotisme.com • Ⓜ Blanche

Perfectly placed among all the sex shops and shows of Pigalle is the **Musée de l'Erotisme**. It's more sincere than smutty: the ground floor and first floor are awash with phalluses, fertility symbols and intertwined figurines from all over Asia, Africa and pre-Columbian Latin America, while the European pieces tend to the satirical, with lots of naughty nuns and priests caught in compromising situations. There's also plentiful cabaret memorabilia and screens showing vintage pornography. The upper floors are devoted to generally excellent temporary exhibitions on themes such as Paris's historic *maisons closes*, or brothels. A few steps west, the photogenic **Moulin Rouge** still thrives on place Blanche. Once Toulouse-Lautrec's inspiration, it's now a shadow of its former self (see box below).

Avenue Frochot

Ⓜ Blanche

One of the city's most elegant *villas* (private streets), **avenue Frochot**, leads off place Pigalle itself. Ordinary mortals are kept out by a digicoded gate, so you'll never get to

---

PARIS CABARETS

For many foreigners, entertainment in Paris is still synonymous with cabaret, especially that mythical name, Pigalle's **Moulin Rouge**, at 82 boulevard de Clichy (☎01 53 09 82 82, Ⓦ moulinrouge.fr). Unlike the **Folies Bergère**, further south at 32 rue Richer (☎08 92 68 16 50, Ⓦ foliesbergere.com), which has gone for a mixed programme of music and magic shows, the *Moulin Rouge* still trades on its bare-breasted, cancanning "Doriss Girls". The show is as glitzy and kitsch as you'd expect, full of high-tech special effects and nodding feathers, and audiences are mainly made up of package tourists whose deal includes a ticket (otherwise around €100, or from €150 with dinner). For similar alternatives, try the **Lido** (116bis av des Champs-Elysées, 8e; ☎01 40 76 56 10, Ⓦ lido.fr), best known for its "Bluebell Girls" – and, these days, its "Lido Boys" too – and its high-tech, Vegas-style shows. At the **Crazy Horse** (12 av George V, 8e; ☎01 47 23 32 32, Ⓦ lecrazyhorseparis.com), performances are relatively arty – and nude.

The crowds are thinner at the pair of tiny **transvestite cabarets** on rue des Martyrs, just up from Pigalle métro. At its best, *Chez Michou*, at no. 80 (☎01 46 06 16 04, Ⓦ michou.fr), is like a scene from an Almodóvar film, with singing transvestites masquerading as various female celebrities, but you'll need to know French pop culture to get much out of it. *Chez Madame Arthur*, at no. 75bis (☎01 42 54 15 92), is similar. Both can be outrageously camp good fun, or rather desperate on a quiet night, and your bill is likely to be larger than you might expect; dinner menus (not obligatory) start at around €100.

see Jean Renoir's house at no. 7. Still, the facade of the house beside the gate at the south end is worth the detour: it's a giant, Art Deco, stained-glass take on Hokusai's famous print of Mount Fuji being engulfed by a tidal wave. It owes its existence to a cabaret that stood here in the 1920s, Le Shangaï, and looks particularly splendid at dusk, when it's lit from behind.

Place St-Georges

Ⓜ St Georges

The handsome centrepiece of the **9ᵉ** is the circular **place St-Georges**. The central fountain – still with its horse trough – is topped by a bust of Paul Gavarni, a nineteenth-century cartoonist who made a speciality of lampooning the mistresses that were *de rigueur* for bourgeois males of the time. This was the mistresses' quarter – they were known as *lorettes*, after the nearby church of **Notre-Dame de Lorette**, built in the 1820s in the Neoclassical style. On the east side of place St-Georges, the **Hôtel de la Païva** was built in the 1840s in an extravagant French Renaissance style for Thérèse Lachman, a famous Second Empire courtesan who married a Marquis. On the west side, the **Hôtel Thiers** was destroyed by the Communards in 1871 but quickly rebuilt; it now houses the Dosne-Thiers foundation, with a huge library specializing in nineteenth-century French history.

The Nouvelle Athènes

Ⓜ St-Georges

The heart of the 9ᵉ arrondissement was first developed in the early nineteenth century as a fashionable suburb. It was soon dubbed the **Nouvelle Athènes**, or New Athens, after the Romantic artists and writers who came to live here made it the centre of a minor artistic boom. **Place Toudouze** and **rues Clauzel**, **Milton** and **Rodier** are worth wandering along for their elegantly ornamented facades. A short distance southwest of St-Georges, a passageway off rue Taitbout leads through to the serene **square d'Orléans**, an 1829 development which aped Regency London and attracted Chopin, Alexandre Dumas *fils* and George Sand as early residents. Some of the fine townhouses of the original Nouvelle Athènes scheme can still be spotted just to the west, along **rue de la Tour des Dames**.

Sainte-Trinité

Ⓜ Trinité d'Estienne d'Orves

As it cuts its bustling way towards the relatively down-at-heel commuter hub of the Gare St-Lazare, **rue St-Lazare** passes the bulbous church of **La Sainte-Trinité**. Its single, over-size French Renaissance-style tower is its most exciting feature. Inside, the vast space under the barrel vault feels cold and sterile – hard to imagine that the deeply spiritual composer Olivier Messiaen was organist here for the best part of half a century.

Musée de la Vie Romantique

16 rue Chaptal, 9ᵉ • Daily except Mon 10am–6pm, closed public hols • Entry price varies during exhibitions, otherwise free • ☏ 01 55 31 95 67 • Ⓜ St-Georges/Blanche/Pigalle

To get the full flavour of the neuvième's nineteenth-century heyday, make for the **Musée de la Vie Romantique** in the house of the painter Ary Scheffer. He was art tutor to Louis-Philippe's children (and upstairs are a number of his hideously sentimental aristocratic portraits) but he is more renowned today for his friendships with the writer George Sand and her lover, Frédéric Chopin, who used to give private, improvised concerts here. The shuttered building, standing at the end of a private alley, is a delightful surprise, with its tree-shaded, courtyard rose garden where you can take tea on sunny days. The interior preserves the rich colours of a typical bourgeois home of the nineteenth century. The ground floor displays fine furnishings and objets once owned by George Sand – who you might think of as France's George Eliot, though she was still more unconventional, what with her cross-dressing and serial

12

taking of lovers. There are family portraits, jewels, locks of hair and a cast of Chopin's exquisite left hand.

Musée Moreau

Rue de la Rochefoucauld, 9ᵉ • Daily except Tues 10am–12.45pm & 2–5.15pm • €5 • ☎ 01 48 74 38 50, ⊛ www.musee-moreau.fr • Ⓜ St-Georges/Blanche/Pigalle

The design of the eccentric little **Musée Gustave Moreau** was conceived by the artist himself, to be carved out of the house he shared with his parents for many years, and you can visit their tiny, stuffy apartment rooms, crammed with furniture and trinkets. His fantastical Symbolist paintings get a whole lot more room – two huge, studio-like spaces connected by a beautiful spiral staircase – but the effect is no less cluttered. Moreau's canvases hang cheek-by-jowl, every surface crawling with figures and decorative swirls – literally crawling in the case of *The Daughters of Thespius* – or alive with deep colours and provocative symbolism, as in the museum's *pièce de résistance*, *Jupiter and Semele*. For all the rampantly decadent symbolism, some viewers haven't been quite convinced that he wasn't more than an oddball pedant. Degas, for one, commented that Moreau was "a hermit who knows the train timetable".

The 10ᵉ and the Goutte d'Or

The rue du Faubourg-Poissonnière separates the 9ᵉ from its grittier twin, the **10ᵉ (dixième) arrondissement**. At its upper end the **northern stations** dominate, while to the south lies the gritty but fascinating quarter of the **faubourgs St-Denis** and **St-Martin**. In the far north, just inside the 18ᵉ, east of Montmartre, lies the African quarter of the **Goutte d'Or**. The prettier eastern end of the arrondissement, on the far side of the Canal St-Martin, is covered in Chapter 13.

The northern stations

Ⓜ Gare du Nord/Gare de l'Est

The life of the 10ᵉ is coloured by the presence of the big **northern stations**. Most travellers scarcely give them a glance, intent on hurrying off to more salubrious parts of the city, but the station buildings are in fact very beautiful, closer to Classical orangeries in style than icons of the industrial age. The **Gare du Nord** (serving all places north, including the high-speed train lines to Germany and London) was built by the architect Hittorff in the early 1860s, and is aggressively dominated by its three giant arches, crowned by eight statues representing the original terminus towns, from Amsterdam and Berlin to Vienna and Warsaw. Facing the boulevard de Strasbourg, the slightly earlier **Gare de l'Est** (serving northeastern and eastern France, and Eastern Europe) is more delicate, though when its central arch was open to the elements, as it was when originally built, the steam and smoke billowing out would have had a powerful effect.

The area around the stations is mostly gritty and unappealing. Beside the Gare de l'Est, however, a high wall encloses the gardens of **square Villemin** (entrance on rue des Récollets and avenue de Verdun), which provides a welcome green haven. The garden once belonged to a convent, the **Couvent des Récollets**, one much-restored, seventeenth-century wing of which still stands on rue du Faubourg-St-Martin. Further east again, the **Canal St-Martin** (see p.198) is an even more tranquil place to escape the city hustle. Just south of the Gare de l'Est, the **church of St-Laurent** has a handsome choir dating from the fifteenth century. Thanks to Haussmann, who thought its original facade irritatingly off-centre, the church's Gothic-looking west front actually dates from the same era as the Gare du Nord.

The faubourgs

The southern end of the 10ᵉ arrondissement is its liveliest, a poor but vibrant quarter that has become home to Indian, black African and Near Eastern communities as well as, in recent years, a small vanguard of young, trendy Parisians. The two main thoroughfares, the rue du Faubourg-St-Denis and rue du Faubourg-St-Martin, bear the names of the **faubourgs**, or suburbs, that once stood just outside the town walls. For once, you can still get a vivid sense of the old city limits, as two triumphal arches stand marooned by traffic at either end of the boulevard St-Denis. The **Porte St-Denis** was erected in 1672 to celebrate Louis XIV's victories on the Rhine – below the giant letters spelling out Ludovico Magno, or "Louis the Great", are the bas-reliefs *The Crossing of the Rhine* (on the south side) and *The Capture of Maastricht* (on the north). With France's

THE 10e & GOUTTE D'OR

RESTAURANTS
Chez Casimir	1
Flo	4
Julien	7
Le Martel	3
Pooja	5
Zerda Café	8

CAFÉS & WINE BARS
| L'Enchotte | 2 |
| Le Réveil du Dixième | 6 |

SHOPS
| Jamin-Puech | 2 |
| Tessa Delpech | 1 |

0   200
metres

BARS & LIVE MUSIC
Chez Jeannette	4
New Morning	3
Olympic Café	1
Le Pompon	2

ACCOMMODATION
Hôtel de Lille	2
Mercure Paris	
Terminus Nord	1

northern frontier secured, Louis ordered Charles V's city walls to be demolished and replaced by leafy promenades; they became known as the *boulevards* after the Germanic word for an earth rampart, a *bulwark*. Some 200m east, the more graceful **Porte St-Martin** was built two years after its sibling, in celebration of further victories in Limburg and Besançon. Louis planned a veritable parade of these arches, but the military misadventures of the latter part of his reign were hardly worth celebrating.

Musée de l'Eventail

2 bd de Strasbourg, 10ᵉ • Mon–Wed 2–6pm; closed Aug • €6 • ☎ 01 42 08 90 20, Ⓦ annehoguet.fr/musee • Ⓜ Strasbourg-St-Denis

The fascination of the **Musée de l'Eventail** is that it's more working atelier than museum. In a small suite of period rooms on the first floor of an ordinary Haussmann building, Anne Hoguet continues the family tradition of fan-making, working almost exclusively on commission for customers from the worlds of haute couture or theatre. There is always an exhibition drawing on a selection of the museum's thousand-strong collection of fans, both historic – some date back to the 1720s – and contemporary. Of course, you can always commission a fan yourself, and ready-made models can be had for as little as €10.

Rue du Faubourg-St-Denis and around

At its lower end, the **rue du Faubourg-St-Denis** is full of charcuteries, butchers, greengrocers and ethnic delicatessens, as well as a number of restaurants, including the historic **brasseries** *Julien* and *Flo* (see p.291). The latter is tucked away in an attractive old stableyard, the cour des Petites-Ecuries, one of a number of hidden lanes and covered *passages* that riddle this corner of the city. The best known is the glazed-over **passage Brady**, the hub of Paris's "Little India", lined with Indian barbers', grocers' shops and restaurants. The *passage* runs through to **rue du Faubourg-St-Martin**, crossing the busy boulevard de Strasbourg and coming out just south of the impressive neo-Gothic **town hall** of the 10ᵉ arrondissement. Rue des Petites-Ecuries, one block north, is known for the large jazz and world music club, the *New Morning* (see p.306), while on the next street north again, at 18 rue de Paradis, is the magnificent mosaic and tiled facade of Monsieur Boulanger's Choisy-le-Roi **tileworks** shop; you can peer through the gate at the peacock tails and flamingos adorning the stairs and floors.

The Goutte d'Or

Ⓜ Barbès-Rochechouart/Château-Rouge

The wide, grotty boulevard de la Chapelle forms the northern boundary of the 10ᵉ arrondissement, its only beacon the gloriously delapidated **Théâtre des Bouffes du Nord** (see p.313), energetically run by British director Peter Brook from 1974 to 2011. Immediately north of the boulevard, the poetically named *quartier* of the **Goutte d'Or** stretches between boulevard Barbès and the Gare du Nord rail lines. The setting for Zola's classic novel of gritty realism, *L'Assommoir*, its name – the "Drop of Gold" – comes from a vineyard which stood here in medieval times. After World War I, when large numbers of North Africans were imported to restock the trenches, it gradually became an immigrant ghetto.

For years, the streets languished in a lamentable state of decay, but a major renovation programme has dramatically changed the area's character – rue des Gardes has even become "fashion street", lined with city hall-subsidized design boutiques. The *quartier* has changed ethnically, too, and is now predominantly the home of West African and Congolese people, rather than North Africans, and there are south-Asian, Haitian, Kurdish and other communities as well.

Marché Dejean and around

Ⓜ Château-Rouge

On the rue de la Goutte d'Or you could seek out one of the city's **Wallace fountains** (see box, p.181), on the corner with the rue de Chartres, but the main sight is a few steps north on rue Dejean, where the **Marché Dejean** (daily except Sun afternoon & Mon) thrums with shoppers, including lots of women in brightly coloured West African dress. You can pick up imported African beers and drinks and, if you're self-catering, vegetables like plantain, yam and taro root. Another more general market takes place in the mornings twice weekly (Wed & Sat) underneath the métro viaduct on the **boulevard de la Chapelle**.

Most of the *quartier*'s cafés and bars tend to be turned towards their own communities, but the *Olympic Café*, a fine bar, café-theatre and world music venue on rue Léon (see p.300), very much looks outward.

Batignolles

Ⓜ Place de Clichy/Brochant

West of Montmartre cemetery, in a district bounded by the St-Lazare train lines, marshalling yards and avenue de Clichy, lies the "village" of **Batignolles** – sufficiently

● ACCOMMODATION	
Hôtel Eldorado	1

● CAFÉS & RESTAURANTS	
Le Bistrot des Dames	2
Fuxia	1
Wepler	3

● BAR	
Cyrano	1

conscious of its uniqueness to have formed an association for the preservation of its *caractère villageois*. Its heart is the attractive **place du Dr Félix Lobligeois,** framing the elegant Neoclassical church of **Ste-Marie-des-Batignolles** – worth a peek inside if only for the extraordinary trompe l'oeil Assumption scene behind the altar, in which Mary apparently rockets up through the ceiling. On the corners of the *place*, a handful of modern bars and restaurants attracts the young, bourgeois parents of the neighbourhood while, behind, the green **square des Batignolles** is filled with pushchairs and handsome old plane trees. The former can now trundle just northwest towards the newly extended **Parc Clichy-Batignolles,** an ecologically designed public park created on land recovered from the railway.

The poet Verlaine was brought up on the **rue des Batignolles**, which runs southeast past the *mairie* of the 17ᵉ arrondissement to the junction with **rue des Dames**. This narrow but lively thoroughfare winds its way east from the flamboyant food and clothes market of the **rue de Lévis** (daily except Mon), beside the Villiers métro stop, to the avenue de Clichy. Just below lies the traffic- and neon-filled roundabout of the **place de Clichy,** dominated by its Pathé cinema and classic old brasserie, *Wepler* (see p.292). Northeast of Ste-Marie-des-Batignolles, the long **rue des Moines** runs past a bustling and covered market, the **Marché des Batignolles,** into an increasingly working-class area.

The pet cemetery

4 Pont de Clichy, Asnières-sur-Seine • Daily except Mon: mid-March to mid-Oct 10am–6pm; rest of year till 4.30pm • €3.50 • ⓘ 01 40 86 21 11, Ⓦ asnieres-sur-seine.fr • Ⓜ Mairie-de-Clichy

Right at the frontier of the 17ᵉ, under the *périphérique*, lies the little-visited **Cimetière des Batignolles,** with the graves of André Breton, Verlaine and Blaise Cendrars (ⓂPorte-de-Clichy). A great deal more curious is the **Cimetière des Chiens,** a **pet cemetery** hidden away on a former islet that is now attached to the north bank of the Seine at Asnières. It's outside the city proper but accessible on métro line 13 to Mairie-de-Clichy, from where it's about fifteen minutes' walk due north along rue Martre, then left at the far end of the Pont de Clichy. Most of the cemetery's tiny graves, some going back as far as 1900, belong to beloved pets, and come adorned with photos, plastic flowers and visiting cats from the adjacent sanctuary. The inscriptions are telling: "26 years of complicity and shared tenderness"; "Cheated by people; by my dog – NEVER". Some of the more exotic tombs are dedicated to the 1920 Grand National winner, a St Bernard named Barry who saved the lives of snow-disoriented travellers over forty years of service, and that Hollywood megastar of the 1920s – the German shepherd Rin Tin Tin.

Eastern Paris

The Canal St-Martin, running from Bastille in the south to the place de la Bataille de Stalingrad in the north, effectively marks the boundary between central and eastern Paris. The area east of the canal is traditionally the home of the working classes, although redevelopment has inevitably shifted older populations further out into the suburbs. Today, the stretch along the canal is a much sought-after, hip neighbourhood. Further east, in Ménilmontant and Belleville, rents remain relatively low, attracting students and artists who have created a thriving alternative scene. These districts have also been settled by sizeable ethnic populations, especially North Africans, Malians, Turks, Chinese and people from the former Yugoslavia, making it one of the most diverse and cosmopolitan areas of the city.

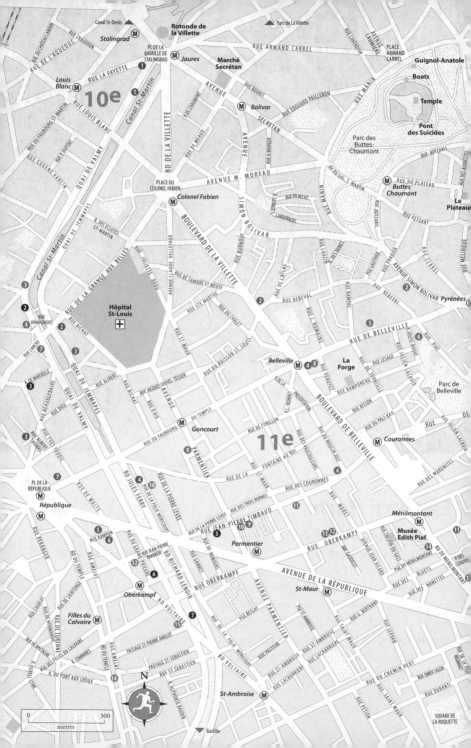

CANAL ST-MARTIN, MENILMONTANT & BELLEVILLE

CAFÉS & WINE BARS
Les 400 Coups	1
L'Atmosphère	3
Chez Prune	7
Le Faitout	2
Aux Folies	8
La Mère Lachaise	13

RESTAURANTS
L'Auberge Pyrénées Cévennes	10
Le Baratin	6
Le Châteaubriand	9
Chez Imogène	12
Ile de Gorée	11
Lao Siam	5
Le Repaire de Cartouche	14
Restaurant de Bourgogne	4

SHOPS
Antoine et Lili	2
Attica	7
Ganachaud	4
Lulu Berlu	6
Du Pain et Des Idées	3
La Petite Maison dans la Villette	1
Thé-Troc	5

ACCOMMODATION
D'Artagnan	7
Le Citizen Hôtel	2
Le Général Hôtel	5
Jules Ferry	4
Hôtel de Nevers	6
Hôtel du Nord	3
Peace and Love Hostel	1

BARS, CLUBS & LIVE MUSIC
L'Alimentation Générale	9
L'Autre Café	10
Babel Café	14
Bataclan	15
La Bellevilloise	8
Café Charbon	13
Café Chéri(e)	2
Le Cannibale	6
Favela Chic	7
Aux Folies	4
Le Jemmapes	3
Lou Pascalou	11
Maroquinerie	5
Le Nouveau Casino	12
Point Ephémère	1

13

Earlier settlers were the French rural poor, who moved into the old villages of Belleville, Ménilmontant and Charonne during the Industrial Revolution in the mid-nineteenth century. These populations supplied the people-power for the many insurrections in the nineteenth century, including the short-lived Commune of 1871, with the centre and west battling to preserve the status quo against the oppressed, radical east. Indeed, for much of the nineteenth century, the establishment feared nothing more than the "descente de Belleville" – the descent of the mob from the heights of Belleville. It was in order to contain this threat that so much of the Canal St-Martin, a natural line of defence, was covered over by Baron Haussmann in 1860.

Today, only a few reminders of these turbulent times survive, such as the Mur des Fédérés in **Père-Lachaise cemetery** recording the deaths of 147 Communards, and a few streets bearing the names of popular leaders. Some of the old working-class character of the district lives on in places: narrow streets and artisans' houses survive in Belleville, Ménilmontant and off the Canal St-Martin. Much of the area, however, has undergone redevelopment over the last few decades. Crumbling, dank and insanitary houses were replaced by shelving-unit apartment blocks in the 1960s and 1970s, giving way in recent years to more imaginative and attractive constructions. The biggest development has been the conversion of the old meat-market area of **La Villette** in the 1980s into a futuristic science museum and park.

The Canal St-Martin and around

Completed in 1825, the **Canal St-Martin** was built so that river traffic could shortcut the great western loop of the Seine around Paris. As it happened, it also turned out to be a splendid natural defence for the rebellious quarters of eastern Paris: the canal was spanned by six swing-bridges, which could easily be drawn up to halt the advance of government troops. Napoléon III's solution was simply to cover over the lower stretch in the latter half of the nineteenth century; the canal now runs underground at the Bastille, emerging after 2.5km near the rue du Faubourg-du-Temple, and continuing up to the **place de la Bataille de Stalingrad**.

The southern stretch of the Canal St-Martin

Ⓜ Jacques-Bonsergent

The northern reaches of the exposed canal still have a slightly industrial feel, but the southern part, along the **quai de Jemmapes** and **quai de Valmy**, has a great deal of charm, with plane trees lining the cobbled *quais*, and elegant high-arched footbridges punctuating the spaces between the locks, from where you can still watch the odd barge slowly rising or sinking to the next level. Lining this stretch are cool cafés, such as *Chez Prune* (see p.292), and stylish boutiques, the most eye-catching of which is Antoine et Lili (see p.326), with its candy-coloured frontages. Inevitably, having acquired a certain cachet, the district has attracted property developers, and bland apartment blocks have elbowed in among the traditional, mid-nineteenth-century residences. One of the older buildings, at 102 quai de Jemmapes, is the **Hôtel du Nord**, so named because the barges that once plied the canal came from the north. Made famous by Marcel Carné's film of the same name, starring Arletty and Jean Gabin, it now thrives as a bar-restaurant. Sunday is one of the best days to come for a wander, as

---

CANAL BOAT TRIPS

A leisurely way of seeing the Canal St-Martin is to take a boat trip between the Port de l'Arsenal, opposite 50 boulevard de la Bastille, 12ᵉ (Ⓜ Bastille), and the Bassin de la Villette, 13 quai de la Loire, 19ᵉ (Ⓜ Jaurès), north of the Canal St-Martin. **Paris Canal** (see p.341) also runs trips between the Musée d'Orsay, quai Anatole-France, 7ᵉ (RER Musée d'Orsay) and the Parc de la Villette (Ⓜ Porte-de-Pantin).

13

THE MONTFAUCON GALLOWS

Long ago, **rue de la Grange-aux-Belles**, on the north side of the Hôpital St-Louis, was a dusty track leading uphill, past fields, en route to Germany. Where no. 53 now stands, a path led to the top of a small hillock. Here, in 1325, on the king's orders, an enormous **gallows** was built, consisting of a plinth 6m high, on which stood sixteen stone pillars each 10m high. These were joined by chains, from which executed malefactors were hanged in clusters. They were left there until they disintegrated, by way of example, and they stank so badly that when the wind blew from the northeast they reached the nostrils of the still far-off city. The practice continued until the seventeenth century. Bones and other remains from the pit into which they were thrown were found during the building of a garage in 1954.

the *quais* are closed to traffic and given over to rollerbladers and cyclists. It's especially lively in summer when people hang out along the canal's edge and on the café terraces.

Hôpital St-Louis and around

Ⓜ Jacques-Bonsergent/Goncourt

Some of the side streets off the canal are worth exploring, such as **rue des Vinaigriers**, a little south of the **square Villemin gardens**, where a Second Empire shop front bears fluted wooden pilasters crowned with capitals of grapes and a gilded Bacchus. At no. 35, Poursin has been making brass buckles and harnesses for horses since 1830 and preserves its old wooden interior.

Just across the canal from rue des Vinaigriers is one of the finest buildings in Paris, the early seventeenth-century **Hôpital St-Louis**, built in the same style as the elegant place des Vosges in the Marais. Although it still functions as a hospital, you can walk into its quiet central courtyard and admire the elegant brick-and-stone facades and steep-pitched roofs that once sheltered Paris's plague victims – the original purpose for which it was built.

Boulevard Richard-Lenoir

Ⓜ Bastille/Breguet-Sabin/Richard-Lenoir

The wide boulevard built over the covered section of the canal, boulevard **Richard-Lenoir**, is attractively landscaped all down its centre, dotted with arched footbridges reminding you of the water flowing underground. It's well worth a wander on Thursday and Sunday mornings in particular, when a big traditional **food market**, known for its choice range of regional produce, sets up on the lower stretch near the place de la Bastille.

The Rotonde and around

Ⓜ Stalingrad/Jaurès

The Canal St-Martin goes underground at the busy **place de la Bataille de Stalingrad**, dominated by the Neoclassical **Rotonde de la Villette**, a handsome stone rotunda fronted with a portico, inspired by Palladio's Villa La Rotonda in Vicenza. This was one of the toll houses designed by the architect Ledoux as part of Louis XVI's scheme to tax all goods entering the city. At that time, every road out of Paris had a customs post, or *barrière*, linked by a 6m-high wall, known as "Le Mur des Fermiers-Généraux" – a major irritant in the run-up to the Revolution. Cleaned and restored, the *rotonde* is used for occasional exhibitions and has a restaurant. Backing the toll house is an elegant aerial stretch of métro, supported by Neoclassical iron and stone pillars. The area has a slightly dodgy reputation at night, as it's a known haunt of drug dealers.

Bassin de la Villette

Ⓜ Stalingrad/Riquet/Laumière

Beyond the Rotonde de la Villette the canal widens out into the **Bassin de la Villette**, built in 1808. The recobbled docks area bears few traces of its days as France's premier

13

port, its dockside buildings now offering **canal boat trips** (see p.340) and housing a multiplex cinema, the **MK2** (see p.309), which has screens on both banks, linked by shuttle boat. On Sundays and public holidays people stroll along the *quais*, jog, cycle, play boules, fish or take a rowing boat out in the dock. In August, as part of the Paris Plage scheme (see p.320), you can rent canoes and pedaloes. The area has benefited from a clean-up and is rapidly gentrifying, with new bars, restaurants and the hip *St Christopher's* hostel (see p.263), housed in a converted boat hangar, all opening recently, though it retains a slightly industrial, rough-around-the-edges feel.

At rue de Crimée a hydraulic lift bridge with huge pulleys, rather fun to watch in action, marks the end of the dock and the beginning of the Canal de l'Ourcq, built in 1802 to bring drinking water to Parisians and to link two branches of the Seine. If you keep to the south bank on quai de la Marne, you can cross directly into the Parc de la Villette.

Le Centquatre

104 rue d'Aubervilliers, 19ᵉ • Tues–Sat 11am–8pm, Sun 11am–7pm • Free entry to the main hall • ☎ 01 53 35 50 00, ⊕ 104.fr • Ⓜ Riquet

West of the basin de la Villette, in one of the poorest parts of the 19ᵉ, a former grand nineteenth-century funeral parlour has been converted into a huge arts centre, with two performance spaces and numerous artists' studios covering some 39,000 square

metres. Its main performance space, the central *nef curial*, is an impressive hall, with high glass roof, grey-painted ironwork and exposed brick walls, though it can feel somewhat chilly and forlorn on a quiet weekday. The centre has taken a while to find its feet; its original lofty aim of being a place of exchange between artists and the public seems to have been quietly laid to rest, and it now has a dynamic new director, José Manuel Gonçalvès, whose programme includes exhibitions and installations, dance (Maguy Marin was here recently) and theatre, with an emphasis on presenting "avant-premières" of new plays and extended runs of sell-out performances from other theatres. The complex also houses a good bookshop, charity and fair-trade shops, a café and first-rate restaurant (*Les Grandes Tables du 104*), and La Maison des Petits, a supervised play area for 0- to 5-year-olds with plenty of activities such as painting and crafts. Numbers are limited to thirty at a time, so there can be a wait to get in.

Parc de la Villette

ⓦ villette.com • Ⓜ Porte-de-la-Villette/Porte-de-Pantin

All the meat for Paris used to come from the slaughterhouses in **La Villette**, an old village that was annexed to the city in the mid-nineteenth century. Slaughtering and butchering, and industries based on the meat markets' by-products, provided plenty of jobs for its dense population, whose recreation time was spent betting on cockfights, skating or swimming, and eating in the numerous local restaurants famed for their fresh meat. In the 1960s, vast sums of money were spent building a huge new abattoir. Yet, just as it neared completion, the emergence of new refrigeration techniques rendered the centralized meat industry redundant. The only solution was to switch course entirely; billions continued to be poured into La Villette in the 1980s, with the revised aim of creating a mind-blowing **music, art and science complex**.

The end result, the **Parc de la Villette**, which opened in 1986, is enormous in scope and volume. There's so much going on here, most of it stimulating and entertaining, but it's all so disparate and disconnected, with such a clash of styles, that it can feel more overwhelming than inspiring. According to the park's creators, this is all intentional, and philosophically justified. It was conceived by Bernard Tschumi as a futuristic "activity" park that would dispel the eighteenth- and nineteenth-century notion of parks and gardens as places of gentle and well-ordered relaxation. Instead of unity, meaning and purpose we're offered a deconstructed landscape: the whole is broken down into its parts. There's something vaguely disconcerting about the setting. The 900m straight **walkway**, with its wavy shelter and complicated metal bridge across the Canal de l'Ourcq, seems to insist that you cover the park from end to end, and there's something too dogmatic about the arrangement of the bright red **follies**, like chopped-off cranes, each slightly different but all spaced exactly 120m apart.

The Cité des Sciences et de l'Industrie

Tues–Sat 10am–6pm, Sun 10am 7pm • €8 includes admission to Explora, certain temporary exhibitions and the Louis-Lumière 3D Cinema • ☏ 01 40 05 70 00, ⓦ cite-sciences.fr • Ⓜ Porte-de-la-Villette

The park's dominant building is the enormous **Cité des Sciences et de l'Industrie**, an abandoned abattoir redesigned by architect Adrien Fainsilber and transformed into a high-tech museum. Four times the size of the Pompidou Centre, from the outside it appears fortress-like, despite the transparency of its giant glass walls beneath a dark blue lattice of steel, reinforced by walkways that accelerate out towards the Géode across a moat level with the underground floors. Once you're inside, however, the solidity of first impressions is totally reversed by the three themes of water (around the building), vegetation (in the greenhouses) and light – which floods the building from vast skylights as well as the glass facade.

This is the science museum to end all science museums, and worth visiting for the interior of the building alone: all glass and stainless steel, crow's nests and cantilevered

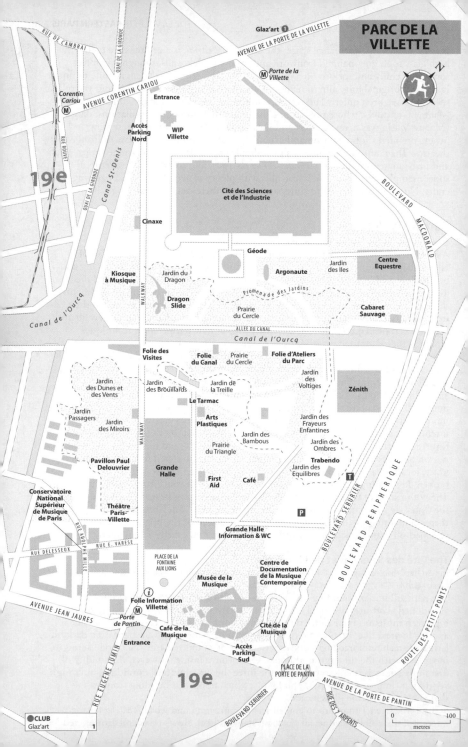

VISITING THE PARC DE LA VILLETTE

The Parc de la Villette is accessible from Ⓜ Porte-de-la-Villette at the northern end by avenue Corentin-Cariou and the Cité des Sciences et de l'Industrie; from the Canal de l'Ourcq's quai de la Marne to the west; or from Ⓜ Porte-de-Pantin on avenue Jean-Jaurès at the southern entrance by the Cité de la Musique. There's an **information centre** at the southern entrance, which will help you get your bearings, and plenty of restaurants and cafés. The park's key attractions are listed below.

CITE DES SCIENCES ET DE L'INDUSTRIE

A huge science museum, with a special section for children, the **Cité des Enfants**. The complex also includes the **Cinaxe** cinema which shows 3D films, the **Géode** Imax film theatre and a decommissioned naval submarine, the **Argonaute**.

CITE DE LA MUSIQUE

The city's music academy, which puts on regular concerts (see p.316) and incorporates a superb museum covering the history of Western music.

GARDENS

As well as large expanses of lawn, the park has ten themed gardens, including the Garden of Mirrors, of Shadows and of Dunes, all linked by a walkway called the Promenade des Jardins. See p.349.

ENTERTAINMENT

The park has a number of distinguished music, arts and theatre venues.
Cabaret Sauvage map p.202. A venue for live music and avant-garde circus performances.
Festival du Cinéma en Plein Air On summer nights you can join the crowds lounging on the acres of grass known as "prairies" for an open-air film screening (see p.309).
Grande Halle map p.202. The elegant old iron-framed beef market hall hosts large-scale art exhibitions and the annual Villette Jazz festival in September (see p.320).
Le Tarmac map p.202. A small theatre specializing in works from French-speaking parts of the world such as Tahiti and Togo; also hosts dance, film and readings. See p.313.
Théâtre Paris-Villette map p.202. A theatre that encourages young talent and puts on mostly contemporary works. See p.313.
Trabendo map p.202. A live music venue for jazz, world music and rock.
Zénith map p.202. Rock concerts are staged at this 6000-seat concert hall.

platforms, bridges and suspended walkways, the different levels linked by lifts and escalators around a huge central space open to the full 40m height of the roof. It may be colossal, but you are more likely to lose yourself mentally rather than physically, and come out after several hours reeling with images and ideas about DNA, quasars, bacterial reproduction, curved space or rocket launching. Entry to the building itself is free, as is entry to some of the facilities within – the cafés, aquarium, *médiathèque* and viewing of documentaries (in French) in the Salle Jean-Painlevé and in the auditorium. The ticket for Explora (the permanent exhibition) is valid all day, but for four entries only. The complex includes the **Cité des Enfants**, specifically designed for children (see p.354).

Explora

Cité des Sciences • Tues–Sat 10am–6pm, Sun 10am–7pm • Included in €8 Cité des Sciences ticket

The **Explora** exhibition space is set across the top two floors of the Cité des Sciences (pick up a plan in English from the welcome desk on level 0) and includes both temporary shows and a permanent exhibition divided into twenty units, many accompanied by English translations. These cover a variety of subjects, among them water, the universe, automobiles, aeronautics, energy, images, genes, sound, mathematics, light and matter, and there's also a section on current scientific developments. As the name suggests, the emphasis is on exploring, and the means used are interactive computers, multimedia displays, videos, holograms and games.

13

On **level 1**, a classic example of chaos theory introduces the **maths section**; La Fontaine Turbulente is a wheel of glasses rotating below a stream of water in which the switch between clockwise and anticlockwise motion is unpredictable beyond two minutes. In **Les Sons** (sounds), you can watch a video of an X-rayed jaw and throat talking, or sit in a cubicle and feel your body tingle with physical sensations as a rainstorm crashes around you. Videos in **L'homme et les gènes** trace the development of an embryo from fertilization to birth, while in **Images** you can use computer simulation to manipulate the *Mona Lisa*'s smile.

On **level 2**, the **Jeux de Lumière** is a whole series of experiments to do with colour, optical illusions, refraction and the like. You can have your head spun further by a session in the **planetarium** (around six shows daily; €3 supplement).

Back on the ground floor, the **Cinéma Louis-Lumière** shows short stereoscopic (3D) films every half-hour or so, for which you'll have to queue. General documentaries in French only and more serious scientific documentaries are shown in **Salle Jean-Painlevé** (level -1; free).

Médiathèque

Cité des Sciences **Médiathèque** Levels -1 & -2 Tues noon–7.45pm, Wed–Sun noon–6.45pm • Free **Cité des Métiers** Level 1 Tues–Fri 10am–6pm, Sat noon–6pm • Free • ⓜPorte-de-la-Villette

In the **Médiathèque**, a multimedia library, you can select from over four thousand films (some in English) at individual consoles, as well as consult educational software, books and magazines. On level -1 the **Cité des Métiers** provides free access to information on finding work, changing careers, training, creating your own employment, and working conditions in different countries. It even offers an on-the-spot consultancy with a careers adviser. Finally, on the lowest floor (-2), you can eat and drink beside an **aquarium** filled with Mediterranean sea life.

The Géode and around

Géode Tues–Sun 10.30am–8.30pm; hourly shows • €10.50 • ☎ 01 40 05 79 99, ⓦ lageode.fr **Argonaute** Tues–Sat 10.30am–5.30pm, Sun 11am–6.30pm • €3 **Cinaxe** Tues–Sun 11am–1pm & 2–5pm; screenings every 15min • €5.40

In front of the museum complex floats the **Géode**, a bubble of reflecting steel dropped from an intergalactic boules game into a pool of water that ripples with the mirrored image of the Cité. Inside, the sphere holds a screen for Imax and 3D films, not noted for their plots but a great visual experience. Beside the Géode, you can clamber around a real 1957 French military submarine, the **Argonaute**, and view the park through its periscope. The **Cinaxe**, between the Cité and the Canal St-Denis, combines 70mm film shot at thirty frames a second with seats that move, so that a bobsleigh ride down the Cresta Run, for example, not only looks unbelievably real, but feels it, too.

The Cité de la Musique

☎ 01 44 84 44 84, ⓦ cite-musique.fr • ⓜPorte-de-Pantin

Crossing the Canal de l'Ourcq south of the Géode, a walkway leads past the Grande Salle to the **Cité de la Musique**, housed in two complexes either side of the Porte-de-Pantin entrance. To the west, the waves and funnels, irregular polygons and non-parallel lines of the Conservatoire de Paris, the city's music academy, make abstract sense: windows in sequences like musical notation; the wavy roof, which, according to the architect, Christian de Portzamparc, is like a Gregorian chant, but could equally suggest the movement of a dancer or a conductor's baton; and the crescendo of the rising curves of the facade.

The wedge-shaped complex to the east contains the public spaces, which include the excellent Musée de la Musique, the chic *Café de la Musique*, a music and dance information centre, and a concert hall whose ovoid dome rises like a perfect soufflé from the roof line. The harsh semi-exterior element of a girdered "arrow" pointing down to the entrance arch pretending to be another red folly hides an unexpectedly sensual interior. A glass-roofed arcade spirals round the auditorium, the combination of pale-blue walls, a subtly sloping floor and the height to the ceiling creating a sense of calm.

13

The Musée de la Musique

Cité de la Musique • Tues–Sat noon–6pm, Sun 10am–6pm • €8 • ⓂPorte-de-Pantin

The **Musée de la Musique** presents the history of music from the end of the Renaissance to the present day, both visually, exhibiting some 4500 instruments, and aurally, via headsets (available in English; free) and interactive displays. Glass cases hold gleaming, beautiful instruments – jewel-inlaid crystal flutes and a fabulous lyre-guitar, made in Paris in the early 1800s, are some impressive examples. The instruments are presented in the context of a key work in the history of Western music; as you step past each case, the headphones are programmed to emit a short scholarly narration, followed by a delightful concert. It's a truly transporting – and educational – experience to gaze at the grouping of harps, made in Paris between 1760 and 1900, and hear an excerpt of music as heavenly as the instruments you're looking at.

The museum also includes an **auditorium** holding regular concerts, in addition to a huge archive of documents and sound recordings, and spaces for workshops and films.

Belleville

ⓂBelleville/Pyrénées/Jourdain/Télégraphe

The old village of **Belleville**, only incorporated into the city in 1860, is strung out along the western slopes of a ridge that rises steadily from the Seine at Bercy to an altitude of 128m near the place des Fêtes, the highest point in Paris after Montmartre. "Belle" is not the first adjective that springs to mind when describing Belleville, with its many bland apartment blocks, but there are pockets of charm here and there, especially around the attractive **Parc des Buttes-Chaumont** and **Parc de Belleville**. It's home to what is probably one of the most diverse populations in the city: a mix of traditional working class, various ethnic communities and a good number of students and artists, drawn to the area by the availability of affordable and large spaces, ideal for *ateliers*. The best opportunity to view local artists' work is during the **Journées portes ouvertes ateliers d'artistes de Belleville** at the end of May (for dates see ⓦateliers-artistes-belleville.org), when around 240 artists living or working in Belleville open their doors to the public.

Rue de Belleville and around

Belleville's main artery is **rue de Belleville**. Its lower end is liveliest, with numerous Chinese restaurants and *traiteurs* doing a brisk trade, while adjoining **boulevard de Belleville** is home to Algerian pastry shops, grocers and *shisha* cafés. The boulevard is lined with dramatic new architecture, employing jutting triangles, curves and the occasional reference to the roof lines of nineteenth-century Parisian blocks. It's particularly lively on Tuesday and Friday mornings when the **market** sets up, stretching the whole length of the boulevard. Kosher food shops and cafés, belonging to Sephardic Jews from Tunisia, are also in evidence here and on **rue Ramponeau**, running parallel to the rue de Belleville. It was at the junction of rue Ramponeau and rue de Tourtille that the very last barricade of the Commune was defended single-handedly for fifteen minutes by the last fighting Communard in 1871. A combative spirit lives on here at **La Forge** (ⓦlaforgedebelleville.fr), nos. 23–25, an abandoned smithy squatted by artists in the 1990s, whose cause was successfully taken up by local community associations. It now houses around twenty artists' studios, open to the public during the Journées portes ouvertes (see above) and for other occasional exhibitions.

13 Parc de Belleville

Maison de l'Air April–Sept Wed 1.30–5pm, Sat 1.30–6.30pm; rest of year Wed & Sat 1.30–5pm • Free • ⓜ Pyrénées/Couronnes

A turn off rue de Belleville onto the cobbled **rue Piat** will take you past the beautiful wrought-iron gate of the jungly **Villa Otoz** to the **Parc de Belleville**, created in the mid-1990s. From the terrace at the junction with rue des Envierges, there's a fantastic view across the city, especially at sunset. At your feet, the small park descends in a further series of terraces and waterfalls. There's a little exhibition/educational centre geared towards children in particular, the **Maison de l'Air**, with lots of information on air quality and meteorology, including live satellite pictures of the weather across Europe.

Around the park

A path crosses the top of the Parc de Belleville past a minuscule vineyard and turns into steps that drop down to **rue des Couronnes** (which leads back to boulevard de Belleville). Some of the adjacent streets are worth a wander for a feel of the changing times – rue de la Mare, rue des Envierges, rue des Cascades – with two or three beautiful old houses in overgrown gardens, alongside new housing that follows the height and curves of the streets and *passages* between them.

The upper stretch of rue de Belleville is not as distinctive as its lower end and could be the busy main street of any French provincial town, with its boulangeries and charcuteries. On the wall of no. 72, a plaque commemorates the birth of the legendary chanteuse **Edith Piaf**; the story goes that she was born under a street lamp just here. One of Piaf's favourite hangouts is not far from here, at 105 rue du Faubourg-du-Temple, on rue de Belleville's busy lower extension: *La Java*, a former *bal musette* venue whose original dancehall interior is still intact.

Parc des Buttes-Chaumont

Daily: May & mid-Aug to Sept 7am–9.15pm; June to mid-Aug till 10.15pm; Oct–April till 8.15pm • Free • ⓜ Buttes-Chaumont/Botzaris

The delightful, hilly **Parc des Buttes-Chaumont**, north of the Belleville heights, was constructed under Haussmann in the 1860s to camouflage what until then had been a desolate warren of disused quarries, rubbish dumps and shacks. Out of this unlikely setting, a park was created – there's a grotto with a cascade and artificial stalactites, and a picturesque lake from which a huge rock rises up, topped with a delicate Corinthian temple. You can cross the lake via a suspension bridge, or take the shorter **Pont des Suicides**. This, according to Louis Aragon, the literary grand old man of the French Communist Party, "before metal grilles were erected along its sides, claimed victims even from passers-by who had had no intention whatsoever of killing themselves but were suddenly tempted by the abyss" (*Le Paysan de Paris*). You can go boating on the lake, and, unusually for Paris, you're not cautioned off the grass.

There are some rather desirable residences around the park, especially to the east, between rue de Crimée and **place de Rhin-et-Danube**; little cobbled *villas* (mews) lined

---

CLAUDE CHAPPE AND THE RUE DU TELEGRAPHE

The rue du Télégraphe, running south off the eastern end of rue de Belleville alongside the Cimetière de Belleville, is named in memory of Claude Chappe's invention of the **optical telegraph**. Chappe first tested his device here in September 1792, in a corner of the cemetery. When word of his activities got out, he was nearly lynched by a mob that assumed he was trying to signal to the king, who was at that time imprisoned in the Temple (see box, p.103). Eventually, two lines were set up, from Belleville to Strasbourg and the east, and from Montmartre to Lille and the north. By 1840, it was possible to send a message to Calais in three minutes, via 27 relays, and to Strasbourg in seven minutes, using 46 relays. Chappe himself did not live to see the fruits of his invention; his patent was contested in 1805 and, distraught, he threw himself into a sewer (his grave is in nearby Père-Lachaise).

with ivy-strewn houses, their gardens full of roses and lilac trees, can be found here, off rue Miguel-Hidalgo, rue du Général-Brunet, rue de la Liberté, rue de l'Egalité and rue de Mouzaïa.

Le Plateau

33 rue des Alouettes, 19ᵉ • Wed–Fri 2–7pm, Sat & Sun noon–8pm • Free • ⓦ fracidf-leplateau.com • ⓜ Jourdain

One block south of the Parc des Buttes-Chaumont is a small contemporary arts centre, **Le Plateau**, set up after a vigorous campaign by local residents who successfully acquired the space after fighting off property developers. Exhibitions tend to focus on experimental, cutting-edge French and international artists.

Ménilmontant

ⓜ Ménilmontant

Like Belleville, much of **Ménilmontant** aligns itself along one straight, steep street, the **rue de Ménilmontant** and its lower extension rue Oberkampf. Although run-down in parts, its popularity with artists and young professionals, or *bobos* (*bourgeois-bohémiens*), has helped to revitalize the area. Alternative shops and cool bars and restaurants have elbowed in among the grocers and cheap hardware stores, especially along **rue Oberkampf** and its parallel street **rue Jean-Pierre Timbaud**, the city's most vibrant nightlife hub (see p.301). The upper reaches of rue de Ménilmontant, above rue Sorbier, are quieter, and looking back you find yourself dead in line with the rooftop of the Pompidou Centre, a measure of how high you are above the rest of the city.

Musée Edith Piaf

5 rue Crespin-du-Gast, 11ᵉ • Mon–Thurs 1–6pm; closed Sept • Donation • Admission by appointment only on ☎ 01 43 55 52 72 • ⓜ Ménilmontant/St-Maur

Further west, across boulevard de Ménilmontant, is the **Musée Edith Piaf**. Piaf was not an acquisitive person; the few clothes (yes, including a little black dress), letters, toys, paintings and photographs that she left are almost all here, along with every one of her recordings. The venue is a small flat lived in by her devoted friend Bernard Marchois, who will show you around and gladly answer any questions (in French).

Père-Lachaise cemetery and around

Main entrance on bd de Ménilmontant • Mon–Fri 8am–5.30pm, Sat 8.30am–5.30pm, Sun 9am–5.30pm • Free • ⓦ pere-lachaise.com • ⓜ Père-Lachaise/Phillipe-Auguste

Final resting place of a host of French notables, as well as some illustrious foreigners, **Père-Lachaise** is one of the world's largest and most famous cemeteries. Sited on a hill commanding grand views of Paris, it's a bit like a miniature town, with its grid-like layout, cast-iron signposts and neat cobbled lanes – a veritable "city of the dead". It's surely also one of the most atmospheric cemeteries, an eerily beautiful haven, with terraced slopes and magnificent old trees (around six thousand of them) spreading their branches over the moss-grown tombs as though shading them from the outside world.

Finding individual graves can be a tricky business. Our **map** (see p.208) and the free plans given out at the entrance will point you in the right direction, but it's worth buying a slightly more detailed one as it's easy to get lost; the best one is published by Editions Métropolitain Paris (around €2) and should be available in the newsagents and florists near the **main entrance** on boulevard de Ménilmontant.

Père-Lachaise was opened in 1804 and turned out to be an incredibly successful piece of land speculation. Nicolas Frochot, the urban planner who bought the land, persuaded the civil authorities to have **Molière**, **La Fontaine**, **Abélard** (see box, p.45) and **Héloïse** reburied in his new cemetery, and it began to acquire cachet, but it really took off when Balzac set the last scene of his 1835 novel *Le Père Goriot* here.

13

Ironically, Frochot even sold a plot to the original owner for considerably more than the price he had paid for the entire site. Even today, rates are extremely high.

Chopin, Jim Morrison and Oscar Wilde

Among the most visited graves is that of **Chopin** (Division 11), who has a willowy muse mourning his loss and is often attended by groups of Poles laying wreaths and flowers in the red and white colours of the Polish flag.

Swarms also flock to the grave of ex-Doors lead singer **Jim Morrison** (Division 6), who died in Paris in 1971 at the age of 27. Once graffiti-covered and wreathed in marijuana fumes, it has been cleaned up and is watched over by a security guard, though this

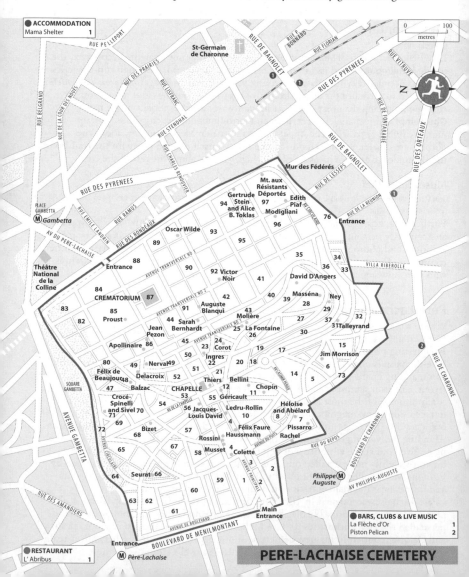

● ACCOMMODATION
Mama Shelter   1

● BARS, CLUBS & LIVE MUSIC
La Flèche d'Or   1
Piston Pelican   2

● RESTAURANT
L' Abribus   1

PERE-LACHAISE CEMETERY

13

hasn't stopped fans placing flowers, candles and cigarette butts on his tomb and scribbling messages in praise of love and drugs on other graves, and trees, nearby. In fact things got so bad some years ago that relatives of undistinguished Frenchmen interred nearby signed a petition asking for the singer's body to be exhumed and sent home, but the grave, unlike many here, is on a perpetual lease, so Jim is here to stay.

Another tomb that attracts many visitors is **Oscar Wilde**'s (Division 89), the base of which is covered in graffiti and lipstick kisses left by devoted fans. It's topped with a sculpture by Jacob Epstein of a Pharaonic winged messenger (sadly missing its once prominent member, which was last seen being used as a paper weight by the director of the cemetery). The inscription behind is a grim verse from *The Ballad of Reading Gaol*.

Writers and musicians

Many other musicians repose near Chopin, among them Bellini, Cherubini, the violinist Kreutzer, whose commemorative column leans precariously to one side, and the more recently deceased French jazz pianist, Michel Petrucciani. Rossini is honoured with a spot on the *avenue principale*, though in fact his remains have been transferred to his native Italy.

Most of the celebrated dead have unremarkable tombs. Femme fatale **Colette**'s tomb, close to the main entrance in Division 4, is very plain, though always covered in flowers. The same holds true for the divine **Sarah Bernhardt**'s (Division 44) and the great chanteuse **Edith Piaf**'s (Division 97). **Marcel Proust** lies in his family's black-marble, conventional tomb (Division 85). Just across the way is the rather incongruous-looking **Crematorium** (Division 87), crudely modelled on the Aghia Sophia in Istanbul, with domes and minarets. Here among others of equal or lesser renown lie the ashes of Max Ernst, Georges Perec, Stéphane Grappelli and American dancer Isadora Duncan, who was strangled when her scarf got tangled in the rear wheel of her open-top car. Maria Callas has a plaque here, too, though her ashes were removed and scattered in the Aegean.

Artists

Among other illustrious representatives of the arts, **Corot** (Division 24) and **Balzac** (Division 48) both have fine busts, as does poet **Alfred de Musset**, near Rossini on the *avenue principale*, and buried, according to his wishes, under a willow tree. **Delacroix** lies in a sombre sarcophagus in Division 49, while **Jacques-Louis David**'s heart rests in Division 56 (the rest of him is buried in Belgium, where he died). His pupil **Ingres** reposes in Division 23. **Géricault** reclines on cushions of stone (Division 12), paint palette in hand, his face taut with concentration; below is a sculpted relief of part of his best-known painting *The Raft of the Medusa*. Close by is the relaxed figure of **Jean Carriès**, a model-maker, in felt hat and overalls, holding a self-portrait in the palm of his hand.

In Division 96, you'll find the grave of **Modigliani** and his lover Jeanne Herburtene, who killed herself in crazed grief a few days after he died in agony from meningitis. Impressionist painter **Camille Pissarro** lies among the sober, unadorned tombs of the Jewish plot near the main entrance, as does the beautiful nineteenth-century actress **Rachel**, known for one of the briefest love-letter exchanges in history; after seeing her on stage, Prince de Joinville sent her his card with the note "Où? Quand? Combien?", to which Rachel scribbled back, "Chez toi. Ce soir. Pour rien."

Politicians

Notable politicians include **Félix Faure** (on the *avenue principale*, Division 4), French president, who died in the arms of his mistress in the Elysée palace in 1899; draped in a French flag, his head to one side, he cuts rather a romantic figure. **Auguste Blanqui**, after whom so many French streets are named, lies in Division 91. Described by Karl Marx as the nineteenth century's greatest revolutionary, he served his time in jail – 33 years in

13

IMMODEST MONUMENTS

In contrast to the many modest monuments marking the tombs of the famous, in Division 48 a now-forgotten French diplomat, **Félix de Beaujour**, is marked with an enormous tower, rather like a lighthouse. To the north in Division 86, one **Jean Pezon**, a lion-tamer, is shown riding the pet lion that ate him. In Division 71, two men lie together hand in hand – **Croce-Spinelli and Sivel**, a pair of balloonists who went so high they died from lack of oxygen. In Division 92, journalist **Victor Noir** – shot at the age of 22 in 1870 by Prince Napoléon for daring to criticize him – is portrayed at the moment of death, flat on his back, fully clothed, his top hat fallen by his feet. However, it's not as a magnet for anti-censorship campaigners that his tomb has become famous, but as a lucky charm – a prominent part of his anatomy has been worn shiny by the touch of infertile women, hoping for a cure.

all – for political activities that spanned the 1830 Revolution to the Paris Commune. Karl's daughter, **Laura Marx**, and her husband **Paul Lafargue**, who committed suicide together in 1911, lie south from Blanqui's grave, in Division 76.

War memorials and the Mur des Fédérés
Monuments to collective, violent deaths have the power to change a sunny outing to Père-Lachaise into a much more sombre experience. In Division 97, in what's become known as the "coin des martyrs", you'll find memorials to the victims of the Nazi concentration camps, to executed Resistance fighters and to those unaccounted for in the genocide of World War II. The sculptures are relentless in their images of inhumanity, of people forced to collaborate in their own degradation and death.

Marking one of the bloodiest episodes in French history is the **Mur des Fédérés** (Division 76), the wall where the last troops of the Paris Commune were lined up and shot in the final days of the battle in 1871. A total of 147 men were killed, after a frenetic chase through the tombstones, and the remains of around a thousand other Communards were brought here and thrown into a grave-pit. The wall soon became a place of pilgrimage for the Left, and remains so today. The man who ordered the execution, Adolphe Thiers, lies in the centre of the cemetery in Division 55.

Charonne
Ⓜ Porte de Bagnolet/Gambetta

Just south of Père-Lachaise cemetery, with its perfect little Romanesque church and the cobbled street of rue St-Blaise, **Charonne** retains its village-like atmosphere. **St-Germain-de-Charonne**, in place St-Blaise, has changed little, and its Romanesque belfry not at all, since the thirteenth century. It's one of only two Paris churches to have its own graveyard (the other is St-Pierre in Montmartre); several hundred Communards were buried here after being accidentally disinterred during the construction of a reservoir in 1897. Elsewhere in Paris, charnel houses were the norm, with the bones emptied into the catacombs as more space was required. It was not until the nineteenth century that public cemeteries appeared on the scene, the most famous being Père-Lachaise.

Opposite the church of St-Germain-de-Charonne, the old cobbled village high street, **rue St-Blaise**, pedestrianized to place des Grès, was once one of the most picturesque in Paris, and still has a measure of charm, with its wooden shuttered houses, cafés and artists' *ateliers*.

Bagnolet
From the top of rue St-Blaise, on rue de Bagnolet, heading southwest will lead you into the heart of the cool, diverse and swiftly developing **Bagnolet** district. A great place for an evening drink, Bagnolet has a collection of bohemian bars, the grungy-electro-chic club *La Flèche d'Or* (see p.304) and one of the city's most hyped concept hotels, the Philippe Starck-designed *Mama Shelter* (see p.261).

BOIS DE BOULOGNE

Western Paris

Western Paris consists of the well-manicured 16e and 17e arrondissements, often referred to as the Beaux Quartiers. The area is mainly residential with few specific sights as such, the chief exception being the Musée Marmottan, known for its impressive collection of Monets. The northern half of the 16e, towards place Victor-Hugo and place de l'Etoile, is leafy though still distinctly metropolitan in feel. The southern part, around the old villages of Auteuil and Passy, is particularly pleasant for strolling. It has an almost provincial air, with its tight knot of streets and charming *villas* – leafy lanes of attractive old houses, fronted with English-style gardens, full of roses, ivy and wisteria. Although they're often closed to non-residents, should you find the access gate open, no one seems to mind if you wander in.

Auteuil and **Passy** were only incorporated into the city in 1860, and soon became the capital's most desirable districts. Well-to-do Parisians commissioned new houses here, and as a result the area is rich in fine examples of early twentieth-century architecture: Hector Guimard, designer of the swirly green Art Nouveau métro stations, worked here, and there are some rare Parisian examples of work by interwar architects Le Corbusier and Mallet-Stevens, who created the first "Cubist" buildings.

14 Auteuil

Ⓜ Eglise d'Auteuil

The **Auteuil** district is now completely integrated into the city, but there's still a villagey feel about its streets, and it has some charming little *villas* not to mention some notable examples of early twentieth-century architecture. The ideal place to start an exploration of Auteuil is the **Eglise d'Auteuil** métro station. Nearby are several of Hector Guimard's **Art Nouveau** buildings: at 34 rue Boileau, 8 avenue de la Villa-de-la-Réunion, 41 rue Chardon-Lagache, 142 avenue de Versailles and 39 boulevard Exelmans.

Rue Boileau to the avenue de Versailles

The house at no. 34 **rue Boileau** was one of Guimard's first commissions, in 1891. To reach it from the Eglise d'Auteuil métro, head directly west along rue d'Auteuil for 200m, then turn left (south) into Boileau. A high fence and wisteria obscure much of the view, but you can see some of the decorative tile-work under the eaves and around the doors and windows. Further down the street, just before you reach boulevard Exelmans, the Vietnamese embassy at no. 62 successfully combines 1970s Western architecture with the traditional Vietnamese elements of a pagoda roof and earthenware tiles. Continue south for 0.5km along rue Boileau beyond boulevard Exelmans, turn right onto rue Parent de Rosan and you'll find a series of enchanting *villas* off to the right, backing onto the Auteuil cemetery.

Rue Boileau terminates on avenue de Versailles, where you can turn left and head back to the métro via the Guimard apartment block at no. 142 (1905), with its characteristic Art Nouveau flower motifs and sinuous, curling lines. It's just by the Exelmans crossroads (on the #72 bus route). You can then cut across the **Jardin de Ste-Périne**, once the rural residence of the monks of Ste Geneviève's abbey, established here in 1109, to get back to the métro. The entrances to the garden are opposite 135 avenue de Versailles and alongside the hospital on rue Mirabeau, just north of the rue Chardon-Lagache junction.

Rue de la Fontaine and around

The old village high street, **rue d'Auteuil**, runs west to **place Lorrain**, which hosts a Saturday market. From here **rue de la Fontaine** runs northeast to the Radio-France building and has Guimard buildings at nos. 14, 17, 19, 21 and 60. No. 14 is the most famous: the "Castel Béranger" (1898), with exuberant Art Nouveau decoration in the bay windows, the roof line and the chimney. At no. 65 there's a huge block of artists' studios by Henri Sauvage (1926) with a fascinating colour scheme, bearing signs of a Cubist influence. Alternatively, head up rue du Dr-Blanche for the cool, rectilinear lines of Cubist architects Le Corbusier and Mallet-Stevens (see p.214).

Musée de Radio-France

116 av du Président Kennedy, 16ᵉ • Undergoing renovation until 2012 • Mon–Fri 10–11am & 2.30–4pm • €5 • ☎ 01 56 40 15 16, Ⓦ radiofrance.fr • RER Av-du-Prés-Kennedy–Maison-de-Radio-France/Ⓜ Ranelagh

The **Maison de Radio-France** is the national radio headquarters. It offers free concerts and the **Musée de Radio-France**, which illustrates the history of broadcasting. It was undergoing renovation at the time of writing, but should open again in 2012.

AUTEUIL BUS ROUTES

Handy bus routes for exploring Auteuil are the #52 and the #72. The #52 runs between ⓂOpéra in the centre and ⓂBoulogne-Pont-de-St-Cloud near the Parc des Princes, stopping at rue Poisson en route, while the #72's route extends between ⓂHôtel-de-Ville in the Marais and ⓂBoulogne-Pont-de-St-Cloud, stopping en route by the Exelmans crossroads near some of Guimard's buildings on avenue de Versailles.

14

Villa Montmorency and Villa La Roche

Villa la Roche 8–10 square du Dr-Blanche, 16ᵉ • Mon 1.30–6pm, Tues–Thurs 10am–6pm, Fri & Sat 10am–5pm; closed Aug • €3 • ☎ 01 42 88 75 72 • ⓂJasmin

Just off place Lorrain, in rue Poussin (on the #52 bus route), carriage gates open onto **Villa Montmorency**, one of the grander *villas* – more like an exclusive estate, built in the grounds of a former château. Jean-Jacques Rousseau, André Gide and Victor Hugo all lived in this one over the years. Behind it, in a cul-de-sac off rue du Dr-Blanche, are **Le Corbusier**'s first private houses (1923), the Villa Jeanneret and the Villa La Roche, now in the care of the Fondation Le Corbusier. You can visit **Villa La Roche**, built in strictly Cubist style, very plain with strip windows, the only extravagance a curved frontage. The houses look commonplace enough now from the outside, but were a great contrast with anything that had gone before, and once you're inside, the spatial play still seems ground-breaking. The interior is sparsely furnished, but originally the walls would have been hung with the outstanding collection of modern art built up by the financier Raoul Albert La Roche, for whom the *villa* was built. In recent restoration work the walls have been repainted in the original colours – soothing greys, creams and blues, which Le Corbusier was fond of using in his easel painting.

Rue Mallet-Stevens

ⓂJasmin

Heading north along rue du Dr-Blanche and off to the right, the tiny **rue Mallet-Stevens** was built by the architect of the same name in Cubist style. The original proportions of the houses were altered by the addition of three storeys in the 1960s, but you can still see the architectural intention of sculpting the entire street space as a cohesive unit. Continue to the end of rue du Dr-Blanche, turn left and then right onto boulevard de Beauséjour; a shortcut immediately opposite rue du Ranelagh across the disused Petite Ceinture rail line takes you to shady avenue Raphaël, which runs alongside the pretty **Jardin du Ranelagh** (with a rather engaging sculpture of the fabulist La Fontaine with an eagle and fox) and on to the Musée Marmottan.

The Musée Marmottan

2 rue Louis-Boilly, 16ᵉ • Tues–Sun 10am–7pm, Thurs till 8pm • €10 • ☎ 01 44 96 50 33, ☞ marmottan.com • ⓂMuette

The **Musée Marmottan** is best known for its excellent collection of **Monet paintings**, bequeathed to the museum by the artist's son. Among them is *Impression, soleil levant*, a canvas from 1872 of a misty Le Havre morning, whose title the critics usurped to give the Impressionist movement its name. The painting was stolen from the gallery in October 1985, along with eight others. After a police operation lasting five years, the paintings were discovered in a villa in southern Corsica, and were put back on show with greatly increased security. There's also a dazzling selection of canvases from Monet's last years at Giverny, showing the increasingly abstract quality of the artist's later work, including several *Nymphéas* (Water lilies), *Le Pont japonais*, *L'Allée des rosiers* and *Le Saule pleureur*, where rich colours are laid on in thick, excited whorls and lines.

The collection also features some of Monet's contemporaries – Manet, Renoir and **Berthe Morisot**. Morisot, who lived most of her life in Passy and is buried in the Cimetière de Passy, is particularly well represented, with two rooms devoted to her wonderfully summery canvases; her work is characterized by vigorous, almost aggressive, brushwork, seen to best effect in paintings such as *Branches of an orange tree* (1889) and *Garden at Bougival* (1884).

In addition, the museum displays some splendid examples of First Empire pomposity: chairs with golden sphinxes for armrests, candelabra of complicated headdresses and twining serpents, and a small and beautiful collection of thirteenth- to sixteenth-century **manuscript illuminations** – look out for the decorated capital R framing an exquisitely drawn portrait of St Catherine of Alexandria.

14

West of Auteuil

West of Auteuil lie some attractive gardens, including the **Jardin des Serres d'Auteuil**, the municipal greenhouses and gardens that supply the city with its plants and flowers, as well as the beautiful **Jardins Albert Kahn**, with pretty French and Japanese gardens and an intriguing museum of early colour photographs from around the world.

Jardin des Poètes and Jardin des Serres d'Auteuil

Jardin des Poètes Daily 9am–6pm • Free **Jardin des Serres d'Auteuil** Daily 10am–6pm, closes 5pm in winter • Free • ⓜPorte-d'Auteuil

West of place de la Porte d'Auteuil are two gardens: the **Jardin des Poètes**, with its entrance on avenue du Général Sarrail, and the adjoining **Jardin des Serres d'Auteuil**, its main entrance at 3 avenue de la Porte d'Auteuil (or you can enter from the Jardin des Poètes). You can't escape the traffic noise completely, but the Jardin des Poètes is extremely tranquil. Famous French poets are each remembered by a verse (of a mostly pastoral nature) engraved on small stones surrounded by little flowerbeds. A statue of Victor Hugo by Rodin stands in the middle of this very informal garden. Approaching the Auteuil garden and the greenhouses (*serres*) from the Jardin des Poètes, you pass delightful potting sheds with rickety wooden blinds. Then you're into a formal garden, beautifully laid out around the big old-fashioned metal-frame greenhouses. Among them is a palm house containing two hundred tropical species and a greenhouse devoted entirely to flora rarely seen outside their native New Caledonia. There may also be a special exhibition on – azaleas in April, for example.

Stade Roland Garros and the Tenniseum

Tenniseum 2 av Gordon Bennett, 16ᵉ • Wed, Fri, Sat & Sun 10am–6pm • €7.50 • ☎01 47 43 48 48, ⓦfft.fr/roland-garros/musee/le-musee-de-la-fft • ⓜPorte-d'Auteuil

Directly beyond the Jardin des Serres d'Auteuil is the **Stade Roland Garros**, venue for the French tennis championships (see p.347). **Le Tenniseum** fills you in on the history of the game and its development from *jeu de paume*, or "real tennis"; Paris boasted over a hundred real tennis courts under Henri IV, while in Orléans in 1656 students were spending so much time hitting a ball around that the only way to get them back to their studies was to close the courts down. Most of the rest of the museum is given over to photos and footage of mainly French tennis stars, such as René Lacoste and Yannick Noah, and there's a multimedia centre, where you can see archive films dating from 1897 to the present day.

Jardins et Musée Albert Kahn

10–14 rue du Port, Boulogne-Billancourt • Daily 11am–7pm, Oct–April till 6pm • Garden and museum €3 • ☎01 55 19 28 00, ⓦalbert-kahn.fr • ⓜBoulogne-Pont-de-St-Cloud/Marcel-Sembat

The **Jardins et Musée Albert Kahn**, to the south in the suburb of Boulogne-Billancourt, consists of a very pretty garden and a small museum dedicated to temporary exhibitions of "*Les Archives de la Planète*" – photographs, many in colour, and films collected by banker and philanthropist Albert Kahn between 1909 and 1931. Kahn wanted to record human activities and ways of life that he knew would soon disappear for ever. His aim in the design of the garden was to combine English, French, Japanese and other styles to demonstrate the possibility of a harmonious, peaceful world. It's an enchanting place, with rhododendrons and camellias under blue cedars, a rose garden, an espaliered orchard, a forest of Moroccan pines, streams with Japanese bridges beside pagoda teahouses, Buddhas and pyramids of pebbles. A palm hothouse has been turned into a chic *salon de thé*, serving such delights as pear liqueur and *marrons glacés* sorbet.

Passy

14

Northeast of Auteuil, the area around the old village of **Passy** offers scope for a good meandering walk, from La Muette métro, through old streets like rue de l'Annonciation, to Balzac's house, and through more cobbled streets to the Seine and Pont de Bir-Hakeim near Passy métro.

From **La Muette** métro, head east along the old high street, **rue de Passy**, past an eye-catching parade of boutiques, until you reach **place de Passy** and the crowded but leisurely café terrace of *Le Paris Passy*. From the *place*, stroll southeast along cobbled, pedestrianized **rue de l'Annonciation**, a pleasant blend of down-to-earth and genteel well-heeled which gives more of the flavour of old Passy. You may no longer be able to have your Bechstein repaired here or your furniture lacquered, but the food shops that now dominate the street have delectable displays guaranteed to make your mouth water.

Maison de Balzac

47 rue Raynouard, 16ᵉ • Tues–Sun 10am–6pm • Free • ☎ 01 55 74 41 80 • RER Av-du-Prés-Kennedy–Maison-de-Radio-France/ⓂPassy

The **Maison de Balzac** is a delightful little house with pale-green shutters and a decorative iron entrance porch, tucked away down some steps in a tree-filled garden. Balzac moved to this secluded spot in 1840 in the hope of evading his creditors. He lived under a pseudonym, and visitors had to give a special password before being admitted. Should any unwelcome callers manage to get past the door, Balzac would escape via a back door and go to the river via a network of underground cellars. It was here that he wrote some of his best-known works, including *La Cousine Bette* and *Le Cousin Pons*.

The museum preserves his study, writing desk and monogrammed cafetière – frequent doses of caffeine must have been essential during his long writing stints, which could extend up to sixteen or eighteen hours a day for weeks on end. One room is devoted to the development of ideas for the creation of a monument to Balzac, resulting in the famously blobby Rodin sculpture of the writer; caricatures of the sculpture by cartoonists of the time are on display. Other exhibits include letters to Mme Hanska, whom he eventually married after an eighteen-year courtship, and a highly complex family tree of around a thousand of the four thousand-plus characters that feature in his *Comédie Humaine*. Outside, the shady, rose-filled garden is a serene haven and a pleasant place to dally on wrought-iron seats amid busts of the writer.

Rue Berton and around

ⓂPassy/La Muette

Behind the Maison de Balzac, reached via some steps descending from rue Raynouard, **rue Berton** is a cobbled path with gas lights still in place, blocked off by the heavy security of the **Turkish embassy**. The building, an eighteenth-century château, was once the home of Marie-Antoinette's friend, the Princesse de Lamballe, who met a grisly fate at the hands of revolutionaries in 1792. Later, it became a private asylum where the pioneering Dr Blanche treated patients with nervous disorders. The poet Gérard de Nerval was admitted in 1854, driven insane partly by the task of translating Goethe's *Faust* into French. Four years later, Charles Gounod, while working on the score for his opera *Faust*, based on Nerval's translation, was also treated here. And in 1892, Guy de Maupassant, suffering serious mental illness brought on by syphilis, was committed; he died here a year later. Get a better view of the building from **rue d'Ankara**, reached by heading down avenue de Lamballe, then left into avenue du Général-Mangin.

Musée du Vin and around

5 square Charles Dickens, 16ᵉ • Daily except Mon 10am–6pm • €11.90, admission includes a glass of wine • ☎ 01 45 25 63 26,
Ⓦ museeduvinparis.com • Ⓜ Passy

From rue d'Ankara, head northeast along avenue Marcel-Proust, turn right and then left onto rue Charles Dickens and follow it until it hits rue des Eaux, where fashionable Parisians used to come in the eighteenth century for the therapeutic benefits of the once-famous iron-rich Passy waters. Today, the street is enclosed by a canyon of moneyed apartments, which dwarf the eighteenth-century houses of **square Charles Dickens**. In one of these houses on the square, burrowing back into the cellars of a vanished, fourteenth-century monastery which produced wine until the Revolution, is the **Musée du Vin**, an exhibition of viticultural bits and bobs about as exciting as flat champagne, though the cellar bar is an atmospheric place for a glass of wine or lunch. Extensive stone-vaulted cellars and passages lead off from here to the ancient quarry tunnels – not visitable – from which the stone for Notre-Dame was hewn.

14

Back on rue Raynouard, head northeast to place du Costa-Rica, take the first right into rue de l'Alboni and go down the steps into square Alboni, a patch of garden enclosed by tall apartment buildings. Here the métro line emerges from what used to be a vine-covered hillside for the Passy stop, before rumbling out across the river by the **Pont de Bir-Hakeim**, the distinctive bridge featured in the racy Bertolucci film *Last Tango in Paris*, starring Marlon Brando. From here, you can hop onto Passy métro or cross the bridge and head north along the water to the Eiffel Tower about 500m along.

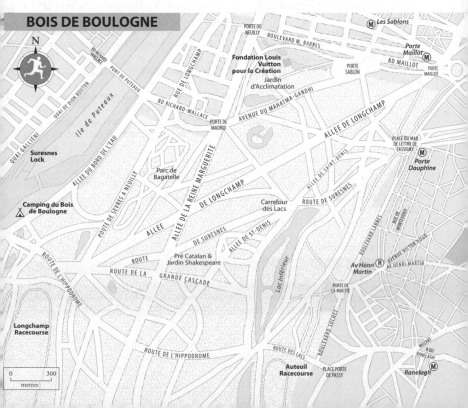

Bois de Boulogne

Ⓜ Porte Maillot/Porte Dauphine/bus #244

The **Bois de Boulogne** was designed by Baron Haussmann and supposedly modelled on London's Hyde Park – though it's a very French interpretation. The *bois*, or "wood", of the name is somewhat deceptive, though the extensive parklands do contain some remnants of the once great Forêt de Rouvray. The Bois was the playground of the wealthy, especially in the nineteenth century, although it also established a reputation as the site of illicit sex romps. Today's unions are no less disreputable – the area is a favoured haunt for prostitutes and accompanying kerb-crawlers who, despite an obvious police presence and the night-time closure of certain roads, still do business along its periphery. Accompanying the sex trade is a certain amount of crime; the park is a very unwise choice for a midnight promenade.

By day, however, the Bois de Boulogne is a delightful retreat from the city. While entry to the park as a whole is free, there are several attractions within it that have entry fees or limited opening times: the **Jardin d'Acclimatation**, which is aimed at children (see p.349); the beautiful floral displays of the **Parc de Bagatelle**; and the **racecourses** at Longchamp and Auteuil. You can also partake of a wealth of activities: there's a **riding** school, a **bowling** alley, 14km of **cycling** routes, **boating** on the Lac Inférieur, and more. The best, and wildest, part for **walking** is towards the southwest corner.

Fondation Louis Vuitton pour la Création

Av du Mahatma-Gandhi, Bois de Boulogne • Ⓜ Porte-Maillot

Inside the Jardin d'Acclimatation, a new Frank Gehry-designed contemporary art centre, the **Fondation Louis Vuitton pour la Création**, is due to open at the end of 2013. It's sure to be worth visiting, as much for the building itself as the art: Gehry's plan is for an impressive, light-filled glass structure dubbed the Cloud of Glass, designed to house the collection of the richest man in France, Bernard Arnault, CEO of the luxury goods company LVMH.

Parc de Bagatelle

Bois de Boulogne • Daily: March 9am–6.30pm; April & Sept 9am–8pm; May–Aug 9am–9pm • €5 • Ⓜ Porte-Maillot, then bus #244, which takes you to the entrance on allée de Longchamp; there's also an entrance on route de Sèvres à Neuilly

The **Parc de Bagatelle** comprises a range of garden styles from French and English to Japanese, and its most famous feature is the stunning **rose garden** of the charming Château de Bagatelle. It was designed and built in just over sixty days in 1775 as a wager between Comte d'Artois and his sister-in-law Marie-Antoinette, who said it could not be achieved in less than three months. The best time for the roses is June, while in other parts of the garden there are beautiful displays of tulips, hyacinths and daffodils in early April, irises in May and water lilies in early August. The park's attractive orangerie is the setting for candlelit recitals of Chopin's music during the Festival de Chopin in late June (see p.319).

Jardin Shakespeare

Bois de Boulogne • Daily 2–4pm • Free • Ⓜ Porte-Maillot

In the middle of the Bois de Boulogne, the Pré Catalan park is famous for its huge two-hundred-year-old copper beech tree and the prestigious *Pré Catalan* restaurant. Also here is the **Jardin Shakespeare**, where you can study the herbs, trees and flowers referred to in the Bard's plays; in summer, open-air Shakespeare plays and French classics are staged here.

LA DEFENSE

The suburbs

"The suburbs", in French, doesn't at all mean what it means in English. In the imagination of those safely ensconced *intra-muros*, or within the historic centre defined by the old city walls, the *banlieue* is no sleepily conservative ring of dormitory towns, but a dangerous belt populated by Reds, rioters and juvenile delinquents. It's true that politically, ethnically and economically, the outskirts of Paris are almost the reverse of the centre. The architecture of the *banlieue* is utterly different too, characterized by *cités* (high-rise housing estates) and industrial estates, with few historic vestiges – and little, at first glance, to attract the visitor. The suburbs do have a handful of quite extraordinary sights, however, and two in particular attract hordes of visitors.

The **St-Ouen market**, a segregated empire of antiques and curios, sprawls just outside the official city limits, beyond the so-called "plain of Montmartre". Then there's **Versailles**, an overwhelming monument to the reigns of Louis XIV, who built it, and Louis XVI, whose furniture now fills it; it sits in its own vast landscaped park on the very edge of the Paris conurbation, southwest of the city. A pleasingly elegant and little-visited alternative is the château of **Malmaison**, west of Paris, which preserves the exquisite Empire furnishings of Napoleon's wife, Joséphine, along with her delightful gardens. North of the city, at the centre of the most fascinating and troubled suburb of them all, stands the proud basilica of **St-Denis**, which was the birthplace of the Gothic style, and the burial place of almost all the French kings. To the west, the great landmark is the **Grande Arche**, the huge centrepiece of Paris's gleaming modern business district, **La Défense**. Whether the various suburban museums deserve your attention will depend on your degree of interest in the subjects they represent: air and space travel at **Le Bourget**; contemporary art in Vitry-sur-Seine's **Mac/Val**; and the authoritative collection of china at **Sèvres**.

15

Paris has long kept its suburbs at arm's length, keeping its eyes shut and holding its nose, but in 2009, Nicolas Sarkozy revealed ambitious – or hubristic, depending on your point of view – plans for his **presidential legacy**. Paris would be transformed into an eco-friendly metropolis dubbed "Le Grand Pari'" (see box, p.376); it would embody "truth, beauty and grandeur". In the short term, expect better transport links with central Paris; in the long term, don't hold your breath.

All of the sights listed in this section are easily accessible by RER, métro and bus. Sights further afield, for which you'll need to take a train or have access to a car, are covered in Chapter 16. For other attractions in the Ile-de-France region, the tourist office – Espace du Tourisme d'Ile-de-France; ⓦnouveau-paris-ile-de-france.fr in the Carrousel du Louvre (see p.38) – is a good source of information.

La Défense

Ⓜ/RER Grande-Arche-de-la-Défense

A thicket of glass and concrete towers, **La Défense**, just west of the city, is Paris's prestige **business district**. Over a hundred thousand people commute here daily during the week, and it's often a popular and animated place at weekends, too – at least by day. Fifty years on from its beginnings, a new wave of building is taking place. There's the sleek EDF building on place de la Défense, and the brand new, forearm-like **Tour Phare**, a sinuous skyscraper by American architect Thom Mayne that is designed to rival the Eiffel Tower in height and to wear its green credentials on its sleeve, in the form of a wind farm on the roof. A panoramic restaurant is planned for the opening in 2015.

La Grande Arche

ⓦ grandearche.com • Ⓜ/RER Grande-Arche-de-la-Défense

Built in 1989 to honour the bicentenary of the Revolution, and in conscious tribute to the Arc de Triomphe, **La Grande Arche** is an astounding structure: a 112m, white marble, hollow cube that's large enough to enclose Notre-Dame with ease. It closes the western axis of the Voie Triomphale (see p.6), albeit positioned at a slight angle so as to allow an uninterrupted view from its offices all the way to the Louvre's similarly askew Cour Carrée, 8km away. The architect was a little-known Danish professor, Johann Otto von Spreckelsen, whose previous projects amounted to no more than three churches and a house, and who tragically died before the arch's completion. The only thing that slightly mars its perfect form – or softens its brutality, depending on your point of view – is the lift scaffolding and a fibreglass "cloud" canopy, suspended within the hollow. Sadly, the thrillingly transparent lifts have been closed since an accident in 2010. The views from steps that lead up to the base of the arch, however, are just as

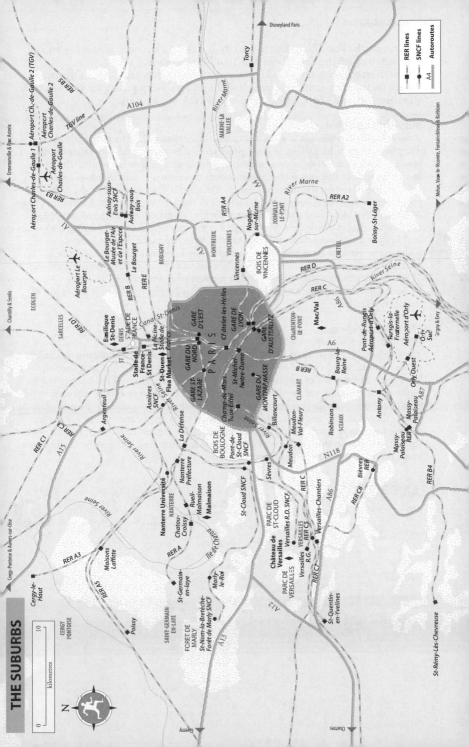

THE SUBURBS

0 kilometres 10

CERGY PONTOISE

N

Disneyland Paris

Torcy

A104

MARNE-LA VALLÉE

River Marne

RER B5

TGV line

Ermenonville & Parc Astérix

Aéroport Ch.-de-Gaulle 1 Aéroport Ch.-de-Gaulle 2 (TGV)
Aéroport Charles-de-Gaulle 2
Aéroport Charles-de-Gaulle

Aéro-ort Charles-de-Gaulle 1

RER B3

IV

RER B

Chantilly & Senis

ÉCOUEN

SARCELLES

RER D1

ST-

Aéroport Le Bourget

Le Bourget-Musée de l'Air et de l'Espace

Le Bourget

BOBIGNY

Aulnay-sous-Bois SNCF

Aulnay-sous-Bois

RER A4

River Marne

RER A2

Boissy-St-Léger

MONTREUIL

VINCENNES

Vincennes

Nogent-sur-Marne

JOINVILLE-LE-PONT

CRÉTEIL

BOIS DE VINCENNES

RER D

RER C

River Seine

Mac'Val

A86

CHARENTON-LE-PONT

A6

Bourg-la-Reine

Pont-de-Rungis Aéroport d'Orly

Rungis-la-Fraternelle

Aéroport d'Orly

Orly-Sud

Grigny & Evry

Melun, Vaux-le-Vicomte, Fontainebleau & Barbizon

Basilique St-Denis

STADE DE FRANCE

ST-DENIS

Canal St-Denis

La Plaine St-Denis

Stade de France

St-Ouen
Flea Market

Asnières SNCF

Argenteuil

RER C1

A15

River Seine

La Défense

Île de la Cité

Nanterre Préfecture

NANTERRE

Nanterre Université

Chatou-Croissy

Ruell-Malmaison

Malmaison

RER A

St-Cloud SNCF

Sèvres

Meudon

Meudon-Val-Fleury

Billancourt

Pont-de-St-Cloud SNCF

BOIS DE BOULOGNE

Robinson

SCEAUX

Antony

Massy-Palaiseau

Massy-Palaiseau RER

A87

Clamart

RER B

N118

A86

Bièvres RER

RER C8

RER B4

PARC DE ST-CLOUD

Versailles R.D. SNCF

Versailles RER C5

VERSAILLES R.G.

Château de Versailles

PARC DE VERSAILLES

RER C

Versailles-Chantiers

A12

St-Quentin-en-Yvelines

St-Rémy-Lès-Chevreuse

Cergy-le-Haut

CERGY PONTOISE

Maisons Laffitte

RER A3

RER A5

Poissy

St-Germain-en-laye

SAINT-GERMAIN-EN-LAYE

FORÊT DE MARLY

St-Nom-la-Bretèche-Forêt de Marly SNCF

Marly-le-Roi

Cergy-Pontoise & Auvers-sur-Oise

A13

Giverny

Chartres

GARE DU NORD
GARE DE L'EST
GARE ST LAZARE
Châtelet-les-Halles
GARE DE LYON
GARE D'AUSTERLITZ
St-Michel Notre-Dame
GARE DU MONTPARNASSE
Champ-de-Mars Tour Eiffel
P A R I S
River Seine

RER lines
SNCF lines
A4 Autoroutes

good: down the Voie Triomphale to the city and along a second, less well-known axis that leads through the Eiffel Tower and Tour Montparnasse.

The **closest station** to the Grande Arche is Ⓜ/RER Grande-Arche-de-la-Défense, though for the most dramatic approach to the arch it's worth getting off a stop early, at Ⓜ Esplanade-de-la-Défense, from where it's a twenty-minute walk.

Musée de La Défense

15 place de la Défense • Daily 10am–6pm, Sat till 7pm • Free • Ⓦ ladefense.fr/cat/tourisme • Ⓜ/RER Grande-Arche-de-la-Défense

The main artery of La Défense is the pedestrianized **Esplanade du Général de Gaulle**, bristling with shiny office towers, apartment blocks and modern artworks. The best in-depth guide to this area is the little **museum** downstairs at **Info Défense**, an information centre on the main place de la Défense. It displays some of the early projects that were put forward for La Défense in the 1930s, such as Le Corbusier's huge *Metropolis*-like high-rises, and the gigantic Victory Angel once considered in place of the Grande Arche. While here, you can pick up a map that shows all La Défense's main buildings and outdoor **sculptures** – of which there are around fifty altogether.

The oldest work of art is just behind, perched on a concrete plinth in front of a coloured plastic water sculpture: Barrias's bronze *La Défense de Paris*, dating from the 1880s and depicting a soldier defending a woman who symbolizes Paris. It commemorates the **defence of Paris** against the Prussians in 1870 and is the origin of the district's name.

The CNIT building

Ⓜ/RER Grande-Arche-de-la-Défense

The first building to go up at La Défense was the undulating **CNIT building**, to the right of the Grande Arche, erected in the 1950s as a trade exhibition centre and the first intimation of the area's modernist architectural future. The floor of the hangar-like building, all gleaming granite, is softened by slender bamboo trees; the serious activity takes place off in the far corners, where it seems every major computer company has an office. There's also a Fnac store, and a selection of cafés and brasseries. Across the way sprawls **Les Quatre Temps shopping centre**, one of the biggest of its ilk in Europe with some 250 shops on three levels. On the south side of the arch is the globe of the **Dôme Imax**, one of the world's largest cinema screens.

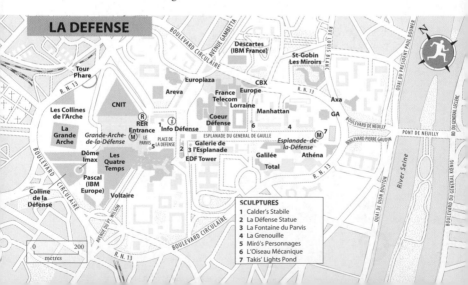

VERSAILLES PRACTICALITIES

To **get to Versailles**, take the RER line C5 to Versailles-Rive Gauche (40min; €2.90 single); turn right out of the station then take the first left onto avenue de Paris, which leads to the palace – a five-minute walk. The château is **open** throughout the year, except on Mondays, public holidays and during occasional state events. You can buy separate tickets to the **Grands Appartements** of the château and Marie-Antoinette's estate (including the Trianons), but it's probably worth buying the **Passeport Versailles** (Nov–March €16; April–Oct Mon–Fri €18, weekends €25 for "spectacle" days), a day-pass that gives access to all the main sights. Note that all tickets are free to under-18s and EU residents under 26, all year round – with the exception of admission to the Grandes Eaux and Jardins Musicaux events. You can buy tickets online at Ⓦ chateauversailles.fr, and print them out yourself; alternatively, pick them up from any branch of Fnac (see p.330) or the tourist offices at the Carrousel du Louvre (see p.38). Tickets are also available on arrival at the château itself, but you will need to queue for them.

A number of **guided tours** (prices vary) are available throughout the day, including English-language tours, which take you to wings of the palace that can't otherwise be seen; they can all be booked in the morning at the information point – turn up reasonably early to be sure of a place. It's well worth taking at least one tour, if only for the guides' commentaries, which are usually extremely well informed – though some anecdotes should be taken with a pinch of salt. Don't set out to see the whole palace in one day – it's not possible.

15

Versailles

RER Versailles-Rive Gauche

Twenty kilometres southwest of Paris, the distinctly royalist town of Versailles has grown up around the **Château de Versailles**, the vast palace built for Louis XIV. Consumed with envy of his finance minister's château at Vaux-le-Vicomte (see p.238), the king was determined to outdo him. He recruited the same design team – architect Le Vau, painter Le Brun and gardener Le Nôtre – and ordered something a hundred times the size. With its 700 rooms, 67 staircases and 352 fireplaces, Versailles is the apotheosis of French regal indulgence. Even if the self-aggrandizing decor of the "Sun King" is not to your liking, the palace's historical significance and anecdotes will enthral, and its park and gardens are a delight.

Château de Versailles

Ⓦ chateauversailles.fr • RER Versailles-Rive Gauche

Under its founder and master, Louis XIV, the Château de Versailles was the headquarters of every arm of the state, and the entire court of around 3500 nobles lived in the palace – in a state of unhygienic squalor, according to contemporary accounts. Construction began in 1664 and lasted virtually until Louis XIV's death in 1715, after which the château was abandoned for a few years before being reoccupied by Louis XV in 1722. It remained a residence of the royal family until the Revolution of 1789, when the furniture was sold and the pictures dispatched to the Louvre. Thereafter Versailles fell into ruin until Louis-Philippe established his giant museum of French Glory here; it still exists, though most is mothballed. In 1871, during the Paris Commune, the château became the seat of the nationalist government, and the French parliament continued to meet in Louis XV's opera building until 1879. Restoration only began in earnest between the two world wars, but today it proceeds apace, the château's management scouring the auction houses of the world in the search for original furnishings from Louis XVI's day. Ironically, they have been helped in the task by the efforts of the revolutionaries, who inventoried all the palace's furnishings before they were auctioned off in 1793–94, a process that took a year.

The Grands Appartements

Daily except Mon 9am–6.30pm, Nov–March till 5.30pm • €15, including audioguide; EU citizens under 26 free

The rooms you can visit without a guide are known as the **Grands Appartements**, and were used for all the king's official business – which meant all his daily life, as

Louis XIV was an institution as much as a private individual. His risings and sittings, comings and goings, were minutely regulated and rigidly encased in ceremony, attendance at which was an honour much sought after by courtiers. The route leads past the **royal chapel**, a grand structure that ranks among France's finest Baroque creations. From there, a procession of gilded drawing rooms leads to the king's throne room and the dazzling **Galerie des Glaces** (Hall of Mirrors), where the Treaty of Versailles was signed after World War I. Under the golden barrel ceiling, with its paintings by Charles Le Brun showing the glories of Louis XIV, Georges Clemenceau finally won his notorious "war guilt" clause, which blamed the entire conflict on German aggression. The *galerie* is best viewed at the end of the day, when the crowds have departed and the setting sun floods it from the west, across the park. More fabulously rich rooms, this time belonging to the **queen's apartments**, line the northern wing, beginning with the queen's bedchamber, which has been restored exactly as it was in its last refit of 1787, with hardly a surface unadorned with gold leaf. At the end of the visit, the staircase leads down to the **Hall of Battles**, whose oversize canvases unashamedly blow the trumpet for France's historic military victories; be thankful that most of the rest of Louis-Philippe's historical museum is out of bounds.

15

The park and gardens
Gardens daily 8am–8.30pm, Nov–March till 6pm • Free with château ticket, €8 during "spectacles"

You could spend the whole day just exploring the **gardens** at Versailles. Beyond the great Water Parterres designed by André Le Nôtre, with their statues symbolizing the rivers of France, geometrically planned walks and gardens stretch out on all sides. There are countless statues of nymphs and gods, fifty fountains, 34 pools and of course the cruciform Grand Canal, on which entire naval battles were re-created for the amusement of the court. The outer limits of the estate are known as the park, and are made up of woods and fields grazed by sheep; the northernmost area is part of the Domaine de Marie-Antoinette (see p.226), and visitable on a separate ticket.

Distances in the park are considerable. If you can't manage them on foot, you could hop on the **petit train**, which shuttles between the terrace in front of the château and the Trianons (€3.50 one way); it runs about every fifteen minutes in summer. Another option is to hire a **buggy**, for which you'll need a driving licence. You can rent **bikes** at the Grille de la Reine, Porte St-Antoine and by the Grand Canal, and **boats** on the Grand Canal, next to a pair of **café-restaurants**. There are plenty of little kiosks where you can get takeaway sandwiches, too.

THE SPECTACLES

On the busiest days of the year, the gardens play host to what the French call a "*spectacle*": that is, the authorities turn the fountains on, to the tune of piped classical music. The dates are complex, and worth checking online, but broadly the **Grandes Eaux Musicales** run on weekends from April to October, with Tuesdays added in late May and June, and Thursdays in June and July; operating hours are 11am–noon & 3.30–5.30pm (or 11am–noon & 2.30–4pm on the Tuesday dates). The less exciting **Jardins Musicaux** features the piped music without the fountains, and takes place on Tuesdays from April to mid-May and from July to late October (10am–6.30pm). On *spectacle* days, the *passeport* ticket price goes up to €25. Alternatively, you can buy a separate ticket for the Grandes Eaux Musicales for €8, or €7 for the Jardins Musicaux.

For the **Grandes Eaux Nocturnes**, the fountains play at night, and are sumptuously lit up. This event runs on Saturdays from mid-June to early September (the exact dates are worth checking online), starting at 9pm; the ticket costs a spectacular €22. It's preceded by a separate *spectacle* dubbed La Sérénade, in which musicians and dancers perform in the Galerie des Glaces at sunset; a combined ticket with the Grandes Eaux Nocturnes costs €38.

The Domaine de Marie-Antoinette

Château de Versailles park • Daily except Mon noon–6.30pm, Nov–March till 5.30pm • €10 • RER Versailles-Rive Gauche

Hidden away in the northern reaches of the park is the **Domaine de Marie-Antoinette** (Marie-Antoinette's estate), the queen's country retreat, centred on the Petit Trianon palace, where she could find some relief from the stifling atmosphere and etiquette of the court. Here she commissioned some dozen or so buildings, sparing no expense and imposing her own style and tastes throughout (and gaining herself a reputation for extravagance that wouldn't do her any favours in the long run). She also had a bucolic park created in the fashionable English style, and a miniature farm. The whole estate has been undergoing restoration funded by the Swiss watchmakers Breguet for several years, reviving a link with the queen that goes back to 1783 when Breguet's founder was commissioned to make her a watch with workings so complex that it was never completed in her lifetime.

The Petit Trianon

15

The estate's centrepiece is the elegant and restrained Neoclassical **Petit Trianon** palace, built by Gabriel in the 1760s for Louis XV's mistress, Mme de Pompadour, and given to Marie-Antoinette by her husband Louis XVI as a wedding gift. The interior boasts a fine stone and wrought-iron staircase, sculpted wood panelling, period furniture and the intriguing *cabinet des glaces montantes*, the queen's elegant pale-blue salon, fitted with sliding mirrors that could be moved by a sophisticated mechanism to conceal the windows, creating a more intimate space.

The Grand Trianon

Included in the ticket for the Domaine de Marie-Antoinette is the Italianate, pink-marble **Grand Trianon** palace, a little to the west, designed by Hardouin-Mansart in 1687 as a "country retreat" for Louis XIV. Its two wings are linked by a colonnaded portico, with formal gardens to the rear. Napoleon stayed here intermittently between 1805 and 1813 and had the interior refurbished in Empire style. Nowadays it's often used by the French president when entertaining foreign dignitaries.

The gardens and Hameau de la Reine

West of the Petit Trianon are the formal gardens (**Jardins à la française**), dotted with pavilions such as the octagonal **Pavillon français** with its gold and marble interior and frieze of sculpted swans, ducks and other wildfowl – which would have been farmed on the estate. More impressive still is the deceptively plain-looking **Petit Théâtre**, built for the queen in 1778–79, so that she could perform before the king and members of her inner circle, often taking the role of a shepherdess or maid. To the east lies the impossibly picturesque **Jardin anglais**, with its little winding stream, grassy banks dotted with forget-me-nots and daisies, classical temple (Le Temple d'Amour), fake waterfall and grotto with belvedere. Further east again lies the equally enchanting, if rather bizarre, **Hameau de la Reine**, a play village and thatch-roofed farm where Marie-Antoinette could indulge the fashionable Rousseau-inspired fantasy of returning to the natural life. The farm is stocked with cows, goats, pigs and hens – much to the delight of children.

Versailles town

The distinctly elegant town of **VERSAILLES** sits right up against the château gates. Its centrepiece is **place Notre-Dame**, which has a lively food market (Tues, Fri & Sun 7.30am–2pm). The surrounding streets are full of buzzy cafés, and the little cobbled **rue du Bailliage** and adjoining **passage de la Geôle** are lined with over fifty antique shops (Fri, Sat & Sun 10am–7pm; ⓦantiques-versailles.com), selling anything from tin soldiers to books, paintings and ceramics. Versailles is a markedly royalist, conservative town, but it does preserve a building dear to the heart of Republicans, the **Salle du Jeu de Paume**, rue du Jeu de Paume (April–Oct Sat & Sun 12.30–6.30pm; free). It was at this tennis court that the representatives of the Third Estate set the Revolution in progress, and sealed the fate of the French monarchy.

Potager du Roi

Rue du Maréchal Joffre, Versailles • Jan–March, Tues & Thurs 10am–1pm; April–Oct Tues–Sun 10am–6pm; Nov & Dec Tues & Thurs 10am–6pm, Sat 10am–1pm • April–Oct Tues–Fri €4.50, Sat & Sun €6.50; Nov–March €3 • ⓦ potager-du-roi.fr

To reach the **Potager du Roi**, or king's kitchen-garden, turn right as you exit the Château de Versailles' main gate and it's a five-minute signposted walk away. Put aside any thoughts of allotments: this is a walled area the size of a small farm. It was run by Louis XIV's head gardener, Jean-Baptiste La Quintinie, who managed to produce strawberries and melons in March and asparagus in December, and gave the king gardening lessons. Today, a statue of the great man – La Quintinie, that is – stands on the raised terrace watching over his plot, a great sunken square of espaliered fruit trees and geometrically arranged vegetables in the lee of the stately church of St-Louis. Some of the 150 varieties of apples and pears, and fifty types of vegetables, are sold in the little farm shop.

Grand Ecurie du Roy

April–Oct shows usually twice daily on Sat & Sun; see website • €25 • ☎ 01 48 39 18 03, ⓦ acadequestre.fr

Opposite the main entrance to the Château de Versailles, the Grand Ecurie du Roy, or royal stables, housed six hundred horses under Louis XIV. It's now the home of the **Académie du Spectacle Equestre**, which puts on highly choreographed theatrical shows of horsemanship at weekends, and some weekday evenings. You can also watch the horses being put through their paces at a morning training session (usually Sat & Sun 11.15am, more frequently during hols; €12).

Château de Malmaison

April–Sept Mon & Wed–Fri 10am–12.30pm & 1.30–5.45pm, Sat & Sun 10am–12.30pm & 1.30–6.15pm; Oct–March closes 30min earlier • €5 • ☎ 01 41 29 05 55, ⓦ www.chateau-malmaison.fr • Ⓜ/RER La Défense, then bus #258 from the bus station (every 30min; 25min) towards St-Germain-en-Laye; from Le Château stop, walk 100m back up av Bonaparte, cross over and take the signposted side road (a 10min walk in all)

According to Napoleon's private secretary, the **Château de Malmaison**, 15km west of central Paris, was "the only place next to the battlefield where he was truly himself". It was the home, after all, of his beloved Joséphine de Beauharnais, who shaped it as a perfect example of the cool First Empire style. After their divorce – Joséphine failed to provide the emperor with an heir – she stayed on, receiving just two visits from the emperor there before her death in 1814.

Visitors today can see the stately official apartments, on the ground floor, which are preserved almost exactly as they were in Joséphine's day. The design fashions reflect imperial interests in Italy and Egypt – which Napoleon was busy conquering at the time Joséphine first began her interior design works here, in 1799. The cloth-hung Salle du Conseil, where Napoleon had ministerial meetings, feels like a luxurious version of a campaign tent; it's now overlooked by a reproduction of Gérard's heartbreakingly lovely portrait of Joséphine, the original of which hangs in the Hermitage. The dining room owes its decor to fashionable interest in Pompeii, and still contains the fabulous, 80-piece gold dinner service used by the Empress. During the Nazi occupation, the imperial chair in the library was rudely violated by the fat buttocks of Reichsmarschall Goering, dreaming perhaps of promotion or the conquest of Egypt. On the top floor, a permanent exhibition shows off a more intimate side of the house's history. You can see Joséphine's collections and effects, including the most personal: her slippers, stockings, lace bonnet and petticoats, along with Napoleon's toothbrush.

15

The park and rose gardens

In Joséphine's time, Malmaison was renowned for its gardens, which nurtured scores of exotic species that had never before flowered in France, such as hibiscus, camellia and the heavenly magnolia soulangeana. They are still very lovely today. Behind the house extends a fine park in the English style, cut through by a picturesque stream and dotted with landmark trees – including a cedar of Lebanon planted by the imperial couple themselves, in 1800. On either side of the front courtyard stand two roseries, a distant echo of Malmaison's legendary collections from the latter half of the nineteenth century. (The question of whether there were roses here in Joséphine's own time, incidentally, is something of a historical mystery, but popular legend has it that the Empress cultivated scores of them herself.) The Roseraie moderne on the north side features repeat-flowering varieties; the Roseraie ancienne, on the south side, has precious old varieties that flower just once, in June. They're decent enough collections, but real enthusiasts will want to make for the Bois de Boulogne's Parc de Bagatelle (see p.218), or the legendary Roseraie de l'Hay, 12km south of Paris (Ⓦroseraieduvaldemarne.com).

15

Sèvres Cité de la Céramique

Museum daily except Tues 10am–5pm • €4.50 • ☎ 01 46 29 22 00, Ⓦ sevresciteceramique.fr • Ⓜ Pont-de-Sèvres

Around 10km southwest of Paris, the ceramic factory at **SEVRES** has been manufacturing some of the world's most renowned **porcelain** since the eighteenth century. The original style, with its painted coloured birds, ornate gilding and rich polychrome enamels, was so beloved by Louis XV's mistress, Madame de Pompadour, that two new colours, *rose Pompadour* and *bleu de roi*, were named after the couple in 1757. The compliment paid off: two years later, when the factory fell into financial trouble, the king bought up all the shares to guarantee its future, and it remained in royal hands until the Revolution. The site is now the **Cité de la Céramique**, which, alongside continuing to produce and sell fine ceramic ware, also houses the third-largest collection of it in the world (after Taipei and Istanbul), with fifty thousand pieces. Inevitably, displays centre on Sèvres ware, but there are also collections of Islamic, Chinese, Italian, German, Dutch and English pieces.

The simplest route is to take the métro to Pont-de-Sèvres, then cross the bridge and spaghetti junction on foot; the museum is the massive building facing the riverbank on your right. An alternative approach would be to take a train from St-Lazare to St-Cloud and head due south for about 1.5km through the **Parc de St-Cloud**, a verdant, landscaped garden the size of a large farm with a fine, geometrical sequence of pools and fountains; the museum stands at the park's southeasternmost corner.

St-Ouen market

Sat–Mon 9am–6.30pm • Ⓦ parispuces.com • Ⓜ Porte-de-Clignancourt/Garibaldi

The **St-Ouen market**, sometimes called the Clignancourt market, is located just outside the northern edge of the 18e arrondissement, in the suburb of St-Ouen. Its popular name of **les puces de St-Ouen**, or the "St-Ouen flea market", dates from the days when secondhand mattresses, clothes and other infested junk was sold here in a free-for-all zone outside the city walls. Nowadays, however, it's predominantly a proper – and very expensive – **antiques** market, selling mainly furniture, but also old zinc café counters, telephones, traffic lights, posters, jukeboxes and so on. Note that it's quieter on wet days and Mondays.

The closest **métro stop** is Porte-de-Clignancourt (line 4), from where it's a five-minute walk up the busy avenue de la Porte-de-Clignancourt, passing under the *périphérique*. Shaded by the flyover, **rue Jean-Henri-Fabre** is the heart of the light-fingered, unofficial fringe area, lined with stalls flogging leather jackets, rip-off DVDs and African souvenirs. Watch your wallet, and don't fall for the gangs pulling the three-card monte or cup-and-hidden-ball scams. For a quieter and scarcely slower approach, make for Garibaldi station on line 13, and approach the market from the north, along rue Kléber, rue Edgar-Quinet and rue des Rosiers.

The markets

The official complex spreads over a dozen separate markets and some two thousand shops. For the chance to buy something you could feasibly carry home by yourself, restrict yourself to one of three markets. Marché **Vernaison** is the oldest in the complex, and its maze-like, creeper-covered alleys are great fun to wander along, threading your way between stalls selling all kinds of bric-a-brac. Marché **Jules-Vallès** is smaller but similar, stuffed with books and records, vintage clothing, colonial knick-knacks and other curiosities. While you won't find any breathtaking bargains, there's plenty to titillate the eye at both. Marché **Malik** stocks mostly discount and vintage clothes and bags, as well as some high-class couturier stuff.

For casual browsing of antiques and curios, try Marché **Dauphine**, whose glazed roof shelters an eclectic mix of decorative antique furniture, vintage fashions and rare books, and Marché **Malassis**, where you'll find all kinds of little boutiques specializing in anything from maritime ephemera or jewellery to imaginatively restored eighteenth-century pieces and twentieth-century designer *objets*. For furnishings, the least expensive is Marché **Paul-Bert**, which offers furniture, china and the like, often unrestored and straight from the auction houses. Marché **Le Passage** has lots of fine

15

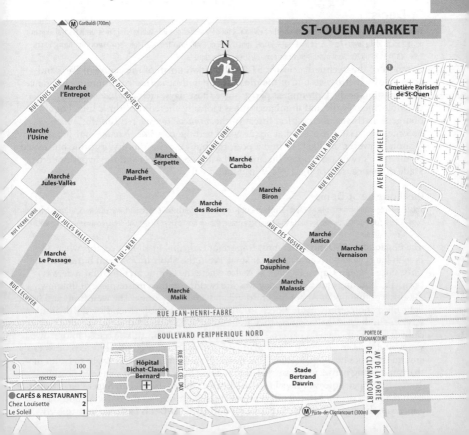

furnishings and objets d'art, including new pieces by contemporary designers and aged gardenware – and some vintage clothes stalls too.

The rest of the markets in the complex are seriously posh clusters of antiques shops, aimed as much at professionals as at private clients. Marché **Biron** is the most luxurious of all, full of eighteenth- and nineteenth-century gilt and crystal. Marché **Antica** and Marché **Cambo** are similar, the latter with an Art Deco area on the gallery level, while Marché **des Rosiers** concentrates on late nineteenth- and early twentieth-century glass, bronzes and ornaments. Marché **Serpette** covers seriously expensive twentieth-century collectors' furnishings, especially Art Deco and Art Nouveau. Marché **l'Entrepôt** houses large-scale antiques, from whole staircases to *boiserie* panelling and cast-iron gates. **L'Usine** is restricted to dealers only.

EATING AND DRINKING	ST-OUEN MARKET

Chez Louisette Allée 10, Vernaison. An old-school *buvette* buried at the end of Marché Vernaison's Allée 10. The great gypsy jazz guitarist, Django Reinhardt, sometimes played here, but these days singers belt out Parisian *chanson* with keyboard backing every Saturday afternoon. The food, famously, is very much not the thing, and the diner-like ambience won't be to all tastes, but it's a kitsch classic. Same hours as market.

Le Soleil 109 av Michelet ☏01 40 10 08 08. For a proper restaurant meal, book a table in advance at *Le Soleil*, where you'll pay upwards of €30 for unfussy but sound *cuisine bourgeoise*. This is where the market dealers come to eat when they've had a good morning. Mon–Wed & Sun noon–2pm, Thurs–Sat noon–2pm & 7.30–10.30pm.

St-Denis

Tourist office St-Denis' tourist office is opposite the basilica at 1 rue de la République. It sells tickets for the St-Denis Festival and can provide maps of the town • April–Sept Mon–Sat 9.30am–1pm & 2–6pm, Sun 10am–1pm & 2–4pm; Oct–March same hours, Sun till 2pm • ☏ 01 55 87 08 70, Ⓦ saint-denis-tourisme.com • Ⓜ St-Denis–Basilique

For most of the twentieth century, **ST-DENIS**, 10km north of the centre of Paris and accessible by métro, was one of the most heavily industrialized communities in France, and a bastion of the Communist party. Since those days, factories have closed, unemployment is rife and immigration has radically altered the ethnic mix. For bourgeois Parisians, the political threat of the *banlieue rouge* ("red suburbs") has become the social threat of what are now dubbed the *banlieue chaude* ("hot suburbs"). Visitors, however, are likely to find a poor but buoyant community, its pride buttressed by the town's twin attractions: the ancient **basilica of St-Denis** and the hypermodern **Stade de France**, seat of the 1998 World Cup final.

Basilique de St-Denis

1 place de la Légion d'Honneur, St-Denis • April–Sept Mon–Sat 10am–6.15pm, Sun noon–6.15pm; Oct–March Mon–Sat 10am–5pm, Sun noon–5.15pm; closed during weddings and funerals, and for extra services on feast days • €7 • Ⓦ saint-denis.monuments-nationaux.fr • Ⓜ St-Denis–Basilique

The **Basilique de St-Denis** is the most important cathedral in all France. It is where the French kings were both crowned (ever since Pepin the Short in 754) and buried (all but three since Hugues Capet, in 996). It is also where the Gothic architectural style was born. The building as it stands today was the twelfth-century masterpiece of unknown masons working under Abbot Suger, friend and adviser to kings. The west front and high, light-filled choir clearly made a deep impression on the bishops attending the dedication service – in the next half-century they went on to build most of the great Gothic cathedrals in France on its pattern. The innovative design can still be traced in the lowest storey of the choir, notably the ambulatory space, which allowed pilgrims to process easily around the relics held in the choir. The novel rib vaulting allowed the walls to be no more than an infilling between a stone skeleton, making huge, luminous windows possible. Today, the upper storeys of the choir are still airier than they were in Suger's day, having been rebuilt in the mid-thirteenth century, at the same time as the nave. A good way to appreciate the atmosphere in the basilica is during the **St-Denis Festival** (June to early

July; ☎01 48 13 06 07, ⓦfestival-saint-denis.com), when it plays host to top-flight classical concerts, with an emphasis on choral music.

The necropolis

You enter the **necropolis** via a separate entrance in the south portal. Immediately on the left is the bizarre sight of the bare feet of **François 1er** and his wife Claude de France peeking out of their enormous Renaissance memorial. Beside the steps to the ambulatory lies **Charles V**, the first king to have his funeral effigy carved from life, on the day of his coronation in 1364. Alongside him is his wife Jeanne de Bourbon, clutching the sack of her own entrails to her chest – a reminder that royalty was traditionally eviscerated at death, the flesh boiled away from the bones and buried separately.

The **ambulatory** itself is a beautiful double-aisled design raised on the revolutionary pointed or ogival vaults, and richly lit by some of St-Denis' original stained glass, including the famous Tree of Jesse window immediately behind the altar. Just up the south steps and around to the right, a florid Louis XVI and a busty **Marie-Antoinette** – often graced by bouquets of flowers – kneel in prayer; the pious scene was sculpted in 1830, long after their execution.

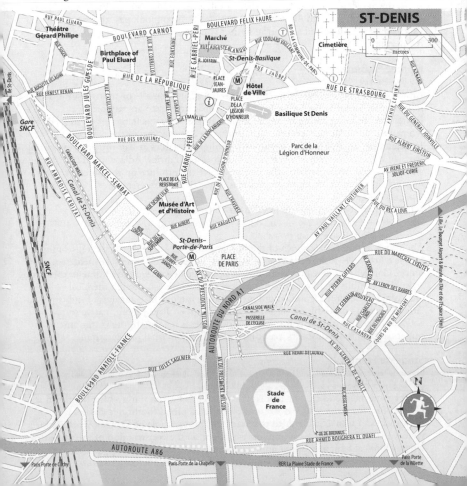

THE LEGEND OF ST DENIS

The first church at St-Denis was probably founded by an early (mid-third-century) Parisian bishop known by the name of St Denis, or St Dionysius in English. The legend goes that after he was decapitated for his beliefs at Montmartre – supposedly so-called because it is the "Mount of the Martyr" – he picked up his own head and walked all the way to St-Denis, thereby indicating the exact spot where his abbey should be built. It's not in fact all that far – just over 5km – though as a friend of Edward Gibbon's once remarked, "The distance is nothing, it's the first step that counts".

On the north side of the ambulatory you pass the effigy of the sixth-century king **Clovis I**, a canny little German who wiped out Roman Gaul and turned it into France, with Paris for a capital. His effigy was actually executed some six hundred years after his death; alongside is another Merovingian, Childebert I, whose twelfth-century effigy is the earliest in the basilica. On the right of the northern steps, the tomb of **Henri II** and **Catherine de Médicis** was boldly designed by Primaticcio in the style of a Classical temple: kneeling on top are sculptures by Germain Pilon of the royal couple as living souls; down below, you can just see their soulless, decaying corpses. Just beyond is the memorial to **Louis XII** and **Anne de Bretagne**; again, if you look past the graceful Renaissance structure and allegorical figures you'll see the pain-wracked bodies of the royal couple.

Marché St-Denis

Ⓜ St-Denis–Basilique

Although the centre of St-Denis still retains traces of its small-town origins, the area immediately abutting the basilica has been transformed into an extraordinary fortress-like housing and shopping complex, where teenagers hang out on mopeds and women shop for African groceries. The thrice-weekly **market**, in the main place Jean-Jaurès (Tues, Fri & Sun mornings), peddles vegetables at half the price of central Parisian markets, as well as cheap curios, clothes and fabrics. Adjacent, off rue Dupont, are the covered *halles*, a multi-ethnic affair where the produce on the butchers' stalls – ears, feet, tails and bladders – shows this is not rich folks' territory.

Musée d'Art et d'Histoire de la Ville de St-Denis

22bis rue Gabriel-Péri, St-Denis • Mon, Wed & Fri 10am–5.30pm, Thurs 10am–8pm, Sat & Sun 2–6.30pm • €5 • ☎ 01 42 43 05 10, Ⓦ musee-saint-denis.fr • Ⓜ St-Denis–Porte-de-Paris

About five minutes' walk south of the St-Denis basilica is the distinctly left-leaning **Musée d'Art et d'Histoire de la Ville de St-Denis**, housed in a former Carmelite convent on rue Gabriel-Péri. The quickest route is along rue de la Légion d'Honneur, then third right. The exhibits on display are not of spectacular interest, though the local archeology collection is good, and there are some interesting paintings of industrial landscapes and an exhibition on the Communist poet, Paul Éluard, native son of St-Denis. The one unique collection is of documents relating to the Commune: posters, cartoons, broadsheets, paintings, plus an audiovisual presentation.

Stade de France

Daily: school-term tours depart 11am, 1pm, 3pm & 5pm; school holidays hourly 10am–5pm • €12 • Ⓦ stadefrance.com • Ⓜ St-Denis–Porte-de-Paris

Just beyond the métro stop St-Denis–Porte-de-Paris (or ten minutes further down rue Gabriel-Péri from the Musée d'Art et d'Histoire), a broad footbridge crosses the motorway and Canal St-Denis to the **Stade de France**, scene of France's World Cup victory in 1998. At least €430 million was spent on the construction of this stadium, whose elliptical structure is best appreciated at night when lit up. If there isn't a match or a mega-event on, you can visit its grounds, facilities and small museum.

15

The St-Denis canal towpath

From the northern side of the Stade de France's footbridge it's possible to walk back to Paris all the way along the **canal towpath**. There are decaying, semi-abandoned stretches where it may feel as if you're not supposed to be there, but press on regardless and you'll eventually fetch up at Porte de la Villette, after no more than two hours. The walk is only picturesque in patches, but it's a fascinating way to probe Paris's rusting underbelly.

Le Bourget

Musée de l'Air et de l'Espace 5km east of St-Denis at Le Bourget airport • Tues–Sun 10am–6pm, Oct–March till 5pm • Free • ☎ 01 49 92 70 00, ⓦ museeairespace.fr • From central Paris, take the RER from Gare du Nord to Le Bourget station, then bus #152 to the museum

Five kilometres east of St-Denis, a short hop up the A1 motorway, is **Le Bourget** airport. Until the development of Orly in the 1950s it was Paris's principal gateway, and is closely associated with the exploits of pioneering aviators – Lindbergh landed here after his epic first flight across the Atlantic. Today Le Bourget is used only for internal flights, while some of the older buildings have been turned into a museum of powered flight, the **Musée de l'Air et de l'Espace**.

15

Mac/Val

Place de la Libération, 94400 Vitry-sur-Seine • Tues–Sun noon–7pm • €5, under-18s free • ☎ 01 43 91 64 20, ⓦ macval.fr • ⓜPorte-de-Choisy then bus #183 (the bus stop is right by the métro entrance on av de Choisy), direction Orly Terminal Sud, and get off at the Musée Mac/Val stop (a 15min journey)

Mac/Val, south of Paris in Vitry-sur-Seine, is a sleek, icebox-white slice of architectural contemporary cool, somehow deposited in the suburbs. With its edgy exhibitions of French art from the last fifty years, drawn from a distinguished, thousand-piece-strong collection, it's even luring Parisians away from the centre. Artists exhibited here include Daniel Buren, Jean Dubuffet, video artists Jean-Luc Vilmouth and Pierre Huyghe, and Christian Boltanski, known for his large-scale installations on themes related to the Holocaust. The collection houses some excellent works from the younger generation, too: look out for video artists Bertrand Lamarche and Melik Ohanian. The bookshop in the foyer is well stocked, and there's a restaurant on the ground floor.

Day-trips from Paris

In the further reaches and beyond the boundaries of Ile-de-France lie exceptional towns and sights that are still accessible as day-trips from Paris, and are worth making the effort to visit. An excursion to Chartres can seem a long way to go just to see one building; but then you'd have to go a very long way indeed to find a building to beat it. Of the châteaux that abound in this region, we describe only a select few: Chantilly, with its wonderful art museum; Vaux-le-Vicomte, the envy of Louis XIV; and Fontainebleau, the most elegant of Renaissance palaces. Monet's garden at Giverny, the inspiration for all his water lily canvases, is perennially popular; it's bright and vibrant in spring, hauntingly melancholy in autumn.

Chantilly

People mostly visit **CHANTILLY**, a small town 40km north of Paris, to watch horses race and to see Italian art in the romantic château, which rises from the centre of a lake amid a forested park. The town's famed, supersweet Chantilly cream provides an extra enticement. The horses are hard to miss: scores of thoroughbreds can be seen thundering along the forest rides of a morning, and two of the season's classiest flat races are held here – the Jockey Club and the Prix de Diane, held on the first and second Sunday in June. The **château** has a fabulous art collection, and stables almost as grand as the main building, and you can try Chantilly cream in the café in the Hameau, the rustic faux-village within the château grounds.

Château de Chantilly

Daily except Tues: château April–Oct 10am–6pm, Nov–March 10.30am–5pm; park April–Oct 10am–8pm, Nov–March 10.30am–6pm • Pass Domaine with Musée Vivant du Cheval €20; château and park only €13; park only €6 • ☏ 03 44 27 31 80, ⓦ chateaudechantilly.com

The Chantilly estate has been the powerbase of two of the most powerful clans in France: first to the Montmorencys, then, through marriage, to the Condés. The present, mostly late nineteenth-century **château** replaced a palace, destroyed in the Revolution, which had been built for the Grand Condé, who smashed Spanish military power on behalf of the infant king, Louis XIV, in 1643. It's a beautiful structure, surrounded by what's more a lake than a moat, looking out in a romantic manner over a formal arrangement of pools and gardens created by the busy André Le Nôtre, the designer of the gardens at Versailles (and indeed at every other seventeenth-century château with pretensions to grandeur). In summer, you can rent rowboats on the Grand Canal.

16

Musée Condé

The **Musée Condé**, which occupies the nineteenth-century Grand Château, harbours one of the greatest collections of Classical art in France. Stipulated to remain exactly as organized by Henri d'Orléans, the son of France's last king and the donor of the château, the arrangement is madly crowded by modern standards, and yet immensely satisfying, as the pictures almost seem to spark ideas off each other. Some highlights can be found in the Rotunda – Piero di Cosimo's allegorical *Simonetta Vespucci* and Raphael's *Virgin of Loreto* – and in the Sanctuary, with Raphael's tiny *Three Graces* displayed alongside Filippo Lippi's *Esther and Assuerius*. But the highlight must be the octagonal and gorgeously red-walled Tribune, where Botticelli's resplendently fertile *Autumn* seems to rival Ingres' astoundingly sexy *Venus Anadyomene*, and works by Delacroix, Poussin and Van Dyck crowd in all around.

Chapelle and Cabinet des Livres

Alongside the Musée Condé, you can visit two of the château's rooms freely on the main entrance ticket. The **chapel** exists primarily to glorify the bronze and marble mausoleum of Henri II de Bourbon, father of Le Grand Condé; one of the two statues contains the

---

USEFUL INFORMATION FOR DAY-TRIPS

At the end of each individual account you'll find information on how to get there. Return train tickets cost €10–30, depending on how far you're going. For Fontainebleau and usually Chantilly as well, you can save a few euros by buying a combined train and château entry ticket ("Forfait Loisirs") at the station before you leave. To check times of specific trains, contact the national train carrier, the SNCF (☏ 08 92 30 83 08, ⓦ sncf-voyages.com), or the transport group for the Paris region, Transilien (ⓦ transilien.com); RER and métro routes can be consulted at RATP (ⓦ ratp.fr). **Tourist Information** on the region surrounding Paris, the Ile-de-France, can be found at ⓦ new-paris-ile-de-france.co.uk.

hearts of all the Princes de Condé. The inlaid wooden *boiseries*, brought here from the Château of Ecouen, are particularly fine, too. The **library** displays a perfect facsimile – and browsable, digitized version – of the fabulous **Les Très Riches Heures du Duc de Berry**. This is the most celebrated of all the medieval Books of Hours, and the museum's single greatest treasure. The illuminated pages illustrating the months of the year with representative scenes from contemporary (early 1400s) rural life – like harvesting and ploughing, sheep-shearing and pruning – are richly coloured and drawn with a delicate naturalism.

Appartements Privés

A free, forty-minute guided tour (French only) will take you round the private apartments of the Princes de Condé, on the first floor of the sixteenth-century wing known as the Petit Château. The tour mostly shows off superb furnishings, but there is a rare highlight: the exquisite *boiseries* panelling the walls of the newly restored **Singerie**, or Monkey Gallery, wittily painted with allegorical stories in a pseudo-Chinese style. A grand parade of canvases in the long gallery depicts the many battles won by the Grand Condé. A second guided tour (€6) takes you round the elegant but surprisingly intimate ground-floor apartments of the Petit Château, which belonged to the château's last private owners, the Duc and Duchesse d'Aumale. It was they who bequeathed the château to the Institut de France (see p.133), its

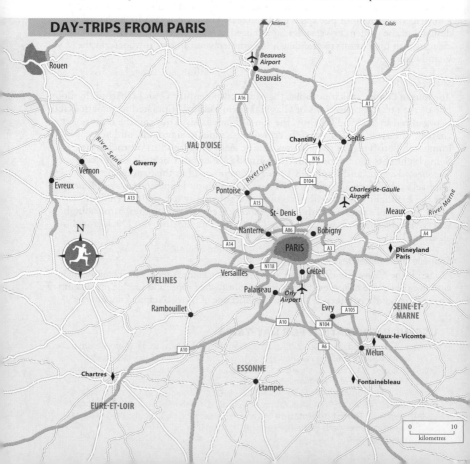

DAY-TRIPS FROM PARIS

A MAN OF HONOUR

Chantilly is perhaps most famous as the venue for a single notorious incident: **the suicide of Vatel**. The story is widely retold to illustrate the otherworldly moral code of the *ancien régime*. Major-domo to the nobility, (supposed) inventor of Chantilly cream and orchestrator of financier Fouquet's fateful supper party in 1661 (see p.238), François Vatel was justifiably proud of his status. In April 1671, the Prince de Condé set him to organize a feast for three thousand guests, in honour of Louis XIV. On the opening evening, two tables went without meat thanks to unexpected arrivals. "I cannot endure such a humiliation," Vatel was heard to say, over and over again. At four in the morning, the distraught maître d' was seen wandering the corridors of the palace, where he met a fish supplier with two baskets of fish "Is that all there is?" he asked, in horror. Not knowing that Vatel had sent for supplies from all over France, the man replied "Yes". Dishonoured, Vatel played the Roman and ran upon his sword.

present owners. The Duc d'Aumale had little reason to cling to it, in fact, as he was not actually a Condé, but the fifth son of King Louis-Philippe, and inherited the château through his godfather, Louis VI Henri, who had lost all six of his children – the eldest son was actually murdered on the orders of Napoleon, in 1804. The Duc d'Aumale's inheritance was doubly surprising as the old Condé was only induced to change his will by his mistress, a former prostitute named Sophia Dawes, who was also suspected of having murdered him, after the 74-year-old prince was found hanging from his bedroom window (not here, but in another château, at St-Leu), strung up by two knotted handkerchiefs.

16

The Musée Vivant du Cheval

7 rue Connétable, 60500 Chantilly • Museum closed for renovation until 2014, check website for updated opening hours • €11, or €20 combined ticket with Château de Chantilly and park (€29.50 with ticket to Spectacle Equestre) • ☎ 03 44 27 31 80, ⓦ museevivantducheval.fr

Five minutes' walk back towards town along the drive of the Château de Chantilly stands the colossal stable block, the **Grandes Ecuries**, looking out towards the racetrack. The building was erected at the beginning of the eighteenth century by the incumbent Condé prince, who believed he would be reincarnated as a horse and wished to provide fitting accommodation for 240 of his future relatives. The actual museum part of the **Musée Vivant du Cheval** is shut for restoration until 2014, but the vast, barrel-vaulted main hall still has stalls for horses of different breeds from around the world. In the central ring a specialist team of riders and trainers put on an equestrian demonstration show, **"Chevaux en fête"**, of the Spanish Riding School type, or the more elaborate, choreographed Spectacle Equestre. Shows are mostly twice daily (11am & 2.30pm, except Tuesdays), with the Spectacle mostly taking place on weekend afternoons in summer – there is a programme throughout the year, so check online.

Potager des Princes

17 rue Faisanderie, 60500 Chantilly • Mid-March to Oct daily except Tues 2–7pm • €8.50 • ☎ 03 44 57 39 66, ⓦ potagerdesprinces.com

Set 400m down from the Grandes Ecuries stables, one block north of the main rue du Connétable, the lush **Potager des Princes**, or "kitchen garden of the princes", is more than merely meticulously planted herbs and vegetables – though it is that, in the best French tradition. There are also fountains set amid beds of flowers, a Japanese garden and bamboo maze, and a luscious orchard, which was designed for the Grand Condé by the ubiquitous Le Nôtre. Children may be more excited by the collection of rare hens, ducks and pheasants, the "rabbit village", and the goats, gambolling beside the garden of exotic plants.

ARRIVAL AND DEPARTURE

By train Four or five trains daily serve Chantilly Gouvieux station (30min), departing from Paris's Gare du Nord – on the main Grandes Lignes level, not the downstairs level serving the suburbs – on the line to Creil. Free buses to the town centre (line 15) usually wait right outside the station; you have to get off by the Grandes Ecuries and walk 500m to the château gates. It's arguably more pleasant to take a direct, half-hour stroll along a signposted, beech-shaded footpath; turn right outside the station, then almost immediately left at the roundabout along the av des Aigles; you'll pass the racetrack about a third of the way along.

By car Chantilly is less than an hour's drive north on the A1 motorway; exit 7, signposted Chantilly, takes you in quick succession via the D16 and D1017 onto the D924A, which you follow for 8km through the forest up to the château gate.

Vaux-le-Vicomte

Mid-March to mid-Nov daily 10am–6pm • €14, €16 including Appartements Privés de Fouquet; garden only €8 • ☎ 01 64 14 41 90, Ⓦ vaux-le-vicomte.com

Of all the great mansions within reach of a day's outing from Paris, the Classical château of **Vaux-le-Vicomte**, 46km southeast of Paris, is the most architecturally harmonious, the most aesthetically pleasing and the most human in scale. It stands isolated in the countryside amid fields and woods, and its gardens make a lovely place to picnic.

The château was built between 1656 and 1661 for **Nicolas Fouquet**, Louis XIV's finance minister, by the finest design team of the day – architect Le Vau, painter-designer Le Brun and landscape gardener Le Nôtre. The result was magnificence and precision in perfect proportion, and a bill that could only be paid by someone who occasionally confused the state's accounts with his own. Fouquet, however, had little chance to enjoy his magnificent residence. On August 17, 1661, he invited the king and his courtiers to a sumptuous housewarming party. Three weeks later he was arrested – by d'Artagnan of Musketeer fame – charged with embezzlement, of which he was certainly guilty, and clapped into jail for the rest of his life. Thereupon, the king stripped the château of most of its furnishings, and carted off the design trio to build his own Versailles.

By 1875, the château had passed through a series of incompetent aristocratic hands and had fallen into a state of utter dereliction. It was bought by Alfred Sommier, a French industrialist, who made its restoration and refurbishment his life's work. It was finally opened to the public in 1968. Today, work continues on restoring more and more public rooms to their original grandeur.

The château and gardens

Candlelight illumination of state rooms and gardens early May to early Oct Sat 8pm–midnight • €17 including château entry after 2pm (château closes 6–8pm)

Seen from the entrance, the **château** is a rather austerely magnificent pile surrounded by an artificial moat. It's only when you go through to the south side, where the gardens decline in measured formal patterns of grass and water, clipped box and yew, fountains and statuary, that you can look back and appreciate the very harmonious and very French qualities of the building – the combination of steep, tall roof and bulbous central dome with classical pediment and pilasters.

The interior is opulent, and its main artistic interest lies in the work of **Le Brun**. He was responsible for the two fine **tapestries** in the entrance, made in the local workshops set up by Fouquet specifically to adorn his house, and subsequently removed by Louis XIV to become the famous Gobelins works in Paris (see p.172). Le Brun also painted numerous **ceilings**, notably in Fouquet's bedroom, the Salon des Muses, his *Sleep* in the Cabinet des Jeux, and the so-called "king's bedroom", whose decor is the first example of the ponderously grand style that became known as Louis XIV. Other points of interest are the cavernous **kitchens**, which have not been altered since construction, and a room displaying letters in the hand of Fouquet, Louis XIV and other notables. One, dated November 1794 (mid-Revolution), addresses the incumbent Duc de Choiseul-Praslin as *tu*. "Citizen," it says, "you've got a week to hand over one hundred thousand pounds…", and signs off with "Cheers and brotherhood".

The **Musée des Equipages** in the stables comprises a collection of horse-drawn vehicles, complete with model horses. On Saturday evenings in summer the **state rooms** and gardens are illuminated with two thousand candles, as they probably were on the occasion of Fouquet's fateful party, with classical music in the gardens adding to the effect. The **fountains** and other waterworks can be seen in action on the second and last Saturday of the month (April to early Nov only; 3–6pm).

ARRIVAL AND DEPARTURE	VAUX-LE-VICOMTE
By train There are half-hourly services from the Gare de Lyon as far as Melun (25min), from where a shuttle-bus service (€7 return) covers the journey to the château – but only at weekends (and only Saturdays from June to August), and only serving some trains; check ⓦ vaux-le-vicomte.com for up-to-date timetables. On	weekdays, you'll have to take a taxi for the last 7km (around €15 one way); there's a rank at the train station, with numbers to call if there are no taxis waiting. **By car** Vaux-le-Vicomte is 7km east of Melun, which is itself 46km southeast of Paris by the A4 autoroute (exit Melun-Sénart) or a little further by the A6 (exit Melun).

Fontainebleau

Daily except Tues 9.30am–6pm, Oct–March till 5pm • €10 • ☎ 01 60 71 50 70, ⓦ musee-chateau-fontainebleau.fr

The **château of Fontainebleau**, 60km south of Paris, was once a mere hunting lodge in the magnificent forest that still surrounds it. Its transformation into an extravagantly luxurious palace only took place in the sixteenth century on the initiative of François I, who imported a colony of Italian artists to carry out the decoration, most notably Rosso Fiorentino, Primaticcio and Niccolò dell'Abate. The palace continued to enjoy royal favour well into the nineteenth century; Napoleon spent huge amounts of money on it, as did Louis-Philippe. And, after World War II, when it was liberated from the Germans by General Patton, it served for a while as Allied military HQ in Europe. The town has since become the seat of the prestigious INSEAD business school – a hothouse for future directors of Tesco and the like.

16

The château

The **buildings**, unpretentious and attractive despite their extent, have none of the unity of a purpose-built residence like Vaux-le-Vicomte. In fact, their chief architectural delight is the gloriously chaotic profusion of styles. From the expanse of the **Cour du Cheval Blanc**, built as a humble *basse cour* or working courtyard in the 1530s, you progress up a seventeenth-century horseshoe staircase into a confusion of wings, courtyards and gardens. At the very heart of the palace, the secretive and splendidly asymmetrical **Cour Ovale** conceals a twelfth-century fortress keep, jarringly but pleasingly flanked by fine Renaissance wings on either side.

The palace's highlights, however, are the sumptuous **interiors** worked by the Italians, chiefly the dazzlingly frescoed **Salle de Bal** and the celebrated **Galerie François I**, which is resplendent in gilt, carved, inlaid and polished wood, and adorned down its entire length by intricate stucco work and painted panels covered in vibrant Mannerist brushwork. The paintings' Classical themes all celebrate or advocate wise kingship, and had a seminal influence on the development of French aristocratic art and design.

The Petits Appartements and museums

Petits Appartements • Call on the day for timetables of guided tours • €6.50 • ☎ 01 60 71 50 60

Utterly contrasting in style is the sober but elegant decor of Napoleon's **Petits Appartements**, the private rooms of the emperor, his wife and their intimate entourage. You have to buy a separate ticket to join the (obligatory) guided tour, but a tour of the **Musée Napoléon** – which displays a wide variety of souvenirs, some very personal, some official – is included in the main château ticket. The tour of the **Musée Chinois** shows off the Empress Eugénie's private collection of Chinese and Thai objets d'art in their original Second Empire setting; you also get to visit the Empress's breathtaking private theatre.

The gardens and the Forest of Fontainebleau

The **gardens** are equally splendid and in the summer months you could splash about on the Etang des Carpes, an ornamental lake with a Classical pavilion as its island centrepiece; you can't swim but you can rent boats. If you want to escape into the relative wilds, head for the surrounding **Forest of Fontainebleau**, which is full of walking and cycling trails, all marked on Michelin map #106 (*Environs de Paris*). Its rocks are a favourite training ground for Paris-based climbers.

ARRIVAL AND DEPARTURE   FONTAINEBLEAU

By train it's forty minutes from the Gare de Lyon to Fontainebleau-Avon station, from where shuttle buses take you to the château gates in fifteen minutes. Getting to Fontainebleau from Paris is straightforward. **By car** it's 16km from the A6 autoroute (exit Fontainebleau).

Chartres

When King Philippe-Auguste visited **CHARTRES** to mediate between church and townsfolk after the riots of October 1210, the cathedral chapter noted that "he did not wish to stay any longer in the city but, so as to avoid the blasphemous citizens, stayed here only for one hour and hastened to return". Chartres' modern visitors often stay little longer, but if you've come all the way from Paris, a journey of 80km, the modest charms of the little town at the cathedral's feet may persuade you to linger. One of the world's most astounding buildings, the cathedral is best experienced early or late in the day, when the low sun transmits the stained-glass colours to the interior stone and the quiet scattering of people leaves the acoustics unconfused.

The cathedral

Cloître Notre-Dame, 28000 Chartres • Daily 8.30am–7.30pm • Free • ☎ 02 37 21 75 02, ⓦ diocesechartres.com/cathedrale

Built between 1194 and 1260, the Gothic **cathedral** was one of the quickest ever constructed and, as a result, preserves a uniquely harmonious design. An earlier Romanesque structure burnt down in 1194, but the church's holiest relic – the **Sancta Camisia**, supposed to have been the robe Mary wore when she gave birth to Jesus – was discovered three days later, miraculously unharmed. It was a sign that the Virgin wanted her church lavishly rebuilt, at least so said the canny medieval fundraisers. Thereafter, hordes of pilgrims stopped here on their way south to the shrine of Santiago de Compostela in Spain, and the church needed to accommodate them with a sizeable crypt, for veneration of the relic, and a nave large enough to sleep hundreds – the sloping floor evident today allowed for it to be washed down more easily.

The interior

The geometry of Chartres cathedral is unique in being almost unaltered since its consecration, and virtually all of its stained glass is original – and unsurpassed – thirteenth-century work. Many of the windows in the nave were donated by craft guilds and merchants, whose symbols can often be seen in the bottommost pane. Some of the stories fit the donors' work, such as the carpenters' window showing Noah's ark. The superb, largely twelfth-century "**Blue Virgin**" window, in the first bay beyond the south transept, is filled with a primal image of the Virgin that has been adored by pilgrims for centuries. The **choir screen**, which curves around the ambulatory, depicts scenes from the lives of Christ and the Virgin. Its sculptor, Jehan de Beauce, was also responsible for the design of the Flamboyant Gothic north spire.

Chartres may be the best-preserved medieval cathedral in Europe, but if a group of medieval pilgrims suddenly found themselves here they would be deeply dismayed. Since their time, the sculptures on the exterior portals have lost their bright paint and gilt, while the walls have lost the whitewash that once so well reflected the stained-glass windows. Worse still, the high altar has been brought down into the body of the church, among the hoi polloi, and chairs cover up the **labyrinth** on the floor of the nave (except on Fridays between Easter and October, when you can trace its 200m-long route all the way to the centre), whose diameter is the same size as that of the rose window above the main doors.

Outside, hosts of sculpted figures stand like guardians at each entrance portal. Like the south tower and spire which abuts it, the mid-twelfth-century Royal Portal actually survives from the earlier Romanesque church, and it's interesting to compare its relatively stylized figures with the more completely Gothic sculptures on the north and south porches, completed half a century later.

The north tower and the gardens

North tower May–Aug Mon–Sat 9.30am–noon & 2–5.30pm, Sun 2–5.30pm; Sept–April Mon–Sat 9.30am–noon & 2–4.30pm, Sun 2–4.30pm • €7

Crowds permitting, it's worth climbing the three hundred steps up the **north tower** for its bird's-eye view of the sculptures and structure of the cathedral. The **gardens** behind

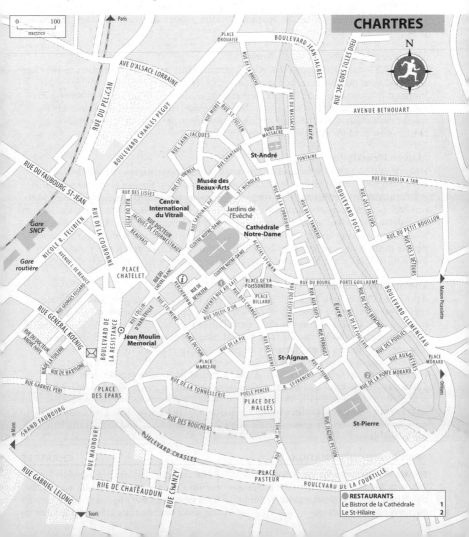

the cathedral, meanwhile, are a perfect spot for contemplation of the flying buttresses. There are a couple of paying extras, including the crypt and a collection of ecclesiastical treasures, but they're relatively unimpressive.

Centre International du Vitrail and Musée des Beaux-Arts

Centre International du Vitrail 5 rue du Cardinal-Pie, 28000 Chartres • Mon–Fri 9.30am–12.30pm & 1.30–6pm, Sat 10am–12.30pm & 2.30–6pm, Sun 2.30–6pm • €4 • ☎ 02 37 21 65 72, Ⓦ centre-vitrail.org **Musée des Beaux-Arts** 29 Cloître Notre-Dame, 28000 Chartres • May–Oct Mon & Wed–Sat 10am–noon & 2–6pm, Sun 2–6pm; Nov–April Mon & Wed–Sat 10am–noon & 2–5pm, Sun 2–5pm • €3.20 • ☎ 02 37 90 45 80

Occasional exhibitions of stained glass take place in the **Centre International du Vitrail**, a foundation devoted to sustaining and promoting the art form. The half-timbered building was once a medieval wine and grain store, and has a handsomely vaulted interior. The **Musée des Beaux-Arts**, in the rather gorgeous former episcopal palace just north of the cathedral, has some beautiful tapestries, a room full of the works of French Fauvist Vlaminck, as well as the Spanish Baroque painter Zurbarán's *St Lucy*. It puts on good temporary exhibitions.

The river and Collégiale de St-André

Behind the Musée des Beaux-Arts, rue Chantault leads past old townhouses to the river Eure and Pont du Massacre. You can follow this reedy river lined with ancient wash houses downstream along rue de la Tannerie, or upstream via rue du Massacre on the right bank. On the latter route, the cathedral appears from time to time through the trees; closer at hand, on the left bank, is the Romanesque **Collégiale de St-André**, a church now used for art exhibitions and concerts.

Maison Picassiette

22 rue du Repos, 28000 Chartres • April Mon & Wed–Sat 10am–noon & 2–5pm, Sun 2–5pm; May, June & Sept Mon & Wed–Sat 10am–noon & 2–6pm, Sun 2–6pm; July & Aug Mon & Wed–Sat 10am–6pm, Sun 2–6pm; Oct Sat 10am–noon & 2–6pm, Sun 2–6pm • €5.20

A left turn at the southern end of rue de la Tannerie, then third right, will bring you to one of Chartres' more eccentric tourist attractions. Over almost thirty years, the **Maison Picassiette** was coated with mosaics using bits of broken pottery and glass by a local road-mender and cemetery caretaker, Raymond Isidore. "I took the things that other people threw away", as he put it, before he died in 1964. The result was mocked by locals in Isidore's time, but is a quirky yet moving example of Christian Naïve art.

The medieval town

At the end of rue de la Tannerie, the bridge over the river brings you back to Chartres' **medieval town**. At the top of rue du Bourg there's a turreted staircase attached to a house, and at the eastern end of place de la Poissonnerie, a carved salmon decorates a sixteenth-century building. The **food market** takes place on place Billard and rue des Changes, and there's a **flower market** on place du Cygne (Tues, Thurs & Sat).

At the edge of the old town, on the corner of rue Collin-d'Harleville (to the right if you're coming up from the station), stands a memorial to **Jean Moulin**, Prefect of Chartres until he was sacked by the Vichy government in 1942. When the Germans occupied the town in 1940, Moulin refused to sign a document attributing Nazi atrocities to Senegalese soldiers in the French army. He later became De Gaulle's number one man on the ground, coordinating the Resistance, and died at the hands of Klaus Barbie in 1943.

ARRIVAL AND INFORMATION   CHARTRES

By train Services run from the Gare du Montparnasse at least every hour on weekdays, but note that there are slightly fewer trains at weekends, especially on Sundays; the journey takes roughly one hour.

By car Chartres is 91km from Paris, around 1hr 15min by car. From the *périphérique*, follow the A6B autoroute, then follow the signs just after Villejuif and L'Haÿ-les-Roses that lead you via the E50 onto the A10 near Massy. Follow the signs onto the A11 near Orsay, and follow this to Chartres, coming off at junction 2.

Tourist office Mid-April to mid-Oct Mon–Sat 9.30am–6.30pm, Sun 10am–5.30pm; mid-Oct to mid-April Mon–Sat 9am–6pm, Sun 9.30am–5pm; ☏ 02 37 18 26 26, ⊛ chartres-tourisme.com. The tourist office is five minutes' walk from the train station, by the cathedral.

EATING AND DRINKING

Le Bistrot de la Cathédrale 1 Cloître Notre-Dame ☏ 02 37 36 59 60. This pocket wine bar and *bistrot* has a perfect spot right opposite the cathedral, and it doesn't waste it, with simple dishes like "poule au pot Henri IV", a good selection of Loire wines, friendly service and a summer *terrasse* outside. Small list of *plats* on the blackboard, for around €17. Closed Wed.

St-Hilaire 11 rue du Pont St-Hilaire ☏ 02 37 30 97 57. The genteel *St-Hilaire* serves refined regional cuisine (*menus* from €27) in a sweet little upstairs dining room. Closed Mon & Sun.

Giverny

84 rue Claude Monet, 27620 Giverny • April–Oct daily 9.30am–6pm • €8 • ☏ 02 32 51 28 21, ⊛ fondation-monet.fr

Claude Monet considered his **gardens at Giverny** to be his greatest masterpiece. They're way out in Normandy, 65km from Paris in the direction of Rouen, but well worth the trip. Monet lived in Giverny from 1883 till his death in 1926, painting and repainting the effects of the changing seasonal light on the gardens he laid out between his house and the river. Every month from spring to autumn has its own appeal, but May and June, when the rhododendrons flower round the lily pond and the wisteria bursts into colour over the famous Japanese bridge, are the prettiest months to visit – though you'll have to contend with crowds photographing the water lilies and posing on the bridge. **Monet's house** stands at the top of the gardens, an idyllic pastel-pink building with green shutters. Inside, the rooms are all painted different colours, exactly as they were when Monet lived here, and the painter's original collection of Japanese prints, including wonderful works by Hokusai and Hiroshige, still hangs on the walls.

16

Musée des Impressionnismes

99 rue Claude Monet, 27620 Giverny • April–Oct Tues–Sun 10am–6pm • €6.50 • ☏ 02 32 51 94 65, ⊛ www .museedesimpressionnismesgiverny.com

Just up rue Claude Monet from the gardens is the **Musée des Impressionnismes**, which puts on exhibitions of works not just by Impressionists but by artists influenced by the movement. The museum owes its existence to the circle of American artists drawn to Giverny by Monet's fame, but its exhibitions are far from parochial: shows have included "Bonnard in Normandy" and "Impressionism along the banks of the Seine".

ARRIVAL AND DEPARTURE   GIVERNY

By train Without a car, the easiest approach to Giverny is by train to Vernon from Paris-St-Lazare (4–5 daily; 45min). At St-Lazare, follow signs to the mainline "Grandes Lignes" platforms, and get your ticket from the main office, signposted "Espace de Vente", or the yellow machines; the Ile-de-France counter is for suburban services only. Buses meet each train for the 6km ride to the gardens (€4 return; 20min) – make sure you walk straight there off the train, as it does fill up on busy days. You can also take a taxi (€15), rent a bicycle at the station (€14 for the day; it's best to reserve in advance: ☏ 02 32 21 16 01) or simply walk (1hr): cross the river and turn right on the D5; take care as you enter Giverny to follow the left fork, otherwise you'll make a long detour to reach the garden entrance.

By car If you're driving, Giverny is an hour's jaunt from Paris; take the A13, direction Vernon/Giverny to exit 14.

Disneyland Paris

Children will love Disneyland Paris – there are no two ways about it. What their minders will think of it is another matter, though a cartoon moment will still cadge a smile from most grown-ups, and you can terrify yourself on a roller coaster at any age. At a distance of just 25km east of Paris, it's easy to visit as a day-trip. The complex is divided into three areas: Disneyland Park, the original Magic Kingdom, with most of the big rides; Walt Disney Studios Park, a more technology-based attempt to re-create the world of cartoon film-making, along with a few rides; and the restaurant complex of Disney Village. There's also the vast discount shopping mall – sorry, "village" – of La Vallée Outlet (see p.327); regular park shuttles connect it to the Disney hotels.

INFORMATION

17

Opening hours Depending on the season and whether it's a weekend, the parks open from 10am to anywhere between 7pm and 11pm at Disneyland Park, or between 6pm and 7pm at Walt Disney Studios.

Admission 1-day 1-park €54/49; 1-day Hopper €68/61; 2-day Hopper €113/102; 3-day Hopper €140/126. Children aged 3–11 pay the reduced tariff given here, while under-3s go free. Prices may drop a little in the low season (Oct–March, excluding holidays).

Tickets To avoid queuing, buy tickets online (ⓦ disneylandparis.com), from tourist offices (see p.38), or from any métro and RER line A and B station – the latter gives you a "passeport" including the RER ticket. The one-day one-park pass allows you to visit either the main Disneyland Park or the Walt Disney Studios Park, but you can't swap between them; you can come and go during the day, however. With a Hopper pass or passe-partout you can move freely between both areas. If you buy a two- or three-day Hopper you don't have to use it on consecutive days.

Access The nearest station is Marne-la-Vallée/Chessy RER; you step straight out onto a central plaza. Ahead lies Disney Village, and a hundred metres or so to the right are the two main gates: the nearest leads past the landmark *Disneyland Hotel* to Disneyland Park, the farther one to Walt Disney Studios Park. All hotels except *Hotel New York* are too far away to walk to comfortably with luggage, but free yellow buses run from the bus station in the central plaza; the hotel name is shown on the front of each bus. Drivers can go straight to the hotel or to the parking areas (€8 per day).

Information At Disneyland Park, you enter underneath Main Street Station, on the internal railroad system; information is available at City Hall to the left. Information at Walt Disney Studios Park can be found at Studio Services, by the entrance. Luggage can be left in "Guest Storage" lockers near the park entrances (€1.50); there are also lockers at Marne-la-Vallée/Chessy station.

Contact details UK ⓣ 0844 800 8111, France ⓣ 01 60 30 60 65, ⓦ disneylandparis.com

Disabled access The *Disabled Visitors Guide* is available from City Hall in Disneyland Park, or Studio Services in Walt Disney Studios Park; alternatively, visit ⓦ visit .disneylandparis.co.uk/disabled-visitors. Staff aren't allowed to lend assistance in getting into and out of the less accessible rides, but all toilets, shops and restaurants are wheelchair accessible. You can rent wheelchairs (€6.50; €150 deposit) in Town Square, in Disneyland Park – the building on the right as you exit Main Street Station. Given the relative dearth of benches, visitors who can normally manage without a chair might appreciate having one.

Babies and small children You can rent pushchairs (€6.50; €150 deposit if you move between parks) from the same place as wheelchairs (see above). There are two Baby Care centres: next to *Plaza Gardens* restaurant in Disneyland Park, and beside Studio Services in Walt Disney Studios Park.

There's not much that's French at Disneyland – for that, try the Parc Astérix (see p.351) – though Sleeping Beauty's Castle is partly based on an illustration in the medieval manuscript *Les Très Riches Heures du Duc de Berry* (see p.236), and there's the odd crêpe stand – otherwise, the food in the resort is almost always American, and often disappointing. The commentaries or scripts in the more theatrical attractions are almost always in French, however, with translated summaries displayed on a board. In the most audience-focused attractions, you'll find an English-language headset to don.

The **best time to go** is a term-time weekday, when you'll probably get round every ride you want, though queuing for and walking between rides is purgatorial in wet or very cold weather. At other times, long waits for the popular rides are common in the middle of the day, though the most popular attractions use the "Fastpass" pre-booked timeslot scheme (see box, p.248).

If you're doing a lot of planning in advance, the official website ⓦ dlrpmagic.com is worth a look. It has videos and reviews of rides, full restaurant listings, up-to-date minimum height regulations, and so on.

Disneyland Park

The introduction to Disneyland Paris is **Main Street USA**, a mythical vision of a 1900s American town. It leads from Town Square, just beyond the entrance turnstiles, up to **Central Plaza**, the hub of the park. Clockwise from Main Street are Frontierland, Adventureland, Fantasyland and Discoveryland. The **castle**, directly opposite Main Street across Central Plaza, belongs to Fantasyland. A steam-train **Railroad** runs round the park with stations at each "land" and at the main entrance.

17

The listings (see pp.247–250) cover all but the most minor rides, with some warnings about suitability, though it's difficult to tell what one child will find exhilarating and another upsetting. For the youngest kids, **Fantasyland** is likely to hold the most thrills. There are no height restrictions here, and rides are mostly gentle. Each of the other three themed areas offers a landmark roller coaster and a theme; **Adventureland** sports tropical, pirate-themed sets, **Frontierland** is set in the Wild West, while **Discoveryland** emphasizes technology and the Space Age. There are few green patches, though Adventureland has a few tree-shaded nooks and crannies, and you could try the seats by the river in Frontierland. Opportunities for afternoon naps, certainly, are limited; renting a pushchair (see p.245) for even an older child might be a good idea.

Main Street USA
Main Street is really just a giant mall for Disney sponsors only. See if you can get down it without buying one of the following: a balloon, a hat with your name embroidered

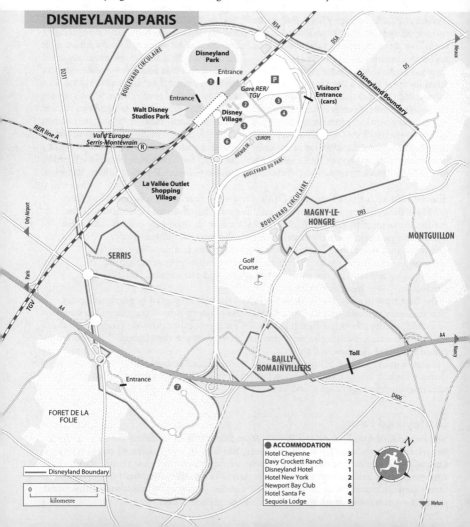

DISNEYLAND PARIS

● ACCOMMODATION	
Hotel Cheyenne	3
Davy Crockett Ranch	7
Disneyland Hotel	1
Hotel New York	2
Newport Bay Club	6
Hotel Santa Fe	4
Sequoia Lodge	5

Disneyland Boundary

0   1
kilometre

17

THE PARADES

The all-dancing, all-costumed **Shows** and **Parades** are some of the most popular events in both parks. Timing a visit to a popular ride to coincide with a big show is a clever idea, but if you have kids they will no doubt force you to press against the barriers for the ultimate Disney event. Timetables are handed out with maps as you enter the park; make sure you catch at least one show. The headline **Once Upon A Dream** parade takes place at 7.15pm in summer, with the **Fantillusion** parade followed by fireworks at 10.25pm. One of the best parade vantage spots is on the queuing ramp for It's a Small World, right by the gates through which the floats appear. From here, the parade progresses, very slowly, to Town Square. The best seating is in front of the Fantasyland Castle, one of the points where the floats stop and the characters put on a performance. The parade floats represent all the top box-office Disney movies and characters, from Mickey and Minnie Mouse to the *Toy Story* team and the *Pirates of the Caribbean* crew. Everyone waves and smiles, and characters on foot shake hands with the kids who've managed to get to the front.

on it, an ice cream, silhouette portraits of your kids, the *Wall Street Journal* of 1902, a Donald Duck costume, some muffins and a complete set of Disney characters in ceramics, metal, plastic, rubber or wool. Leaving Main Street is quickest on foot (crowds permitting), although omnibuses, trams, horse-drawn streetcars and fire trucks are always on hand, plus the Disney *pièce de résistance*, the Railroad, for which **Main Street Station** has the longest queues.

RIDES

DISCOVERYLAND

L'Astroport Services Interstellaires A videogame arcade. Some games have an interactive element: you can distort a photo of your own face, for instance (then buy it).

Autopia Miniature futuristic cars to drive on rails. Good fun, especially for little kids, but there's no possibility of any race-day stratagems. Minimum height to drive is 1.32m.

Buzz Lightyear Laser Blast An interactive cart ride through a black-light universe, inspired by *Toy Story 2*. You shoot at threatening space creatures, helping Buzz and his friendly three-eyed Martians save the galaxy. Good for little kids. Uses Fastpass.

Captain EO *Star Wars* meets the King of Pop in this 1986 3D film (17min; in English) produced by George Lucas, starring Michael Jackson on a mission to save the world – with the help of some snazzy song and dance routines. Some scenes may frighten younger children.

Les Mystères du Nautilus A stroll through a mock-up of the *Nautilus* submarine – Captain Nemo's vessel in *20,000 Leagues Under the Sea*. What's supposed to impress you is the faithfulness of the decor to the original Disney set, though there is a fishy surprise inside.

Orbitron The "rockets" on this ride go round and round fairly slowly and go up (at your control) to a daring 30 degrees above the horizontal. Suitable for small kids and for those who dislike more violent rides.

Space Mountain Mission 2 The star attraction provides 1.3G of horrifying speed and a moment of weightlessness, all in an elaborately lit ambience, with meteor storms and rushing star clusters. Minimum height 1.32m, and

pregnant women and people with health problems are advised not to ride. Uses Fastpass.

Star Tours Giddy, simulated ride in a spacecraft (with sixty other people all in neat rows) piloted by friendly, incompetent C-3PO of *Star Wars* fame. The projection of what you're supposed to be careering through is actually from the film, which pleases fans. Minimum height 1.02m. Pregnant women and those with health problems are advised not to board. Uses Fastpass.

FANTASYLAND

Alice's Curious Labyrinth A giant maze with surprises. There are passages that only those under 1m can pass through and enough false turns and exits to make it a decent enough labyrinth. Takes maybe ten minutes, with the option to exit at the halfway point.

Blanche-Neige et les Sept Nains This *Snow White and the Seven Dwarfs* ride takes you through lots of menacing moving trees, swinging doors and cackling witches, re-creating scenes from the classic Disney film. Can frighten smaller kids.

Le Carrousel de Lancelot A stately merry-go-round, whose every horse has its own individual medieval equerry in glittering paint.

Casey Jr – Le Petit Train du Cirque This charming little circus train chugs around rolling landscaped gardens behind *Le Pays des Contes de Fées*. Not too fast, not too slow, it's just right for little ones.

Dumbo the Flying Elephant Dumbo and his clones provide a safe, slow, aerial ride in which you can regulate the rise and fall of the revolving elephants with a lever. One

17

of the most popular rides in Fantasyland, with queues to match, though it only lasts a measly 25 seconds.

It's a Small World This is a quintessential Disney experience; there's one in every Disneyland, and Walt considered it to be the finest expression of his corporation's philosophy. Your boat rides through a polystyrene and glitter world, with animated dolls in national/ethnic/tribal costumes dance beside their most famous landmarks or landscapes, singing the song *It's a Small World*. Some children seem to enjoy the sugar-coated fantasy.

Mad Hatter's Teacups Great big whirling teacups slide past each other on a chequered floor. Not a whizzy ride, but fun for younger ones.

Le Pays des Contes de Fée A boat ride through cleverly miniaturized fairy-tale scenes: *Alice in Wonderland*, *Pinocchio*, etc. Fine for little kids.

Peter Pan's Flight The very young seem to really enjoy this jerky "flight" above Big Ben and the lights of London to Never-Never Land. Very popular. Uses Fastpass.

Sleeping Beauty's Castle The castle stands at the entrance to Fantasyland, just off the central plaza at the end of Main Street. There's little to see inside other than a few bits of plasticky vaulting, stained glass and cartoon tapestries, though a huge animated dragon lurks in the dungeon.

Les Voyages de Pinocchio A rattling, swervy wagon ride through a string of beautifully re-created scenes from *Pinocchio*; some are dimly lit and faintly menacing.

Adventure Isle Not a ride, but a sort of playground of caves, bouncy bridges, huge boulders, trees, tunnels and waterfalls built on two small islands in the middle of Adventureland. Parents of over-tired children and those who need a break from the queues should not underestimate the thrill of just being able to wander around unfettered.

La Cabane des Robinson The 27m mock banyan tree at the top of Adventure Isle is one of Disneyland Paris's most obsessively detailed and most enjoyable creations, complete with hundreds of thousands of (false) leaves and blossoms. It's reached by walkways and a series of more than 170 steps, so it's best avoided by pram-pushers and toddler-haulers.

Indiana Jones and the Temple of Peril A fast roller coaster along rattling train tracks through a classic Indy landscape. Moderately violent, and renowned for its 360-degree loop, though it's no Space Mountain. The minimum height for the ride is 1.40m. Children under around 8 years old, pregnant women and people with health problems should steer clear. Uses Fastpass.

Le Passage Enchanté d'Aladdin A sedate meander on foot through a colourful Oriental-style passageway takes you past animated scenes from *Aladdin*, featuring the genie, the flying carpet and some truly insistent theme music.

Pirates of the Caribbean This satisfyingly long ride is one of the finest, consisting of an underground ride on water and down waterfalls, past scenes of evil piracy. The animated automata are the best yet – be warned that they set small children whimpering and crying immediately. Battles are staged across the water, skeletons slide into the deep, parrots squawk, chains rattle and a treasure-trove is revealed.

La Plage des Pirates The ladders, walkways, climbing ropes and slides at this nautical-themed adventure playground give kids a great chance to run off steam, in the shadow of Captain Hook's pirate ship. It's divided into two different areas: one for 3–6s, the other for 7–9s.

FRONTIERLAND

Big Thunder Mountain A proper scream-out-loud funfair thrill, this is a roller coaster mimicking a runaway mine train round a "mining mountain". There are wicked twists and turns, sudden tunnels and hairy moments looking down on the water, but no violent upside-down or corkscrew stuff. Minimum height 1.02m; not suitable for small children. Uses Fastpass.

The Chaparral Theater Shows seasonal theatrical spectaculars featuring all the usual Disney suspects. Times are displayed outside and on the programme handed out with the main park map.

Legends of the Wild West A series of models, displays and mocked-up rooms commemorating characters and scenes from the gold-rush days of

---

QUEUES AND FASTPASS

Energy-sapping, one-hour waits for the popular rides are pretty standard during school holidays and on summer weekends. Don't be fooled by the length of the visible queues; they often snake for a further 100m or more inside. Realistic wait times are posted at the entry to most rides (eg 20 minutes, 50 minutes). Bring sun hats or umbrellas, and make sure your kids have all been to the toilet recently before you begin to queue as, once you're in, it's very hard to get out; keep snacks and drinks handy, too. A number of rides use the **Fastpass** scheme, in which you insert your entry card into a ticket machine by the entrance to the ride; the machine then spews out a time at which you should come back and join the much shorter Fastpass queue. You're only allowed one Fastpass ticket at a time, unless you have a **VIP Fastpass** (given to guests staying in certain hotel suites) or a **Premium Fastpass** (available for €80 from City Hall and Studio Services), which both offer unlimited access to all Fastpass lanes.

17

America's Wild West, all housed in Fort Comstock, a replica log-built stockade.

Phantom Manor *Psycho*-style house on the outside and Hammer Horror Edwardian mansion within. Holographic ghosts appear before cobweb-covered mirrors and ancestral portraits, but nothing actually jumps out and screams at you. Probably too frightening for young children nevertheless.

Pocahontas Indian Village This Native-American-themed adventure playground is nicely sited by the water, providing a welcome spot for parents to sit down and recharge their batteries while their offspring play on the slides, bridges, climbing areas and tepees.

River Rogue Keelboats A guided ten-minute keelboat ride around the lake. The attraction's recent relaunch was delayed for a full year when authorities decreed that the helmsmen would require full French boating licenses. At least you know you're in safe hands.

Rustler Roundup Shootin' Gallery There's a fee (€2) for this attraction, apparently because without some check people stay for hours and hours shooting infrared beams at fake cacti.

Thunder Mesa Riverboat Landing A rather pointless cruise around the lake, but the paddleboat steamer is carefully built to offer lots of antique-style curiosities, and it's fun to watch the roller coaster rattle around the rocks of Big Thunder Mountain.

Woody's Roundup Village Ranch-style buildings given over to photo backdrops, drinks kiosks and *Toy Story* memorabilia.

Walt Disney Studios Park

The **Walt Disney Studios Park** complex rather lacks the mega-rides offered by its older, larger neighbour, and as a result it's less busy: the queues are shorter and it's easier to meet characters as the area is smaller. And in some ways this side of the park is a more satisfying affair, focusing on what Disney was and is still renowned for – animation. You can try your hand at drawing, there are mock film and TV sets where you can be part of the audience, and the special effects and stunt shows are impressive in their way, although probably not as impressive as just going to the movies. And there are two thrilling rides: the corkscrew-looping, Metal-playing white-knuckler of the **Rock 'n' Roller Coaster Starring Aerosmith**, and the plummeting elevator of the **Tower of Terror**.

RIDES AND SHOWS

Animagique Disney characters in full fluffy costumes act out classic scenes from Disney films.

Armageddon Special Effects Your group of fifty or so is ushered into a circular chamber decked out as a space station. As meteors rush towards the screens on all sides, the whole ship seems about to break up. Less cynical children may find the whole experience overwhelming.

Art of Disney Animation You progress through two mini-theatres, one showing famous moments from Disney cartoons, the next with a "cartoonist" having a conversation with an on-screen animated creation, explaining to the creature how it came to look as it did. In the lobby area, children are taught to draw identical Mickey Mouse faces.

Cars Quatre Roues Rallye *Cars*-inspired ride on the lines of a destruction derby. The ride is real enough, though sedate – the hell-raising element is engineered using special effects.

Cinémagique A theatrical screening of a century of movie moments, with actors appearing to jump into and out of the on-screen action, helped by special effects.

Crush's Coaster The theme of this gentle and very popular coaster is taken from *Finding Nemo*. You're taken into a virtual underwater world on the back of a turtle, then into a minute-long roller-coaster section which isn't especially fast but features an unusual spinning mechanism. Minimum height 1.07m.

Flying Carpets Over Agrabah A good, solid fairground ride where the carpet-shaped cars wheel around the central lamp for a disappointingly short time. Very popular with smaller children, especially the lever which makes their carpet rise up and down. Uses Fastpass.

Moteurs...Action! Stuntshow Spectacular Decked out like a Mediterranean village, a big arena is the scene for some spectacular stunts: jumping rally cars, sliding motorbikes, leaping jet skis, stuntmen falling from heights and so on. Various timed shows throughout the day.

Playhouse Disney Live on Stage A lively, smiley stage show drawn from the TV series, featuring costumed characters aimed at littler ones: Mickey, the Little Einsteins, Handy Manny. Seating is on the floor.

RC Racer A half-pipe roller coaster: you're shuttled back and forth and up and down an upended semicircle till you're begging to get off. Minimum height 1.20m.

Rock 'n' Roller Coaster Starring Aerosmith A real heart-stopper, reaching 5G at one point. There are corkscrews, loops and violent lurches, and the whole thing takes place in a neon-lit and hard-rock-soundtracked darkness that makes it all the more alarming. It's all over in less than two minutes. Minimum height 1.2m; entirely unsuitable for small children. Uses Fastpass.

17

Slinky Dog Zig Zag Spin This fairly gentle ride takes you round and round on an undulating track pulled by said Slinky Dog.

Stitch Live! A theatrical-type experience in which children talk and play with the virtual reality alien Stitch who, despite being on-screen, manages to interact with the audience.

Studio 1 For "boulevard of dreams", read "row of shops and restaurants". Not a ride, though it's listed on the map.

Studio Tram Tour Behind the Magic An electric tram takes you on a sedate circuit of various bits and pieces of film set. The high point is the halt among the Wild West rocks of Catastrophe Canyon – sit on the left for the scariest ride.

Toy Soldiers Parachute Drop Hanging in a group of bucket seats under a giant umbrella, you're repeatedly lifted up and dropped – not all that fast, but from fairly high up. Minimum height 0.81m.

Twilight Zone Tower of Terror Exciting ride in which you "enjoy" the sensation of free-falling in the lift of a classic, crumbling Hollywood hotel. Not actually physically demanding, though the Twilight Zone video might scare some, and it does turn your stomach upside down. Minimum height 1.02m. Uses Fastpass.

Disney Village

The **Disney Village** entertainment and restaurant complex, opposite the Marne-la-Vallée/Chessy RER and train stations, is basically a street lined with expensive shops and restaurants. The work of architect Frank Gehry, it looks like a circus tent that has had its top carried off by a bomb, with a pedestrian street driven through the middle of it. "Buffalo Bill's Wild West Show" (cowboys and Indians charging round a ring on horseback, with slapstick routines and dancing Disney characters) and rides on the Panoramagique tethered balloon await you, alongside *Annette's Diner*, the *Rainforest Café* and a host of other themed restaurants. You'll find real, French food – and pasta, and sausages – at *King Ludwig's Castle* (two-course menu €20). There's live outdoor music on summer nights, IMAX and multiplex cinemas, and lots of sideshows.

When you're nearing exhaustion from so much enchantment, you can return to your **hotel** (see opposite) and have a sauna, jacuzzi or whirlpool dip and be in bed in time to feel fresh and fit to meet Mickey and Minnie again over breakfast. In the hotel area of the resort, you can play **golf** (27-hole course), skate (in winter), sail (in summer) and jog on a special "health circuit", though these activities can be expensive.

ARRIVAL

From London by train There are direct Eurostar trains to Disneyland, but it can sometimes be less expensive to change onto the TGV at Lille; all these trains arrive at Marne-la-Vallée/Chessy station, right outside the main entrance. If you're coming straight from the airport, there are shuttle buses from both Charles de Gaulle and Orly, taking 45 minutes from both airports (roughly every 30min from 8.30am–7.45pm; see ⓦ vea.fr/uk for timetables and pick-up points). Tickets cost €18 one way, but children under 12 pay €13, and under-3s go free. There is a Beauvais airport shuttle, but it takes over 2hr 30min and costs €30.

ROLLER COASTERS

Each of the park's areas, apart from the tinies-focused Fantasyland, centres on its roller coaster. The runaway train on Frontierland's **Big Thunder Mountain** and the mine-carts of Adventureland's **Indiana Jones and the Temple of Peril: Backwards!** are fast and exciting, but the emphasis is on thrills rather than sheer terror. **Space Mountain Mission 2**, in Discoveryland, and the **Rock 'n' Roller Coaster Starring Aerosmith**, over in the Walt Disney Studios section, are a different matter altogether, and you'll need a strong constitution to enjoy the upside-down loops, corkscrews and terrifying accelerations.

All four rides have different height restrictions, and as you queue for the latter two you'll be bombarded with warnings to discourage pregnant women or people with neck or back problems. Heed them! You can avoid queues on all of them by using the Fastpass scheme, and arriving early can also be a good strategy, but be warned: the experience can be so intense that the park's gentler rides may seem disappointing. Children, in particular, may want to return again and again.

OVERNIGHT PACKAGES

17

If you plan to stay at a Disneyland hotel, it's much cheaper to book a special accommodation and entry package. Visit an agent, or book through Disney, either online or on ☎0844 576 5504 in the UK, ☎0825 300 222 in France, or ☎00 33 1 60 30 60 53 from other countries.

From Paris by train Take RER line A (from Châtelet-Les Halles, Gare-de-Lyon or Nation) to Marne-la-Vallée/Chessy station, which is right next to the train terminal, and opposite the main park gates. The journey takes around forty minutes and costs €6.70 single (children under 10 half-price, under-4s free). You can get Mobilis travel cards, including Disneyland Paris (see p.25).

By car The park is a 32km drive east of Paris along the A4; take the Porte de Bercy exit off the *périphérique*, then follow "direction Metz/Nancy", leaving at exit 13 for *Ranch Davy Crockett* or exit 14 for Parc Disneyland and the hotels. From Calais follow the A26, changing to the A1, the A104 and finally the A4.

ACCOMMODATION

Disney's six themed **hotels** are a mixed bag of kitsch designed by some of the world's leading architects – Michael Graves, Antoine Predock, Robert Stern and Frank Gehry. For all the dramatically themed exteriors and lobbies, the rooms are much the same inside: comfortable, huge and soulless. **Prices** vary hugely according to season and which package you book – there are almost always offers. Free bright-yellow shuttle buses run between the hotels and the single stop for the train station and both park entrances.

Hotel Cheyenne Along with the *Sante Fe*, the *Cheyenne* is broken up into attractively small units: the film-set buildings of a Western frontier town, complete with wagons, cowboys, a hanging tree and scarecrows. With its Wild West theme and bunk beds in all the rooms, this is a good hotel for children – and it's usually relatively inexpensive.

Davy Crockett Ranch The budget option: self-catering bungalows and log cabins (4–6 people) in a wooded, Wild West-themed setting – there's even a high-wire tree-top assault course. The ranch is a fifteen-minute drive from the park, with no shuttle service laid on, so you'll need your own transport.

Disneyland Hotel Situated right over the entrance to the park with wings to either side, the large, frilly, pastel-pink *Disneyland Hotel* is decked out in glitzy Hollywood style. It's the most upmarket and best located by far.

Hotel New York Outside, the hotel is a plasticky, postmodern attempt at conjuring up the New York skyline,

while the furnishings within are pseudo Art Deco with lots of apples. Comfortable, and towards the top of the range. In winter, the outdoor ice rink makes it a good option for children.

Newport Bay Club This "New England seaside resort circa 1900" spreads like a game of dominoes. Blue-and-white-striped canopies over the balconies fail to give it that cosy guesthouse feel, but some rooms have the benefit of looking out over the lake.

Hotel Santa Fe Accommodation takes the form of smooth, mercifully unadorned, imitation sun-baked mud buildings in various shapes and sizes. Between them are tasteful car wrecks, a cactus in a glass case, strange geological formations and other products of the distinctly un-Disney imagination of New Mexican architect Antoine Predock. Usually relatively inexpensive.

Sequoia Lodge Built around the theme of the "mountain lodge" typically found in the national parks of the western United States, but on a giant scale.

CAMPING

To really economize, you could camp at the nearby *Camping du Parc de la Colline*, route de Lagny, 77200 Torcy (☎01 60 05 42 32, ⊛camping-de-la-colline.com), which is open all year; prices vary throughout the year, but a family of four staying in two tents will usually pay under €50.

EATING AND DRINKING

There are opportunities to eat throughout both parks, as well as in Disney Village. As you'd expect, there's a lot of pricey American junk food, though the fixed price, "all-you-can-eat" buffet-style restaurants are not a bad deal, with their large salad bars. The free programmes usually offer discount coupons; consider booking ahead (at City Hall or Studio Services, or on ☎01 60 30 40 50), as all restaurants fill up quickly at lunch and dinner time. Adults can drink wine or beer at any of the park's restaurants. Officially, you're not supposed to bring in full-on picnics, but Goofy won't turn nasty if he sees you eating a sandwich.

Accommodation

Accommodation is not, on the whole, Paris's strong point. At the luxury end, things are sumptuous enough, and there are a fair few boutique hotels with stunning design and locations, and sometimes views that could make your heart skip a beat. Unless you stumble upon a promotional deal, however, prices at the top end are stratospheric, and even in the better three- and four-star establishments, rooms are typically cramped. Americans, especially, are often shocked by the square footage. If you're unlucky enough to be at the back of the building, overlooking the courtyard, rooms can be dark as well, though at least you're spared the street noise. There are, however, a few genuine gems, and many places where the welcome, the style or the location easily outweighs the lack of space.

ESSENTIALS

Reservations The best hotels are typically booked up well in advance, especially in the spring and autumn peak seasons. It's wise to reserve a room as early as you can, particularly if you fancy staying in one of the more characterful places. You can simply call – all receptionists speak some English – but bear in mind that more and more hotels offer online booking as well, sometimes at discounted prices. In fact, it's always worth asking for a discount on the advertised rate; in August and from November to March (apart from Christmas) you can often negotiate reductions of ten to twenty percent or more. If you book by phone, many places will ask for a credit card number, others for written or faxed confirmation.

Online reservation services The tourist office offers a free online reservation service (Ⓦ parisinfo.com), with good discounts on many hotels. The online agency Ⓦ ratestogo.com offers discounts on last-minute bookings. **Tourist offices** If you find yourself stuck on arrival, the main tourist office (see p.38) at rue des Pyramides and the branches at the Gare de Lyon and Eiffel Tower will find you a room in a hotel or hostel free of charge.

Hotel breakfasts Breakfast (*petit déjeuner*) is sometimes included (*compris*) in the room price but is normally extra (*en sus*) – around €6–12 per person. Always make it clear whether you want breakfast or not when you take the room. Either way, it's usually an indifferent continental affair of croissant/baguette, orange juice and coffee.

18

HOTELS

One of the best central **areas for budget-priced hotels** is the 10ᵉ, especially around place de la République. Quieter districts, further out, where you can get some good deals are the 13ᵉ and 14ᵉ, south of Montparnasse, and the 17ᵉ and 20ᵉ, on the western and eastern sides of the city respectively. Our hotel recommendations are listed by area, following the same chapter divisions used in the guide. Most hotels have a selection of rooms – singles, doubles, twin-bedded and triples – at different prices, which can fluctuate widely throughout the year. In our listings we give approximate **prices for a standard double in high season**, based on what you're likely to actually pay rather than the quoted rack rate, and also cite tariffs for **single rooms** where these are particularly good value.

THE ISLANDS

Henri IV 25 place Dauphine, Ile de la Cité, 1ᵉʳ ☎ 01 43 54 44 53, Ⓦ henri4hotel.fr; Ⓜ Pont-Neuf/Cité; map p.42. An ancient, slightly ramshackle cheapie on a beautiful square right in the centre of Paris, with fifteen basic rooms spread over five storeys (no lift); it's worth paying a bit extra for a renovated en-suite room. Book well in advance. **€60**

Hôtel de Lutèce 65 rue St-Louis-en-l'Ile, 4ᵉ ☎ 01 43 26 23 52, Ⓦ paris-hotel-lutece.com; Ⓜ Pont-Marie; map p.42. This narrow seventeenth-century townhouse, located on the most desirable island in France, has 23 tiny but appealing wood-beamed en suites in shades of terracotta and cream. All have been renovated in a contemporary style, and come with modern, sparkling-white bathrooms. **€205**

BOOKING A HOTEL ROOM

The **star system** provides some clues as to the pretensions of a hotel, but little else – a two-star hotel might have lovely rooms but fail to be awarded a third star because its staff don't speak enough languages, or its foyer is small. A double room in an old-fashioned two-star will cost between €75 and €150, depending on season and location, though don't expect much in the way of decor at the lower end of the scale. For something with a bit more class – whether that means a touch of design, smooth efficiency or a minibar – you'll pay in the region of €120–240. At the luxury end of the scale the sky's the limit, with prices above €400 not uncommon – though internet and off-season deals in such places can work out at dramatically less than the official price. It is possible to find a double room in a central location for around €50–75, though at this level you will probably have to accept a room with just a sink (*lavabo*) and a shared bathroom on the landing (*dans le palier*).

Within one hotel, **rooms** can vary hugely, and it's well worth asking what's available – almost all hoteliers speak at least enough English to get by. Rooms at the back, overlooking an internal courtyard (*côté cour/jardin*) can be dark; rooms on the street (*côté rue*) tend to be larger and lighter, but noise can be a problem if there isn't double-glazing. Certain standard terms recur: *douche/WC* and *bain/WC* mean that you have a shower or bath as well as toilet in the room. A room with a *grand lit* (double bed) is invariably cheaper than one with *deux lits* (two separate beds). Many hotels offer *de luxe* or *supérieure* rooms as well as those in a *standard* or *classique* class; a superior room in a less expensive hotel can often be better value than a standard one in a pricier establishment.

18

THE CHAMPS-ELYSEES AND AROUND

Le 123 123 rue du Faubourg-St-Honoré, 8e ☎01 53 89 01 23, ⓦastotel.com; ⓜSt-Philippe-du-Roule; map p.62. A giant puffball light greets you in the lobby of this stylish hotel, five minutes' walk from the Champs-Elysées. Rooms are a good size with high ceilings, laminate floors and bathtubs. Each one has at least one antique – a chaise longue, nest of tables or desk – to take the edge off the minimalism. **€170**

Hôtel Arioso 7 rue d'Argenson, 8e ☎01 53 05 95 00, ⓦarioso-hotel.com; ⓜMiromesnil; map p.62. Set on a quiet side-street, about fifteen minutes' walk from the Champs-Elysées, this is a charming, comfy four-star hotel set in a solid Haussmann-era block, run by courteous and helpful staff. The 28 rooms are small, especially the cheaper ones, but cosily decorated with quality furnishings and slightly busy fabrics; some of the more expensive rooms have jasmine-strewn balconies looking onto a pretty little tiled interior courtyard. The gleaming-white bathrooms are stocked with Occitane products. **€160**

Le Bristol 112 rue du Faubourg St-Honoré, 8e ☎01 53 43 43 00, ⓦhotel-bristol.com; ⓜMiromesnil; map p.62. Arguably the city's most luxurious and spacious hotel, *Le Bristol* remains discreet and warm, with consistently good service. A number of the rooms come with Gobelins tapestries and private roof gardens, and a sumptuously designed new wing has been recently added. There's also a large colonnaded interior garden, plus the inevitable swimming pool and gourmet restaurant. **€670**

Hôtel Lancaster 7 rue de Berri, 8e ☎01 40 76 40 76, ⓦhotel-lancaster.fr; ⓜGeorge-V; map p.62. The rooms in this elegantly restored nineteenth-century townhouse retain original features and are chock-full of Louis XVI and rococo antiques, but with a touch of contemporary chic. The hotel was the pied-à-terre for the likes of Garbo, Dietrich and Sir Alec Guinness, and is still a favourite hide-out today for those fleeing the paparazzi. A small interior zen-style garden and pleasant service make for a relaxing stay, and there's an excellent restaurant too. **€520**

Hôtel Le Lavoisier 21 rue Lavoisier, 8e ☎01 53 30 06 06, ⓦhotellavoisierparis.com; ⓜSt Augustin; map p.62. A traditional, comfortable hotel in a Haussmann-era townhouse, on a quiet side-street, around fifteen minutes' walk from the Champs-Elysées. The good-sized, slightly old-fashioned rooms are decorated in tones of red and yellow and graced with the odd antique. There's a cosy breakfast room downstairs in the basement, and the comfortable reception area with sofas is a nice place to linger. Official rates start at €255 for a double, but regular discounted internet deals are available. **€160**

L'Hôtel Pergolèse 3 rue Pergolèse, 16e ☎01 53 64 04 04, ⓦhotelpergolese.com; ⓜArgentine; map p.62. This classy four-star boutique hotel, now owned by Best Western, is in a tall, slender building on a quiet side-street near the Arc de Triomphe. The decor is contemporary – light wood furniture, cool colours, chic styling – but without chilliness; sofas and friendly service add a cosy touch. Rooms face the street or the internal courtyard and vary in size; some are quite poky. Most are comfortable and well appointed, however, with great designer bathrooms. **€126**

Hôtel de Sers 41 av Pierre 1er de Serbie, 8e ☎01 53 23 75 75, ⓦhoteldesers.com; ⓜGeorge-V; map p.62. A chic and luxurious hotel, just off the Champs-Elysées, offering restrained rooms with rosewood furnishings, Italian-marble bathrooms and decor in white, grey, deep reds and pinks; facilities include CD/DVD players and huge Bang & Olufsen TVs. The two suites (from €660) on the top floor have fabulous panoramic terraces. **€460**

Hôtel de la Trémoille 14 rue de la Trémoille, 8e ☎01 65 52 14 00, ⓦwww.tremoille.com; ⓜAlma-Marceau; map p.62. A swanky four-star boasting understated rooms with harmonious decor and shimmering black-and-white bathrooms; room service is delivered through a specially designed hatch to avoid disturbing guests. There's also a revamped spa and gym. **€340**

THE TUILERIES AND LOUVRE

★ **Hôtel Brighton** 218 rue de Rivoli, 1er ☎01 47 03 61 61, ⓦparis-hotel-brighton.com; ⓜTuileries; map p.72. An elegant hotel, dating back to the late nineteenth century, with faux marble columns in the reception area and airy, high-ceilinged rooms. The "classic" rooms, with internal views and striped blue-and-white walls, are fine if nothing special; the "superior" rooms are much better, particularly those on the upper floors, with magnificent views of the Tuileries gardens and nice touches such as double sinks in the bathrooms. **€180–220**

Costes 239 rue St-Honoré, 1er ☎01 42 44 50 00, ⓦhotelcostes.com; ⓜTuileries; map p.72. A favourite with media and fashion folk, this luxury hotel, marrying Second Empire style with all up-to-date amenities, is postmodern decadence perfected. Beautiful people saunter about plush red-velvet interiors under dim lighting, making you feel you're in an elite, invitation-only French bordello. The service, however, is variable. **€550**

Hôtel Meurice 228 rue de Rivoli, 1er ☎01 44 58 10 10, ⓦlemeurice.com; ⓜTuileries; map p.72. Palatial opulence in the style of Louis XVI, with unsurpassed vistas over Paris and superlative en suites, as you'd expect for the price. You'll be so busy having tea in the winter garden or taking a Turkish bath that the delights of Paris just on your doorstep are likely to go ignored. Special deals are sometimes available online from around €400. **€700**

Le Relais Saint-Honoré 308 rue St-Honoré, 1er ☎01 42 96 06 06, ⓦrelaissainthonore.com; ⓜTuileries; map p.72. A snug little hotel, set in a stylishly renovated seventeenth-century townhouse. The neat, tastefully furnished rooms have painted wooden beams and pretty floral fabrics; rooms with door numbers ending in two are smaller than the others. Facilities include free wi-fi and flat-screen TVs, and service is excellent. **€213**

★ **Hôtel Thérèse** 5–7 rue Thérèse, 1er ☎01 42 96 10 01, ⊛hoteltherese.com; Ⓜ Palais-Royal-Musée-du-Louvre; map p.72. A very attractive boutique hotel, run by helpful and courteous staff, on a quiet street within easy walking distance of the Louvre. Rooms are small, pared-down and stylish, with nice prints and dark-wood fittings. Book in advance as it's very popular, especially during the fashion shows. **€170**

THE GRANDS BOULEVARDS AND PASSAGES

Appi Hôtel 158 rue St-Denis, 2e ☎01 42 33 35 16, ⊛appihotel.com; Ⓜ Réaumur-Sébastopol; map p.72. In the midst of the St-Denis red-light district, the budget-priced *Appi* offers surprisingly stylish, airy (if small), rooms with exposed beams, laminate flooring and minimalist decor. Those on the top floor even have a vaguely New York loft feel. Note, however, that there's no lift or air-conditioning, the cheapest rooms have no en suites, and it can get noisy at night. Free internet. **€50**

Hôtel Chopin 46 passage Jouffroy, 9e; entrance on bd Montmartre, near rue du Faubourg-Montmartre ☎01 47 70 58 10, ⊛hotelbretonnerie.com; Ⓜ Grands-Boulevards; map p.72. A charming, quiet hotel set in an atmospheric period building at the end of a picturesque 1850s *passage*. Rooms are pleasantly furnished, though the cheaper ones are on the small side and a little dark. **€96**

★ **Hôtel Mansart** 5 rue des Capucines, 1er ☎01 42 61 50 28, ⊛paris-hotel-mansart.com; Ⓜ Opéra/Madeleine; map p.72. This gracious hotel is just a stone's throw from the *Ritz*, but with rooms at a fraction of the price, and while they're not quite in the luxury bracket they're very agreeably decorated in Louis XIV style. It's worth asking to see a few rooms, as three in the standard class have balconies (at no extra cost) and some have huge bathrooms. The more expensive rooms (€345) look out onto place Vendôme. **€145**

BEST BUDGET HOTELS

You don't have to spend a fortune to get a decent, or even better-than-decent, room in Paris. Here are our top choices for under €100 – and in some cases, much less.

Hôtel Bonséjour Montmartre See p.260
Hôtel Chopin See above
Hôtel Marignan See p.258
Hôtel Port-Royal See p.259
Hôtel de la Porte Dorée See p.257
Hôtel Tiquetonne See above

Hôtel Tiquetonne 6 rue Tiquetonne, 2e ☎01 42 36 94 58, ☐01 42 36 02 94; Ⓜ Etienne-Marcel; map p.72. Located on a characterful pedestrianized street a block away from Montorgueil street market and around the corner from the rue St-Denis red-light district, this excellent-value budget hotel in a 1920s building offers old-fashioned charm. Colour clash notwithstanding, the rooms – accessed via a creaking lift or a spiral staircase – are nice enough and well maintained: many are quite spacious, though the walls are thin. Non-en-suite rooms come with a sink and bidet. **€40**

★ **Hôtel Vivienne** 40 rue Vivienne, 2e ☎01 42 33 13 26, ⊛hotel-vivienne.com; Ⓜ Grands-Boulevards/Bourse; map p.72. A ten-minute walk from the Louvre, this friendly, family-run place does the essentials well: the cheery rooms are very clean, good sized and come with modern facilities; some also have internet capability, and the foyer also has a terminal with free access for guests. **€98**

BEAUBOURG AND LES HALLES

Hôtel du Cygne 3–5 rue du Cygne, 1er ☎01 42 60 14 16, ⊛cygne-hotel-paris.com; Ⓜ Etienne-Marcel; map p.85. A six-storey seventeenth-century townhouse, with a measure of charm, is the setting for this friendly budget hotel, harbouring twenty very small, cheerily decorated rooms. There's no lift, just a narrow twisty staircase. It's on a lively pedestrianized street in the heart of the Les Halles district, so can get a little noisy at night. Five singles are available from €65 a night. **€90**

Relais du Louvre 19 rue des Prêtres St-Germain l'Auxerrois, 1er ☎01 40 41 96 42, ⊛relaisdulouvre .com; Ⓜ Palais-Royal-Musée-du-Louvre; map p.85. An intimate hotel with eighteen rooms set on a quiet backstreet opposite the church of St-Germain l'Auxerrois; you can admire the church's flying buttresses from the front-facing rooms. The rooms have rich fabrics, old prints, period furniture, Turkish rugs and Indian paintings. There are also two comfy suites and an apartment on the top floor. All rooms have flat-screen TV and wi-fi. The relaxed atmosphere and charming service attract a repeat clientele. **€175**

★ **Hôtel Saint-Merry** 78 rue de la Verrerie, 4e ☎01 42 78 14 15, ⊛hotel-saintmerry.com; Ⓜ Rambuteau; map p.85. "Unique" is a much overused word, but perfectly appropriate when describing this quirky little hotel, where you can indulge your Gothic medieval fantasies in a former presbytery attached to the Eglise St-Merri. There are ten wonderfully atmospheric rooms and two suites, all featuring dark-wood furniture, exposed stone walls and wrought iron; room 9, incorporating a flying buttress, no less, is the most popular. **€160**

THE MARAIS

Hôtel Bourg Tibourg 19 rue du Bourg-Tibourg, 4e ☎01 42 78 47 39, ⊛bourgtibourg.com; Ⓜ Hôtel-de-Ville; map p.96. Oriental meets medieval, with a dash of

18

18

Second Empire, at this sumptuously designed boutique hotel. Rooms are tiny, but cosseted with rich velvets, silks and drapes; those on the fifth floor have their own mini balconies, and there's an opulent breakfast area. Although frequented mainly by business and fashion-industry travellers, the hotel would make a perfect romantic hideaway. **€250**

★ **Hôtel de la Bretonnerie** 22 rue Ste-Croix de la Bretonnerie, 4e 🕾 01 48 87 77 63, 🖤 bretonnerie.com; Ⓜ Hôtel-de-Ville; map p.96. A charming place with a range of individually designed rooms, all decorated with exquisite care with quality fabrics, oak furniture and, in some cases, four-poster beds. The beamed attic rooms on the fourth floor, and the split-level or dual-bathroom suites (from €200) are particularly appealing. The location's perfect for exploring the Marais, though front-facing rooms may suffer from street noise at night. **€145**

Caron de Beaumarchais 12 rue Vieille-du-Temple, 4e 🕾 01 42 72 34 12, 🖤 carondebeaumarchais.com; Ⓜ Hôtel-de-Ville; map p.96. Named after the eighteenth-century French playwright Beaumarchais, who would have felt quite at home here: all the furnishings – the original engravings and Louis XVI furniture, not to mention the piano in the foyer – evoke the refined tastes of high-society pre-Revolution Paris. Rooms overlooking the courtyard are petite, while those on the street are more spacious, some with a small balcony, others with chandeliers. Book at least a month in advance. **€145**

Hôtel Central Marais 33 rue Vieille-du-Temple, 4e 🕾 01 48 87 56 08, 🖤 hotelcentralmarais.com; Ⓜ Hôtel-de-Ville; map p.96. The only self-proclaimed gay hotel in Paris, whose famously popular gay bar, *Le Central*, is just downstairs. There are just seven boxy rooms; six have shared facilities and one has en-suite bath and WC, but all cost the same. The entrance is on rue Ste-Croix-de-la-Bretonnerie; ask at the bar if no one's at reception. **€89**

Grand Hôtel Jeanne d'Arc 3 rue de Jarente, 4e 🕾 01 48 87 62 11, 🖤 hoteljeannedarc.com; Ⓜ St-Paul; map p.96. A recent makeover has brightened up this old Marais townhouse, just off lovely place du Marché-Ste-Catherine. The small, simple, clean en-suite rooms have yellow, orange or mauve walls and often clashing carpets and duvets, but it all seems to work. The triple at the top has nice views over the rooftops. **€92**

Grand Hôtel du Loiret 8 rue des Mauvais-Garçons, 4e 🕾 01 48 87 77 00, 🖤 hotel-du-loiret.fr; Ⓜ Hôtel-de-Ville; map p.96. A simple budget hotel, grand in name only. The rooms are very small, but acceptable for the price; the cheaper ones have a washbasin only, the more expensive ones have either a shower or bath; all have TV. The two rooms (one quad and one twin) on the top floor have distant views of Sacré-Coeur. There are a number of basic single rooms with shared facilities for €70. **€80**

CHIC BOUTIQUE HOTELS

The loveliest hotels aren't always five-star palaces. Here are our favourite small, sometimes quirky, boutique hotels.
La Belle Juliette See p.258
Hôtel Bourg-Tibourg See p.255
Le Général Hôtel See p.261
L'Hôtel See p.258
Hôtel Particulier Montmartre See p.260
Hôtel du Petit Moulin See below
Hôtel Thérèse See p.255

Hôtel de Nice 42bis rue de Rivoli, 4e 🕾 01 42 78 55 29, 🖤 hoteldenice.com; Ⓜ Hôtel-de-Ville; map p.96. A well-run six-storey establishment, with a delightful old-world charm: its small, pretty rooms have Indian-cotton bedspreads, carved wooden wardrobes, elaborate wallpaper and gilded mirrors. The rue de Rivoli is very busy, though double glazing helps to block out most of the traffic noise. **€110**

Hôtel Pavillon de la Reine 28 place des Vosges, 4e 🕾 01 40 29 19 19, 🖤 pavillon-de-la-reine.com; Ⓜ Bastille; map p.93. A perfect honeymoon or romantic-weekend getaway in a beautiful ivy-covered mansion secreted away off the place des Vosges. It preserves an intimate ambience, with friendly, personable staff. The rooms mostly have a distinctively 1990s "hip hotel" feel, and could probably use a makeover. **€330**

Hôtel du Petit Moulin 29–31 rue de Poitou, 3e 🕾 01 42 74 10 10, 🖤 hoteldupetitmoulin.com; Ⓜ St-Sébastien-Froissart/Filles-du-Calvaire; map p.96. Inside a former bakery, the *Alice in Wonderland*-style polka-dot carpet guides you around this exquisite Christian Lacroix-designed boutique hotel. The designer's hallmark *joie de vivre* reigns in the seventeen rooms, each a fusion of different styles, from elegant Baroque to Sixties kitsch via raunchy bordello; shocking pinks and lime greens give way to *toile de Jouy* prints, while pod chairs rub up alongside antique dressing tables and old-fashioned bathtubs. There's also a stylish bar. **€190**

Hôtel Picard 26 rue de Picardie, 3e 🕾 01 48 87 53 82, 🖶 hotel.picard@wanadoo.fr; Ⓜ Temple/République; map p.93. In a quiet Marais street, this family-run two-star is gradually being renovated. Rooms are very basic and rather spartan, but the beds are comfy, the staff are pleasant and there's a good breakfast for €4.50. The cheapest doubles have a washbasin, with a shower on the landing (an extra €3). It's best to specify if you want a non-smoking room. You get a ten-percent reduction if you produce your Rough Guide. **€53**

Hôtel Sévigné 2 rue Malher, 4e 🕾 01 42 72 76 17, 🖤 le-sevigne.com; Ⓜ St-Paul; map p.96. A pleasant family-run budget hotel set in a narrow townhouse, with small, simple rooms in shades of pale yellow and red, and modern tiled bathrooms. Double glazing helps muffle the traffic noise from nearby rue de Rivoli. Good value for the area. **€86**

Hôtel St-Louis Marais 1 rue Charles-V, 4ᵉ ☎01 48 87 87 04, ⓦsaintlouismarais.com; ⓜSully-Morland; map p.96. Formerly part of the seventeenth-century Célestins Convent, this characterful place retains its period feel, with stone walls, exposed beams (or in some cases painted-on beams) and tiled floors. Standard rooms are very small and have private showers, while superior ones are larger and have bathtubs; all have flat-screen TVs. The hotel has a less appealing annexe round the corner. A major plus is the hotel's location on a very quiet road, just a short walk from the Marais action, with the Left Bank easily accessible too. **€115**

BASTILLE AND AROUND

★ **Hôtel Marais Bastille** 36 bd Richard-Lenoir, 11ᵉ ☎01 48 05 75 00, ⓦmaraisbastille.com; ⓜBréguet-Sabin/Bastille; map p.108. Part of the Best Western chain and handily located for both the Marais and Bastille, this 37-room hotel has recently undergone a stylish refurbishment by interior designer Michel Jouannet. The rooms are small but bright, done out in beige, taupe and moss green, with splashes of orange; bathrooms are modern, with white and black granite fittings. Free wi-fi is available in the rooms, and there's an attractive breakfast area and small courtyard. The rack rate is €195 for a double, but internet offers can bring the price down to €105, making this a really good deal. **€105**

Nouvel Hôtel 24 av du Bel Air, 12ᵉ ☎01 43 43 01 81, ⓦnouvel-hotel-paris.com; RER/ⓜNation; map p.108. A quiet, family-run hotel, with a faintly provincial air and small but neat and tidy rooms, each with private shower or bath, TV and phone. Some overlook the lovely garden (no. 9 opens directly onto it), where you can eat breakfast in the shade of a medlar tree. The obliging owners provide a personal touch. It's a bit out of the way, but the nearby RER gets you into the centre in no time. **€90**

★ **Hôtel de la Porte Dorée** 273 av Daumesnil, 12ᵉ ☎01 43 07 56 97, ⓦhoteldelaportedoree.com; ⓜPorte-Dorée; map p.108. A considerable step above the two-star norm: all rooms have private shower or bath, cable TV, comfy beds and pleasant decor. It's been refurbished with care and taste by an American–French family; traditional features such as ceiling mouldings, fireplaces and the elegant main staircase have been retained and many of the furnishings are antique. The owners have taken steps to make it more eco-friendly, too. Bastille is seven minutes away by métro or a pleasant twenty-minute walk along the Promenade Plantée. The public rate for a double is €130, but special internet deals are available from €59. **€59**

Le Quartier Bercy Square 33 bd de Reuilly, 12ᵉ ☎01 44 87 09 09, ⓦlequartierhotels.com; ⓜDaumesnil/Dugommier; map p.108. A worthy addition to Paris's stable of design hotels, *Le Quartier* is located in a cool, untouristy neighbourhood. The sleek en suites are small – some are tiny – but perfectly formed, with lots of smooth curves and subdued lighting, and there are thoughtful features like tea/coffee makers. Staff can be a little haughty, but are generally fine. **€140**

QUARTIER LATIN

Hôtel du Commerce 14 rue de la Montagne-Ste-Geneviève, 5ᵉ ☎01 43 54 89 69, ⓦcommerceparishotel.com; ⓜMaubert-Mutualité; map p.120. There's not much to like about this budget hotel but if you need to stay very centrally on a small budget, it fits the bill precisely. Boxy, flimsy and often noisy rooms range from washbasin-only cheapies (€55) up to simple en suites (around €70) and three- and four-bed rooms. No credit cards. **€55**

★ **Hôtel Degrés de Notre-Dame** 10 rue des Grands Degrés, 5ᵉ ☎01 55 42 88 88, ⓦlesdegreshotel.com; ⓜSt-Michel/Maubert-Mutualité; map p.120. Just ten rooms make up this welcoming and superbly idiosyncratic hotel, so you'll need to book well in advance. The building is ancient and the rooms all very different, with prices corresponding to size. Unique, personal touches are everywhere: hand-painted murals of clouds, antique mirrors, ancient beams and curious nooks and crannies. Perhaps the loveliest room of all is the one under the roof, which has its own stairs. **€120**

★ **Hôtel Esmeralda** 4 rue St-Julien-le-Pauvre, 5ᵉ ☎01 43 54 19 20, ⓦhotel-esmeralda.fr; ⓜSt-Michel/Maubert-Mutualité; map p.120. Dozing in an ancient house on square Viviani, this ancient hotel offers a deeply old-fashioned feel, with simple en-suite rooms (€100) – a few of them with unrivalled views of Notre-Dame. Not always perfectly tidy, and there are plenty of worn corners and few mod cons (you'll have to take the rickety stairs) but it's utterly charming. There are a few singles (€75) at the back. **€100**

Familia Hôtel 11 rue des Ecoles, 5ᵉ ☎01 43 54 55 27, ⓦfamiliahotel.com; ⓜCardinal-Lemoine/Maubert-Mutualité/Jussieu; map p.120. Friendly, family-run hotel in the heart of the *quartier*. Rooms are small but full of character, with beams, elegant *toile de Jouy* wallpaper and pretty murals; some top-floor rooms have views of nearby Notre-Dame, and others have their own balcony with table and chairs. The slightly more expensive *Minerva*, a three-star next door, has the same owners. **€100**

★ **Hôtel des Grandes Ecoles** 75 rue du Cardinal-Lemoine, 5ᵉ ☎01 43 26 79 23, ⓦhotel-grandes-ecoles.com; ⓜCardinal-Lemoine; map p.120. A cobbled private alleyway leads through to a big surprise: a large and peaceful garden, right in the heart of the Quartier Latin. The rooms are pretty in a modest sort of way, with floral wallpaper and old-fashioned furnishings, and the welcome is homely and sincere. Reservations are taken three months

18

in advance, on the 15th of the month; don't be even a day late, as it fills up fast. **€145**

Hôtel des Grands Hommes 17 place du Panthéon, 5ᵉ ☎01 46 34 19 60, ⓦhotelsdesgrandshommes.com; ⓂMaubert-Mutualité/RER Luxembourg; map p.120. There's a certain magnificence here: half the thirty rooms look out over the Panthéon (€430) and the Empire styling is distinctly luxurious. But it's a friendly hotel at heart, and often offers up to 50 percent discounts on the official rate. **€270**

Hôtel Marignan 13 rue du Sommerard, 5ᵉ ☎01 43 54 63 81, ⓦhotel-marignan.com; ⓂMaubert-Mutualité; map p.120. This budget hotel has been in the same family for three generations, and is totally sympathetic to the needs of rucksack-toting foreigners, with free laundry, ironing and wi-fi, plus a room to eat your own food in – plates, fridge and microwave provided – and rooms for up to five people; the cheapest have shared bathrooms. Simple enough, but one of the better bargains in town, with breakfast thrown in. **€60**

★ **Hôtel Résidence Henri IV** 50 rue des Bernardins, 5ᵉ ☎01 44 41 31 81, ⓦresidencehenri4.com; ⓂMaubert-Mutualité; map p.120. Set back from busy rue des Ecoles on a cul-de-sac, this hotel is discreet and elegant. The eight rooms are classically styled, and some have original features like fireplaces; all have miniature kitchenettes. **€150**

Hôtel St-Jacques 35 rue des Ecoles, 5ᵉ ☎01 44 07 45 45, ⓦparis-hotel-stjacques.com; ⓂMaubert-Mutualité/Odéon; map p.120. This pretty hotel in the heart of the district combines original nineteenth-century features, including a wrought-iron staircase and decorative ceiling mouldings, with modern comforts. The rooms are spacious, some with sashes draping the beds, plush velvet settees and balconies offering great views of the Panthéon. **€125**

Select Hôtel 1 place de la Sorbonne, 5ᵉ ☎01 46 34 14 80, ⓦselecthotel.fr; ⓂCluny-Sorbonne; map p.120. Situated right on the *place*, this fairly large hotel has a stylish feel, with exposed stone walls matched with modern furnishings. The more appealing rooms with views onto the square attract a hefty mark-up (€245). Efficiently run, with helpful, pleasantly unsnooty staff. **€195**

ST-GERMAIN

Hôtel de l'Abbaye 10 rue Cassette, 6ᵉ ☎01 45 44 38 11, ⓦhotelabbayeparis.com; ⓂSt-Sulpice; map p.134. An atmosphere of hushed, luxurious calm presides over this hotel – there's even a fair-sized courtyard garden and conservatory out back. Rooms are characterized by swathes of flowery fabric and brass fittings. **€260**

★ **La Belle Juliette** 92 rue du Cherche-Midi, 6ᵉ ☎01 42 22 97 40, ⓦlabellejuliette.com; ⓂRue-du-Bac; map p.134. This beautifully designed four-star boutique hotel opened in 2011. All its spacious rooms look out onto one of the quietest and most charming roads in the Left Bank, and the decor brings high-concept arty touches to classic, late-eighteenth-century elegance – and makes it work. Has its own spa and tearoom. Check the website for deals (from around €220). **€300**

Hôtel du Danube 58 rue Jacob, 6ᵉ ☎01 42 60 34 70, ⓦhoteldanube.fr; ⓂRue-du-Bac; map p.134. Refined but friendly hotel in a very posh area, with a luxuriantly floral decor. The standard rooms are small and fairly attractive, but the *supérieures* (€210) are the ones to go for: unusually large, each with a pair of handsome, tall windows. **€155**

L'Hôtel 13 rue des Beaux-Arts, 6ᵉ ☎01 44 41 99 00, ⓦl-hotel.com; ⓂMabillon/St-Germain-des-Prés; map p.134. Extravagantly styled and fashionable designer hotel, with twenty sumptuous rooms accessed by a wonderful spiral staircase, and with a tiny pool in the basement. Oscar Wilde died here, "fighting a duel" with his wallpaper, and he's now remembered in a room with a "Wilde" theme. **€250**

Hôtel Louis II 2 rue St-Sulpice, 6ᵉ ☎01 46 33 13 80, ⓦhotel-louis2.com; ⓂSt-Sulpice; map p.134. A great location between the Odéon and the Jardin du Luxembourg means that it isn't cheap, but the warm, plush decor lives up to the price. It's more Louis XIV than Louis II, with plenty of gilt and old wood furniture – plus flat-screen TVs, a/c and free wi-fi. **€195**

★ **Hôtel Michelet-Odéon** 6 place de l'Odéon, 6ᵉ ☎01 53 10 05 60, ⓦhotelmicheletodeon.com; ⓂOdéon; map p.134. The accommodation here is a bargain when you're so close to the Jardin du Luxembourg – and the rooms facing onto the *place*, especially the corner ones, are attractive, and slightly larger than the usual shoebox. A few triples, quads and apartments are also available. **€120**

Hôtel de Nesle 7 rue de Nesle, 6ᵉ ☎01 43 54 62 41, ⓦhoteldenesleparis.com; ⓂSt-Michel; map p.134. Eccentric, offbeat hotel with historical- or literary-themed rooms, some decorated with wacky cartoon murals you'll either love or hate. Rooms are tiny, and not bursting with freshness, but inexpensive for the astoundingly central location. **€75**

Hôtel Odéon Saint-Germain 13 rue St-Sulpice, 6ᵉ ☎01 43 25 70 11, ⓦparis-hotel-odeon.com; ⓂSt-Sulpice/Odéon; map p.134. Old-fashioned luxury: flowers, antique furniture, some four-poster beds and elegant designer fabrics. The service is excellent, and the location splendid: right between the boulevard St-Germain and the Jardin du Luxembourg. Internet deals can be as little as half the official rate. **€280**

Relais Christine 3 rue Christine, 6ᵉ ☎01 40 51 60 80, ⓦrelais-christine.com; ⓂOdéon/St-Michel; map p.134. This deeply romantic four-star hotel is in a sixteenth-century building set around a deliciously hidden courtyard. At this level, it's well worth paying the 20 percent premium for one of the *supérieure* rooms. **€300**

Relais Saint-Sulpice 3 rue Garancière, 6ᵉ ☎01 46 33 99 00, ⓦrelais-saint-sulpice.com; Ⓜ St-Sulpice/St-Germain-des-Prés; map p.134. Set in a beautiful, aristocratic townhouse on a side street immediately behind St-Sulpice's apse, this is a discreetly classy hotel with well-furnished rooms painted in cheery Provençal colours. The rooms at the front have a view, and are a little more expensive. Comes with all mod-cons, including a sauna off the dining room. **€180**

Hôtel Stanislas 5 rue du Montparnasse, 6ᵉ ☎01 45 48 37 05, ⓦstanislas-hotel.com; Ⓜ Notre-Dame-des-Champs/St-Placide; map p.134. This friendly, family-run two-star is closer to the bright lights of Montparnasse – you can hear the rumble of the métro – than the chichi north of St-Germain, but the price is correspondingly good value. Rooms are basic but clean and welcoming enough, in a frumpily provincial sort of way. **€73**

Hôtel de Verneuil 8 rue de Verneuil, 6ᵉ ☎01 42 60 82 14, ⓦhotelverneuil.com; Ⓜ St-Germain-des-Prés; map p.134. Cosy hotel in the quiet riverbank quarter between St-Germain and the Musée d'Orsay. Beams and pretty print wallpapers add a touch of class, and there's a/c in all the rooms. It's worth paying the modest premium for a larger one, at around €185. Popular with Americans, so book well in advance. **€155**

THE EIFFEL TOWER QUARTER

Hôtel du Champ-de-Mars 7 rue du Champ-de-Mars, 7ᵉ ☎01 45 51 52 30, ⓦhotelduchampdemars.com; ⓂEcole-Militaire; map p.148. In a handsome area just off the rue Cler market, this good-value hotel has a comforting neighbourhood feel. The rooms are small but cosy, with colourful fabrics adorning the bedheads, curtains and chairs. **€100**

★ **Hôtel du Palais Bourbon** 49 rue de Bourgogne, 7ᵉ ☎01 44 11 30 70, ⓦhotel-palais-bourbon.com; ⓂVarenne; map p.148. This substantial, handsome old three-star in the hushed, posh district near the Musée Rodin offers unusually spacious and prettily furnished double rooms. As befits a homely, family-run hotel, there are parquet floors and lots of period details – but there's also a/c

---

CLASSIC PARIS LUXURY

If want to splash out, Paris is the place to do it. Check out our favourite luxury hotels, many of which offer great deals at weekends or out of season.

Le Bristol See p.254
Hôtel Costes See p.254
Hôtel Lancaster See p.254
Hôtel Meurice See p.254
Relais Christine See opposite
Hôtel de Sers See p.254
Hôtel Sezz See p.262

---

in all rooms. Family rooms are available, as well as a few miniature, unmodernized singles (€110). **€150**

MONTPARNASSE AND THE 14ᵉ

Hôtel de la Loire 39bis rue du Moulin Vert, 14ᵉ ☎01 45 40 66 88, ⓦhoteldelaloire-paris.com; ⓂPernety/Alésia; map p.160. Behind the pretty blue shutters lies a homely family hotel. The rooms may be a little tired but are good value. Those in the annexe, which runs the length of the garden – a bonus in itself – are on the dark side. **€75**

Hôtel Mistral 24 rue de Cels, 14ᵉ ☎01 43 20 25 43, ⓦhotel-mistral-paris.com; ⓂPernety/Alésia; map p.160. Welcoming and decently refurbished hotel on a very quiet street, with a little courtyard garden and breakfast room behind. The good-value rooms come with showers and shared WC facilities (€70), or en suite (€95). **€70**

Solar Hôtel 22 rue Boulard, 14ᵉ ☎01 43 21 08 20, ⓦsolarhotel.fr; ⓂDenfert-Rochereau; map p.160. This modern, budget hotel maintains a determinedly ecological spirit, from its breakfasts to its waste water. The rooms are unfussy and comfortable, at an excellent price, which includes breakfast, though those in the annexe are much less appealing. **€59**

THE 15ᵉ

Hôtel de l'Avre 21 rue de l'Avre, 15ᵉ ☎01 45 75 31 03, ⓦhoteldelavre.com; ⓂLa-Motte-Picquet-Grenelle; map p.170. Within striking distance of the Eiffel Tower, this cheery, good-value hotel lies just off the rue du Commerce – but you could be forgiven for thinking you were in the provinces. The fresh, pastel-coloured rooms have floral accents and wicker furniture, and some have balconies over the garden. **€90**

Hôtel Printemps 31 rue du Commerce, 15ᵉ ☎01 45 79 83 36, ⓔhotel.printemps.15e@wanadoo.fr; ⓂEmile-Zola/La-Motte-Picquet-Grenelle; map p.170. Cheap furnishings and ageing decor don't stop this being a reasonable budget choice for its neighbourhood location and friendly welcome. The nicer rooms have small balconies, and it's popular with backpackers. Doubles €50 with bathroom, €40 with shared facilities. **€40**

THE 13ᵉ AND AROUND

La Manufacture 8 rue Philippe de Champagne, 13ᵉ ☎01 45 35 45 25, ⓦhotel-la-manufacture.com; ⓂPlace-d'Italie; map p.173. The fifty-odd rooms at this smart, welcoming hotel are trimmed in warm colours. Helpful staff, wooden flooring and rooms looking onto the handsome *mairie* almost justify the price. **€145**

★ **Hôtel Port-Royal** 8 bd Port-Royal, 5ᵉ ☎01 43 31 70 06, ⓦhotelportroyal.fr; ⓂGobelins; map p.173. Actually located at the edge of the 5ᵉ arrondissement, this is a one-star hotel at its best. This discreet address has been in the same family since the 1930s. Double rooms (€78.50)

18

18

are fairly large, immaculately clean and attractive; fifteen rooms are available with shared bathroom facilities (€52.50). It's located out at the southern edge of the *quartier*, at the rue Mouffetard end of the boulevard, but near the métro. No credit cards. **€52.50**

Résidence Les Gobelins 9 rue des Gobelins, 13e ☎01 47 07 26 90, ⊛hotelgobelins.com; ⊛Gobelins; map p.173. A pleasantly old-fashioned, quiet and well-run establishment within walking distance of the Quartier Latin's rue Mouffetard. With its large, simple but comfortable rooms, this is a well-known bargain, so book far in advance. **€95**

Hôtel Tolbiac 122 rue de Tolbiac, 13e ☎01 44 24 25 54, ⊛hotel-tolbiac.com; ⊛Tolbiac; map p.173. This big but friendly budget hotel has been refitted as a kind of budget designer option, with bright but hastily applied paintwork, cool, stripy bedlinen and double-glazing on all but the top floors. There's free parking and wi-fi, it's well run, and the prices are low: €50 with shared facilities, or €60 en suite, with some basic singles at €35. The drawback is the situation on a noisy junction, quite a way from any action. **€50**

★ **Le Vert-Galant** 41 rue Croulebarbe, 13e ☎01 44 08 83 50, ⊛vertgalant.com; ⊛Gobelins; map p.173. Set on a quiet backwater overlooking the verdant square René-le-Gall, with a large garden behind, this family-run hotel seems to belong to a provincial French town rather than Paris – they'll even do your laundry and let you park your car on site, and in the evening you can eat downstairs at the enjoyable *Auberge Etchegorry*. The rooms are modern but pleasantly airy; those giving onto the garden come with French windows and kitchenettes (up to €130). **€90**

MONTMARTRE

Hôtel des Arts 5 rue Tholozé, 18e ☎01 46 06 30 52, ⊛montmartrehotel.com; ⊛Abbesses/Blanche; map p.180. Manages that rare combination of homeliness and efficiency, with courteous staff, and the family dog lolling by the reception desk. Rooms are fairly small and a little bland, but cosy and well maintained – and the topmost "superior" ones have great views. The location – on a romantically sloping, cobbled street in the heart of the Abbesses quarter, opposite a classic arts cinema – is just fantastic. The superior rooms, which have views, are usually around €150. **€80**

★ **Hôtel Bonséjour Montmartre** 11 rue Burq, 18e ☎01 42 54 22 53, ⊛hotel-bonsejour-montmartre.fr; ⊛Abbesses; map p.180. Set in a romantic location on a quiet, untouristy street on the slopes of Montmartre, this hotel is run by friendly owners, and the rooms, which are basic but clean and relatively spacious, are one of Paris's best deals – €54 for a simple double room with just a sink (and bearable shared shower facilities), or €66 with a private shower. Ask for the corner rooms 23, 33, 43 or 53, which have balconies. **€54**

★ **Ermitage Hôtel** 24 rue Lamarck, 18e ☎01 42 64 79 22, ⊛ermitagesacrecoeur.fr; ⊛Lamarck-Caulaincourt/Château-Rouge; map p.180. One of the highest-altitude hotels in Paris, this discreet family-run establishment has rooms that seem to be caught in time, decorated with florals in deep colours and antique objets d'art. Only a stone's throw from the Sacré-Coeur, but it's best to approach via ⊛Anvers and the *funiculaire* to avoid the steep climb. No credit cards. **€100**

★ **Hôtel Particulier Montmartre** 23 av Junot, 18e ☎01 53 41 81 40, ⊛hotel-particulier-montmartre.com; ⊛Abbesses/Lamarck-Caulaincourt; map p.180. An exceptional hotel for a treat – or perhaps a honeymoon retreat, given its secluded location in a garden off a private *passage* just back from one of Paris's most exclusive streets. Set in an elegant Neoclassical mansion, this utterly discreet boutique hotel has just five rooms, all large and très designer – provocatively so, in some cases. You can often get deep discounts, especially during the week in summer. **€390**

THE 9e

★ **Hôtel Amour** 8 rue Navarin, 9e ☎01 48 78 31 80, ⊛hotelamourparis.fr; ⊛Pigalle; map p.180. Designer hotel for Bohemians, with old parquet and a deliberately sleazy Pigalle porn theme: there's a Mickey Mouse with a giant phallus by the reception desk. Every room is different – one is all black with disco balls above the bed – but none has phone or TV, and all have iPod speakers: the two hyper-designed *supérieures* and duplexes cost €215–250. There's a spacious dining area, a private terrace where you can entertain up to fifteen, a vodka bar and an achingly cool clientele. You're paying for fashion and atmosphere here, not service. Some love it. **€155**

★ **Hôtel Langlois** 63 rue St-Lazare, 9e ☎01 48 74 78 24, ⊛hotel-langlois.com; ⊛Trinité; map p.180. This utterly genteel hotel feels as if it has scarcely changed in the last century, though it has all the facilities you'd expect of a two-star, plus excellent service. Every room is different, but they're all large and handsome with high ceilings, antique furnishings, fireplaces and other period details. Some have enormous bathrooms. There are only 27 rooms, so book well in advance. **€150**

Hôtel Lorette 36 rue Notre-Dame de Lorette, 9e ☎01 42 85 18 81, ⊛astotel.com; ⊛St-Georges; map p.180. With its handsome location by elegant place St-George, nicely situated between Opéra and Montmartre, this Best Western feels refreshingly unlike a chain, though staff are very professional. The warm, friendly, moderately stylish rooms are all well sized. **€120**

Perfect Hotel 39 rue Rodier, 9e ☎01 42 81 18 86, ⊛paris-hostel.biz; ⊛Anvers; map p.180. This friendly, well-kept budget hotel on a lively street lined with restaurants sees many return visitors. The rooms (without bath €58, otherwise €72) are simple and decent, though the walls are notoriously paper-thin. Definitely a cut above a youth hostel, for just a few euros more. **€58**

THE NORTHERN STATIONS

Hôtel de Lille 2 rue de Montholon, off 87 rue du Faubourg Poissonnière, 9ᵉ ☎01 47 70 38 76; Ⓜ Poissonnière; map p.191. If you want a basic, inexpensive hotel near the Gare du Nord, you won't find much better than this. The rooms are airy, clean and fairly large, with double glazing and decent carpets: en-suite doubles cost €51, or €38 with sinks and shared bathroom facilities (showers €5). The welcome is sleepy but genuine. **€38**

Mercure Paris Terminus Nord 12 bd de Denain, 10ᵉ ☎01 42 80 20 00, Ⓦ mercure.com; Ⓜ Gare du Nord; map p.191. Massive, professionally-run three star right opposite the Gare du Nord, with its own enormous – and gorgeous – 1920s brasserie on the ground floor. It's reliable enough, though the rooms are definitely variable in quality, as are the prices, with doubles costing up to €260 according to demand. **€100**

BATIGNOLLES

★ **Hôtel Eldorado** 18 rue des Dames, 17ᵉ ☎01 45 22 35 21, Ⓦ eldoradohotel.fr; Ⓜ Rome/Place-de-Clichy; map p.193. Not quite the golden kingdom, but a superb address nonetheless. Idiosyncratic and enjoyable, this hotel has its own little wine bar and an attractive annexe in a detached house at the back of its sizeable courtyard garden. The en-suite rooms (€76–85) are charmingly decorated, with bright colour schemes offsetting the vintage furnishings and the old hotel fittings that are fast disappearing from Paris. A few simple shared-bath rooms are also available (€39 single, €65 double). **€65**

EASTERN PARIS: REPUBLIQUE AND THE CANAL ST-MARTIN

Le Citizen Hotel 96 quai de Jemmapes, 10ᵉ ☎01 83 62 55 50, Ⓦ lecitizenhotel.com; Ⓜ Jacques Bonsergent; map p.196. On the banks of the Canal St-Martin, the *Citizen* is a new, eco-friendly design hotel with only twelve rooms, including one suite (€249) and one apartment (€399). The Zen-style decor of light wood, clean lines and predominantly white, blue and grey tones makes for nice airy rooms, all of which have windows overlooking the canal. The cheaper rooms are compact, the more expensive are twice as big and have a little sitting area and desk. A nice touch is the free iPads that come with each room. You can have a simple breakfast for €5.50 or something more substantial for

COOL ON A BUDGET

Want a cool interior, without the celebrity designer and associated price-tag? Here are some of the most stylish hotels in the city that won't break the bank.
Le Citizen Hôtel See below
Hôtel Degrés de Notre-Dame See p.257
Hôtel Eldorado See below
Mama Shelter See below
Hôtel Marais Bastille See p.257
Le Quartier Bercy Square See p.257

18

€12.50. It's worth checking the website for last-minute special deals which can bring the price down to around €120 for a double. **€179**

Le Général Hôtel 5–7 rue Rampon, 11ᵉ ☎01 47 00 41 57, Ⓦ legeneralhotel.com; Ⓜ République; map p.196. This cool boutique hotel, run by young staff and located on a fairly peaceful road, is a lesson in restrained modern design. The bright, airy, compact rooms have spotless bathrooms (complete with rubber ducks) and rosewood furnishings. Facilities include a sauna and fitness centre, and the breakfast area turns into a bar in the evenings. **€186**

Hôtel de Nevers 53 rue de Malte, 11ᵉ ☎01 47 00 56 18, Ⓦ hoteldenevers.com; Ⓜ Oberkampf/République; map p.196. The entrance to this one-star is patrolled by two smoky-grey cats. Needless to say, there's no room to swing one, but otherwise these are for the most part decent, cheerful, if basic, rooms – the best are the en-suite doubles at the front, though there's a bit of traffic noise; courtyard-facing rooms are dark and poky. When it's working, a rickety 1930s lift rumbles its way between the floors. The cheaper rooms have only a washbasin and access to a shower on the landing. **€62**

★ **Hôtel du Nord** 47 rue Albert Thomas, 10ᵉ ☎01 42 01 92 10, Ⓦ hoteldunord-leparivelo.com; Ⓜ Jacques Bonsergent/République; map p.196. A pretty ivy-strewn entrance leads into a cosy reception and 23 rooms, all different and tastefully, if simply, decorated. The cheaper ones look onto the courtyard and tend to be a little smaller and darker. Four rooms have a bath, the rest have showers, and a family room is available for €105. A small lift serves the six floors. The owner, a cycling enthusiast, has ten bicycles available for guests to use for free. A simple breakfast (€7.50) with home-made jams is served in a cosy basement room. **€69**

BAGNOLET

★ **Mama Shelter** 109 rue de Bagnolet, 20ᵉ ☎01 43 48 48 48, Ⓦ mamashelter.com; Ⓜ Alexandre-Dumas; map p.208. One of the most talked about hotels in Paris, *Mama Shelter*, owned by Club Med founders the Trigano family, justifies the hype. Philippe Starck-designed, with

18

an industrial-chic theme, the 172 rooms are also extremely good value. The sharp en suites come with an arty graffiti motif on the carpets and ceilings, swanky bathrooms, iMacs, free wi-fi, and decorative superhero masks. An excellent bar-restaurant with live music at weekends, sun terrace and top-notch service complete the package. The cheapest deals are available via the website. **€89**

WESTERN PARIS

Hameau de Passy 48 rue Passy, 16ᵉ ☎ 01 42 88 47 55, Ⓦ paris-hotel-hameaudepassy.com; Ⓜ Muette/Passy; map p.213. An utterly peaceful, modern hotel with a country sensibility, set back from the main street. While the rooms are on the small side, they get lots of natural light and are pleasantly decorated in white, orange and green hues. Faultless service is assured by a charming, polyglot

staff, and there's free wi-fi in all the rooms. The official rack rate is €153, but great internet deals are often available from as little as €58. **€58**

Hotel Sezz 6 av Frémiet, 16ᵉ ☎ 01 56 75 26 26, Ⓦ hotelsezz.com; Ⓜ Passy; map p.213. No humble receptionist, but a "personal assistant" welcomes you to this sleek boutique hotel, hidden behind a nineteenth-century facade on a quiet street near the place de Passy. The rooms are decorated with sober minimalism, veering on the austere (slate-grey stone walls, black wooden flooring, glass partitions and chrome furnishings), but with splashes of colour providing a touch of warmth. The standard rooms are smallish; the suites come with huge bathtubs big enough for two, and all rooms have flat-screen TVs, free wi-fi and CD/DVD player. Within easy walking distance of the Eiffel Tower. **€335**

APARTMENTS AND BED AND BREAKFAST

If you're staying for more than a few days, renting an **apartment** can transform a stay in Paris. Apartments tend to be more attractively styled than the average Parisian hotel, and they can make you feel that little bit like a local. **Apartment-hotels** – a hotel made up of mini-apartments each with its own self-contained kitchen – may be useful alternatives for families or visitors on an extended stay. Staying on a **bed and breakfast** basis in a private house is also worth considering if you want to get away from the more impersonal setup of a hotel, and is a reasonably priced option. The following is a list of recommended organizations. Prices given are per night, unless specified otherwise. In addition, see the reviews of the *Hôtel Résidence Henri IV*, 5ᵉ (see p.258), the *Hôtel Michelet-Odéon*, 6ᵉ (see p.258) and *Le Vert-Galant*, 13ᵉ (see p.260), which all offer apartments or rooms with kitchenettes as well as standard rooms.

Air BnB Ⓦ airbnb.com. San Francisco-based dotcom which allows owners of private houses to rent out rooms or apartments in their homes – and there are scores of "hosts" in Paris, some with beautiful apartments, many in trendier areas of town. Based on trust, and user feedback. From **€40**

Alcôve & Agapes ☎ 01 44 85 06 05, Ⓦ bed-and-breakfast-in-paris.com. A family-run bed-and-breakfast organization that has a good selection of rooms on its books, most accommodating couples, but some able to welcome families. Some hosts offer extras, such as French conversation, wine tasting or cookery classes. From **€85**

Citadines Ⓦ citadines.com. A Europe-wide chain of apartment-hotels. Most of its sixteen Paris establishments are centrally located and offer high-standard, comfortable accommodation consisting of compact self-contained studios and apartments sleeping up to six, with well-equipped kitchen and bathroom. Offers all the usual amenities of a three-star hotel, plus parking, laundry facilities and the option of breakfast. Studios sleeping two cost from around €160 a night, apartments for four €175, though they sometimes have special offers and there are lower rates for long stays. **€160**

Coach House Rentals Paris ☎ 06 15 28 90 26, Ⓦ rentals.chsparis.com. Agency for forty-odd private

apartments, mostly second homes, and around half studios or one-beds – though there are larger apartments too. The admin charge for linen, utilities, etc isn't cheap at €75, but you're met at the apartment by an English-speaking agent and there's a helpline, should you need it. They can arrange airport cars, too. A minimum five-night stay is required. **€125**

France Lodge 2 rue Meissonier, 17ᵉ ☎ 01 56 33 85 80, Ⓦ apartments-in-paris.com. Offers bed-and-breakfast rooms and apartments inside and outside Paris. Prices start at €40 for a single or €60 for a double, plus a €15 booking fee. They can usually find something last minute, but reserve well in advance to be sure of something more special. They can also organize accommodation in furnished apartments by the week (from €400) or month (from €900). **€60**

Good Morning Paris 43 rue Lacépède, 5ᵉ ☎ 01 47 07 28 29, Ⓦ goodmorningparis.fr. Bed-and-breakfast accommodation (130 rooms in total) in central Paris. You have to stay at least two nights but there's no reservation fee – payment in full confirms your booking. **€79**

Lodgis 47 rue de Paradis, 10ᵉ ☎ 01 70 39 11 11, Ⓦ lodgis.com. A well-run agency with over a thousand furnished studios and flats on its books. Most places are available by the week, but some will consider shorter stays. **€440** per week.

Paris B and B ☎1-800 872 26 32 , ⓦparisbandb.com. US-based online bed-and-breakfast booking service. The rooms are on the luxurious side, with apartments from $120. Payment in $US only. Minimum three-night stay. **$90**

HOSTELS

The best **hostels** in Paris offer fantastic, central locations at prices that only a handful of budget hotels can match. The smarter, cleaner, quieter places tend to be run by institutions, and are often aimed at groups. The funkier, livelier ones are usually the independents, but they often suffer from unenthusiastic staff – which impacts on the welcome and the cleanliness. There are a few exceptions, of course: group hostels with real character, and independents with charm. The main downsides of hostels are noise and the lockout, with rooms closed "for cleaning" for hours in the middle of the day.

18

GROUP AND INSTITUTIONAL HOSTELS

D'Artagnan 80 rue Vitruve, 20ᵉ ☎01 40 32 34 56, ⓦfuaj.org; ⓜPorte-de-Bagnolet; map p.196. This colourful, modern HI hostel is the largest in France with 440 beds and lots of facilities including a small cinema, restaurant and bar, internet access and a swimming pool nearby. It's located on the eastern edge of the city near Bagnolet, which has some good bars. You have to vacate the rooms between 11am and 3pm for cleaning. Doubles and rooms for three to five are available at just a few euros more per head than the dorm rate. It's very popular, so get here early or book online or by phone on the central reservations number: ☎01 44 89 87 27. Dorms **€27**

BVJ Louvre 20 rue Jean-Jacques-Rousseau, 1ᵉʳ ☎01 53 00 90 90, ⓦbvjhotel.com; ⓜLouvre/Châtelet-Les-Halles; map p.72. More than 60 years old, with 200 beds, the well-run *BVJ Louvre* attracts a young student crowd from around the world, but the clean four- to ten-bed dorms have a somewhat institutional feel. Accommodation ranges from single rooms to dorms sleeping eight, and there's a restaurant (daily except Sun). Dorms **€29**, doubles **€70**

BVJ Paris Quartier Latin 44 rue des Bernardins, 5ᵉ ☎01 43 29 34 80, ⓦbvjhotel.com; ⓜMaubert-Mutualité; map p.120. Typically institutional BVJ hostel, but spick and span and in a very central location. Dorm beds (€29), plus singles (€49) and doubles (€70), all with shared toilet. Dorms **€29**, doubles **€70**

★ **Le Fauconnier** 11 rue du Fauconnier, 4ᵉ ☎01 42 74 23 45, ⓦmije.com; ⓜSt-Paul/Pont-Marie; map p.96. One of three hostels run by MIJE, all in the Marais. *Le Fauconnier* is in a superbly renovated seventeenth-century building with a courtyard. With a 1am curfew, MIJE hostels are not for party animals. Breakfast is included. Dorms (€30 per person) sleep four to eight, and there are also some single (€49) and double rooms with shower. Dorms **€30**, doubles **€72**

Le Fourcy 6 rue de Fourcy, 4ᵉ ☎01 42 74 23 45; ⓜSt-Paul; map p.96. Another excellent MIJE hostel (same prices and deal as *Le Fauconnier*, above). Housed in a beautiful mansion, this one has a small garden and an inexpensive restaurant. Doubles and triples are available, as well as dorms. Dorms **€30**, doubles **€72**

Foyer International d'Accueil de Paris Jean Monnet 30 rue Cabanis, 14ᵉ ☎01 43 13 17 00, ⓦfiap.asso.fr; ⓜGlacière; map p.160. A huge, efficiently run hostel in a fairly sedate area a couple of métro stops south of the Quartier Latin. Offers singles (€59), doubles (€79) and dorms (€27–35, depending on number of beds). Facilities include a disco; ideal for groups. Dorms **€27–35**, doubles **€79**

Foyer Tolbiac 234 rue Tolbiac, 13ᵉ ☎01 44 16 22 22, ⓦfoyer-tolbiac.com; ⓜGlacière; map p.173. Large place catering to working women aged 18–25 only, offering spartan but pleasant private rooms for short or long stays. The excellent facilities include kitchens on every floor, wi-fi, programmes of activities and welcome parties. Singles **€31**

Jules Ferry 8 bd Jules Ferry, 11ᵉ ☎01 43 57 55 60, ⓦfuaj.org; ⓜRépublique; map p.196. Pleasant but relatively small (100 beds) HI hostel in an old Haussmann-era apartment building in a good location near République and the ever more trendy Canal St-Martin. Reserve online or at ☎01 44 89 87 27. Dorms **€25**

Maubuisson 12 rue des Barres, 4ᵉ ☎01 42 74 23 45, ⓦmije.com; map p.96. A MIJE hostel (see *Le Fauconnier*) in a magnificent medieval building on a quiet street. Shared use of the restaurant at nearby *Le Fourcy*. 1am curfew. Breakfast included. Dorms only, sleeping four. Dorms **€30**

Maurice Ravel 6 av Maurice-Ravel, 12ᵉ ☎01 44 75 60 00, ⓦcisp.fr; ⓜPorte-de-Vincennes/Porte-Dorée; map p.108. Aimed at groups, this institutional hostel, run by the Centres Internationaux de Séjours de Paris, is some distance from central Paris, but near the lovely Bois de Vincennes. There's a self-service *resto* and outdoor swimming pool in summer. Rooms range from eight-bed dorms to twins and singles (€41.20); all share shower rooms. CISP has another hostel in a park near the Porte-d'Italie, at the southern end of the 13ᵉ. Dorms **€21.80**, twins **€61**

★ **St Christopher's Paris** 68–74 quai de la Seine, 19ᵉ ☎01 40 34 34 40, ⓦst-christophers.co.uk/paris-hostels; ⓜCrimée/Laumière; map p.200. Massive, new hostel housed in an eye-catching, renovated former boat hangar overlooking the water of the Bassin de la Villette – some way from the centre. Rooms sleep six to eight and are pleasant enough in a functional, cabin-like way, and there's a great bar,

18

inexpensive restaurant, café, book exchange, internet access and dozens of activities on offer. Mostly dorms, plus a few twins and doubles; prices fluctuate on a day-to-day basis, but always include breakfast. Dorms €31, doubles €44

INDEPENDENT HOSTELS
Auberge International des Jeunes 10 rue Trousseau, 11ᵉ ☎ 01 47 00 62 00, ⓦ aijparis.com; Ⓜ Ledru-Rollin; map p.108. Just about the cheapest dorm beds in Paris are to be found here; as you would expect, the three- and four-bed dorms are pretty spartan, facilities are thin on the ground and you have to vacate the rooms between 11am and 4pm. Nevertheless, it's friendly and well located. Dorms €19

Hôtel Caulaincourt Square 2 square Caulaincourt (by 63 rue Caulaincourt), 18ᵉ ☎ 01 46 06 46 06, ⓦ caulaincourt.com; Ⓜ Lamarck-Caulaincourt; map p.180. Hostel and hotel at the very top of Montmartre with a shabby but useful dormitory section; good value for the location – a few rooms have expansive views – though travellers' reports are variable. Dorms €29, doubles €80

★ **Oops** 50 av des Gobelins, 13ᵉ ☎ 01 47 07 47 00, ⓦ oops-paris.com; Ⓜ Gobelins; map p.173. This "design hostel", opened in 2007, is decorated in bright colours and funky patterns. Service is no better than at most hostels, but all dorms are en suite, there's free wi-fi, a/c and a basic breakfast included, and it's open 24 hours. Unexceptional

location, but it's just a couple of métro stops south of the Quartier Latin. Dorms from €23, doubles €60

Peace and Love Hostel 245 rue La Fayette, 10ᵉ ☎ 01 46 07 65 11, ⓦ paris-hostels.com; Ⓜ Jaurès; map p.196. Tucked away at the top end of the 10ᵉ, just off the trendy Canal St-Martin, this hostel has recently been renovated, with showers in every room. Doubles and triples cost a few euros more than dorms. The bargain-priced bar that's open till 2am gives a clue to the style of the place. Open 24hr. Dorms €23

★ **Le Village Hostel** 20 rue d'Orsel, 18ᵉ ☎ 01 42 64 22 02, ⓦ villagehostel.fr; Ⓜ Anvers; map p.180. Set in an attractively renovated nineteenth-century building with a view of the Sacré-Coeur from the terrace. Good facilities (sheets included, kitchen available). Dorms from €28, doubles and twins from €70

Woodstock Hostel 48 rue Rodier, 9ᵉ ☎ 01 48 78 87 76, ⓦ woodstock.fr; Ⓜ Anvers/St-Georges; map p.180. A grungey, party-oriented backpacker hostel, with its own bar. The standards are far from high, but then neither is the price: there's a €3 supplement at weekends and for a double room. Dorms from €22

Young and Happy Hostel 80 rue Mouffetard, 5ᵉ ☎ 01 47 07 47 07, ⓦ youngandhappy.fr; Ⓜ Monge/Censier-Daubenton; map on p.120. Noisy, basic and studenty hostel in a lively location. Dorms, with shower, sleep four to ten. Dorms €30, twins €45

CAMPING

The least expensive option is, of course, camping. There's only one option anywhere near the centre, and another close to Disneyland; the other **campsites** in the region are way out of town. For a full list, contact the tourist office.

Camping du Bois de Boulogne Allée du Bord-de-l'Eau, 16ᵉ ☎ 01 45 24 30 00, ⓦ campingparis.fr; Ⓜ Porte-Maillot then bus #244 to Moulins Camping; the bus doesn't run in the evening, but a shuttle bus is laid on in summer; see map p.217. Currently being renovated, with the addition of cottages and caravans, this is the most central campsite, with space for over 400 tents, next to the Seine in the Bois de Boulogne, and usually booked out in summer. The ground is pebbly, but the site is well equipped. Prices start at €18 for a tent

with two people in high season; bungalows for four to six people are from €115 (in high season) per night.

Camping la Colline Route de Lagny, Torcy ☎ 01 60 05 42 32, ⓦ camping-de-la-colline.com; RER line A4 to Torcy, then take a shuttle bus. Wooded lakeside site to the east of the city near Disneyland (with an inexpensive minibus shuttle), offering rental of anything from luxury tents to bungalows; erecting your own tent costs from €26.80 per night for two people.

CAFÉ DE L'INDUSTRIE, BASTILLE

Cafés and restaurants

The French seldom separate the major pleasures of eating and drinking, and there are thousands of establishments in Paris where you can do both. A restaurant may call itself a brasserie, *bistrot*, café or indeed restaurant; equally, a café can be a place to eat, drink, listen to music, dance or even watch theatre. To simplify matters, we've split our listings for each area into two parts: under cafés and wine bars, you'll find venues we recommend primarily for daytime or relaxed evening drinks, or perhaps a snack or light meal; under restaurants, you'll find any establishment we recommend for a full meal. Most cafés and some wine bars remain open until fairly late at night and are perfect for a beer, glass of wine or *digestif*; if you're looking for cocktails, pints or full-on nightlife, however, you'll need to head for the bars and clubs (see p.295).

The traditional Paris **café**, with zinc bar, tobacco-stained ceiling and neon lights, is slowly giving way to a lounge-bar look, with comfy velvet chairs, music, designer lighting – and of course a ban on smoking. Yet some cafés are still resolutely traditional in decor, and remain one of the mainstays of Parisian society, places where people come to gossip and discuss, pose and people-watch, or simply read a book. In our "**cafés**" category, we've included all kinds of venues which we recommend primarily as places where you'd want to come and have a drink, but don't forget that most cafés also serve **food**, from the simple pastries, *tartines* (open sandwiches) and toasted sandwiches often available in more basic places, to the dishes and full meals served in the larger cafés and **café-brasseries** – usually salads, a *plat du jour* (daily special), and perhaps a limited- or no-choice two-course *formule*. Alongside cafés, we've listed **wine bars** or *bistrots à vin* which may offer cheeses, cold meats and regional dishes to go with their fine wines by the glass. Also included in this category, you'll find genteel **salons de thé** (tearooms), typically serving tea, pastries and light meals.

Most visitors come to Paris with an appetite, and high expectations. This is, after all, the city that invented the **restaurant**, and indeed fine cooking. But while the city's celebrity art-chefs relentlessly pursue perfection, and the avant-garde operates at the very cutting edge of gastronomy, the **cuisine** at the average Parisian restaurant or simpler, more local **bistrot** is surprisingly conservative. It is *cuisine bourgeoise*, not *gastronomique*, meaning homely meats in sauces, for the most part. Being comfortingly *correcte* is often judged as more important than exhibiting gourmet flair, and quality and precision are typically valued over inventiveness and experimentation. As such the real engines of the contemporary restaurant scene are the smaller local restaurants and *bistrots*, often run by committed enthusiasts for good food and wine whose stars tend to rise and fall in line with the exacting standards of their Parisian clientele. Still more conservative are the Parisian institutions, the old-time **brasseries** and historic restaurants whose owners and chefs rarely dare to meddle with a decor – or indeed a style of cooking – that has been enjoyed by Parisians and visitors for generations. It's useful to look up a few **food and drink terms** (see pp.384–388).

ESSENTIALS

PRICES

Prices have to be displayed in every **café** by law, usually without the fifteen percent service charge added, but detailing separately the prices for consuming at the bar (*au comptoir*), sitting down (*la salle*), or on the terrace (*la terrasse*) – each progressively more expensive. Addresses in the smarter or more touristy arrondissements set costs soaring and you'll generally pay more on main squares and boulevards than on backstreets. At almost all cafés and bars, you're presented with a small bill along with your drinks, which you settle when you leave.

In **restaurants** there is often a choice between one or more **fixed-price menus** (simply called *le menu* in French – the French word for "menu" in the English sense is *la carte*), where the number of courses for the stated price is fixed and the choice accordingly limited. Lunchtime *menus* are particularly good value, typically priced at less than €25 even at quite classy restaurants, and as little as €12 for two courses at good inexpensive places. Top-notch gastronomic restaurants, too, typically offer a lunch *menu* for roughly half the price of the full evening experience. Eating out in the evening has become expensive; at most decent restaurants you'll usually pay €30 or more for a three-course meal. Often the best value is to be found at some of the smaller, cutting-edge *bistrots*, where the choice might be limited (or nonexistent) but the quality of the food is usually excellent. If you just want a main course it's worth looking out for the *plat du jour* (chef's daily special). Eating *à la carte*, of course, gives you access to everything on offer, though you'll pay a fair bit more. The *à la carte* prices we give are generally for an average three-course meal with half a bottle of wine. **Service** is legally included in your bill at all restaurants, bars and cafés, but you may want to leave an optional **tip** (see box, opposite). House **wines** are usually inexpensive, but a bottle of something interesting will usually add at least €20 to the bill, and potentially much, much more for a good bottle in a more expensive place.

RESTAURANT OPENING HOURS AND RESERVATIONS

Restaurant and *bistrot* **opening hours** are usually noon until 2pm, and 8pm until around 10pm. The **latest time** at which you can walk into a restaurant and order is generally about 9.30 or 10pm, although once ensconced you can often remain well into the night. **Brasseries** serve quicker meals and at most hours of the day; they also serve meals later than

WAITERS, THE BILL AND TIPPING

Waiters in Paris are considered to be professionals, and are paid as such, so **tipping** is a matter of leaving a few coins, perhaps €2 or so, depending on the service. Many speak English and are eager to help, practise and/or show off, so try not to be offended if they shrug off your attempts in French. And never call a waiter *garçon*, whatever you were taught in school – *Monsieur, Madame/Mademoiselle* or *s'il vous plaît* or *excusez-moi* are de rigueur. To ask for the bill, the phrase is *l'addition, s'il vous plaît*.

restaurants, often till midnight or 1am, and because of this are popular places for a post-theatre or opera dinner. Hours – last orders – are stated in the listings. After 9pm or so, some restaurants serve only *à la carte* meals, which invariably work out more expensive than eating the set menu.

For the more upmarket or trendy places, and at weekends, it's wise to make **reservations** – usually easily done on the same day, except for the most fashionable or gastronomically renowned places, for which you will need to book well in advance. At the elite, Michelin-starred end of the market, you'd be advised to **dress up**, too. Some more formal restaurants even insist on men wearing a tie.

COFFEE AND TEA

Coffee is invariably made properly. *Un café* or *un express* is an espresso, *une noisette* is an espresso with a dash of milk and *un crème* is a coffee with hot milk (you can get either a *grand crème* or a smaller, *petit crème*). In the morning you could also ask for *un café au lait* – espresso in a large cup or bowl filled up with hot milk. *Un déca*, decaffeinated coffee, is widely available. *Chocolat chaud* (hot chocolate) can also be had in any café. Drinkers of **tea** (*thé*), nine times out of ten, have to settle for Lipton's teabags, served black. You can have a slice of lemon (*citron*) with it, or ask for milk, "*un peu de lait frais*". *Tisanes* or *infusions* are the generic terms for **herbal teas**. Common ones are *verveine* (verbena), *tilleul* (lime blossom), *menthe* (mint) and *camomille*.

SOFT DRINKS

Boulangeries often stock the usual chilled fizzy drinks – *limonade, Coca, Orangina* – as well as canned fruit juices. At cafés, bottled fruit juices and **soft drinks** are expensive; better value is a freshly squeezed *citron pressé*: lemon juice served in the bottom of a long ice-filled glass, with a jug of water and a sugar bowl. Particularly French are the various **sirops**, diluted with water to make cool, eye-catching drinks with traffic-light colours, such as *menthe* (peppermint) and *grenadine* (pomegranate).

Bottles of **mineral water** (*eau minérale*) are widely drunk, from the best-selling, naturally sparkling Badoit to the most obscure spa product. Ask for *eau gazeuse* for sparkling, *eau plate* (pronounced "platt") for still. That said, there's not much wrong with the tap water, which will always be brought free to your table if you ask for *une carafe d'eau du robinet*.

WINE

Wine is the thing to drink in Paris; it's certainly a lot cheaper than the alternatives. The astringent whites of the northern Loire – Quincy, Reuilly and Sancerre – have long been Parisian favourites. A *kir*, a white wine with a dash of *cassis* (blackcurrant liqueur), is a popular *apéritif*, sometimes with champagne instead of white wine – *un kir royal*. The annual release of the new red wine from the Beaujolais on November 15 – "*le Beaujolais Nouveau est arrivé*" – is a much-heralded event. Champagne is drunk as much for simple pleasure as celebration.

In less expensive **restaurants** you can usually get a fairly good house wine by the *pichet* (carafe) – ask for *un quart* or *un demi*, a quarter- or half-litre. There is currently a vogue for less well-known *vins du pays* (country wines), but you'll find the top-quality AOC (Appellation d'Origine Contrôlée) bottles on most menus. Wine is usually only included as part of a set-price meal on the most expensive tasting *menus*, where different wines are matched with each course.

BEER

Beers are usually Belgian, German or Alsatian lagers, typically Kronenbourg. Most Parisians simply order *une pression*, or a glass of draught beer, but to be precise you could ask for *un demi* (25cl). For a wider choice of draughts and artisan bottled beers you need to go to the special beer-drinking establishments, or the English- and Irish-style pubs found in abundance in Paris (see Chapter 20).

APERITIFS, BRANDIES AND LIQUEURS

A characteristically French **apéritif** is the aniseed-flavoured *pastis* – Pernod and Ricard are the most common brands – which turns cloudy when diluted with water and ice cubes (*glaçons*). As for the harder stuff, there are dozens of **eaux de vie** (brandies distilled from fruit) and **liqueurs**, in addition to the classic Cognacs or Armagnac. Measures are generous, but they don't come cheap; the same applies for imported spirits like whisky, usually referred to as *scotch*.

ETHNIC CUISINE

It's telling that out of the almost ten thousand restaurants in the city, an astonishing ninety percent or so feature primarily French cooking. That said, an openness to spicing and **overseas techniques and ingredients** – typically

19

BREAKFAST AND BRUNCH

Most cafés advertise **snacks** or *un casse-croûte* (a quick bite), but even when they don't they may be able to make you up a filled baguette or a *tartine* on request. This is generally the best way to eat **breakfast**, and works out cheaper than the rate charged by most hotels (typically around €8–12). In the mornings, you may see a basket of croissants or some hard-boiled eggs on the counter. The drill is to help yourself – the waiter will keep an eye on how many you've eaten and bill you accordingly. **Brasseries** are also possibilities for cups of coffee, eggs, snacks and other breakfast-type food, while the concept of **le brunch** has taken Paris by storm in recent years, becoming a Sunday institution in areas like the Marais; most places serve it from around midday to 4 or 5pm.

TOP FIVE BRUNCH SPOTS

Chez Casimir See p.291
Drouant See p.272
L'Entrepôt See p.285

Le Loir dans la Théière See p.275
A Priori Thé See p.272

19

Asian – has been pioneered by young chefs in the last decade or so. Often working in smaller restaurants in the outer arrondissements, these rising stars are well worth seeking out and offer some of the city's most exciting cuisine at very affordable prices. The quality and profile of **ethnic restaurants** is ever-growing, too (see box, p.290).

VEGETARIAN CUISINE

Paris's gastronomic reputation is largely lost on **vegetarians**, who mostly have to subsist on salads, omelettes and cheeses. In most restaurants, even if there are apparently meat-free dishes, they'll come garnished with *lardons* (diced bacon), *anchois* (anchovies) or *jambon* (ham). That said, some of the

newer, more innovative places will often have one or two vegetarian dishes on offer, and ethnic restaurants are a good bet. *Salons de thé*, too, offer lighter fare such as soups and quiches or flans (*tartes*), which may be vegetarian. It's also possible to put together a meal at even the most meat-oriented brasserie by choosing dishes from among the starters and soups, or by asking for an omelette.

Useful French phrases to help you along are *Je suis végétarien(ne)* ("I'm a vegetarian") and *Il y a quelques plats sans viande*? ("Are there any non-meat dishes?"). The few purely vegetarian restaurants that do exist tend to be based on a healthy diet principle rather than haute cuisine, but at least you get a choice; they usually have a few options for **vegans**, too.

THE ISLANDS

CAFÉS AND WINE BARS

Berthillon 31 rue St-Louis-en-l'Ile, Ile St-Louis, 4ᵉ; Ⓜ Pont-Marie; map p.42. *Berthillon* serves some of the best ice cream in Paris, in all sorts of unusual flavours – salted butter caramel is a highlight. Also available at other island sites listed on the door. Wed–Sun 10am–8pm.

Taverne Henri IV 13 place du Pont-Neuf, Ile de la Cité, 1ᵉʳ; Ⓜ Pont-Neuf; map p.42. Once a favourite haunt of Yves Montand and Simone Signoret, this old-style wine bar is at its buzziest at lunchtime, when it's usually full of lawyers from the nearby Palais de Justice. You can get reasonably priced plates of meats and cheeses, as well as *tartines* (open sandwiches with a choice of cheeses, hams, pâté and *saucisson*). Mon–Fri 11.30am–9.30pm, Sat noon–5pm; closed Aug.

RESTAURANTS

Mon Vieil Ami 69 rue St-Louis-en-l'Ile, 4ᵉ ☎ 01 40 46 01 35; Ⓜ Pont-Marie; map p.42. Owned by top Alsatian chef

Antoine Westermann, this charming little *bistrot* serves bold, zesty cuisine, with an emphasis on well-prepared vegetables, and the wine list includes a fine selection of Alsatian vintages. The contemporary decor of warm chocolate tones and frosted-glass panels makes a stylish backdrop, and the long communal *table d'hôtes* down one side creates a nice convivial atmosphere. There's a €43 three-course *menu*; the bargain *plat du jour* is €13. Wed–Sun noon–2pm & 7–10pm.

Le Relais de l'Isle 37 rue St-Louis-en-l'Ile, Ile St-Louis, 4ᵉ ☎ 01 46 34 72 34; Ⓜ Pont-Marie; map p.42. Eight small tables are crammed into the ground floor of this cosy, candlelit jazz-restaurant with several more on a wooden mezzanine balcony. You'll pay around €30 for three courses, with mains like rabbit in prune sauce – but it's the ambience that really makes it special: the convivial atmosphere, the pianist tinkling away, and the chef occasionally popping out from the kitchen to join in. Wed–Sun noon–3pm & 7–11pm.

CLOCKWISE FROM TOP LEFT TOKYO EAT (P.284); CAFÉ DE LA MOSQUEE (P.279); L'ARPEGE (P.285)>

19

THE CHAMPS-ELYSEES

CAFÉS AND WINE BARS

Le Café Jacquemart-André 158 bd Haussmann, 8ᵉ; Ⓜ St-Philippe-du-Roule/Miromesnil; map p.62. Part of the Musée Jacquemart-André (see p.66) but with independent access, this is the most sumptuously appointed *salon de thé* in the city. Huge tapestries adorn the walls, Louis XV consoles display fine pastries, and ladies with parasols and men in ruffs look down over a trompe l'oeil balustrade from a wonderful ceiling fresco by Tiepolo. €9 for tea and pastry, set lunch €16.50. Daily 11.45am–5.30pm.

Le Dada 12 av des Ternes, 17ᵉ; Ⓜ Ternes; map p.62. The *Dada*'s sunny terrace is a pleasant spot for a drink, drawing in a lively after-work crowd in the evenings, while at lunchtime locals stream in for hearty servings of *steak frites* or huge salads. There's a more intimate, low-lit room upstairs with leather stools. Set lunch €20. Mon–Sat 8am–2am, Sun 8am–8pm.

Le Fouquet's 99 av des Champs-Elysées, 8ᵉ ☎ 01 47 23 70 60; Ⓜ George-V; map p.62. Dating from 1899, *Le Fouquet's* (you pronounce the "t") is the favourite venue for celebrations after the annual César film awards and is now such a well-established watering hole for the rich and famous that it's been classified a Monument Historique. You can sit out on the terrace, a prime spot for people-watching, or sink into a red velvet banquette in the plush café-brasserie. Coffee €9, mains around €30. Daily 8am–midnight.

RESTAURANTS

Al Ajami 58 rue François 1ᵉʳ, 8ᵉ ☎ 01 42 25 38 44; Ⓜ George-V; map p.62. This top-notch Lebanese restaurant is a branch of the venerable *Al Ajami* in Beirut. Meat dishes include croquettes of minced lamb pounded together with cracked wheat and grated onion, a rarity on any menu outside the Middle East. There's plenty for vegetarians, too: tabbouleh and *shanklish* (goat's cheese in olive oil chopped with tomato and onion), done to perfection; and exquisite *foul madames* (an Egyptian dish of broad beans cooked with lemon and garlic) and *fattayer* (pastry triangles filled with spinach). *Menus* range from €16 at lunch to the €48 *dégustation*. You can expect to pay around €55 *à la carte*. Daily noon–midnight.

Lasserre 17 av Franklin D. Roosevelt, 8ᵉ ☎ 01 43 59 11 61, Ⓦ restaurant-lasserre.com; Ⓜ Franklin-D.-Roosevelt; map p.62. A classic, haute-cuisine two-Michelin-starred restaurant with a beautiful *belle époque* dining room, decorated with flower-draped balustrades and fine ceiling frescoes – at the end of each meal and on balmy summer nights the roof is rolled back, with much rumbling and whirring, to reveal the Paris sky. The excellent cuisine is presided over by chef Christophe Moret, trained by Alain Ducasse; signature dishes include a sublime duck à l'orange and pigeon André Malraux, named after the Resistance hero and writer who used to dine here almost every day. Evening *menus* cost €150 or €185, though the lunchtime

menu is cheaper at €75. Mon–Wed & Sat 7–10pm, Thurs & Fri noon–2pm & 7–10pm; closed Aug.

La Maison de l'Aubrac 37 rue Marbeuf, 8ᵉ ☎ 01 42 89 66 09; Ⓜ Franklin-D.-Roosevelt; map p.62. Large photographs of prize-winning cattle from the restaurant's own farm in the Auvergne leave you in little doubt as to what to expect at this all-night restaurant, with its cosy, ranch-style wooden cubicles: very meaty country cuisine, such as *pot-au-feu* and sausage with *aligot* (creamy mashed potato and cheese), while the most carnivorous of cravings should be satisfied by the *trilogie de viande* (*salade de boeuf*, *steak tartare* and *faux filet grillé sauce béarnaise*). There's also an impressive thousand-plus wines to choose from, with several available by the glass. Mains cost around €25. Daily 24hr.

La Maison Blanche 15 av Montaigne, 8ᵉ ☎ 01 47 23 55 99, Ⓦ maison-blanche.fr; Ⓜ Alma-Marceau; map p.62. The cool white decor of the aptly named *Maison Blanche*, at the top of the Théâtre des Champs-Elysées, exudes sophistication, though it's the views of the city skyline from the restaurant's floor-to-ceiling windows that really impress. The refined cuisine is inventive and blends unusual flavours (such as collared dove with caramelized turnips, Sichuan pepper and liquorice morello syrup). The prices may take some swallowing (set menus at €69 and €110), but it's a stylish place for a special night out. Lunch (€40–55) tends to attract a mainly business clientele. On Saturday it turns into a club later on. Mon–Fri noon–2pm, Sat & Sun 8–10pm.

Pierre Gagnaire Hôtel Balzac, 6 rue Balzac, 8ᵉ ☎ 01 58 36 12 50, Ⓦ pierre-gagnaire.com; Ⓜ George-V; map p.62. Regularly judged among the top ten restaurants in the world by *Restaurant* magazine, *Pierre Gagnaire* is a gastronomic adventure. The *menu dégustation* (€265) has nine courses, featuring such treats as sea bass, Breton prawns, pomegranate, lychee, white cabbage and passion fruit (and that's just one course). *A la carte* will set you back around €300, lunch €105. Mon–Fri noon–1.30pm & 7.30–9.30pm, Sun 7.30–9.30pm.

Plaza-Athénée Hôtel Plaza-Athénée, 25 av Montaigne, 8ᵉ ☎ 01 53 67 65 00, Ⓦ plaza-athenee-paris.com; Ⓜ Alma-Marceau; map p.62. To mark its tenth anniversary in 2010, Alain Ducasse revamped his three-Michelin-starred restaurant, going for a "back-to-basics" approach – avoiding overly fussy dishes and instead emphasizing the quality and purity of ingredients. The decor, too, is understated, with plain tableware, but also hints of luxury in the huge chandeliers and shimmering embroidered screens by designer Patrick Jouin. Despite the simpler approach, you can still expect such delights as lobster and caviar or scallops with white truffles. From around €230 per head *à la carte*, €360 for the tasting menu. Mon–Wed 7.45–10.15pm, Thurs & Fri 12.45–2.15pm & 7.45–10.15pm; closed mid-July to mid-Aug.

GOURMET RESTAURANTS

With its concentration of top **gourmet restaurants**, Paris is the perfect place to splurge on the meal of a lifetime. Two of the most eminent haute-cuisine chefs at the moment are young Pascal Barbot at *L'Astrance* (see p.294) and Yannick Alléno at *Le Meurice* (see p.272), both awarded three Michelin stars for their bold and innovative cuisine. Also highly rated is Alain Ducasse, who swept like a tidal wave through the world of French cuisine in the early 1990s and hasn't looked back; his headline restaurants include the one at the *Plaza-Athénée* hotel (see opposite), and another halfway up the Eiffel Tower, *Le Jules Verne* (see p.285). Other greats include *Pierre Gagnaire* (see opposite), known for his experimental "molecular cuisine", and the more traditional *Taillevent* (see below). Over on the Left Bank, you'll find two relatively unusual establishments: *Hélène Darroze* (see p.283) stands out in having a female chef, while Alain Passard's remarkable *L'Arpège* (see p.285) eschews most meat in favour of superb fish and vegetable dishes.

Prices at most of these restaurants are often cheaper if you go at midday during the week, and some offer a set lunch *menu* for around €90. In the evening, prices average about €200, and there's no limit on the amount you can pay for top wines.

Recently, some of the star chefs have made their fine cuisine more accessible to a wider range of customers by opening up less expensive, more casual, but still high-quality establishments. Alain Ducasse, for example, also runs the restaurants *Spoon* (see below) and *Le Relais du Parc* (see p.294) and *Aux Lyonnais bistrot* (see p.273). Hélène Darroze has her tapas-style *Salon d'Hélène* (see p.283). Beneath the main restaurant, Pierre Gagnaire oversees the seafood restaurant *Gaya Rive Gauche* (see p.283), while Guy Savoy has his rôtisserie, *L'Atelier Maître Albert* (see p.280).

19

Le Relais de l'Entrecôte 15 rue Marbeuf, 8ᵉ; ⓂFranklin-D.-Roosevelt; map p.62. Don't worry that a menu isn't forthcoming here – there isn't one. The only dish is *steak frites*, widely considered the best in Paris and served with a delicious sauce, the ingredients of which are a closely guarded secret. Make sure you leave room for seconds. The set price of €24.80 includes a salad starter; desserts, such as profiteroles or crème brûlée, are around €6 extra. No reservations are taken so you may have to queue, or arrive early. There's a second branch at 20bis rue St-Benoit, 6ᵉ (ⓂSt-Germain-des-Prés). Daily noon–2.30pm & 7–11.30pm.

Spoon 14 rue de Marignan, 8ᵉ ☎01 40 76 34 44, ⓦspoon.tm.fr; ⓂFranklin-D.-Roosevelt; map p.62. This fashionable *bistrot* has been inspired by star chef Alain Ducasse's travels, and while this could have led to an incoherent menu, Ducasse avoids any potential pitfalls with aplomb: dishes include *ceviche*, spit-roast spare ribs in

a tandoori sauce and chocolate pizza. Aim to get one of the cute window seats and expect to pay around €80 a head without wine. Mon–Fri 12.15–2.30pm & 7.30–10.30pm; closed mid-July to mid-Aug.

Taillevent 15 rue Lamennais, 8ᵉ ☎01 44 95 15 01, ⓦtaillevent.com; ⓂGeorge-V; map p.62. One of Paris's finest gourmet restaurants. The Provençal-influenced cuisine of Alain Solivérès is outstanding, with the emphasis on the classic rather than the experimental; sample dishes include spelt risotto with frogs' legs, and saddle of lamb with braised artichokes in wine. The contemporary decor of light-wood panelling and pale greys and beiges is soothing and unobtrusive, and the supremely charming waiters manage to make you feel like special guests. Eating *à la carte*, count on around €140; the tasting menu costs €190, and there's also a set lunch for €80. Wine ranges from around €30 a bottle up to €2000 for a 1934 Château Haut-Brion. Mon–Fri 12.15–2.30pm & 7.15–11pm; closed Aug.

THE TUILERIES

CAFÉS AND WINE BARS

Angélina 226 rue de Rivoli, 1ᵉʳ; ⓂTuileries; map p.72. This grand *salon de thé*, with its murals, gilded stuccowork and comfy leather armchairs, does one of the best hot chocolates in town – a generous jugful with whipped cream on the side is enough for two. The other house speciality is the Mont Blanc, a chestnut cream, meringue and whipped cream dessert. It's also a good place for breakfast, with a wide range of pastries. Mon–Fri 8am–7pm, Sat & Sun 9.15am–7pm; closed Tues in July & Aug.

Le Rubis 10 rue du Marché-St-Honoré, 1ᵉʳ; ⓂPyramides; map p.72. Very small and crowded, this is

one of the oldest wine bars in Paris, known for its excellent wines – mostly from the Beaujolais and Loire regions – and homemade *rillettes* (a kind of pork pâté). The faded sign and peeling paint just add to the charm. Mains around €10. Mon–Fri noon–10pm, Sat 9am–3pm; closed for around a week mid-Aug.

RESTAURANTS

L'Ardoise 28 rue du Mont Thabor, 1ᵉʳ ☎01 42 96 28 18; ⓂTuileries; map p.72. A modern *bistrot* with a friendly atmosphere (the chef frequently pops out of the kitchen to greet diners) and an imaginative take on the classics: think langoustine ravioli, scallops in their shells with herb butter, and banana and caramel crème brûlée. Some dishes, however, can lack a real punch. Three-course *menu* €35. Tues–Sat noon–2.30pm & 6.30–11pm, Sun 6.30–11pm; closed first three weeks in Aug.

Le Meurice *Hôtel Meurice*, 228 rue de Rivoli, 1ᵉʳ ☎01 44 58 10 55, ⊚meuricehotel.com; ⓂTuileries/Concorde; map p.72. This sumptuous three-Michelin-starred restaurant, decorated by Philippe Starck in Louis XVI style, complete with ornate gildings and marble, wows diners with chef Yannick Alléno's adventurous cuisine. You might start with foie gras "iodized" in sugar bread, followed by veal sweetbreads with chestnuts, and finish with melted meringue with pink grapefruit and green apple jelly. *Menu dégustation* €240, lunch menu €90, *à la carte* around €210, with drinks extra. Mon–Fri 12.30–2pm & 7.30–10pm.

★ Mini Palais Av Winston Churchill, 8ᵉ ☎01 42 56 42 42, ⊚minipalais.com; map p.62. ⓂChamps-Elysées-Clemenceau. At the Grand Palais's revamped restaurant, you can either sit in the large, sleek dining room decorated in muted browns and greys or out on the grand colonnaded terrace. Triple-Michelin-starred chef Eric Fréchon oversees the menu, a mix of French classics and more international dishes such as chicken satay and beef with pak choy. There are some lovely touches such as warm gougère bread offered as soon as you arrive, and the desserts are sublime. You can also just come for a snack, or a drink at the bar; food is served all day, and the service is friendly and, mostly, efficient. Mains range from €15 to €35, snacks start at €8 (cheese platter). Daily 10am–2am.

GRANDS BOULEVARDS

CAFÉS AND WINE BARS

Café de la Paix Corner of place de l'Opéra and bd des Capucines, 9ᵉ; ⓂOpéra; map p.72. The last survivor of the great nineteenth-century cafés that once lined the Grands Boulevards, the *Café de la Paix* is something of a historic monument, counting Zola, Maupassant, Tchaikovsky and Oscar Wilde among its past habitués. It's difficult to choose whether to sit in the sumptuously gilded, frescoed interior or watch the world go by from the splendid *terrasse*, with views of the Opéra Garnier. Either way, it's a great place for a special treat. Drinks start from €6 for an espresso; the plat du jour is €27 or try the excellent *soupe à l'oignon* for €17. Daily 9am–11.30pm.

Ladurée 16 rue Royal, 8ᵉ; Ⓜ Madeleine; map p.72. This tearoom's melt-in-your-mouth macaroons are legendary – the chocolate and blackcurrant ones are the best – while the light-as-air meringues and *millefeuilles* are almost as good. When you're done with the cakes, sit back and enjoy the luxurious interior of gilt-edged mirrors and ceiling frescoes, and count the Hermès scarves. Mon–Sat 8.30am–7pm.

Legrand Filles et Fils Galerie Vivienne, 4 rue des Petit-Champs/1 rue de la Bourse, 2ᵉ; ⓂBourse; map p.72. Attached to the wine and food emporium (see p.334) of the

same name, *Legrand* attracts an older crowd with its reserved atmosphere, weekly-rotating selection of wines (glasses from around €6) and fine cheeses and olives. You can also select a bottle from the extensive cellar and drink it at the bar. Mon–Sat noon–7pm.

RESTAURANT

Drouant 16–18 place Gaillon, 2ᵉ ☎01 42 65 15 16; ⓂOpéra; map p.72. Legendary restaurant *Drouant*, the setting for the annual Goncourt prize, was stylishly revamped some years ago and taken over by Michelin-starred chef Antoine Westermann. The main courses are well prepared, but it's really the starters and desserts that steal the show – you're served four of each in small portions, so you get a lovely variety of tastes and flavours. Starters cost €25, mains €30 (€20 at lunch), desserts €15, and there's a lunchtime *menu* for €44 and a *plat du jour* for €18. The fine weekend brunch at €35 includes the usual eggs, ham, smoked salmon and pastries, but also tasty extras such as fromage blanc, a soup – gazpacho, maybe – and a glass of Crémant d'Alsace (Alsatian sparkling wine). In fine weather, you can sit outside on the charming, secluded *terrasse*. Daily noon–3pm & 7pm–midnight.

PASSAGES AND PALAIS-ROYAL

CAFÉS AND WINE BARS

Le Bar de l'Entracte Corner of rue Montpensier and rue Beaujolais, 1ᵉʳ; ⓂPalais Royal-Musée-du-Louvre; map p.72. Theatre people, bankers and journalists drop in for a quick snack in this almost-traffic-free spot. Fills up to bursting before and after performances at the Palais-Royal theatre just down the road; you can scarf down a pre-theatre *tartine* and glass of wine for around €8, otherwise *plats* cost from €11. Mon–Fri 10am–2am, Sat & Sun noon–midnight.

A Priori Thé 35 Galerie Vivienne, 2ᵉ ☎01 42 97 48 75; ⓂBourse; map p.72. An attractive little *salon de thé* in a charming *passage*, with some tables in the arcade itself. You can get crumbly home-made scones or cheesecake and tea, plus more substantial dishes at lunch, and the copious weekend brunch (€30; best to book) includes mini-scones and fromage blanc with honey. Mon–Sat 9am–6pm, Sun noon–6.30pm.

★ Verlet 256 rue St-Honoré, 1ᵉʳ; ⓂPalais-Royal-Musée-du-Louvre; map p.72. The intoxicating aroma of more than 30 types of coffee from all over the world, including gourmet options like Jamaican Blue Mountain, greet you inside this long-established coffee merchant's

CAFÉ CULTURE

The boulevards Montparnasse and St-Germain, on the Left Bank, are the historic haunts of **café society**. There you'll find the *Select*, *Coupole*, *Closerie des Lilas*, *Deux Magots* and *Flore* – the erstwhile hangouts of Apollinaire, Picasso, Hemingway, Sartre and de Beauvoir, and mostly still popular today with the Parisian intelligentsia. The more contemporary café culture is found on the Right Bank, around the Canal St-Martin and Oberkampf, where many cafés have become buzzing venues for exhibitions, live music and DJs.

and café, with its wood furnishings, green-leather benches and caddies lining one wall. If you're having trouble deciding, opt for one of the house's own rich and smoky blends; there's a good selection of teas and light snacks, too. Mon–Sat 9.30am–6.30pm.

RESTAURANTS

Bistrot des Victoires 6 rue de la Vrillière, 1er ☎ 01 42 61 43 78; Ⓜ Bourse; map p.72. Located just behind the chic place des Victoires, but very reasonably priced for the area, this charming, old-fashioned *bistrot* with zinc bar, mustard-coloured walls, globe lamps and dark-purple banquettes serves good old standbys such as *confit de canard* and *poulet rôti* for around €10, as well as huge salads and *tartines* (€8.50) – try the hearty *savoyarde* one (with bacon, potatoes and gruyère). Sunday brunch for €15.50. Daily 9am–11pm.

★ **Gallopin** 40 rue Notre-Dame-des-Victoires, 2e ☎ 01 42 36 45 38; Ⓜ Bourse; map p.72. An utterly endearing old brasserie, with all its original brass and mahogany fittings and a beautiful painted glass roof in the back room. The place heaves at lunchtime with journalists, bankers and glamorous Parisiennes. The classic French dishes, especially the *foie gras maison*, are well above par; *menus* range from €23 to €36. Daily noon–midnight.

Le Grand Véfour 17 rue de Beaujolais, 1er ☎ 01 42 96 56 27, ☒ grand-vefour.com; Ⓜ Pyramides/Bourse; map p.72. The carved wooden ceilings, frescoes, velvet hangings and late eighteenth-century chairs haven't changed since

Napoleon brought Joséphine here. Considering the luxury of the cuisine, the lunchtime *menu* for €88 is a steal, but go *à la carte* and the bill could easily top €220. Mon–Thurs 12.30–2pm & 7.30–10pm, Fri 12.30–2pm; closed Aug.

Higuma 32bis rue Ste Anne, 1er ☎ 01 47 03 38 59; Ⓜ Pyramides; map p.72. The pick of the numerous Japanese canteens in this area, *Higuma* serves up cheap and filling staples like pork *katsu* curry, *yaki udon* and *gyosa*. Sit at the counter and watch the chefs at work from close quarters, or cram onto one of the tiny tables further back. It's very popular and you may have to queue at lunchtime. *Menus* €11–12.50. Daily 11.30am–10pm.

Aux Lyonnais 32 rue St-Marc, 2e ☎ 01 42 96 65 04; Ⓜ Bourse/Richelieu-Drouot; map p.72. This venerable old *bistrot*, with its *belle époque* tiles and mirrored walls, preserves a lovely old-fashioned ambience and serves classic Lyonnais cuisine, perfectly executed under the direction of star chef Alain Ducasse. Specialities include *quenelles* (light and delicate fish dumplings) and turbot with salsify. Service is friendly and there's a buzzy atmosphere. Three-course *menu* €32. Tues–Fri noon–2pm & 7.30–10pm, Sat 7.30–10pm.

Le Vaudeville 29 rue Vivienne, 2e ☎ 01 40 20 04 62; Ⓜ Bourse; map p.72. There's often a queue to get a table at this lively, late-night Art Deco brasserie, attractively decorated with marble and mosaics. Dishes include tuna steak with chorizo and lamb with *boulangère* potatoes. Mains around €20. Daily noon–3pm & 7pm–1am; breakfast Mon–Sat 7–11am.

SENTIER

CAFÉS AND RESTAURANTS

Le Dénicheur 4 rue Tiquetonne, 2e ☎ 01 42 21 31 03; Ⓜ Etienne-Marcel; map p.72. This tiny café-restaurant, run by a nice couple, is a hotch-potch of wacky decor: turquoise-coloured walls, bright-blue globes hanging from the ceiling, garden gnomes in the window and old *carte orange* photocards lining the walls. Salads are the main event here, though you can find lasagne, ravioli, gazpacho and *tartines* too for around €12. Weekend brunch for €19. Tues–Sat noon–3pm & 6.30–11.30pm, Sun noon–5pm.

Dilan 13 rue Mandar, 2e ☎ 01 40 26 81 04; Ⓜ Les Halles /Sentier; map p.72. An excellent-value, popular Kurdish restaurant, with stone walls, kilims strewn liberally across the benches and taped Kurdish music playing in the

background. You could start perhaps with the melt-in-your-mouth *babaqunuc* (stuffed aubergines) or *boreks* (feta cheese pastries), followed by delicious *beyti* (spiced minced beef wrapped in pastry, with yoghurt, tomato sauce and bulgar wheat). Mains cost from €13; around €11 for half a litre of Kurdish Yakut wine. The set lunch at €12.50 is a bargain for the area. Mon–Sat noon–2.30pm & 7.30–11pm.

Frenchie 5 rue du Nil, 2e ☎ 01 40 39 96 19; Ⓜ Sentier; map p.72. Grégory Marchand, who worked in New York and with Jamie Oliver at *Fifteen* in London (where he was known, predictably, as "Frenchie"), set up this tiny restaurant, with simple decor of exposed bricks and industrial lighting, in 2009 and quickly became the talk of

19

the town. Using only the freshest ingredients, he offers a limited-choice €38 set menu that features French classics with an international twist, such as braised lamb with aubergines, spinach and lemon confit. Book well in advance; call between 3 and 5pm on a weekday. Mon–Fri 7–10.30pm.

BEAUBOURG AND LES HALLES

CAFÉS AND WINE BARS

Café Beaubourg 43 rue St-Merri, 4e; ⓜRambuteau/ Hôtel-de-Ville; map p.85. It's showing its age a little now, but this stylish café, bearing the trademark sweeping lines of designer Christian de Portzamparc, still has cachet and is unbeatable for people-watching on the Pompidou Centre's piazza. A tea or coffee costs €6, snacks such as *Croque-Monsieur* around €12. Mon–Thurs & Sun 8am–1am, Sat 8am–2am.

Le Café des Initiés 3 place des Deux-Ecus, 1er; ⓜChâtelet-Les-Halles/Louvre; map p.85. A smart yet intimate and comfortable café, with dark-red leather banquettes, wooden floor, arty photos on the wall and a popular terrace. Locals gather round the zinc bar or tuck into tasty dishes such as grilled king prawns and steak *tartare* (around €16) and home-made apple crumble. It's also a good spot for an evening drink. Daily 7am–2am.

A la Cloche des Halles 28 rue Coquillière, 1er; ⓜChâtelet-Les-Halles/Louvre; map p.85. The bell hanging over this little wine bar is the one that used to mark the end of trading in the market halls, and though the decor has undergone a makeover, it's still a locals' favourite and has a great ambience. You are assured of some very fine wines, best accompanied by the *jambon d'Auvergne* or one of their delectable cheeses, all very reasonably priced. Mon–Fri 11am–10pm, Sat 11am–5pm.

Le Cochon à l'Oreille 15 rue Montmartre, 1er; ⓜChâtelet-Les-Halles/Etienne-Marcel; map p.85. This classic little wooden café-bar, with its raffia chairs outside and scenes of fruit and veg stalls on ceramic tiles inside, dates from Les Halles' days as a market, and appears not to have changed in that time. The intellectual conversation is accompanied by Coltrane and other bebopping jazz greats. Mon–Sat 6pm–2am.

Dame Tartine 2 rue Brisemiche, 4e; ⓜRambuteau/ Hôtel-de-Ville; map p.85. Overlooking the Stravinsky fountain, with pleasant outdoor seating under shady plane trees, this popular café serves cheap and tasty open toasted sandwiches and soups, and there's a special set menu for children. Daily noon–11.30pm.

Le Petit Marcel 63 rue Rambuteau, 4e; ⓜRambuteau; map p.85. A bustling, unpretentious place with tiled floors and ceiling, mirrors, friendly staff, a jazz soundtrack and about eight square metres of drinking space. There's a dining area, too, where you can get cheap and filling dishes such as sausages with mustard. Mains around €13. No credit cards. Daily 10am–1am.

RESTAURANTS

Georges Centre Georges Pompidou, 4^e ☎01 44 78 47 99; ⓜRambuteau/Hôtel-de-Ville; map p.85. On the top floor of the Pompidou Centre, this cool, ultra-minimalist restaurant with outdoor terrace commands stunning views over the rooftops of Paris and makes a stylish place for lunch or dinner; the fluid aluminium-swathed interior calls to mind a Frank Gehry museum. The perfectly acceptable cuisine, with plenty of meat, fish and pasta options, is not cheap (mains €24–40), but then that's not the chief reason you come. Reservations are a must for dinner. Daily except Tues noon–1am.

Le Gros Minet 1 rue des Prouvaires, 1er ☎01 42 33 02 62; ⓜChâtelet-Les-Halles; map p.85. A welcoming little restaurant, reminiscent of the old Les Halles market days, popular with families and cluttered with knick-knacks including china cats, military caps, trilby hats and an ice-hockey stick. The menu has simple, reliable fare such as beef brochettes, cassoulet, *magret de canard* and crème caramel. *Menus* €14.50–23.50. Tues–Sat noon–2pm & 7.30–11.30pm.

Au Pied de Cochon 6 rue Coquillière, 1er ☎01 40 13 77 00; ⓜChâtelet-Les-Halles; map p.85. Since first opening its doors in 1946, *Au Pied de Cochon* has become a Les Halles institution – and it knows it. Still, this brasserie is worth a visit for extravagant middle-of-the-night pork chops, fresh lobster and, of course, pigs' trotters. *Menus* from €27. Daily 24hr.

La Robe et le Palais 13 rue des Lavandières St-Opportune, 1er ☎01 45 08 07 41; ⓜChâtelet; map p.85. Small, busy *restaurant à vins* serving traditional

---

MOST INNOVATIVE *BISTROTS*

Many of Paris's most talked about chefs now work not in Michelin-starred palaces but in *bistrots* – relatively relaxed, smaller restaurants, often in outlying neighbourhoods, where the specials may be chalked up on a board and the focus is very much on the food, not service or decor. At the following, you'll find some of the most exciting cooking in town.

Le Châteaubriand See p.293
Frenchie See p.273
Le Gaigne See p.277
La Gazzetta See p.279
Le Timbre See p.286
Yam'Tcha See opposite

cuisine and a *tête*-boggling selection of 250 wines *au compteur* (priced according to how much you consume). Although the food here can be tough on your cholesterol level, it is excellently prepared, and you'll want to take your time eating and soaking up the cool ambience of old Paris. Dishes include home-made foie gras, *risotto du champignon* and *grosse côte de cochon noir*, a delicious cut of the once-endangered Gascogne-bred boar, available in only a few Paris restaurants. Reckon on around €40 a head for three courses without wine. Mon–Sat noon–2.30pm & 7.30–11pm.

★ **La Tour de Montlhéry (Chez Denise)** 5 rue des Prouvaires, 1ᵉʳ ☎01 42 36 21 82; ⓜLouvre-Rivoli/Châtelet; map p.85. An old-style, late-night Les Halles *bistrot*, packed with diners sitting elbow to elbow at long tables tucking into substantial meaty French dishes, such as *daube* of beef, *andouillette* (tripe sausages) and haddock

in a *beurre blanc* sauce with perfectly cooked chips. Mains cost around €25. Mon–Fri noon–3pm & 7.30pm–5am; closed mid-July to mid-Aug.

Yam'Tcha 4 rue Sauval, 1ᵉʳ ☎01 40 26 08 07; ⓜLes Halles; map p.85. Opened in 2009 and already awarded a Michelin star, this pocket-sized restaurant, with barely twenty covers, has quickly garnered high praise for its original, delicate Chinese cuisine, with French influences. The limited-choice menu might include roast duck breast with Sichuan-style aubergines, followed by melting meringue with moscatel grapes and lychee with shiso (a herb, similar to mint) sorbet. Lunch for €50, dinner €85. For around €25 extra you can choose to have each course accompanied by specially selected teas, or you can just opt for wine. You currently need to book around two months in advance. Wed–Sat 12.15–1.30pm & 7.30–10pm, Sun 12.15–1.30pm; closed Aug.

19

CENTRAL MARAIS

CAFÉS AND WINE BARS

L'As du Falafel 34 rue des Rosiers, 4ᵉ; ⓜSt-Paul; map p.96. The sign above the doorway of this falafel shop in the Jewish quarter reads "*Toujours imité, jamais égalé*" ("always copied, but never equalled"), a boast that few would challenge, given the queues outside. Falafels to take away cost €5, or pay a bit more and sit in the buzzing little dining room. Mon–Thurs & Sun noon–11.30pm, Fri noon–3pm.

Café Martini 11 rue du Pas-de-la-Mule, 4ᵉ; ⓜSt-Paul/Chemin Vert; map p.93. Just off elegant place des Vosges, but much more down-to-earth and patronized mostly by locals, this relaxing little café with low, wood-beamed ceiling, stone walls and taped jazz in the background is run by friendly staff and offers low prices: *tartines* €7; soup €5; cocktails €6. Happy hour 7–10pm. Live jazz on Mon from 6.30pm, quiz on Wed eve. Mon 6pm–2am, Tues–Sat noon–2am, Sun noon–8pm.

L'Ebouillanté 6 rue des Barres, 4ᵉ; ⓜHôtel-de-Ville; map p.96. In nice weather, this two-storey café spills onto a picturesque, cobbled street behind the church of St-Gervais. You can choose from an extensive choice of drinks, from home-made hot chocolate to iced fruit cocktails, as well as salads and crêpes (€14); try one with a goat's cheese and raisin filling. Tues–Sun noon–10pm, till 9pm in winter.

Le Loir dans la Théière 3 rue des Rosiers, 4ᵉ; ⓜSt-Paul; map p.96. A long-established *salon de thé* decorated with antique toys and *Alice in Wonderland* murals. It's a popular spot for meeting friends and lounging about on comfy leather sofas, while feasting on enormous portions of delicious home-made cakes or vegetarian quiches. €9 for tea and cake. It's best to get here early for the fine Sunday brunch (€19.50), as queues often stretch out the door. Daily 9.30am–7pm.

Mariage Frères 30 rue Bourg-Tibourg, 4ᵉ ☎01 42 72 28 11; ⓜHôtel-de-Ville; map p.96. The ultimate tearoom, serving over six hundred varieties; a little book accompanies the menu and describes each one. The tea is perfectly brewed and arrives in a huge metal-insulated teapot. The pastries, including excellent fruit tarts and scones with *gelée extra de thé* (tea jelly), go down very nicely, too. The decor is elegant and faintly colonial – rattan chairs and potted palms – while service is by handsome white-suited waiters. Reckon on around €18 for tea and pastries. Brunch is also available at weekends, though is a little steeply priced at €29–39. Daily noon–6.30pm.

Pozzetto 39 rue du Roi de Sicile, 4ᵉ; ⓜHôtel-de-Ville; map p.96. One of the city's best ice-cream parlours, selling proper Italian *gelato* – including the very moreish Sicilian pistachio flavour – which is made fresh every day; if you're having trouble choosing, just ask for a free taster first. You can get authentic Italian coffee here too, a real rarity in Paris. Daily 10am–midnight.

BEST BRASSERIES

The grand nineteenth-century brasseries are restaurants now, not beer taverns, but many have preserved their globe lamps, brass fittings and leather banquettes. The food is unshowy, but these are some of Paris's most atmospheric places to eat.
Bofinger See p.278
Brasserie Lipp See p.283
Gallopin See p.273
Julien See p.291
Vagenende See p.284

19

RESTAURANTS

Breizh Café 109 rue Vieille du Temple, 4e ☎ 01 42 72 13 77; Ⓜ St-Paul; map p.96. A Breton café, with sister outposts in Cancale and Tokyo, serving the best crêpes in the Marais (and arguably the city), with traditional fillings like ham and cheese, as well as more exotic options such as smoked herring, which you can wash down with one of twenty different ciders. Leave room for dessert, as Valrhona chocolate is used in the sweet crêpes. It's very popular, so book ahead. Wed–Sun noon–11pm; closed three weeks in Aug.

Café des Musées 49 rue de Turenne, 3e ☎ 01 42 72 96 17; Ⓜ Chemin Vert; map p.93. An attractive old bistro (with a less appealing basement room) popular with locals drawn by the reasonably priced, hearty fare, such as *parmentier gourmand de faisan* (basically shepherd's pie made with pheasant), *steak frites*, terrines and crème caramel. There's always a vegetarian dish on the menu too, usually a *cocotte de légumes* (roast seasonal veg). It's a nice relaxed place with friendly staff and a buzzy atmosphere. The evening set menu is a bargain €20, otherwise mains cost around €19. Mon–Sat noon–3pm & 7–11pm, Sun 7–11pm. Also open for breakfast Mon–Fri 8am–noon, Sat & Sun 10.30am–noon.

Chez Marianne 2 rue des Hospitalières-St-Gervais, 4e ☎ 01 42 72 18 86; Ⓜ St-Paul; map p.96. A Marais institution, this homely place with cheery red awnings specializes in Middle Eastern and Jewish delicacies at very reasonable prices. A platter of mezze that might include tabbouleh, aubergine purée, chopped liver and hummus starts at €12, and the wines are inexpensive too. There are two small dining rooms and outside seating in fine weather. Bookings are taken for the evenings only. Turn up early at weekend lunchtimes, as it gets very busy. Daily noon–midnight.

L'Enoteca 25 rue Charles-V, 4e ☎ 01 42 78 91 44; Ⓜ St-Paul; map p.96. A fashionable Italian *bistrot à vins* in an old Marais building. If you take your Italian wine seriously this is the place to come; the list runs to 22 pages and features over 400 varieties, with an ever-changing selection available by the glass. Food doesn't take a back seat either; choose from an array of *antipasti*, fresh pasta or more substantial dishes like stuffed courgettes or *cochon de lait* (spit-roasted pork). Menus at €29 and €44. Mon–Sat noon–2.30pm & 7.30–11.30pm, Sun 12.30–3pm & 7.30–11.30pm; closed one week in Aug.

Le Potager du Marais 22 rue Rambuteau, 4^e ☎ 01 42 74 24 66; Ⓜ Rambuteau; map p.96. A tiny, good-value vegetarian restaurant, with only 25 covers at a long communal table. The ingredients are all organic and there's plenty for vegans and those with gluten allergies, too. Dishes include goat's cheese with honey, "crusty" quinoa burger and ravioli with basil. Two-course menu for €20, three courses €25. Daily noon–3pm & 7pm–11pm.

HAUT MARAIS

CAFÉS AND WINE BARS

Café Charlot 38 rue de Bretagne, 3e; Ⓜ Filles-du-Calvaire; map p.93. You'll need to fight for a seat on the terrace of this white-tiled retro-chic café (a former boulangerie), which bursts at the seams on weekends with local hipsters and in-the-know tourists. The food – a mix of French and American standards – is not that special, but it's a great place for a drink and a spot of people-watching. Daily 7am–2am.

Le Progrès 1 rue de Bretagne, 3e; Ⓜ Filles-du-Calvaire; map p.93. Cool, black-leather-jacketed types prop up the zinc bar or bag the terrace tables of this hip corner café, with its traditional decor of mustard-coloured walls and mosaic floor. It's especially popular at *apéritif* time, but also makes a good spot for relaxing with a coffee and newspaper in the morning. Mon–Sat 8am–2am.

RESTAURANTS

404 69 rue des Gravilliers, 3e ☎ 01 42 74 57 81; Ⓜ Arts-et-Métiers; map p.93. A very popular and trendy Moroccan restaurant, with a pricey menu and a lanterned, dimly lit interior that screams colonialist romance. The standard North African fare here is good enough, but it's the Casbah fetish ambience you're paying for. Reckon on around €40 exclusive of drinks. Their famed Berber Brunch (€21) requires reservations (Sat & Sun noon–4pm). Daily noon–midnight.

Ambassade d'Auvergne 22 rue du Grenier St-Lazare, 3e ☎ 01 42 72 31 22; 🖥 ambassade-auvergne.com; Ⓜ Rambuteau; map p.93. Suited, mustachioed waiters serve scrumptious Auvergnat cuisine that would have made Vercingétorix proud. There's a *menu* for €28, but you may well be tempted by some of the house specialities, like the *blanquette d'agneau* (white Roquefort lamb stew). Among the after-dinner treats are a plate of cheeses, including the region's brittle, pungent Cantal, as well as divine profiteroles. Reservations recommended. Daily noon–2pm & 7.30–10pm; closed last two weeks in Aug.

Chez Nénesse 17 rue Saintonge, 3e ☎ 01 42 78 46 49; Ⓜ Filles-du-Calvaire; map p.96. Steak in bilberry sauce, scallops with endive and figs stuffed with cream of almonds are just some of the delights on offer at this simple, welcoming restaurant, along with home-made chips on Thursday lunchtimes. Look out for the restaurant's own comic strip in the window. Mains around €18, *plat du jour* €10. Mon–Fri noon–2.30pm & 8–10.30pm; closed Aug.

Chez Omar 47 rue de Bretagne, 3e ☎ 01 42 72 36 26; Ⓜ Arts-et-Métiers; map p.93. You can't reserve at this popular North African couscous restaurant, but it's no hardship to wait for a table at the bar, taking in the handsome old brasserie decor, fashionable crowd and spirited atmosphere. Portions are copious and the couscous light and fluffy. The *merguez* (spicy sausage) costs €16, or go all-out for the royal (€25), though don't expect to have any room afterwards for the sticky cakes passed round on a large platter. No credit cards. Mon–Sat noon–2.30pm & 7–11.30pm, Sun 7–11.30pm.

L'Estaminet Marché des Enfants Rouges, 3ᵉ ☎01 42 72 28 12; ⓜArts-et-Métiers; map p.96. An inexpensive family-friendly place in a buzzing foodie market: sit on the picnic tables outside to soak up the atmosphere and choose from tasty dishes such as moussaka, oysters (in season), soup, charcuterie platters, salads and lots of ice cream. Service is amiable, if a little overwrought. *Plat du jour* €12, Sunday brunch €20. Breakfast served till 11.30am. Free wi-fi. Tues–Sat 9am–8pm, Sun 9am–3pm.

Le Gaigne 12 rue Pecquay, 3ᵉ ☎01 44 59 86 72, ⓦrestaurantlegaigne.fr; ⓜRambuteau; map p.96. Run by young chef Mickaël Gaignon, this small contemporary bistro with only nine tables set against a muted decor of pale browns and mauves, serves beautifully presented, inventive cuisine, with a slant towards fish. Desserts are a bit more hit and miss. It's certainly good value, at €42 for the five-course tasting menu, or €59 with specially chosen accompanying wines. Tues–Sat 12.15–2pm & 7.30–10.30pm.

★ **Pramil** 9 rue du Vertbois, 3ᵉ ☎01 42 72 03 60; ⓜTemple/Arts-et-Métiers; map p.93. An elegant, petite restaurant with simple decor, serving a short but appetizing menu of classic French and more unusual dishes, such as cauliflower "cake", squash soup with a dollop of foie gras ice cream, and raspberry and red pepper tart. The wine list (from €26) is small but well chosen. Jovial chef Alain Pramil emerges from the kitchen at the end of the meal to greet diners. The set dinner for €30 (lunch €20) is excellent value considering the standard of cuisine. Tues–Sat noon–2pm & 7.30–10pm, Sun 7.30–10pm.

BASTILLE

CAFÉS AND WINE BARS

L'Armagnac 104 rue de Charonne, 11ᵉ; ⓜCharonne; map p.108. The red sofas at this unpretentious café-bar, which have an appealingly lethargic air, are ideal for a reasonably priced daytime coffee, lunchtime snack or late-night drink. Mon–Fri 7.30am–1.30am, Sat 10am–1am, Sun 10am–midnight.

Café des Anges 66 rue de la Roquette, 11ᵉ; ⓜBastille; map p.108. A friendly, low-key corner café hung with old photos, great for cheap and filling dishes – burgers, veggie lasagne, salads and quiches – and a popular place for evening drinks. Mon–Sat 8am–2am.

★ **Café de l'Industrie** 16 rue St-Sabin, 11ᵉ; ⓜBastille; map p.108. One of the best of the Bastille cafés, packed out at lunch and in the evening. There are rugs on the scuffed wood floor, solid old tables, potted palms, mounted rhinoceros heads, old black-and-white photos on the walls and a young, unpretentious crowd enjoying the comfortable absence of minimalism. Mains, such as roast chicken, sausage and mash or linguine with pesto, from €9. Daily 10am–2am.

LE SNACKING, TAKEAWAYS AND PICNICS

Parisians are steadily abandoning the traditional sit-down lunch for "le snacking", and new snack and **sandwich bars** are springing up to service the demand. **Cojean** (17 bd Haussmann and many other branches; ⓦcojean.fr) is one successful example of this sleek new breed, serving home-made soups and gourmet salads. Traditional sandwiches such as the humble *sandwich jambon fromage* (cheese and ham) are of course still widely available; the chain *Paul* is reliable and easily found in railway stations and on main shopping streets.

Boulangeries are also a good source of traditional takeaway fare – most sell savoury quiches and flans as well as breads and cakes. For picnics, head for a **charcuterie** or the delicatessen counter in a good supermarket, or *traiteurs* such as Fauchon (see box, p.332). Although specializing in cooked meats like hams and pâtés, most charcuteries also stock an excellent range of dressed salads and side dishes. You buy by weight, by the slice (*tranche*) or by the carton (*barquette*). Asian delis, especially Chinese, are a popular alternative in Paris. Alternatively, try the city's most specialized and luxurious food shops (see pp.332–334).

For **takeaway** hot food, the indigenous offering is the **crêperie**, which sells *galettes* (wholewheat pancakes) and *gaufres* (waffles) as well as sweet and savoury crêpes. More common are Turkish or North African **kebab shops**, the latter also serving couscous, which you can choose to have with *merguez* (spicy sausage), chicken or lamb, or indeed *royale* – with all three. Couscous always comes with a spicy, tomato-rich vegetable soup, while kebabs are usually served in pitta bread with *frites* (French fries). Middle Eastern falafel with salad is very popular in the Jewish quarter (see p.99).

19

Pause Café 41 rue de Charonne, corner of rue Keller, 11ᵉ; ⓜLedru-Rollin; map p.108. Or maybe "Pose Café" – given its popularity with the *quartier*'s young and fashionable (sunglasses are worn at all times) who bag the pavement tables at lunch and *apéritif* time. Service is predictably insouciant. *Plats du jour* around €12.50. Mon–Sat 8am–2am, Sun 9am–8pm (brunch noon–3pm).

RESTAURANTS

Le Bistrot du Peintre 116 av Ledru-Rollin, 11ᵉ ☎01 47 00 34 39; ⓜLedru-Rollin; map p.108. A charming, traditional *bistrot*, where small tables are jammed together beneath faded Art Nouveau frescoes and wood panelling. The emphasis is on meaty Auvergnat cuisine, with mains for around €17. Mon–Sat 7am–2am, Sun 10am–8pm.

Bofinger 7 rue de la Bastille, 4ᵉ ☎01 42 72 87 82; ⓜBastille; map p.108. This popular fin-de-siècle brasserie has a splendid, perfectly preserved coloured-glass dome and is frequented by opera-goers and tourists. Specialities are seafood and steaming dishes of sauerkraut. Set menu from €27.50. Mon–Fri noon–3pm & 6.30pm–1am, Sat & Sun noon–11pm.

Chez Paul 13 rue de Charonne, corner of rue de Lappe, 11ᵉ ☎01 47 00 34 57; ⓜBastille; map p.108. Housed in a wonky corner building, *Chez Paul* is a throwback to an older Bastille, with faded furnishings, black-and-white tiles on the floor and a real mix of customers. Food is traditional (*pot-au-feu*, Chateaubriand, sardines and so on) and affordable, and the ambience very congenial. Mains from €18.50. Daily noon–2.30pm & 7.15pm–12.30am.

FAUBOURG ST-ANTOINE AND AROUND

CAFÉS AND WINE BARS
Le Baron Rouge 1 rue Théophile-Roussel, corner of place d'Aligre market, 12ᵉ; ⓜLedru-Rollin; map p.108. Also known affectionately as *Le Baron Bouge*, this popular *bar à vins* is as close as you'll find to the spit-and-sawdust saloon stereotype of the old movies. Stallholders and shoppers from the nearby Marché Aligre gather here for a light lunch or an *apéritif* during the day, especially on Sundays, with a younger crowd appearing later on, when you can listen to jazz and funk. If it's crowded, join the locals outside standing around the wine barrels and lunching on *saucisson*, mussels or Cap Ferrat oysters washed down with a glass of Muscadet. Not to be missed. Tues–Fri 10am–2pm & 5–10pm, Sat 10am–10pm, Sun 10.30am–3.30pm.

Chez Prosper 7 av du Trône, 11ᵉ; ⓜNation; map p.108. Indulge yourself with a decadent Nutella tiramisu (€6.90) or pear and chocolate tart, order a coffee or a glass of wine and while away the afternoon with a paper at this attractive, popular café on the edge of place de la Nation. Daily 8.30am–1am.

Jacques Mélac 42 rue Léon-Frot, 11ᵉ ☎01 43 70 59 27; ⓜCharonne; map p.108. Somewhat off the beaten track (between Père-Lachaise and place Léon-Blum), this is a highly respected and atmospheric *bistrot à vins* set in an oak-beamed former greengrocer's. The eponymous owner is an attraction in his own right, and even makes his own wine – the solitary vine winds round the front of the shop – and plays host to some renowned fêtes when grapes are harvested. There are excellent meats, cheeses and wines from his native Aveyron in eastern France, though don't expect to find any Bordeaux, as he doesn't like them. Mains around €16. Tues–Sat 9am–4pm & 7.45–11pm; closed Aug.

Paris-Hanoï 74 rue de Charonne, 11ᵉ ☎01 47 00 47 59; ⓜCharonne; map p.108. The exterior could do with a smarten-up, but then staff at this cheap Vietnamese canteen are probably too busy serving quality, inexpensive stir-fries, noodles, soups and *bun cha* to a steady stream of diners to do much about it. Count on around €15 a head for a full meal. No credit cards. Mon–Sat noon–2.30pm & 7–10.30pm; closed Aug.

Waly Fay 6 rue Godefroy-Cavaignac, 11ᵉ ☎01 40 24 17 79; ⓜCharonne/Faidherbe-Chaligny; map p.108. An overgrown pot plant hides the entrance to this West African restaurant with a cosy, stylish atmosphere, the dim lighting, rattan and old, faded photographs creating an intimate, faintly colonial ambience. Smart young Parisians are here to dine on perfumed, richly spiced stews, plantain fritters, jumbo prawns and other delicacies at a moderate cost (mains around €15). Mon–Fri noon–2pm & 7.30–11pm, Sun brunch noon–5pm; closed two weeks in Aug.

La Ruche à Miel 19 rue d'Aligre, 12ᵉ; ⓜLedru-Rollin; map p.108. The mouthwatering array of pistachio, almond, walnut and honey cakes at the entrance to this little Algerian teashop, on the rue d'Aligre market street, entices in many a passer-by. The best accompaniment to the cakes is mint tea, made with real mint and served in the traditional way. Seating is at low brass tables with comfy benches and pouffes. Around €10 for tea and two cakes. Couscous served at lunch. Tues–Sun 9am–7.30pm.

RESTAURANTS
★ **A la Biche au Bois** 45 av Ledru-Rollin, 11ᵉ ☎01 43 43 34 38; ⓜGare de Lyon; map p.108. The queues leading out through the conservatory at the front are a strong indicator of the popularity of this restaurant, which mixes charming service with keenly priced, well-produced food served in generous quantities. The house speciality is a huge, rich *coq au vin*, and in winter game features heavily on the menu. Four-course *menu* (including cheese) €29. Mon 7–11pm, Tues–Fri noon–2pm & 7–11pm; closed four weeks July–Aug.

HISTORIC CAFÉS

The grand Parisian cafés and tearooms are beloved institutions. Many preserve not just their wonderful decor, but the spirit that has sustained them over a century. Here are the city's most atmospheric establishments.

Angélina See p.271
Café de la Paix See p.272
Le Flore See p.282
Le Fouquet's See p.270
Ladurée See p.272
Le Select See p.285

Bistrot Paul Bert 18 rue Paul Bert, 11ᵉ ☎01 43 72 24 01; ⓂFaidherbe-Chaligny; map p.108. A quintessential Parisian *bistrot*, with the menu chalked up on the board, little wooden tables and white tablecloths, tobacco-stained ceiling, and old posters and paintings on the mustard-coloured walls. A mix of locals and visitors flock here for the cosy, friendly ambience and high-quality simple fare such as *poulet rôti* as well as more sophisticated dishes like guineafowl with morel mushrooms. Save room for one of the substantial desserts, such as the perfectly cooked Grand Marnier soufflé. The dinner *menu* is €34, with a few supplements, and there's an excellent wine list. Tues–Sat noon–2pm & 7.30–11pm; closed Aug.

L'Encrier 55 rue Traversière, 11ᵉ ☎01 44 68 08 16; ⓂLedru-Rollin; map p.108. The simple interior of exposed brick walls and wood beams complements the good-value, homely fare served by pleasant staff in this little restaurant near the Viaduc des Arts. The kitchen opens into the centre of the room, creating a welcoming, convivial ambience. The menu has a slight southwestern influence and might include goose breast in honey or steak and morel mushrooms. Lunchtime *menu* from €12.50, evening *menus* at €19.50 and €24. Mon–Fri noon–2.15pm & 7.30–11pm, Sat 7.30–11pm.

★ **La Gazzetta** 29 rue de Cotte, 12ᵉ ☎01 43 47 47 05; ⓂLedru-Rollin; map p.108. A nonchalantly stylish place, with sleek Art Deco decor, dim lighting, romantic ambience and imaginative, well-executed food. The five-course menu is fixed and the portions are on the dainty side, but at €39 (or €52 for seven courses) it's a bargain

when you consider the quality of the food. You might start with oysters, rosehip *sablé*, broad beans and peas, followed by perfectly cooked lamb, topped off with not just one, but two divine desserts. The appealing wine list includes offerings from Italy and Spain, as well as France. Service is discreet and attentive. Tues–Sat noon–2.30pm & 8–11pm.

Le Mansouria 11 rue Faidherbe-Chaligny, 11ᵉ ☎01 43 71 00 16; ⓂFaidherbe-Chaligny; map p.108. Look out for the elaborately carved Islamic-style doors at this excellent and elegant Moroccan restaurant, which dishes up superb couscous, tajines, pigeon *pastilla* and spicy *harira* soup. Menus €30–46, mains €17–19. Mon & Tues 7.30–11.30pm, Wed–Sat noon–2pm & 7.30–11.30pm; closed two weeks in Aug.

Le Train Bleu Gare de Lyon, 12ᵉ ☎01 43 43 09 06, ⓦle-train-bleu.com; ⓂGare-de-Lyon; map p.108. It would be hard to imagine a better prelude to a journey down to the sunny Côte d'Azur than a meal at *Le Train Bleu*, but a halt at this sumptuous *belle époque* establishment is a must even if you're not going anywhere. The decor is straight out of a bygone golden era – everything drips with gilt, and chandeliers hang from high ceilings frescoed with scenes from the Paris–Lyon–Marseille train route; to add to the spectacle, huge windows give onto the arriving and departing trains below. The traditional French cuisine has a hard time living up to all this, but is more than acceptable, if rather overpriced. Set *menu* from €55, including half a bottle of wine. If you just want a glimpse at the decor you could go for coffee and cake (around €17), or have a drink in the comfy bar. Restaurant: daily 11.30am–3pm & 7–11pm. Bar: Mon–Fri 7.30am–11pm, Sat & Sun 9am–11pm.

★ **Au Vieux Chêne** 7 rue du Dahomey, 11ᵉ ☎01 43 71 67 69; ⓂFaidherbe-Chaligny; map p.108. A very fine restaurant with fresh flowers, shelves heaving with books and smart service. The kitchen shows considerable flair: you could try smoked haddock on a bed of carrots and lentils with a lemon-butter sauce, followed by a perfect *tarte tatin*. The three-course set menus – €18 at lunch and €33 at dinner – are a steal considering the quality of the food. Mon–Fri noon–2pm & 8–10.30pm; closed last week in July and first two in Aug.

THE QUARTIER LATIN

CAFÉS AND WINE BARS

Café des Arts corner of place Contrescarpe and rue Lacépède, 5ᵉ; ⓂMonge; map p.120. Slightly less pricey and much more authentic than its touristy neighbours, but the location on this café-packed square is arguably the best, with its south-facing *terrasse*. Daily 8am–2am.

★ **Café de la Mosquée** 39 rue Geoffroy-St-Hilaire, 5ᵉ; ⓂMonge; map p.120. Drink mint tea and eat sweet cakes

beside the courtyard fountain and fig trees of the Paris mosque – a haven of calm. The indoor salon has a beautiful North African interior, where delicious tajines and authentic couscous are served for around €15 and up. There's even a hammam-massage-meal option for €58. Daily 9am–midnight.

★ **Café de la Nouvelle Mairie** 19 rue des Fossés-St-Jacques, 5ᵉ; ⓂCluny-La Sorbonne/RER Luxembourg; map

19

19

p.120. Sleek café-wine bar with a relaxed feel generated by its university clientele (note that it's shut at weekends). At lunch, and on Tuesdays and Thursday evenings, it serves good, straightforward dishes ranging from linguine to a rich beef *daube*; otherwise it's *assiettes* of cheese or charcuterie (all around €13). On sunny days or warm nights the outside tables on the picturesque square are delightful. No credit cards. Mon, Wed & Fri 8am–8pm, Tues & Thurs 8am–11pm.

L'Ecritoire 3 place de la Sorbonne, 5ᵉ; ⓜCluny-La Sorbonne/RER Luxembourg; map p.120. This classic university café is right beside the Sorbonne, and has outside tables by the fountain. Good for a coffee and people-watching. Daily 7am–midnight.

★ **La Fourmi Ailée** 8 rue du Fouarre, 5ᵉ; ⓜMaubert-Mutualité; map p.120. Simple, filling fare is served in this former feminist bookshop, now a slow-paced *salon de thé*. A high, mural-painted ceiling, a book-lined wall and background jazz contribute to the atmosphere. Around €12–16 for a *plat*, or €8 for a quiche. Daily noon–midnight.

Les Pipos 2 rue de l'Ecole-Polytechnique, 5ᵉ; ⓜMaubert-Mutualité/Cardinal-Lemoine; map p.120. Old bar in a long-established position opposite the gates of the former *grande école*, with a decor that's heavy on old wood and a local clientele. Serves wines from €5 a glass along with simple plates of Auvergnat charcuterie and cheese (€7–15), and the odd steak. Mon–Sat 8.30am–2am; closed two weeks in Aug.

Le Reflet 6 rue Champollion, 5ᵉ; ⓜCluny-La Sorbonne; map p.120. This artsy cinema café has a strong flavour of the *Nouvelle Vague*, with its scruffy black paint, lights rigged up on a gantry and rickety tables packed with film-goers and chess players. Perfect for a drink either side of a film at one of the arts cinemas on rue Champollion, perhaps accompanied by a *croque*, steak, quiche or salad from the very short list of blackboard specials (€9–13). Daily 10am–2am.

★ **Le Verre à Pied** 118bis rue Mouffetard, 5ᵉ; ⓜMonge; map p.120. Deeply old-fashioned market bar where traders take their morning glass of wine at the bar, or sit down to eat a *plat du jour* for around €10. Some have been doing it so long they've got little plaques on their tables, but they welcome visitors stopping by. Tues–Sat 9am–8.30pm, Sun 9am–3.30pm.

RESTAURANTS

L'Atelier Maître Albert 1 rue Maître Albert, 5ᵉ ☎01 56 81 30 01; ⓜMaubert-Mutualité; map p.120. One of chef-entrepreneur Guy Savoy's ventures, this rôtisserie has a decor that's like a contemporary designer's take on a medieval château. It's a fitting backdrop for the speciality of spit-roast meats, though you can also find lighter dishes on the menu such as spit-roast sole with a fennel gratin, or a delicious starter of marinated tuna with carrot and seafood jelly. There are lunch *menus* at €25 and €32, but you'll pay

double that for dining *à la carte*. Mon–Wed noon–2.30pm & 6.30–11.30pm, Thurs & Fri noon–2.30pm & 6.30pm–1am, Sat 6.30pm–1am, Sun 6.30–11.30pm.

★ **Brasserie Balzar** 49 rue des Ecoles, 5ᵉ ☎01 43 54 13 67; ⓜMaubert-Mutualité; map p.120. This classic, high-ceilinged brasserie is an institution among the literary intelligentsia of the Quartier Latin. The decor isn't jaw-droppingly glamorous, but the feel is almost intimidatingly Parisian – though if you're unlucky, or choose to eat early, the tourist clientele can spoil the Left Bank mood. Eating *à la carte* could cost upwards of €40, but you can have steak tartare or garnished sauerkraut – garnished with copious amounts of pork and sausage, that is – for €22, and a glass of *kir* for €5. Daily 8am to 11.45pm.

★ **Le Buisson Ardent** 25 rue Jussieu, 5ᵉ ☎01 43 54 93 02; ⓜJussieu; map p.120. Generous helpings of first-class cooking with vivacious touches: *velouté* of watermelon followed by lamb noisettes with a fennel and blue cheese fondant, perhaps. The high-ceilinged, panelled and muralled dining room is grand but the atmosphere is never less than convivial – and there's a cosy back room with banquettes. Lunch *menu* €16, dinner €27–33. Reservations recommended. Mon–Fri noon–2pm & 7.30–10pm, Sat 7.30–10pm; closed two weeks in Aug.

Les Cinq Saveurs d'Anada 72 rue du Cardinal-Lemoine, 5ᵉ ☎01 43 29 58 54; ⓜCardinal-Lemoine; map p.120. Airy and informal restaurant serving decent organic, vegetarian and macrobiotic food. Try the creative meat-substitute dishes (around €14–18), such as tofu soufflé, *confit* of tempeh with ginger, or seitan with celeriac and basil. Tues–Sun noon–2.30pm & 7–10.30pm.

L'Ecurie 58 rue de la Montagne Ste-Geneviève, 5ᵉ ☎01 46 33 68 49; ⓜMaubert-Mutualité/Cardinal-Lemoine; map p.120. Shoe-horned into a former stables on a particularly lovely corner of the Montagne Ste-Geneviève, this family-run restaurant is bustling and very lovable. Outside tables and the cellar below provide a few extra seats, but not many, so book ahead. Expect well-cooked meat dishes served without flourishes – grilled with chips, mostly – for less than €17, and simple starters and desserts for around €5. Lunch menu at €11. Mon & Wed–Sat noon–3pm & 7pm–midnight, Tues & Sun 7pm–midnight.

Les Fontaines 9 rue Soufflot, 5ᵉ ☎01 43 26 42 80; RER Luxembourg; map p.120. The dated brasserie-cum-diner decor looks unpromising from the outside, but the welcome inside this family-run place is warm and genuine, and the cooking is in the same spirit, with honest French meat and fish dishes such as *blanquette de veau* or game in season. Starters around €8, mains €18, *menu* €30. Daily noon–3pm & 7.30–11pm.

Le Jardin des Pâtes 4 rue Lacépède, 5ᵉ ☎01 43 31 50 71; ⓜJussieu; map p.120. Delicious home-made pasta

BEST-VALUE SET LUNCH MENUS

A lunchtime set menu often gives you the chance to sample top-quality food without paying a fortune. These restaurants offer what the French call "rapport qualité-prix" – or serious gastronomic bang for your buck.

L'Avant Goût See p.287
Le Baratin See p.293
Hélène Darroze See p.283
Pramil See p.277
Le Pré Verre See p.281
Taillevent See p.271

made with all manner of freshly ground organic grains, and served with wonderful flourishes and garnishes. The room is stylish, fresh-feeling and airy – almost like a conservatory – and you'll pay no more than €14 for a plate of pasta. Daily noon–2.30pm & 7–11pm.

Perraudin 157 rue St-Jacques, 5ᵉ ☎01 46 33 15 75; RER Luxembourg; map p.120. One of the classic *bistrots* of the Left Bank, featuring solid home cooking. The 1900s atmosphere is thick with Parisian and international chatter floating above the brightly lit, packed-in, gingham-clad tables. There's a midday *menu* at €16, while in the evening it costs €31, or you can eat *à la carte* (around €12–25 for a main). Daily noon–2pm & 7–10.30pm; closed Aug.

Le Petit Pontoise 9 rue de Pontoise, 5ᵉ ☎01 43 29 25 20; ⓜMaubert-Mutualité; map p.120. This relaxed, young *bistrot* is as authentically Parisian as you can get this close to the river: lace café curtains, little wooden tables, a bar in one corner and simple specials on the blackboard – perhaps a salad of haricot beans with prawns, steak *en croûte* and duck breast. The wines are good, and the puddings outstanding. Expect to pay around €50 a head. Mon–Fri & Sun noon–2.30pm & 7.30–10.30pm, Sat 7.30–10.30pm.

Pho 67 59 rue Galande, 5ᵉ ☎01 45 25 56 69; ⓜMaubert-Mutualité; map p.120. A beacon of South Asian authenticity in this desperately touristy area. The Vietnamese proprietors work away in an open kitchen, preparing a good range of reasonably priced dishes; go for the famous and filling *pho* soup (€13), made with tender French steak. Mon 7–11.30pm, Tues–Sun noon–3pm & 7–11.30pm.

★ **Le Pré Verre** 8 rue Thénard, 5ᵉ ☎01 43 54 59 47; ⓜMaubert-Mutualité; map p.120. This sleek, modern and furiously popular *bistrot à vins* has a great wine menu, as you'd expect, but the food is just as interesting. The blackboard lists are dotted with unusual ingredients and spices – maybe swordfish on poppy seeds and artichokes, chicken with avocado and ginger, or roast bananas in an amazing chilli syrup. The evening *menu* is €29.50 – stunning value for the quality – while the lunchtime two-courser costs just €13.50, including a glass of wine and coffee. Tues–Sat noon–2pm & 7.30–10.30pm; closed three weeks in Aug.

Le Reminet 3 rue des Grands-Degrés, 5ᵉ ☎01 44 07 04 24; ⓜMaubert-Mutualité; map p.120. This artful but friendly little *bistrot*-restaurant shows its class through small touches: snowy-white tablecloths, gilt mirrors and fancy chandeliers liven up the simple dining room, while imaginative sauces grace high-quality traditional French ingredients: how about a fricasée of guineafowl with foie gras and gingerbread jus? Gastronomic *menu* at €55, but you can get away with two courses *à la carte* for less, and there are lunch menus at under €15. Daily noon–3pm & 7.30–11.30pm; closed two weeks in Aug.

Ribouldingue 10 rue St-Julien le Pauvre, 5ᵉ ☎01 46 33 98 80; ⓜMaubert-Mutualité; map p.120. If you baulk at lamb's tongues, artichoke-stuffed trotters and beef cheek, stay away: it's almost all offal here. But it's cooked with care and flair, accompanied by hearty sides like nutmeg-rich *pommes dauphinoise*, and followed by gorgeous puddings – such as a herby Chartreuse ice cream. The service is discreet and the ambience, in a narrow, wood-panelled dining room, surprisingly upmarket for the *quartier*. Evening menu at €32. Tues–Sat noon–2pm & 7–11pm.

Tashi Delek 4 rue des Fossés-St-Jacques, 5ᵉ ☎01 43 26 55 55; RER Luxembourg; map p.120. Elegantly styled Tibetan restaurant serving Himalayan regional dishes ranging from robust, warming noodle soups to the addictive, ravioli-like *momok* and a salty, soupy yak-butter tea. Evening *menus* are €17 and €23. Mon–Sat noon–2.30pm & 7–11pm; closed two weeks in Aug.

19

ST-GERMAIN

CAFÉS AND WINE BARS

L'Assignat 7 rue Guénégaud, 6ᵉ ☎01 43 54 87 68; ⓜPont-Neuf; map p.134. Zinc counter, bar stools, bar football and young regulars from the nearby art school in an untouristy café close to the quai des Augustins. Honest *plats du jour* and hearty *gratins* for around €10. Mon–Sat 9am–11pm, food served noon–3pm; closed July.

L'Avant Comptoir 9 carrefour de l'Odéon, 6ᵉ; ⓜOdéon; map p.134. Micro-wine bar and *sandwicherie* serving crêpes, sandwiches and great hams, cheeses and hors d'oeuvres. Vaguely like an old-fashioned hole-in-the-wall tapas bar, with standing room for a handful only. Daily noon–11pm.

Bar du Marché 75 rue de Seine, 6ᵉ; ⓜMabillon; map p.134. This thrumming café, where the *serveurs* are cutely kitted out in flat caps and aprons, is a fashionable place for a pre-dinner *kir*. Admittedly, you pay a little extra for the colours and smells of the rue de Buci market on the doorstep. Daily 7am–2am.

Bistrot des Augustins 39 quai de Grands Augustins, 6ᵉ; ⓜSt-Michel; map p.134. Intimate, friendly wine bar conveniently located on the river bank near the Pont-Neuf. Serves good charcuterie, salads and hot *gratins*, all for around €10, as well as filling *tartines* – perfect with a glass of wine. Daily 10am–midnight.

★ **Café de la Mairie** 8 place St-Sulpice, 6ᵉ; ⓜSt-Sulpice; map p.134. A peaceful, pleasant café on the sunny north side of the square, opposite St-Sulpice church and with lots of outside tables. Perfect for basking with a coffee or an *apéritif*, and admiring the neighbourhood's beautiful people. Mon–Sat 7am–2am.

La Crèmerie 9 rue des Quatre Vents, 6ᵉ ☎01 45 54 99 30; ⓜOdéon; map p.134. Infectiously passionate wine merchants store in a beautiful old dairy shop, with just a couple of tables where they serve intimate, high-quality tapas-style meals. The emphasis is on produce, not cooking, so expect cheeses, charcuterie, and fine desserts, all with wines to match. You can pay anything from €30, but it's likely to be much more, with wine. There are also less formal, "apéro" sessions, where you pay €10 for a few pâtés and hams to go with the wines you order by the glass or bottle. Mon–Sat 10.30am–10pm; meals served Tues–Thurs noon–1.30pm & 7.30–8.30pm, Fri & Sat 1–2.30pm & 7.30–8.30pm; tapas sessions Mon 4–8pm, Tues–Sat 5–7.30pm.

Les Etages St-Germain 5 rue de Buci, 6ᵉ; ⓜMabillon; map p.134. Bastion of boho trendiness at the edge of the rue de Buci street market, with outside and overhead heaters for winter days. Good for a lunchtime coffee and, later on, a great spot for people-watching over a glass of beer (€4) or a cocktail (see p.299). Daily noon–2am.

★ **Le Flore** 172 bd St-Germain, 6ᵉ; ⓜSt-Germain-des-Prés; map p.134. The great rival and immediate neighbour of *Les Deux Magots*, with a trendier and distinctly more Parisian clientele. There's a unique hierarchy: tourists on the terrace, beautiful people inside, intellectuals upstairs. Sartre, de Beauvoir, Camus and Marcel Carné used to hang out here – and there's still the odd organized reading or debate. Equally enjoyable for a (fabulous) morning hot chocolate (€6.80), a lunchtime omelette (€10), a late-afternoon coffee (just short of €5) or an after-dinner drink. Daily 7am–1.30am.

Ladurée 21 rue Bonaparte, 6ᵉ; ⓜSt-Germain-des-Prés; map p.134. The latest outpost of *Ladurée*'s tearoom mini-empire has a lovely pale-green murralled conservatory at the back of the shop where elegant locals sip fine teas and eat pink macaroons till they're bursting out of their matching Chanel suits. Mon–Fri 8.30am–7.30pm, Sat 8.30am–8.30pm, Sun 10am–7.30pm.

La Palette 43 rue de Seine, 6ᵉ; ⓜOdéon; map p.134. This former Beaux Arts student hangout is now frequented by art dealers and their customers, though it's still very relaxed. The decor is superb, including, of course, a large selection of paint-spattered palettes hanging on the walls. There's a roomy *terrasse* outside, and a short menu of lunchtime specials. Mon–Sat 9am–2am.

Au Petit Suisse 16 rue de Vaugirard, 6ᵉ; RER Luxembourg/ⓜCluny-La Sorbonne; map p.134. The perfect retreat from the Jardin du Luxembourg, with everything you'd want in a café: outdoor terrace; in-house *tabac*; two-hundred-year history; Art Deco interior; menu of sandwiches, salads and decent *plats du jour*; and a mezzanine level that's made for people-watching. Mon–Sat 7am–midnight, Sun 7am–11.30pm.

Au Vieux Colombier 65 rue de Rennes, 6ᵉ; ⓜSt-Sulpice; map p.134. An attractive Art Deco café on the corner of rue du Vieux-Colombier, with a big, curving zinc bar, ice-cream-cone lights and stained-green wooden

---

STUDENT RESTAURANTS

Students of any age are eligible for subsidized meals at the **university restaurants** under the direction of CROUS de Paris. They're mostly on the Left Bank, plus one in the Bastille area; you can find a complete list at ⓦcrous-paris.fr. You need to obtain a Carte Crous, available from the particular restaurant of your choice; just turn up during opening hours, buy a Carte (€2; bring your student ISIC card as proof of status), charge it up, and then get your meal. Not all serve evening meals, and most are closed at weekends and outside term time (details are given on the website). Though the food is less than wonderful, it's certainly filling, and you can't complain about the price: meals cost €3.

You'll find student restaurants at the following locations: 31 rue Geoffroy St-Hilaire, 5ᵉ (Mon–Fri 11am–2.30pm; ⓜCensier-Daubenton/Jussieu); 39 av Georges-Bernanos, 5ᵉ (daily 11.30am–2pm & 6.30–8pm; RER Port-Royal); 12 place du Panthéon, 5ᵉ (daily 8am–6pm; RER Luxembourg); 45 rue des Sts-Pères, 6ᵉ (Mon–Fri 8am–6pm; ⓜSt-Germain-des-Prés); 5 rue Mazet, 6ᵉ (Mon–Fri 11.30am–2pm; ⓜOdéon); 3 rue Mabillon, 6ᵉ (daily 11.30am–2pm & 6–8pm; ⓜMabillon); 92 rue d'Assas, 6ᵉ (Mon–Fri 11am–2.30pm; RER Port-Royal/ⓜNotre-Dame-des-Champs); 45 bd Diderot, 12ᵉ (Mon–Fri 11.30am–2pm; ⓜGare de Lyon/Reuilly-Diderot).

window frames. Perfect for a coffee break while shopping. Mon–Sat 8am–midnight, Sun 11am–7.30pm.

RESTAURANTS

Allard 41 rue St-André-des-Arts, 6ᵉ ☎ 01 43 26 48 23; ⓂOdéon; map p.134. Expect the menu at this proudly unreconstructed Parisian restaurant to be meaty and rich rather than sophisticated or imaginative and you'll be very satisfied. The atmosphere is unimpeachably antique: if it wasn't for the almost exclusively international clientele, you could be dining in another century. Evening menu €34. Daily noon–2pm & 7.30–11.30pm.

★ **L'Atlas** 11 rue de Buci, 6ᵉ ☎ 01 40 51 26 30; ⓂMabillon; map p.134. Despite a few Art Deco details, the decor at L'Atlas is functional rather than classic, but that's half the charm of this unpretentious market brasserie, and you can sit outside beside the oyster sellers, watching the street bustle. Good seafood, and simple, meaty main dishes from €14–26. Daily 6.30am–1am, food served 11.30am–midnight.

Au Babylone 13 rue de Babylone, 7ᵉ ☎ 01 45 48 72 13; Ⓜ Sèvres-Babylone; map p.134. Madame has run this tiny restaurant for almost fifty years, and Monsieur for fifteen longer still, and the gingham paper tablecloths, old lamps and pictures, and hanging flower baskets have buckets of old-fashioned charm. The €23 set three-courser (which comes with a drink) is similarly unreconstructed, with good meaty classics such as andouillette, blanquette de veau and rôti de porc. Mon–Sat noon–2pm; closed Aug.

★ **Brasserie Lipp** 151 bd St-Germain, 6ᵉ ☎ 01 45 48 53 91; ⓂSt-Germain-des-Prés; map p.134. One of the most celebrated of all the classic Paris brasseries, and the haunt of the very successful and very famous, Lipp has a wonderful 1900s wood-and-glass interior. There are decent plats du jour, including the famous choucroute (sauerkraut), for €22, but gastro-exploring à la carte gets expensive. Daily noon–2am, food served noon–11.45pm.

Le Comptoir du Relais St-Germain 9 carrefour de l'Odéon, 6ᵉ ☎ 01 44 27 07 97; ⓂOdéon; map p.134. Celebrated Parisian chef Yves Camdeborde has all the foodies lining up to eat here. The headline food is ambitious bistrot fare – lobster bisque with mushroom duxelles, tournedos de boeuf with a céleri and girolle mousseline, and there's a €55 tasting menu – but you could order up some charcuterie, a salade niçoise (€18) or a simple souris d'agneau (€19) and watch St-Germain sashay by. Prepare to queue and expect patchy service. School holidays: daily noon–11pm; no reservations. School terms: Mon–Fri noon–6pm, with a single, reserved sitting (gastronomic menu only) at 8.30pm; Sat & Sun noon–11pm (no reservations).

★ **L'Epi Dupin** 11 rue Dupin, 6ᵉ ☎ 01 42 22 64 56; Ⓜ Sèvres-Babylone; map p.134. This friendly bistrot in an untouristy corner reliably serves up what Parisians really want: high-quality, seasonal food with imaginative touches,

but nothing too crazy: perhaps Jerusalem artichokes in a langoustine emulsion, scallops with an orange-cream risotto, or a perfect lamb shoulder. The decor is relaxed and contemporary, and there are two sittings – go for the second if you want to take your time. Menus at €34 and €48, or €24 at lunch. Mon 7–11pm, Tues–Fri noon–3pm & 7–11pm.

L'Epigramme 9 rue de l'Eperon, 6ᵉ ☎ 01 44 41 00 09; ⓂOdéon; map p.134. Rough stone walls, a terracotta floor, mirrors with the menu written on them and a window onto the kitchen indicate the emphasis here: quality French cooking, stripped bare of pretensions. The dining room is tiny, the red plush chairs comfy, the reputation high and the prices reasonable (from around €40 in the evening, plus wine), so book well ahead. Tues–Sun noon–2.30pm & 7.30–11.30pm.

Ferrandaise 8 rue de Vaugirard, 6ᵉ ☎ 01 43 26 36 36; ⓂSt-Germain-des-Prés; map p.134. Don't be misled by the arty photos of Ferrandaise-breed cows on the walls: it's about more than beef at this restaurant near the Jardin du Luxembourg. You might choose a rich Ferrandaise blanquette de veau, but you could have a beetroot and celeriac glacé starter, oven-steamed pike-perch, and spiced strawberries in red wine. The ambience is airy and relaxed, with high ceilings and stone walls. Lunch menu €15, evening menu €32. Mon 7.30–10.30pm, Tues–Thurs noon–2pm & 7.30–10.30pm, Fri noon–2pm & 7.30–11pm, Sat 7.30–11pm.

Gaya Rive Gauche 44 rue du Bac, 6ᵉ ☎ 01 45 44 73 73; ⓂSt-Germain-des-Prés; map p.134. A wall covered in metal scales hints at the theme at this hyper-designed, upscale mini-restaurant: fish. It's a satellite of the empire of celebrity chef Pierre Gagnaire, so you'll find plenty of his trademark, Asian-tinged invention: pressé of skate with a Bloody Mary sauce, prawns in turmeric with rhubarb mousse and soy shoots, grilled swordfish on a bed of caramel, soya and Asian mushrooms. For gastro-cuisine, the prices aren't all that inflated: around €90 a head with wine, or weekday lunch at €48. Mon–Fri noon–2.45pm & 7.30–11pm, Sat 7–11.30pm.

★ **Hélène Darroze** 4 rue d'Assas, 6ᵉ ☎ 01 42 22 00 11; ⓂSt-Sulpice/Sèvres-Babylone; map p.134. Beneath celebrity chef Hélène Darroze's remarkable high-end Restaurant d'Hélène (evening menu €125, or €175 with wines), the more relaxed, ground-floor Salon d'Hélène offers some superbly imaginative dishes. She draws on her native Basque cuisine – hence the tapas portions – and on international influences too: imagine hake cooked in mother of pearl with white asparagus, sauce vierge and egg, plus caviar from Aquitaine. Neither the lack of windows, the oddly Japanese decor nor the hideous tableware should put you off; this is some of the best-value gastronomy in Paris: lunch menu at €28 up to an evening tasting menu at €85. Tues–Sat 12.30–2.30pm & 7.30–10.30pm; closed Aug.

19

TOP *TERRASSES*

A Parisian terrasse can be anything from a few chairs squeezed along a narrow pavement to a grand space under a glass canopy. Here's our pick of the finest places in Paris for outdoor eating and drinking.

CAFÉS

Café Charlot See p.276
Le Café des Initiés See p.274
Café de la Mairie See p.282
Café de la Mosquée See p.279
L'Entrepôt See opposite
L'Eté en Pente Douce See p.287
La Palette See p.282
Pause Café See p.278
Le Progrès See p.276
Chez Prune See p.292
Le Sancerre See p.288

RESTAURANTS

L'Atlas See p.283
Le Bistrot des Dames See p.292
Le Comptoir du Relais St-Germain See p.283
Drouant See p.272
Maison de l'Amerique Latine See below
Mini Palais See p.272
Le Moulin de la Galette See p.290
Pavillon Montsouris See p.286
Le Relais du Parc See p.294

19

Maison de l'Amerique Latine 271 bd St-Germain, 6ᵉ ☎01 49 54 75 10; ⓜSolférino; map p.134. Although it's part of the Latin American cultural institute, don't expect anything Latino about the restaurant (except a few Argentinian wines): this is rather superior French cooking. The draw, however, is the romantic outdoor setting amid expansive eighteenth-century gardens (summer only), with candles gracing white tablecloths in the evening. Set menu only: lunchtime €37, evening €55. April to late July & late August to Sept Mon–Fri noon–2pm & 7–10.30pm; Oct–March Mon–Fri noon–2pm; closed late July and early Aug.

Le Petit St-Benoît 4 rue St-Benoît, 6ᵉ ☎01 42 60 27 92; ⓜSt-Germain-des-Prés; map p.134. Another of the tobacco-stained St-Germain institutions, all rickety wooden tables and brass train-carriage-style coat racks, this restaurant is packed with international visitors seeking the authentic Parisian experience. Serves the sort of hearty, meaty, unsophisticated comfort food your *grand-mère* would cook: try a hard-boiled egg (€2.50) then *hachis parmentier* – known to lesser mortals as shepherd's pie (€12). Mon–Sat noon–2.30pm & 7–10.30pm; closed Aug.

La Tourelle 5 rue Hautefeuille 6ᵉ ☎01 46 33 12 47; ⓜSt-Michel; map p.134. This splendidly medieval little *bistrot*, named after the stone *échauguette* tower outside, is packed into a low-ceilinged, stone-walled room. The meaty cuisine is simple and traditional in the best sense

– they make terrines out of what wasn't finished the day before. Service is considerate – the owner may offer to change your wine if you prefer something in a different style – and the two-course lunch and three-course evening *menus* are good value at €13 and €23 respectively. No bookings are taken, so you'll just have to turn up and wait. Mon–Fri noon–1.45pm & 7–10pm, Sat 7–10pm; closed Aug.

Vagenende 142 bd St-Germain, 6ᵉ ☎01 43 26 68 18; ⓜMabillon; map p.134. This Art Nouveau marvel is registered as a historic monument, all mirrors, marble pillars, chandeliers and dark wood that has been polished for decades to a lustrous glow. Serves surprisingly unfussy, meaty brasserie dishes such as *coq au vin* and *pot-au-feu*, plus seafood specials. Mains and good-value *menu* both at around €20. Daily noon–11.30pm.

Ze Kitchen Galerie 4 rue des Grands-Augustins, 6ᵉ ☎01 44 32 00 32; ⓜSt-Michel; map p.134. Halfway between restaurant and trendy art gallery in atmosphere, with zany modern abstracts on the walls and a designer kitchen on open display. The food mixes Mediterranean with surprising Asian flavours: octopus with lime jam among the marinated fish starters, *gnocchi* with a Thai pistou in the pasta course, and grilled *confit* pigeon with a tamarind *jus* as a main. Expect to pay around €70 for three courses, without wine. Mon–Fri noon–2.30pm & 7–11pm, Sat 7–11pm.

TROCADERO

CAFÉS AND RESTAURANTS

Aux Marchés du Palais 5 rue de la Manutention, 16ᵉ ☎01 47 23 52 80; ⓜléna; map p.148. Simple, traditionally styled *bistrot*, with sunny tables on the pavement opposite the side wall of the Palais de Tokyo. There's always a good *entrée* and *plat du jour* – you might find a creamy broccoli *velouté* followed by Charolais steak

or prawn risotto. The prices are a little elevated – count on around €35 a head without wine – but then there's nothing half as satisfying anywhere nearby. Mon–Fri noon–2.30pm & 7.30–10.30pm, Sat 7.30–10.30pm; closed for three weeks in Aug.

Tokyo Eat/Tokyo Self Palais de Tokyo, 16ᵉ ☎01 47 20 00 29; ⓜléna/Alma-Marceau; map p.148. The restaurant inside the Site de Création Contemporaine is a self-consciously cool place to eat, with its futuristic, colourful decor, arty clientele and Mediterranean fusion menu; mains cost €15–30. The quality is a bit patchy, however, and the prices somewhat inflated. The *Tokyo Self* café is a reliable bet for a drink and a snack, and has a more dressed-down vibe. Tues–Sun noon–11pm, bar till 2am.

THE 7ᵉ

CAFÉ

Café du Marché 38 rue Cler, 7ᵉ ☎01 47 05 51 27; ⓂLa-Tour-Maubourg; map p.148. Big, busy café-brasserie serving excellent-value meals, with a *plat du jour* for around €11 that's as fresh-tasting as you'd expect, given the position in the middle of the rue Cler market. Outdoor seating, or covered-over terrace in winter. Mon–Sat 7am–midnight, Sun 7am–4pm.

RESTAURANTS

★ **L'Arpège** 84 rue de Varenne, 7ᵉ ☎01 45 05 09 06; ⓂVarenne; map p.148. Alain Passard is one of France's truly great chefs – and he pushes boundaries here by giving vegetables (all from his own *potager*) the spotlight, though you'll also find lobster, salmon and pigeon on his menus. He can turn a simple hen's egg into a culinary symphony of textures, tastes and temperatures, and dishes such as grilled turnips with chestnuts or duck with black sesame and orange brandy are just astounding. Pricing, of course, is fierce, with lunch (€120) and evening (€320) *menus*. Reserve well in advance and dress up. Mon–Fri noon–2.30pm & 7.30–10.30pm.

★ **Au Bon Accueil** 14 rue de Monttessuy, 7ᵉ ☎01 47 05 46 11; ⓂDuroc/Vaneau; map p.148. Huddled in the shadow of the Eiffel Tower, rue de Monttessuy is something of a gastro-street, and this is one of the most enjoyable restaurants on it. In a relaxed, modern *bistrot* setting, you might enjoy well-turned-out dishes like a delicate salad of prawns, salmon and lemon verbena, followed by a perfectly cooked veal liver with Jerusalem artichoke purée. There are a few outside tables. Lunch *menu* at €28; in the evening expect to pay €50 with wine. Mon–Fri noon–2.30pm & 7–10.30pm, Sat 7–10.30pm; closed Sat in Aug.

La Fontaine de Mars 129 rue St-Dominique, 7ᵉ ☎01 47 05 46 44; ⓂLa Tour-Maubourg; map p.148.

Heavy, pink-checked tablecloths, leather banquettes, attentive service: this restaurant offers a quintessentially French atmosphere. The food is reliable, meaty southwestern food: think snails, *magret de canard* and delicious Basque *boudin* sausages. There are lovely outside tables opposite the old stone fountain, too: no wonder President Obama ate here. Starters at €11–15, *plat du jour* €20, carafe of Beaujolais €12. Daily noon–2.30pm & 7.30–11pm.

Le Jules Verne Pilier Sud, Eiffel Tower, 7ᵉ ☎01 45 55 61 44 🌐lejulesverne-paris.com; ⓂBir-Hakeim; map p.148. Dining halfway up the Eiffel Tower is enough of a draw in itself, but now that Alain Ducasse's team are in charge, the ultra-luxe (but not overly heavy) gastronomic food and smart decor match the setting. Best at dinner (€200, plus wine), but cheaper for a weekday lunch (a mere €85). Reserve months in advance (online only), dress up, and don't expect a window table. Daily noon–2pm & 7–10pm.

Au Pied de Fouet 45 rue de Babylone, 7ᵉ ☎01 47 05 12 27; ⓂSt-François-Xavier/Sèvres-Babylone; map p.148. An atmospheric little place – just four tables and no reservations – where the specials are written up on the mirror. Think home-made *confit* of duck, basil ravioli, or haddock fillet with slivers of cabbage. Under €20 for a full meal. Mon–Sat noon–2.30pm & 7–10pm; closed Aug.

Le P'tit Troquet 28 rue de l'Exposition, 7ᵉ ☎01 47 05 80 39; ⓂEcole Militaire; map p.148. This tiny family restaurant has a discreetly nostalgic feel, with its ornate zinc bar along the back wall topped by an old brass coffeepot. Serves well-judged, traditional, seasonal cuisine to the diplomats of the *quartier*. On the evening *menu du marché* (€33) you might find a wild boar terrine or endive tart, followed by seven-hour lamb with thyme, or red mullet from Brittany. Mon & Sat 6–10.15pm, Tues–Fri noon–2pm & 6–10.30pm; closed first three weeks in Aug.

19

MONTPARNASSE AND THE 14ᵉ

CAFÉS AND WINE BARS

★ **L'Entrepôt** 7–9 rue Francis-de-Pressensé, 14ᵉ; ⓂPernety; map p.160. Lively, innovative arts cinema with a spacious, ultra-relaxed, glazed-in café and outside seating in the little courtyard. Great Sunday brunch, *plats du jour* for under €20 and frequent concerts in the evening. Mon–Sat noon–midnight.

Le Select 99 bd du Montparnasse, 6ᵉ; ⓂVavin; map p.160. If you want to visit one of the great Montparnasse cafés, as frequented by Picasso, Matisse, Henry Miller and F.

Scott Fitzgerald, make it this one. It's the most traditional of them all, the prices aren't over-inflated, and it's on the sunny side of the street. Only the brasserie-style food is disappointing. Daily 7am–2am, Fri & Sat till 4am.

RESTAURANTS

Aquarius 40 rue de Gergovie, 14ᵉ ☎01 45 41 36 88; ⓂPernety/Plaisance; map p.160. This laidback vegetarian restaurant serves wholesome if unspectacular meals. Mobiles hang from the ceiling, the art on the walls is

19

for sale, and there's a tiny kitchen knocking out nut roast, Mexican chilli and lasagne – all under €15. Mon–Sat noon–2.30pm & 7–10.30pm.

Crêperie Josselin 67 rue du Montparnasse, 14ᵉ ☎01 43 20 93 50; ⓂMontparnasse; map p.160. Montparnasse is traditionally the Breton quarter of Paris, and this crêperie couldn't be any more traditionally Breton: heavy wood furniture, lace, Breton porcelain and a super-abundance of crêpes – reputedly the best in the city. Tues–Fri 11.30am–3pm, Sat noon–midnight, Sun noon–11pm; closed Aug.

A Mi Chemin 31 rue Boulard, 14ᵉ ☎01 45 39 56 45; ⓂDenfert-Rochereau; map p.160. This is exactly why you'd head away from the centre of Paris: in the charming rue Daguerre neighbourhood, you'll find this resolutely local *bistrot* with a tiled floor, red banquettes and food that's unshowy but spot on. The short blackboard menu lists classics such as kidneys in mustard sauce alongside more adventurous dishes such as spiced duck *pastilla*. Around €30–40 a head, with carafes of excellent house wine for €12–16. Mon–Sat noon–2pm & 7–10.30pm.

Pavillon Montsouris 20 rue Gazan, 14ᵉ ☎01 43 13 29 00; RER Cité-Universitaire; map p.160. A treat for summer days. Sit on the famed terrace or in the elegant conservatory overlooking the park, and choose from a menu featuring lots of excellent lighter dishes – perhaps crab, foie gras and gracefully sauced fish dishes. Single *menu* at €49. Daily noon–2.30pm & 7.30–10.30pm; Sept–March closed Sun evening.

La Régalade 49 av Jean-Moulin, 14ᵉ ☎01 45 45 68 58; ⓂAlésia; map p.160. Diners at Bruno Doucet's renowned *bistrot* are packed cheek-by-jowl onto banquettes and wooden café chairs, and the service can be slow, but that's all part of the joy of this old-fashioned-style place, with its tiled floor, old framed pictures on the walls and hearty "amuse bouche" of help-yourself home-made pâté. Dishes sound deceptively simple – beautifully sauced meats and fish, for the most part – but the standard €32 *prix fixe* delivers a memorable meal, and for once the wines aren't marked up with the cooking. Mon 7.30–11.30pm, Tues–Fri noon–2.30pm & 7.30–11.30pm; closed mid-July to mid-Aug.

La Rotonde 105 bd du Montparnasse, 6ᵉ ☎01 43 26 48 26; ⓂVavin; map p.160. One of the grand old Montparnasse establishments, frequented in its time by the full roll-call of prewar artists and writers, and of course Lenin and Trotsky. Since those days it has moved well upmarket, gaining a plush decor of red velvet and brass, and is now best visited for a reliable French meal, served at almost any time of day or night. Starters like veal carpaccio or six oysters at €10–14, mains such as rump steak or lamb shoulder at €30. Daily 7.30am–2am; food served noon–12.30am.

★ **Le Timbre** 3 rue Ste-Beuve, 6ᵉ ☎01 45 49 10 40; ⓂVavin/Notre-Dame-des-Champs; map p.160. "The Postage Stamp" deserves its name: operating from one minuscule corner of a tiny dining room, British chef Chris Wright somehow produces top-rate French food. You might have sardine toast then lamb shoulder, or cuttlefish with chorizo and a perfect *croustillant* of beef cheek – followed by a heavenly cornet of jasmine cream. Expect to pay around €40 a head. It's fast gaining a reputation, so book well ahead. Mon–Sat noon–1.30pm & 7.30–10.30pm.

THE 15ᵉ AND AROUND

CAFÉ

Tea and Tattered Pages 24 rue Mayet, 6ᵉ; ⓂDuroc; map p.170. Set at the edge of the 6ᵉ arrondissement, this secondhand English-language bookshop is rather a long way from anywhere, but inside you can have tea and cakes, chat to the staff in English and browse through a very good selection of English books. Mon–Sat 11am–7pm, Sun noon–6pm; closes for part of the summer.

RESTAURANTS

Le Café du Commerce 51 rue du Commerce, 15ᵉ ☎01 45 75 03 27; ⓂEmile-Zola; map p.170. There aren't quite "a thousand covers", which was the name for this popular brasserie when it opened in 1922, but it's still a buzzing, dramatic place to eat, with the tables set on three storeys of galleries running round a central patio. Honest, high-quality meat is the speciality, with steaks from Limousin cows bought whole, but there's always a fish and vegetarian dish too. Expect to pay

€15–20 for a main course, though the €14 three-course lunch *menu* is always a bargain. Daily noon–3pm & 7pm–midnight.

★ **L'Os à Moelle** 3 rue Vasco da Gama, 15ᵉ ☎01 45 57 27 27; ⓂLourmel; map p.170. The highlight of chef Thierry Faucher's relaxed *bistrot* is the €35 *menu*, which brings you six courses showing off the most rewarding side of traditional French cuisine – from Jerusalem artichoke and black truffle soup, via scallops and giant snails to satisfying steaks. There's an inexpensive lunch *menu*, or you could make your way across the road to 181

TOP 5 VEGETARIAN RESTAURANTS

Aquarius See p.285
L'Arpège See p.285
Les Cinq Saveurs d'Anada See p.280
Au Grain de Folie See p.288
Le Potager du Marais See p.276

rue de Lourmel, where *La Cave de l'Os à Moelle* (☎01 45 57 28 88/28) is a no-frills offshoot with two communal tables where you can enjoy a €20 *menu* of the same exciting food. The ethos is self-service; you help yourself to a steaming pot of stew and cut your own slice of terrine. Reserve well in advance at both. Tues–Thurs noon–2pm & 7–11pm, Fri–Sun noon–2pm & 7pm–midnight; closed last three weeks in Aug.

THE 13ᵉ AND AROUND

RESTAURANTS

L'Avant Goût 26 rue Bobillot, 13ᵉ ☎01 53 80 24 00; ⓜPlace-d'Italie; map p.173. Small neighbourhood restaurant with a big reputation for excitingly good modern French cuisine – try the rich, spicy signature dish of *pot-au-feu* – and wines to match. Cool, contemporary decor and presentation, with a swish clientele relaxing on bright red leather banquettes. Superb-value lunch *menu* at €14, and evening *menu* at €31. Tues–Sun 12.30–2pm & 7.45–10.45pm; closed three weeks in Aug.

★ **Le Bambou** 70 rue Baudricourt, 13ᵉ ☎01 45 70 91 75; ⓜTolbiac; map p.173. Tiny Asian-quarter restaurant crammed with punters, French and Vietnamese alike, tucking into sublimely fresh-tasting Vietnamese food. Serves giant, powerfully flavoured *pho* and *Bun bo Hue* soups, packed with beef and noodles, for €8, as well as a full menu of vermicelli, stir-fry and grilled specialities for a couple of euros more. Last orders at 10.30pm, but you can stay till midnight. Expect to wait for a table. Tues–Sun 11.45am–3.30pm & 6.45–10.30pm.

★ **Chez Gladines** 30 rue des Cinq-Diamants, 13ᵉ ☎01 45 80 70 10; ⓜCorvisart; map p.173. This tiny, Basque-run corner *bistrot* is always warm, welcoming and packed with young people. Excellent wines and hearty Basque and southwest dishes – the mashed/fried potato is a must and goes best with *magret de canard*, and there are giant salads for €9. Less than €20 for a (very) full meal. Mon & Tues noon–3pm & 7pm–midnight, Wed–Sun noon–3pm & 7pm–1am.

Coco de Mer 34 bd St-Marcel, 5ᵉ ☎01 47 07 06 64; ⓜSt-Marcel; map p.173. Actually located down at the southeastern end of the 5ᵉ, this Réunionnais restaurant offers (fake) palm trees, happy-island music, a table in a sand pit and some of the best Indian Ocean food in the city. Try the heavenly grilled red snapper cooked in garlic and passion-fruit sauce (€20). Full meals for around €35, plus wine. Mon 7.30pm–midnight, Tues–Sat noon–3pm & 7.30pm–midnight; closed Aug.

Lao Lane Xang 2 102 av d'Ivry, 13ᵉ ☎01 58 89 00 00; ⓜTolbiac; map p.173. This is the newest and trendiest of a trio of bustling family restaurants, offering gastronauts a relative novelty: Laotian cuisine. It's not quite Vietnamese, nor Thai, though an aromatic cold beef salad or prawn and lime soup (all dishes around €7–10) won't be unfamiliar. Try the *panaché* of Laotian specialities (lunch €11, a more elaborate evening version €22), including the delicious pork sausage. The two older restaurants, with their cosy wood partitions, are just across the street. Book at any of them, or expect to wait. Mon, Tues & Thurs–Sun noon–3pm & 7pm–11pm.

La Mer de Chine 159 rue Château des Rentiers, 13ᵉ ☎01 45 84 22 49; ⓜTolbiac; map p.173. This upmarket, elegant Chinese restaurant in a quiet neighbourhood attracts politicians and celebrities. Its light, fresh food is influenced by the delicate Teocheow cuisine, which emphasizes poached and steamed fish and vegetables. Expect to pay at least €40 a head. Mon & Wed–Sun noon–2.30pm & 7pm–12.30am; closed for part of July.

Le Temps des Cerises 18–20 rue Butte-aux-Cailles, 13ᵉ ☎01 45 89 69 48; ⓜPlace-d'Italie/Corvisart; map p.173. Truly welcoming restaurant – it's run as a co-op – with elbow-to-elbow seating and a daily choice of unexceptional but hearty French dishes that ranges from *cassoulet* and black pudding to fillet of ling with artichoke cream. Expect to pay around €30 a head. Mon–Fri 11.45am–2.15pm & 7.30–11.45pm, Sat 7.30pm–11.45pm.

Tricotin Kiosque de Choisy, 15 av de Choisy, 13ᵉ ☎01 45 85 51 52 & 01 45 84 74 44; ⓜPorte-de-Choisy; map p.173. *Tricotin's* "kiosque", glazed in like a pair of overgrown fish tanks, is just set back from the broad avenue de Choisy, next to the Chinese-signed *McDonald's*. Its two restaurants cover much the same ground, and cover it well, but no. 1 (closed Tues) specializes in Thai and grilled dishes, while no. 2 has a longer list of Vietnamese, Cambodian and steamed foods. *Plats complets* cost around €7, but you could multiply dishes and spend around €25. Daily 9am–11.30pm.

MONTMARTRE AND THE 9ᵉ

CAFÉS AND WINE BARS

Café des Deux Moulins 15 rue Lepic, 18ᵉ; ⓜBlanche; map p.180. Apart from its big poster of Amélie (she waited tables here in the film), and its smattering of trendy twenty-somethings and tourists, this diner-style café is back to what it was before the film: a down-to-earth neighbourhood hangout, preserved in a charming 1950s interior. Sunday brunch is popular. Mon–Sat 7am–2am, Sun 8am–2am.

L'Eté en Pente Douce 23 rue Muller, 18ᵉ ☎01 42 64 02 67; ⓜChâteau-Rouge; map p.180. A useful Montmartre lunch or coffee spot, with chairs and tables set out on a terrace alongside the steps leading up to Sacré-Cœur. The food ranges from a decent goat's cheese and fig salad to heavier French *plats*, all at around €13. Daily noon–midnight.

19

BEST CHEAP EATS

The title says it all. Here is our pick of places where you can eat splendidly for between €10 and €20.

Le Bambou See p.287
Bistrot des Victoires See p.273
La Cantine Merci See p.292
Chez Gladines See p.287
Higuma See p.273
Lao Siam See p.293
Paris-Hanoï See p.278

19

★ **La Fourmi Café** 74 rue des Martyrs, 18e; ⓂPigalle/Abbesses; map p.180. Fashionable, vibrant, high-ceilinged café-bar full of edgily beautiful young Parisians drinking coffee by day and cocktails at night. Popular pre-club venue, with DJs later on. Unexceptional snacks, salads and light meals served at lunchtime. Mon–Thurs 8am–2am, Fri & Sat 8am–4am, Sun 10am–2am.

Aux Négociants 27 rue Lambert (corner of rue Custine), 18e ☎01 46 06 15 11; ⓂChâteau-Rouge; map p.180. An intimate and friendly *bistrot à vins* with a selection of well-cooked *plats*, home-made charcuterie and excellent Loire wines by the glass. It's wise to book if you plan to eat – count on around €25 for a full meal, without wine. The clientele is resolutely local, with a smattering of arty-intellectual types. Mon–Fri noon–2.30pm & 7–10.30pm; closed Aug.

Le Progrès 1 rue Yvonne Le Tac, 18e; Ⓜ Abbesses/Anvers; map p.180. Generous glazed windows overlook this crossroads at the heart of Abbesses, making this café something of a lighthouse for the young *bobos* (bourgeois-bohemians) of Montmartre. By day a simple, relaxed café serving reasonably priced meals and salads (€13–17), by night a pub-like venue. The café *Le Carrousel*, opposite, boasts a south-facing terrace for sunny days. Daily 9am–2am.

Le Refuge 72 rue Lamarck, 18e; ⓂLamarck–Caulaincourt; map p.180. If you're shocked by how touristy Montmartre has become, a refuge is exactly what this classic café-brasserie provides – and it's right by the Lamarck–Caulaincourt métro. The tiled decor hasn't changed much in a hundred years, and the clientele is resolutely local. Offers simple, reasonably priced dishes. Daily 7am–2am.

Le Relais de la Butte 12 rue Ravignan, 18e; ⓂAbbesses; map p.180. Come for the outdoor café tables on an expansive terrace, with its amazing views over Paris. The drinks come with a moderate mark-up, but don't bother with the overpriced, indifferent food. Daily 8.30am–midnight.

Le Sancerre 35 rue des Abbesses, 18e; ⓂAbbesses; map p.180. A well-known hangout for the young and trendy of all nationalities under the southern slope of Montmartre, with a row of outside tables perfect for watching the world go by. The food can be disappointing, though. Daily 7am–2am.

Un Zèbre à Montmartre 38 rue Lepic, 18e; ⓂAbbesses; map p.180. This buzzy, popular little bar somehow crams in a restaurant alongside, which serves generous portions of good French food. Expect to pay around €30–40, with wine. The clientele is young, friendly and predominantly local. Daily 9am–2am, food served noon–11.30pm.

RESTAURANTS

Café Burq 6 rue Burq, 18e ☎01 42 52 81 27; ⓂAbbesses; map p.180. Ultra-relaxed bar-*bistrot* serving (from 8pm to midnight) zesty-flavoured dishes such as an asparagus *velouté*, veal with lime cream sauce or honey-roast camembert. You'll jostle elbows with a trendy young clientele, whose noisy conversation competes with the DJ soundtrack. Mon–Sat 7pm–2am.

Casa Olympe 48 rue St-Georges, 9e ☎01 42 85 26 01; ⓂSt-Georges; map p.180. Dominique Versini, aka Olympe, is that rare thing: a female chef running her own *bistrot* in Paris. Her food is even more exceptional: bold meats – from veal foot to pig's head via spiced pigeon breast – with sunny, herby, powerful Corsican sauces and accents. At under €45, the set *menu* is a bargain for serious cooking like this. The ambience is classy but not stuffy, with leather banquettes down one wall and a blackboard list of daily specials. Mon–Fri noon–2pm & 7.45–11pm; closed Aug and first 2 weeks of May.

L'Entracte 44 rue d'Orsel, 18^e ☎01 46 06 93 41; Ⓜ Abbesses/Anvers; map p.180. Tucked down beside the Charles Dullin theatre, this is a taste of old Montmartre, the friendly owner presiding over a tiny room filled with paintings and pot plants accumulated over the last few decades. The food is homely in the proper sense – everything is prepared fresh – and there's a good choice of honest French starters (around €9), from pâté to crudités via marinated mackerel. The list of mains (€20) is admirably short, including just one fish dish, one *plat du jour* and a few steaks. Wed–Sat noon–2pm & 7–10.30pm, Sun noon–2pm.

Au Grain de Folie 24 rue de la Vieuville, 18e ☎01 42 58 15 57; ⓂAbbesses; map p.180. Tiny, simple and inexpensive organic and vegetarian place decked out with a few prayer flags and the like. Tues 7.30–10.30pm, Wed–Sat 11.30am–2.30pm & 7.30–10.30pm, Sun 12.30–2.30pm.

Le Mono 40 rue Véron, 18e ☎01 46 06 99 20; ⓂAbbesses; map p.180. Welcoming, family-run Togolese restaurant. Mains (around €13) are mostly grilled fish or

ETHNIC RESTAURANTS

Our selection of Paris's **ethnic restaurants** can only scratch the surface of what's available. **North African** places can be found throughout the city. **Indo-Chinese** restaurants are also widely scattered, with notable concentrations around avenue de la Porte-de-Choisy in the 13ᵉ and in the Belleville Chinatown. At the south end of rue du Faubourg-St-Denis, there are numerous good snack bars and restaurants – mainly **Turkish and Kurdish** in rue d'Enghien and rue de l'Echiquier, and **Indian, Pakistani and Bangladeshi** around passage Brady. The majority of the city's **Greek** eateries are tightly corralled in the area around rue de la Huchette, in the 5ᵉ, and are mostly garish and overpriced – the better places are elsewhere in the city.

AFRICAN (WEST AND CENTRAL)
Ile de Gorée West African. See p.292
Le Mono Togolese. See p.288
Waly Fay West African. See p.278

INDIAN
Pooja See opposite

INDIAN OCEAN
Coco de Mer See p.287

ITALIAN
L'Enoteca See p.276
Fuxia See p.292
Le Jardin des Pâtes See p.280

INDO-CHINESE
Le Bambou Vietnamese. See p.287
Lao Lane Xang 2 Laotian. See p.287
Lao Siam Thai and Laotian. See p.293
La Mer de Chine Chinese. See p.287
Paris-Hanoï Vietnamese. See p.278
Pho 67 Vietnamese. See p.281
Tricotin Thai, Vietnamese, Chinese and Cambodian. See p.287
Yam'Tcha Chinese-French. See p.275

JAPANESE
Higuma See p.273

JEWISH
L'As du Falafel See p.275
Chez Marianne See p.276

KURDISH
Dilan See p.273

LEBANESE
Al Ajami See p.270

NORTH AFRICAN
404 Moroccan. See p.276
Café de la Mosquée North African. See p.279
Chez Omar North African. See p.276
Le Mansouria Moroccan. See p.279
Le Martel Moroccan. See opposite
La Ruche à Miel Algerian. See p.278
Zerda Café North African. See opposite

TIBETAN
Tashi Delek See p.281

meat served with sour, hot sauces – try the delicious *akoboudessi* – a fried African fish in sauce with rice or cassava meal on the side. Starters (€7) include a Scotch bonnet-rich stuffed crab; for dessert, think rum-flambéed bananas. Enjoyable Afro atmosphere, with Afro-print tablecloths, *soukous* on the stereo and Togolese carvings on the walls. Daily except Wed 7–11pm; closed Aug.

Le Moulin de la Galette 83 rue Lepic, 18ᵉ ☎01 46 06 84 77; ⓂBlanche/Abbesses; map p.180. Eating in one of the last surviving Montmartre windmills might seem irresistible – never mind that the real, famous Moulin de la Galette is just down the street. It's spacious and welcoming inside, with wooden tables jostling together and a pleasant garden arbour out back. The food is classic French with a few modestly ambitious touches: duck with honey and Sauternes, roast bream with leeks and ginger. Two-course lunch at €19 (until 5pm), or expect to pay around €40–60 a head at dinner. Daily noon–11.30pm.

A la Pomponnette 42 rue Lepic, 18ᵉ ☎01 46 06 08 36; ⓂBlanche/Abbesses; map p.180. A genuine old Montmartre *bistrot*, with posters, drawings and zinc-top bar. The traditional French food is reliably decent, with a *menu* at €34 (€21 at lunch); otherwise it will cost you €35–50 *à la carte*. Mon 7–11.45pm, Tues–Sat noon–3pm & 7–11.45pm; closed 2 weeks in Aug.

Refuge des Fondus 17 rue des Trois Frères, 18ᵉ ☎01 42 55 22 65; ⓂAbbesses; map p.180. The €18 *menu* here gets you a hearty fondue – *bourguignonne* (meat) or *savoyarde* (cheese) – and your personal *biberon*, or baby bottle, full of wine. This idea is unflaggingly popular with a raucous young Parisian crowd, who squeeze onto the banquette tables and enthusiastically add to the zany graffiti on the walls. Daily 7pm–2am.

Le Relais Gascon 6 rue des Abbesses, 18ᵉ ☎01 42 58 58 22; ⓂAbbesses; map p.180. Serving hearty, filling meals all day, this two-storey restaurant (upstairs is cosier) provides a welcome blast of straightforward Gascon

19

heartiness in this alternately trendy, run-down and touristy part of town. The enormous hot salads cost €12.50, and there are equally good-value *plats* and lunch *menus*. Daily 10am–2am; food noon–midnight.

Le Restaurant 32 rue Véron, 18ᵉ ☎01 42 23 06 22; ⓂAbbesses; map p.180. Airy and arty little corner restaurant whose decor and clientele seem to follow the same fashion for distressed chic. There are a few adventurous flavours – vanilla cream with the veal shoulder, figs and coriander with the roast duck – but most of the food is surprisingly unpretentious, and comes in good-sized portions. The two-course evening *menu* costs €24. Daily noon–2.30pm & 7–11.30pm.

THE 10ᵉ AND GOUTTE D'OR

CAFÉS AND WINE BARS

L'Enchotte 11 rue de Chabrol, 10ᵉ; ⓂGare-de-l'Est; map p.191. A pleasantly ramshackle wine bar opposite the St-Quentin market, with tobacco-stained paintwork and a simple tiled floor. Inexpensive cheese and charcuterie to go with your *rouge ordinaire*, as well as a few more substantial dishes. Mon–Fri noon–2.30pm & 7.30–10.30pm; closed last two weeks of Aug.

Le Réveil du Dixième 35 rue du Château-d'Eau, 10ᵉ; ⓂChâteau-d'Eau; map p.191. A welcoming, unpretentious wine bar opposite the covered market. Serves inexpensive glasses of wine, *casse-croûte* plates of ham or cheese (€6–12), and honest *plats* like *andouille* or *cuisse de canard* (around €15). Mon–Fri 7.30am–midnight, Sat 10am–4pm; closed Aug.

RESTAURANTS

★ **Chez Casimir** 6 rue de Belzunce, 10ᵉ ☎01 48 78 28 80; ⓂGare-du-Nord; map p.191. It's astonishing that so good a restaurant can exist this close to the Gare du Nord. This no-frills *bistrot* with a surprisingly lovely corner situation, opposite a church, offers perfectly cooked *cuisine bourgeoise* at bargain prices: haddock carpaccio, monkfish with green and white asparagus and a sauce of morel mushrooms, then rhubarb and raspberry chocolate costs scarcely more than €30. The Sunday "brunch" (€25) is an adventure – think an astonishing smorgasbord of dishes from fish soup to pork casserole, not eggs and ham. The chef-owner, Thierry Breton, offers a more adventurous, Breton-flavoured *menu* at the slightly pricier but still excellent *Chez Michel*, two doors down, at no. 10 (☎01 44 53 06 20). Mon–Fri noon–2pm & 7.30–10.30pm, Sat & Sun 10am–7pm.

Flo 7 cour des Petites-Ecuries, 10ᵉ ☎01 47 70 13 59; ⓂChâteau-d'Eau; map p.191. Hidden away down what was once Louis XIV's stableyard, this old-time Alsatian brasserie is so handsome that even the very patchy service and crammed-in clientele can't quite spoil the experience. You're served (or not served) by old-fashioned waiters in ankle-length aprons. Fish and seafood form the backbone of the menu – look out for the winter specialities of hot oysters in champagne sauce, and salt pork with lentils. It's not cheap or particularly sophisticated, but there are reasonably priced *menus* from €25. Daily noon–3pm & 7pm–1.30am; last food orders at midnight; closed Aug.

★ **Julien** 16 rue du Faubourg-St-Denis, 10ᵉ ☎01 47 70 12 06; ⓂStrasbourg-St-Denis; map p.191. Part of the same enterprise as *Flo*, with an even more splendid decor – all globe lamps, hat stands, white linen, brass and polished wood, with frescoes of flowery Art Deco maidens surveying the scene. The cuisine (and prices) is similar to *Flo*'s, minus the seafood, and with a few seasonal specialities. Again, it's not a place for a cosy, romantic meal, but the surroundings provide a real feeling of spectacle. Daily noon–3pm & 7pm–1am; last service 12.30am; closed Aug.

Le Martel 3 rue Martel, 10ᵉ ☎01 47 70 67 56; ⓂChâteau-d'Eau; map p.191. Aimed at the trendy loft-living types who have recently moved into the *quartier*, *Le Martel* has a smart, classic French *bistrot* decor of zinc bar, polished wood banquettes and dark cream walls, with ultra-low lighting and soft, sometimes trancey music adding stylish touches. The menu is mainly Moroccan, with a few salads and French staples. Couscous is good, but there's more opportunity for culinary flair with the savoury-sweet *pastilla* or the tajines – all under €20. Good Maghreb wines from €20. Mon–Fri noon–2.30pm & 7.30–11pm, Sat until 11.30pm.

Pooja 91 passage Brady, 10ᵉ ☎01 48 24 00 83; ⓂStrasbourg-St-Denis/Château-d'Eau; map p.191. In a glazed *passage* that is Paris's own slice of the Indian subcontinent, *Pooja* is slightly pricier and sometimes slightly more elaborate than its many neighbours, and has more outside (well, *passage*-side) seating. Lunch *formule* for €12; evening *menus* €18–25. Daily noon–3pm & 7–11pm.

Zerda Café 15 rue René Boulanger, 10ᵉ ☎01 42 00 25 15; ⓂRépublique/Strasbourg St-Denis; map p.191. Always one of the contenders for the title of best authentic couscous in Paris, this restaurant also offers a fairly authentically North African decor, with decorative tiles and carvings set out like an internal courtyard. Serves Moroccan tajines (around €14) and delicious Tunisian *ojja* (a kind of ratatouille, with eggs, *merguez* or prawns) as well as Algerian-style couscous (€14–18), and a big selection of wines from the Maghreb. Mon & Sat 7–11pm, Tues–Fri noon–2.30pm & 7–11pm.

19

BATIGNOLLES

CAFÉS AND RESTAURANTS

Le Bistrot des Dames 18 rue des Dames, 17e ☎01 45 22 13 42; ⓂPlace de Clichy; map p.193. The food at this friendly, bric-a-brac strewn *bistrot* is modern Mediterranean fare – clam linguine, chicken supreme with chorizo – but the draw is the cosy conviviality, and generous garden seating at the back. Starters under €10, mains €14–20. Mon–Fri noon–3.30pm & 7pm–2am, Sat & Sun noon–2am.

Fuxia 69 place du Docteur Félix-Lobligeois, 17e ☎01 42 28 07 79; ⓂRome/Brochant; map p.193. This is an Italian café-deli chain, but the corner location here is particularly appealing, and there are lots of outdoor tables. The food is unfussy, filling and very fresh, with lots of vegetarian choices. Choose from the blackboard list of pasta and salad specials (€10–15), or go for the giant bruschetta platter, served on a wooden board. Daily 10am–1am; food served Mon–Fri 11am–3pm & 7–11.30pm, Sat & Sun noon–11.30pm.

Wepler 14 place de Clichy, 18^e ☎01 45 22 53 24; ⓂPlace-de-Clichy; map p.193. Now over a hundred years old, and still a beacon of conviviality amid the hustle of place de Clichy. Its clientele has moved upmarket (*menus* €20 and up) since it was depicted in Truffaut's *Les 400 Coups*, but as palatial brasseries go, *Wepler* has remained unashamedly *populaire*. Serves honest brasserie fare and classic seafood platters (from €32). Daily noon–12.30am, café from 8am.

19

EASTERN PARIS: CANAL ST-MARTIN AND REPUBLIQUE

CAFÉS AND WINE BARS

L'Atmosphère 49 rue Lucien-Sampaix, 10e; ⒨Gare-de-l'Est; map p.196. Lively bar-restaurant with decent, good-value midday and evening *plats*, on a pleasant corner beside the Canal St-Martin. Tables on the towpath on sunny days, and live music on Sun afternoons, with an alternative flavour. Daily 9.30am–2am.

Chez Prune 36 rue Beaurepaire, 10^e ☎01 42 41 30 47; ⒨Jacques-Bonsergent; map p.196. Named after the owner's grandmother (a bust of whom is inside), friendly, laidback *Chez Prune* is popular with an arty and media crowd, who bag the outside tables overlooking the canal. Lunchtime dishes around €14; evening snacks like platters of cheese or charcuterie around €11. Daily 10am–2am.

RESTAURANTS

L'Auberge Pyrénées Cévennes 106 rue de la Folie Méricourt, 11e ☎01 43 57 33 78; ⒨République; map p.196. Make sure you come hungry to this friendly family-run little place serving hearty portions of country cuisine. Highly recommended are the garlicky *moules marinières* for starters and the superb *cassoulet*, served in its own copper pot. Three-course *menu* €30. Mon–Fri noon–2pm & 7–11pm, Sat 7–11pm.

La Cantine Merci 111 bd Beaumarchais, 11e; ⒨St-Sébastien-Froissart; map p.93. Come early or be prepared to queue for a seat at one of the long communal tables in this cool concept store's lower-floor "canteen". Pick of the short menu, with its emphasis on healthy, fresh ingredients, are the "grandes salads" (€14, smaller ones for €9) and the home-made risotto (€10.50). It's family-friendly, with a *menu enfant* and high-chairs. Mon–Sat noon–4pm.

Chez Imogène Corner of rue Jean-Pierre-Timbaud and rue du Grand-Prieuré, 11e ☎01 48 07 14 59; ⒨Oberkampf; map p.196. A great little crêperie in a wood-beamed dining room: you could start with a home-made blini and smoked salmon, followed by a *savoyarde* crêpe (with a cheese, potato, onion and ham filling), and finish with a sweet crêpe, perhaps flambéed apple in Calvados. A *kir breton* (cider with cassis) is the perfect accompaniment. Lunch *menus* from €9.50, dinner €16. Mon 7–10.30pm, Tues–Sat 12.30–2.30pm & 7–10.30pm.

Ile de Gorée 70 rue Jean-Pierre-Timbaud, 11e ☎01 43 38 97 69; ⒨Couronnes; map p.196. A small West African place with colourful decor. Try the spicy stuffed crab for starters, followed by the filling Colombo Cabri (curried goat stewed with carrots and aubergines). There's often live Senegalese music in the evening. Mains cost around €16. Mon–Sat 7pm–midnight.

Au Rendez-Vous de la Marine 14 quai de la Loire, 19e ☎01 42 49 33 40; ⒨Jaurès; map p.200. Busy, successful old-time restaurant on the east bank of the Bassin de la Villette – but no water view – renowned for its fish, desserts and copious portions. You can get a really good meal for €35, not including wine. Paella is a speciality, but you have to order it a day in advance. A sociable clientele means that you might also make some friends. Tues–Sat noon–2pm & 8–10.30pm.

WHERE THE LOCALS EAT

If you want good food at reasonable prices, ask a local. Here's our pick of the restaurants where you'll find more Parisians than visitors.

Le Café du Commerce See p.286
Café des Musées See p.276
Au Clocher du Village See p.294
Jacques Mélac See p.278
A Mi Chemin See p.286
L'Os à Moelle See p.286
Le Repaire de Cartouche See opposite

Le Repaire de Cartouche 8 bd des Filles du Calvaire, 11ᵉ ☎01 47 00 25 86; Ⓜ Filles du Calvaire; map p.196. Reputedly the house where eighteenth-century brigand Cartouche once hid away, this simple, rustic-style restaurant is a popular bolthole with locals, who come for the excellent, classic French cuisine and the exceptional wine list of over 400 vintages. Around €45 a head for three courses, wine from around €25 a bottle. Tues–Fri noon–2pm & 7.30–11pm, Sat 7.30–11pm; closed Aug.

Restaurant de Bourgogne 26 rue des Vinaigriers, 10ᵉ ☎01 46 07 07 91; Ⓜ Jacques-Bonsergent; map p.196. The menu (*steak frites*, duck à l'orange, snails) holds few surprises at this homely local diner, but everything is done well and at very low prices. Despite the changing nature of the area, it still retains a strong local character, and lively conversation fills the dining room. Three-course *menu* €16. Book ahead for Sat dinner. Mon–Fri noon–2.15pm & 7.30–11pm, Sat 7.30–11pm; closed last week July to third week Aug.

BELLEVILLE, OBERKAMPF, MENILMONTANT AND BAGNOLET

CAFÉS AND WINE BARS

Les 400 Coups 12bis rue de la Villette, 20ᵉ ☎01 40 40 77 78, ⓦ les400coups.eu; Ⓜ Jourdain; map p.196. A light and airy, contemporary café-restaurant, that's particularly welcoming to families, providing a play area for under-8s and board games for older children. The house speciality is a fragrant chicken tajine and couscous; there's also the standard *confit de canard* as well as more exotic options such as spicy samosas, while the children's menu (€11) might include meat balls and rice with beetroot and carrots (or chips). Two-course lunch for €13.50, Sunday brunch €22. It's best to book at weekends. Check out the website for children's workshops and mini jazz and classical music concerts. Wed–Sun 10.30am–6pm, Sat until 9pm.

Le Faitout 23 av Simon Bolivar, 19ᵉ; Ⓜ Pyrénées; map p.196. A characterful, arty café-restaurant, with nice old café decor, high ceilings and a horseshoe-shaped bar. It's a good place for an *apéritif* or a daytime stop, when you can linger over a *café sirop* (coffee sweetened with Monin syrup), take down a book from the shelf or play a game of draughts. The traditional food is decent too, with the *plat du jour* around €10 and evening *menu* €25. Daily 7am–1.30am.

Aux Folies 8 rue de Belleville, 20ᵉ; Ⓜ Belleville; map p.196. Once a café-théâtre where Edith Piaf and Maurice Chevalier sang, *Aux Folies* offers a real slice of Belleville life; its outside terrace and long brass bar, with mirrored tiles, pinball machine and broken window panes held together with sticking tape, are packed day and night with a mixed, cosmopolitan crowd, enjoying cheap beer, cocktails and mint tea. Daily 6.30am–1am.

La Mère Lachaise 78 bd Ménilmontant, 20ᵉ ☎01 47 97 61 60; Ⓜ Père-Lachaise; map p.196. The sunny terrace of this trendy bar-restaurant, popular with students and *bobos* (bourgeois-bohemians), makes a good place for a drink after a visit to Père-Lachaise, or check out its cosy interior bar, with retro-chic decor of painted wood and wrought-iron lamps. The restaurant serves classic dishes and cheeseburgers (mains €12–15). Mon–Sat 8am–2am, Sun 9am–1am.

RESTAURANTS

L'Abribus 56 rue de Bagnolet, 20ᵉ; Ⓜ Alexandre Dumas; map p.208. A neighbourhood *bistrot* with offbeat decor: surreal, eye-like protrusions drooping from the ceiling, a large metal lizard attached to one of the stone walls and miscellaneous mechanical items dotted around. Giant, inexpensive portions of couscous with *merguez* sausage, beef, lamb or chicken (€9) are the speciality, as well as cheese and meat platters. Daily 8am–midnight.

★ **Le Baratin** 3 rue Jouye-Rouve, 20ᵉ ☎01 43 49 39 70; Ⓜ Pyrénées/Belleville; map p.196. At first glance there's little to distinguish *Le Baratin* from any other local *bistrot à vins*: the chalkboard menu, tiled floor and black-and-white photos are all in place. But the stellar cooking by Argentine chef Raquel Carena and fine selection of organic wines elevate it above the competition. The €16 three-course lunch *menu* might include a thick bean soup, a melt-in-the-mouth *daube* of beef and a quivering crème caramel. In the evenings, count on around €40 a head. It's best to book for both lunch and dinner. Tues–Fri noon–1am, Sat 8pm–1am; closed first week of Jan & three weeks in Aug.

★ **Le Châteaubriand** 129 av Parmentier, 11ᵉ ☎01 43 57 45 95; Ⓜ Goncourt; map p.196. One of the stars of the Paris dining scene, innovative Basque chef Inaki Aizpitarte has created an avant-garde *bistrot* that's booked out every evening (and lunchtime, too). The menu changes daily, featuring dishes such as mackerel ceviche with pear sorbet, and oyster soup with red fruits and beetroot. There's excellent Iberico ham and chorizo, too. Lunch costs €20, the dinner set menu (five courses with no choices) €50. If you don't have a booking for the evening you could try turning up for the second seating at around 10pm (for which there is no reservation). Tues–Fri noon–2pm & 8–10.30pm, Sat 8–10.30pm.

Lao Siam 49 rue de Belleville, 19ᵉ ☎01 40 40 09 68; Ⓜ Belleville; map p.196. The surroundings are nothing special, but the excellent Thai and Lao food, very popular with locals, makes up for it. Dishes from €10. Mon–Fri noon–3pm & 6–11.30pm, Sat & Sun noon–12.30am.

19

AUTEUIL AND PASSY

CAFÉS AND WINE BARS

La Gare 19 chaussée de la Muette, 16e ☎01 42 15 15 31; ⓜMuette; map p.213. This former train station has been turned into an elegant restaurant-bar, which boasts a huge, sunny dining room and serves, among other things, a popular €21–23 lunch *menu*. You can sit out on the attractive terrace on sunny days, and the bar upstairs (which often has samba, soul and house music DJs in the evenings) is well worth a look. Restaurant: daily noon–3pm & 7pm–midnight. Bar: daily noon–2am.

RESTAURANTS

L'Astrance 4 rue Beethoven, 16^e ☎01 40 50 84 40; ⓜPassy; map p.213. Triple-Michelin-starred chef Pascal Barbot's *L'Astrance* produces some of the city's most exciting cuisine. The exquisite dishes might include avocado and crab ravioli with almond oil; foie gras and mushroom *millefeuille* with lemon *confit* and hazelnut oil; or lemongrass and pepper sorbet. The pleasantly contemporary dining room seats only 26 and bookings are notoriously hard to get; try at least a month in advance. Lunch *menus* €70 and €120 (with wine pairings included, €200), dinner €210 (with wine pairings, €330). Tues–Fri 12.15–1.30pm & 8.15–9pm; closed Aug.

Au Clocher du Village 8bis rue Verderet, 16e ☎01 42 88 06 38; ⓜEglise d'Auteuil; map p.213. There is indeed something villagey about the setting of this charming café-restaurant, with its terrace shaded by chestnut trees and the church chiming out the hours across the way. Run by a laidback patron (he doesn't seem to mind the odd pampered poodle sitting on the comfy banquettes), the kitchen turns out nicely prepared *confit de canard* and other French standards, plus salads and more unusual offerings such as omelette with figs. Mains from €8.50. Tues–Sat noon–2.30pm & 7–10.30pm.

Le Relais du Parc 59 av Raymond Poincaré, 16e ☎01 44 05 66 10; ⓜVictor Hugo; map p.213. At this chichi restaurant in a chichi area, celebrated chef Alain Ducasse's menu revolves around fish, beef, lamb, vegetables and fruit in imaginative permutations, such as milk-fed lamb with spring vegetables, or "American-style" angler fish with Madras rice. In the summer meals are served outdoors in a lovely garden. Lunch *menu* €45, dinner around €75 a head. Tues–Sat noon–2.30pm & 7.30–10.30pm.

La Table Lauriston 129 rue Lauriston, 16e ☎01 47 27 00 07; ⓜTrocadéro; map p.213. A slightly older, well-off crowd usually dines at this traditional *bistrot* run by chef-to-the-stars Serge Rabey. Game terrine with chanterelle mushrooms and *poularde fondante au vin jaune* (chicken croquettes with Arbois wine) are indicative of the upscale dishes here, and be sure to taste their famed *Baba au rhum*. You'll easily spend €50–60 per person, but the *cuisine bourgeoise* is excellent. Mon–Fri noon–2.30pm & 7.15–10pm, Sat 7.30–10.30pm.

19

NEW MORNING JAZZ CLUB

Bars, clubs and live music

Paris's fame as the quintessential home of decadent, hedonistic nightlife has endured for centuries. That reputation seems only to grow stronger, fuelled by a vibrant bar and club scene – much has been learned from the city's energetic gay community – and a world-leading music programme, from rock and world music to jazz and electro. The city's strength in live music is partly a reflection of its absorption of immigrant populations. Paris has no rivals in Europe for the variety of world music to be discovered; Algerian, West and Central African, Caribbean and Latin American sounds are represented in force. Hip-hop is popular, both imported and home-grown, though you're unlikely to hear it in bars and clubs, where house and techno still rule, mixed in with good-time Mediterranean, Latin and African flavours.

Jazz fans are in for a treat, too, with all styles from New Orleans to current experimental to be heard. Then there's French **chanson**, a tradition long associated with Paris, particularly during the war years through cabaret artists like Edith Piaf, Maurice Chevalier and Charles Trenet, and in the 1960s with poet-musicians as diverse as Georges Brassens, Jacques Brel and Serge Gainsbourg. *Chanson* is currently undergoing something of a revival, with excellent showcase evenings in restaurants and bars. For a relaxed taste of the nightlife of the past, head for one of the old suburban eating-and-drinking venues known as *guinguettes* (see p.341).

ESSENTIALS

Information To find out **what's on**, get hold of one of the city's **listings magazines** (see p.38). If you want more in-depth coverage, try the *Bons Plans* listings (in French) in the monthly magazine *Nova* (ⓦnovaplanet .com). The best way to find out about the latest club nights is to head to a specialist music shop (see p.331), or pick up flyers – or word-of-mouth tips – in one of the city's trendier shops and cafés.

Venues Events at **major concert venues** are advertised on billboards and posters throughout the city. On June 21 the *Fête de la Musique* sees live bands and free concerts of

every kind of music on street corners and at venues throughout the city (see p.319).

Tickets Concert tickets, whether rock, jazz or *chanson* (or indeed classical), can be obtained at the venues themselves, though it's easier to get them through agents like Fnac (see p.330) or Virgin Megastore (see p.331).

Getting home Given the difficulty of finding a taxi after hours (see p.26), many clubbers use Vélib' bikes to get home, or keep going until the métro starts up at around 5.30am, while the hard core move on to one of the city's *after* events.

BARS

20

The city's liveliest venues for **night-time drinking**, places that stay open late and maybe have DJs or occasional live music, are rounded up here, under "**bars**". Also included are the more vibrant, late-opening **cafés**, Alsatian/German-type **beer cellars**, imported Irish/English **pubs**, American-style **cocktail bars** plus informal **bar-clubs**. You'll find lower-key and more relaxed cafés listed in the "Cafés and restaurants" chapter (see pp.265–294), while full-on nightclubs, with entry fees and proper sound systems, are reviewed separately under "Clubs" (see p.302).

THE CHAMPS-ELYSEES AND AROUND

Flûte L'Etoile 19 rue de l'Etoile, 17ᵉ; ⓜTernes/Charles-de-Gaulle-Etoile; map p.62. A classy champagne bar, with a wide selection of bubbly available by the glass. Downstairs is a tiny bar and a bigger mezzanine, with comfy red velour seats, an intimate spot for a tête-à-tête. There's often live jazz on a Wednesday from 8pm. Daily 5pm–4am (Sun & Mon until 2am).

Pershing Lounge Pershing Hall, 49 rue Pierre Charron, 8ᵉ; ⓜGeorge-V; map p.62. The hip, minimalist *Pershing Hall Hotel*'s lounge bar is a delightful retreat from the bustle of the city, with its 30m-high vertical garden, planted with exotic vegetation. It's a bit of a jetsetters' hangout, with cocktails priced to match (€19 and upwards). Daily 6pm–2am.

Sir Winston 5 rue de Presbourg, 16ᵉ; ⓜKléber/Charles-de-Gaulle-Etoile; map p.62. Churchill's eyes would surely have lit up on perusing the drinks menu at this large British–Indian-themed bar-restaurant, with its fifty kinds of whisky (from €8.50) and numerous martini cocktails (€10). There are plenty of cosy corners for chilling out, with comfy leather chesterfields and snug booths dimly lit by Indian lanterns. Evenings see DJ sets with a world-music slant. Daily 9am–2am (Thurs–Sat till 4am).

GRANDS BOULEVARDS AND AROUND

Bar Costes *Hôtel Costes*, 239 rue St-Honoré, 1ᵉʳ; ⓜConcorde/Tuileries; map p.72. A favourite haunt of fashionistas and film and media stars, this is a decadently romantic place for an *apéritif* or late-night drinks amid opulent nineteenth-century decor of red velvet, swags and columns, set around an Italianate courtyard draped in ivy and atmospherically lit at night. Dress up if you want to get in, and don't expect too much deference from the ridiculously good-looking staff. Cocktails from around €20. Daily till 2am.

Bar Hemingway *Ritz Hôtel*, 15 place Vendôme, 1ᵉʳ; ⓜTuileries/Opéra; map p.72. Hemingway first came here with F. Scott Fitzgerald in the 1920s at a time when he was too poor to buy his own drinks. Once he'd made his money, he returned here frequently to spend it; with a classic decor of warm wood panelling, stately leather chairs and deferential, suited barmen, it's easy to see why. The walls are now plastered with photos of Hemingway from all stages of his life, great for soaking up his mystique. Sip the famed dry martinis or choose from a large selection of malt whiskies. There's very little on the drinks list under €20, but it's a good venue for a special occasion. Daily 6.30pm–2am.

Le Café Noir 65 rue Montmartre, 2ᵉ; ⓂLes Halles/ Sentier; map p.72. Despite the name, it's the colour red that predominates in this cool little corner café, with papier-mâché globes, mirrors covered with stickers, and theatre and concert posters in the windows. It's great for an *apéritif* or late-night drink, when the music and ambience hot up and it's standing room only at the bar. DJ Thurs & Fri. Mon–Fri 8.30am–2am, Sat 4pm–2am.

La Conserverie 37bis rue du Sentier, 2ᵉ; ⓂBonne Nouvelle; map p.72. This stylishly converted *atelier* on a quiet backstreet arguably mixes the city's most original cocktails; you could try, for example, the champagne and balsamic vinegar mojito, or perhaps more appealingly the Du Maurier, a mix of rum, lemon juice, champagne and raspberries, which comes with rock candy on the side (you place it on your tongue as you drink). The food, too, goes beyond the usual charcuterie platters, and includes Petrossian smoked salmon, caviar and foie gras, which you can consume on appropriately decadent low, soft sofas at candlelit tables. Cocktails around €10. Mon–Fri 6pm–2am, Sat 7pm–2am.

De La Ville Café 34 bd de la Bonne Nouvelle, 10ᵉ; ⓂBonne-Nouvelle; map p.72. The grand staircase, gilded mosaics and marble columns hint at this bar's former incarnation as a bordello. It draws in crowds of pre-clubbers, who sling back a mojito or two under the multicoloured awning, before moving on to one of the area's clubs; tellingly, absinthe is listed as an *apéritif*. On weekends, well-known DJs spin the disks till the early hours. Daily 11am–2am.

Kitty O'Shea's 10 rue des Capucines, 2ᵉ; ⓂOpéra; map p.72. A favourite haunt of expats, and a decent stab at an Irish bar, with excellent Guinness, Magners and reasonably priced down-home meals like Irish stew and fish and chips. Anglo-Irish football and rugby matches are shown on the big screens, and there's live music on Sun evenings. Daily noon–1.30am.

Le Tambour 41 rue Montmartre, 2ᵉ; ⓂSentier; map p.72. A dusty local habitués' bar, eccentrically furnished with recycled street signs, old paving stones and the like. A throwback to the old Les Halles market days and still keeping long hours. Drinks are reasonably priced, and there are hearty salads and snacks available, as well as fuller meals, with mains like pigs' trotters around €15. Daily 6pm–6am.

BEAUBOURG AND LES HALLES

Le Fumoir 6 rue de l'Amiral-Coligny, 1ᵉʳ ☎01 42 92 00 24; ⓂLouvre-Rivoli; map p.85. An Old Fashioned would be an appropriate choice at this sedate bar, where animated chatter from the thirty-something crowd rises above the mellow jazz soundtrack and the clink of cocktail shakers. You can browse the international press and there's also a restaurant at the back, complete with library. Cocktails from €9. Happy hour 6–8pm. Daily 11am–2am.

Kong 5th floor, 1 rue du Pont-Neuf, 1ᵉʳ ☎01 40 39 09 00, ⓦkong.fr; ⓂPont-Neuf; map p.85. The last episode of *Sex and the City* was set in this über-cool, Philippe Starck-fashioned bar/restaurant above the flagship Kenzo building. While the gorgeous *demoiselles* meeting the lift will let you in, you might get ignored by the bartenders – and everyone else – if you can't claim the right pedigree. The decor is new Japan meets old: geisha girls and manga cartoons. Booths eerily beam holograms of heads of models who glare at you as you sip your €16 cocktail. The separate restaurant upstairs is under an impressive glass roof, with views over the Seine. The so-so Asian-influenced food (around €60 per head) includes dishes such as black cod with miso. Restaurant daily 10.30am–2am, with brunch on Sun; bar same hours except Fri & Sun until 3am.

Au Trappiste 4 rue St-Denis, 1ᵉʳ; ⓂChâtelet; map p.85. Over 140 draught beers include Jenlain, France's best-known *bière de garde*, Belgian Blanche Riva and Kriek from the Mort Subite (Sudden Death) brewery – ask for a taster if you can't decide – plus very good *moules frites* and various *tartines*. Or, if you've just come to drink, go all out for the giraffe, a table cask bong filled to the brim with three litres of beer. Mon–Thurs noon–2.30am, Fri–Sun noon–4am.

THE MARAIS

★ **Andy Wahloo** 69 rue des Gravilliers, 3ᵉ; ⓂArts-et-Métiers; map p.93. This very popular bar decked out in original Pop Art-inspired Arabic decor is fairly quiet during the week but gets packed to the gills at weekends. You can get yummy mezze appetizers until midnight (the *guassâa* is a good assortment) and the bar serves mojitos and a few original cocktails, including the Wahloo Special (rum, lime, ginger, banana and cinnamon; €10). DJs play a wide range of dance music, Moroccan rock and Algerian raï. Tues–Sat 5.30pm–2am.

La Belle Hortense 31 rue Vieille du Temple, 4ᵉ ☎01 48 04 71 60; ⓂSt-Paul; map p.96. Named after a Jacques Roubaud novel, this cross between a bookshop and a wine bar predictably attracts literary types. It also publishes its own magazine and hosts regular readings, book signings and other events, which are well worth attending if your French is up to it. Mon–Wed 5pm–2am, Thurs & Fri 4pm–2am, Sat 1pm–2am, Sun 1pm–midnight.

La Perle 78 rue Vieille du Temple, 3ᵉ; ⓂSt-Paul; map p.96. An Emperor's New Clothes kind of place that maintains a *très cool* reputation and is always packed with an arty, indie crowd knocking back cheap beer and spilling onto the pavement in the warmer months. Mon–Fri 6am–2am, Sat & Sun 8am–2am.

Le Petit Fer à Cheval 30 rue Vieille du Temple, 4ᵉ; ⓂSt-Paul; map p.96. A very attractive, minuscule *bistrot*/bar with original fin-de-siècle decor, including a

20

marble-topped bar in the shape of a horseshoe (*fer à cheval*). It's a popular drinking spot, with good wine, and you can snack on sandwiches or simple *plats* in the little back room, furnished with old wooden métro seats. Mon–Fri 9am–2am, Sat & Sun 11am–2am; food served noon–midnight.

Quiet Man 5 rue des Haudriettes, 4e ☎ 01 48 04 02 77, ⓦ thequietman.eu; ⓜ Rambuteau; map p.96. Live traditional Celtic music is played by troubadours nightly downstairs at this tiny Irish pub, which also boasts a dartboard and good pints of Guinness, Kilkenny and Murphy's. Lots of locals, but does pull in its share of the tourist crowd as well. Happy hour 5–8pm, music begins shortly thereafter. Daily 5pm–2am.

Stolly's 16 rue Cloche-Perce, 4^e; ⓜ St-Paul; map p.96. Tiny, no-nonsense, almost exclusively Anglo bar with very friendly atmosphere and broadcasts of all major sporting events, washed down with pints of Guinness, Grolsch and the wonderfully named Cheap Blond, plus a wide selection of spirits and cocktails (from €7). Daily 4.30pm–2am, happy hour 5–8pm.

La Tartine 24 rue de Rivoli, 4^e; ⓜ St-Paul; map p.96. This traditional bar's been given a fresh lick of paint and a subtle spruce-up, while retaining a distinctive Art Nouveau feel. It draws a refreshing mix of students, pensioners, fashionistas and workmen, as well as the odd tourist. Glasses of wine from €4, plus light meals including, of course, *tartines*. Daily 8am–2am.

BASTILLE AND AROUND

★ **Café de l'Industrie** 16 rue St-Sabin, 11e; ⓜ Bastille. See p.277.

Le Lèche-Vin 13 rue Daval, 11e; ⓜ Bastille; map p.108. The owners of this kitsch bar appear to have ransacked a church for the decor. The statue of Mary with a cross (and an AIDS ribbon) in the window is certainly eye-catching;

BEST BARS FOR DJS AND DANCEFLOORS

You don't have to go to a full-on club to dance in Paris. At these bars, things get moving later on, with either live bands or DJs providing the sounds.

L'Alimentation Générale See p.301
Café Chéri(e) See p.301
Le Carmen See opposite
Chez Georges See opposite
De La Ville Café See p.297
La Fourmi Café See p.300
La Mezzanine de l'Alcazar See opposite
Olympic Café See p.300
Piston Pélican See p.302
Le Pompon See p.300

---

the pics in the toilet, on the other hand, are far from pious. Gets packed very quickly at night with a young, cosmopolitan crowd. Happy hour 6–10pm. Daily 6pm–2am.

★ **Les Marcheurs de Planète** 73 rue de la Roquette, 11e ⓦ lesmarcheursdeplanete.com; ⓜ Voltaire; map p.108. Good old-fashioned Parisian atmosphere, with an effortlessly cool, vaguely retro vibe: chess tables, a hat stand, various musical instruments, posters covering the walls and a wild-haired owner are all present and correct. More than a hundred wines are on offer, plus excellent cheeses and charcuterie dishes. Live music on Thurs at 10pm. Tues–Sun 5.30pm–2am.

SanZSanS 49 rue du Faubourg-St-Antoine, 11^e; ⓜ Bastille; map p.108. The gothic get-up of red velvet, oil paintings and chandeliers make this bar popular with a young crowd, especially on Friday and Saturday evenings, when DJs play rare groove and funky/Brazilian house. Drinks are reasonably priced. Mon noon–3am, Tues–Sun noon–5am.

QUARTIER LATIN

Le Bateau Ivre 40 rue Descartes, 5^e; ⓜ Cardinal-Lemoine; map p.120. Small, dark and ancient, this studenty bar is just clear of the Mouffetard tourist hotspot, though it attracts a fair number of Anglos in the evenings, especially after about 10pm. If it's packed out, the *Pub River* next door is less appealing but more spacious. Daily 6pm–2am.

Curio Parlor 16 rue des Bernardins, 5e; ⓜ Maubert-Mutualité; map p.120. This secretive – spot the entrance if you can – pocket cocktail bar is much patronized by Paris's gilded youth, who loll fashionably on the comfy velvet sofas, while DJs play in the designer-dressed basement. Expensive and glossy. Tues–Thurs & Sun 6pm–2am, Fri & Sat 6pm–4am.

Le Pantalon Bar 7 rue Royer-Collard, 5^e; RER Luxembourg; map p.120. This archetypal student dive sports weathered mirrors and graffiti-covered walls, and serves very cheap drinks, especially at happy hour – happy two hours, to be precise, starting at 5.30pm. Daily 5.30pm–2am.

Le Piano Vache 8 rue Laplace, 5^e; ⓜ Cardinal-Lemoine; map p.120. This venerable little bar has a laidback, grungy atmosphere, and is crammed with students drinking cheapish beer at small tables. Mon–Fri noon–2am, Sat 6pm–2am.

★ **Aux Trois Mailletz** 56 rue Galande, 5e; ⓜ St-Michel; map p.120. Deep in perhaps the most unappealingly touristy quarter of the city is a historic jazz/cabaret bar. By day a café-resto, it unwinds into a relaxed and raucous piano bar by night. But the main draw is the cabaret show in the basement, featuring outrageous performances and serious world music artists: the cabaret starts from 8.30pm and is best booked in advance (☎01 43 54 42 94). Daily 11am–5am.

★ **Le Violon Dingue** 46 rue de la Montagne-Ste-Geneviève, 5ᵉ; ⓜMaubert-Mutualité; map p.120. Long, dark, student pub that's also popular with young international students, though it's much quieter in summer. Noisy and friendly, with English-speaking bar staff and cheap drinks. The cellar bar stays open until 4.30am on busy nights. Tues–Sat 7pm–4am.

ST-GERMAIN

★ **Le 10** 10 rue de l'Odéon, 6ᵉ; ⓜOdéon; map p.134. Peeling art-exhibition posters line the walls of this small, dark bar, and the theme is continued in the atmospherically vaulted cellar bar. Famed for its cheap *pichets* of sangria and party atmosphere, especially among the international student/traveller crowd. Daily 6pm–2am.

Bar du Marché 75 rue de Seine, 6ᵉ; ⓜMabillon; map p.134. This former market café is just as satisfying and just as busy at night as by day. Expect animated conversation rather than banging techno, and kir rather than cocktails. Daily 7am–2am.

Bistrot des Augustins 39 quai des Grands Augustins, 5ᵉ; ⓜSt-Michel; map p.134. This friendly albeit touristy pocket café (see p.282) transforms itself by night into a raucous and excitable micro-venue, with local, wine-swilling patrons spilling out onto the pavement. Good stop-off on a romantic, Seine-side walk. Daily 10am–midnight.

★ **Chez Georges** 11 rue des Canettes, 6ᵉ; ⓜMabillon; map p.134. This dilapidated wine bar is one of the few authentic addresses in an area dominated by big, noisy theme pubs (you'll find plenty in the vicinity if you're in the market). The young, studenty crowd gets good-naturedly rowdy later on in its atmospheric, vaulted cellar bar. Tues–Sat 2pm–2am; closed Aug.

Les Etages St-Germain 5 rue de Buci, 6ᵉ; ⓜMabillon; map p.134. Fashionably distressed café-bar, with a downstairs level open to the street – prime for posing. Upstairs, you can lounge around on dog-eared armchairs, chilling out with a relatively reasonably priced cocktail (around €8). Daily noon–2am.

Lutetia Bar 45 bd Raspail, 6ᵉ; ⓜSèvres-Babylone; map p.134. This discreet and classy bar deep in the interior of the grand *Hôtel Lutetia* is a pleasant sanctum, though drinks are expensive (around €20). Offers genteel jazz piano, live, every evening from 7pm and soft-focus jazz concerts Wed–Sat at 10.15pm. The hyper-modern smoking room is a sight in itself. Daily 10am–1am.

La Mezzanine de l'Alcazar 62 rue Mazarine, 6ᵉ; ⓜOdéon; map p.134. Both decor and clientele are *très design* at this cool, monied cocktail bar, set on a mezzanine level overlooking Terence Conran's *Alcazar* restaurant. It's reassuringly expensive at around €12 for a drink, with

champagne at €80 a bottle. Most nights start off relaxed and finish with feverish dancing, the harder core moving downstairs to *WAGG* club (see p.303). DJs Wed–Sat. Daily 7pm–2am.

La Palette 43 rue de Seine, 6ᵉ; ⓜOdéon; map p.134. This traditional café-bar (see p.282) heaves with a fashionable but chattily relaxed crowd till late, and has one of the best outdoor *terrasses* in the city — ranks of tables beneath heaters (in winter) in a quiet micro-square. Great for an *apéro* or two. Mon–Sat 9am–2am.

★ **Prescription** 23 rue Mazarine, 6ᵉ; ⓜOdéon; map p.134. Very trendy on the well-dressed and well-funded Anglo/Euro-trash scene, this small, exclusive cocktail bar hides a glamorously plush interior behind its artfully blank facade. Like an ultra-designer hotel bar earlier in the evening, turning into a madhouse later on. One for the beautiful people. Tues–Thurs 8am–2am, Fri & Sat 8pm–4am.

MONTPARNASSE AND SOUTHERN PARIS

L'Entrepôt 7–9 rue Francis-de-Pressensé, 14ᵉ; ⓜPernety; map p.160. See p.285.

La Folie en Tête 33 rue Butte-aux-Cailles, 13ᵉ; ⓜPlace-d'Italie/Corvisart; map p.173. Its corner spot is a little set back from the main Butte-aux-Cailles action, but this friendly and distinctly lefty café-bar is a classic of the *quartier*. The walls are littered with bric-a-brac and musical instruments, the tables and stools with young locals. Occasional gigs, but mostly it's world music, laidback underground beats or a young singer-songwriter's latest album on the sound system. Mon–Sat 7pm–2am, Sun 7pm–midnight.

Le Merle Moqueur 11 rue Butte-aux-Cailles, 13ᵉ; ⓜPlace-d'Italie/Corvisart; map p.173. Classic narrow, shop-front-style Butte-aux-Cailles bar, which once saw the Paris debut of Manu Chao. It maintains an alternative edge, though most days serves up 1980s French rock CDs and home-made flavoured rums to young Parisians. If you don't fancy the playlist, try the very similar *Le Diapason*, two doors along, where the sounds can be more varied. Daily 5pm–2am.

Le Rosebud 11bis rue Delambre, 14ᵉ; ⓜVavin; map p.160. A hushed, faintly exclusive bar just off the boulevard Montparnasse where the thirty-something-plus clientele keeps up the prewar arty traditions of the area – Sartre and his crew used to drink here. The white-jacketed barmen, who seem to date from the same era as the decor, serve up wonderful, traditional cocktails – think martinis rather than Sex on the Beach – for around €12. Daily 7pm–2am; closed Aug.

MONTMARTRE AND NORTHERN PARIS

★ **Le Carmen** 34 rue Duperré, 9ᵉ; ⓜPigalle; map p.180. Somehow, this astonishingly beautiful cocktail bar occupies the grand, high-ceilinged reception rooms of

20

Georges Bizet's old house. You'll feel like you're at the ball from *La Traviata*, except the music is provided by edgy DJs, and everyone's drinking designer cocktails (bespoke, and stunningly good; €12–15). There's a sofa in a giant birdcage and imaginatively alternative events from classical piano soirées to a book club – as well as all the gigs and parties. Daily 8pm–2am.

Chez Camille 8 rue Ravignan, 18ᵉ; ⓜAbbesses; map p.180. *Très chouette* (cool in a charming sort of way) is how locals have been describing this little bar for years. In a great location on the slopes of the Butte, with a small outdoor seating space, the clientele is typical of the location – young and trendy, but laidback too. Tues–Sat 9am–2am, Sun 9am–2am.

★ **Chez Jeannette** 47 rue du Faubourg St-Denis, 10ᵉ; ⓜChâteau-d'Eau; map p.191. For the bourgeois-bohemians flooding into the 10ᵉ, this corner café is a kind of nexus. Beneath the high ceilings, the decor is genuine prewar vintage, but the clientele is right up to the minute: all iPhones and asymmetric haircuts. Makes a feature of candlelit *soirées*, but they never turn off the laidback sounds. Daily 8am–2am.

Cyrano 3 rue Biot, 17ᵉ; ⓜPlace de Clichy; map p.193. This sympathetically ramshackle café-bar, with its superb *belle époque* gold mosaics and mirrors, is a Clichy institution. Outside here (and outside its neighbour, *L'Entracte*, two doors along), a young, noisy, theatrical crowd gathers in the evenings. Mon–Fri 9am–2am, Sat 4pm–2am, Sun 4pm–midnight.

La Fourmi Café 74 rue des Martyrs, 18ᵉ; ⓜPigalle/Abbesses; map p.180. The long bar and high-ceilinged spaciousness draw the discerning *bobos* of Abbesses and the 10ᵉ for *before* (pre-club) cocktails, to the sounds of electro-lounge. Mon–Thurs 8am–2am, Fri & Sat 8am–4am, Sun 10am–2am.

★ **Olympic Café** 20 rue Léon, 10ᵉ ⓦrueleon.net; ⓜChâteau-Rouge; map p.191. In the heart of the poor and peeling Goutte d'Or, this lefty, boho café-restaurant pumps out life and energy like a lighthouse, its big rainbow peace flag looking down on a faintly grungey 1930s Art Deco interior. In the evening, the local young bohemians can eat African *plats* cooked to European tastes (*poulet yassa* or *beef mafé* for around €8), but the main draw is the basement venue's music programme (Tues–Sat), covering anything from African rock to klezmer, Bulgarian folk and French *chanson*. Tues–Sun 5pm–2am.

Le Pompon 39 rue des Petits-Ecuries, 10ᵉ; ⓜAbbesses; map p.191. Ultra-trendy bar from the high-profile team behind the high-class nightclub *Le Baron*, though up in this boho quarter the clientele is more web-designer than designer suit. Chandeliers and exposed brick, wood panelling and DJs. Daily 7pm–2am.

Le Progrès 1 rue Yvonne Le Tac, 18ᵉ; ⓜAbbesses/Anvers; map p.180. See p.288.

Au Rendez-Vous des Amis 23 rue Gabrielle, 18ᵉ; ⓜAbbesses; map p.180. Halfway up the Butte, this small, ramshackle, community-spirited hangout is a magnet for Montmartre locals, and is especially popular with the young, arty and alternative-leaning. Daily 8.30am–2am.

Le Sans Souci 65 rue Jean-Baptiste Pigalle, 9ᵉ; ⓜPigalle; map p.180. This otherwise fairly ordinary corner café has become a key meeting-point for the fashionable bourgeois-bohemians of the quarter. Fairly low-key and friendly, until the DJs get going and the crowds gather outside. Mon–Sat 9.30am–2am.

Un Zèbre à Montmartre 38 rue Lepic, 18ᵉ; ⓜAbbesses; map p.180. See p.288.

EASTERN PARIS: CANAL ST-MARTIN AND AROUND

L'Abracadabar 123 av Jean-Jaurès, 19ᵉ; ⓜLaumière ⓦabracadabar.fr; map p.200. Tucked away in the far reaches of the 19ᵉ, this popular little music bar pulsates with live rock, ragga, funk, blues, jazz and techno most evenings, drawing a mixed crowd of students and thirty-somethings. Hundreds of photos of past guests are pegged up on washing lines and strung across the bar. Music usually starts at 9pm and there's sometimes a small entry fee of €2/3. Daily 6pm–2am, Thurs–Sat till 5am.

Bar Ourcq 68 quai de la Loire, 19ᵉ ⓦbarourcq.free.fr; ⓜLaumière; map p.200. With its turquoise facade and large windows looking out onto the canal *quai*, this popular bar really comes into its own in the warmer months when you can sit out on the quayside, or borrow the bar's set of *pétanques*. It also has a cosy interior with sofas and cushions. Drinks are very reasonably priced. DJs Fri, Sat & Sun. Summer Wed & Thurs 3pm–midnight, Fri & Sat 3pm–2am, Sun 3–10pm; winter Sat 3pm–2am, Sun 3–9.30pm.

Belushi's Bar *St Christopher's Inn*, 159 rue de Crimée, 19ᵉ ❶01 40 34 34 40; ⓜJaurès/Laumière/Stalingrad; map p.200. Popular with both backpackers and locals, this hostel bar occupies a great spot overlooking the water and offers cheap drinks (beer or a glass of wine from €2.50) and food such as sandwiches or waffles. Live Premiership matches and DVDs are screened, and there are often gigs, karaoke sessions, theme nights and DJ sets both in the bar and in the club downstairs. Happy hour daily 6–8pm. Bar daily 7pm–1am; club Wed–Sat 9pm–2am.

Le Jemmapes 82 quai de Jemmapes, 10ᵉ; ⓜJacques-Bonsergent; map p.196. In the summer this neighbourhood resto-bar and boho hangout is well known for letting its patrons cross the road to nip at their drinks (from plastic cups) along the banks of the canal. The standard French cuisine is good, but the lure here is the hipster atmosphere. Beer from €3. Daily 11am–2am.

★ **Point Ephémère** 200 quai de Valmy, 10ᵉ ⓦpointephemere.org; ⓜJaurès/Louis Blanc;

20

CLASSY COCKTAILS

Stylish surroundings and fancy drinks; here's our pick of Paris's American-style cocktail bars.

Bar Hemingway See p.296
La Conserverie See p.297
Curio Parlor See p.298
Le Fumoir See p.297
Lutetia Bar See p.299
Prescription See p.299

map p.196. A great energetic atmosphere pervades this young, creative space for music, dance and visual arts set in a former canal boathouse. There are frequent concerts, with a wide range of bands playing rock, hip-hop, indie, jazz and more, while the rotating art exhibitions range from the quotidian to the abstract. There's always interesting multilingual conversation going on around the bar, and you can even get a decent cheeseburger or bagel in the restaurant looking out onto the canal. Mon–Sat noon–2am, Sun 1–9pm (later if there's a concert).

BELLEVILLE, MENILMONTANT/ OBERKAMPF AND BAGNOLET

L'Alimentation Générale 64 rue Jean-Pierre Timbaud, 11ᵉ; ⓦ alimentation-generale.net; ⓂParmentier; map p.196. Despite its name and attractive traditional facade, this is not the local grocer's shop, but one of Oberkampf's hottest nightlife spots, with a global line-up of live music ranging from Afro-rock to Italian folk. A DJ usually takes over later and there's room for dancing. There's sometimes a cover charge of €10 that includes the first drink. Daily 6pm–2am.

L'Autre Café 62 rue Jean-Pierre Timbaud, 11ᵉ; ⓂParmentier; map p.196. Amid the heaving throng of bars on this popular nightlife stretch, this attractive fin-de-siècle café-bar-restaurant stands slightly apart, perhaps because it seems to welcome all comers and has no trace of pretension, and yet still has a great vibe. It also stands out for its size – it's very spacious, with high ceilings, a long zinc bar, small café tables and comfy leather banquettes. Drinks are reasonably priced, and the food isn't bad either, especially if you stick to the blackboard specials, which might include *boeuf bourguignon* (around €10). It's also a great place to while away time during the day, browsing the newspapers or taking advantage of the free wi-fi. Daily 8am–2am.

Babel Café 109 bd de Ménilmontant, 11ᵉ ⓦmyspace .com/babelcafeparis; ⓂMénilmontant; map p.196. A small, convivial *café-concerts*, slightly off the main Oberkampf drag and especially popular with locals, who crowd in after work to relax over sangria or pints of beer

and charcuterie platters. It has an interesting programme of live music, usually acoustic, including Moroccan oud and classical Persian. Concerts start at 8pm. Tues–Sat 5pm–2am.

★ **La Bellevilloise** 19–21 rue Boyer, 20ᵉ ⓦ labellevilloise.com; ⓂGambetta/Ménilmontant; map p.196. There's always something interesting going on at this former workers' co operative, dating back to 1877, now a dynamic bar, club, live concert venue and exhibition space, all rolled into one. It also hosts film festivals, and vintage and organic markets. Its cool bar-restaurant, *La Halle aux Oliviers*, with real olive trees dotted about beneath a glass roof, makes an attractive place for a drink, dinner (around €15 for mains such as cheeseburger and fries or vegetable tajine), or jazz brunch on Sunday (€29). The basement club and live music venue hosts some exciting bands, playing anything from Afro jazz to Balkan beats. Opening times vary, but generally: Wed & Thurs 7pm–1am, Fri 7pm–2am, Sat 6pm–2am, Sun 11.30am–midnight.

Café Charbon 109 rue Oberkampf, 11ᵉ; ⓂSt-Maur/ Parmentier; map p.196. The place that pioneered the rise of the Oberkampf bar scene in the mid-1990s is still going strong and continues to draw in a young, fashionable, mixed crowd day and night. Part of its allure is the attractively restored *belle époque* decor, with high ceilings, mirrors, comfy booths and dangling lights. Happy hour daily 5–7pm. Sun–Thurs 9am–2am, Fri & Sat 9am–4am.

Café Chéri(e) 44 bd de la Villette, 19ᵉ ⓦlecafecherie .blogspot.com; ⓂBelleville; map p.196. A cool DJ bar, with scruffy red interior and popular terrace, where local hipsters sit at their laptops or read during the day, or drop in for drinks after work and stay long into the night. Drinks are reasonably priced. Music, from hip-hop to indie, Thurs–Sat nights. Daily 8am–2am.

Le Cannibale 93 rue Jean-Pierre Timbaud, 11ᵉ ☎01 49 29 00 40; ⓂCouronnes; map p.196. The sight of a copy of Goya's gory painting *Saturn Devouring His Son* hanging above the bar (after which the place is named) creates a certain frisson as you walk in the door of this arty bar-restaurant, a handsome *belle époque* former brasserie. Locals chill out to a soundtrack of electro lounge, or tuck into *burgers and chips* in the dining area. There's usually live music (often *chanson*, jazz funk or Cuban) on Sundays from 6pm. Daily 8am–2am.

Aux Folies 8 rue de Belleville, 20ᵉ; ⓂBelleville; map p.196. See p.293.

Lou Pascalou 14 rue des Panoyaux, 20ᵉ; ⓂMénilmontant; map p.196. A trendy but friendly place with a zinc bar and sunny terrace, this local boho hangout is a great weekend find for the area, especially if you're interested in leaving with your eardrums intact. Be sure to try some of their delicious mint tea – over a ponderous

20

game of chess if you fancy it. You can also choose from a wide range of reasonably priced beers, bottled and on tap. There's an interesting programme of live music, such as gypsy jazz and *chanson*, on Sundays at 6.30pm, and a DJ livens things up on Friday and Saturday nights. Daily 9am–2am.

Piston Pélican 15 rue de Bagnolet, 20e ⓦ pistonpelican .com; ⓜ Alexandre-Dumas; map p.208. This friendly local joint, with its assortment of chipped mirrors, posters and pop culture memorabilia, has an appealingly eclectic soundtrack, featuring rock, Eighties pop and the odd drum'n'bass anthem. Live bands, playing anything from jazz rock to klezmer, are given a platform at the weekend, often followed by a DJ. The food – light meals such as quiche and soup – is good too. Happy hour daily 5–8pm. Mon–Fri 8.30am–2am, Sat 10am–2am, Sun 4pm–1am.

CLUBS

Paris's **club** scene moves ever further away from huge monster-clubs rammed every weekend with techno-heads to fast-changing, esoteric programmes, often put on at smaller venues. Where once deep house ruled, you can now find hip-hop, r'n'b, electro-lounge, rock and more alternative sounds. The clubs listed below attract some of the trendiest or biggest crowds, but the style of music and the general vibe really depend on who's running the "*soirée*" on a particular night. Some showcase occasional live acts, too. It's worth checking the listings for **live music** venues (see opposite), which tend to hold DJ-led sessions after hours, and the **gay and lesbian** club listings (see p.358). Note too that lots of **bars** (see pp.296–302) bring in DJs for weekend nights.

OPENING HOURS AND ENTRANCE FEES

Most clubs **open** between 11pm and midnight, sometimes earlier if the venue is hosting a gig or live event first, but venues rarely warm up before 1am or 2am. It's worth dressing up, especially for the cooler clubs, some of which operate very snooty door policies. Most **entry prices** include one free drink (*consommation*), and may vary from night to night.

CLUB LISTINGS

★ **Batofar** Opposite 11 quai François Mauriac, 13e ⓣ 01 56 29 10 33, ⓦ batofar.org; ⓜ Quai de la Gare; map p.173. This old lighthouse boat moored at the foot of the Bibliothèque Nationale is a small but classic address. The programme is alternative electro, techno, hip-hop, whatever – with the odd experimental funk night or the like thrown in to mix it up a bit. Head to the deck and check out the views if you need a time-out. Popular for after-sunrise *after* events on the first Sunday of the month (till noon). Entry €5–12. Mon–Sat 11pm–6am, first Sun of the month 6am–noon.

Favela Chic 18 rue du Faubourg du Temple, 11e ⓣ 01 40 21 38 14, ⓦ favelachic.com/paris; ⓜ République; map p.196. Brazilian restaurant with seriously popular Latino club alongside. Attracts a fairly glam Euro-trashy crowd, but there are plenty of goodtimers to make sure things don't get too posey. Free entry Tues–Thurs, €10 Fri & Sat. Mon–Thurs 8pm–2am, Fri & Sat 8pm–4am.

Glaz'art 7–15 av de la Porte de la Villette, 19^e ⓣ 01 40 36 55 65, ⓦ glazart.com; ⓜ Porte de la Villette; map p.202. Artsy, alternative-leaning venue that's serious about its music – hugely eclectic range of live acts and DJ sets covering everything from punk to jungle. Quite a trek from the centre, but it's spacious and in summer there's a glorious outdoor "beach". Entry €10–20. Times vary, but weekend club nights usually 11pm–5am.

La Machine du Moulin Rouge 90 bd de Clichy, 18^e ⓣ 01 53 41 88 89, ⓦ lamachinedumoulinrouge.com; ⓜ Blanche; map p.180. Beside the fabled Moulin Rouge, this club has a concert space, a dedicated dancefloor known as "La Chaufferie" and a glitzy bar. A touch of trashy hedonism lifts it above the usual monster club. Entry €10–20. Club 11pm–6am, often with gigs before.

Le Montana 28 rue St-Benoît, 6e; ⓜ St-Germain-des-Prés; map p.134. This small, exclusive and distinctly beautiful mini-club is achingly jet-set, and so celebrity-packed it doesn't need a publicly listed phone number. You'll have to look the part to get in, and feel the part to enjoy it. No entry fee, but expensive drinks. Mon–Sat 11pm–5am.

★ **Le Nouveau Casino** 109 rue Oberkampf, 11e ⓣ 01 43 57 57 40, ⓦ nouveaucasino.net; ⓜ Parmentier; map p.196. Right behind *Café Charbon* (see p.301) lies this excellent venue. An interesting, experimental line-up of live gigs makes way for a relaxed, dancey crowd later on, with music ranging from electro-pop or house to rock. There's a good sound system and ventilation, but not much space. Entry price €5–12, depending on whether you reserve online and the time you arrive. Fri & Sat midnight–5am.

Point Ephémère 200 quai de Valmy, 10e; ⓜ Jaurès/ Louis Blanc; map p.196. See p.300.

Le Redlight 34 rue du Départ, 14e ⓣ 01 42 79 94 53, ⓦ leredlight.com; ⓜ Montparnasse-Bienvenüe; map p.160. The house is hard rather than happy at this large club, thus pulling in a largely but not exclusively gay crowd. If it all gets too much, the second dancefloor is sometimes – only sometimes – a little more relaxed. Entry €20–25. Fri & Sat midnight–11am.

★ **Rex Club** 5 bd Poissonnière, 2e ☎01 42 36 28 83, ⓦrexclub.com; ⓜBonne-Nouvelle; map p.72. The iconic *Rex* is the clubbers' club: spacious and serious about music, which is strictly electronic, notably techno, played through a top-of-the line sound system. Refreshingly, not a style-fest. Attracts big-name DJs too. Entry up to €20. Wed–Sat 11.30pm–6am.

La Scène Bastille 2bis rue des Taillandiers, 11e ☎01 48 06 50 70 (restaurant reservations: ☎01 48 06 12 13), ⓦla-scene.com; ⓜBastille; map p.108. Club, concert venue and restaurant all rolled into one, in a converted warehouse, snazzily refurbished in plush colours. The eclectic music policy embraces anything from house and electro to zouk and hip-hop, with regular gay nights, and live bands earlier on. Entry €8–12. Mon–Thurs & Sun 7.30pm–midnight, Fri & Sat till 6am; closed Aug.

★ **Scopitone** 5 av de l'Opera, 1^e ☎01 42 60 64 45, ⓦscopitoneclub.com; ⓜPyramide/Palais Royale; map p.72. Currently one of the cooler small clubs in town, pulling in a designer-scruffy Parisian crowd. The entrance fee varies, with gigs earlier on, and lots of free nights. Club sessions mostly around midnight–5am.

Showcase Below Pont Alexandre III, 8e ☎01 45 61 25 43, ⓦshowcase.fr; ⓜChamps-Elysées–Clemenceau; map p.62. This superclub, facing onto the river, has a 1500 capacity, slick decor and a fun but sometimes pretentious crowd – increasingly less-so as the trends move on. Electronica, particularly techno, is the order of the day, with Chloe from Paris regularly on the decks. Dress up to get in, or sign up online. Entry up to €20. Fri & Sat 10pm–dawn, Sun 11am–3pm.

★ **Social Club** 142 rue Montmartre, 2^e ☎01 40 28 05 55, ⓦparissocialclub.com; ⓜBourse/Grands Boulevards; map p.72. Despite the forbidding black exterior, and interior, this unpretentious yet cool club is packed with a mixed clientele, from local students to lounge lizards. Here, it's all about the music, with everything from electro to jazz and hip-hop to ska on the playlist. Entry ranges from nothing up to €20. Wed 11.30pm–3am, Thurs–Sat 11pm–6am.

WAGG 62 rue Mazarine, 6e ☎01 55 42 22 01, ⓦwagg .fr; ⓜOdéon; map p.134. Adjoining Terence Conran's flashy *Alcazar* restaurant and bar, the *WAGG* puts on Seventies "Carwash" nights on Friday, and disco and funk on Saturday. Sundays see Latin flavours, with salsa classes from 3.30–5.30pm. Entry €12. Fri & Sat 11pm–6.45am, Sun 5pm–midnight.

20

ROCK AND WORLD MUSIC

Most of the **venues** listed below are primarily concert venues, though some double up as clubs on certain nights, or after hours. A few of them will have live music all week, but the majority host bands on just a couple of nights. Admission prices vary depending on who's playing. Note that the most interesting **clubs** tend to host gigs earlier on; watch out for the programmes at *Le Nouveau Casino* (see opposite) and *Social Club* in particular (see p.304). Jazz venues, too, often branch into other genres such as world music and folk – *New Morning* is a classic example.

ROCK AND WORLD MUSIC VENUES

Le Bataclan 50 bd Voltaire, 11^e ☎01 43 14 00 30, ⓦle-bataclan.com; ⓜOberkampf; map p.196. Classic pagoda-styled ex-theatre venue (seats 1200) with one of the best and most eclectic line-ups covering anything from international and local dance and rock musicians – Pete

Doherty, Fleet Foxes and Paolo Nutini for example – to *chanson*, comedy and techno nights. The Follivores and Crazyvores Saturday gay club nights are currently hugely popular.

Café de la Danse 5 passage Louis-Philippe, 11e ☎01 47 00 57 59, ⓦcafedeladanse.com; ⓜBastille; map

---

MUSIC ON TV AND RADIO

The private **TV** channel Canal Plus broadcasts big European concerts, while M6 has some late-night music programmes, as well as numerous video clips during the day. Arte, the Franco-German highbrow channel (after 7pm), shows contemporary opera productions and documentaries on all types of music.

Of the local **radio** stations, Radio Nova (ⓦnovaplanet.com; 101.5 MHz) plays the best cross-section of what's new, from house to hip-hop, and broadcasts updates on the latest and coolest club nights, or *soirées*. The high-class, eclectic station FIP (ⓦsites.radiofrance.fr/chaines/fip/accueil; 105.1 MHz) has plenty of jazz, but also recherché rock, French *chanson* and world music. Oüi FM (ⓦouifm.fr; 102.3 MHz) is the all-day rock radio; techno and house can be heard on the station Radio FG (ⓦradiofg.com; 98.2 MHz); and Radio Classique carries classical music (ⓦradioclassique.fr; 101.1 MHz). France-Musiques (ⓦfrancemusique.com; 91.7 MHz) offers classical, contemporary, jazz and opera. Under strict language laws, forty percent of pop music played by any radio station in primetime has to be French, and there's a dire Parisian radio station playing only French music, Chante France (ⓦchantefrance.com; 90.9 MHz).

p.108. Rock, pop, world, folk and jazz music played in an intimate and attractive space. Open for concerts only.

La Cigale 120 bd de Rochechouart, 18ᵉ ☎ 01 49 25 81 75, ⊛ lacigale.fr; ⓂPigalle; map p.180. Formerly playing host to the likes of Mistinguett and Maurice Chevalier, since 1987 and a Philippe Starck renovation this historic, 1400-seater Pigalle theatre has become a leading venue for pop, rock and indie acts, especially French and other continental European bands.

Le Divan du Monde 75 rue des Martyrs, 18ᵉ ☎ 01 40 05 06 99, ⊛ divandumonde.com; ⓂAnvers; map p.180. A youthful venue in a café whose regulars once included Toulouse-Lautrec. It runs one of the city's most diverse and exciting programmes, ranging from techno to Congolese rumba, with dancing till dawn at the weekends.

La Flèche d'Or 102bis rue de Bagnolet, corner of rue des Pyrénées, 20ᵉ ☎ 01 44 64 01 02, ⊛ flechedor.fr; ⓂPorte-de-Bagnolet/Alexandre-Dumas (it's a fifteen -minute walk from both); map p.208. Housed in the old Bagnolet station on the defunct *petite ceinture* railway, this bar and live music venue has a punkish atmosphere, with throngs of bikers, clubbers, musos, students and aspiring trend-setters. They are drawn by an eclectic music programme – indie-pop, ska, rock,

chanson and punk – which has made it one of the hottest tickets in town (gigs up to €15 extra). Mon–Thurs 8pm–2am, Fri & Sat 8pm–6am.

Maroquinerie 23 rue Boyer, 20ᵉ ☎ 01 40 33 35 05, ⊛ lamaroquinerie.fr; ⓂGambetta; map p.196. This smallish concert venue is the downstairs part of a trendy arts centre. The line-up is anything from folk and jazz to metal and hip-hop, with a particularly good selection of French musicians.

Point Ephémère 200 quai de Valmy, 10ᵉ ☎ 01 40 34 02 48, ⊛ pointephemere.org; ⓂJaurès; map p.196. Run by an arts collective in a disused warehouse, this superbly dilapidated venue lives up to its reputation as a nexus for alternative and underground performers of all kinds. There are gigs most nights, covering anything from electro to Afro-jazz via folk-rock. In the warmer months you can take your drinks outside, and sit on the banks of the canal.

Social Club 142 rue Montmartre, 10ᵉ ☎ 01 40 28 05 55, ⊛ parissocialclub.com; ⓂBourse/Grands Boulevards; see p.72. This smallish but high-profile venue has one of the most intriguing programmes in the city – folk and African acts find space alongside big indie rockers, with DJs from midnight.

JAZZ, BLUES AND *CHANSON*

Jazz is well established in Paris (see box below), and the genre is still alive and well, with a good selection of clubs plying all styles from New Orleans to current experimental. There are plenty of **festivals**, too, especially in the summer (see pp.318–320). **Gypsy jazz** (*jazz manouche*), pioneered by Django Reinhardt, is particularly in vogue at the moment; carrying on the tradition are musicians such as Romane and the Ferré brothers. Other jazz names to look out for are saxophonist Didier Malherbe; violinist Didier Lockwood; British-born but long-time Paris resident, guitarist John McLaughlin; pianist Alain Jean-Marie; clarinettist Louis Sclavis; and accordionist Richard Galliano, who updates the French *musette* style. All of them can be found playing small gigs, regardless of the size of their reputations. *Bistrots* and bars are a good place to catch gypsy jazz, as well as French traditional *chanson*. **Gigs** aren't usually advertised in the press, but you'll see posters in the venues themselves. In addition to the places listed here, it's also worth checking out *Café de la Danse* (see p.303) for occasional *chanson* or jazz concerts.

JAZZ IN PARIS

Jazz has long enjoyed an appreciative audience in France, especially since the end of World War II, when the intellectual rigour and agonized musings of bebop struck an immediate chord of sympathy in the existentialist hearts of the *après-guerre*. Charlie Parker, Dizzy Gillespie, Miles Davis – all were being listened to in the 1950s, when in Britain their names were known only to a tiny coterie of fans.

Gypsy guitarist **Django Reinhardt** and his partner, violinist Stéphane Grappelli, whose work represents the distinctive and undisputed French contribution to the jazz canon, had much to do with the genre's popularity. But it was also greatly enhanced by the presence of many front-rank black American musicians, for whom Paris was a haven of freedom after the racial prejudice of the States. Among them were the soprano sax player **Sidney Bechet**, who set up a legendary partnership with French clarinettist Claude Luter, and Bud Powell, whose turbulent exile partly inspired the tenor man played by Dexter Gordon (himself a veteran of the Montana club) in the film *Round Midnight*.

MAINLY JAZZ

L'Atelier Charonne 21 rue de Charonne, 11ᵉ ☎01 40 21 83 35, ⓦateliercharonne.com; ⓜLedru-Rollin/ Bastille; map p.108. This sleek bar-restaurant is a good place to hear traditional performers, as well as new upcoming musicians, including two of Django Reinhardt's descendants, David and Noé Reinhardt. Booking ahead for their dinner concert (€19.90 for one course, €29.90 for three courses) reserves you a table with a view of the stage. There's also a separate bar area with limited views of the performers. Concerts are at 9pm (Monday to Saturday), and on Sundays there's a *jazz manouche* jam session from 6pm to 8pm. Mon–Sat 8pm–midnight, Sun 6pm–midnight.

Le Baiser Salé 58 rue des Lombards, 1ᵉʳ ☎01 42 33 37 71, ⓦlebaisersale.com; ⓜChâtelet; map p.85. The "salty kiss" is a small, crowded upstairs room with live music every night from 10pm – usually jazz, *chanson*, rhythm & blues, fusion, reggae or Brazilian. There are free jam sessions on Mondays, and the downstairs bar is great for just chilling out. Admission €13–20. Daily 5pm–6am, with most sets starting at 9.30pm.

Caveau de la Huchette 5 rue de la Huchette, 5ᵉ ☎01 43 26 65 05, ⓦcaveaudelahuchette.fr; ⓜSt-Michel; map p.120. A wonderful slice of old Parisian life in an otherwise touristy area. There's live jazz, usually trad and big band, to dance to on a floor surrounded by tiers of benches, and a bar decorated with caricatures of the barman drawn on any material to hand. Sun–Thurs €12, Fri & Sat €14; drinks from €6. Sun–Wed 9.30pm–2.30am, Thurs–Sat 9.30pm–dawn.

Au Duc des Lombards 42 rue des Lombards, 1ᵉʳ ☎01 42 33 22 88, ⓦducdeslombards.com; ⓜChâtelet/ Les-Halles; map p.85. Modern, stylish club with performances every night from 9pm. This is the place to hear jazz piano, blues, ballads and fusion, often played by big names. Most gigs €25 or €30. Daily until 3am, with a free jam session at midnight on Fri & Sat.

Instants Chavirés 7 rue Richard-Lenoir, Montreuil ☎01 42 87 25 91, ⓦinstantschavires.com; ⓜRobespierre. Avant-garde jazz joint close to the Porte de Montreuil. A place where musicians go to hear each other play, its reputation has attracted subsidies from both state and local authorities. Admission €12. Tues–Sat 8.30pm–1am; concerts at 9pm.

Jazz Club Lionel Hampton *Hôtel Méridien Etoile*, 81 bd Gouvion-St-Cyr, 17ᵉ ☎01 40 68 30 42, ⓦjazzclub-paris .com; ⓜPorte-Maillot. Inaugurated by Himself, this is a first-rate jazz venue, with big-name musicians. No entry fee but first drink from €27, refills €16. Mon–Sat 7pm–2am, with concerts at 10pm.

New Morning 7–9 rue des Petites-Ecuries, 10ᵉ ☎01 45 23 51 41, ⓦnewmorning.com; ⓜChâteau-d'Eau; map p.191. Housed in a former printing press, this is the place where the big international names come to play, and it attracts true aficionados. Often standing room only. Blues and world music, too. Admission around €22. Usually Mon–Sun 8pm–1.30am (concerts start at 9pm).

Le Sunset/Le Sunside 60 rue des Lombards, 1ᵉʳ ☎01 40 26 46 20, ⓦsunset-sunside.com; ⓜChâtelet-Les-Halles; map p.85. Two clubs in one: *Le Sunside* on the ground floor features mostly traditional jazz, whereas the downstairs *Sunset* is a venue for electric and fusion jazz. The *Sunside* concert usually starts at 8.30 or 9pm and the *Sunset* at 10pm. Attracts the likes of pianist Alain Jean-Marie and saxophonist Turk Mauro. Admission €12–30. Daily 8pm–2.30am.

MAINLY *CHANSON*

Casino de Paris 16 rue de Clichy, 9ᵉ ☎01 49 95 99 99, ⓦcasinodeparis.fr; ⓜTrinité; map p.180. This decaying, once-plush casino in one of the seediest streets in Paris is a venue for all sorts of performances – from *chanson* to cabaret to poetry combined with flamenco guitar. Check the listings magazines under "Variétés" and "Chanson". Tickets from €30. Most performances start at 8.30pm.

Au Lapin Agile 22 rue des Saules, 18ᵉ ☎01 46 06 85 87, ⓦau-lapin-agile.com; ⓜLamarck-Caulaincourt; map p.180. This historic old haunt of Apollinaire, Utrillo and other Montmartre artists – the "nimble rabbit" – has been reinvented as a *chanson* club. Visitors sit packed in on the benches round the walls of the ancient back room, listening to some cabaret and poetry but mostly *chanson*. €24 including one drink, students €17 (except Sat). Tues–Sun 9pm–2am.

Au Limonaire 18 Cité Bergère, 9ᵉ ☎01 45 23 33 33, ⓦlimonaire.free.fr; ⓜGrands-Boulevards; map p.72. Tiny backstreet venue, perfect for Parisian *chanson* nights, showcasing young singers and zany music/poetry performances. Dinner at 8pm guarantees a seat for the show at 10pm; otherwise you'll be crammed up against the bar, if you can get in at all. Tues–Sat 6pm–2am, Sun till 7pm.

La Magique 42 rue de Gergovie, 14ᵉ ☎01 45 42 26 10, ⓦaumagique.com; ⓜPernety; map p.160. A bar and "*chanson* cellar" with traditional French *chanson* performances by lesser-known acts during the week. At weekends the owner takes to the piano. Admission around €5, and drinks are reasonably priced. Wed–Sat 8pm–2am; concerts usually at 9pm or 10pm.

Les Trois Baudets 64 bd de Clichy, 18ᵉ ☎01 42 62 33 33, ⓦlestroisbaudets.com; ⓜBlanche/Pigalle; map p.180. This historic theatre was refitted in 2009 as a venue dedicated to the art of *chanson*, and has found a proud place on the Pigalle nightlife scene. It specializes in developing young, upcoming French musicians, so concerts are something of a lucky dip, but admission is often free or relatively inexpensive at €12–15. The venue is intimate (250 seats), and there are often *after* events with DJs at the lively bar/restaurant. Tues–Sat from 6.30pm.

CINEMATHEQUE

Film, theatre and dance

Cinema-lovers in Paris have a choice of around three hundred films showing in any one week, taking in contemporary French movies, classics from all eras and international offerings. The city also has a vibrant theatre and dance scene, with highly innovative, cutting-edge domestic productions jostling with the best shows touring or transferring from across Europe. The famous cabarets, unfortunately – places such as the Lido and Moulin Rouge (see box, p.188) – thrive off group bookings for an expensive dinner-and-show formula, and retain none of the bawdy atmosphere depicted in Toulouse-Lautrec's sketches or Baz Luhrmann's film. Listings for all films and stage productions are detailed in *Pariscope* (see p.38) and other weeklies, with brief résumés or reviews. Venues with wheelchair access will say "accessible aux handicapés".

21

FILM

Paris remains one of the few cities in the world in which you can expect not only serious entertainment but a serious film education from the programmes of regular – never mind specialist – cinemas. Independent movie houses, especially in the Quartier Latin, continue to resist the popcorn-touting clout of the big chains, UGC and Gaumont, by screening classic and contemporary films. If your French is up to it, you can watch your way through the entire careers of individual directors in the **mini-festivals** held at many independents, notably the Action chain, the Escurial, the Entrepôt and Le Studio 28. Even if you have no French at all, it's easy to find **v.o.** (*version originale*) films, both modern and classic. The unappealing alternative is **v.f.** (*version française*) – which means the film has been dubbed into French. It's mostly used for blockbusters, and you'll find these films mostly in the mega-cinemas around Montparnasse station, the Grands Boulevards and Champs-Elysées.

PROGRAMMES AND TICKETS

Séances (**programmes**) start between 1 and 3pm at many places, sometimes as early as 9am, and usually continue through to the early hours. **Tickets** rarely need to be purchased in advance, and they're cheap by European standards. Prices are mostly around €9, with the lowest prices at the smaller, independent cinemas. Almost all venues have reductions for students and the unemployed, at least from Monday to Thursday, while some matinée *séances* also carry discounts. For long-termers, UGC, MK2 and Gaumont sell various booklets of tickets and subscriptions, and some independents offer a *carte de fidélité*, or loyalty card. All Paris's cinemas are non-smoking.

CINEMATHEQUES AND CULTURAL INSTITUTIONS

Cultural institutions and embassies often have their own cinema programmes and screenings: the **Pompidou Centre**, place Georges-Pompidou, 4ᵉ (ⓜRambuteau; ☎01 44 78 12 33, ⓦcentrepompidou.fr), runs particularly good programmes. In addition, some of the city's **foreign institutes** host occasional screenings, so if your favourite director is a Hungarian, a Swede or a Korean, check what's on at those countries' cultural centres. These are listed in *Pariscope* along with other cinema clubs and museum screenings under *"Séances exceptionnelles"*, and are usually cheaper than ordinary cinemas.

Cinémathèque Française 51 rue de Bercy, 12ᵉ ☎01 71 19 33 33, ⓦcinematheque.fr; ⓜBercy. For the seriously committed film-freak, this is the best movie venue in Paris. Along with a dedicated museum of cinema (see p.114), you

get a choice of around two dozen different films and shorts every week, many of which would never be shown commercially – and it's all packaged in an incredible building designed by Frank Gehry. Tickets for films are only €6.50.

Forum des Images 2 rue du Cinéma, Porte St-Eustache, Forum des Halles; ☎01 44 76 63 00, ⓦforumdesimages .fr; ⓜChâtelet-Les Halles. This refitted hall puts on some fine festivals (including the Gay and Lesbian Film Festival) and director-led talks and sessions, and shows several films (or projected videos) daily on its five screens (€5). Its really unique feature, however, is the Salle des Collections: either individual terminals with digital access to the (huge) archive, or private, rentable screens for up to seven people (Tues–Fri 1–10pm, Sat & Sun 2–10pm; €5 per person, per 2hr session).

CINEMAS

★ **L'Arlequin** 76 rue de Rennes, 6ᵉ ☎01 45 44 28 80, ⓦlesecransdeparis.fr; ⓜSt-Sulpice. Owned by Jacques Tati in the 1950s, then by the Soviet Union as the Cosmos cinema until 1990, L'Arlequin has now been renovated and is once again *the* cinephile's palace in the Latin Quarter. There are special screenings of classics every Sun at 11am, followed by debates in the café opposite.

Le Champo 51 rue des Ecoles, 5ᵉ ☎01 43 54 51 60, ⓦlechampo.com; ⓜCluny-La-Sorbonne/Odéon. Scruffy little cinema at the foot of rue Champollion. Runs themed *v.o.* programmes over a week or more, featuring Stanley Kubrick, perhaps, or Jacques Tati.

★ **L'Entrepôt** 7–9 rue Francis-de-Pressensé, 14ᵉ ☎01 45 40 07 50, ⓦlentrepot.fr; ⓜPernety. One of the best alternative Paris cinemas, which has been keeping

NEW FILM PROJECTS

New cinemas and film foundations are springing up all over Paris. The **Fondation Jérôme Seydoux-Pathé** is scheduled to open in 2014, after a Renzo Piano-directed renovation of the old Cinéma Rodin – whose facade was sculpted by Rodin, no less – at 73 av des Gobelins, 13ᵉ (ⓦfondation-jeromeseydoux-pathe.com); it'll be primarily a research centre for scholars and students, but there are plans for a small screen too. At the time of writing, a multi-screen, architecturally high-concept art-house cinema, **Cinélilas**, is nearing completion on the edge of the 20ᵉ, by the Porte des Lilas. The industry, meanwhile, is celebrating work having started on the **Cité Européene du Cinéma**, a huge new studio complex in the Pleyel quarter of the suburb of St-Denis.

cine-addicts happy for years with its three screens dedicated to the obscure, the subversive and the brilliant, as well as its bookshop and bar/restaurant (see p.285).

L'Escurial Panorama 11 bd de Port-Royal, 13ᵉ 🕿 01 47 07 28 04, 🌐 lesecransdeparis.fr; Ⓜ Gobelins. Combining plush seats, a big screen, and more art than commerce in its programming policy, this cinema is likely to be showing a French classic on the small screen and the latest offering from a big-name director – French, Japanese or American – on the panoramic screen (never dubbed).

Grand Action 5 rue des Ecoles, 5ᵉ 🕿 01 43 54 47 62, 🌐 legrandaction.com; Action Ecoles, 23 rue des Ecoles, 5ᵉ 🕿 01 43 25 72 07, 🌐 actioncinemas.com (both Ⓜ Cardinal-Lemoine/Maubert-Mutualité); Action Christine Odéon, 4 rue Christine, 6ᵉ 🕿 01 43 25 85 78; Ⓜ Odéon/St-Michel. The Action group specializes in new prints of old classics and screens contemporary films from around the world. A *carnet* of ten tickets costs €45.

Le Grand Rex 1 bd Poissonnière, 2ᵉ 🕿 08 92 68 05 96, 🌐 legrandrex.com; Ⓜ Bonne-Nouvelle. The ultimate 1930s public movie-watching experience, though more often than not, the programme features blockbusters – dubbed, if the film is foreign. The Big Rex has an Art Deco facade, a ceiling of glowing stars and a kitsch, Hollywood-meets-Baroque cityscape inside its 2750-seater, three-storey Grande Salle.

Le Louxor 170 bd de Magenta, 10ᵉ 🌐 paris-louxor.fr; Ⓜ Barbès-Rochechouart. This legendary 1920s cinema became a massive gay disco in the 1980s, but is currently being renovated, and should be open for business – with its splendid ancient Egyptian decor renewed – in 2013.

Lucernaire 53 rue Notre-Dame-des-Champs, 6ᵉ 🕿 01 42 22 26 50, 🌐 lucernaire.fr; Ⓜ Notre-Dame-des-Champs/ Vavin. An art complex with three screening rooms, two theatres, an art gallery, bar and restaurant. Shows old arty movies and undubbed current films from around the world.

Max Linder Panorama 24 bd Poissonnière, 9ᵉ 🕿 08 92 68 50 52, 🌐 maxlinder.com; Ⓜ Bonne-Nouvelle. Opposite Le Grand Rex, and with almost as big a screen (though a mere 560 seats), this Art Deco cinema always shows films in the original language and has state-of-the-art sound.

MK2 Bibliothèque 128–162 av de France, 13ᵉ 🕿 08 92 69 84 84, 🌐 mk2.com; Ⓜ Bibliothèque/Quai de la Gare. Brand new, and right behind the Bibliothèque Nationale, this is an architecturally cutting-edge cinema with a very cool café and fourteen screens showing a varied range of French films – mostly new, some classic – and *v.o.* foreign movies.

MK2 Quai de la Seine 14 quai de la Seine, 19ᵉ 🕿 08 92 69 84 84, 🌐 mk2.com; Ⓜ Jaurès/Stalingrad. On the banks of the Bassin de la Villette. Part of the MK2 chain but distinctive in style – it's covered in famous cinematic quotes and has a varied, art-house repertoire.

Le Nouveau Latina 20 rue du Temple, 4ᵉ 🕿 01 42 78 47 86, 🌐 lenouveaulatina.com; Ⓜ Hôtel-de-Ville. Specializes in Latin American, Portuguese, Italian and Spanish films, usually in *v.o.*, and has a restaurant and art gallery, with music and dance events.

Le Nouvel Odéon 6 rue de l'Ecole de Médecine, 6ᵉ 🕿 01 45 55 48 48, 🌐 nouvelodeon.com; Ⓜ Odéon/Cluny-La Sorbonne. The renovated Racine Odéon is now an elegant minimalist treat, with (bright orange, and numbered) seats bookable online, and an enticing programme.

⭐ **La Pagode** 57bis rue de Babylone, 7ᵉ 🕿 01 45 55 48 48; Ⓜ François-Xavier. The most beautiful of the city's cinemas, built in Japanese style at the turn of the last

---

FILM FESTIVALS

The **International Festival of Women's Films**, held around late March to early April, is organized by the Maison des Arts in Créteil, on place Salvador Allende (🕿 01 49 80 38 98, 🌐 filmsdefemmes.com; Ⓜ Créteil-Préfecture). At around the same time of year, Magic Cinéma (rue du Chemin-Vert, 93000 Bobigny; 🌐 magic-cinema.fr) runs the festival **Théâtres au Cinéma**, which takes place in the suburb of Bobigny, to the northeast of the city; it concentrates on the links between literature and cinema. In early July, twenty independent cinemas across the city give themselves over for a fortnight to the **Festival Paris Cinéma** (🌐 pariscinema.org), featuring previews of the year to come and celebrations of individual countries' and directors' work.

During the summer, the Parc de la Villette (Ⓜ Porte-de-Pantin) organizes the **Festival du Cinéma en Plein Air** (🕿 01 40 03 75 75, 🌐 villette.com, or see the unofficial fansite, 🌐 cinema .arbo.com). Films are shown most nights (usually Tues–Sun from mid-July to late August at around 10pm, unless it's raining). Entry is free, but you have to pay €7 if you want to hire a deck chair; most people just bring a bottle and blanket and hang out until the sun goes down. There's a great communal feeling as everyone falls quiet and turns to face the big screen at the same time. On weekends throughout August, the lovely **Cinéma au Clair de Lune festival** (🌐 forumdesimages.fr) shows films on a set theme – 2009's was the films of Claude Berri, 2010's was films with a Parisian backdrop – screened in various one-off locations in parks and squares, and projected onto the sides of buildings, mostly; films start at 9.30pm, as long as it's not raining, and entry is free. During the week-long **Printemps du Cinéma** (🌐 printempsducinema.com), usually in late March, cinema tickets are sold at a flat rate of €3.50, across the city.

PARIS ON FILM

Parisians have treated **cinema** as their own private art form ever since the first projection by the **Lumière** brothers'"Cinematograph" at the Parisian *Grand Café du Boulevard des Capucines* in 1895. The 1930s were the golden age of French cinema, as stars of musicals and theatres invaded the cinemas, many of them on liberally censored film vehicles that helped create the French reputation for naughtiness. Meanwhile, more artistically minded *auteurs* were scripting, directing and producing moody, often melodramatic films. The key figure was **Jean Renoir**, son of the Impressionist painter Auguste Renoir. For Parisian scenes, check out his left-wing *Le Crime de Monsieur Lange* (1935), set in a print shop in the then-crumbling Marais. The movement known as Poetic Realism grew up around Renoir and the director Marcel Carné, who made the Canal St-Martin area of Paris famous in *Hôtel du Nord* (1938), a film that starred Arletty, a great populist actress of the 1930s and 40s. Arletty and Poetic Realism reached their apogee in Carné's wonderful *Les Enfants du Paradis* (1945), set in the theatrical world of nineteenth-century Paris, with a script by the poet Jacques Prévert.

Post war, Renoir continued to make great films: his *French CanCan* (1955) is *the* film about the *Moulin Rouge* and the heyday of Montmartre. Like the vast majority of prewar films, however, even those with Parisian backdrops, it was all shot in the studio. An exception to this was Claude Autant-Lara's wartime comedy *La Traversée de Paris* (1956), which follows Jean Gabin smuggling black-market goods across the city. From 1959, however, the directors of the **Nouvelle Vague** ("New Wave") took their new, lightweight cameras out onto the streets, abandoning the big studio set-pieces in favour of a fluid, métro-savvy style. Among the seminal works of the movement, **Les Quatre Cents Coups** (1959), by François Truffaut, and **A Bout de Souffle** (1959), by Jean-Luc Godard, both have contemporary Paris as their real star. But perhaps the strongest collaborations between the city and the directors of the Nouvelle Vague are *Paris Vu Par* (*Six in Paris*; 1965), a collection of six shorts by the key figures of the genre; and the quirky *Zazie dans le Métro* (1961), which is only outdone for its Parisian locations by Agnès Varda's *Cléo de 5 à 7* (1962), which depicts two hours in the life of a singer as she moves through the city – mainly around Montparnasse.

Following the success of Claude Berri's *Jean de Florette* (1986), French films concentrated on glossy "heritage" movies. Few did Paris any favours, although there were a couple of notable exceptions: Jean-Pierre Jeunet's *Un long dimanche de fiançailles* (2004) re-created the city – including the market pavilions of Les Halles – during World War I, while Bernardo Bertolucci's *Innocents*, or *The Dreamers* (2003), was set in the radical Paris of 1968. In

complete contrast, the **Cinéma du Look** movement captured a cool, image-conscious version of Paris in films like Léos Carax's *Les Amants du Pont-Neuf* (1991), though its bridge was actually a set in the south of France; Jean-Jacques Beinelx's *Diva* (1981), which takes in the Bouffes du Nord theatre (18ᵉ); Luc Besson's *Nikita* (1990), with its classic scene in the railway restaurant *Le Train Bleu* (12ᵉ), and Besson's *Subway* (1985), filmed largely in the Auber métro station (15ᵉ).

As the early energy of the Cinéma du Look petered out in the 1990s, Paris was again depicted in a more meditative and less frenetic style. Krzysztof Kieslowski's *Three Colours: Blue* (1993) featured Juliette Binoche as the perfect melancholy Parisian – and had her swimming in the Pontoise swimming pool (5ᵉ). The premise of Cédric Klapisch's *Chacun cherche son chat* (1995) – *When the cat's away* – was the perfect excuse for a classic exploration of the Bastille quarter in the full, mid-1990s swing of restoration. Far edgier is Mathieu Kassovitz's **La Haine** (1996), an original portrayal of exclusion and racism in the Paris métro and *banlieue*. Kassovitz also had big international hits as an actor in the Jeunet-directed film *Amélie* (2001) – which relaunched Montmartre, especially the area around Abbesses métro, as an international tourist destination – and in Gaspar Noé's utterly shocking *Irréversible* (2002), which follows two bourgeois-bohemian Parisians as they are drawn into a nightmare underworld. Two recent films are virtual love-letters to the city. Cédric Klapisch's *Paris* (2008) is a touching ensemble-piece seen largely from Romain Duris's Montmartre balcony window and *Paris je t'aime* (2006) is a fine series of twenty interlinked shorts focusing on different kinds of love; each is shot by a different director, and each linked thematically to a different *quartier* of the city.

For **American films** with classic Paris locations, look no further than: Vincente Minnelli's musical *An American in Paris* (1951), featuring Gene Kelly and Leslie Caron dancing on the *quais* of the Seine – a scene hilariously taken off in Woody Allen's *Everyone Says I Love You* (1996); Billy Wilder's *Love in the Afternoon* (1957); Stanley Donen's musical *Funny Face* (1957) and his comic thriller *Charade* (1963), featuring Cary Grant and Audrey Hepburn; Roman Polanski's nightmarish *Frantic* (1988); Richard Linklater's utterly romantic *Before Sunrise* (1995) and its sequel, *Before Sunset* (2004), both featuring Ethan Hawke and Julie Delpy as transatlantic lovers living out a one-night Parisian fantasy; and Doug Liman's upmarket thriller, *The Bourne Identity* (2002).

For more **information on cinema** in France, the English-language website ⓦ filmsdefrance .com has excellent listings of French films, searchable by year or by name, as well as directors' and actors' biographies. The best Parisian source of information on films is the Les Halles **Forum des Images** (see p.00).

21

century to be a rich Parisienne's party place, and recently restored. The wall panels of the Salle Japonaise auditorium are embroidered in silk, golden dragons and elephants hold up the candelabra, and a battle between warriors rages on the ceiling. Shows a mix of art films and documentaries, as well as commercial movies in *v.o.*

★ **Reflet Medicis** 3, 5, 7 & 9 rue Champollion, 5e ☎01 43 54 42 34, ⓦlesecransdeparis.fr; ⓂCluny-La-Sorbonne/Odéon. A cluster of inventive little cinemas, tirelessly offering up rare screenings and classics, including frequent retrospective cycles covering great directors, both French and international (always in *v.o.*). The small cinema café *Le Reflet*, on the other side of the street, is a little-known cult classic in itself.

Le Studio 28 10 rue de Tholozé, 18e ☎01 46 06 36 07, ⓦcinemastudio28.com; ⓂBlanche/Abbesses. In its early days, after one of the first showings of Buñuel's *L'Age d'Or*, this was done over by extreme right-wing Catholics who destroyed the screen and the paintings by Dalí and Ernst in the foyer. The cinema still hosts avant-garde premieres, followed occasionally by discussions with the director, as well as regular festivals.

Le Studio des Ursulines 10 rue des Ursulines, 5e ☎01 56 81 15 20, ⓦstudiodesursulines.com; RER Luxembourg. Screens and sometimes premieres avant-garde movies, art films and documentaries, often followed by in-house debates with the directors and actors.

THEATRE

Looking at the scores of métro posters advertising theatre in Paris, you might think bourgeois farces starring gurning celebrities you've never heard of form the backbone of French theatre. To an extent, that's true, though the classics – Molière, Corneille and Racine – are also staple fare, and well worth a try if your French is up to it. You can get by with quite basic French at one of the performances of plays by the postwar generation of Francophone dramatists, such as Anouilh, Genet, Camus, Ionesco and Samuel Beckett. For non-French-speakers, the most rewarding theatre in Paris is likely to be the genre-busting, avant-garde, highly styled and radical kind best represented by director **Patrice Chéreau** and **Ariane Mnouchkine** and her **Théâtre du Soleil**, based at the Cartoucherie in Vincennes.

The best time of all for theatre-lovers to come to Paris is for the **Festival d'Automne** from mid-September to mid-December (see p.320), an international celebration of all the performing arts, which attracts stage directors of the calibre of the American Robert Wilson and Canadian Robert Lepage.

BUYING TICKETS

Booking well in advance is essential for new productions and all shows by the superstar directors. **Prices** are mostly in the range of €20–40; inexpensive previews are advertised in *Pariscope*, etc, and there are weekday discounts at some places for students. Most theatres are closed on Sunday and Monday, and during August.

The easiest place to get **tickets** to see a stage performance

in Paris is from one of the Fnac shops (see p.330) or Virgin Megastore (see p.331). If you buy online at ⓦfnac.com or ⓦvirginmega.fr you can pick up tickets from a branch or get them sent; Fnac also lets you print them out at home. At ⓦtheatreonline.com you're given a reference number which you present to the box office half an hour before the performance to claim your tickets. Same-day tickets with a fifty-percent discount and a small commission are available

---

CAFÉ-THEATRE

Although literally a revue, monologue or mini-play performed in a place where you can drink, and sometimes eat, **café-théâtre** is probably less accessible than a Racine tragedy at the Comédie Française – the humour or dirty jokes, wordplay, and allusions to current fads, phobias and politicians can leave even a fluent French-speaker in the dark, but to give it a try, head for one of the main venues concentrated around the Marais. The spaces are small, though you have a good chance of getting in on the night during the week, and tickets are likely to be cheaper than at standard theatres.

Blancs-Manteaux 15 rue des Blancs-Manteaux, 4e ☎01 48 87 15 84, ⓦblancsmanteaux.fr; ⓂHôtel-de-Ville/Rambuteau. The programme includes revues, plays, stand-up comedy and *chanson* evenings. As well as hosting established names, it encourages new talent and has been the launch pad for a number of French stars.

Café de la Gare 41 rue du Temple, 4e ☎01 42 78 52 51, ⓦcdlg.org; ⓂHôtel-de-Ville/Rambuteau. This place retains a reputation for novelty and specializes in stand-up comedy and comic plays.

Point Virgule 7 rue Ste-Croix-de-la-Bretonnerie, 4e ☎01 42 78 67 03, ⓦlepointvirgule.com; ⓂHôtel-de-Ville/St-Paul. With a policy for giving unknown performers a go, this is a place where you can sometimes strike lucky, sometimes not.

from the **half-price ticket kiosks** (ⓦkiosquetheatre
.com) on place de la Madeleine, 8ᵉ, opposite no. 15, and on
the Esplanade de la Gare du Montparnasse, 14ᵉ (Tues–Sat
12.30–8pm, Sun 12.30–4pm), but queues can be long and
the tickets are likely to be for the more commercial plays.

VENUES

★ **Bouffes du Nord** 37bis bd de la Chapelle, 10ᵉ
☎01 46 07 34 50, ⓦbouffesdunord.com; Ⓜ La Chapelle.
Ground-breaking theatre director Peter Brook resurrected
the derelict Bouffes du Nord in 1974 and was based here
until 2011, mounting experimental works, most famously
his nine-hour *Mahabharata* in 1985. The theatre's two new
young French directors, Olivier Mantel and Olivier Poubelle,
are likely to continue Brook's innovative approach. The
theatre also hosts top-notch chamber music recitals.

★ **Cartoucherie** Route du Champ-de-Manœuvre,
12ᵉ; Ⓜ Château-de-Vincennes. This ex-army munitions
dump is home to several cutting-edge theatre companies:
the Théâtre du Soleil (see opposite; ☎01 43 74 24 08,
ⓦtheatre-du-soleil.fr); the French–Spanish troupe,
Théâtre de l'Epée de Bois (☎01 43 08 39 74, ⓦepeedebois
.com); the Théâtre de la Tempête (☎01 43 28 36 36,
ⓦla-tempete.fr); the Théâtre du Chaudron (☎01 43 28 97
04); and the Théâtre de l'Aquarium (☎01 43 74 99 61,
ⓦtheatredelaquarium.com).

Comédie Française 2 rue de Richelieu, 1ᵉʳ ☎01 44 58 15
15, ⓦcomedie-francaise.fr; Ⓜ Palais-Royal. This venerable
national theatre is *the* venue for the French classics: chiefly
tragedies and comedies by Molière, Racine and Corneille, but
also twentieth-century greats. There are three theatres: the
Théâtre du Vieux-Colombier, 21 rue du Vieux-Colombier, 6ᵉ;
the mini Studio-Théâtre, under the Louvre, accessed via the
Carrousel; and the headquarters, next to the Palais Royal – the
Salle Richelieu or "Maison de Molière", as it's dubbed.

Maison des Arts de Créteil Place Salvador-Allende,
Créteil ☎01 45 13 19 19, ⓦmaccreteil.com; Ⓜ Créteil-
Préfecture. As well as hosting the International Festival of
Women's Films (see box, p.309), the Maison des Arts de
Créteil also serves as a lively suburban theatre, with a
festival in February/March of multicultural and cutting-
edge performances, known as Festival Exit.

MC93 1 bd Lénine, Bobigny ☎01 41 60 72 60, ⓦmc93
.com; Ⓜ Pablo-Picasso. MC93 succeeds with highly
challenging productions, and regularly invites foreign
directors.

★ **Odéon Théâtre de l'Europe** 1 place Paul-Claudel,
6ᵉ ☎01 44 85 40 40, ⓦtheatre-odeon.fr; Ⓜ Odéon. This
Neoclassical state-funded theatre puts on contemporary
plays by top directors such as Robert Wilson, as well as
version originale productions by well-known foreign
companies. During May 1968, the theatre was occupied by
students and became an open parliament with the backing
of its directors, Jean-Louis Barrault (of Baptiste fame in *Les*

Enfants du Paradis) and Madeleine Renaud, one of the
great French stage actresses. Since then it has been
splendidly restored.

Le Tarmac Parc de la Villette, 211 av Jean-Jaurès, 19ᵉ
☎01 40 03 93 90, ⓦletarmac.fr; Ⓜ Porte de Pantin. Set
in an old dining hall once used by the cattle market traders
of La Villette, this small theatre houses the Théâtre
International de la Langue Française and specializes in
works from French-speaking parts of the world such as
Tahiti and Togo.

Théâtre des Amandiers 7 av Pablo-Picasso, Nanterre
☎01 46 14 70 00, ⓦnanterre-amandiers.com; RER
Nanterre-Préfecture and theatre shuttle bus. Renowned
for innovative and avant-garde productions, such as a six-
hour adaptation of Dostoevsky's *Possessed*.

Théâtre des Artistic-Athévains 45bis rue Richard-
Lenoir, 11ᵉ ☎01 43 56 38 32, ⓦartistic-athevains.com;
Ⓜ Voltaire. Small company heavily involved in community
and educational theatre.

Théâtre de la Bastille 76 rue de la Roquette, 11ᵉ
☎01 43 57 42 14, ⓦtheatre-bastille.com; Ⓜ Bastille.
One of the best places for new work and fringe productions.

Théâtre du Châtelet Place du Châtelet, 4ᵉ ☎01 40 28
28 40, ⓦchatelet-theatre.com; Ⓜ Châtelet. The vogue
for musicals is growing in Paris, and the Théâtre du Châtelet
is the best place to see them. It brings over Broadway and
West End hits, such as *Sweeney Todd*, performed in 2011 to
much acclaim.

Théâtre de l'Est Parisien 159 av Gambetta, 20ᵉ
☎01 43 64 80 80, ⓦtheatre-estparisien.net;
Ⓜ St-Fargeau. Well respected for its experimental work.

Théâtre de la Huchette 23 rue de la Huchette, 5ᵉ
☎01 43 26 38 99, ⓦtheatre-huchette.com;
Ⓜ St-Michel. Almost sixty years on, this intimate little
theatre, seating ninety, is still showing Ionesco's *La
Cantatrice Chauve* (*The Bald Prima Donna*; 7pm) and *La
Leçon* (8pm), two classics of the Theatre of the Absurd.

Théâtre National de Chaillot Palais de Chaillot, place
du Trocadéro, 16ᵉ ☎01 53 65 30 00, ⓦtheatre-chaillot
.fr; Ⓜ Trocadéro. Puts on an exciting programme and often
hosts foreign productions; Deborah Warner and Robert
Lepage are regular visitors.

Théâtre National de la Colline 15 rue Malte-Brun,
20ᵉ ☎01 44 62 52 52, ⓦcolline.fr; Ⓜ Gambetta. Known
for its modern and cutting-edge productions.

Théâtre de l'Opprimé 78 rue du Charolais, 12ᵉ
☎01 43 45 81 20, ⓦtheatredelopprime.com;
Ⓜ Reuilly-Diderot. This small theatre puts on mostly
contemporary plays, and is inspired by the ideas of
Brazilian director Augusto Boal.

Théâtre Paris-Villette Parc de la Villette, 211 av Jean-
Jaurès, 19ᵉ ☎01 40 03 72 23, ⓦtheatre-paris-villette
.com; Ⓜ Porte de Pantin. Showcases contemporary work
by young, up-and-coming playwrights.

21

21

DANCE FESTIVALS

Major festivals combining theatre, dance, mime, classical music and its descendants include the **Festival Exit** in February/March in Créteil (📞maccreteil.com); **Les Etés de la Danse** in July (📞01 40 28 28 40, 🌐lesetesdeladanse.com) at the Théâtre du Châtelet; **Paris Quartier d'Eté** from mid-July to mid-August (📞01 44 94 98 00, 🌐quartierdete.com); the **Festival Agora** at the Pompidou Centre's IRCAM in June (🌐ircam.fr); and the **Festival d'Automne** from mid-September to mid-December (📞01 53 45 17 00, 🌐festival-automne.com).

DANCE

The status of **dance** in Paris received a major boost with the inauguration in 2004 of the **Centre National de la Danse**, a long-overdue recognition of the importance of the art form in a nation that boasts six hundred companies. While Paris has few home-grown companies, it regularly hosts the best contemporary practitioners. As well as international names like Merce Cunningham, **notable companies** worth looking out for are Compagnie Maguy Marin and troupes from Régine Chopinot, Jean-Claude Gallotta, Catherine Diverrès and Angelin Preljocaj.

As for **ballet**, the principal stage is at the restored Opéra Garnier, home to the Ballet de l'Opéra National de Paris, directed by Brigitte Lefèvre. It still bears the influence of Rudolf Nureyev, its charismatic, controversial director from 1983 to 1989, and frequently revives his productions. Plenty of space and critical attention are also given to **tap**, **tango**, **folk** and **jazz dancing**, and to international traditional dance troupes. There are also a dozen or so black African companies in Paris and the fashionable Japanese butoh, as well as several Indian dance troupes, the Ballet Classique Khmer, and many more.

VENUES

Centre Mandapa 6 rue Wurtz, 13e 📞01 45 89 01 60, 🌐centre-mandapa.fr; Ⓜ️Glacière. Mainly hosts (and gives lessons in) classical Indian dance, but also showcases other Asian music and dance traditions.

⭐ **Centre National de la Danse** 1 rue Victor Hugo, Pantin 📞01 41 83 27 27, 🌐cnd.fr; Ⓜ️ Hoche/RER Pantin. Converted from a disused 1970s monolith in the suburb of Pantin into an airy, high-tech space, the national centre for dance is devoted mainly to promoting dance through training, workshops and exhibitions. Also stages performances and masterclasses, and has a huge archive and multimedia library.

Maison des Arts de Créteil Place Salvador-Allende, Créteil 📞01 45 13 19 19, 🌐maccreteil.com; Ⓜ️Créteil-Préfecture. Home base of the innovative Compagnie Montalvo-Hervieu, founded in 1988 by José Montalvo, and Dominique Hervieu; their entertaining shows combine every genre going – hip-hop, ballet, break-dancing – against a backdrop of video images and accompanied by a soundtrack of music ranging from Vivaldi to Fat Boy Slim.

⭐ **Opéra de Paris Garnier** Place de l'Opéra, 9e 📞08 36 69 78 68, 🌐opera-de-paris.fr; Ⓜ️Opéra. This glittering, extravagantly decorated *palais* is the main home of the Ballet de l'Opéra National de Paris and the place to see ballet classics.

Pompidou Centre Entrance rue Beaubourg, 4e 📞01 44 78 16 25, 🌐centrepompidou.fr; Ⓜ️Rambuteau/RER Châtelet-Les-Halles. The Grande Salle in the basement is used for dance performances by visiting companies.

Regard du Cygne 210 rue de Belleville, 20e 📞01 43 58 55 93, 🌐leregarducygne.com; Ⓜ️Place-des-Fêtes. Innovative and exciting new work is performed here. One of the centre's best-known events is its series of "Sauvages", in which virtually anyone can perform for the public.

Théâtre des Abbesses 31 rue des Abbesses, 18e 📞01 42 74 22 77, 🌐theatredelaville-paris.com; Ⓜ️Abbesses. Sister company to the Théâtre de la Ville, with a more adventurous programme, including international dance.

Théâtre de la Bastille 76 rue de la Roquette, 11e 📞01 43 57 42 14, 🌐theatre-bastille.com; Ⓜ️Bastille. As well as more traditional dance, there are also dance and mime performances by young dancers and choreographers.

Théâtre des Champs-Elysées 15 av Montaigne, 8e 📞01 49 52 50 50, 🌐theatrechampselysees.fr; Ⓜ️Alma-Marceau. This prestigious venue occasionally hosts major foreign troupes and stars such as Sylvie Guillem.

Théâtre du Châtelet Place du Châtelet, 4e 📞01 40 28 28 40, 🌐chatelet-theatre.com; Ⓜ️Châtelet. Though mainly used for classical concerts and opera, it also hosts top-notch visiting ballet companies such as the Mariinsky, as well as more commercial contemporary dance acts.

Théâtre de la Cité Internationale 21 bd Jourdan, 14e 📞01 43 13 50 50, 🌐theatredelacite.com; RER Cité Universitaire. An exciting theatre and dance venue; hosts performances during the Festival d'Automne.

Théâtre National de Chaillot Palais de Chaillot, place du Trocadéro, 16e 📞01 53 65 30 00, 🌐theatre-chaillot.fr; Ⓜ️Trocadéro. Innovative and top-quality dance from France's leading choreographers, as well as regular slots by foreign superstars such as William Forsythe.

⭐ **Théâtre de la Ville** 2 place du Châtelet, 4e 📞01 42 74 22 77, 🌐theatredelaville-paris.com; Ⓜ️Châtelet. The biggest contemporary dance venue in the city, specializing in avant-garde productions by companies working with the top European choreographers, such as Anne Teresa De Keersmaeker.

OPERA GARNIER

Classical music and opera

Classical music, as you might expect in this Neoclassical city, is alive and well and will continue to flourish with the opening of a grand new concert hall in March 2014: Jean Nouvel's 2400-seat Philharmonie de Paris auditorium in La Villette (see ⓦphilharmoniedeparis.com) will have state-of-the-art acoustics, and will be home to the city's top orchestra, the Orchestre de Paris, under its director Paavo Järvi. The Paris Opéra, with its two homes, puts on a fine selection of opera and ballet, from core repertoire to new commissions, and there's an energetic contemporary music scene based at the Cité de la Musique at La Villette, and IRCAM, near the Pompidou Centre. The Fête de la Musique on June 21 is a day of music-making throughout the capital; orchestras play in the Palais Royal courtyard, buskers take to the streets and the big music venues stage free concerts.

22

ESSENTIALS

Tickets Ticket prices for classical concerts vary considerably, depending on the seat, venue and event; opera, ballet and celebrity performers attract considerably higher prices, while churches and museums tend to be relatively inexpensive. You might pay anything from €5 (for a recital in a small church, or a restricted-view seat in a big venue) to €150 for a stalls seat in a big-name opera, but most seats are in the €15–40 range. Tickets can almost always be bought online; for big names you may find overnight queues at the actual box office.

Festivals The city hosts a good number of music festivals, which vary from year to year (see pp.318–320). For more details, pick up the current year's festival schedule from any of the tourist offices or the Hôtel de Ville, 29 rue du Rivoli, 4ᵉ (ⓂHôtel-de-Ville).

Listings The quality monthly magazine *Diapason* is devoted to the music scene and can usually be picked up at concert venues, while listings can be found online at Ⓦconcertclassic.com.

CLASSICAL MUSIC

Besides the Orchestre de Paris, Paris's other main orchestra is the Orchestre National de France, under the baton of Daniele Gatti. **Early music** has a dedicated following in Paris. The capital's most respected Baroque ensemble is William Christie's Les Arts Florissants, renowned for their exciting renditions of Rameau's operas and choral works by Lully and Charpentier. The highly regarded Marc Minkowski, another champion of French Baroque music, also conducts regularly in the capital.

Contemporary and electronic work flourishes, too. Regular concerts are given at IRCAM, a vast laboratory of acoustics and "digital signal processing", funded by the state and headed for many years by renowned composer Pierre Boulez, a pupil of Olivier Messiaen, the grand old man of modern French music who died in 1992. Although Boulez no longer conducts IRCAM's acclaimed Ensemble Intercontemporain (Ⓦensembleinter.com), now based at the Cité de la Musique, it still bears its creator's stamp and is committed to performing new work.

CONCERT VENUES

The following venues and churches host regular concerts, but note that many other museums and churches put on occasional events too; *Pariscope* (see p.38) has details.

AUDITORIUMS AND THEATRES

Cité de la Musique 221 av Jean-Jaurès, 19ᵉ ☎01 44 84 44 84 for the Salle des Concerts, Ⓦcite-musique.fr; ⓂJaurès; map p.202. Adjustable concert hall with seating for 800–1200 listeners depending on the programme, which can cover anything from traditional Korean music to the contemporary sounds of the Ensemble Intercontemporain. Performances also in the museum amphitheatre with the occasional airing of instruments from the museum.

Conservatoire National Supérieur de Musique et de Danse de Paris 209 av Jean-Jaurès, 19ᵉ ☎01 40 40 46 46, Ⓦcnsmdp.fr; ⓂPorte-de-Pantin; map p.200. Debates, masterclasses and free performances from the conservatoire's students.

IRCAM (Institut de Recherche et Coordination Acoustique/Musique) 1 place Igor Stravinsky, 4ᵉ ☎01 44 78 48 43, Ⓦircam.fr; ⓂHôtel-de-Ville; map p.85. IRCAM, the experimental music laboratory set up by Pierre Boulez, hosts regular concerts on site and also in the main hall (Grande Salle) of the nearby Pompidou Centre and at the Théâtre des Bouffes du Nord.

Maison de Radio France 116 av du Président-Kennedy, 16ᵉ ☎01 56 40 15 16, Ⓦradio-france.fr; ⓂPassy; map p.213. Radio station France Musique programmes an excellent range of classical music,

operas, jazz and world music and sometimes puts on free concerts – just turn up half an hour in advance to claim your *carton d'invitation*.

Salle Gaveau 45 rue de la Boétie, 8ᵉ ☎01 49 53 05 07, Ⓦsallegaveau.com; ⓂSt-Augustin; map p.62. This atmospheric and intimate concert hall, built in 1907, is a major venue for piano recitals by world-class players, as well as chamber music recitals and full-scale orchestral works.

Salle Pleyel 252 rue du Faubourg-St-Honoré, 8ᵉ ☎01 42 56 13 13, Ⓦsallepleyel.fr; ⓂConcorde; map p.62. This distinguished concert hall, dating back to 1927, re opened in autumn 2006 after a highly acclaimed renovation; acoustics are much improved and the Art Deco reception hall has been restored to full splendour. The Orchestre de Paris (Ⓦorchestredeparis.com) currently performs here most frequently, along with visiting international performers such as Martha Argerich and Jessye Norman.

Théâtre des Champs-Elysées 15 av Montaigne, 8ᵉ ☎01 49 52 50 50, Ⓦtheatrechampselysees.fr; ⓂAlma-Marceau; map p.62. Two-thousand-seater historic Modernist theatre with sculptures by Bourdelle and paintings by Vuillard. Opened in 1913, it held the premiere of Stravinsky's *Rite of Spring,* whose modernity scandalized Paris. Now home to the Orchestre National de France and Orchestre Lamoureux, it also hosts international superstar conductors and ballet troupes, and has a vigorous operatic programme. Offers bargain tickets for seats with no view at all, but you can pay up to €150 or so for star performers.

Théâtre Musical de Paris Théâtre du Châtelet, 1 place du Châtelet, 1ᵉʳ ☎01 40 28 28 40, ⓦchatelet-theatre .com; ⓂChâtelet; map p.85. A prestigious concert hall with a varied programme of high-profile operas, ballets, concerts, musicals and solo recitals. Wide range of tickets from around €10.

CHURCHES AND MUSEUMS

Archives Nationales Hôtel de Soubise, 60 rue des Francs-Bourgeois, 3ᵉ ☎01 40 20 09 32; ⓂRambuteau; map p.96. Chamber music recitals every Sat, usually at 6pm. Tickets at €6 and €12.

Auditorium du Louvre Musée du Louvre (Pyramide entrance), 1ᵉʳ ☎01 40 20 55 00, ⓦlouvre.fr; ⓂLouvre-Rivoli/Palais-Royal-Musée-du-Louvre; map p.49. Midday and evening concerts of chamber music in the auditorium. Tickets from €6.

Eglise de la Madeleine Place de la Madeleine, 8ᵉ ☎01 42 50 96 18; ⓂMadeleine; map p.72. Organ recitals and choral concerts. Tickets from €20.

Musée Carnavalet 23 rue de Sévigné, 3ᵉ ☎01 40 53 89 15; ⓂSt-Paul; map p.96. Mainly chamber music from the

Baroque period, held in one of the museum's elegant salons. Tickets €15 and 20.

Musée National du Moyen Age 6 place Paul Painlevé, 5ᵉ ☎01 53 73 78 16, ⓦmusee-moyenage.fr; ⓂCluny-La-Sorbonne; map p.120. Regular evening concerts of little-known medieval music (tickets €16), as well as "L'heure musicale" – 45 minutes of medieval music on Sundays at 4pm and Mondays at 12.30pm (€6).

Musée d'Orsay 1 rue de Bellechasse, 7ᵉ ☎01 40 49 47 50, ⓦmusee-orsay.fr; ⓂSolférino/RER Musée d'Orsay; map p.134. Varied programme of midday and evening recitals of chamber music in the auditorium. Tickets €12–32.

St-Julien-le-Pauvre 23 quai de Montebello, 5ᵉ ☎01 42 26 00 00; ⓂSt-Michel; map p.120. Mostly chamber music and choral recitals. Tickets €15–23.

St-Séverin 5 rue des Prêtres St-Séverin, 5ᵉ ☎01 48 24 16 97; ⓂSt-Michel; map p.120. Varied programmes, with tickets from €15.

Sainte-Chapelle 4 bd du Palais, 1ᵉʳ ☎01 42 77 65 65; ⓂCité; map p.42. A fabulous setting for mainly Mozart, Bach and Vivaldi classics. €29–44.

22

OPERA

The Opéra National de Paris has two homes: the **Palais Garnier** and the newer **Opéra Bastille**. After a run of radical and challenging performances under Gérard Mortier, its new director, Nicolas Joel, has returned to a more conventional mainstream repertoire. **Tickets** (€5–180) for both venues can be booked online at ⓦopera-de-paris.fr or on ☎08 92 89 90 90; the more popular productions sell out within days of tickets becoming available – which happens online first. For last-minute tickets it's worth joining the queue early in the day at the venues themselves; unfilled seats are also sold at a discount to students five minutes before the curtain goes up.

Both opera and recitals, usually of the more glossy, popular kind, are occasionally staged at the city's major multi-purpose **performance venues**, especially the Palais des Congrès (programmes listed at ⓦviparis.com), but also the Olympia rock venue (ⓦolympiahall.com) and even the Stade de France stadium (ⓦstadefrance.fr); these large-scale events are usually well advertised throughout the city.

VENUES

Opéra Bastille 120 rue de Lyon, 12ᵉ ⓦoperadeparis .fr; ⓂBastille; map p.108. Opened in 1989, the city's new opera house hasn't been entirely successful. The design is unlovable and opinions differ over the acoustics. The stage, at least, is well designed and allows the auditorium uninterrupted views, and there's no doubting the high calibre of the Bastille orchestra. Most performances sell out.

Opéra Comique 5 rue Favart, 2ᵉ ☎08 25 01 01 23, ⓦopera-comique.com; ⓂRichelieu-Drouot; map p.72. The Opéra Comique has been going from strength to strength since the appointment of its dynamic director Jérôme Deschamps. Deschamps has taken the theatre back to its roots, concentrating on the rich, yet largely forgotten (in some cases with good reason) French opera of the nineteenth century, reviving such obscure

composers as Hérold and Auber, with largely successful and surprising results.

Opéra Garnier Place de l'Opéra, 9ᵉ ⓦoperadeparis.fr; ⓂOpéra; map p.72. An evening in this opulent nineteenth-century opera house, used for ballets and smaller-scale opera productions, is unforgettable. While views from some of the side seats can be poor, the acoustics are excellent.

Théâtre Musical de Paris (part of the Théâtre du Châtelet) 1 place du Chatelet, 1ᵉʳ ☎01 40 28 28 40, ⓦchatelet-theatre.com; ⓂChâtelet; map p.85. To the dismay of Paris's musical elite, though with much popular acclaim, director Jean-Luc Choplin has broadened out the Châtelet's repertoire to include more popular performances, especially musicals such as *My Fair Lady* and *Sweeney Todd*, a genre relatively unfamiliar to French audiences.

NUIT BLANCHE

Festivals and events

Paris hosts an impressive roster of festivals and events. The city's most colourful jamborees are Bastille Day, on July 14, and the summer-long Paris Plage, but throughout the year there's invariably something on. If it's not one of the big exhibitions, it'll be one of the arts events subsidized by the ever-active town hall or culture ministry. The tourist office produces a biannual "Saisons de Paris – Calendrier des Manifestations", which gives details of all the mainstream events; otherwise check listings in other Paris magazines (see p.38) such as *Pariscope*, or look up "What's on" at ⦿parisinfo .com. Many Parisian *quartiers* like Belleville, Ménilmontant and Montmartre have open-door weeks when artists' studios are open to the public – keep an eye open for posters and flyers. The following listings give a selection of the most important or entertaining festivals and events in the Paris calendar.

JANUARY

Salon du Jouet et du Jeu (mid-Jan) The latest in multimedia and board games (ⓦ salon-du-jeu.fr).

FEBRUARY

Rétromobile (early Feb) Hundreds of classic cars at the Parc des Expositions, Porte de Versailles (ⓦ retromobile.fr).
Chinese New Year (mid-Feb) Paris's Chinese community brings in the New Year in the heart of Chinatown around avenue d'Ivry in the 13ᵉ.
Salon de l'Agriculture (end Feb to early March) The biggest agricultural show in the world at the Parc des Expositions, Porte de Versailles (ⓦ salon-agriculture.com).

MARCH

Paris Fashion Week (first week of March) The fashion event of the year. Technically for professionals only, but surely there's a door left ajar somewhere (ⓦ modeaparis.com).
Banlieues Bleues (early March to early April) International jazz festival in the towns of Seine-St-Denis – Blanc-Mesnil, Drancy, Aubervilliers, Pantin, St-Ouen and Bobigny (ⓦ banlieuesbleues.org).
Festival of the Imagination (early March to early June) Performances and exhibitions from lesser-known cultures from all over the world (ⓦ mcm.asso.fr).
Poets' Springtime (second week of March) Thousands of readings, debates, lectures and workshops on the art of *la poésie* (☎ 01 53 80 08 80, ⓦ printempsdespoetes.com).
Festival Exit (end March) International festival of contemporary dance, performance and theatre at Créteil (ⓦ maccreteil.com).
Festival de Films des Femmes (end March/early April) Major women's film festival out at Créteil (ⓦ filmsdefemmes.com).

APRIL

Poisson d'Avril (April 1) April Fools' Day with media spoofs and kids sticking paper fishes on the backs of the unsuspecting.
Foire du Trône (April to early June) Centuries-old funfair with an actual freak show located in the Pelouse de Reuilly (Bois de Vincennes, 12ᵉ; ⓦ foiredutrone.com).
Marathon International de Paris (mid-April) The Paris Marathon departs from place de la Concorde and arrives at the Hippodrome de Vincennes 42km later. There's also a half-marathon in March (ⓦ parismarathon.com).
Foire de Paris (end April/beginning of May) Food, wine, house and home fair at the Parc des Expositions, Porte de Versailles (ⓦ foiredeparis.fr).

MAY

Fête du Travail (May 1) May Day. Everything closes and there are marches and festivities in eastern Paris and around place de la Bastille.

Printemps des Rues (early May) Free street performances in the areas of La Villette, Gambetta, Nation and République (ⓦ leprintempsdesrues.com).
Course des Garçons de Café (mid-May) Jacketed waiters and waitresses hightail with their trays in an 8km marathon beginning at the Hôtel de Ville (ⓦ waitersrace.com).
La Nuit des Musées (usually third Saturday in May) Most of Paris's museums stay open till around midnight, many putting on workshops, talks, concerts, etc (ⓦ nuitdesmusees.culture.fr).
Quinzaine des Réalisateurs (mid-May) Public screenings in the Forum des Images of films from the Cannes alternative film festival (ⓦ quinzaine-realisateurs.com).
Internationaux de France de Tennis (last week May and first week June) The French Open tennis championships at Roland Garros (ⓦ rolandgarros.com).

JUNE

Jazz in the Parc Floral (May–July) Big jazz names give free concerts in the Parc Floral at the Bois de Vincennes (ⓦ parisjazzfestival.fr).
Festival Agora (early June) Contemporary theatre/dance/music festival organized by IRCAM and the Pompidou Centre (ⓦ ircam.fr).
Foire St-Germain (June & July) Concerts, antique fairs, poetry and exhibitions in the 6ᵉ (ⓦ foiresaintgermain.org).
Journées d'Architectures à vivre (second and third weekend of June) More than 400 houses designed by modern architects across the country are opened up to the public (ⓦ journeesavivre.fr).
Festival de Chopin (mid-June to July) Chopin recitals by candlelight, held in the Orangerie de Bagatelle, in the Bois de Boulogne (ⓦ frederic-chopin.com).
Festival de St-Denis (last two weeks June) Classical and world-music festival with opportunities to hear music in the Gothic St-Denis Basilica (ⓦ festival-saint-denis.com).
Fête de la Musique (June 21) Live bands and free concerts throughout the city (ⓦ fetedelamusique.culture.fr).
Gay Pride (late June) Lesbian and Gay Pride march (ⓦ marche.inter-lgbt.org).
Fête du Cinéma (end June) A superb opportunity to view a wide range of films from classics to the cutting-edge in French and foreign cinema. Buy one full-price ticket and you can see any number of films during the weekend-long festival for €3 (ⓦ feteducinema.com).

JULY

La Goutte d'Or en Fête (one week late June/early July) Music festival of rap, reggae and raï with local and international performers in the Goutte d'Or district, 10ᵉ (ⓦ gouttedorenfete.org).
Bastille Day (July 14 and evening before) The 1789 surrender of the Bastille is celebrated with parades of tanks down the Champs-Elysées, fireworks and concerts. On the

23

23

evening of the 13th, there's dancing in the streets around Bastille to good French bands, and "Bals Pompiers" parties rage inside every fire station – rue Blanche and rue des Vieux-Colombiers are known to be among the best.

Paris Quartier d'Eté (mid-July to mid-Aug) Cinema, dance, music and theatre events around the city (W quartierdete.com).

Festival de Cinéma en Plein Air (mid-July to end Aug) Thousands turn up at dusk every night for free, open-air, classic cinema at the Parc de la Villette (W villette.com or W cinema.arbo.com).

Paris Plage (mid-July to mid-Aug) A popular initiative in which 3km of the Seine *quais* are closed to traffic and transformed into mini-beaches, complete with imported sand, palm trees, parasols and sun-loungers. There's also a beach on the Left Bank, in front of the Bibliothèque Nationale (13ᵉ), and you can muck about in boats on the Bassin de la Villette. The Stade de France stadium is taken over by swimming, sailing, volleyball, and more. There are free concerts on Friday and Saturday evenings (W paris.fr).

Arrivée du Tour de France Cycliste (third or fourth Sun in July) The Tour de France cyclists cross the finishing line in the avenue des Champs-Elysées (W letour.fr).

AUGUST

Cinéma au Clair de Lune (throughout Aug) Open-air screenings of films shot in Paris on a giant screen that tours the arrondissements (W forumdesimages.fr).

Fête de l'Assomption (Aug 15) A procession from Notre-Dame around the Ile de la Cité.

SEPTEMBER

Fête de l'Humanité (second or third weekend in Sept) Sponsored by the French Communist Party and *L'Humanité* newspaper, this large annual three-day event, north of Paris at La Courneuve, features food and drink (all cheap), plus music and crafts from every corner of the globe. Each French regional Communist Party section has a restaurant tent; French and foreign bands play on an open-air stage; and the event ends on Sunday night with a firework display (W humanite.fr/fete_huma). Ⓜ La Courneuve, then special shuttle bus.

Villette Jazz Festival (early to mid-Sept) One of the city's best jazz festivals, with music played by legendary greats and local conservatory students, held in the park and Grande Halle at La Villette (W villette.com).

Biennale des Antiquaires (third week of Sept) The city's largest antiques show, held at the Grand Palais with everything from coins and stamps to art, furniture and jewellery (W bdafrance.eu).

Festival d'Automne (mid-Sept to late Dec) Major festival of contemporary theatre, music, dance and avant-garde arts (W festival-automne.com).

Techno Parade (mid-Sept) One of the highlights of the Rendez-vous Electroniques festival, attracting hundreds of thousands. Floats with sound systems parade from place de la République to Pelouse de Reuilly (W technopol.net).

Journées du Patrimoine (third weekend Sept) A France-wide event where normally off-limits buildings – like the Palais de l'Elysée where the President resides – are opened to a curious public. Details in local press and on W journeesdupatrimoine.culture.fr.

OCTOBER

Prix de l'Arc de Triomphe (first weekend in Oct) Horse flat-racing at Longchamp (W prixarcdetriomphe.com).

Fêtes des Vendanges (early Oct) The bacchanalian grape harvest festival in the Montmartre vineyard, at the corner of rue des Saules and rue St-Vincent (W fetedesvendangesdemontmartre.com).

Nuit Blanche (first or second Sat in Oct) All-night cultural events at unusual venues (W paris.fr).

Foire Internationale d'Art Contemporain (FIAC) (late Oct) International contemporary art fair taking place over several days at the Grand Palais (W fiacparis.com).

Salon du Chocolat (end Oct) International chocolatiers flock to Paris Expo, and there are tastings and even a chocolate fashion parade (W salonduchocolat.fr).

NOVEMBER

Festival les Inrocks (early Nov) "Les Inrocks" features big acts playing at various venues around town – anything from Lily Allen to Joan as Police Woman, by way of lots of French bands (W lesinrocks.com).

Paris Photo (mid-Nov) Held at the Grand Palais, this is one of the best events anywhere for seeing some of the world's greatest photography, from early works to modern masterpieces. November also sees photographic exhibitions held in museums, galleries and cultural centres throughout the city (W parisphoto.fr).

DECEMBER

Patinoire de l'Hôtel de Ville (early Dec to end Feb) Ice-skating rink in front of the town hall, with a smaller rink for younger children. Free entry but you pay €5 to rent skates (W paris.fr).

Great Wines Fair (mid-Dec) Held at the Carrousel du Louvre, this wine festival allows would-be sommeliers to taste vintages for next to nothing (W grandtasting.com).

Noël (Dec 24–25) Christmas eve is a huge affair all across France, and of much more importance than the following day. Both Notre-Dame and Eglise de la Madeleine hold midnight Mass services; arrive early to get a seat (doors open at 10pm, ceremony begins at 10.30pm).

Le Nouvel An (Dec 31) New Year's Eve means dense crowds of out-of-towners on the Champs-Elysées, fireworks at the Champs de Mars and super-elevated restaurant prices everywhere.

AGNES B.

Shops and markets

Paris is almost as fabled among shoppers as it is among lovers. From the flagship "concept stores" of Europe's glitziest couture houses to the humblest of neighbourhood bakeries, you'll find an obsession with quality and style, and a fierce pride in detail. That ribbon on a package from the bakery, for instance, will always be just so. Supermarkets and chains have made advances in the city, but Parisians, for the most part, remain fiercely loyal to local traders and independently owned shops. Whether you can afford to buy or not, some of the most entertaining and memorable experiences of a trip to Paris are to be had for free just browsing in small boutiques, their owners proudly displaying their cache of offbeat items, particular passions and mouthwatering treats.

ESSENTIALS

Opening hours Many shops in Paris stay open all day Monday to Saturday. Most tend to close comparatively late – 7 or 8pm as often as not. Some smaller businesses close for up to two hours at lunchtime, somewhere between noon and 3pm.

Shopping tours If you feel overwhelmed by the wealth of opportunities for retail therapy, head for a company like Chic Shopping (☎06 14 56 23 11, ⒲chicshoppingparis.com), which runs shopping-themed tours (from €100 per person) in English around different Parisian neighbourhoods.

Sunday trading Most shops are closed on Sunday (Sunday trading laws remain strict) and some on Monday as well. That said, many food shops, such as boulangeries, will open on Sunday morning, and shops in seven tourist zones are allowed to open on Sundays, generally around 1.30–7pm. This exception gives these areas – some of which are also pedestrianized on that day – a pleasant, relaxed buzz. The Sunday zones are: the Butte Montmartre, around Abbesses (18ᵉ): the Marais, between place des Vosges and rue des Francs-Bourgeois (3ᵉ–4ᵉ); the Viaduc des Arts (12ᵉ); rue d'Arcole, on the Ile de la Cité (4ᵉ); boulevard St-Germain (6ᵉ); rue de Rivoli (1ᵉʳ); and the Champs-Elysées (8ᵉ).

VAT It's worth researching VAT reimbursement for non-EU citizens (see p.37).

CLOTHES

Milan, New York and London may have their supporters, but Paris remains the world capital of **fashion**. As a tourist, you may not be able to get into the haute couture shows, but there's nothing to prevent you trying on fabulously expensive creations – as long as you can brave the intimidatingly chic assistants and the awesome chill of the marble portals. But if it's actual shopping you're interested in, the box below gives general pointers on the best areas to browse, while the listings review some of the most promising addresses in the city. As long as there's a strong euro, visitors from outside the eurozone will find shopping relatively expensive. **Sales** are held twice a year, beginning in mid-January and mid-July and lasting a month – though the best lines in the best sizes usually go within the first couple of days. Ends of lines and old stock from the couturiers are sold year round in "stock" **discount** shops (see p.327), or at La Vallée Outlet, inside the frontiers of Disneyland (see p.327).

DEPARTMENT STORES AND HYPERMARKETS

Paris's two largest **department stores**, Printemps and Galeries Lafayette, are right next door to each other near the St-Lazare station, and between them there's not much they don't have. Both stores offer a ten-percent discount for tourists on all red-dot items, which includes almost all the big brands; pick up a tourist discount card in your hotel, at the main tourist office or at the welcome desk at either store. Their main rival is Le Bon Marché, over on the Left Bank.

Bazar de l'Hôtel de Ville (BHV) 52–64 rue de Rivoli, 4ᵉ; ⓜHôtel-de-Ville; map p.96. Only two years younger than Le Bon Marché and noted in particular for its DIY department, artists' materials and craft kits, menswear department and cheap self-service restaurant overlooking the Seine. For lighter refreshment, hunt out the cosy *Bricolo Café* in the downstairs DIY department, done out like an old-fashioned workshop. The store is less elegant in appearance than some of its rivals, but pretty good value

WHERE TO SHOP IN PARIS

The most distinctive and unusual shopping possibilities are in the smartly renovated nineteenth-century **arcades**, or *passages*, in the **2ᵉ and 9ᵉ arrondissements**, which harbour the kind of outlets that make shopping an exciting expedition rather than a chore. On the streets proper, the square kilometre around **place St-Germain-des-Prés** is hard to beat; to the north of the square, the narrow streets are lined with antiques shops and arts and interior design boutiques, while to the south you'll find every designer clothing brand you can think of, Parisian or otherwise.

The aristocratic **Marais**, the hip **Bastille** *quartier* and northeastern Paris (**Oberkampf** and the **Canal St-Martin**) have filled up with dinky little boutiques, interior design stores, arty and specialist shops and galleries. For Parisian **haute couture**, the traditional bastions are avenue Montaigne, rue François 1ᵉʳ, and the upper end of **rue du Faubourg-St-Honoré** in the 8ᵉ, while **Les Halles** is good for high-street fashion.

Place de la Madeleine is the place to head for luxury **food** stores, such as Fauchon and Hédiard. For essentials, the cheapest **supermarket** chain is Ed l'Epicier. Other last-minute or convenience shopping is probably best done at Fnac shops (for books and records), the big department stores (for high-quality merchandise) and Monoprix (for basics). A selection of **toy shops**, and shops selling children's clothes and books, is detailed in Chapter 26.

for money. Mon, Tues, Thurs & Fri 9.30am–7.30pm, Wed 9.30am–9pm, Sat 9.30am–8pm.

★ **Le Bon Marché** 38 rue de Sèvres, 7e Ⓦ lebonmarche.com; Ⓜ Sèvres-Babylone; map p.134. The world's oldest department store, founded in 1852 and now run by the luxury goods empire LVMH. It's smaller, calmer and classier than Galeries Lafayette and Printemps, and has an excellent kids' department and a legendary food hall (see box, p.324). Mon–Wed & Sat 10am–8pm, Thurs & Fri 10am–9pm.

Galeries Lafayette 40 bd Haussmann, 9e Ⓦ www .galerieslafayette.com; Ⓜ Havre-Caumartin; map p.72. The store's forte is high fashion, with two floors given over to the latest creations by leading designers; the third floor is almost entirely dedicated to lingerie, plus there's a large children's clothes section on the fourth floor. Then there's a host of big names in men's and women's accessories, a huge parfumerie, and a branch of *Angélina salon de thé*, all under a superb 1912 dome. Just down the road at no. 35 is Lafayette Maison, consisting of five floors of quality kitchenware, linens and furniture. Mon–Sat 9.30am–8pm, Thurs till 9pm.

Printemps 64 bd Haussmann, 9e Ⓦ printemps.com; Ⓜ Havre-Caumartin; map p.72. The main store recently underwent a €180m revamp and has gone more upmarket, stocking a bigger range of high-end brands. It has an excellent three-floor womenswear department, plus a whole floor devoted to shoes and one to accessories. The sixth-floor brasserie is right underneath the beautiful Art Nouveau glass dome. Next door is a huge men's store; the Paul Smith-designed *World Bar* on the top floor is a perfect spot for a shopping break. Mon–Sat 9.35am–8pm, Thurs till 10pm.

Tati 4 bd Rochechouart, 18e Ⓦ tati.fr; Ⓜ Barbès; map p.180. Hugely successful budget department store chain with a distinctive pink-gingham logo, selling reliable and cheap clothing, among a host of other items. A staple for seekers of seriously low prices. Mon–Fri 10am–7pm, Sat 9.15am–7pm.

CLASSIC STYLE

agnès b. 6 & 10 rue du Vieux Colombier, 6e Ⓜ St-Sulpice, map p.134; 2, 3 & 6 rue du Jour, 1er Ⓜ Châtelet-Les-Halles; map p.72. Born in Versailles, this queen of understatement favours cool, simple staples. While the line has expanded into watches, sunglasses and cosmetics, her clothing remains chic, timeless and, best of all, relatively affordable. (Pronounced "ann-yes bay" in French.) Mon–Sat 10.30am–7.30pm.

★ **APC** 38 rue Madame, 6e Ⓜ St-Sulpice, map p.134; 112 rue Vieille du Temple, 3e Ⓜ St-Paul, map p.96; APC Surplus, 20 rue André del Sarte, 18e Ⓜ Barbès-Rochechouart, map p.180. This major chain is perfect for young, urban basics. Simple cuts and fabrics, but still effortlessly classic in that Parisian way. The main shop is on rue Madame, but there's also a branch in the Marais, while

APC Surplus sells discounted over-stock fare. Rue Madame Mon–Sat 11am–7.30pm; rue Vieille du Temple, Mon–Sat 11.30am–8pm, Sun 1.30–7.30pm; APC Surplus Mon–Sat 12.30–7.30pm, Sun 1.30–7.30pm.

Ba&sh 22 rue des Francs-Bourgeois, 3e; Ⓜ St-Paul; map p.96. Barbara Boccara and Sharon Krief produce modern, chic women's clothes in quality materials such as silk and cashmere. Their hallmarks are slouchy tops, short tunic dresses and leather jackets, with most items in the €100–200 range. Mon–Sat 11.30am–7pm, Sun 1–7pm.

Comptoir des Cotonniers 30 rue de Buci, 6e Ⓜ Mabillon, map p.134; 33 rue des Francs-Bourgeois, 4e Ⓜ St-Paul, map p.96; 41 rue des Abbesses, 18e Ⓜ Abbesses, map p.180. Utterly reliable little chain stocking comfortable, well-cut women's basics that nod to contemporary fashions without being modish. Trousers, shirts and dresses for around €100. Has around thirty branches in Paris. Mon 11am–7pm, Tues–Sat 10am–7.30pm.

Et Vous 46 rue du Four, 6e; Ⓜ St-Germain-des-Prés; map p.134. With blouses and cardigans in natural fabrics as well as retro T-shirts and leather jackets, this Paris-based brand is a good stop for a mother-and-daughter shopping trip. It's inexpensive – linen trousers and a lambswool cardigan might set you back around €80. The menswear line is similarly casual yet classic: think v-neck knits and raw cotton shirts. Also stocks like-minded brands such as Petit Bateau, Christophe Sauvat, Leon & Harper and Mason's. Branches throughout the city. Mon–Sat 10.30am–7pm.

Isabel Marant 16 rue de Charonne, 11e; Ⓜ Bastille; map p.108. Marant has established an international reputation for her feminine and flattering clothes, such as elegantly tapered trousers and ruffled, floaty tops and tea dresses. She also has a second, more affordable line, called Étoile. Mon–Sat 10.30am–7.30pm.

Kabuki 25 rue Etienne-Marcel, 1er; Ⓜ Etienne-Marcel; map p.72. A one-stop store for all your Prada, Issey Miyake and Calvin Klein needs. There's a men's store two doors down the road selling similar designer brands. Mon–Sat 10.30am–7.30pm.

Maje 92 rue des Martyrs, 18e; Ⓜ Abbesses; map p.180. This Paris-based brand has stores throughout the city and offers utterly Parisian clothes: relaxed, slightly Bohemian but always elegant. Prices are fairly affordable, and this Montmartre branch offers discounted lines from last season. Mon–Sat 10am–6pm.

Patricia Louisor 16 rue Houdon, 18e; Ⓜ Abbesses; map p.180. Vibrant and sassy, but springing from a solid base of classic Parisian style. Trousers, skirts and jumpers all come in at around €70–120. Mon–Sat noon–8pm, Sun 1–8pm.

★ **Paul & Joe** 62–66 rue des Sts-Pères, 7e Ⓜ Sèvres-Babylone, map p.134; 46 rue Etienne-Marcel, 2e Ⓜ Sentier, map p.72. The clothes here are quintessentially French: quirky but not overly showy, cool but not overly

24

radical, feminine but with an edge – for men and women alike. As long as you've got a slim, French-style figure to match, Paul & Joe will magically transform you into a chic young Parisian. There are half a dozen branches in Paris, but these two are the ones that stock the men's, women's and trendier, cheaper diffusion line, Paul & Joe Sister. Mon–Sat 10.30am–7.30pm.

Samy Chalon 24 rue Charlot, 3ᵉ; ⓜFilles-du-Calvaire; map p.96. Cairo-born Samy Chalon creates original, vibrantly coloured knitted jumpers, cardigans and dresses for women, using cashmere, alpaca and mohair. Prices start at around €175. Tues–Sat 11am–7pm.

Sonia by Sonia Rykiel 6 rue de Grenelle, 6ᵉ; ⓜSt-Sulpice; map p.134. Sonia Rykiel's daughter Nathalie has started up this less expensive (roughly €185–350) offshoot of the Rykiel brand. Younger and more everyday in feel, but still with the signature Gallic stripes and flounces, and hot colours. Mon–Sat 10.30am–7pm.

Sonia Rykiel 175 bd St-Germain, 6ᵉ; ⓜSt-Germain-des-Prés; map p.134. Unmistakably Parisian designer who brought out her first line when the soixante-huitards threw Europe into social revolution. Her multi-coloured designs – especially those stripy sweaters – are still all the rage, as is her "Sonia" diffusion line. Mon–Sat 10.30am–7pm.

★ **Spree** 16 rue de la Vieuville, 18ᵉ; ⓜAbbesses; map p.180. The hip, feminine clothing collection at this gallery-like boutique is led by individual designers such as Vanessa Bruno, Isabel Marant and Christian Wijnants, and there are often a few vintage pieces, as well as bigger-brand lines (APC and Comme des Garçons, for instance), accessories and even furniture. Clothing mostly falls in the €150–350 range. Mon & Sun 3–7pm, Tues–Sat 11am–7.30pm.

Vanessa Bruno 25 rue St-Sulpice, 6ᵉ; ⓜOdéon; map p.134. Bright, breezy and effortlessly beautiful women's fashions – trainers/sneakers, dresses and bags – with a hint of updated hippy chic. Around €240 for a top or skirt. Mon–Sat 10.30am–7.30pm.

YSL 32 (men) & 38 (women) rue du Faubourg-St-Honoré, 8ᵉ ⓜConcorde, map p.62; 6 place St-Sulpice (women), 6ᵉ ⓜSt-Sulpice/Mabillon, map p.134. When Yves Saint Laurent retired in 2002, he closed shop on his revered couture line and passed the baton over to Tom Ford, who initially designed this prêt-à-porter spin-off. Now run by ex-Prada man Stefano Pilati, the line has been modernized once again. Classic monochrome chic remains the staple for men. Mon 11am–7pm, Tues–Sat 10.30am–7pm.

Yves Andrieux et Vincent Jalbert 55 rue Charlot, 3ᵉ; ⓜFilles-du-Calvaire; map p.93. It's hard to believe these elegant and beautiful clothes (each piece is unique, and costs from around €400) were made from something so

CLOTHES SHOPPING IN THE FASHION CAPITAL

For designer prêt-à-porter, the **department stores** Galeries Lafayette and Printemps (see p.323) have unrivalled selections; if you're looking for a one-stop hit of Paris fashion, this is probably the place to come.

For couture and seriously expensive designer wear, make for the wealthy, manicured streets around the **Champs-Elysées**, especially avenue François 1ᵉʳ, avenue Montaigne and **rue du Faubourg-St-Honoré**. Younger designers have colonized the lower reaches of the latter street, between rue Cambon and rue des Pyramides. In the heart of this area, luxurious **place Vendôme** is the place to come for serious jewellery.

One notch down in terms of price is the appealingly compact area around **St-Sulpice** métro, on the Left Bank. You'll find a host of pretty upscale French clothing brands on rues du Vieux Colombier, de Rennes, Madame, de Grenelle (expensive brands and, especially, designer shoes – think Prada and Christian Louboutin) and du Cherche-Midi (good for bags, lingerie and more shoes); the chichi department store, Le Bon Marché, is a stone's throw away, on rue de Sèvres.

On the eastern side of the city, around the **Marais** and **Bastille**, the clothes, like the residents, are younger, cooler and more relaxed. For the former, the free bilingual Le Marais shopping guide, available from numerous Marais boutiques, including Trazita, 25 rue de Blancs Manteaux, is a useful resource. Chic boutiques line the Marais' main shopping street, **rue des Francs-Bourgeois**, and particularly rues Charlot, de Saintonge and de Poitou in the Haut Marais. Young, trendy designers and hippie outfits congregate on Bastille's **rue de Charonne** and **rue Keller**.

At the more alternative and avant-garde end of the spectrum, there's a good concentration of trendy high-street names and one-off designer boutiques at the foot of Montmartre – try rues des Martyrs, des Trois Frères, de la Vieuville, Houdon and Durantin. For more streetwise clothing, the **Forum des Halles** and surrounding streets are good places to browse. **Rue Etienne-Marcel** and pedestrianized **rue Tiquetonne** are good for young, trendy fashion boutiques.

24

utilitarian as recycled army uniforms from the 50s. The tailored jackets and long coats are particularly stylish and pair well with the flouncy skirts made from recycled parachutes and tents. A more affordable range of attractive bags and brooches, made out of floral vintage fabrics, is also available. Mon–Fri 10am–1pm & 2–7pm, Sat 11am–7pm.

★ **Zadig & Voltaire** 1 & 3 rue du Vieux Colombier, 6ᵉ ⓂSt-Sulpice, map p.134; discount "stock" shop at 22 rue du Bourg-Tibourg, 4ᵉ ⓂHôtel-de-Ville, map p.96. The women's clothes at this small, moderately expensive chain are pretty and feminine, and similar in style to agnès b. – the shop's just opposite too – only with a more wayward flair. Mon–Sat 10.30am–7.30pm.

TRENDY AND AVANT-GARDE

Le 66 66 av des Champs-Elysées, 8ᵉ; ⓂGeorge V; map p.62. Three linked glass-walled shops with a great selection of high-end streetwear labels such as Evisu, Raf Simons, American Retro and Acne for both men and women. Jeans from €100, T-shirts from €50. Daily 11am–8pm.

★ **Anne Willi** 13 rue Keller, 11ᵉ; ⓂLedru-Rollin/ Voltaire; map p.108. Completely original pieces of clothing that respect classic French sartorial design. The pieces are in gorgeous, luxurious fabrics and run the gamut from layered, casual-chic sets to one-piece geometric studies of the body. Prices from €60 upwards. Also stocks cute clothes for kids. Mon 2–8pm, Tues–Sat 11.30am–8pm.

Antoine et Lili 95 quai de Valmy, 10ᵉ ⓂRépublique, map p.196; 51 rue des Francs-Bourgeois, 4ᵉ ⓂSt-Paul, map p.96. Quirky Parisian institution, with a flagship store whose signature lurid-pink frontage lights up the Canal St-Martin. There are other branches across the city. Sells women and children's clothes, best described as ethnic revisited, with a dose of camp and an emphasis on fun fabrics and patterns. Prices mostly well under €100. You'll find inexpensive gifts, accessories and homeware, too. Quai de Valmy Mon & Sun 11am–7pm, Tues–Sat 11am–8pm; rue des Francs-Bourgeois Mon–Fri 10.30am–7.30pm, Sat 10.30–8pm, Sun 11am–7.30pm.

Cancan 30 rue Henry Monnier, 9ᵉ; ⓂPigalle; map p.180. In the last couple of years a handful of boutiques have sprung up on rue Monnier, all stocking choice selections of women's clothes by French *créateurs* – Cancan usually has some quirky, stylish dresses that won't break the bank and that you won't find back home. Tues–Sat 11.30am–7.30pm.

Colette 213 rue St-Honoré, 1ᵉʳ ⓦcolette.fr; ⓂTuileries; map p.72. This cutting-edge concept store, combining high fashion and design, and complete with photo gallery and exhibition space, has become something of a tourist attraction. When you've finished sizing up the Pucci

underwear, Stella McCartney womenswear and Sonia Rykiel handbags, you could head for the cool Water Bar, with its 80 different kinds of H₂O, including Brazilian Petropolis Paulista, Corsican Orezza and a limited-edition Evian. Mon–Sat 11am–7pm.

Comme des Garçons 54 rue du Faubourg-St-Honoré, 8ᵉ; ⓂConcorde; map p.62. Led by Tokyo-born Rei Kawakubo, this popular high-end label favours novel tints and youthful, asymmetric cuts that defamiliarize the body. Mon–Sat 10am–7pm.

Heaven 16 rue du Pont Louis-Philippe, 4ᵉ; ⓂSt-Paul; map p.96. English-bred Lea-Anne Wallis has a wild streak, designing luxurious clothing, sometimes brash, but sometimes classically elegant, for men and women. Her husband, Jean-Christophe Peyrieux, handles a small designer lighting section. Tues–Sat 11am–7.30pm, Sun 2–7.30pm.

Lanvin 15–22 rue du Faubourg-St-Honoré, 8ᵉ; ⓂConcorde; map p.62. The designs of this originally Breton label often incorporate idiosyncratic characteristics like taffeta trench coats, satin capes and removable cuffs and collars. Mon–Sat 10am–7pm.

Pigalle 7 rue Henry Monnier, 9ᵉ; ⓂSt-Georges; map p.180. Cool boutique selling "selected clothing" to the bobos of the *quartier*: VANS and Comme des Garçons for the boys, designer names you mightn't yet have heard of for the girls. From around €130 for a shirt to dresses and men's jackets in the €300s. Tues–Sat noon–8pm, Sun 2–8pm.

Roxan 25 rue Lepic, 9ᵉ (plus other branches in local area); ⓂPigalle; map p.180. With a few shops clustered around Abbesses and so-called SoPi ("South Pigalle"), this boutique brand stocks designer jeans and pretty little cardigans, as well as daywear from popular brands like American Vintage (around €70), See by Chloé and Filippa K (around €300 for a dress). Tues–Sun 10.30am–7.30pm.

Swildens 22 rue de Poitou, 3ᵉ; ⓂSt-Sébastien-Froissart; map p.96. Womenswear designer Juliette Swildens makes well-cut, affordable clothes, with a hint of rock'n'roll. Typical pieces are off-the-shoulder smocks, slouchy sweatshirts, baggy harem pants and layered knits (prices in the €100–200 range). Mon–Sat 10am–7.30pm.

Tessa Delpech 7 rue des Gardes, 18ᵉ; ⓂBarbès-Rochechouart; map p.191. In the middle of the edgy Goutte d'Or, the municipality sponsors the boutiques of young Parisian designers and seamstresses, turning this small, undistinguished street into the *rue de la mode*. This is where you come to get something unique without paying a fortune. Tessa Delpech has a very bright, feminine and Monroe-ish look; she works *sur mésure*. The neighbouring boutiques offer a wide range of styles and attitudes, though mostly aimed at a young, fashion-conscious clientele. Mon–Sat 11am–7pm.

Y-3 47 rue Etienne-Marcel, 2ᵉ; ⓂBourse; map p.72. Japanese designer Yohji Yamamoto's hook-up with Adidas has led to a collection of on-trend sports and casual clothes, with the trainers/sneakers (well over €100) the stand-out creations. Mon–Sat 11am–7pm.

DISCOUNT

A number of dedicated "stock" shops (short for *déstockage*) sell end-of-line and last year's models at thirty- to fifty-percent **reductions**. Before you get too excited, however, remember that thirty percent off €750 still leaves a hefty bill – not that all items are this expensive. The best times of year to join the scrums are after the new collections have come out in January and October.

La Clef des Marques 124 bd Raspail, 6e; ⓂVavin; map p.160. Huge store with a wide choice of inexpensive brand-name clothes for men and women; also lots of lingerie and children's clothes. Mon 12.30–7pm, Tues–Sat 10.30am–7pm.

Défilé de Marques 171 rue de Grenelle, 7e; ⓂLa Tour-Maubourg; map p.148. This outlet sells a wide choice of designer clothes for women – as returned unsold from the big-name boutiques. Labels from Chanel to YSL via Givenchy and Prada, for around €300–700 for jackets, half that for shoes. Tues–Sat noon–8pm.

★ **Le Mouton à Cinq Pattes** 8 rue St-Placide, 6e; ⓂSèvres-Babylone; map p.134. Names such as Gaultier and lots of Italian brands can be found among the racks of discounted (around €60 for a shirt, €120 for a dress) last-season's clothes, though labels are often cut out so you'll have to trust your judgement. Mon–Sat 10am–7pm.

La Vallée Inside Disneyland Paris boundary; Ⓦlavalleevillage.com; map p.246. Mall designed to look like a village, best for discounted designer labels. Mon–Fri & Sun 10am–7pm, Sat 10am–8pm.

SECONDHAND AND RETRO

The **rétro** outlets mostly have unsold factory stock from the 1950s and 1960s, though some shops specialize in expensive high-fashion articles from as far back as the 1920s. These vintage shops generally differ from *dépôts-vente*, stores selling secondhand designer gear for hundreds of euros off retail. Plain **secondhand** stuff is referred to as *fripe* – not especially interesting compared

with London or New York. A great place to look is the Porte de Montreuil flea market (see p.337).

Alternatives 18 rue du Roi-de-Sicile, 4e; ⓂSt-Paul; map p.96. Vintage meets designer at this fantastic shop where you can perfect *le look parisien* with fashionable labels and lesser-known brands. The clothes here are often straight off the bodies of runway models. Tues–Sat 1–7pm.

Chezel 59 rue Condorcet, 9e; ⓂPigalle; map p.180. One of the best of three or four (the others come and go) little shops on this street that specialize in vintage fashion. Prices from €30 to easily five times that for a classic – and some serious designerwear finds its way here. Tues–Sun 1–8pm.

Free "P" Star 8 rue Ste-Croix-de-la-Bretonnerie, 4e ⓂSt-Paul, map p.96; 61 rue de la Verrerie 4e ⓂHôtel-de-Ville, map p.85. A tiny, popular vintage clothing shop, with racks of Lacoste polo shirts, 1970s floral dresses, inexpensive Levi's, army surplus and leather jackets. Many items in the €10–30 range. Rue Ste-Croix-de-la-Bretonnerie Mon–Sat noon–11pm, Sun 2–10pm; rue de la Verrerie Mon–Sat 11am–9pm, Sun 2–9pm.

Kiliwatch 64 rue Tiquetonne, 2e; ⓂEtienne-Marcel; map p.72. No problem coming up with an original clubbing outfit here: rails of new cheap'n'chic streetwear and a slew of trainers/sneakers meet the best range of unusual secondhand clothes and accessories in Paris. Resale here includes army surplus, lumberjack bomber jackets and retro streetwear. It's also *the* place to buy jeans for men, with no fewer than fifteen brands stocked. Mon 2–7pm, Tues–Sat 10am–7pm.

L'Occaserie 19 & 30 rue de la Pompe, 16e; 16 & 21 rue de l'Annonciation, 16e; and 14 rue Jean Bologne, 16e; Ⓦoccaserie.com; all ⓂMuette/Passy; all map p.213. Specialists in secondhand haute couture – Dior, Prada, Cartier and the like. "Secondhand" doesn't mean cheap though: Chanel suits are around €720, Louis Vuitton handbags €300. Tues–Sat 11am–7pm.

Réciproque 89, 92, 93–97, 101 & 123 rue de la Pompe, 16e Ⓦreciproque.fr; ⓂPompe; map p.213. A similar series of shops to L'Occaserie, this is slightly more chichi and better for couture, with finds like Christian Lacroix,

24

HOW TO SHOP PARIS-STYLE

Parisian shopkeepers aren't the most fawning of individuals, but by making an early effort to win them over, your shopping experience can become much more pleasant and successful. A respectful "*Excusez-moi de vous déranger, Madame* (or *Monsieur…*")" will go a long way. Sauntering into a boutique with a designer shopping bag already in tow – evidence that you're not merely window-shopping – has also been known to work wonders on the customer service front. Failing that, you could try the Parisian approach: demand precisely what you want and expect service, not friendliness. In smaller shops, especially food shops where there's a queue, it's traditional to greet everyone in the shop with a polite "*Bonjour Messieurs-Dames*" on entry, but it's not exactly common in the big city.

Moschino and Manolo Blahnik. Women's design at no. 93–95; accessories and coats for men at no. 101; more accessories and coats for women at no. 123. Tues–Sat 11am–7pm.

Vintage Désir 32 rue des Rosiers, 4e; ⓜSt-Paul; map p.96. Don't be put off by the haphazard, somewhat overwhelming nature of this vintage clothing shop, jam-packed with checked shirts, 1980s woolly jumpers, cowboy boots, leather jackets, patterned dresses and skirts, silk scarves, fur hats and tangled heaps of belts and bags. Stamina and determination are a must, but it's worth the effort if you want to take home something unique. With belts for €5 and dresses for €10, it's surprisingly inexpensive, too. Daily 11am–9pm.

Violette & Léonie 27 rue de Poitou & 1 rue de Saintonge, 3e ⓦvioletteleonie.com; ⓜFilles-du-Calvaire/St-Sébastien-Froissart; map p.96. Two secondhand shops that look so smart you'd think they were designer boutiques. Perhaps that's part of their success – that and their decent range of stock, from high-end labels to H&M and Zara. You can also buy online. Mon 1–7.30pm, Tues–Sat 10.30am–7.30pm.

24

SHOES
The French on the whole tend to have smaller, narrower feet, so women (and men) in need of wider sizes may find themselves out of luck in this department. In addition to the shops mentioned below, just walk down rue Grenelle and rue du Cherche-Midi in the 6^e, or rue du Meslay in the 3^e, for a great choice of shoe shops.

Autour du Monde 8 rue des Francs-Bourgeois, 4^e; ⓜSt-Paul; map p.96. Stocks cute canvas pumps by Bensimon in colours such as lime green, orange and pink, though you can't beat the classic white (from around €30). Mon–Sat 11am–7.30pm, Sun 2–7pm.

Freelance 30 rue du Four, 6e; ⓜMabillon; map p.134. From leather to feathers, this very popular, free-spirited shoe shop attracts the young and extremely funky, though you can expect to pay from €200 upwards. Mon–Sat 10am–7pm.

★ **Repetto** 22 rue de la Paix, 2e ⓦrepetto.com; ⓜOpéra; map p.72. This long-established supplier of ballet shoes, which has shod ballet stars from Margot Fonteyn to Sylvie Guillem, has branched out to produce attractive ballerina pumps in assorted colours, much coveted by the fashion crowd. Mon–Sat 9.30am–7.30pm.

Shinzo 39 rue Etienne-Marcel, 1er; ⓜEtienne-Marcel; map p.72. Limited and collectors' editions of all the major trainer/sneaker brands at good prices. Mon–Sat 10.30am–7pm.

LINGERIE
In general, for lingerie you're best off at the department stores, where you can find an array of fine French brands from Princesse Tam Tam (at the lower end) to Eres (great for swimwear) and Chantal Thomass (high end), but there are also some stand-out, one-off addresses.

Le Boudoir de Marie 47bis rue d'Orsel, 18e; ⓜAbbesses; map p.180. This imaginative boutique makes and sells sexy but artful lingerie: think pink gingham with soigné embroidered cherries, or bold-print silks and vintage fabrics offset by lace. It's all limited edition, and they offer a made-to-measure service with a fortnight's turnaround. Also nighties, masks, garters, corsets and other titillations. Prices start at around €100. Tues–Sat 11am–7pm.

Cadolle 4 rue Cambon, 1er; ⓜConcorde; map p.72. This fabled family has produced couture lingerie and corsets for generations – though this is the ready-to-wear boutique, where you can pick up an exquisite bra and culottes for a mere €200 or so. Mon–Sat 11am–7pm.

Princesse Tam Tam 4 rue de Sèvres 6e; ⓜSt-Sulpice; map p.134. A French lingerie brand, Princesse Tam Tam pulls off that typical French trick of making fashionable but simultaneously classic pieces. In the market since the 1930s, it's still very much in touch with its roots so you'll find vintage-style silk slips (€60) and underwear sets (€80), but always in the latest season's colours. Several branches in Paris, and in all the main department stores. Mon–Fri 10am–7.30pm, Sat 10am–8pm.

Sabbia Rosa 71–73 rue des Sts-Pères, 6e; ⓜSt-Germain-des-Près; map p.134. Supermodels' lingerie – literally, they shop here – at supermodel prices. All made in France using natural materials – lots of silk – and in genteel but feminine pastel shades. An ensemble will cost upwards of €150 – you could easily pay three times that. Mon–Sat 10am–7pm.

ACCESSORIES AND JEWELLERY
Anthony Peto 56 rue Tiquetonne, 2e; ⓜEtienne-Marcel; map p.72. This largely men's *chapelier* is loaded with fedoras, top hats, panamas and fezzes done in wool and cotton plaid, tweed, velour and fur. Run by friendly, helpful staff. Most of the fancier hats run at around €100. Mon–Sat 11am–7pm.

Cécile et Jeanne 49 av Daumesnil, 12e; ⓜGare-de-Lyon; map p.108. Innovative jewellery design from local artisans in one of the Viaduc des Arts showrooms (see p.112). Many pieces under €100. Mon–Fri 10am–7pm, Sat & Sun 2–7pm.

Entrée des Fournisseurs 8 rue des Francs-Bourgeois, 4e; ⓜSt-Paul; map p.96. Everything you might need to make clothes yourself, including buttons, ribbons, fabrics, patterns and knitting equipment. Mon 2–7pm, Tues–Sat 10.30am–7pm.

Harpo 19 rue Turbigo, 2e ⓦharpo-paris.com; ⓜEtienne-Marcel; map p.72. Specializing in turquoise Native American-style jewellery, this popular shop sells necklaces, bracelets, rings, clasps, bolas and headgear in

BEST PARISIAN PERFUMERIES

Annick Goutal 12 place St-Sulpice, 6ᵉ; ⓜSt-Sulpice; map p.134. Though Goutal has passed on, the business is still in the family, continuing to produce her exquisite perfumes, all made from natural essences and presented in old-fashioned, ribbed-glass bottles. The bestselling fragrance is Eau d'Hadrien, a heady blend of citrus fruits and cypress. There's also a range for men, including Eau de Monsieur, a delicious lemony amber scent. This is the original branch. From €67 for 50ml eau de toilette. Mon–Sat 10am–7pm.

Belle de Jour 7 rue Tardieu, 18ᵉ, ⓦbelle-de-jour.fr; ⓜAbbesses/Anvers; map p.180. Beautiful, deeply old-fashioned shop selling perfume bottles, both new and vintage. From €8 for an inexpensive mini gift-bottle to €500 (or more) for the serious antiques – which range from eighteenth-century to utterly desirable Art Nouveau numbers. Tues–Fri 10.30am–1pm & 2–7pm, Sat 10.30am–1pm & 2–6pm.

Editions de Parfums Frédéric Malle 37 rue de Grenelle, 7ᵉ ⓦeditionsdeparfums.com; ⓜRue-du-Bac; map p.134. All the perfumes at this deliciously serious boutique have been created by "authors", which means professional parfumeurs working under their own name through this "publishing house". A 50ml bottle costs upwards of €100, but you're buying a genuine work of art, and getting seriously expert advice too. Mon noon–7pm, Tues–Sat 11am–7pm; closed two weeks in Aug.

Séphora 70 av des Champs-Elysées, 8ᵉ ⓦsephora.com; ⓜFranklin-D.-Roosevelt; map p.62. A huge perfume and cosmetics emporium, stocking every conceivable brand. There are lots of testers, and you can get free makeovers and beauty consultations. There are branches throughout the city, but this is the flagship store. Mon–Sat 10am–midnight, Sun 11am–midnight.

every imaginable shape and size, much of it for under €100. Mon–Fri 9am–7pm, Sat noon–7pm.

Hermès 24 rue du Faubourg-St-Honoré, 8ᵉ; ⓜConcorde; map p.62. Luxury clothing and accessory store. Come here for the ultimate silk scarf – at a price. Mon–Sat 10am–6.30pm.

Hervé Chapelier 1bis rue du Vieux-Colombier, 6ᵉ ⓦherve-chapelier.com; ⓜSt-Sulpice; map p.134. Often imitated, rarely matched, these classic bags are striped in two-tone to never go out of fashion. Priced affordably from €20 to €150. Mon–Sat 10am–7pm.

Jamin-Puech 61 rue d'Hauteville, 10ᵉ ⓦjamin-puech.com; ⓜPoissonnière; map p.191. An exquisite range of beautifully crafted bags (from around €225) in brightly coloured leather, crepe silk and other luxury fabrics. Tues–Sat 10.30am–7pm.

Marie-Hélène de Taillac 8 rue de Tournon, 6ᵉ ⓦmariehelenedetaillac.com; ⓜOdéon; map p.134. Sophisticated contemporary jewellery, mixing vivid, bold-coloured precious and semi-precious stones with deep, antique-looking gold in excitingly patterned designs. Expensive: even a tiny butterfly earring is over €500. Mon–Sat 11am–7pm.

Marie Mercié 23 rue St-Sulpice, 6ᵉ; ⓜSt-Sulpice; map p.134. This grande dame of chapellerie sells a glamorous collection of plaid, felt and fur hats for all occasions – but you're looking at wedding hats, really – at €250 and up. Mon–Sat 11am–7pm.

★ **Maroquinerie Saint Honoré** 334 rue St-Honoré, 1ᵉʳ; ⓜPyramides/Tuileries; map p.72. An unexpected find on one of the city's most exclusive shopping streets, this bargain shop sells very stylish French-made leather handbags (around €80 and up). Mon–Sat 10.30am–6.30pm.

L'Oeuf 9 rue Clauzel, 9ᵉ ⓦloeufparis.com; ⓜSt-Georges; map p.180. Trendy "concept" store selling ironic, retro-tinged accessories: anything from feather earrings to old-school Casio watches in bright colours, plus keyrings, jewellery, bags and "South Pigalle" branded T-shirts. Good for gifts for dotcom types. Tues–Sat noon–8pm.

MATERNITY

Paris is an excellent place to shop for maternity wear. Streets to check out include rue Guichard in the 16ᵉ and boulevard Raspail in the 7ᵉ, each with no fewer than five different boutiques for expectant mums.

1 et 1 font 3 9 rue Guichard, 16ᵉ ⓦ1et1font3.com; ⓜVictor-Hugo; map p.213. Small, blissful shop with a stylish selection of maternity wear, both casual and semi-formal. Most pieces cost around €100. Mon–Sat 10.30am–7pm.

En Attendant Bebe 2 rue Guichard, 16ᵉ ⓦenattendantbebe.fr; ⓜLa Muette; map p.213. Fairly sophisticated place selling relaxed but stylish maternity clothes under the logo "nine months that look like me". Many items under €100. Mon 2–7pm, Tues–Sat 10.30am–7.30pm.

ART

Paris has literally hundreds of **art galleries**, and for an idea of who is being exhibited where, look up details in *Pariscope* under "Expositions", or *L'Officiel des Spectacles* under "Galeries". The commercial art galleries (see box, p.100) are concentrated in the 8e, especially in and around avenue Matignon; in the Haut Marais; on rue Quincampoix, near the Pompidou Centre; around Bastille; and in St-Germain. A new crop of next-generation conceptual art galleries is located in rue Louise-Weiss in the 13e, just west of the new Bibliothèque Nationale de France-Mitterrand. Entry to commercial galleries is free.

ARTISTS' MATERIALS

Comptoir des Ecritures 35 rue Quincampoix, 4e ⓦcomptoirdesecritures.com; Ⓜ Rambuteau; map p.85. A delightful shop entirely devoted to the art of calligraphy, with an extensive collection of paper, pens, brushes and inks. Also runs lessons and mounts exhibitions. Tues–Sat 11am–7pm.

Dubois 20 rue Soufflot, 5^e ⓦdubois-paris.com; RER Luxembourg; map p.120. In the same great apothecary-style building since the mid-1800s, the Dubois family still offers an excellent selection of art supplies and paints alongside very knowledgeable service. Mon 10am–12.30pm & 2–7pm, Tues–Sat 9.30am–7pm.

Papier Plus 9 rue du Pont-Louis-Philippe, 4e ⓦpapierplus.com; Ⓜ St-Paul; map p.96. Fine-quality, colourful stationery, including notebooks, travel journals, photo albums and artists' portfolios. Several other fine stationers cluster on the same street. Mon–Sat noon–7pm.

Sennelier 3 quai Voltaire, 7e; Ⓜ St-Germain-des-Prés; map p.134. Serious, old-fashioned art suppliers, with some beautiful and reasonably priced sketch books. Mon 2–6.30pm, Tues–Sat 10am–12.45pm & 2–6.30pm.

FILM POSTERS

Ciné-Images 68 rue de Babylone, 7e ⓦcine-images .com; Ⓜ Sèvres-Babylone; map p.148. Suitably located right opposite the famous Pagode cinema, this classy shop sells original and mainly French film posters. Prices range from €30 for something small and recent to €15,000 for the historic advert for the Lumière brothers' *L'Arroseur Arrosé*. Tues–Fri 10am–1pm & 2–7pm, Sat 2–7pm.

BOOKS AND MUSIC

24

The most atmospheric areas for **book shopping** are the Seine *quais*, with their rows of new and secondhand bookstalls perched against the river parapet, and the narrow streets of the Quartier Latin.

ENGLISH-LANGUAGE BOOKS

English-language bookshops function as a home-away-from-home for expats, often with readings from visiting writers, and sometimes handy noticeboards for flat-shares, language lessons and work.

Abbey Bookshop 29 rue de la Parcheminerie, 5^e; Ⓜ St-Michel; map p.120. A Canadian bookshop round the corner from Shakespeare & Co, with lots of secondhand British and North American fiction, knowledgeable and helpful staff – and free coffee. Mon–Sat 10am–7pm.

Galignani 224 rue de Rivoli, 1er; Ⓜ Concorde; map p.72. Claims to be the first English bookshop established on the Continent way back in 1802. Stocks a good range, including fine art and children's books. Mon–Sat 10am–7pm.

Red Wheelbarrow 22 rue St-Paul, 4e ⓦwww .theredwheelbarrow.com; Ⓜ St-Paul; map p.96. A small, friendly bookshop, stocking a good selection of general fiction, history and children's books. Occasional readings and musical *soirées*. Mon 10am–6pm, Tues–Sat 10am–7pm, Sun 2–6pm.

Shakespeare & Co 37 rue de la Bûcherie, 5e ⓦshakespeareandcompany.com; Ⓜ St-Michel; map p.120. A cosy and very famous literary haunt (see p.119); getting the stamp in your book is something of a ritual. Has the biggest selection of secondhand English books in town, and lots of new stock, especially Paris-related. Every Monday there are readings or signings, and there's a library upstairs where you can sit and read for as long as you like. Mon–Fri 10am–11pm, Sat & Sun 11am–11pm.

★**Village Voice** 6 rue Princesse, 6^e ⓦvillagevoicebookshop.com; Ⓜ Mabillon; map p.134. A welcoming re-creation of a neighbourhood bookstore, with a good two-storey selection of contemporary fiction and non fiction, and a decent list of British and American poetry and classics. Frequent readings and author events. Mon 2–7pm, Tues–Sat 10am–7.30pm, Sun noon–6pm.

WH Smith 248 rue de Rivoli, 1er; Ⓜ Concorde; map p.72. The Parisian outlet of the British chain stocks a wide range of new books, newspapers and magazines, plus a small selection of British food for anyone feeling homesick (eg Marmite and baked beans). Mon–Sat 9am–7pm, Sun 12.30–7pm.

GENERAL FRENCH BOOKS

For general French titles, the biggest and most convenient shop has to be the Fnac in the Forum des Halles, but it'd be a pity to miss out on the slightly chaotic Left Bank experience at Gibert Jeune.

Fnac Forum des Halles, niveau 2, Porte Pierre-Lescot, 1er Ⓜ/RER Châtelet-Les-Halles, map p.85; 77–81 bd St-Germain, 6e Ⓜ Odéon/St-Michel/Cluny-La Sorbonne, map p.134; 74 av des Champs-Elysées, 8e Ⓜ Franklin-D. Roosevelt, map p.62; ⓦfnac.com. Fnac is France's leading retail chain for books, CDs and electronic equipment – as well as for concert and sports events tickets. The shops offer supermarket-style discounting, but the range of books and music extends into the higher brow. Lots of comics, guidebooks and maps. Forum des Halles and bd St-Germain Mon–Sat 10am–8pm; Champs-Elysées Mon–Sat 10am–11.45pm, Sun noon–11.45pm.

Gallimard 15 bd Raspail, 7ᵉ; ⓂSèvres-Babylone; map p.134. Most French publishers operate their own flagship bookshops, and Gallimard's boulevard Raspail store is one of the greats. Daily 10am–7pm.

Gibert Jeune 10 place St-Michel, 5ᵉ; ⓂSt-Michel; map p.120. There's a fair English-language and discounted selection at this branch of the classic Quartier Latin student/academic bookshop. A vast selection of French books can be found in the other seven branches, all scattered around the place. A real institution. Mon–Sat 9.30am–7.30pm.

Gibert Joseph 26 bd St-Michel, 5ᵉ; ⓂSt-Michel; map p.120. Neighbour and rival of the very similar Gibert Jeune group, with new and secondhand English books for sale at this branch. Mon–Sat 10am–8pm.

ART AND ARCHITECTURE BOOKS

★ **Artcurial** 7 Rond-Point des Champs-Elysées, 8ᵉ; ⓂFranklin-D.-Roosevelt; map p.62. The best art bookshop in Paris, set in an elegant townhouse. Sells French and foreign editions, and there's also a gallery, which puts on interesting exhibitions, and a stylish café. Mon–Sat 10.30am–7pm; closed two weeks in Aug.

La Hune 170 bd St-Germain, 6ᵉ; ⓂSt-Germain-des-Prés; map p.134. A good general French range, but the main selling point – apart from its fifty-year history as a Left Bank arts institution – is the art, design, fashion and photography "image" collection on the first floor. Mon–Sat 10am–11.45pm, Sun 11am–7.45pm.

Librairie le Moniteur 7 place de l'Odéon, 6ᵉ; ⓂOdéon; map p.134. Entirely dedicated to architecture, contemporary and historical, with books in English as well as French. There's even an in-house magazine devoted to public building projects. There's also a branch inside the Cité de l'Architecture, 16ᵉ (see p.154). Mon–Sat 10am–7pm.

COMICS (BANDES DESSINEES)

Album 8 rue Dante, 5ᵉ ⓦalbum.fr; ⓂMaubert-Mutualité; map p.120. Serious collection of French BDs, some of them rare editions with original artwork. This block of rue Dante houses no fewer than five separate comic-book shops. Mon–Sat 10am–8pm.

Thé-Troc 52 rue Jean-Pierre-Timbaud, 11ᵉ; ⓂParmentier; map p.196. The friendly owner publishes *The Fabulous Furry Freak Brothers* in French and English (he's a friend of the author of the famous Seventies comics, who lives nearby). There are other comic books and memorabilia on sale, too, as well as a wide selection of teas and teapots, secondhand records, jewellery and assorted junk. The

attached *salon de thé* (until 7pm) is comfy, colourful and restful, with board games. Mon–Sat 10am–8pm.

FILM AND PHOTOGRAPHY BOOKS

La Chambre Claire 14 rue St-Sulpice, 6ᵉ; ⓂOdéon; map p.134. Photography specialist selling art-house titles, style guides and instruction manuals, as well as a good number of English-language books. Sells photographs too. Tues–Sat 10.30am–7pm.

Ciné Reflet 14 rue Monsieur le Prince, 6ᵉ; ⓂOdéon; map p.134. This specialized and rather serious little shop has an excellent collection of books on cinema, many but not all in French, as well as pieces of film memorabilia. Mon–Sat 1–8pm.

MUSIC

Rue Keller and **rue des Taillandiers**, in the 11ᵉ (ⓂBastille), have a wide range of offbeat record shops selling current trends. For mainstream records, Fnac (with numerous branches, eg 26 av des Ternes, 17ᵉ ⓂTernes; Mon–Sat 10am–8pm) usually has the best prices (see opposite). If you're after musical equipment, try around rues Victor-Massé, Douai, Houdon and other streets in the **Pigalle** area, which are full of instrument and sound-system shops.

Analog Collector 13 rue Charles V, 4ᵉ ⓦanalog-collector.com; ⓂSt-Paul; map p.96. Stocks a fine collection of classical music and jazz on vinyl. Mon–Fri 1–7pm.

Crocodisc 40–42 rue des Ecoles, 5ᵉ ⓦcrocodisc.com; ⓂMaubert-Mutualité; map p.120. Folk, Oriental, Afro-Antillais, raï, funk, reggae, salsa, hip-hop, soul and country. New and secondhand, at some of the best prices in town. Tues–Sat 11am–7pm; closed first two weeks in Aug.

Librairie Musicale de Paris 68bis rue Réaumur, 3ᵉ; ⓂRéaumur-Sébastopol; map p.93. Huge selection of music books, from Baroque oratorios to heavy metal, some in English. Tues–Sat 10.15am–7pm.

Maison Sauviat 124 bd de la Chapelle, 18ᵉ; ⓂBarbès-Rochechouart; map p.180. Wonderful shop that's been going strong since the 1920s. Now specializing in North and West African and Middle Eastern music. Mon–Sat 9.45am–6.45pm.

Paul Beuscher 15–27 bd Beaumarchais, 4ᵉ ⓦpaul-beuscher.com; ⓂBastille; map p.93. A music department store that's been around for more than a hundred years. Instruments, scores, books, recording equipment, etc. Amazing sales in spring. Mon 2–7pm, Tues–Sat 10.15am–7pm.

Virgin Megastore 52 av des Champs-Elysées, 8ᵉ ⓂFranklin-D.-Roosevelt, map p.62; also Carrousel du Louvre, under the Louvre, 1ᵉʳ ⓂPalais-Royal-Musée-du-Louvre. This is one of the biggest music stores in the

24

country, and also houses a concert-booking agency. Champs-Elysées Mon–Sat 10am–midnight, Sun noon–midnight; Louvre Mon & Tues 10am–8pm, Wed–Sun 10am–9pm.

TRAVEL BOOKS

Attica 106 bd Richard Lenoir, 11ᵉ ⓦattica.fr; ⓂOberkampf; map p.196. All the books, CD-ROMS, dictionaries and DVDs you could possibly need to learn any number of the two hundred languages represented at this language-learning hub. Online ordering enables you to hit the books before hitting the road. Tues–Sat 10am–7pm.

Institut Géographique National (IGN) 107 rue La Boétie, 8ᵉ ⓦign.fr; ⓂSt-Philippe-Roule; map p.62. The official (and best) source for maps of France, and indeed the entire world, plus guidebooks, satellite photos, old maps of Paris and raised relief maps of the mountainous regions of France. Mon–Fri 9.30am–7pm, Sat 11am–12.30pm & 2–6.30pm.

Librairie Ulysse 26 rue St-Louis-en-l'Ile, 4ᵉ ⓂPont-Marie/Sully-Morland; map p.42. A tiny bookshop, piled from floor to ceiling with new and secondhand travel books and run by a friendly English-speaking owner. Mon noon–6.30pm, Tues–Fri 11am–7pm, Sat 11am–6.30pm.

FOOD AND DRINK

Paris has resisted the march of mega-stores with admirable resilience. Almost every *quartier* still has its charcuterie, boulangerie and weekly market, while some streets, such as rue Cler, in the 7ᵉ, and rue des Martyrs, in the 9ᵉ, are literally lined with grocers', butchers' shops delicatessens, pâtisseries, cheese shops, and wine-merchants. Buying food at these places is an aesthetic experience, a feast for the eyes quite as much as the palate. Our listings, below, are for **specialist food shops**, many of which are veritable palaces of gluttony and fairly expensive, while **street markets** are detailed in a separate section at the end of this chapter. **Food halls** to equal that of Harrods are to be found at Fauchon, Hédiard and the Grande Epicerie (see box below). In addition, there are one-product specialists for whom gourmets will cross the city: Poilâne or Ganachaud for bread; Barthélémy for cheese; La Maison de l'Escargot for snails. As for buying food inexpensively, you will be best off shopping at the street markets or supermarkets – though save your bread- and cake-buying at least for the local boulangerie and pâtisseries. Useful **supermarkets** with branches throughout Paris are Franprix, Monoprix and Ed l'Epicier; this last is particularly cheap.

BREAD

Ganachaud 226 rue des Pyrénées, 20ᵉ; ⓂGambetta; map p.196. Although father Ganachaud has left the business, his three daughters continue his work, and the bread is still out of this world. The cakes, especially the almond pastries, are also well worth sampling. Tues–Sat 7.30am–8pm.

Du Pain et Des Idées 34 rue Yves Toudic, 10ᵉ ⓦdupainetdesidees.com; ⓂJacques Bonsergent; map p.196. Christophe Vasseur, a former fashion-industry sales executive, was named the best baker in Paris in 2008, and a visit here quickly reveals why: heavenly baguettes, brioches, pastries and the signature *pain des amis*, a nutty flatbread. Mon–Fri 6.45am–8pm.

★ **Poilâne** 8 rue du Cherche-Midi, 6ᵉ; ⓂSèvres-Babylone; map p.134. The source of the famous "Pain Poilâne" – a bread baked using traditional methods (albeit

---

FOODIE HEAVEN: GOURMET GROCERIES

Any list of food shops in Paris has to have at its head three palaces:

Fauchon 24–30 place de la Madeleine, 8ᵉ ⓦfauchon.fr; ⓂMadeleine; map p.72. An amazing range of extravagantly beautiful groceries, exotic fruit and vegetables, charcuterie, wines both French and foreign – almost anything you can think of, all at exorbitant prices. The quality is assured by blind testing, which all suppliers have to submit to. Just the place for presents of tea, jam, truffles, chocolates, exotic vinegars, mustards and so forth. There's also a *traiteur* and a restaurant. Mon–Wed 10am–7.30pm, Thurs 10am–9pm, Fri 10am–8pm, Sat 9.30am–8pm.

La Grande Epicerie 38 rue de Sèvres, 7ᵉ; ⓂSèvres-Babylone; map p.134. This edible offshoot of the famous Bon Marché department store may not be

quite as nakedly epicurean as Fauchon and Hédiard, but it's still a fabulous emporium of fresh and packed foods. Popular among choosy Parisians, moneyed expats (for its country-specific favourites) and gastro-tourists alike. Mon–Sat 8.30am–9pm.

Hédiard 21 place de la Madeleine, 8ᵉ ⓦhediard.fr; ⓂMadeleine; map p.62. The aristocrat's grocer since the 1850s, with sales staff as deferential as servants, as long as you don't try to reach for items yourself. Superlative quality in their coffees, spices and conserves. There's also a restaurant upstairs, and several smaller branches around the city, including one at 31 av Georges V, 8ᵉ (ⓂGeorges-V). Mon–Sat 8.30am–9pm.

ramped up on an industrial scale) as conceived by the late, legendary Monsieur Poilâne himself. Mon–Sat 7.15am–8.15pm.

CHARCUTERIE

★ **Le Comptoir de la Gastronomie** 34 rue Montmartre, 1er; Ⓜ Les Halles/Etienne-Marcel; map p.72. The walls of this lovely old-fashioned shop are stacked high with wine bottles, foie gras, *saucisses*, preserves and hams. There's also a fine little restaurant attached, ideal for a lunchtime snack. Mon–Sat noon–midnight.

Aux Ducs de Gascogne 111 rue St-Antoine, 4e; Ⓜ St-Paul; map p.96. Excellent range of high-quality charcuterie and foie gras, as well as enticing – and expensive – deli goods ranging from little salads to caviar. Mon–Sat 10am–8pm.

Flo Prestige 42 place du Marché-St-Honoré, 1er; Ⓜ Pyramides; map p.72. All sorts of delicacies, plus wines, champagne and exquisite ready-made dishes. Daily 8am–11pm.

Labeyrie 6 rue Montmartre, 1er; Ⓜ Châtelet-Les-Halles; map p.72. Specialist in products from the Landes region: Bayonne hams, goose and duck pâtés, and conserves. Tues–Fri 11am–2pm & 3–7pm.

Maison de la Truffe 19 place de la Madeleine, 8e; Ⓦ maison-de-la-truffe.com; Ⓜ Madeleine; map p.62. Truffles, of course, both *noires*, from France, and *blanches*, from Italy – either way upwards of €1500 per 400g. Also sells roe, foie gras and similar delicacies. You can try before you buy at the attached restaurant, but bring a second credit card for backup. Mon–Sat 9.30am–9pm.

CHEESE

Androuet 134 rue Mouffetard, 5e; Ⓜ Censier-Daubenton; map p.120. One of four fine cheese shops on the rue Mouffetard, all offering wonderful selections, beautifully displayed. This one is part of a small, highly regarded chain. Tues–Fri 9.30am–1pm & 4–7pm, Sat 9.30am–7.30pm, Sun 9.30am–1.30pm.

Barthélémy 51 rue de Grenelle, 7e; Ⓜ Rue-du-Bac; map p.134. Purveyors of carefully ripened and meticulously stored seasonal cheeses to the rich and powerful. Can arrange home delivery. Tues–Fri 8.30am–1pm & 4–7.15pm, Sat 8.30am–1.30pm & 3–7pm; closed Aug.

Fromagerie Alléosse 13 rue Poncelet, 17e Ⓦ fromage-alleosse.com; Ⓜ Ternes; map p.62. A connoisseur's selection of high-quality cheeses, including Brie from Champagne, creamy Brillat-Savarin, nutty-flavoured Mont d'Or and an enormous variety of goat's cheeses. Mon–Thurs 9am–1pm & 4–7pm, Fri & Sat 9am–7pm, Sun 9am–1pm.

CHOCOLATES AND PATISSERIES

La Bague de Kenza 106 rue St-Maur, 11e; Ⓜ St-Maur; map p.108. An Algerian pâtisserie full of enticing cakes

made of dates, orange, pistachios, figs, almonds and other tasty ingredients. There's also a little *salon de thé* attached. Mon–Sat 10am–8pm.

★ **Chocolaterie Jacques Genin** 133 rue de Turenne, 3e; Ⓜ St-Sébastien-Froissart; map p.93. After many years supplying chocolates to Paris's top restaurants, Jacques Genin finally opened his own shop in 2008. A wonderful selection of chocolates, caramels, nougats and pastries are on offer, and don't miss the ganaches; flavours include coffee, raspberry and szechuan pepper. Daily 11am–9pm.

★ **Debauve et Gallais** 30 rue des Sts-Pères, 7e; Ⓜ St-Germain-des-Prés/Sèvres-Babylone; map p.134. This beautiful shop specializing in chocolate and elaborate sweets has been around since chocolate was taken as a medicine – and an aphrodisiac. Mon–Sat 9am–7pm.

Jean-Paul Hévin 231 rue St-Honoré, 8e; Ⓜ Tuileries; map p.72. One of the best chocolatiers in Paris, with a sleek shop displaying an array of elegantly presented tablets of chocolate, all bearing little descriptions of their aroma and characteristics, as if they were fine wines. Upstairs is a stylish *salon de thé* serving delicious chocolate cakes. Mon–Sat 10am–7.30pm.

★ **Joséphine Vannier** 4 rue Pas de la Mule, 4e; Ⓜ Bastille; map p.93. This marvellous chocolatier sells chocolate shaped into accordions, violins, books, Eiffel Towers and Arcs de Triomphe – exquisite creations, almost too beautiful to eat. Prices are reasonable, too, from around €17. Tues–Sat 11am–1pm & 2–7pm.

Pâtisserie Stohrer 51 rue Montorgueil, 2e; Ⓜ Sentier; map p.72. Bread, pâtisseries, chocolate and charcuterie have been produced here since 1730. Come to discover what *pain aux raisins* should really taste like. Daily 7.30am–8pm; closed first two weeks in Aug.

HERBS, SPICES AND OILS

G. Detou 58 rue Tiquetonne, 2e; Ⓜ Etienne-Marcel; map p.72. Friendly épicerie that gets packed to the gills on Saturdays. Kilos of spices, nuts and chocolate, plus the usual *confit* and foie gras. Mon–Sat 8.30am–6.30pm.

Izraël 30 rue François-Miron, 4e; Ⓜ St-Paul; map p.96. A cosmopolitan emporium of goodies from all round the globe: vinegars, oils, spices and mustards. Tues–Fri 9.30am–1pm & 2.30–7pm, Sat 9.30am–7pm.

Maille 6 place de la Madeleine, 8e; Ⓜ Madeleine; map p.72. Founded in 1747, Maille is best known for its Dijon mustard, but it also makes 28 other varieties, plus all kinds of flavoured vinegars and hand-painted mustard pots. Mon–Sat 10am–7pm.

ASIAN AND HEALTH FOOD

Rendez-Vous de la Nature 96 rue Mouffetard, 5e; Ⓜ Censier-Daubenton; map p.120. One of the city's

24

largest and most comprehensive health-food stores, with everything from organic produce to herbal teas. Tues–Sat 9.30am–7.30pm, Sun 9.30am–1pm.

Tang Frères 168 av de Choisy, 13ᵉ Ⓜ Place d'Italie, map p.173; 48 av d'Ivry, 13ᵉ Ⓜ Olympiades, map p.173. The original and classic "Chinese" supermarket – though the Tang brothers actually came from Laos originally, and their shop sells Southeast Asian goods as much as, if not more than, Chinese. At no. 188 there's also a deli-restaurant, *Tang Gourmet*, which does fast business in lunchtime noodles. Daily 11am–8pm.

HONEY

Les Abeilles 21 rue Butte-aux-Cailles, 13ᵉ; Ⓜ Corvisart/ Place-d'Italie; map p.173. Honey from all over France and further afield, sold from a barrel by an experienced beekeeper. Around €3 for a 250g pot, though you'll pay almost double for the Miel de Paris – harvested from beehives across the city. You can save 50 cents by bringing your own (best sterilized) jar. Tues–Sat 11am–7pm.

Les Rûchers du Roy 37 rue du Roi de Sicile, 4ᵉ; Ⓜ St-Paul; map p.96. Well-priced and original flavoured honeys, honey jams, honey sweets and some interesting apitherapy products meant to cure digestive and cardiovascular ailments. Tues–Sun 2–8pm.

SALMON, SNAILS AND CAVIAR

Autour du Saumon 60 rue François-Miron, 4ᵉ; Ⓜ St-Paul; map p.96. Salmon especially, but eels, trout and all things fishy as well, plus a delightful little restaurant in which to taste it all. There are also several other branches around the city. Mon–Sat 10am–10.30pm, Sun 11am–8pm.

Caviar Kaspia 17 place de la Madeleine, 8ᵉ Ⓦ lamaisonkaspia.com; Ⓜ Madeleine; map p.62. Blinis, smoked salmon and Beluga caviar, all of which can also be sampled in the plush upstairs restaurant. Mon 10am–midnight, Tues–Sat 10am–1am.

La Maison de l'Escargot 79 rue Fondary, 15ᵉ; Ⓜ Dupleix; map p.170. As the name suggests, this place specializes in snails: they even sauce them and re-shell them while you wait. Tues–Sat 9.30am–7pm; closed mid-July to Sept.

TEA AND COFFEE

Mariage Frères 30 rue du Bourg-Tibourg, 4ᵉ; Ⓜ Hôtel-de-Ville; map p.96. Hundreds of teas, neatly packed in tins, line the floor-to-ceiling shelves of this 100-year-old tea emporium. There's also a classy *salon de thé* (see p.272) on the ground floor. Daily 10.30am–7.30pm.

★ **Verlet** 256 rue St-Honoré, 1ᵉʳ; Ⓜ Palais-Royal-Musée-du-Louvre; map p.72. An old-fashioned *torréfacteur* (coffee merchant), one of the best known in Paris, selling both familiar and less-common varieties of coffee and tea from around the world. There's also a tearoom, perfect for a pick-me-up. Mon–Sat 9am–7pm.

WINE AND BEER

Nicolas and Le Repaire de Bacchus are the best of the chains, with branches across the city.

Le Baron Rouge 1 rue Théophile-Roussel, 12ᵉ; Ⓜ Ledru-Rollin; map p.108. A good selection of dependable lower-range French wines, with wines by the glass from around €1.50. Very drinkable Merlot at around €3 a litre, if you bring your own containers. Tues–Fri 10am–2pm & 5–10pm, Sat 10am–10pm, Sun 10.30am–3.30pm.

Les Caves Augé 116 bd Haussmann, 8ᵉ Ⓦ cavesauge .com; Ⓜ St-Augustin; map p.62. This old-fashioned, wood-panelled shop is the oldest *cave* in Paris, dating back to 1850, and sells around six thousand French and foreign wines made from organic grapes. Mon 1–7.30pm, Tues–Sat 9am–7.30pm.

Caves Michel Renaud 12 place de la Nation, 12ᵉ; Ⓜ Nation; map p.108. Established in 1890 and purveying superb-value French and Spanish wines, champagnes and Armagnac. You can also buy a bottle of Green Muse, a special unsweetened absinthe from southwestern France. Mon 3–8.30pm, Tues–Sat 9.30am–1pm & 2.30–8.30pm, Sun 10am–1pm.

Les Caves St-Antoine 95 rue St-Antoine, 4ᵉ; Ⓜ St-Paul; map p.96. A small, amicable outfit, selling almost exclusively French wines. Tues–Fri 9am–1pm & 3–8pm, Sat 9am–8pm, Sun 9am–1pm.

La Crèmerie 9 rue des Quatre-Vents, 6ᵉ; Ⓜ Odéon; map p.134. See p.282.

Lavinia 3–5 bd de la Madeleine, 8ᵉ; Ⓜ Madeleine; map p.72. The largest wine and spirits store in Europe. The modern interior displays thousands of bottles of wines from over 43 countries, and the wine cellar holds some of the rarest bottles in the world. The attached wine library and bar/restaurant allow you to read up, then drink up. Mon–Fri 10am–8pm, Sat 9am–8pm.

Legrand Filles et Fils Galerie Vivienne, 4 rue des Petit Champs/1 rue de la Banque, 2ᵉ Ⓦ caves-legrand.com; Ⓜ Bourse; map p.72. An established wine merchant, dating back more than a hundred years, with an extensive cellar, as well as quality truffles, foie gras and chocolates, plus a wine bar (see p.272). Mon 11am–7pm, Tues–Fri 10am–7.30pm, Sat 10am–7pm.

De Vinis Illustribus 48 rue de la Montagne Ste-Geneviève, 5ᵉ; Ⓜ Maubert-Mutualité; map p.120. Connoisseur Lionel Michelin set up shop twenty years ago in this ancient wine cellar. He still specializes in very old and very rare vintages but is just as happy selling you an €8 bottle of Coteaux du Languedoc and orating eloquently on its tannins. Tues–Sat 2pm–7pm.

FURNITURE AND HOMEWARE

A selection of the best shops specializing in objects for the **home**, as well as **furniture** stockists, are listed below. Also worth checking out are the shops at the art and design museums, and the streets around Bastille, with a high concentration of stores specializing in particular periods. For kitchenware, rue Montmartre, just north of Les Halles, is a great place to start looking, with no fewer than three superb options. Also try the kitchen sections at BHV (see p.322) and Lafayette Maison (see p.323) for great selections of cookware and cutlery.

ANTIQUES

Galerie Patrick Séguin 5 rue des Taillandiers, 11e Ⓦ patrickseguin.com; ⓂBastille; map p.108. A fine collection of furniture and objects from the 1950s, including pieces by Le Corbusier and Jean Prouvé, though not everything is for sale. Tues–Sat noon–7pm.

Louvre des Antiquaires 2 place du Palais-Royal, 1er Ⓦ louvre-antiquaires.com; ⓂPalais-Royal-Musée-du-Louvre; map p.72. An enormous antiques and furniture hypermarket where you can pick up anything from a Mycenaean seal ring to an Art Nouveau vase – for a price. Tues–Sun 11am–7pm; closed Sun in July and Aug.

Lulu Berlu 2 rue du Grand-Prieuré, 11e Ⓦ luluberlu .com; ⓂOberkampf; map p.196. Crammed with twentieth-century toys and curios, most in their original packaging. There's a particularly good collection of 1970–90s favourites, including Doctor Who, Star Wars, Planet of the Apes and Batman, and they also do a good range of new toys. Mon–Sat 11am–7.30pm.

Au Petit Bonheur la Chance 13 rue St-Paul, 4e; ⓂSt-Paul; map p.96. A tiny shop stacked high with antique kitchenware, such as very French-looking teatowels, café-au-lait bowls, storage jars, dainty lace handkerchiefs and door-number plaques. Mon & Wed–Sat 11am–1pm & 2.30–6pm, Sun 2.30–6pm.

FABRICS

Dominique Picquier 10 rue Charlot, 3e; ⓂFilles-du-Calvaire/St-Sébastian-Froissart; map p.96. "A tribute to nature in the city" is how this textile designer describes her beautiful fabrics printed with striking graphic patterns. Picquier also does an attractive range of accessories, including tote bags and purses (from €30). Mon & Sat 2.30–7.30pm, Tues–Fri 11am–7.30pm.

Marché St-Pierre 2 rue Charles-Nodier, 18e; ⓂAnvers; map p.180. Five floors offering a huge range of (mostly inexpensive) fabrics. Fashion buyers can be spotted browsing here, but it's well worth a visit even if you're not buying. Mon–Sat 10am–6.30pm.

HOMEWARE

Astier de Villatte 173 rue St-Honoré, 1er; ⓂPalais Royal; map p.72. You feel as if you've just walked into your grandmother's kitchen on entering this delightful shop with its dark-wood floorboards and cabinets, all displaying stylish ceramic dinnerware (pieces from around €35). Mon–Sat 11am–7pm.

Colette 213 rue St-Honoré, 1er Ⓦ colette.fr; ⓂTuileries; map p.72. See p.326.

Merci 111 bd Beaumarchais, 3e; St-Sébastien-Froissart; map p.93. Flowers, bed linen, throws, kitchenware, Annick Goutal fragrances, secondhand books and clothes (some specially designed for the store by leading designers such as Stella McCartney) are all sold under the glass roof of this very hip and original concept store: all profits go to charity. Mon–Sat 10am–7pm.

Résonances 9 cour St-Emilion, 12e Ⓦ resonances.fr; ⓂCour St-Emilion; map p.113. Stylish kitchen and bathroom accessories, with an emphasis on French design. Covetable items include elegant wine decanters and a white porcelain hot-chocolate maker. Daily 11am–9pm.

Sam 35 rue de Bretagne, 3e; ⓂFilles-du-Calvaire/St-Sébastian-Froissart; map p.96. A modern design shop selling lamps, gadgets and many quirky items such as pig-shaped chopping boards. A good place for gifts. Mon–Sat 10.30am–8pm, Sun 10.30am–3pm.

★ **Le Viaduc des Arts** 9–129 av Daumesnil, 12e; ⓂBastille/Gare de Lyon; map p.108. Practically the entire north side of the street is dedicated to an extremely high standard of skilled workmanship and craft. Each arch of this old railway viaduct houses a shop front and workspace for the artists within, who produce contemporary metalwork, ceramics, tapestry, sculpture and much more. Most shops Mon–Sat 10.30am–7.30pm.

KITCHENWARE

A. Simon 48–52 rue Montmartre, 2^e; ⓂEtienne-Marcel; map p.72. A huge collection of anything and everything for the kitchen, including a wide range of cast-iron and copper cookware, and fine glassware. Bovida, at no. 36, and MORA, at no. 13, are the big rivals on the street. Mon 1.30–6.30pm, Tues–Sat 9am–6.30pm.

E. Dehillerin 18–20 rue Coquillière, 1er Ⓦ e-dehillerin .fr; ⓂChâtelet-Les-Halles; map p.72. This nineteenth-century institution, in business since 1820, is laid out like a traditional ironmonger's: narrow aisles, no fancy displays, prices buried in catalogues, but good-quality stock of knives, slicers, peelers, presses and assorted cookware, many of restaurant quality at reasonable prices. A great selection of very durable copper and pewter pans. Mon 9am–12.30pm & 2–6pm, Tues–Sat 9am–6pm. **La Vaissellerie** 80 bd Haussmann, 8e ⓜHavre-Caumartin, map p.62; also 85 rue de Rennes, 6e ⓜRennes, and 79 rue St-Lazare, 9e ⓜTrinité. Simple, inexpensive French crockery, mostly in white, but they also stock the cheerful bright-yellow Chocolat Menier and Banania ranges. Mon–Sat 9.30am–7pm.

SPECIALIST SHOPS

Abdon 6 bd Beaumarchais, 11e; ⓜChemin-Vert; map p.108. New and secondhand photographic equipment. If they don't have what you're looking for, try the half-dozen other camera shops on the same street. Tues–Sat 9.30am–12.30pm & 1.30–6.30pm.

Archives de la Presse 51 rue des Archives, 3^e; ⓜRambuteau; map p.96. A fascinating shop for a browse, trading in old French newspapers and magazines. The window always has a display of outdated newspapers corresponding to the current month, and there's pile upon pile of old magazines inside, with vintage *Vogues* giving a good insight into the changing fashion scene. Mon–Sat 10.30am–7pm.

L'Artisanat Monastique 68bis av Denfert-Rochereau, 14^e; ⓜDenfert-Rochereau/RER Port Royal; map p.160. An unusual address in an odd location – the vaulted basement of a hospice run by nuns. All the products on sale are handmade by French monks or nuns, and run the gamut from religious kitsch to beautifully old-fashioned clothes for young children, and from fine beeswax cleaning products to herbal unguents and Chartreuse liqueurs. Mon–Fri noon–6.30pm, Sat 2–7pm.

★ **Boîte à Musique Anna Joliet** Jardin du Palais Royal, 9 rue de Beaujolais, 1er; ⓜPalais-Royal-Musée-du-Louvre; map p.72. A delightful, minuscule boutique selling every style of music box, from inexpensive self-winding toy models to grand cabinets costing thousands of euros. Parisians have long loved mechanical instruments, and many of these play old favourites such as *La Vie en Rose* and *Chim-Chimney*. Prices begin at around €50. Mon–Sat 10am–7pm.

Dam Boutons 46 rue d'Orsel, 18^e ⓦdamboutons.com; ⓜPigalle; map p.180. Over ten thousand buttons, from the out-there to the traditional, in a friendly, old-fashioned little Montmartre shop. Mon 1.30–6.30pm, Tues–Sat 10.30am–1pm & 1.30–6.30pm.

★ **Deyrolle** 46 rue du Bac, 6e ⓦdeyrolle.com; ⓜRue-du-Bac; map p.134. Extraordinary, historic palace of taxidermy – as much a sight as a shop (see p.142). From €15 for a box of butterflies or fossils to €45,000 for a (naturally deceased) polar bear. Mon 10am–1pm & 2–7pm, Tues–Sat 10am–7pm.

Le Pot à Tabac 28 rue de la Pépinière, 8e; ⓜSt-Augustin; map p.62. This shop sells a classy selection of pipes, cigars and tobacco, as well as an enormous choice of international cigarettes. Daily 7.30am–7.30pm.

Trousselier 73 bd Haussmann, 8e; ⓜSt-Augustin; map p.62. Described in French *Vogue* as *the* artificial flower shop. Every conceivable species of flora fashioned from man-made fibre, from a simple basket of roses to more decadent and pricey arrangements. Also does a good selection of tableware, such as very French-looking espresso cups (€25), and attractive picnic hampers (€35). Mon–Sat 10.30am–7pm.

MARKETS

Paris's **markets** are a grand spectacle. Most are resolutely French, their produce forming an enduring tie between the city and that great national obsession: *terroir*, or land. But you'll also find intoxicating ethnic markets: on the fringes of the 18e, Africa predominates; Southeast Asia in the 13e arrondissement. Other street markets are dedicated to secondhand goods (the *marchés aux puces*), clothes and textiles, flowers, birds, books and stamps. Several of the markets listed below are also described in the guide.

BOOKS AND STAMPS

Marché du Livre Ancien et d'Occasion Pavillon Baltard, Parc Georges-Brassens, rue Brancion, 15e; ⓜPorte-de-Vanves; map p.160. Up to 60 stalls selling secondhand and antiquarian books. Sat & Sun 9am–6pm, though best in the morning.

Marché aux Timbres Junction of avs Marigny & Gabriel, on the north side of place Clemenceau in the 8e; ⓜChamps-Elysées-Clemenceau; map p.62. *The* stamp market in Paris, attracting professional dealers as well as individual sellers. You can also buy postcards and phonecards here. Thurs, Sat, Sun & hols 10am–7pm.

CLOTHES AND FLEA MARKETS

Porte de Montreuil Av de Porte de Montreuil, 20e; ⓜPorte-de-Montreuil. Cheap new clothes now dominate what was the best market for secondhand clothes; still cheapest on Mondays when weekend leftovers are sold off. Also old furniture, household goods and assorted junk. Sat, Sun & Mon 7.30am–5pm.

Puces de Vanves Av Georges Lafenestre/av Marc Sangnier, 14^e ⓦpucesdevanves.typepad.com; ⓜPorte-de-Vanves; map p.160. The best choice for bric-a-brac and little Parisian knick-knacks. Professionals deal alongside weekend amateurs. Sat & Sun

24

7am–1pm, or till around 3pm on av Georges Lafenestre.

St-Ouen/Porte de Clignancourt 18e; map p.229. By far the biggest and most visited flea market (see p.228).

FLOWER MARKETS

Place Lépine Ile de la Cité, 1er; ⓂCité; map p.42. On Sundays, the flower market is augmented with birds and pets. Daily 8am–7pm.

Place de la Madeleine 8e; ⓂMadeleine; map p.62. Flowers and plants. Tues–Sun 8am–7.30pm.

Place des Ternes 8e; ⓂTernes; map p.62. Flowers and plants. Tues–Sun 8am–7.30pm.

FOOD MARKETS

At the top end of the **food market** scale, you'll find lavish arrays in rue de Lévis in the 17e and rue Cler in the 7e. The real **street markets** include a scattering in the Left Bank – especially place Maubert and place Monge – along with bigger ones at Montparnasse, in boulevard Edgar-Quinet and opposite Val-de-Grâce in boulevard Port-Royal. The largest is in rue de la Convention, in the 15e. A selection is given below; a full list of food markets can be found at ⓌØparis.fr (search for "Les marchés Parisiens"). For a different feel and more exotic **foreign produce**, take a look at the Mediterranean/Oriental displays on rue Dejean and rue d'Aligre. Markets usually start up between 7am and 8am and tail off between 1pm and 2.30pm, although a few are afternoon-only.

Aguesseau Place de la Madeleine, 8e; ⓂMadeleine; map p.62. Tues & Fri.

Alésia Rue de la Glacière and rue de la Santé, 13e; ⓂGlacière; map p.173. Wed & Sat.

Alibert Rue Alibert by the Hôpital St-Louis, 10e; ⓂGoncourt; map p.196. Sun 7am–3pm.

Auguste-Blanqui Bd Blanqui between place d'Italie and rue Barrault, 13e; ⓂCorvisart; map p.173. Fri & Sun.

Batignolles Rue de Turin and rue des Batignolles, 8e; ⓂRome; map p.193. Organic produce. Sat 8.30am–1pm.

Baudoyer Place Baudoyer, 4^e ⓂHôtel-de-Ville; map p.96. Wed 3–8.30pm & Sat 7am–3pm.

Belleville Bd de Belleville, 11e; ⓂBelleville; map p.196. Tues & Fri.

Bercy Place Lachambaudie, 12e; ⓂCour St-Emillion; map p.113. Wed & Sun.

Boulevard de Grenelle Rue Lourmel, 15e. ⓂLa-Motte-Picquet; map p.170. Wed & Sun.

Brancusi Place Brancusi, 14e; ⓂGaîté; map p.160. Specialist organic market. Sat 9am–3pm.

Charonne Rue de Charonne & rue Dumas, 11e; ⓂAlexandre Dumas; map p.108. Wed & Sat.

Convention Rue de la Convention, 15e; ⓂConvention; map p.170. Tues, Thurs & Sun.

Dejean Rue Dejean, 18e; ⓂChâteau-Rouge; map p.191. African foods. Tues–Sun.

★ **Edgar-Quinet** Bd Edgar-Quinet, 14^e; ⓂEdgar-Quinet; map p.160. Food market Wed & Sat mornings, art and crafts market Sun roughly 10am–dusk.

Enfants-Rouges 39 rue de Bretagne, 3e; ⓂFilles-du-Calvaire; map p.96. Tues–Sat 8am–1pm & 4–7.30pm, Sun 9am–1pm.

Ledru-Rollin Av Ledru-Rollin between rue de Lyon and rue de Bercy, 12e; ⓂGare de Lyon; map p.108. Thurs & Sat.

Maubert Place Maubert, 5e; ⓂMaubert-Mutualité; map p.120. Tues & Thurs 7am–2.30pm, Sat 7am–3pm.

★ **Monge** Place Monge, 5e; ⓂMonge; map p.120. Wed & Fri 7am–2.30pm, Sun 7am–3pm.

Montorgueil Rue Montorgueil & rue Montmartre, 1er; ⓂChâtelet-Les-Halles/Sentier; map p.72. Tues–Sat 8am–1pm & 4–7pm, Sun 9am–1pm.

Mouffetard Rue Mouffetard, 5e; ⓂCensier-Daubenton; map p.120. Tues–Sun.

Père-Lachaise Bd de Ménilmontant, between rue des Panoyaux and rue des Cendriers, 11e; ⓂMénilmontant; map p.196. Tues & Fri.

Place d'Aligre 12e; ⓂLedru-Rollin; map p.108. Tues–Sun until 1pm.

Popincourt Bd de Port-Royal, near Val-de-Grâce, 5e; RER Port-Royal; map p.160. Tues, Thurs & Sat.

★ **Raspail/Marché Bio** Bd Raspail, between rue du Cherche-Midi & rue de Rennes, 6e; ⓂRennes; map p.134. Organic market with herbal remedies and produce. Also known as the Marché Bio. Tues & Fri.

★ **Richard Lenoir** Bd Richard Lenoir, 11e; ⓂBastille; map p.108. An authentic Parisian street market, with lots of regional produce. Thurs & Sun.

Rue Cler 7e; ⓂEcole-Militaire; map p.148. Tues–Sun 8.30am–noon.

St-Germain Rue Mabillon, 6e; ⓂMabillon; map p.134. Tues–Fri 8am–1pm & 4–8pm, Sat 8am–1.30pm & 3.30–8pm, Sun 8am–1.30pm.

St-Honoré Place du Marché St-Honoré, 1er; ⓂPyramides; map p.72. Wed 3–8.30pm, Sat 7am–3pm.

St-Martin 31–33 rue du Château-d'Eau, 10e; ⓂChâteau-d'Eau; map p.191. Covered market. Tues–Fri 9am–1pm & 4–7.30pm, Sat 9am–7.30pm, Sun 9am–1.30pm.

St-Quentin 85bis bd Magenta, 10e; ⓂGare-de-l'Est; map p.191. Tues–Fri 9am–1pm & 4–7.30pm, Sat 9am–1pm & 3.30–7.30pm, Sun 8.30am–1.30pm.

Saxe-Breteuil Av de Saxe, 7e; ⓂSégur; map p.148. Thurs & Sat.

24

JOSEPHINE BAKER POOL

Activities and sports

If you've had enough of following crowds through museums or wandering through the city in the blazing sun or pouring rain, then it may just be time to do what the Parisians do. There are ice rinks to fall over on, libraries to settle down in, fine wines to taste and some genuinely beautiful swimming pools to dive into. Hammams, or Turkish baths, are particularly loved by Parisians, and range from the luxuriously chichi to the pungently authentic. The more active can rent a bike, take a boat trip, view the city from a balloon, learn the tricks of the gourmet chef at a cookery school, or simply play a few rounds of boules. There's a world-leading array of spectator sports on offer, too, from football to horse racing, though the highlight of the city's calendar is, of course, the triumphal arrival of cycling's Tour de France in July.

25

ESSENTIALS

Listings and information *Pariscope* has useful listings of sports facilities, pools, hammams and so on (under "Sport et bien-être"). Information on municipal facilities is available from the Hôtel de Ville (see ⓦ paris.fr) or at individual arrondissements' *mairies*. For details of current sporting events, try the daily sports paper *L'Equipe*. It's also worth keeping an eye on events at the Palais Omnisports Paris-Bercy (see p.347), a major venue for all sports, including athletics, cycling, show jumping, ice hockey, ballroom dancing, judo and motocross.

BOAT TRIPS AND BALLOON RIDES

Seeing Paris by **boat** is one of the city's most enduring experiences – and a lot of fun. Seeing it **from the air** is arguably even better.

BATEAUX-MOUCHES

Bateaux-Mouches Boat trips start from the Embarcadère du Pont de l'Alma, on the Right Bank in the 8ᵉ (ⓣ 01 42 25 96 10, ⓦ bateaux-mouches.fr; ⓜ Alma-Marceau. Many a romantic evening walk along the *quais* has been rudely interrupted by the sudden appearance of a bulging Bateau-Mouche, with its dazzling floodlights and blaring commentaries. One way of avoiding the problem is to get on one yourself. You may not be able to escape the trite narration, but the rides certainly give a glamorous close-up view of the classic buildings along the Seine. The rides, which usually last an hour, run roughly every thirty minutes to hourly, depending on the season. Summer departures are 10.15am–11pm, winter 10.15am–9pm. Tickets cost €10, or €5.50 for children aged 4–12, and over-60s. You're probably best off avoiding the overpriced lunch and dinner trips, for which "correct" dress is mandatory (€50 for lunch, from €95 for dinner).

OTHER RIVER-BOAT TRIPS

The main **competitors** to the Bateaux-Mouches are: Bateaux Parisiens Notre-Dame, quai de Montebello, 5ᵉ (ⓣ 08 25 01 01 01; ⓜ St-Michel); Bateaux-Parisiens Tour Eiffel, Port de la Bourdonnais, 7ᵉ (ⓣ 08 25 01 01 01; ⓜ Trocadéro); Bateaux-Vedettes de Paris, Port de Suffren, 7ᵉ (ⓣ 01 44 18 19 50; ⓜ Bir-Hakeim); and Bateaux-Vedettes du Pont-Neuf, Square du Vert-Galant, 1ᵉʳ (ⓣ 01 46 33 98 38; ⓜ Pont-Neuf). They're all much the same, and can be found detailed in *Pariscope* under "Croisières" in the "Visites-Promenades" section and in *L'Officiel des Spectacles* under "Promenades" in the "A Travers Paris" section. An alternative way of riding on the Seine – one in which you are spared the commentary – is the **Batobus** (ⓣ 08 25 05 01 01, ⓦ batobus.com), a river transport system operating nearly all year round (see p.26).

CANAL TRIPS

Canauxrama Less overtly touristy than the river trips, Canauxrama boats (ⓣ 01 42 39 15 00, ⓦ canauxrama.com) chug up and down between the Port de l'Arsenal (opposite 50 bd de la Bastille, 12ᵉ; ⓜ Bastille) and the Bassin de la Villette (13 quai de la Loire, 19ᵉ; ⓜ Jaurès) on the Canal St-Martin. From May to September, there are daily departures at 9.45am and 2.45pm from La Villette and at 9.45am and 2.30pm from the Port de l'Arsenal; departure times vary outside the summer months. At the Bastille end is a long, spooky tunnel from which you eventually surface in the 10ᵉ arrondissement. The ride lasts around two and a half hours – not bad for €16 (students €12 on weekdays, under-12s €8.50, under-4s free).

GREAT VIEWS OF THE CITY

Few cities present such a uniform skyscape as Paris. Looking down on the ranks of seven-storey apartment buildings from above, it's easy to imagine the city as a lead roofed plateau split by the leafy canyons of the boulevards and avenues. Spires, towers and parks – not to mention multicoloured art museums and glass pyramids – stand out all the more against the solemn grey backdrop. Fortunately, many of Paris's tall buildings provide access to wonderful **rooftop views**. The following are some of the best in town:

Arc de Triomphe (see p.61): look out on an ocean of traffic and enjoy impressive vistas of the Voie Triomphale.

Eiffel Tower (see p.146): the classic, best at night.

Institut du Monde Arabe (see p.130): sip mint tea on the rooftop overlooking the Seine.

Notre-Dame (see p.44): perch among the gargoyles.

Parc André-Citroën (see p.168): a tethered balloon rises 150m above this quirky park.

Parc de Belleville (see p.206): watch the sun set over the city.

Pompidou Centre (see p.84): a stunning backdrop to modern art.

Sacré-Coeur (see p.185): this puffball dome soars over Montmartre.

Tour Montparnasse (see p.159): stand eye to eye with the Eiffel Tower.

Catamaran of Paris-Canal A more stylish vessel for exploring the canal, the catamaran runs trips between the Musée d'Orsay (quai Anatole-France by the Pont Solférino, 7ᵉ; ⓂSolférino) and the Parc de la Villette (La Folie des Visites Guidées, on the canal by the bridge between the Grande Salle and the Cité des Sciences, 19ᵉ; ⓂPorte-de-Pantin), which also last two and a half hours. It departs from the Musée d'Orsay at 9.30am and from Parc de la Villette at 2.30pm. Trips run from mid-March to mid-November and cost €18, 12–25s and over-60s €15, 4–11s €11; to book, call ☎01 42 40 96 97.

PARIS BY BALLOON

After Paris from the water, the next step up is Paris from the air. You can opt to go up in a **hot-air balloon** with France Montgolfières (☎08 10 60 01 53, ⓦfranceballoons.com). Cost is approximately €185–230, depending on the length of the trip and whether it's midweek or a weekend. A much cheaper option (around €10), and nearly as panoramic, is the huge tethered balloon in the Parc André-Citroën (see p.168), which ascends daily to 150m.

TEA DANCES AND GUINGUETTE

For many years, the classic way to fill the afternoon hours was at a **bal musette** – a traditional, working-class knees-up, usually to the tune of an accordion (*musette*) band. The nearest equivalent these days is the **tea dance**, or *thé dansant* – a much more genteel (or camp) experience. One of the best known is that held at the former *guinguette*, Balajo (see p.110), every Thursday afternoon (3–7pm; ⓦbalajo.fr). Other tea dances are held by different promoters on a monthly or occasional basis. Absolutely free and splendidly relaxed are the open-air dances held on Sunday afternoons throughout the summer on the lawns by the **Kiosque de Musique** at the Parc de la Villette (see p.201), and on the waterfront alongside the Bassin de la Villette (19ᵉ), the latter being an imaginative offshoot of the Paris Plage programme (see p.320).

For the ultimate Parisian retro experience, head for a traditional riverbank **guinguette**. You can usually eat homely French food, but the real draw is the band. Families, older couples and trendy young things from the city sway with varying degrees of skill to foxtrots, tangos and lots of well-loved accordion numbers – especially good for a Sunday afternoon.

Chalet du Lac Facing the Lac de St-Mandé, Bois de Vincennes, 11ᵉ ☎01 43 28 09 89; ⓂSt-Mandé-Tourelles. Dances take place in the afternoons (2.30–7.30pm; women €7, men €11) and evenings (8.30pm–1am or later; women €9, men €15–18) on Thurs, Fri and Sat, but it's best to save yourself for the elegant evening Sunday Grand Bal (3pm–1am; €15), when a live band helps smooth out your footwork. The restaurant serves brasserie classics.
Chez Gégène 162bis quai de Polangis, Joinville-le-Pont ☎01 48 83 29 43, ⓦchez-gegene.fr; RER Joinville-le-Pont. Just the other side of the Bois de Vincennes from the Chalet du Lac, this is a genuine *guinguette* established in the 1900s, though the band mixes in pop anthems with the accordion classics. There's a decent restaurant, but the time to come is on Saturday nights (daily 9pm–2am) and Sunday afternoons (3–7pm), when a live band plays ballroom classics and traditional French numbers. Admission €16 for non-diners. April–Dec.
Guinguette de l'Île du Martin-Pêcheur 41 quai Victor-Hugo, Champigny-sur-Marne ☎01 49 83 03 02; RER A2 to Champigny-sur-Marne. Traditional and charming *guinguette* situated on an island in the River Marne. Entry free, optional dinner around €30. Dancing roughly May to Aug (Sat 9.30pm–2am, Sun 2–6pm, but phone to check).
Le Tango 13 rue au Maire, 3ᵉ ☎01 42 72 17 78; ⓂArts-et-Métiers. Gay- and lesbian-oriented tea dances take place most Sunday afternoons (6–11pm), as well as on Friday and Saturday nights (10.30pm–5am; €8).

LIBRARIES

The city's **libraries** naturally provide the perfect environment for a quiet moment, and some have beautiful interiors. For English-language books, the American Library's collection is unrivalled. Paris also has a library of films, the **vidéothèque**, where getting out a movie and watching it on the spot is as easy as taking out a book. Some of the collections below require non-residents without a library card to buy day-passes (around €3). You can find information on the city's 64 municipal libraries organized by arrondissement at ⓦparis-bibliotheques.org.

American Library in Paris 10 rue du Général-Camou, 7ᵉ ☎01 53 59 12 60, ⓦamericanlibraryinparis.org, ⓂEcole-Militaire. Hundreds of American magazines and newspapers and 130,000 books, plus readings, children's story hours and other events. Day-pass €12, weekly €25, annual €100. Free wi fi internet access; otherwise book a (free) slot in advance on one of their computers. Used book sales on the first Sat of the month. Tues–Sat 10am–7pm, Sun 1–7pm.

Bibliothèque des Femmes Marguerite Durand 79 rue Nationale, 13ᵉ ☎01 53 82 76 77, ⓂNationale/Tolbiac. A feminist library with books, journals, photos, posters and original manuscripts and letters. Tues–Sat 2–6pm.
Bibliothèque Forney Hôtel de Sens, 1 rue du Figuier, 4ᵉ ☎01 42 78 14 60; ⓂPont Marie. Medieval building filled with volumes on fine and applied arts. Tues, Fri & Sat 1.30–7pm, Wed & Thurs 10am–7.30pm.

25

Bibliothèque Historique de la Ville de Paris Hôtel Lamoignon, 24 rue Pavée, 4ᵉ ☎01 44 59 29 40; ⓜSt-Paul. Sixteenth-century mansion housing centuries of texts and picture books on the city. Mon–Sat 10am–6pm.

Bibliothèque Mazarine Institut de France, 23 quai de Conti, 6ᵉ ☎01 44 41 44 06, ⓦbibliotheque-mazarine .fr; ⓜSt-Michel. History of France and of religion. The setting, in a magnificent seventeenth-century building, with fine views across the Seine to the Louvre, is the real lure here. ID required. Mon–Fri 10am–6pm; closed first 2 weeks in Aug.

Bibliothèque Nationale François Mitterrand Quai François-Mauriac, 13ᵉ ☎01 53 79 59 59, ⓦbnf.fr; ⓜQuai-de-la-Gare/Bibliothèque-François Mitterrand. The elephantine national library (see p.176) with two levels, one for the public, the other for accredited researchers. Hosts a large number of exhibitions. €3.50 for a day-pass; bring ID. Public reading rooms Tues–Sat 10am–8pm, Sun 1–7pm; closed second half of Sept.

Bibliothèque Ste-Geneviève 10 place du Panthéon, 5ᵉ ☎01 44 41 97 97; RER Luxembourg. Reference library with beautiful murals in the foyer and a gorgeous reading room built around an iron skeleton. You have to register first; bring ID and a photo. Mon–Sat 10am–10pm.

BIFI Cinémathèque Française, 51 rue de Bercy, 12ᵉ ☎01 71 19 32 32, ⓦbifi.fr; ⓜLedru-Rollin. The Bibliothèque du Film encompasses magazines, books, stills, posters, videos and DVDs. €3.50 day-pass. Mon & Wed–Fri 10am–7pm, Sat 1–6.30pm.

BPI Centre Georges Pompidou, 3ᵉ ⓦbpi.fr; ⓜRambuteau. The vast Bibliothèque Publique d'Information collection includes the foreign press, videos and a language lab to brush up on your French. Free. Mon & Wed–Fri noon–10pm, Sat & Sun 11am–10pm.

Vidéothèque Forum des Images, 2 rue du Cinéma, Porte St-Eustache, Forum des Halles, 1ᵉʳ ☎01 44 76 62 00, ⓦforumdesimages.net; RER Châtelet-Les-Halles/ ⓜChâtelet. For a small entry fee you can watch any of the four films screened each day and, in the Salle Pierre Emmanuel, make your own selection from thousands of film clips, newsreel footage, commercials, documentaries, soaps and the like, from 1896 to the present day. All the material is connected to Paris in some way. Tues–Fri 12.30–11.30pm, Sat & Sun 2–11.30pm.

COOKERY AND WINE COURSES

Paris is, of course, the perfect place to get to grips with French gastronomy and wines. There are a large number of institutions offering **courses**, including those below.

Atelier des Sens 40 rue Sedaine, 11ᵉ ☎01 40 21 08 50, ⓦatelier-des-sens.com; ⓜBastille. This unstuffy school has just two kitchens, but offers a host of courses (including many on weekday evenings and Sundays) ranging from "sauces" and "sushi" to events focusing on individual French regions or single, seasonal ingredients. The sessions are in French, but they can organize English-language classes for groups of five or more. Classes are capped at twelve people, and cost €70–110.

Le Cordon Bleu 8 rue Léon-Delhomme, 15ᵉ ☎01 53 68 22 50, ⓦlcbparis.com; ⓜVaugirard/Convention. This international chain of cookery schools offers bilingual demonstrations followed by tastings (morning or afternoon sessions; 24hr advance booking; from €45), or day-long hands-on sessions (some in English, two weeks' advance booking required; €160).

Promenades Gourmandes 38 rue de Notre-Dame de Nazareth, 3ᵉ ☎01 48 04 56 84, ⓦpromenades gourmandes.com; ⓜTemple. At the other end of the scale from the Cordon Bleu school is this one-woman show, run by Paule Caillat, who speaks flawless English. You take a trip to the market then back to the kitchen for a multi-course demonstration, with lots of hands-on work. This level of personal attention doesn't come cheap: the half day costs €280; the full day (€390) includes a three-hour walking tour of local food and wine shops.

GYMS, FITNESS CLUBS AND EXERCISE CLASSES

You'll find any number of aerobics classes, dance workouts and anti-stress fitness programmes in Paris, along with yoga, t'ai chi and martial arts. Many **gyms** organize their activities in courses or require a minimum month's or year's subscription (chains like Garden Gym and Gymnase Club are financially prohibitive), but if your last meal has left you feeling the need to shed a few kilos, here are some options.

Aquaboulevard 4 rue Louis-Armand, 15ᵉ ☎01 40 60 10 00, ⓦaquaboulevard.com; ⓜBalard/Porte-de-Versailles/RER Bd-Victor. The biggest in town, with a state-of-the-art fitness centre containing 250 weight-training machines and offering 120 fitness lessons, squash and tennis courts, a climbing wall, golf, aquatic diversions (see opposite), hammams, dancefloors, shops and restaurants. To gain access to the full range of facilities, including the gym, you're supposed to be accompanied by a member, but exceptions are sometimes made. €20 for a day-pass. Mon–Thurs 9am–11pm, Fri 9am–midnight, Sat 8am–midnight, Sun 8am–11pm.

Ashtanga Yoga Paris 5 rue Morand, 11ᵉ ☎01 45 80 19 96 ⓦashtangayogaparis.fr; ⓜCouronnes/Parmentier. A bilingual yoga studio run by a Franco-Canadian couple. Two decent-sized practice rooms have been cleverly squeezed into a typical Parisian apartment building and a Japanese Zen garden fills the courtyard below. €16 for a one-hour class, €45 for a week-long pass, with classes held throughout the day, every day. The trainee-taught community classes, for those of lesser means, are held a few times a week, and are a bargain at €5. Bring your own mat or hire one for €2. You can just turn up for a class, but call or email first to get the door code.

Centre de Danse du Marais 41 rue du Temple, 4ᵉ ☎01 42 72 15 42, ⓦparisdanse.com; ⓜHôtel-de-Ville. Rock'n'roll, tap, ballet, contemporary dance, flamenco – with classes for all standards. Each 90-minute session costs €18, though you must become a member for insurance purposes (€11). Daily 9am–9pm.

Centre Sivananda de Yoga Vedanta 140 rue du Faubourg St-Martin, 10ᵉ ☎01 40 26 77 49, ⓦsivananda .org/paris; ⓜGare de l'Est. Traditional, Hindu and meditation-oriented yoga centre. A first trial lesson is free, otherwise donations of €23–27 are suggested. While speaking French helps, it's not essential.

Club Quartier Latin 19 rue de Pontoise, 5ᵉ ☎01 55 42 77 88, ⓦclubquartierlatin.com; ⓜMaubert-Mutualité. Dance, gym, swimming and squash; €20 day-pass for the pool and gym. Mon–Fri 9am–midnight, Sat & Sun 9.30am–7pm.

Espace Vit'Halles Place Beaubourg, 48 rue Rambuteau, 3ᵉ ☎01 42 77 21 71, ⓦvithalles.fr; ⓜRambuteau. One of the flashiest fitness clubs in the city, with endless classes of every kind, weight rooms, various gyms, a sauna and hammam, and everything else you'd expect. For €20, the day-pass gives access to all of the above. Other branches throughout the city. Mon–Fri 8am–10.30pm, Sat & Sun 10am–7pm.

Gym Suedoise ☎08 05 69 63 00, ⓦgymsuedoise.com. Hour-long "Swedish gym" classes combine aerobics, stretching and simple dance steps, and are something of a craze in Paris. You don't have to be experienced or hyper-fit (or speak French), and can just show up, without booking, to any one of the dozens of inexpensive classes held all over Paris – in school gyms, community centres and even nightclubs. Check the website for your nearest class. €10 per class; no cash – cards only.

SWIMMING POOLS

For €3, you can go swimming in most of Paris's excellent **municipal pools**. If you plan to go swimming a lot, the €24 *carnet* of ten tickets (each good for one entrance) works out to be even cheaper. **Privately run pools**, whether owned by the city or not, are usually more expensive. At weekends, the **opening hours** of most municipal pools are roughly Saturday 7am–6pm, Sunday 8am–6pm. During school terms opening hours are complicated. A general rule is that on weekdays they open for an hour in the early morning and at lunch, then close for the morning and afternoon school sessions, then reopen in the later afternoon until about 6–8pm, though many close completely on Mondays. It's best to ring in advance, or check under "loisirs" then "piscines" on the Mairie's website (ⓦparis.fr). The following are among the best pools.

Les Amiraux 6 rue Hermann-Lachapelle, 18ᵉ ☎01 46 06 46 47; ⓜSimplon. Handsome 1920s pool – as featured in the film *Amelie* – surrounded by tiers of changing cabins. €3.

Aquaboulevard 4 rue Louis-Armand, 15ᵉ ☎01 40 60 10 00, ⓦaquaboulevard.com; ⓜBalard/Porte-de-Versailles/RER Bd-Victor. The private pool and fitness centre has wave machines and some incredible water slides, and there are jacuzzis and a grassy outdoor area. Also see opposite. €25 (€10 for children aged 3–11).

Butte-aux-Cailles 5 place Paul-Verlaine, 13ᵉ ☎01 45 89 60 05; ⓜPlace-d'Italie. Housed in a spruced-up 1920s brick building with an Art Deco ceiling, this is one of the most pleasant swims in the city. There's a children's pool inside, and in summer a 25m heated outdoor pool. €3.

Les Halles Suzanne Berlioux 10 place de la Rotonde, Niveau 3, Porte du Jour, Forum des Halles, 1ᵉʳ ☎01 42 36 98 44; RER Châtelet-Les-Halles/ⓜChâtelet. Very centrally located, this 50m pool sports a glass wall looking through to a tropical garden. €4.

Henry-de-Montherlant 32 bd Lannes, 16ᵉ ☎01 40 72 28 30; ⓜPorte-Dauphine. Two pools, one 25m and one 15m, plus a terrace for sunbathing, a solarium – and the Bois de Boulogne close by. €3.

Jean Taris 16 rue Thouin, 5ᵉ ☎01 55 42 81 90; ⓜCardinal-Lemoine. A 25-metre unchlorinated pool in the centre of the Quartier Latin, and a student favourite. There's a small pool for children and swim groups for those with disabilities. €3.

Josephine Baker Quai François-Mauriac, 13ᵉ ☎01 56 61 96 50; ⓜQuai de la Gare. Eye-catching floating 25m, four-lane pool, moored on the Seine by the Bibliothèque Nationale. Retractable roof for when it rains. Winter €3, summer €5.

Pailleron 32 rue Edouard Pailleron, 19ᵉ ☎01 40 40 27 70; ⓜBolivar. One of the coolest pools in the city – a 1930s Art Deco marvel surrounded by tiers of changing rooms and arched over by a gantrywork roof. During school holidays, it's open late. €3.10, or €4.80 after 8pm.

Pontoise 19 rue de Pontoise, 5ᵉ ☎01 55 42 77 88; ⓜMaubert-Mutualité. Art Deco architecture, a beautiful blue mosaic interior and a 33m pool. Juliette Binoche memorably swam here in the Kieslowski film *Three Colours: Blue*. Pool €4.50. On weekdays outside school terms, there are night sessions until 11.45pm; €10, including sauna access and a fitness class. There are squash courts too – see Club Quartier Latin (above).

25

HAMMAMS

Hammams, or Turkish baths, are one of the unexpected delights of Paris. Much more luxurious than the standard Swedish sauna, these are places to linger and chat, and you can usually pay extra for a massage and a *gommage* – a rubdown with a rubber glove – followed by mint tea to recover. You're given a strip of linen and modest towel on entry, and usually some slippers, but bring your own swimsuit for mixed men-and-women sessions.

Les Bains du Marais 31–33 rue des Blancs-Manteaux, 4ᵉ ☎01 44 61 02 02, ⓦ www.lesbainsdumarais.com; ⓜRambuteau/St-Paul. As much a posh health club as a hammam, with a chichi clientele and glorious interior. Offers facials, massage and haircuts, and you can lounge about in a robe with mint tea and a newspaper. Sauna and steam room entry costs €35 for two hours; massage/ *gommage* is €35 extra. There are exclusive sessions for women (Mon 10am–8pm, Tues 10am–11pm, Wed 10am–7pm) and men (Thurs 10am–11pm, Fri 10am–8pm), as well as mixed sessions (Wed 7–11pm, Sat 10am–8pm, Sun 10am–11pm), for which you have to bring a swimsuit.

Hammam Medina Center 43–45 rue Petit, 19ᵉ ☎01 42 02 31 05, ⓦ hammam-medina.com; ⓜ Laumière. A bit far from the centre, but it's one of the most authentically bustling hammams in the city, attracting locals for traditional mud treatments. €39 hammam and *gommage*; €55 with massage. Women: Mon–Fri 11am–10pm & Sun 9am–7pm; mixed: Sat 10am–9pm.

Hammam de la Mosquée 39 rue Geoffroy-St-Hilaire, 5ᵉ ☎01 43 31 38 20; ⓜ Censier-Daubenton. An old-fashioned public bath, where people come to wash as well as relax, with an atmospheric, vaulted cooling-off room and a marble-lined steam chamber. Good value at €15, though towels are extra, and you can also have a reasonably priced massage and brisk *gommage* (€10 for a 10min session of either). After your bath you can enjoy mint tea and honey cakes around a fountain in the little courtyard café. Women: Mon, Wed, Thurs & Sat 10am–9pm, Fri 2–9pm; men: Tues 2–9pm, Sun 10am–9pm.

Hammam Pacha 17 rue Mayet, 6ᵉ ☎01 43 06 55 55, ⓦ hammampacha.com; ⓜ Duroc. Elegant, women-only hammam which mixes North African details with a swish, contemporary feel. Steam rooms are fairly small, but there's a grand, arcaded cool room, with a long plunge pool. €35; €55 with *gommage*. Mon–Wed, Sat & Sun 11am–8pm, Thurs & Fri 11am–11pm.

ROLLERBLADING AND SKATEBOARDING

Rollerblading has become so popular in Paris that it takes over entire streets most Friday nights from 9.30pm, when expert skaters – up to 15,000 on fine evenings – meet on the esplanade of the Gare Montparnasse in the 14ᵉ (ⓜ Montparnasse) for a demanding **three-hour circuit** of the city; check out ⓦ pari-roller.com for details. A more sedate outing – and a better choice for families – takes place on Sundays, departing at 2.30pm from the place de la Bastille and returning at 5.30pm (ⓦ rollers-coquillages.org). The main outdoor **rollerblading and skateboarding arenas** are on the concourses of the Palais Omnisports Bercy (ⓜ Bercy) and the Palais de Chaillot (ⓜ Trocadéro). The flat areas just beside the place de la Bastille and place du Palais-Royal are also very popular, as well as the central quays of the Seine on Sundays (see box, p.352). The best place to find more **information** and **hire blades** (around €8 for a half-day) is Nomades, 37 boulevard Bourdon, 4ᵉ (☎01 44 54 07 44, ⓦ nomadeshop.com; ⓜ Bastille), which also holds its own events.

ICE-SKATING

In winter, a big **outdoor rink** is set up on place de l'Hôtel-de-Ville, 3ᵉ (Dec–March Mon–Thurs noon–10pm, Fri noon–midnight, Sat 9am–midnight, Sun 9am–10pm; free; ⓜ Hôtel de Ville); you can hire skates (*patins*) for around €5 (bring your passport) and there's a small section cordoned off for children under 6. From early December to February, two small **seasonal rinks** can be found on place Raoul Dautry, 15ᵉ (ⓜ Montparnasse-Bienvenüe), and outside the Bibliothèque Nationale-François Mitterrand (ⓜ Bibliothèque François Mitterrand/Quai de la Gare): entrance is free, though skate hire is €5.

PERMANENT RINKS

Patinoire de Bercy Palais Omnisports, 8 bd de Bercy, 12ᵉ ☎01 40 02 60 60; ⓜ Bercy. Wed 3–6pm, Fri 9.30am–12.30am, Sat 3–6pm & 9.30pm–12.30am, Sun 10am–noon & 3–6pm.

Patinoire Pailleron 32 rue Edouard Pailleron, 19ᵉ ☎01 40 40 27 70; ⓜ Bolivar. School holidays: Mon, Tues & Thurs noon–10pm, Wed 9am–10pm, Fri noon–midnight, Sat 9am–midnight, Sun 10am–6pm; hours vary in term time.

JOGGING

25

For running or **jogging**, the Jardin du Luxembourg, Tuileries and Champ de Mars are particularly popular with Parisians; all provide decent, varied runs, and are more or less flat. If you want to run hills, head for the Parc des Buttes-Chaumont in the 19^e or Parc Montsouris in the 14^e. If you have easy access to them, try the Bois de Boulogne and the Bois de Vincennes, which are the largest open spaces, though both are cut through by a number of roads.

CYCLING

Since 1996 the Mairie de Paris has made great efforts to introduce dedicated **cycle lanes** in the city, though if you prefer cycling in a more natural environment, both the Bois de Boulogne and the Bois de Vincennes have extensive bike tracks: you can pick up Vélib' bikes by the park entrances. "**Paris Respire**", a town hall-sponsored scheme, closes off the following areas on Sundays and public holidays year-round (10am–6pm, some till 8pm in summer), making them popular places for cyclists and rollerbladers to meet up: the right bank of the Seine from the Pont Charles de Gaulle (12^e) to place de la Concorde (8^e); the Left Bank from Pont Royal (1er) to quai Branly (7^e); around rue Mouffetard, rue Descartes and rue de l'Ecole Polytechnique (5^e); in the Marais, around rue des Francs-Bourgeois (3^e/4^e); around rue de la Roquette (11^e; summer only); along and around the Canal St-Martin (10^e); the Sentier quarter (2^e); and Butte Montmartre (18^e).

BIKE SHOPS AND TOURS

Fat Tire Bike Tours 24 rue Edgar Faure, 15^e ☎01 56 58 10 54, ⍟fattirebiketours.com/paris; ⓜDupleix. Friendly, Anglo-run agency offering bike rental and four-hour guided bicycle trips in English, with a choice of day and night tours (€28), and full-day tours to Versailles and Monet's gardens (including train travel). You can just show up at the south pillar of the Eiffel Tower without a reservation for the Paris day (11am) and night (3pm) tours. Good exercise and cheerful camaraderie for people of all ages looking to explore Paris, but don't want to go it alone. Also offers electric Seqway tours (⍟cityseqwaytours.com) and low-key, small-group walking tours. Daily 9am–7pm.
Paris Bike Tour 38 rue de Saintonge, 3^e ☎01 42 74 22 14, ⍟parisbiketour.net; ⓜFilles du Calvaire. Offers

21-speed and mountain bikes, and morning bike delivery to your address, as well as a range of relaxed tours, which take you onto and around the islands (€32). Rental costs €15 a day (€16 at the weekend), or €28 for the whole weekend. Daily 9.30am–6.30pm.
Paris à Vélo C'est Sympa/Vélo Bastille 22 rue Alphonse Baudin, 11e ☎01 48 87 60 01, ⍟parisvelosympa.com; ⓜRichard Lenoir. One of the least expensive (€25 for a weekend, or €50 for a tandem) and most helpful companies for bike rental. Their excellent three-hour tours of Paris – including a Montmartre dawn tour – cost €34, under-26s €28. Mon & Wed–Fri 9.30am–1pm & 2–6pm, Tues 2–6pm, Sat & Sun 9am–7pm.

BILLIARDS AND POOL

Unlike the English version, **billiards** (*billard*) is an original and ancient French game played with three balls and no pockets.

Académie de Billard Clichy-Montmartre 84 rue de Clichy, 9e ☎01 48 78 32 85, ⍟cercleclichy-montmartre .com; ⓜPlace-de-Clichy. The classiest billiard hall in Europe, the decor is all ancient gilded mirrors, high ceilings and panelled walls, and staff in bow ties deliver drinks to your table. Pool, snooker and poker tables are also available. You need to become a member (men €40, women free), so bring a passport. Once inside, tables cost €12–25 an hour, depending on the day. Daily 1pm–5am.

Blue-Billard 111 rue St-Maur, 11e ☎01 43 55 87 21; ⓜParmentier. Cocktails, chess and backgammon as well as billiards, in an arty-intellectual café-bar close to Belleville. €13–15 per hour. Daily 2pm–2am.
Salle de Billard des Halles Niveau -2, 14 rue Porte-du-Jour, Forum des Halles, 1er; ⓜLes Halles/RER Châtelet-Les-Halles. Two French billiard tables and eight pool tables. Daily 1–9pm (noon–10pm in winter).

VELIB' BIKE SCHEME

The easiest way to **rent a bike** in Paris is to use the **Vélib'** scheme (see box, p.26). There are stands beside the major parks. If you're cycling a lot, or want a better bike, it's worth trying other outlets (see above). Prices depend on the type of bike, but are usually about €15–20 a day, or upwards of €50 for a week; you have to leave a variable *caution* (deposit) or your credit-card details. If you want a bike for Sunday, when all of Paris takes to the *quais*, you'll need to book in advance.

25

CHAUFFEUR-DRIVEN TOURS IN A 2CV

A number of companies now offer tours in the nimble little **Citroën 2CV**. The classic, open-top "deux chevaux" was originally designed as an economy vehicle for farmers, but is now a beloved symbol of French identity. The original and still most adaptable company is 4 Roues Sous 1 Parapluie ("4 Wheels under an Umbrella"), which offers a range of tours, from hour-long quickies, with an English-speaking driver suggesting places to which you might want to return, to chauffeur-driven pick-ups from the Eurostar and full-day tours with stops for dinner and wine-tastings. The cars attract interest and even affectionate comments wherever they go. Book on ☎08 00 80 06 31 or online at ⓦ4roues-sous-1parapluie.com. Tours from €19 per person (maximum of 3 people in each car).

BOULES

The classic French game, **boules** (or *pétanque*), is best played or watched at the Arènes de Lutèce (see p.130), Jardin du Luxembourg (see p.138) and the Bois de Vincennes (see p.115). The principle is the same as British bowls but the terrain is always rough – usually gravel or sand, and never grass – and the area much smaller. The metal ball is usually thrown upwards from a distance of about 10m, with a strong backspin in order to stop it skidding away from the wooden marker (*cochonnet*). It's very male-dominated, and socially the equivalent of darts or perhaps pool; there are café or neighbourhood teams and endless championships. On balmy summer evenings it's a common sight in many of the city's parks and gardens.

TENNIS, SQUASH AND TABLE TENNIS

Tennis One of the nicest places to play tennis is on one of the six asphalt courts in the Jardin du Luxembourg (daily 8am–9pm; €6.50 per hour; ⓜNotre-Dame-des-Champs). You can book any of the city's forty or so municipal courts online at ⓦ tennis.paris.fr. In practice, it's often fine to just turn up with your kit and wait on the spot – usually no more than an hour – though as a rule school holidays are generally less busy. Most city courts are in quite good shape; private clubs demand steep membership fees.

Squash There are several dedicated squash centres, including Squash Montmartre, 14 rue Achille-Martinet, 18ᵉ (☎01 42 55 38 30; Mon–Fri 10am–11pm, Sat & Sun

10am–7pm; ⓜLamarck-Caulaincourt), which charges €13 for 40 minutes (you can hire racket and shoes for €5); book two days in advance, or 10 days ahead for evening sessions. Alternatively, the Club Quartier Latin (see p.343) has squash courts for €20–30 per hour.

Table tennis The Mairie provides outdoor table-tennis tables in many of the smaller parks and outdoor spaces in Paris. It's up to you to bring a racket and balls. Some good locations include: Jardin Marco-Polo (6ᵉ), square de la Trinité (9ᵉ), Parc Floral (12ᵉ), Parc Georges-Brassens (15ᵉ), Jardin des Batignolles (17ᵉ) and place des Abbesses (18ᵉ).

ROCK CLIMBING

Mur Mur Pantin 55 rue Cartier Bresson, Pantin ☎01 48 46 11 00, ⓦmurmur.fr; ⓜAubervilliers/RER Pantin. Paris lays claim to one of the world's largest indoor climbing arenas, with some 13,000 square metres

of wall space, as well as a special section for honing your ice-climbing skills. €15, or €8 on weekdays before 2pm for return visits. Mon–Fri 9.30am–11pm, Sat & Sun 9.30am–6.30pm.

SPECTATOR SPORTS

Paris St-Germain (PSG), one of France's richest and most powerful **football** teams, is the only major-league club in the city. The capital's teams also retain a special status in the **rugby**, **cycling** and **tennis** worlds, and **horse racing** is a serious pursuit here.

FOOTBALL AND RUGBY

Parc des Princes 24 rue du Commandant-Guilbaud, 16ᵉ; ⓦleparcdesprinces.fr; ⓜPorte-de-St-Cloud. The capital's main stadium for both **rugby union** and domestic **football** events (*le foot*), and home ground to the first-division Paris football team PSG (Paris St-Germain) and the rugby team, Le Racing. The next-door Stade Jean-Bouin, home to the Stade Français rugby club, hosts most of their

home matches, with the higher-profile clashes being played out in the Parc des Princes. PSG tickets are sold exactly two weeks before any match (and usually sell out within a week); to buy them, call in at the club shop, 27 avenue des Champs-Elysées, 8ᵉ, or contact the club directly on ☎3275 (premium rate) or ⓦpsg.fr. Prices start at around €12.

Stade de France rue Francis de Pressensé in St-Denis ☎08 92 70 09 00, ⓦstadefrance.com; RER

25

THE PARIS MARATHON

The **Paris Marathon** is held in early April over a route from place de la Concorde to Vincennes. If you want to join in, check out ⓦ parismarathon.com, where you can register to run. A half-marathon is held in early March, and "Les 20km de Paris" takes place in mid-October, beginning and ending at the Eiffel Tower (ⓦ 20kmparis.com).

Stade-de-France-St-Denis. Specially built to host the 1998 World Cup, this is the venue for international football matches and Six Nations' Cup rugby matches.

CYCLING

The sport the French are truly mad about is **cycling**, and the biggest event of the French sporting year is the grand finale of the **Tour de France**, which ends in a sweep along the Champs-Elysées in the third week of July with the French president himself presenting the *maillot jaune* (the winner's yellow jersey). However, only very rarely does Paris witness memorable scenes such as those of 1989, when American Greg Lemond snatched the coveted *maillot jaune* on the final day. Other classic long-distance bike races that begin or end in Paris include the 600km **Bordeaux–Paris** in May, the world's longest single-stage race, first held in 1891; the **Paris–Roubaix** in April, instigated in 1896, which is reputed to be the most exacting one-day race in the world; the **Paris–Brussels** in September, held since 1893; and the six-day **Paris–Nice** event in March, covering more than 1100km. The Palais Omnisports Paris-Bercy holds cycling events, including time trials.

TENNIS

Roland Garros Between the Parc des Princes and the Bois de Boulogne, 2 av Gordon-Bennett, 16ᵉ ☎ 01 47 43 48 00, ⓦ rolandgarros.com; Ⓜ Porte-d'Auteuil. The French equivalent of Britain's Wimbledon complex, Roland Garros hosts the **French Tennis Open**, one of the four major events which together comprise the Grand Slam, in the last week of May and first week of June. Tickets need to be reserved online months in advance (usually in late Feb), but you can sometimes pick up tickets for unseeded matches at Roland Garros itself on the day of the tournament, or there's a heavily oversubscribed, official online ticket exchange, Viagogo (ⓦ rolandgarros .viagogo.com).

ATHLETICS AND OTHER SPORTS

Palais Omnisports Paris-Bercy (POPB) 8 bd Bercy, 12ᵉ ☎ 01 40 02 60 60, ⓦ bercy.fr; Ⓜ Bercy. The stadium hosts all manner of sporting events – athletics, cycling, handball, dressage and show-jumping, ice hockey, ballroom dancing, judo and motocross – as well as stadium gigs from the likes of Green Day and Muse. The complex holds 17,000 people, so you've a fair chance of getting a ticket at the door, championships excepted. Otherwise, tickets are sold through the usual outlets: Fnac (see p.330) and Virgin Megastore (see p.331), and online.

HORSE RACING

The **biggest races** are the Grand Prix de l'Arc de Triomphe and the Prix de la République, held on the first and last Sundays in October respectively at Auteuil and Longchamp. In May Auteuil also hosts the Great Paris Steeplechase, the poshest of all French equestrian competitions. The week starting the last Sunday in June sees nine big racing events, at Auteuil, Longchamp, St-Cloud and Chantilly (see p.235). If you want to try your luck with **betting**, any bar or café with the letters PMU will take your money on a three-horse bet, known as *le tiercé*.

St-Cloud Champ de Courses is in the Parc de St-Cloud off allée de Chamillard, Auteuil is off the route d'Auteuil (Ⓜ Porte-d'Auteuil), and Longchamp is off the route des Tribunes (Ⓜ Porte-Maillot and then bus #244, or free shuttle buses on major race days), both in the Bois de Boulogne. Admission costs €3–10: see publications *L'Humanité* or *Paris-Turf* for details. **Trotting races**, with the jockeys in chariots, run from August to September on the route de la Ferme in the Bois de Vincennes.

CAROUSEL, JARDIN D'ACCLIMATATION

Paris for children

The French are extremely welcoming to children on the whole, and Paris's vibrant atmosphere, with its street performers, lively pavement cafés and merry-go-rounds, is certainly family-friendly. The obvious pull of Disneyland aside (covered in Chapter 17), there are plenty of attractions and activities to keep kids happy, from circuses to rollerblading. As you'd expect, museum-hopping with youngsters in Paris can be as tedious as in any other big city, but remember that while the Louvre and Musée d'Orsay cater to more acquired tastes, the Musée des Arts et Métiers, the Pompidou Centre, Parc de la Villette and some of the other attractions listed here will interest children and adults alike. Travelling with a child also provides the perfect excuse to enjoy some of the simpler pleasures of city life – the playgrounds, ice-cream cones and toy shops that Paris seems to offer in abundance.

ESSENTIALS

Peak times It's worth remembering that Wednesday afternoons, when primary school children have free time, and Saturdays are the peak times for children's activities; Wednesdays continue to be child-centred even during the school holidays.

Listings The most useful sources of information for current shows, exhibitions and events are the special sections in the listings magazines: "Enfants" in *Pariscope* and "Pour les jeunes" in *L'Officiel des Spectacles*. The bimonthly *Paris Mômes – môme* is French for "kid" – provides the lowdown on current festivals, concerts, films and other activities for children up to age 12; it's available for free from the tourist office and libraries, or check the website, ⓦ parismomes.fr. The tourist office also publishes a free booklet in French, *Paris-Ile-de-France avec des Yeux d'Enfants*, with lots of ideas and contacts, and there's a children's section on its website ⓦ parisinfo.com. It's worth checking the festivals calendar (pp.318–320), as there are a number of annual events perfect for children, including Paris Plage, Bastille

Day, the Tour de France and the Course des Garçons de Café.

Discounts Many cafés, bars or restaurants offer *menus enfants* (special children's set menus) or are often willing to cook simpler food on request, and hotels tack only a small supplement for an additional bed or cot onto the regular room rate. Throughout the city the RATP (Paris Transport) charges half-fares for 4–10s; under-4s travel free on public transport.

Babysitting Many hotels can organize babysitting; just check when you book. Otherwise, reliable babysitting agencies include Baby Sitting Services, 4 rue Nationale, Boulogne Billancourt 92100 (☎ 01 46 21 33 16, ⓦ babysittingservices.com; from €7 per hour – minimum of two consecutive hours – plus €12.90–15.90 fees). You can also try individual notices at the American Church, 65 quai d'Orsay, 6^e (⓵ Invalides; ⓦ acparis.org), the Alliance Française, 101 bd Raspail, 6^e (⓵ St-Placide; ⓦ www .alliancefr.org), or CIDJ, 101 quai Branly, 15^e (⓵ Bir-Hakeim; ☎ 01 44 49 12 00, ⓦ cidj.com).

26

PARKS, GARDENS AND ZOOS

Younger kids in particular are well catered for by the parks and gardens within the city. Although there aren't, on the whole, any open spaces for spontaneous games of football, baseball or cricket, most parks have an enclosed playground with swings, climbing frames and a sandpit, while there's usually a netted enclosure for older children to play casual **ball games**. The most standard forms of entertainment in parks and gardens are puppet shows and **Guignol**, the French equivalent of Punch and Judy; these usually last about 45 minutes, cost around €3 and take place on Wednesday, Saturday and Sunday afternoons (more frequently during school holidays). Children under 8 seem to appreciate these shows most, with the puppeteers eliciting an enthusiastic verbal response from them; even though it's all in French, the excitement is contagious and the stories are easy enough to follow.

MAJOR PARKS

The Jardin d'Acclimatation In the Bois de Boulogne, by Porte des Sablons (☎ 01 40 67 90 82, ⓦ jardindacclimatation.fr; ⓵ Les Sablons/Porte-Maillot. Daily: May–Sept 10am–7pm; Oct–April 10am–6pm. Adults and children €2.90, under-3s free; rides €2.70, or buy a carnet of 15 tickets for €32. The Jardin d'Acclimatation is a cross between a funfair, zoo and amusement park, with temptations ranging from bumper cars, go-karts, pony and camel rides, sea lions, birds, bears and monkeys, to a magical mini-canal ride (*"la rivière enchantée"*), distorting mirrors, a huge trampoline, scaled-down farm buildings, a puppet theatre and a golf driving range. Also in the park is the Théâtre du Jardin pour l'Enfance et la Jeunesse, which puts on musicals, ballets and poetry readings. There are special attractions on Wednesday, Saturday, Sunday and all week during school holidays, including a little train to take you to the park from ⓵ Porte-Maillot (behind *L'Orée du Bois* restaurant; every 15min, 11am–6pm; €5.60 return, includes admission). Outside the Jardin, in the Bois de Boulogne (see p.218), older children can amuse themselves with mini-golf and bowling, or boating on the

Lac Inférieur. The park offers babysitting services in the summer.

Parc de la Villette In the 19e between avs Jean-Jaurès and Corentin-Cariou (☎ 01 40 03 75 75, ⓦ villette .com; ⓵ Porte-de-Pantin/Porte-de-la-Villette. Daily 6am–1am; admission free. As well as the Cité des Enfants (see p.354) and wide-open spaces to run around or picnic in, the Parc de la Villette has a series of ten themed gardens, some specially designed for kids. All are linked by a walkway called the Promenade des Jardins, indicated on the park's free map. Most popular with children are the Jardin du Dragon, with its huge slide in the shape of a dragon, and the Jardin des Vents et des Dunes (April–Oct daily 10am–8pm; Nov–March Wed, Sat, Sun & school hols 10am till dusk; under-13s only and their accompanying adults), with sandpits, large air-filled cushions that roll like waves and are great for bouncing on, climbing frames, zip wires and tunnels. The park also holds regular workshops and activities for children, such as music, baking and gardening. Full details are given on the website or at the information centre at the Porte de Pantin entrance.

Parc Floral In the Bois de Vincennes, on route du Champ de Manoeuvre (☎ 01 49 57 24 84, ⓦ parcfloral.com;

26

PARIS WITH BABIES AND TODDLERS

You will have little problem in getting hold of **essentials for babies** in Paris. Familiar brands of baby food are available in the supermarkets, as well as disposable nappies (*couches à jeter*), etc. After hours, you can get most goods from late-night pharmacies, though they are slightly more expensive.

Getting around with a pushchair poses the same problems as in most big cities. The métro is especially awkward, with its endless flights of stairs (and few escalators). Buses are much easier, with seats near the front for passengers with young children.

Unfortunately, many of the lawns in Parisian **parks** are out of bounds ("*pelouse interdite*"), so sprawling on the grass with toddlers and napping babies is often out of the question. That said, more and more parks are now opening the odd grassy area to the public, and there are two central spaces that offer complete freedom to sit on the grass: place des Vosges and Parc des Buttes-Chaumont.

Finding a place to **change and feed** a baby is especially challenging. While most of the major museums and some department stores have areas within the women's toilets equipped with a shelf and sink for changing a baby, most restaurants do not. Breastfeeding in public, though not especially common among French women, is, for the most part, tolerated if done discreetly. Few restaurants have high-chairs available for babies and toddlers.

Ⓜ Château-de-Vincennes, then bus #112 or a 10min walk past the Château de Vincennes. April to mid-Sept 9.30am–8pm; mid-Sept to mid-Oct 9.30am–7pm; mid-Oct to March 9.30am–5/6pm; free except from June to Sept Wed, Sat & Sun when entry is €5, €2.50 for 7–26-year-olds, under-7s free. The excellent playground at the Parc Floral has a new attraction, Evasion Verte (see below), as well as slides, swings, ping-pong, quadricycles (from 2pm), mini-golf modelled on Paris monuments (from 2pm), an electric car circuit, and a little train touring all the gardens (April–Oct daily 1–5pm). Tickets for the paying activities are sold at the playground between 2pm and 5.30pm weekdays and until 7pm at weekends; activities stop fifteen minutes afterwards. Note that many of these activities are available from March/April to August only and on Wed and weekends only in Sept and Oct. On Wed at 2.30pm (May–Sept) there are free performances by clowns, puppets and magicians at the Delta amphitheatre. Also in the park is a children's theatre, the Théâtre Astral, which has mime, clowns and other not-too-verbal shows for small children aged 3 to 8, for which you're best off calling ahead and making reservations, as they're popular with school groups (Wed & Sun 3pm, school hols Mon–Fri & Sun 3pm; €7; ☎01 43 71 31 10). There is also a series of pavilions with child-friendly educational exhibitions (free), which look at nature in Paris; the best is the butterfly garden (mid-May to mid-Oct Mon–Fri 1.30–5.15pm, Sat & Sun 1.30–6pm).

Evasion Verte Parc Floral Ⓦ evasion-verte.fr. April–June & Sept–Nov Wed, Easter & Nov hols 1–5pm, Sat & Sun 10am–5pm; July & Aug daily 10am–5pm. Children aged 6 and under 1.40m in height €10, adults and children over 1.40m in height €15; ticket valid for two hours. The Parc Floral's new attraction, "Green Escape", allows you to explore the treetops by walking along rope ladders, swinging on ropes, etc, from tree to tree. You're

attached to a harness and given a brief introduction; you then choose one of three walkways of varying height and difficulty. It's suitable for children over 6; all children under 16 have to be accompanied by an adult.

OTHER PARKS, SQUARES AND PUBLIC GARDENS

All of these assorted open spaces can offer play areas, puppets or, at the very least, a bit of room to run around in, and are open from 7.30 or 8am till dusk, unless otherwise stated.

Arènes de Lutèce Rue des Arènes, 5ᵉ; Ⓜ Place Monge. This great public park, built on what used to be a Roman theatre, has a fountain, sandpit and jungle gyms.

Buttes-Chaumont 19ᵉ ☎01 42 40 88 66; Ⓜ Buttes-Chaumont/Botzaris. Built on a former quarry, these grassy slopes are perfect for rolling down and offer great views. Unusually for Paris there are no "keep off the grass" signs. You'll also find a lake, a waterfall and Guignol shows (see p.349).

Champs-de-Mars 7ᵉ ☎01 48 56 01 44; Ⓜ Ecole-Militaire. Puppet shows Wed, Sat & Sun at 3.15pm & 4.15pm.

Jardin du Luxembourg 6ᵉ ☎01 43 26 46 47; Ⓜ St-Placide/Notre-Dame-des-Champs/RER Luxembourg. A large playground, pony rides, toy boat rental (Wed & Sun), bicycle track, rollerblading rink and puppets. A 45min marionette show takes place Wed & Sat at 3.30pm, Sun at 11am & 3.30pm.

Jardin des Plantes 57 rue Cuvier, 5ᵉ; Ⓜ Jussieu/Monge. Open from 7.30/8am until dusk, it contains a small zoo, the Ménagerie (Mon–Sat 9am–6pm, Sun till 6.30pm; €9, 4–16s, students and under-26s €7, under-4s free), a playground, hothouses and plenty of greenery (see p.128).

Jardins du Ranelagh Av Ingres, 16ᵉ; Ⓜ Muette. Marionettes, cycle track, rollerblading rink and playground.

Jardins du Trocadéro Place du Trocadéro, 16ᵉ; ⓜTrocadéro. Rollerblading, skateboarding and aquarium.

Jardin des Tuileries Place de la Concorde/rue de Rivoli, 1ᵉʳ ☎01 40 20 90 43; ⓜPlace-de-la-Concorde/ Palais-Royal-Musée-du-Louvre. Pony rides, period merry-go-round, marionettes, trampolines, toy sailing boats (Wed & Sun), funfair in July, and more (see p.68)

Parc Georges-Brassens Rue des Morillons, 15ᵉ ☎01 48 42 51 80; ⓜConvention/Porte-de-Vanves. Access the park at the entrance across from 86 rue Brancion. Climbing rocks, puppets, artificial river, playground and scented herb gardens (see p.169).

Parc Monceau Bd de Courcelles, 17ᵉ ☎01 42 67 04 63; ⓜMonceau. Rollerblading rink, and more (see p.66).

Parc Montsouris Bd Jourdan, 14ᵉ; ⓜGlacière/RER Cité-Universitaire. Puppet shows by the lake (Wed & Sat 3.30pm & 4.30pm, Sun 11.30am, 3.30pm, 4.30pm & 5.30pm), a number of playgrounds and a waterfall (see p.167).

Place de la Bastille 11ᵉ ☎08 20 00 39 75; ⓜBastille. In December the square becomes a Christmas fantasyland, with a giant trampoline, carousels, a North Pole market and French Santas.

Place des Vosges 4ᵉ; ⓜBastille/Chemin Vert/St-Paul. The oldest square in Paris (see p.92) has two popular sandpits, a small playground and plenty of space to run around in.

Quai de la Mégisserie 11ᵉ; ⓜPont-Neuf/Châtelet. This riverside stretch is lined with pets for sale (and for petting), including puppies, kittens, rabbits and hamsters.

26

FUNFAIRS AND THEME PARKS

Funfairs Three big funfairs (*fêtes foraines*) are held in Paris each year. The season kicks off in late March with the Foire du Trône in the Bois de Vincennes (running until late May), followed by the funfair in the Tuileries gardens in mid-June to late August, with more than forty rides, including a giant Ferris wheel, and ending up with the Fête à Neu Neu, held near the Bois de Boulogne from early September to the beginning of October. Look up "Fêtes Populaires" under "Agendas" in *Pariscope* for details if you're in town at these times. Very occasionally, rue de Rivoli around ⓜSt-Paul hosts a mini-fairground.

Merry-go-rounds There's usually a merry-go-round at the Forum des Halles, in place de l'Hôtel de Ville and beneath the Tour St-Jacques at Châtelet, with carousels for smaller children on place de la République, at the Rond-Point des Champs-Elysées by avenue Matignon, at place de la Nation, and at the base of the Montmartre funicular in place St-Pierre.

Musée des Arts Forains There is a funfair museum, the privately owned Musée des Arts Forains, on the edge of the Parc de Bercy at 53 avenue des Terroirs de France, 12ᵉ. Located within one of the old Bercy wine warehouses, the museum has working merry-go-rounds as well as fascinating relics from nineteenth-century fairs. Visits, which consist of an hour-and-a-half guided tour and cost €13 (children €5), are by appointment only on ☎01 43 40 16 15; ⓜBercy then bus #24.

PARC ASTERIX

Parc Astérix In Plailly, 38km north of Paris off the A1 autoroute ☎08 26 30 10 40, ⓦparcasterix.fr. Check the website or phone for opening times, as they vary, but generally April–June daily 10am–6pm; July & Aug daily 10am–7pm; Sept & Oct Sat & Sun 10am–6pm; also closed for several days in May. Admission €40 (children aged 3–11 €30, under-3s free), though the

---

EATING OUT WITH KIDS

Restaurants in Paris are usually good at providing small portions or allowing children to share dishes. A number of places listed in the "Cafés and restaurants" chapter (see pp.265–294) offer a *menu enfant*, including *Chez Imogène* (see p.292), *La Cantine Merci* (see p.292) and *Dame Tartine* (see p.274), which also has the advantage of outside tables in a traffic-free environment. A little out of the way, but definitely worth a visit if you're in the Parc des Buttes-Chaumont area is *Les 400 Coups* (see p.293), which has a children's play area, including toy kitchen, and does excellent food. Another good family option is Sunday brunch at *Villa Spicy*, 8 avenue Franklin D. Roosevelt, 4ᵉ (daily noon–midnight; ☎01 56 59 62 59, ⓦspicyrestaurant.com; ⓜFranklin-D.-Roosevelt), with plenty of non-spicy options on the menu (mains €20–27), a clown and activities such as drawing for children.

Slightly healthier than *McDonald's* et al, and very reasonably priced, is the family-friendly, French-style "*fast foude*" chain, *Hippopotamus* (branches throughout the city centre, including 1 bd des Capucines, 2ᵉ; ☎01 47 42 75 70, ⓦhippopotamus.fr; daily 11–5am; €6.90 *menu enfant*; ⓜOpéra); they specialize in *steak frites* and offer toys, games and colouring books to boot. One thing to remember when ordering a steak, hamburger, etc, is that the French will serve it rare unless you ask for it "*bien cuit*".

26

website often has special offers. Parking €8. Disneyland Paris (see Chapter 17) has put all Paris's other **theme parks** into the shade, though **Parc Astérix** (see p.351) – better mind-fodder, less crowded and cheaper – is well worth considering. Interesting historical-themed sections like Ancient Greece, Roman Empire, Gallic Village, the Middle Ages and Old Paris are sure to spark curiosity in your children. A Via Antiqua shopping street, with buildings from every country in the Roman Empire, leads to a Roman town where gladiators play comic battles and dodgem chariots line up for races. In another area, street scenes of Paris show the city changing from Roman Lutetia to the present-day capital. All sorts of rides are on offer, including the Trace du Hourra, a bobsled that descends very fast from high above. Dolphins and sea lions perform tricks for the crowds; there are parades and jugglers; restaurants for every budget; and most of the actors speak English. The easiest way to get here is to take the shuttle bus from the Louvre or Eiffel Tower, which runs in the summer; check website for times (€20, under-12s €16). Alternatively, take the half-hourly shuttle bus (9.30am–6/7pm; €7.50, under-12s €5.50) from RER Roissy-Charles-de-Gaulle (line B).

CIRCUSES AND THEATRE

Language being less of a barrier for smaller children, the younger your kids, the more likely they are to appreciate Paris's many special **theatre** shows and **films**. There's also **mime** and the **circus**, which need no translation.

CIRCUS (CIRQUE)

Circuses, unlike funfairs, are taken seriously in France. They come under the heading of culture as performance art (and there are no qualms about performing animals). Some circuses have permanent venues, of which the most beautiful in Paris is the nineteenth-century Cirque d'Hiver Bouglione (see below). You'll find details of the seasonal ones under "Cirques" in the "Pour les Jeunes" section of *L'Officiel des Spectacles* and under the same heading in the "Enfants" section of *Pariscope*, and there may well be visiting circuses from Warsaw or Moscow.

Cirque Diana Moreno Bormann 112 rue de la Haie Coq, 19ᵉ ☎ 06 10 71 83 50, ⓦ cirquedianamoreno.com; Bus #65 (direction Mairie d'Aubervilliers). A traditional circus, with lion-tamers, elephants, zebras, acrobats, jugglers, trapeze artists – the lot. From €10, children under 4 free. Performances on Wed, Sat and Sun at 3pm throughout the year.

Cirque d'Hiver Bouglione 110 rue Amelot, 11ᵉ ☎ 01 47 00 28 81, ⓦ cirquedhiver.com; Ⓜ Filles-du-Calvaire. This rather splendid, recently restored Second Empire building decorated with pilasters, bas-reliefs and sculpted panels, is the setting for dazzling acrobatic feats, juggling, lion-taming and much else. From the end of October to early March (and TV and fashion shows the rest of the year). The Christmas shows are extremely popular. Tickets €20–50. Shows Wed 2pm, Sat & Sun 2pm & 5pm.

Cirque de Paris Parc des Chantereines, 115 bd Charles-de-Gaulle, Villeneuve-La-Garenne ☎ 01 47 99 40 40, ⓦ journeeaucirque.com; RER Gennevilliers/St-Denis. This dream day out allows you to spend an entire day at the circus (Oct–June Wed, Sun & school hols 10am–5pm; €35, children aged 3–11 from €30, including show and lunch). In the morning you are initiated into the arts of juggling, walking the tightrope, clowning and make-up. You have lunch in the ring with your artist tutors, then join the spectators for the show, after which, if you're lucky, you might be taken round to meet the animals. You can, if you prefer, just attend the show at 2pm (from €20, under-12s from €15), but you'd better not let the kids know what they've missed.

SWIMMING, ROLLERBLADING AND OTHER FAMILY ACTIVITIES

One of the most fun things a child can do in Paris – and as enjoyable for the minders – is to have a wet and wild day at **Aquaboulevard**, a giant leisure complex with a landscaped wave pool, slides and a grassy outdoor park. In addition, many municipal **swimming pools** (see p.343) in Paris have dedicated children's pools.

Cycling and **rollerblading** are other fun undertakings for the whole family. Sunday is the favoured day to be *en famille* on wheels in Paris, when the central *quais* of the Seine and the Canal St-Martin are closed to traffic. One of the most thrilling wheelie experiences is the **mass rollerblading** (see p.344) that takes place on Friday nights and Sunday afternoons (the Sunday outings tend to be family affairs and the pace is a bit slower). Paris à Vélo C'est Sympa (see p.345) has a good range of kid-sized bikes as well as baby carriers and tandems, and they also offer bicycle tours of Paris.

Boules (see p.345) and **billiards** (see p.346) are both popular in Paris and might amuse your teenagers.

CLOCKWISE FROM TOP JARDIN D'ACCLIMATATION (P.349); CIRQUE D'HIVER BOUGLIONE; CRANE, JARDIN DES PLANTES (P.350) >

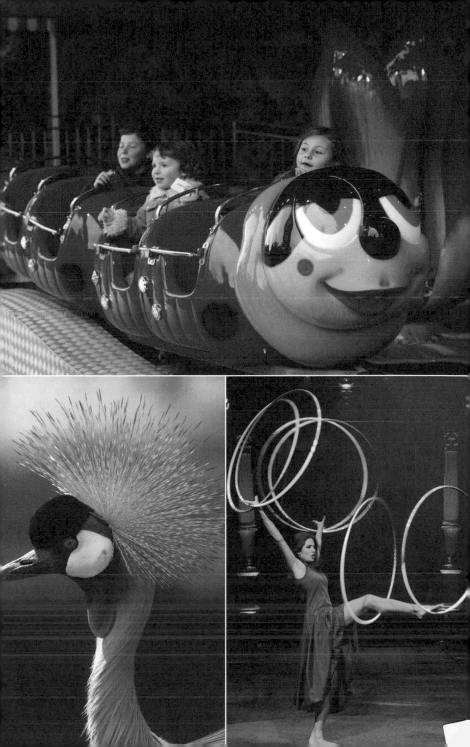

Cirque Pinder Pelouse Reuilly Bois de Vincennes ☎01 45 90 21 25, ⓦcirquepinder.com; ⓂPorte de Charenton/Porte Dorée. This travelling circus has been entertaining French audiences since 1854 with acts featuring performing lions, elephants and camels, clowns and trapeze artists. €15–50. End of Nov to early Jan.

THEATRE AND MAGIC

The "Spectacles" section under "Enfants" in *Pariscope* lists details of magic, mime, dance and music shows. Several **theatres**, in addition to the ones in the Parc Floral and the Jardin d'Acclimatation, specialize in shows for children, and a few occasionally have shows in English.
Au Bec Fin, 6 rue Thérèse, 1ᵉʳ (☎01 42 96 29 35; ⓂPyramides), Blancs-Manteaux, 15 rue des Blancs-Manteaux, 4ᵉ (☎01 48 87 15 84; ⓂHôtel-de-Ville), and Point Virgule, 7 rue Ste-Croix-de-la-Bretonnerie, 4ᵉ (☎01 42 78 67 03; ⓂHôtel-de-Ville) in the Marais have excellent reputations for occasional programming for kids, while Théâtre Dunois, 7

rue Louise Weiss, 13ᵉ (☎01 45 84 72 00, ⓦtheatredunois .org), is dedicated almost solely to children's theatre.
The **magicians' venue**, Le Double-Fond, 1 place du Marché Ste-Catherine, 4ᵉ (☎01 42 71 40 20, ⓦdoublefond .com), has a special children's magic show (€10) every Saturday at 2.30pm and Wednesdays and Sundays at 4.30pm, though there's a lot of chat in French along with the sleight of hand. If your kids are really into magic they should visit the **Musée de la Magie** (see p.105), where a magician performs throughout the day.

CINEMA

There are many **cinemas** showing cartoons and children's films, but if they're foreign they are usually dubbed into French. The Cinémathèque Française (see p.114) screens films for children on Wednesday and Saturday afternoons. Listings of the main Parisian cinemas are given in Chapter 21. At La Villette (see p.201), the Géode IMAX cinema and Cinaxe 3-D cinema will appeal to most children.

MUSEUMS AND SIGHTS

Cité des Enfants Cité des Sciences, Parc de la Villette, 30 av Corentin-Cariou, 19ᵉ ⓦcite-sciences.fr; ⓂPorte-de-la-Villette. Ninety-minute sessions; check online for times; €6 (€8 for over-25s); as sessions are very popular, advance booking online is recommended, or you can book a place (for weekday sessions only) on ☎08 92 69 70 72. The Cité des Enfants, the Cité des Science's special section for children, with sessions for 2–7s and 5–12s, is totally engaging. Kids can touch, smell and feel inside things, play about with water (it's best to bring a change of clothes), construct buildings on a miniature site (complete with cranes, hard hats and barrows), experiment with sound and light, manipulate robots, race their own shadows, and superimpose their image on a landscape. They can listen to different languages by inserting telephones into the appropriate country on a globe, and put together their own television news. Everything, including the butterfly park, is on an appropriate scale, and the whole area is beautifully

organized and managed. If you haven't got a child, it's worth borrowing one to get in here. The rest of the museum is also pretty good for kids, particularly the planetarium, the various film shows, the Argonaute submarine, children's *médiathèque* (Tues noon–7.45pm, Wed–Sun noon–6.45pm; free) and the frequent temporary exhibitions designed for the young. In the Parc de la Villette (see pp. 201–205), there's lots of wide-open green space and a number of playgrounds.
Le Musée en Herbe 21 rue Hérold, 1ᵉʳ ☎01 40 67 97 66, ⓦmusee-en-herbe.com; ⓂLes Halles/Palais-Royal. Daily 10am–7pm; €10. The Musée en Herbe puts on fun, interactive art exhibitions, using jigsaws, dressing-up clothes, etc, designed for children from as young as 2; recent exhibitions have included Keith Haring and Surrealism. They also run popular art workshops that chime in with the exhibitions – some are for toddlers (aged 2 and a half to 4; €10), others for children aged from 5 to 12 (€10).

CHILDREN'S WORKSHOPS

Many museums organize children's **workshops** on Wednesdays, Saturdays and daily throughout the school holidays. The **Musée d'Art Moderne de la Ville de Paris** (see p.156) has special exhibitions and workshops in its children's section (Wed & Sat; entrance 14 av de New-York). Other museums with sessions for kids include the **Musée Carnavalet** (see p.94), **Musée d'Orsay** (see p.142), **Musée de la Mode et du Textile** (see p.59), **Musée des Arts Décoratifs** (see p.58), **Institut du Monde Arabe** (see p.130), **Musée du Quai Branly** (see p.147) and the **Petit Palais** (see p.65).
For the current programme of workshops, look under "Animations" in the "Pour les Jeunes" section of *L'Officiel des Spectacles*, or pick up a copy of Objectif Musée, available from museums.

TOP TEN CHILD-FRIENDLY PARIS SIGHTS

The best treat for children of every age from 2 upwards is undoubtedly the **Cité des Enfants** (see opposite) within the Cité des Sciences, and the Cité des Sciences museum itself, in the Parc de la Villette. However, lots of Paris's main attractions, although not exclusively aimed at children, have much to offer young visitors; here are our top ten recommendations.

Catacombs (see p.165) Older children will probably relish the creepiness of the catacombs, stacked with millions of bones from the city's old charnel houses and cemeteries.

Cinéaqua (see p.154) An impressive new aquarium in the Jardins du Trocadéro, with thousands of exotic fish, and sharks too, in giant fishtanks.

Grande Galerie de l'Evolution (see p.129) Includes a children's discovery room on the first floor with child-level microscopes, glass cases with live caterpillars and moths and a burrow of Mongolian rodents.

Musée d'Art Moderne (p.84) The collections of cutting-edge furniture and gadgets here may well appeal to some teenagers.

Musée Grévin (see p.71) Kids will enjoy the mock-ups here of key events in French history, especially the more grisly ones.

Musée de la Magie (see p.105) Children can have lots of hands-on fun operating quirky automata, experiment with optical illusions and enjoy a magic show.

Musée de la Poupée (see p.87) A must for children who love dolls.

Pompidou Centre (p.84) Includes a special gallery with fun exhibits designed to appeal to children; workshops are also held most Wednesday and Saturday afternoons for kids aged 6 to 12, and sometimes for the whole family.

Planetariums If outer space is your child's prime interest, then bear in mind the planetariums in the Palais de la Découverte (see p.65) and the Cité des Sciences (see p.201).

Sewers (see p.150) Some 500m down, *les égouts* are dank, damp, dripping, claustrophobic and filled with echoes. Entered through a large square manhole, it's a fascinating way to explore the city.

SHOPS

The fact that Paris is filled with beautiful, enticing, delicious and expensive things all artfully displayed is not lost on most children. Toys, gadgets and clothing are all bright, colourful and appealing, while the sheer amount of ice cream, chocolate, biscuits and sweets of all shapes and sizes is almost overwhelming. The only goodies you are safe from are high-tech toys, of which France seems to offer a particularly poor range. A good place to head is rue Vavin, just north of boulevard Montparnasse, in the St-Germain district, and rue de la Villette, in the Parc des Buttes-Chaumont area, both of which have a good concentration of children's shops.

ENGLISH-LANGUAGE BOOKS

Chantelivre 13 rue de Sèvres, 6ᵉ ⓦ chantelivre.com; ⓜ Sèvres-Babylone; map p.134. A huge selection of everything to do with and for children, including good picture books for the younger ones, an English section, and a play area. Mon 1–7.30pm, Tues–Sat 10am–7.30pm, closed mid-Aug.

Galignani 224 rue de Rivoli, 1ᵉʳ; ⓦ galignani.fr; ⓜ Tuileries; map p.72. This long-established English bookshop stocks a decent range of children's books. Mon–Sat 10am–7pm.

Shakespeare & Co 37 rue de la Boucherie, 5ᵉ ⓦ shakespeareandcompany.com; ⓜ Maubert-Mutualité; map p.120. Upstairs there's a comfy children's classics area. Daily noon–midnight.

WH Smith 248 rue de Rivoli, 1ᵉʳ; ⓜ Concorde; map p.72. The first floor of this British bookseller has a very good children's section. Mon–Sat 9am–7.30pm, Sun 1–7.30pm.

TOYS AND GAMES

In addition to the shops below, be sure to check out the superb selection of toys at Le Bon Marché department store (see p.323).

Le Bonhomme de Bois 141 rue d'Alésia, 14ᵉ ⓦ bonhommedebois.com; ⓜ Alésia; map p.160. Perfect little shop with classic wooden cars and dolls, and plush, colourful, floppy-eared stuffed animals. Mon–Sat 10am–7.30pm.

Le Ciel Est à Tout le Monde 10 rue Gay-Lussac, 5ᵉ, RER Luxembourg; map p.120; also 7 av Trudaine, 9ᵉ ⓦ cielestatoutlemonde.free.fr; ⓜ Anvers. The best kite shop in Europe also sells frisbees and boomerangs, and, next door, books, slippers, mobiles and traditional wooden toys. Mon 1–7pm, Tues–Sat 10.30am–7pm.

Les Cousins d'Alice 36 rue Daguerre, 14ᵉ; ⓜ Gaîté/Edgar-Quinet; map p.160. *Alice in Wonderland* decorations, toys, games, puzzles and mobiles, plus a

26

26

general range of books and records. Tues–Sat 10am–1pm & 3–5pm, Sun 11am–1pm; closed Aug.

Amuzilo 34 rue Dauphine, 6ᵉ; Ⓜ Odéon; map p.134. Small, friendly toy shop with a nice selection of wooden toys (some handcrafted in France) for toddlers; marionettes, dolls' house furniture and games for primary-school-aged children. Mon–Sat 10.30am–7.30pm.

Au Nain Bleu 5 bd Malesherbes, 8ᵉ Ⓦ aunainbleu.com; Ⓜ St-Augustin; map p.62. Around since the 1830s, this shop is expert at delighting children with wooden toys, dolls and faux-china tea sets galore. Mon–Sat 10am–6.30pm; closed Mon in Aug.

Puzzles Michèle Wilson 116 rue du Château, 14ᵉ Ⓦ pmw.fr; Ⓜ Pernéty; map p.160. Puzzles galore, with workshop on the premises. Tues–Fri 10am–8pm, Sat 10am–7pm.

Tout s'arrange 11 rue Vavin, 6ᵉ; Ⓜ Notre-Dame-des-Champs; map p.160. A delightfully idiosyncratic miniature boutique selling inexpensive tiny treasures (jewellery, decorations, micro-dollies) handmade using objects found or recycled by the owner, who also makes toys and bags. Mon–Sat 10.30am–7pm.

CLOTHES

Besides the specialist shops listed here, most of the big department and discount stores have children's sections (see Chapter 24). Of the latter, Tati is the cheapest, while Monoprix has decent prices and quality.

Alice à Paris 9 rue de l'Odéon, 6ᵉ Ⓦ aliceaparis.com; Ⓜ Odéon; map p.134. Beautiful, elegant clothes to make your children perfect little Parisians. From babies upward, but best for toddlers and older children. Expensive, but not overpriced. Mon 2–7pm, Tues–Sat 11am–7pm.

Bonpoint 50 rue Etienne-Marcel, 2ᵉ Ⓦ bonpoint.fr; Ⓜ Etienne-Marcel; map p.72. Insanely expensive but utterly elegant outfits for the 0-to-6-year-old going on 24. These are elegant, well-designed clothes mixing traditional children's outfitting with contemporary touches. Prices in the €50–100 range. A half-dozen other branches around the city, and available at Le Bon Marché (see p.323). Mon–Sat 10am–7pm.

Du Pareil au Même 122 rue du Faubourg-St-Antoine, 12ᵉ Ⓦ dpam.fr; Ⓜ Ledru-Rollin; map p.108. Beautiful kids' clothing at very good prices. Gorgeous floral dresses, cute jogging suits and brightly coloured basics. Branches all over Paris. Mon–Sat 10am–7pm.

La Petite Maison dans la Villette 33 rue de la Villette, 19ᵉ; Ⓜ Jourdain; map p.196. A charming shop, with lots of chic little outfits, knitted hats and scarves, floral bags, quilts, children's cutlery sets and little sewing kits. Mon–Sat 10am–7pm.

Les P'tits Bo'Bo 7 rue Clauzel, 9ᵉ; Ⓜ St-Georges; map p.180. A treasure-trove of secondhand but top-quality children's clothing for newborns to 12-year-olds, stocking leading "bourgeois-bohemian" brands like Bonpoint, Bonton, IKKS and Luco, plus internationals Burberry and Finger in the Nose. Also sells used toys and accessories. Tues–Sat 11am–2pm & 3–7pm.

GAY PRIDE MARCH

Gay and lesbian Paris

The focal point of the gay scene is the Marais, whose central street, rue Ste-Croix-de-la-Bretonnerie, has visibly gay-oriented businesses at almost every other address. Indeed, the whole of central Paris has a prevailing culture of tolerance and respect: the city's mayor, for instance, is gay, though this fact barely registers on the political agenda. The high spots on the calendar are the huge annual Gay Pride march, which normally takes place on the last Saturday in June (ⓦmarche.inter-lgbt.org), and the Bal Gay on the eve of Bastille Day (July 13; 10pm–dawn), a wild open-air dance on the quai de la Tournelle, 5ᵉ (ⓜPont-Marie). Gais Musette (ⓦgaismusette.com), an association dedicated to "*danse à deux*", organizes the Carnaval Interlope in mid-February every year; not every one of the thousand revellers comes in disguise, or indeed dances *à deux*, but it's one of the best nights of the year.

27

ESSENTIALS

The gay and lesbian community is well catered for by rights and support organizations and an active **media**. Listed below are a handful of the most useful contacts, along with a couple of classic, gay-oriented **hotels**.

USEFUL CONTACTS

Centre LGBT de Paris 63 rue Beaubourg, 3^e ☎01 43 57 21 47, ⓦcentrelgbtparis.org; ⓂBastille/Ledru-Rollin/Voltaire. The first port of call for information and advice – legal, social, psychological and medical. Also has a good library and puts on small exhibitions. Mon 6–8pm, Tues & Thurs 3.30–8pm, Wed, Fri & Sat 1–8pm.

Inter-LGBT 127 rue Amelot, 11e ☎01 53 01 47 01, ⓦinter-lgbt.org; ⓂSt-Sébastien-Froissart. Actively campaigns for gay rights and organizes the annual pride march.

MAG 106 rue de Montreuil, 11e ☎01 43 73 31 63, ⓦmag-paris.fr; ⓂNation. The Mouvement d'Affirmation des Jeunes Gais et Lesbiennes, a group aimed at young people that organizes a drop-in welcome service (Fri 6–10pm, Sat 4–9pm) as well as occasional tea dances, picnics, and cinema and theatre nights.

Paris Gay Village ⓦparisgaivillage.com. Voluntary association that acts as an alternative tourist office, with inexpensive guided walks and museum visits ("gay Louvre" and "Left Bank lesbians", for example) and a one-hour welcome-to-gay-Paris service.

Pharmacie du Village 26 rue du Temple, 4^e ☎01 42 72 60 71; ⓂHôtel-de-Ville. This gay-run pharmacy is sympathetic to most needs. Mon–Sat 8.30am–9.30pm, Sun 9am–8pm.

THE MEDIA AND WEBSITES

2X ⓦ2xparis.fr. "Deux Fois" aka "Two Weeks" is the premier free gay paper for cultural and nightlife listings, small ads, lonely hearts, services, etc. Comes out every other Thurs and is found in gay venues all over the Marais. Downloadable.

Citegay ⓦcitegay.fr. One of the best national websites (in French), with lots of links, features and contacts.

Les Mots à la Bouche 6 rue Ste-Croix-de-la-Bretonnerie, 4e ☎01 42 78 88 30, ⓦmotsbouche.com; ⓂHôtel-de-Ville; map p.96. The main gay and lesbian bookshop, with exhibition space and meeting rooms; a selection of literature in English, too. Lots of free listings maps and club flyers to pick up, and one of the helpful assistants usually speaks English. Mon–Sat 11am–11pm, Sun 1–9pm.

Paris Gay ⓦparis-gay.com. Major portal for gay tourists visiting Paris. The online *Guide Gay* has lots of reviews of bars, restaurants, clubs, saunas, etc, though the English translations tend to be rather brief.

Têtu ⓦtetu.com. The glossiest and most readable of France's gay (and to a secondary extent, lesbian) monthlies – the name means "headstrong". The pull-out section, "Agenda", is full of contact details, addresses and reviews, though it's not restricted to Paris.

HOTELS

Hôtel de la Bretonnerie 22 rue Ste-Croix de la Bretonnerie, 4^e ☎01 48 87 77 63, ⓦbretonnerie.com; ⓂHôtel-de-Ville. See p.256.

Hôtel Central Marais 33 rue Vieille-du-Temple, 4e ☎01 48 87 56 08, ⓦhotelcentralmarais.com; ⓂHôtel-de-Ville. See p.256.

NIGHTLIFE

In terms of **nightlife**, Paris's "gay village" is the Marais, centred on rue Ste-Croix-de-la-Bretonnerie and spreading up past the Pompidou Centre towards métro Etienne-Marcel. It's not just *Le Central* and the *Open Café* any more – even the selection below only scratches the surface. **Lesbians** don't enjoy a similarly wide selection, but there's a developing scene a few steps south, around rue du roi de Sicile. The old focal point of the 1980s, around Les Halles, still has a few great addresses.

The reputation of wild hedonism in gay **clubs** has spread beyond the gay community and attracted heterosexuals in search of a good time. Consequently, straights are welcome in some gay establishments, especially when in gay company. Don't forget that many if not most mainstream clubs (see p.302) run gay *soirées*, but the best thing is to keep an eye on flyers and ask around in bars. Club **opening hours** are largely irrelevant: they're all pretty empty before at least 1am and keep going till at least dawn – some continue into *after* events well into weekend mornings. **Entry prices** are generally around €10–20, depending on the size of the venue and the popularity of the individual *soirée*.

Ecstasy, cocaine and amphetamines (*ecstasy*; *cocaïne* or *coke*; *amphés* or *speed*) are still an integral part of the scene, and largely sold through contacts – often inside clubs. Similar laws and risks apply in Paris as in most Western countries.

BARS – MAINLY WOMEN

★ **3W-Kafé** 8 rue des Ecouffes, 4e ☎01 48 87 39 26; ⓂHôtel-de-Ville; map p.96. Swish lipstick-lesbian lounge-café. Sophisticated professionals earlier on, but it warms up considerably at weekends, when the cellar bar gets moving. The owners also run *Les Jacasses*, immediately opposite, a lower-key wine bar which does decent tapas, bruschetta and the like. Daily 5.30pm–2am.

La Champmeslé 4 rue Chabanais, 3e ☎01 42 96 85 20; ⓂPyramides; map p.72. Long-established lesbian address, popular among thirty-somethings, though packs everyone in for the live music or cabaret nights from Thursday to Saturday (after 10pm). Holds frequent exhibitions. A good place to begin exploring the scene. Daily 4pm–4am.

★ **Le Troisième Lieu** 62 rue Quincampoix, 4ᵉ ☎01 48 04 85 64; ⓜRambuteau; map p.85. Upbeat new disco-diner offering all things: (inexpensive) cocktail bar, restaurant (with excellent "big salads") and dancing later on at weekends. In all, a welcoming and fairly mixed space, though mainly frequented by *les filles*, and mostly younger ones at that. Daily 6pm–2am.

BARS – MAINLY MEN

Café Cox 15 rue des Archives, 3ᵉ ☎01 42 72 08 00; ⓜHôtel-de-Ville; map p.96. Muscular types up for a seriously good time pack out this loud, neon-coloured bar. Friendly – if your face fits – and has DJs at weekends. Mon–Thurs 12.30pm–2am, Fri–Sun 1.30pm–2am.

★ **Le Duplex** 25 rue Michel-le-Comte, 3ᵉ ☎01 42 72 80 86; ⓜRambuteau; map p.96. Arty little bar that's popular with intellectual or media types for its relaxed and chatty atmosphere. Friendly rather than cruisy. Puts on art exhibitions. Mon–Thurs & Sun 8pm–2am, Fri & Sat 8pm–4am.

Le Free DJ 35 rue Ste-Croix-de-la-Bretonnerie, 4ᵉ ☎01 42 78 26 20; ⓜHôtel-de-Ville; map p.96. This stylish, fairly recent addition to the scene draws the young and *très looké* – beautiful types. It's friendly, though, and features some big sounds (house, disco-funk) in the basement club. Daily 6pm–4am.

L'Open Café 17 rue des Archives, 3ᵉ ☎01 48 87 80 25; ⓜArts-et-Métiers; map p.96. The first gay café-bar to have tables out on the pavement, and they're still there, with overhead heaters in winter. *L'Open* is *the* most famous gay bar in Paris and, as such, it's expensive and quite touristy, but still good fun. Mon–Thurs & Sun 11am–2am, Fri & Sat 11am–4am.

★ **Le Raidd** 23 rue du Temple, 4ᵉ ⓜHôtel-de-Ville; map p.96. One of the city's biggest, glossiest (and most expensive) bars, famous for its beautiful staff, topless waiters and go-go boys' shower shows every hour. Daily 5pm–2am.

CLUBS

Le Club 18 18 rue du Beaujolais, 1ᵉʳ ⓦclub18.fr; ⓜPalais Royal; map p.72. The oldest gay club in Paris, but still fashionable, especially among a friendly, fresh-faced crowd. Tiny, too, which is part of the fun. Entry €10.

CUD 12 rue des Haudriettes, 3ᵉ; ⓜRambuteau; map p.96. The "Classic Up and Down" is just that: bar upstairs, club below. A great, miniature venue for low-key, relaxed dancing with no queues, door policies or overpriced drinks. More for bears than boys, though it's pretty mixed. Free.

Queen 102 av des Champs-Elysées, 8ᵉ ⓦqueen.fr; ⓜGeorge V; map p.62. The gay club of the 1980s has bounced back from its inevitable fall, though it's still a bit packed out with eager provincials – except on the friendly (and officially "overkitsch"), gay-focused Sunday nights. Entry costs vary, from free to €20 on Sun.

Le Rive Gauche 1 rue du Sabot, 6ᵉ ⓦlerivegauche .com; ⓜSt-Germain-des-Prés; map p.134. Currently fashionable among gorgeous young *gamines* on the Saturday girls-only nights (from 11pm; €15), this pocket club is a historic 1970s address (preserving some of its gold mirror-mosaic decor). Friday is Latino night (entry free).

★ **Le Tango** 13 rue au Maire, 3ᵉ ☎01 42 72 17 78; ⓜArts-et-Métiers; map p.93. Unpretentious (and inexpensive) gay and lesbian club with a traditional Sunday-afternoon *bal* from 6pm, featuring slow dances as well as anything from tango to camp disco classics. Turns into a full-on club later on, as well as on Friday nights. Saturdays feature the excellent *Bal de la Boîte à Frissons*, with dancing to accordion music until the legendary "Madison" at 12.30am, after which it's pure fetish costume and disco – and no techno allowed. Entry up to €10.

GYMS, SAUNAS AND BACKROOMS

Paris's proud history as the erotic capital of Europe is reflected in the modern-day plethora of gay **saunas**, **gyms** and full-on **sex clubs**. A handful of stand-out venues are listed here – good first ports of call if you plan to explore the scene in more depth.

VENUES

Le Dépôt 10 rue aux Ours, 3ᵉ ⓦwww.ledepot-paris.fr; ⓜEtienne-Marcel/Rambuteau. This club is allegedly "Europe's biggest backroom", spread over a maze of different rooms and levels, with a laser-streaked, pumping dancefloor. It's usually packed – you'll have to queue for a cubicle. €8.50–13. Daily 2pm–7/8am.

Gym Louvre 7 rue du Louvre, 1ᵉʳ ⓦgymlouvre.com; ⓜLouvre Rivoli. "Le sauna de toutes les tentations", with a serious gym as well as a hammam, cabins, glory-holes and a bar. €7–15. Mon–Sat 9am–2am, Sun noon–2am.

IDM 4 rue du Faubourg Montmartre, 9ᵉ ⓦidm-sauna .com; ⓜGrands Boulevards. Big, cruisey gym and sauna, established for some thirty years, and still going strong with its beautiful clientele, restaurant, basement backroom, and gym. €15–21. Daily noon–1am.

Sun City 62 bd Sébastopol, 3ᵉ ⓦsuncity-paris.fr; ⓜEtienne-Marcel. Luxuriously appointed sauna-gym complex with a kitsch Indian theme. Has a proper swimming pool as well as the obligatory jacuzzis, hammam, fitness suites and so on. €12–20. Daily noon–6am.

27

Contexts

361 History
378 Books
381 French

History

Early humans – and for many millennia their Neanderthal cousins alongside them – first lived in the Paris region some 600,000 years ago, when deer, boar, bears and aurochs roamed the banks of a half-kilometre-wide river. The waters slowly shifted southward before settling in the current bed of the Seine in around 30,000 BC (leaving behind today's Marais or "marsh"). The discovery of 14,000-year-old reindeer-hunter campsites at Pincevent, Verberie and Etiolles, in the Paris basin, suggests that modern humans arrived relatively recently. The oldest encampment yet uncovered, dating back to about 7600 BC, was found by the river in the southwest corner of the modern 15^e arrondissement; it seems to have been a site for sorting flint pebbles. At Bercy, several well-preserved dugout canoes probably date from a marshy fishing and hunting settlement of around 4500 BC.

The Parisii

Mud and water were clearly still major features of the area when the **Gauls** or **Celts** began to settle, probably in the third century BC, as the Roman rendition of their name for the city, **Lutetia** or Lucotetia, is drawn from *luco*, a Celtic root word for "marshland". The local Quarisii or **Parisii** tribe built an oppidum or Iron-Age fort on the eastern part of what is now the Ile de la Cité. The island was originally part of a miniature archipelago of five islets, with two further islets lying to its east (these became the modern Ile St-Louis; another, easternmost island was only joined to the Right Bank at boulevard Morland in 1843). The fort of the Parisii commanded a perfect site: defensible and astride the most practicable north–south crossing point of an eminently navigable river.

Roman Paris

When Julius Caesar's conquering armies arrived in 52 BC, they found a thriving and populous settlement – the Parisii had managed to send a contingent of some eight thousand men to stiffen the Gallic chieftain Vercingétorix's doomed resistance to the invaders. Romanized Lutetia prospered, thanks to its commanding position on the Seine trade route, the river's *nautes*, or boatmen – remembered in the carved pillar now in the Musée du Moyen Age (see p.123) – occupying an important position in civic society. And yet the town was fairly insignificant by **Roman** or even Gaulish standards, with a population no larger than the Parisii's original eight-thousand-strong warband – other Gallo-Roman cities, by contrast, had populations of twenty to thirty thousand. The Romans established their basilica on the Ile de la Cité, but the town lay almost

Third century BC	52 BC	Around 275
A tribe known as the Parisii begins to settle on the Ile de la Cité.	When Julius Caesar's conquering armies arrive they find a thriving settlement of some 8000 people.	St Denis brings Christianity to Paris. He is martyred for his beliefs at Montmartre.

entirely on the Left Bank, on the slopes of the Montagne Ste-Geneviève. Though no monuments of their presence remain today, except the baths by the Hôtel de Cluny and the amphitheatre in rue Monge, their street plan, still visible in the north–south axes of rue St-Martin and rue St-Jacques, determined the future growth of the city.

Roman rule in Gaul disintegrated under the impact of **Germanic invasions** around 275 AD, at about the same time St Denis (see box, p.232) established **Christianity** in the Paris region. Roman Lutetia itself, however, or "Paris", as it was beginning to be called, held out for almost two hundred years. The Emperor Julian was headquartered in the city for three years from 358, during his campaign against the German and Frankish tribes – the latter so-called after the Latin word for "ferocious" – making Paris the de facto capital of the Western Empire. Julian found the climate agreeable, with mild winters and soft breezes carrying the warmth of the ocean, and noted that the water of the Seine was "very clear to the eye".

Franks and Capetians

The marauding bands of **Attila the Hun** were repulsed in 451, supposedly thanks to the prayerful intervention of Geneviève, who became the city's patron saint. (Popular legend has it that Attila had massacred eleven thousand virgins in Cologne, on his way to Paris, and that there weren't enough virgins in the city to make it worth his while.) In any case, the city finally fell to **Clovis the Frank** in 486, the leader of a group of Germanic tribes who traced their ancestors back to Merowech, the son of a legendary sea monster – hence the name of the **Merovingian** dynasty Clovis founded. (This sea-monster story has, if anything, more respectable historical roots than the conspiratorial theory that the Merovingians were the descendants of Jesus and Mary Magdalene.) It was the first but by no means the last time the city would fall to German troops.

Clovis's own conversion to Christianity hastened the Christianization of the whole country. In 511 Clovis's son Childebert commissioned the cathedral of St-Etienne, whose foundations can be seen in the Crypte archéologique under the square in front of Notre-Dame. He also imported the relics of St Vincent to a shrine on the Left Bank. The site slowly grew to become the great monastery at St-Germain-des-Prés, while St-Denis, to the north of the city, became the burial site of the Merovingians from Dagobert I onwards, in the early seventh century.

The endlessly warring, fratricidally minded Merovingians were gradually supplanted by the hereditary Mayors of the Palace, the process finally confirmed by the coronation of Pépin III, "the Short", in St-Denis, in 754. Pépin's heir, Carolus Magnus or "**Charlemagne**", who gave his name to the new Carolingian dynasty, conquered half of Europe and sparked a mini-Renaissance in the early ninth century. Unfortunately for Paris, he chose to live far from the city. Paris's fortunes further plummeted after the break-up of Charlemagne's empire, being repeatedly sacked and pillaged by the **Vikings** from the mid-840s onwards. Finally, in the 880s, **Eudes**, the Comte de Paris, built strong fortifications on the Ile de la Cité, and the Vikings were definitively repulsed. Yet Paris lay largely in ruins, a provincial backwater without power, influence or even a significant population. Only the Right Bank, which lacked the wealthy monasteries of the main city, had escaped the Vikings' depredations. It was to emerge as the heart of a reborn city.

486	768	845–85	987
The city falls to Clovis the Frank. His dynasty, the feuding Merovingians, governs Paris for the next two hundred years or so.	Charlemagne is proclaimed king at St-Denis. Over the next forty years he conquers half of Europe – but spends little time in Paris.	Vikings repeatedly sack Paris.	Hugues Capet, one of the counts of Paris, is elected king of Francia and makes Paris his capital.

LEFT AND RIGHT: A TALE OF TWO RIVER BANKS

During the medieval era, the city's commercial activity naturally centred on the place where goods came in to the city – a trade monopolized by the powerful Watermen's guild of Paris. The chief landing place was the place de Grève, a strip of marshy ground which lay where the Hôtel de Ville now stands, on the Right Bank. The Left Bank's intellectual associations were formed equally early, as students came to study at the two great monasteries of Ste-Geneviève and St-Germain-des-Prés. Europe's pre-eminent scholar, Peter Abélard – famously the lover of Héloïse and the victim of violent castration – taught in Paris in the early twelfth century, and in 1215 a papal licence allowed the official formation of what gradually became the renowned University of Paris, eventually to be known as the **Sorbonne**, after Robert de Sorbon, founder of a college for poor scholars in 1257. By 1300 there were around three thousand students on the Left Bank of the city, protected by ecclesiastical rather than city law. At this time, the Latin used both inside and outside the schools gave the student district its name of the "Latin Quarter".

The medieval heyday

In 987, Eudes' descendant Hugues Capet was crowned king, but the early rulers of the new **Capetian dynasty** rarely chose to live in Paris, despite the association of the monarchy with the city. Regrowth, therefore, was slow, and by 1100, the city's population was only around three thousand. One hundred years later, however, Paris had become the largest city in the Christian world (which it would remain until overtaken by London in the eighteenth century), as well as its intellectual and cultural hub. By the **1320s**, the city's population had swollen again to around a quarter of a million. This unparalleled success rested on the city's valuable river-borne trade and the associated expansion of the **merchant classes**, coupled with thriving **agriculture** in the wider Paris region. Vines and cereals grew to the south, while swathes of rich woodland lay to the east and west, and in the north, between the city and the hill of Montmartre. The economic boom was matched by the growth of the city's university, and protected by the novelty of a relatively strong – and largely Paris-based – monarchy, which gradually brought the surrounding regions under its overlordship. Between them, Louis VI, Louis VII and Philippe-Auguste ruled with confidence for almost all the twelfth century.

Walls and Watermen

To protect his burgeoning city, **Philippe-Auguste** (1180–1223) built the **Louvre fortress** whose excavated remains are now on display beneath the Louvre museum. He also constructed a vast **city wall**, which swung north and east to encompass the Marais, and south to enclose the Montagne Ste-Geneviève – a line roughly traced by the inner ring of modern Paris's 1er–6e arrondissements (though the abbey at St-Germain-des-Prés remained *extra muros*). European contemporaries saw the fortifications as a wonder of the world (even if by Rabelais' time "a cow's fart" would have brought down the walls on the Left Bank), a vital guarantee of the city's security and a convincing proof of the monarchy's long-term ambitions to construct an imperial capital. Famously appalled by the stench of the city's mud as a young man, Philippe-Auguste even began to pave some of the city's streets, though most remained filthy, hopelessly rutted and crowded with people and animals – Louis VI's heir had even been killed when de-horsed by a runaway pig in 1131.

1200s	1330s to 1430s	1429
Paris experiences an economic boom, its university becomes the centre of European learning and King Philippe-Auguste constructs a vast city wall.	The French and English nobility struggle for power in the Hundred Years' War. One year in four is a plague year and Paris's population falls by half.	Joan of Arc attempts to drive the English out of Paris. It is not until 1437 that Charles VII regains control of his capital.

The administration of the city remained in the hands of the monarchy until 1260, when **Louis IX** (St Louis) ceded a measure of responsibility to the *échevins* or leaders of the Paris Watermen's guild (see box, p.363). The city's government, when it has been allowed one, has been conducted ever since from the place de Grève/place de l'Hôtel-de-Ville, and the guild's motto, Sec Fluctuat Nec Mergitur ("Battered, but not sinking"), was later adopted by the city itself.

A city adrift

From the **mid-fourteenth** to **mid-fifteenth centuries**, Paris shared the same unhappy fate as the rest of France, embroiled in the long and destructive **Hundred Years' War**, which pitted the French and English nobilities against each other in a power struggle whose results were misery for the French peasant classes, and penury for Paris. A break in the Capetian line led to the accession of Philippe VI, the first of the **Valois dynasty**, but the legitimacy of his claim on the throne was contested by Edward III of England. Harried by war, the Valois monarchs spent much of their troubled reigns outside their capital, whose loyalty was often questionable. Infuriated by the lack of political representation for merchant classes, the city mayor, or Prévôt des Marchands, **Etienne Marcel**, even let the enemy into Paris in 1357.

Charles V, who ruled from 1364, tried to emulate Philippe-Auguste by constructing a new Louvre and a new city wall that increased Paris's area by more than half again (roughly incorporating what are now the modern 9e–11e arrondissements, on the Right Bank), but the population within his walls was plummeting due to disease and a harsh climate in Europe generally, as well as warfare and political instability. The **Black Death**, which arrived in the summer of 1348, killed some eight hundred Parisians a day, and over the next 140 years one year in four was a plague year. In the fourteenth century, the state and populace alike easily found scapegoats for such ills. Leading knights of the wealthy Templar order were burnt at the stake on the tip of the Ile de la Cité in 1314, and they were followed to their deaths by hundreds of **Jews** falsely accused of poisoning the city's wells. France's Jews were definitively expelled from the kingdom in 1394. Paris had lost two of its most economically productive minorities. Harvests repeatedly failed – icebergs even floated on the Seine in 1407 – and politically, things were no better. Taxes were ruinous, trade almost impossible and government insecure.

In 1422 the Duke of Bedford based his overlordship of northern France in Paris. **Joan of Arc** made an unsuccessful attempt to drive the English out in 1429, but was wounded in the process at the Porte St-Honoré, and the following year the English king, Henry VI, had the cheek to have himself crowned king of France in Notre-Dame. Meanwhile, the Valois kings fled the city altogether for a life of pleasure-seeking irrelevance in the gentle Loire Valley, a few days' ride to the southwest.

Renaissance

In the course of the hundred years leading up to the mid-fifteenth century, Paris's population more than halved. It was only when the English were expelled – from Paris in 1437 and from France in 1453 – that the economy had the chance to recover from decades of devastation. Even so, it was many more years before the Valois monarchs felt

1528	1572	1607
François I transfers the royal court from the Loire to his new palace at the Louvre.	On St Bartholomew's Day, August 25, some 3000 Protestants gathered in Paris are massacred at the instigation of the ultra-Catholic Guise family.	The triumphant monarch Henri IV builds the Pont-Neuf and sets about creating a worthy capital.

able to quit their châteaux and hunting grounds in the Loire and return to the city. Finally, in 1528, **François I** decided to bring back the royal court to Paris, aiming, like Philippe-Auguste before him, to establish a new Rome. Work began on reconstructing the Louvre and building the Tuileries palace for **Catherine de Médicis**, and on transforming Fontainebleau and other country residences into sumptuous Renaissance palaces. An economic boom brought peasants in from the countryside in their thousands, and the city's population surpassed its medieval peak by the 1560s. Centralized planning coughed into life to cope with the influx; royal edicts banned overhanging eaves on houses, and a number of gates were removed from Charles V's walls to improve street congestion. But Paris remained, as Henri II put it, a city of "mire, muck and filth".

The wars of religion

In the second half of the century, war interrupted the early efforts at civic improvement – this time **civil war** between Catholics and Protestants. Paris, which swung fanatically behind the Catholic cause – calls for the establishment of a new Jerusalem quickly replaced the old Roman ideals – was the scene of one of the worst atrocities ever committed against French Protestants. Some three thousand of them were gathered in Paris for the wedding of Henri III's daughter, Marguerite, to Henri, the Protestant king of Navarre. On August 25, 1572, **St Bartholomew's Day**, as many as three thousand Protestants were massacred at the instigation of the noble "ultra-Catholic" Guise family. When, through this marriage, Henri of Navarre became heir to the French throne in 1584, the Guises drove his father-in-law, Henri III, out of Paris. Forced into alliance, the two Henris laid siege to the city in May 1590 – Henri III claiming to love the city more than he loved his own wife (which, given he was a notorious philanderer among both men and women, was almost certainly true). Parisians were quickly reduced – and it wasn't to be for the last time – to eating donkeys, dogs and rats. Five years later, after Henri III had been assassinated and some forty thousand Parisians had died of disease or starvation, Henri of Navarre entered the city as king **Henri IV**. "Paris is worth a Mass", he is reputed to have said, to justify renouncing his Protestantism in order to soothe Catholic sensibilities.

Henri's inheritance

The Paris that Henri IV inherited was not a very salubrious place. It was **overcrowded**: no domestic building had been permitted beyond the limits of Philippe-Auguste's twelfth-century walls because of the guilds' resentment of the unfair advantage enjoyed by craftsmen living outside the jurisdiction of the city's tax regulations. The swollen population had caused an **acute housing shortage** and a terrible strain on the rudimentary water supply and drainage system. It is said that the first workmen who went to clean out the city's cesspools in 1633 fell dead from the fumes. It took seven months to clean out 6420 cartloads of filth that had been accumulating for two centuries. The overflow ran into the Seine, whence Parisians drew their drinking water.

Planning and expansion

As the **seventeenth century** began, Henri IV's government set to work in Paris, regulating street lines and facades, and laying out the splendidly harmonious place

1661–1715	1789	1793
Louis XIV transfers the court to Versailles, but this doesn't stop the city growing in size, wealth and prestige.	Long-standing tensions explode into revolution. Ordinary Parisians, the "sans-culottes", storm the Bastille prison on July 14.	The revolutionaries banish the monarchy and execute Louis XVI. A dictatorship is set up, headed by the ruthless Robespierre.

BOULEVARDS AND AVENUES

Aside from his grand palace at Versailles, just outside Paris (see p.223), Louis XIV's most significant architectural legacy was perhaps the demolition of Charles X's old fortifications to make way for the new **boulevards** – which took their name from the *bulwarks*, or giant earthen ramparts, that they replaced – and the creation of long, tree-lined **avenues** such as the Champs-Elysées, which was laid out in 1667 by the landscape designer Le Nôtre. Avenues and boulevards were to become the defining feature of Paris's unique cityscape.

Royale (later renamed the place des Vosges) and place Dauphine. Most emblematic of all the new construction work, however, was the **Pont-Neuf**, the first of the Paris bridges not to be cluttered with medieval houses. It was a potent symbol of Paris's renewal and architectural daring. After Henri IV was assassinated in 1610 – while caught in his carriage in a seventeenth-century traffic jam on rue de la Ferronnerie – his widow built the **Palais du Luxembourg**, the first step in the city's colonization of the western Left Bank – previously the province of abbeys and churches.

The tradition of grandiose public building initiated by Henri IV perfectly symbolized the bureaucratic, centralized power of the newly self-confident state. The process reached its apogee in the seventeenth century under **Louis XIV**, whose director of architecture promised to fill the city "with so many magnificent buildings that the whole world will look on in wonder". Under the unifying design principles of grace and **Classicism**, the places Vendôme and Victoire were built, along with the sublime Cour Carrée of the Louvre, and half a dozen Italianate Baroque domes.

Grandiose building projects were commissioned as often without royal patronage as with it. The aristocratic *hôtels*, or private mansions, of the **Marais** were largely erected during the seventeenth century, to be superseded early in the **eighteenth century** by the **Faubourg St-Germain** as the fashionable quarter of the rich and powerful. Despite the absence of the court, Paris only grew in size, wealth and prestige, until the writer Marivaux could claim, with some truth, in 1734 that "Paris is the world, and the rest of the earth nothing but its suburbs". By the 1770s and 1780s, conversational *salons*, Masonic lodges, coffee houses or "cafés" and newspapers had opened by the hundreds to serve the needs of the burgeoning **bourgeoisie**, while the Palais Royal became the hub of fashionably decadent Europe – a gambling den, brothel, mall and society venue combined. In 1671, however, Louis repaired with his entire court to a new and suitably vast palace at **Versailles**, declaring it was "the spot where I can most be myself". The monarchy would not return until Louis' grandson, Louis XVI, was brought back at pike-point in 1789.

The poor

Meanwhile, the centre of the city remained a densely packed and unsanitary warren of **medieval lanes and tenements**. And it was only in the years immediately preceding the 1789 Revolution that any attempt was made to clean it up. The buildings crowding the bridges were dismantled as late as 1786. Pavements were introduced for the first time and attempts were made to improve the drainage. A further source of pestilential infection was removed with the emptying of the overcrowded cemeteries into the catacombs. One grave-digger alone claimed to have buried more than ninety thousand

1799	1820s	1830
Army general Napoleon Bonaparte seizes control in a coup and, in 1804, crowns himself emperor in Notre-Dame.	Paris acquires gas lighting and its first omnibus.	After three days of fighting, known as *les trois glorieuses*, Louis-Philippe is elected constitutional monarch.

people in thirty years, stacked "like slices of bacon" in the charnel house of the Innocents, which had been receiving the dead of 22 parishes for eight hundred years.

In 1786 Paris received its penultimate ring of fortifications, the so-called **wall of the Fermiers Généraux**, which roughly followed the line of modern Paris's inner and outer ring of arrondissements. The wall had 57 *barrières* or toll gates (one of which survives in the middle of place Stalingrad), where a tax was levied on all goods entering the city. At its outer edge, beyond the customs tolls, new houses of entertainment sprang up, encouraging a long tradition of Parisians crossing the boundaries of the city proper in search of drink, dancing and other kinds of transgression. It was a tradition that would culminate – and largely die – with the early twentieth-century artistic boom-towns of Montmartre and Montparnasse.

The Revolution

The **Revolution of 1789** was provoked by a financial crisis. Louis XVI had poured money into costly wars and the only way to increase revenue was to tax the clergy and nobility. He couldn't easily impose his will despotically so, for the first time since 1614, he recalled the **Estates General** – a kind of tax-raising parliament made up of representatives of the country's three "estates", or orders: the clergy (the First Estate), the nobility (the Second) and the rest (the Third). In May 1789 each of the three orders presented its grievances to the Crown; the bourgeois delegates representing the Third Estate were particularly resentful and outspoken. Responding to rising tension, Louis XVI began posting troops around Versailles and Paris, as though preparing for a coup to reverse his actions.

Fear of attack by royal troops propelled the Parisian people from the sidelines into the heart of the action. The Parisian electoral assembly entered the Hôtel de Ville, declared itself the municipal government or **Commune**, and set up a bourgeois militia, later to become known as the National Guard. It was supposed to keep order in an agitated city, but actually joined in when a band of ordinary Parisians stormed the **Bastille** prison on July 14. The Parisian working classes, known as the **sans-culottes**, literally "the people without breeches", now became major players in the unfolding drama. As the king gathered troops at Versailles, the deputies of the Third Estate proclaimed themselves the **National Assembly** and threatened to unleash a popular explosion in Paris. The king was forced to recognize the new parliament, which in August 1789 passed the **Declaration of the Rights of Man**, sweeping away the feudal privileges of the old order. Rumours were rife of counter-revolutionary intrigues at the court in **Versailles**, and in October a group of Parisians marched on Versailles and forced the king to return to Paris with them; they installed him in the Tuileries, where he was basically kept prisoner. In 1791 he attempted to flee abroad, but was stopped at Varennes and humiliatingly brought back to Paris.

As France was drawn into a succession of wars with neighbouring states, radical clamours for the overthrow of the king grew. The National Assembly was divided, but in August 1792 the *sans-culottes* rose up again, imprisoned the king and set up an **insurrectionary Commune** at the Hôtel de Ville. Under pressure from the Commune, the Assembly agreed to disband and order elections for a new **Convention** to draw up a new, republican, constitution. Later that month the Convention abolished the

1848	1850s and 1860s	1863
In June, revolution erupts once again. Louis Napoléon Bonaparte, Napoleon's nephew, is elected president. In 1851 he declares himself Emperor Napoléon III.	Baron Haussmann literally bulldozes the city into the modern age, creating long, straight boulevards and squares. The poor are driven out to the suburbs.	At the Salon des Refusés, Manet's proto-impressionist painting *Déjeuner sur l'Herbe* scandalizes all of Paris.

monarchy, set up a republic and convicted the king of treason. He was guillotined on place de la Révolution (now place de la Concorde) in January 1793. Europe was in uproar.

The Terror

The Convention, under the radical **Jacobin** faction, set up a war dictatorship. The Committee of Public Safety, headed by the chillingly ruthless Maximilien **Robespierre**, began the extermination of "enemies of the people", a period known as the *Grande Terreur*. Among the first casualties was **Marie-Antoinette**, who went with calm dignity to the guillotine in October 1793. Over the next few months some further 2600 individuals were executed, including many of the more moderate revolutionaries such as **Danton** whose last words as he went to his death were typical of his proud spirit: "Above all, don't forget to show my head to the people; it's well worth having a look at." **The Terror** finally ended in July 1794 when Robespierre, now widely perceived as a tyrant, was himself arrested by members of the Convention; he suffered the fate he had meted out to so many.

Power was thereafter put into the hands of a more temperate – but fatally weak – five-man **Directory**. The longed-for strong leader quickly emerged in the form of the celebrated General **Napoleon Bonaparte**, who had put down a Royalist insurrection in Paris in October 1795 with the minimum of fuss. In November 1799 he overthrew the Directory in a **coup d'état**. He appointed himself first consul for life in 1802 and **emperor** in 1804.

Napoleon

Napoleon is best known for his incessant **warmongering**, but he also upheld the fundamental reforms of the Revolution. His rights-based Code Civil, or Code Napoléon, long outlasted Napoleon's empire and has been a major influence on legal systems in many other countries. He established the system of education which still endures today, and created an efficient **bureaucracy** that put Paris in still firmer control of the rest of the country. He wanted to make Paris the "capital of capitals", but focused more on public works than monuments: he lined the Seine with two and a half miles of stone *quais*, built three bridges and created canals and reservoirs, providing Paris with its modern water supply. He also built the Arcs de Triomphe and Carrousel, extended for the Louvre, and drew up plans for a temple to the Grande Armée – which later became the church of the Madeleine. He laid out the long and straight rue de Rivoli and rue de la Paix and devised new street-numbering (still in place) – odd on one side, even on the other; where streets ran parallel to the Seine, the numbering followed the flow of the river; in other streets, numbering started at the end nearest the river.

By 1809 Napoleon's conquered territory stretched from southern Italy to the Baltic, an empire much greater than that achieved by Louis XIV or even Charlemagne, but the **invasion of Russia** in 1812 was a colossal disaster. Out of four hundred thousand men (half of whom were conscripts from Napoleon's empire), barely twenty thousand made it back home. In March 1814 an army of Russians, Prussians and Austrians marched into Paris – the first time foreign troops had invaded the city since the English in 1429.

1870	1871	1889
Hundreds die of starvation as the city is besieged by the Prussians.	Paris surrenders in March, but the Prussians withdraw after just three days. In the aftermath, workers rise up and proclaim the Paris Commune. It is speedily and bloodily suppressed by French troops.	The all-new Eiffel Tower steals the show at the Exposition Universelle, or "great exhibition".

Napoleon was forced to abdicate and **Louis XVIII**, brother of the decapitated Louis XVI, was installed as king. In a last desperate attempt to regain power, Napoleon escaped from exile on the Italian island of Elba and reorganized his armies, only to meet final defeat at **Waterloo** on June 18, 1815. Louis XVIII was restored to power.

Restoration and barricades

For the rest of the **nineteenth century** after Napoleon's demise, France was occupied fighting out the contradictions and unfinished business left behind by the Revolution of 1789. Aside from the actual conflicts on the streets of the capital, there was a tussle between the class that had risen to wealth and power as a direct result of the destruction of the monarchy and the survivors of the old order, who sought to make a comeback in the 1820s under the **restored monarchy** of Louis XVIII and Charles X. This conflict was finally resolved in favour of the new bourgeoisie. When Charles X refused to accept the result of the 1830 National Assembly elections, **Adolphe Thiers** – who was to become the veteran conservative politician of the nineteenth century – led the opposition in revolt. Barricades were erected in Paris and there followed three days of bitter street fighting, known as **les trois glorieuses**, in which 1800 people were killed (they are commemorated by the column on place de la Bastille). The outcome of this **July Revolution** was parliament's election of **Louis-Philippe** in August 1830 as constitutional monarch, or *le roi bourgeois*, and the introduction of a few liberalizing reforms, most either cosmetic or serving merely to consolidate the power of the wealthiest stratum of the population.

As the demands of the disenfranchised poor continued to go unheeded, so their radicalism increased, exacerbated by **deteriorating living and working conditions** in the large towns, especially Paris, as the Industrial Revolution got under way. There were, for example, twenty thousand deaths from cholera in Paris in 1832, and 65 percent of the population in 1848 were too poor to be liable for tax. Eruptions of discontent invariably occurred in the capital, with insurrections in 1832 and 1834. When Thiers ringed Paris and its suburbs with a defensive wall (thus defining the limits of the modern city), his efforts soon appeared misdirected. In 1848, the lid blew off the pot. Barricades went up in February, and the **Second Republic** was quickly proclaimed. It looked for a time as if working-class demands might be at least partly met, but in the face of agitation in the streets, the more conservative Republicans lost their nerve, and the nation showed its feelings by returning a spanking reactionary majority in the April elections.

Revolution appeared the only alternative for Paris's radical poor. On June 23, 1848, working-class Paris – Poissonnière, Temple, St-Antoine, the Marais, Quartier Latin, Montmartre – rose in revolt. In what became known as the **1848 Revolution**, men, women and children fought side by side against fifty thousand troops. In three days of fighting, nine hundred soldiers were killed. No one knows how many of the *insurgés* – the insurgents – died. Fifteen thousand people were arrested and four thousand sentenced to prison terms. **Louis Napoléon Bonaparte**, the nephew of Napoleon I, was elected president in November 1848, but within three years he brought the tottering republic to an end by announcing a coup d'état. Twelve months later, he had himself crowned Emperor **Napoléon III**.

1895	1900	1914
Parisians are the first people anywhere in the world to see the jerky cinematic documentaries of the Lumière brothers.	The Métropolitain underground railway, or "métro", is unveiled.	War with Germany calls time on the "belle époque". In September, the Kaiser's armies are just about held off by French troops shuttled from Paris to the front line, only fifteen miles away.

Baron Haussmann

The nearly twenty years of the **Second Empire** brought rapid **economic growth** alongside virulent repression designed to hold the potentially revolutionary underclasses in check. It also brought **Baron Haussmann**, who undertook a total **transformation of the city**. In love with the straight line and grand vista, he drove 135km of broad new streets through the cramped quarters of the medieval city, linking the interior and exterior boulevards, and creating long, straight north–south and east–west cross-routes.

In 1859, all the land up to Thiers' wall of 1840 was incorporated into the city of Paris. A contemporary journalist railed "they have sewn rags onto the dress of a queen", but it was a brave and possibly brilliant decision – and a move that subsequent governments have consistently failed to emulate, leaving Paris's future suburbs to swell energetically but chaotically, then wallow in unregulated and unadorned semi-squalor. Between 1860 and the outbreak of World War I, the population of Paris "beyond the walls", or the **banlieue** as it became known, tripled in size, becoming the home of 1.5 million almost-Parisians. (The city proper had been surpassed in population by London in the eighteenth century; after 1900 it was overtaken by New York too, with Berlin, Vienna and St Petersburg catching up fast.)

The dark side

Haussmann's demolitions were at least in part aimed at workers, and the poor. Barracks were located at strategic points – like the place du Château-d'Eau, now République, controlling the turbulent eastern districts – and the broad boulevards were intended to facilitate cavalry manoeuvres and artillery fire, with angled intersections that would allow troops to outflank any barricades. In other ways, however, **the poor** within the city were largely left to fend for themselves. Some 350,000 Parisians were displaced. The prosperous classes moved into the new western arrondissements, abandoning the decaying older properties. These were divided and subdivided into ever-smaller units as landlords sought to maximize their rents. Sanitation was nonexistent. Water standpipes were available only in the street. Migrant workers from the provinces, sucked into the city to supply the vast labour requirements, crammed into the old villages of Belleville and Ménilmontant. Many, too poor to buy furniture, lived in barely furnished digs or *demi-lits*, where the same bed was shared by several tenants on a shift basis. Cholera and TB were rife. Until 1870 refuse was thrown into the streets at night to be collected the following morning. When in 1884 the Prefect of the day required landlords to provide proper containers, they retorted by calling the containers by his name, Poubelle – and the name has stuck as the French word for "dustbin".

The siege and the Commune

In September 1870, Napoléon III surrendered to Bismarck at the border town of Sedan, less than two months after France had declared war on the well-prepared and superior forces of the **Prussian** state. The humiliation was enough for a Republican government to be instantly proclaimed in Paris. The Prussians advanced and by September 19 were laying **siege** to the capital. Minister of the Interior Léon Gambetta was flown out by hot-air balloon to rally the provincial troops but further balloon

1920s	1940	1942
In the aftermath of war, the decadent *années folles* (or "mad years") of the 1920s rescue Paris's international reputation for hedonism.	In May and June, the government flees Paris, and Nazi soldiers are soon marching down the Champs-Elysées. Four years of largely collaborative fascist rule ensue.	Parisian Jews are rounded up – by other Frenchmen – and shipped off to Auschwitz.

HAUSSMANN'S HARMONIOUS CITY

In half a century, from 1853, much of Paris was rebuilt, transforming an overgrown and insanitary medieval capital into an **urban utopia**. Napoléon III's government provided the force, while banks and private speculators provided the cash. The poor, meanwhile, were either used for labour or cleared out to the suburban badlands.

The presiding genius was the emperor's chief of works, **Baron Haussmann**. In his brave new city, every apartment building was seven storeys high. Every facade was built in creamy limestone, often quarried from under the city itself, with Neoclassical details sculpted around the windows. Every second and fifth floor had its wrought-iron balcony and every lead roof sloped back from the streetfront at precisely 45 degrees. It would all have been inhumanly regular if it hadn't been for the ground-floor shops, which have provided Paris's streets with a more varied face ever since.

The basic Haussmann design proved astonishingly resilient. In the Art Nouveau period, sinuous curves and contours crept across the faces of apartment buildings, and Art Deco and Modernism provided their own, stripped-down facelifts, but still, underneath the new styles, many Parisian buildings followed the basic Haussmannien pattern. The result is a city of rare and enduring harmoniousness.

messengers ended up in Norway or the Atlantic. The few attempts at military sorties from Paris turned into yet more blundering failures. Meanwhile, the city's restaurants were forced to change menus to fried dog, roast rat or peculiar delicacies from the zoos, and death from disease or starvation became an ever more common fate.

The government's half-hearted defence of the city – more afraid of revolution within than of the Prussians – angered Parisians, who clamoured for the creation of a 1789-style Commune. The Prussians, meanwhile, were demanding a proper government to negotiate with. In January 1871, those in power agreed to hold elections for a new National Assembly with the authority to surrender officially to the Prussians. A large monarchist majority, with the conservative Adolphe Thiers at its head, was returned, and on March 1, Prussian troops marched down the Champs-Elysées and garrisoned the city for three days while the populace remained behind closed doors in silent protest. On March 18, amid growing resentment from all classes of Parisians, Thiers' attempt to take possession of the National Guard's artillery in Montmartre (see box, p.185) set the barrel alight. The **Commune** was proclaimed from the Hôtel de Ville and Paris was promptly subjected to a second siege by Thiers' government, which had fled to Versailles, followed by the remaining Parisian bourgeoisie.

The Commune lasted just 72 days, and implemented no lasting reforms. It succumbed to Thiers' army on May 28, 1871, after a week of street-by-street warfare – the so-called *semaine sanglante*, or "Bloody Week" – in which some 25,000 men, women and children were killed, including thousands in random revenge shootings by government troops.

The belle époque

The Commune left great landmarks such as the Tuileries palace and Hôtel de Ville as smoking ruins, but within six or seven years few signs of the fighting remained.

1944	1961	1968
Liberation arrives on August 25, with General de Gaulle motoring up the Champs-Elysées to the roar of a vast crowd.	As France's brutal repression of its Algerian colony reaches its peak, at least two hundred Algerians are murdered by police during a civil rights demonstration.	In May, left-wing students occupying university buildings are supported by millions of striking and marching workers.

Visitors remarked admiringly on the teeming streets, the expensive shops and energetic nightlife. Charles Garnier's Opéra was opened in 1875. Aptly described as the "triumph of moulded pastry", it was a suitable image of the frivolity and materialism of what the British called the "naughty" Eighties and Nineties, and the French called the **belle époque**, or "Age of Beauty". In 1889 the **Eiffel Tower** stole the show at the great Exposition. For the 1900 repeat, the Métropolitain or "**métro**" was unveiled.

The years up to World War I were marked by the unstable but thoroughly conservative governments of the **Third Republic**. On the extreme right, fascism began to make its ugly appearance with Maurras' proto-Brownshirt organization, the Camelots du Roi. Despite – or maybe in some way because of – the political tensions, Paris emerged as the supremely inspiring environment for artists and writers – the so-called Bohemians – both French and foreign. It was a constellation of talents such as Western culture has rarely seen. **Impressionism**, **Fauvism** and **Cubism** were all born in Paris in this period, while French **poets** like Apollinaire, Laforgue, Max Jacob, Blaise Cendrars and André Breton were preparing the way for Surrealism, concrete poetry and Symbolism. **Cinema**, too, first saw the light in Paris, with the jerky documentaries of the Lumière brothers and George Méliès' fantastical features both appearing in the mid-1890s.

War and depression

As a city, Paris escaped **World War I** relatively lightly, with only a brief Zeppelin bombardment in 1916, and heavy shelling from the Germans' monstrous, long-range "Big Bertha" cannon mercifully restricted to the early part of 1918. The human cost was rather higher: one in ten Parisian conscripts failed to return. But Paris remained the world's art – and party – capital after the war, with an injection of foreign blood and a shift of venue from Montmartre to Montparnasse. Indeed, the **années folles** (or "mad years") of the 1920s were among Paris's most decadent and scintillating, consolidating a long-standing international reputation for hedonistic, often erotic, abandon that has sustained its tourism industry for the best part of a century. Meanwhile, work on the dismantling of Thiers' outmoded fortifications progressed with aching slowness from 1919 until 1932 – after which the cleared space languished as a wilderness of shantytowns, or *bidonvilles*, until the construction of the *boulevard périphérique* ring road in the 1960s.

As **Depression** deepened in the 1930s and Nazi power across the Rhine became more menacing, however, the mood changed. Politicized thuggery grew rife in Paris, and the Left united behind the banner of the Popular Front, winning the **1936 elections** with a handsome majority. Frightened by the apparently revolutionary situation, the major employers signed the Matignon Agreement with Socialist Prime Minister Léon Blum. It provided for wage increases, nationalization of the armaments industry, a forty-hour week, paid annual leave and collective bargaining on wages. These reforms were pushed through Parliament, but when Blum tried to introduce exchange controls to check the flight of capital the Senate threw the proposal out and he resigned. The Left returned to opposition, where it remained, with the exception of coalition governments, until 1981.

1969	1973	1998
President de Gaulle loses a referendum, and retires, wounded, to his country house.	Paris's first skyscraper, the Tour Montparnasse, tops out at 56 hideous storeys. The *périphérique* ring road is completed in April.	In July, a multiracial French team wins the World Cup at the new Stade de France, in the suburb of St-Denis.

Fascism and Resistance

The outbreak of war was followed with stunning swiftness by the **Fall of France**. After sweeping across the low countries, the German army broke across the Somme in early June. The French government fled south to Bordeaux, declaring Paris an "open city" in an attempt to save it from a destructive siege. By 14 June, Nazi troops were parading down the Champs-Elysées. During the **occupation** of Paris in **World War II**, the Germans found some sections of Parisian society, as well as the minions of the Vichy government, only too happy to hobnob with them. For four years the city suffered fascist rule with curfews, German garrisons and a Gestapo HQ. Parisian Jews were forced to wear the star of David and in 1942 were rounded up – by other Frenchmen – and shipped off to Auschwitz.

The **Resistance** was very active in the city, gathering people of all political persuasions into its ranks, but with Communists and Socialists, especially of East European Jewish origin, well to the fore. The job of torturing them when they fell into Nazi hands – often as a result of betrayals – was left to their fellow citizens in the fascist militia. Those who were condemned to death – rather than the concentration camps – were shot against the wall below the old fort of Mont Valérien above St-Cloud.

As Allied forces drew near to the city in 1944, the FFI (armed Resistance units) called their troops onto the streets. Alarmed at the prospect of the Left seizing power in his absence, the free French leader, **Général de Gaulle**, urged the Allies to let him press on towards the capital. To their credit, the Paris police also joined in the uprising, holding their Ile de la Cité HQ for three days against German attacks. On August 23, Hitler famously gave orders that Paris should be physically destroyed, but the city's commander, Von Cholitz, delayed just long enough. **Liberation** arrived on August 25 in the shape of General Leclerc's tanks, motoring up the Champs-Elysées to the roar of a vast crowd.

Revolts and demonstrations

Postwar Paris has remained no stranger to political battles in its streets. Violent demonstrations accompanied the Communist withdrawal from the coalition government in 1947. In the Fifties the Left took to the streets again in protest against the colonial wars in Indochina and Algeria. And, in 1961, in one of the most shameful episodes in modern French history, some two hundred Algerians were killed by the police during a civil rights demonstration – a "**secret massacre**", which remained covered by a veil of total official silence until the 1990s.

In the extraordinary month of **May 1968**, a radical, libertarian, leftist movement gathered momentum in the Paris universities. Students began by occupying university buildings in protest against old-fashioned and hierarchical university structures (see box, p.122), but the extreme reaction of the police and government helped the movement to spread until it represented a mass revolt against institutional stagnation that ended up with the occupation of hundreds of factories across the country and a general strike by nine million workers.

Yet this was no revolution. The vicious battles with the paramilitary CRS police on the streets of Paris shook large sectors of the population – France's silent majority – to the core. Right-wing and "nationalist" demonstrations – orchestrated by de Gaulle

2001	2002	2002
Unassuming Socialist candidate, Bertrand Delanoë, is elected Mayor of Paris in March.	Parisians find themselves paying a little extra for their coffees and baguettes with the introduction of the euro, on January 1.	On April 21, far-Right candidate Jean-Marie Le Pen knocks Socialist Lionel Jospin into third place in the first round of presidential elections. Incumbent president Jacques Chirac wins the second round.

– left public opinion craving stability and peace, and a great many workers were satisfied with a new system for wage agreements. Elections called in June returned the Right to power, the occupied buildings emptied and the barricades in the Latin Quarter came down. For those who thought they were experiencing The Revolution, the defeat was catastrophic.

But French institutions and French society had changed – de Gaulle didn't survive a referendum in 1969. His successor, **Georges Pompidou**, only survived long enough to begin the construction of the giant Les Halles development, and the expressways along the *quais* of the Seine. In 1974, he was succeeded by the conservative **Valéry Giscard d'Estaing**, who appointed one Jacques Chirac as his prime minister. In 1976, Chirac resigned, but made a speedy recovery as Mayor of Paris less than a year later.

Corruption and cohabitation

When **François Mitterrand** became president in 1981, hopes and expectations were initially high. By 1984, however, the flight of capital, inflation and budget deficits had forced a complete volte-face, and the Right won parliamentary elections in 1986, with **Chirac** beginning his second term as prime minister, while also continuing as Paris's mayor (he occupied the latter office continuously from 1977 to 1995). This was France's first period of "cohabitation": the head of state and head of government belonging to opposite sides of the political fence. Paris, meanwhile, pursued its own course, with the town halls of all twenty of the city's arrondissements remaining under right-wing control through much of the 1980s. It was a period of widespread corruption, but it didn't stop the city's mayor, **Jacques Chirac**, winning the election as **president** and taking office in May 1995.

That summer, **bombs** planted by an extremist Algerian Islamic group exploded across Paris – a foretaste of what awaited other countries. Discontent was fuelled by a sluggish economy, and routine discrimination. For many blacks or Arabs seeking work, particularly young men, the ring road dividing the city from its suburbs might as well have been a wall of steel. Prime Minister Alain Juppé proposed sweeping **economic liberalization**, which was seen by many as a threat to the founding values of the French republic. Over the course of three weeks in late 1995, some five million people took to the streets. There were typical scenes of **Parisian revolt**: burning tyres and railway sleepers; flying tear-gas canisters, paving stones and petrol bombs; and bands playing for free in place de la République. Chirac and his successors would face similar protests again and again, ultimately frustrating every attempt to alter the course of the French economy.

Cataclysms, demonstrations and heat waves

When France won the **World Cup** in July 1998, change seemed to be in the air. The victory at the new Stade de France in the ethnically mixed Paris suburb of St-Denis, with a multi-ethnic team, prompted a wave of popular patriotism. For once, support for "les bleus" seemed to override all other colour distinctions, and some even thought that Parisians might start being interested in football. Both notions, however, would soon be proved ephemeral.

2002	2003
Mayor Bertrand Delanoë launches Paris's new image by turning three kilometres of river-bank expressway into a summer beach: "Paris Plage" is an immense success.	Following Chirac's spat with George W. Bush over Iraq, US tourists temporarily vanish from the capital. In the summer, temperatures soar above 40 degrees C (104 degrees F).

THE MODERN FACE OF PARIS

Paris changed little up to the late 1960s – all the action took place out in the surburbs. Even the 1970s brown-glass skyscraper of the **Tour Montparnasse** only inspired a law limiting buildings taller than 25m in the city centre. And the demolition of the ironwork marketplace of Les Halles resulted in a conservationist outcry – though it didn't prevent the construction of its replacement, the curved-glass pit of the **Forum des Halles** shopping centre, itself scheduled for replacement now (see p.88). The only postmodern success was the **Pompidou Centre**. Critics called it a giant petrol refinery but Parisians, with a mixture of irony and fondness, dubbed it the Beaubourg – or "Prettytown".

Due largely to the **Grands Projets** of Socialist president François Mitterrand, Paris changed more in the 1980s and 1990s than it had since the era of Eiffel, with I.M. Pei's glass **Pyramide** in the Louvre's courtyard, Jean Nouvel's **Institut du Monde Arabe** and the **Cité de la Musique** at La Villette all becoming well-loved classics. However, there were also some less-successful projects: the **Bibliothèque Nationale** was deemed woefully inadequate for its purpose, while the **Grande Arche de la Défense** feels overweening rather than triumphal. As for the unhappy **Bastille Opéra**, it has been compared to a hospital, an elephant and even, according to Parisophile Edmund White, "a cow palace in Fort Worth".

The most recent adornments to Paris are bold, futuristic structures making ambitious use of glass. The smoothly muscular Tour Phare is rising above the business district of La Défense, the Project Triangle is taking (triangular) shape at the Porte de Versailles and, by 2014 a giant glass roof will transform the once-murky mall of **Les Halles**. Three signature works, meanwhile, are staking bold claims to landmark status: the **Musée du Quai Branly** is a typically clever work by the darling of contemporary French architecture, Jean Nouvel; Jakob Macfarlane's **Cité de la Mode et du Design** has a lime-green glass tube apparently pouring through it; while Frank Gehry's **Fondation Louis Vuitton pour la Création** looks less like the advertised "cloud of glass" than a glazed armadillo which has burst out of its own skin.

A deeper change took place with less fuss when the unassuming Socialist candidate, **Bertrand Delanoë**, was elected Mayor of Paris in March 2001. The fact that this was the first time the Left had won control of the capital since the bloody uprising of the Paris Commune in 1871 was far more of a shock to most Parisians than the fact that he was openly gay. His brief was to end town-hall corruption, tackle crime and traffic congestion, and instil new pride and energy into the city.

France's second cataclysm of the new millennium – not counting the smooth **introduction of the euro** on January 1, 2002 – was the shocking success of the far-Right candidate **Jean-Marie Le Pen** in the first round of the presidential election of spring 2002. On May 1, some 800,000 people packed the boulevards of Paris in the biggest **demonstration** the capital had seen since the student protests of 1968. Two weeks later, in the run-off, Chirac duly triumphed, winning 90 percent of the vote in Paris.

With such a mandate, Chirac and his reformed and renamed UMP party decided to take on the public sector: first pensions and unemployment benefits, then worker-friendly hiring and firing rights, and finally the world-leading health service. Again, hundreds of thousands came out onto the streets in protest. More trouble came when Chirac declared in March 2003 that he would veto any UN resolution that contained an ultimatum leading to **war in Iraq**. The cherished but often fragile Franco-American relationship collapsed, catastrophically, and American tourists seemed to vanish from the capital. That

2005	2007
In late October, disaffected youths riot in the impoverished Paris suburb of Clichy-sous-Bois. Right-wing interior minister, Nicolas Sarkozy, declares a state of emergency.	As Nicolas Sarkozy becomes President, Mayor Delanoë continues his greening of Paris: bus and cycle lanes appear everywhere, as do the new Vélib' rental bikes. Smokers are banished from cafés and restaurants.

LE GRAND PARI': THE FUTURE METROPOLIS

France has long lavished money on its capital, adorning the city centre with grand buildings, cultural institutions and events. Meanwhile, the *banlieue*, or suburbs, have festered as they have grown, kept at arm's length from the centre by the administrative and physical barricade of the *périphérique* ring road.

In 1860, outlying villages such as Belleville and Montmartre were absorbed into the city, and the outer ring of arrondissements was created. Since then, the population of the "agglomeration Parisienne" has swollen to around ten million, and yet the **official city boundaries** have stayed the same. Beyond the *périphérique*, the three administrative *départements* of the "Petite Couronne", the suburban districts encircling Paris, now contain some four million people – twice as many as Paris proper. Yet the city government has no remit to be concerned with them or their affairs. **The poor**, including large numbers of immigrants and their families, are effectively excluded from the city centre. The high-paying, white-collar jobs of the shopping, banking and governmental districts just don't seem to be available to black youths from the "9–3" – as the depressed *département* of Seine St-Denis, officially numbered 93, is known.

While the troubled *cités*, the housing projects of the northern *banlieue*, simmer with discontent, the desirable new towns to the south and west of the city are sucking away Paris's lifeblood: its **population**. There are now 2.1 million people living "intra-muros", or in Paris proper, down from 2.8 million in the late 1950s, and retirees make up fifteen percent of the population. Parisians are regularly alarmed by horrifying statistics such as the fact that the city has lost roughly a quarter of its small food stores in the last decade, or that bakeries are nowhere to be found near the Champs-Elysées. They may be comforted to learn, however, that a city with "only" 159 cheese shops is not yet facing a crisis.

Intent on preventing the "museumification" of Paris, the Mairie has bought up private apartment buildings in the historic centre, to be rented out as **social housing**. Paris is also turning its attention outwards. Construction of the new suburban transport network, **Grand Paris Express**, has begun, with even larger projects afoot. In 2009, the government invited ten leading architectural firms to submit proposals for **Le Grand Pari'**, the greater, greener Paris needed for the future. The architects envisioned new *Grands Axes*, avenues as radical as any bulldozed by Haussmann – but in this case linking city and *banlieue*. Replanted forests would jostle with high-density housing and wind farms, and the rivers and canals be brought back to life. Richard Rogers called for a green network covering the train lines leading out of the northern stations, while Christian de Portzamparc wanted a high-speed elevated train running circles around the ring road. One scheme even had a Greater Paris conurbation following the Seine all the way down to Le Havre. That may never happen. But with climate change, social unrest and economic disturbances all lapping at the city's walls, Paris cannot remain an island much longer.

summer was as heated in reality as politically. Parisian temperatures in the first half of August regularly topped 40°C (104°F) – more than 10°C above the average maximum for the time of year – and **climate change** finally forced its way onto the mainstream agenda.

"Sarko" and Delanoë

In 2004, a new political force emerged in the hyper-energetic if diminutive shape of **Nicolas Sarkozy** – a kind of Margaret Thatcher meets J.F.K, bent on giving France a

2009	2011
Paris contemplates its future with an exhibition of architectural visions for the green mega-city of the future, dubbed "Le Grand Pari'".	In January, Sarkozy offers French heritage sites, including Paris's Hôtel de la Marine, to hotel chains. In May, leading Socialist presidential candidate and IMF President, Dominique Strauss-Kahn is arrested in New York, and charged with rape. At the end of the year, electric Autolib' hire cars appear on the streets of Paris.

dose of neoliberal or "Anglo-Saxon" capitalism. In 2005 and again in 2006 – when students once again occupied the Sorbonne – waves of passionate strikers flooded the city streets, but the more dramatic **civil unrest** began after two teenagers died fleeing what they thought was police pursuit in Clichy-sous-Bois, a run-down area in the Paris *banlieue*. Local **car-burnings** and confrontations with police quickly spread to other Parisian suburbs and then beyond. Night after night, for three weeks, youths across France torched cars, buses, schools, and police and power stations – anything associated with the state. As Interior Minister, "Sarko" demanded that the neighbourhoods were cleaned with power-hoses.

Such right-wing posturing seemed to pay off, and, on May 16, 2007, Nicolas Sarkozy became President. Within a year, he'd separated from his wife and taken up with the model, singer and Euro-jetsetter **Carla Bruni**. Then came the **global financial crisis** of 2008–09. Suddenly, the "Anglo-Saxon" form of market-led, laissez-faire capitalism seemed exactly what French socialists had always said it was: a debt-fuelled castle built on sand. In response, Sarkozy performed an astonishing political about-turn, pledging to wield the power of the state to ensure stability. Strong-state *dirigisme* was back. National reform, again, would have to wait.

Delanoë's new, green Paris

Blithely independent of the national storms, effective reform in the city of Paris has been surging ahead for years. In 2002, **Mayor Bertrand Delanoë** launched Paris's new image. He ordered a 3km length of the river-bank roads to be turned into a public beach for six summer weeks, and encouraged hundreds of museums, bars, restaurants and public buildings to remain open for a city-wide all-night party of live music and performance art in October. **Paris Plage** ("Paris Beach") and the **Nuit Blanche** ("Sleepless Night") are now established parts of the city's calendar.

Meanwhile, less glamorous but further-reaching policies are greening the face of Paris. The smoky fug that once blurred out the city's cafés, restaurants and nightclubs has been entirely blown away by new laws **banning smoking** in public places. **Bus lanes, cycle lanes and pedestrianized areas** have sprung up all over the city; the Batobus ferries are making new use of the river, and will one day be a fully integrated **métro fluvial** service; electric hire cars on the Vélib' model, called **Autolib'**, will be available all around the city; and all-new **tramway lines** are threading through the suburbs and encircling the ring road – which is slowly acquiring a green roof. Best of all, the hop-on, hop-off community bicycles, known as **Vélib'** ("free bike"), are multiplying like rabbits.

Books

GUIDES

David Hampshire and Jim Watson *Living and Working in France*. With almost 500 pages, this accurate and comprehensive guide takes you beyond our advice in "Basics" and deep into the bureaucratic niceties of expat life in France. Usually updated every couple of years. Includes advice on buying property.

Miroslav Sasek *This is Paris*. A kind of illustrated child's travel guide, with enticing facts about the city and beautiful, quirky watercolours and drawings. First published in 1959, but still a brilliant companion (or preparation) for a trip with children.

HISTORY AND POLITICS

Anthony Beevor & Artemis Cooper *Paris After the Liberation: 1944–1949*. Gripping account of a crucial era in Parisian history, featuring de Gaulle, the Communists, the St-Germain scene and Dior's New Look. Five strange, intense years that set the tone for the next fifty.

Robert Cole *A Traveller's History of Paris*. This brief history of the city from the first Celtic settlement to the present day is an ideal starting point – though the current edition stops at 2002.

Larry Collins and Dominique Lapierre *Is Paris Burning?* (out of print). Classic history-as-thriller account of the race to save Paris from the destruction threatened by the retreating Nazis.

Alistair Horne *The Fall of Paris* (Pan) and *Seven Ages of Paris*. Highly regarded historian Alistair Horne's *The Fall of Paris* is a very readable and humane account of the extraordinary period of the Prussian siege of Paris in 1870 and the ensuing struggles of the Commune. His *Seven Ages of Paris* is a compelling (if rather old-fashionedly fruity) account of significant episodes in the city's history.

★ **Andrew Hussey** *Paris, The Secret History*. Delves into some fascinating and little-known aspects of Paris's history, including occultism, freemasonry and the seedy underside of the city. Hussey is concerned above all with ordinary Parisians, and their frequent clashes with authority.

★ **Colin Jones** *Paris: Biography of a City*. Jones focuses tightly on the actual life and growth of the city, from the Neolithic past to the future. Five hundred pages flow by easily, punctuated by thoughtful but accessible boxes on characters, streets and buildings whose lives were

especially bound up with Paris's, from the Roman *arènes* to Zazie's métro. The best single book on the city's history.

Peter Lennon *Foreign Correspondent: Paris in the Sixties* (out of print). Irish journalist Peter Lennon went to Paris in the early 1960s unable to speak a word of French. He became a close friend of Samuel Beckett and was a witness to the May 1968 events.

Lucy Moore *Liberty: The Lives and Times of Six Women in Revolutionary France*. Follows the fervid lives of six influential women through the Revolution, taking in everything from sexual scandal to revolutionary radicalism.

Orest A. Ranum *Paris in the Age of Absolutism*. A truly great work of city biography, revealing how and why seventeenth-century Paris rose from medieval obscurity to become the foremost city in Europe under Louis XIV.

★ **Graham Robb** *Parisians*. This playful, joyfully readable but magnificently researched book tells the story of Paris from 1750 to today, through the eyes of the people who have played key roles in its turbulent life. Among other scenes, Robb shows us Marie-Antoinette fleeing the Tuileries, Napoleon losing his virginity in the Palais Royal, Hitler's day-trip conquerer's tour, and the nasty build-up to the suburban riots of 2005.

Duc de Saint-Simon *Memoirs*. Written by an insider, this compelling memoir of life at Versailles under Louis XIV is packed with fascinating, gossipy anecdotes.

Gillian Tindall *Footprints in Paris*. In this beautifully written and personal micro-history of the Quartier Latin, Tindall reconstructs the intimate lives of a handful of the quarter's residents, both celebrated and obscure, creating an evocative portrait of the city in the nineteenth and twentieth centuries.

CULTURE AND SOCIETY

★ **Marc Augé** *In the Metro*. A philosophically minded anthropologist descends deep into métro culture and his own memories of life in Paris. A brief, brilliant essay in the spirit of Roland Barthes.

Walter Benjamin *The Arcades Project*. An all-encompassing portrait of Paris covering 1830–70, in which the *passages* are used as a lens through which to view Parisian society. Never completed, Benjamin's magnum

opus is a kaleidoscopic assemblage of essays, notes and quotations, gathered under such headings as "Baudelaire", "Prostitution", "Mirrors" and "Idleness".

James Campbell *Paris Interzone*. The feuds, passions and destructive lifestyles of Left Bank writers in 1946–60 are evoked here. The cast includes Samuel Beckett, Boris Vian, Alexander Trocchi, Eugène Ionesco, Jean-Paul Sartre, Simone de Beauvoir, Vladimir Nabokov and Allen Ginsberg.

Rupert Christiansen *Paris Babylon: Grandeur, Decadence and Revolution 1869–1875.* Written with verve and dash, Christiansen's account of Paris at the time of the Siege and the Commune is exuberant and original. Worth reading for its evocative and insightfully chosen contemporary quotations alone – it begins with a delightful 1869 guidebook to "Paris Partout!"

Richard Cobb *Paris and Elsewhere.* Selected writings on postwar Paris by the acclaimed historian of the Revolution, with a personal and meditative tone.

Adam Gopnik *Paris to the Moon.* Intimate and acutely observed essays from the Paris correspondent of the *New Yorker* on society, politics, family life and shopping. Probably the most thoughtful and enjoyable book by an expat in Paris.

★ **Julien Green** *Paris.* Born in Paris in 1900, Green became one of the city's defining writers. This bilingual edition presents twenty-odd short, meditative and highly personal essays on different aspects and *quartiers* of Paris, from Notre-Dame and the 16ᵉ to "stairways and steps" and the lost cries of the city's hawkers. Proust meets travel-writing.

★ **Eric Hazan** *The Invention of Paris.* Utterly compelling psycho-geographical account of the city, picking over its history *quartier* by *quartier* in a thousand *aperçus* and anecdotes. It's a weighty book, but a zesty, lefty bias nicely brings out the passions behind the rebellions and revolutions.

Patrice Higonnet *Paris: Capital of the World.* An extraordinary intellectual investigation of Paris as a kind of mythical capital of culture – or rather a capital of "crime", "art", "sex" and "the modern self". Shows how the idea of Paris inspired and underpinned key cultural epochs, from the Enlightenment and the Revolution to the era of great exhibitions and the Surrealist movement.

J.K. Huysmans *Parisian Sketches.* Published in 1880, Huysmans' fantastical, intense prose pieces on contemporary Paris drip with decadence, and cruelly acute observation. Rhapsodies on "Landscapes" and "Parisian characters" are matched by an exhilaratingly vivid account of the Folies-Bergères. If Manet had been a novelist, he might have produced this.

Ian Littlewood *A Literary Companion to Paris* (out of print). A thorough account of which literary figures went where, and what they had to say about it.

Gertrude Stein *The Autobiography of Alice B. Toklas.* The most accessible of Stein's works, written from the point of view of her long-time lover, is an amusing account of the artistic and literary scene of Paris in the 1910s and 1920s.

Tad Szulc *Chopin in Paris: The Life and Times of the Romantic Composer.* Not much on music, but explores Chopin's relationship with his friends – Balzac, Hugo, Liszt among them – and his lover, George Sand, and their shared life in Paris.

Judith Thurman *Colette: Secrets of the Flesh.* An intelligent and entertaining biography of Colette (1873–1954), highly successful novelist, vaudeville artist, libertine and flamboyant *bon viveur*.

Sarah Turnbull *Almost French: A New Life in Paris.* Funny but mostly painful account of a young Australienne falling in love, moving to Paris and desperately failing to fit in. Acute observation lifts it above chick-lit travel status. A must for would-be expats.

★ **Edmund White** *The Flâneur.* An American expat novelist muses over Parisian themes and places as diverse as the Moreau museum, gay cruising and the history of immigration, as well as the art of being a good *flâneur* – a loiterer or stroller.

William Wiser *The Twilight Years: Paris in the 1930s.* Breathless account of the crazy decade before the war, all jazz nights, scandals, and the social lives of expat poets and painters.

ART AND ARCHITECTURE

André Chastel *French Art.* The great French art historian tries to define what is distinctively French about French art in this insightful and superbly illustrated three-volume work.

Dan Franck *The Bohemians – the Birth of Modern Art: Paris 1900–1930.* Anecdotes and encounters from within the Bohemian demi-monde that gave birth to modern art. Encompasses the Montmartre years, when Picasso hung out with Apollinaire, and the Montparnasse era of André Derain, Man Ray and the Surrealists.

Ross King *The Judgement of Paris: The Revolutionary Decade That Gave the World Impressionism.* High-octane account of the fierce battles in the 1860s and 1870s between the "finishers", the Classical painters of the academic Salons, and the upstart "sketchers" who tried to supplant them with their impressionistic canvases. Focuses on the culture and political atmosphere of the times as much as the art.

Michel Poisson *The Monuments of Paris.* Arrondissement-by-arrondissement survey of Paris's chief buildings, with attractive line drawings and brief notes. Short on contemporary architecture but otherwise fairly comprehensive.

Anthony Sutcliffe *Paris – An Architectural History.* Excellent overview of Paris's changing cityscape, as dictated by fashion, social structure and political power.

FICTION

IN ENGLISH

Helen Constantine (ed) *Paris Tales.* Twenty-two (very) short stories and essays, each chosen for their evocation of a particular place in Paris. From Balzac in the Palais Royal and Colette in Montmartre cemetery, to Perec on the Champs-Elysées and Jacques Réda on the rue du Commerce.

Charles Dickens *A Tale of Two Cities*. Paris and London during the 1789 Revolution and before. The plot is pure, breathtaking Hollywood, but the streets and the social backdrop are very much for real.

Ernest Hemingway *A Moveable Feast*. Hemingway's memoirs of his life as a young man in Paris in the 1920s. Includes fascinating accounts of meetings with literary celebrities Ezra Pound, F. Scott Fitzgerald and Gertrude Stein, among others.

Henry Miller *Tropic of Cancer; Quiet Days in Clichy*. Semi-autobiographical, rage- and sex-fuelled roar through the 1930s Parisian demi-monde; or, "a gob of spit in the face of Art", as the narrator puts it.

George Orwell *Down and Out in Paris and London*. Documentary account of breadline living in the 1930s – Orwell at his best.

Jean Rhys *Quartet*. A beautiful and evocative story of a lonely young woman's existence on the fringes of 1920s Montparnasse society. In the same vein are the subsequent *After Leaving Mr Mackenzie* and *Good Morning, Midnight*, both exploring sexual politics and isolation in the atmospheric streets, shabby hotel rooms and smoky bars of interwar Paris, all in Rhys's spare, dream-like style.

FRENCH (IN TRANSLATION)

★ **Honoré de Balzac** *The Père Goriot*. Biting exposé of cruelty and selfishness in the contrasting worlds of the fashionable faubourg St-Germain and a down-at-heel but genteel boarding-house in the Quartier Latin. Balzac's equally brilliant *Wild Ass's Skin* is a strange moralistic tale of an ambitious young man's fall from grace in early nineteenth-century Paris.

Muriel Barbery *The Elegance of the Hedgehog*. This whimsical, philosophically minded novel, set among the eccentric characters of a Parisian apartment block, sold over a million copies in France. Deftly exposes the pretensions and aspirations of the upper middle classes.

André Breton *Nadja*. First published in 1928, *Nadja* is widely considered the most important and influential novel to spring from the Surrealist movement. Largely autobiographical, it portrays the complex relationship between the narrator and a young woman in Paris.

Louis-Ferdinand Céline *Death on Credit*. Disturbing semi-autobiographical novel recounting working-class Paris through the eyes of an adolescent at the beginning of the twentieth century. Much of it takes place in the passage Choiseul, and its claustrophobic atmosphere is vividly evoked.

Blaise Cendrars *To the End of the World*. An outrageous, bawdy tale of a randy septuagenarian Parisian actress, having an affair with a deserter from the Foreign Legion.

★ **Colette** *Chéri*. Considered Colette's finest novel, *Chéri* brilliantly evokes the world of a demi-monde Parisian courtesan who has a doomed love affair with a man at least half her age.

Didier Daeninckx *Murder in Memoriam*. A thriller involving two murders: one of a Frenchman during the massacre of the Algerians in Paris in 1961, the other of his son twenty years later. The investigation by an honest detective lays bare dirty tricks, corruption, racism and the cover-up of the massacre.

★ **Gustave Flaubert** *Sentimental Education*. A lively, detailed 1869 reconstruction of the life, manners, characters and politics of Parisians in the 1840s, including the 1848 Revolution.

Victor Hugo *Les Misérables*. A long but eminently readable novel by the master. Set among the Parisian poor and low-life in the first half of the nineteenth century, it's probably the greatest treatment of Paris in fiction – unless that title goes to Hugo's haunting (and shorter) *Notre-Dame de Paris*, a novel better known in English as *The Hunchback of Notre-Dame*.

Claude Izner *Murder on the Eiffel Tower*. 1889: a young bookseller falls in love and investigates a series of curious murders. One of the best of a new series of detective stories from the team of bookish sisters known as "Claude Izner".

François Maspero *Cat's Grin* (out of print). Moving and revealing semi-autobiographical novel about a young teenager living in Paris during World War II, with an adored elder brother in the Resistance.

★ **Guy de Maupassant** *Bel-Ami*. Maupassant's *chef-d'oeuvre* is a brilliant and utterly sensual account of corrupt Parisian high society during the *belle époque*. Traces the rake's progress of the fascinating journalist and seducer, Georges Duroy.

Daniel Pennac *Monsieur Malaussène* (out of print). The last in the "Belleville Quintet" of quasi-detective novels set in the working-class east of Paris is possibly the most disturbing, centred on a series of macabre killings. Witty, experimental and chaotic, somewhat in the mode of Thomas Pynchon.

Georges Perec *Life: A User's Manual*. An extraordinary literary jigsaw puzzle of life, past and present, human, animal and mineral, extracted from the residents of an imaginary apartment block in the 17^e arrondissement.

Jean-Paul Sartre *The Age of Reason*. The first in Sartre's *Roads to Freedom* trilogy is probably his most accessible work. A philosophy teacher in wartime Paris's Montparnasse struggles to find both the money for his girlfriend's abortion and the answers to his obsession with freedom.

Georges Simenon *Maigret at the Crossroads* – or any other of the Maigret crime thrillers. The Montmartre and seedy criminal locations are unbeatable. If you don't like crime fiction, go for *The Little Saint*, the story of a little boy growing up in the rue Mouffetard when it was a down-at-heel market street.

★ **Emile Zola** *Nana*. The rise and fall of a courtesan in the decadent times of the Second Empire. As the quintessential realist, Zola is *the* novelist for bringing the seedy, seething reality of nineteenth-century Paris alive; Paris is also the setting for Zola's *L'Assommoir*, *The Masterpiece*, *Money*, *Thérèse Raquin* and *The Debacle*.

French

There's probably nowhere harder to speak or learn French than Paris. Like people from most capital cities, many Parisians speak a kind of hurried slang. Worse still, many speak fairly good English – which they may assume is better than your French. Generations of keen visitors have been offended by being replied to in English after they've carefully enunciated a well-honed question or menu order. Then there are the complex codes of politeness and formality – knowing when to add Madame/Monsieur is only the start of it. Despite this, the essentials are not difficult to master and can make all the difference. Even just saying "Bonjour Madame/Monsieur" and then gesticulating will usually get you a smile and helpful service, even if your efforts to speak French come to nothing. The *Rough Guide French Phrasebook* gives more detail, along with an expanded menu reader.

PRONUNCIATION

One easy rule to remember is that consonants at the end of words are usually silent. Pas plus tard (not later) is thus pronounced "pa-plu-tarr". But when the following word begins with a vowel, you run the two together: pas après (not after) becomes "pazapray".

Vowels are the hardest sounds to get right. Roughly:

a as in hat
e as in get
é between get and gate
è like the ai in pair
eu like the u in hurt
i as in machine
o as in hot
o/au as in over
ou as in food
u as in a pursed-lip, clipped version of toot

More awkward are the combinations in/im, en/em, on/om, un/um at the end of words, or followed by consonants other than n or m. Again, roughly:

in/im like the "an" in anxious
an/am, en/em like "on" said with a nasal accent
on/om like "on" said by someone with a heavy cold
un/um like the "u" in understand

Consonants are much as in English, except that ch is always sh, h is silent, th is the same as t, ll is sometimes pronounced like the y in "yes" when preceded by the letter "i" as in "fille" and "tilleul", w is v, and r is growled (or rolled).

WORDS AND PHRASES

THE TOP TWELVE

yes	oui
no	non
please	s'il vous plaît
thank you	merci
excuse me	pardon/excusez-moi
sorry	pardon, Madame/Monsieur
hello	bonjour
goodbye	au revoir
good morning/afternoon	bonjour
good evening	bonsoir
OK/agreed	d'accord
I (don't) understand	Je (ne) comprends (pas)

KEY WORDS AND PHRASES

French nouns are divided into masculine and feminine. This causes difficulties with adjectives, whose endings have to change to suit the gender of the nouns they qualify. If in doubt, stick to the masculine form, which is the simplest – it's what we have done in the glossary below.

today	aujourd'hui
yesterday	hier
tomorrow	demain
in the morning	le matin
in the afternoon	l'après-midi
in the evening	le soir
now	maintenant
later	plus tard

at one o'clock	à une heure
at three o'clock	à trois heures
at ten-thirty	à dix heures et demi
at midday	à midi
man	un homme
woman	une femme
here	ici
there	là
this one	ceci
that one	cela
open	ouvert
closed	fermé
big	grand
small	petit
more	plus
less	moins
a little	un peu
a lot	beaucoup
half	la moitié
cheap	bon marché/pas cher
expensive	cher
good	bon
bad	mauvais
hot	chaud
cold	froid
with	avec
without	sans

TALKING TO PEOPLE

When addressing people you should always use Monsieur for a man, Madame for a woman, Mademoiselle for a girl – plain "bonjour" by itself is not enough. This isn't as formal as it seems, and it has its uses when you've forgotten someone's name or want to attract someone's attention. "Bonjour" can be used well into the afternoon, and people may start saying "bonsoir" surprisingly early in the evening, or as a way of saying goodbye.

How are you?	Comment allez-vous?/Ça va?
Fine, thanks	Très bien, merci
I don't know	Je ne sais pas
I see!	Ah bon!
Do you speak English?	Vous parlez anglais?
How do you say...	Comment dit-on...
in French?	en français?
What's your name?	Comment vous appelez-vous?
My name is...	Je m'appelle...
I'm English/	Je suis anglais(e)/
Irish/	irlandais(e)/
Scottish/	écossais(e)/
Welsh/	gallois(e)/
American/	américain(e)/
Australian/	australien(ne)/
Canadian/	canadien(ne)/
a New Zealander	néo-zélandais(e)

Can you speak slower?	S'il vous plaît, parlez moins vite
Let's go	Allons-y
See you tomorrow	A demain
See you soon	A bientôt
goodnight	bonne nuit

EMERGENCIES

Leave me alone	Laissez-moi tranquille
Please help me	Aidez-moi, s'il vous plait
Help!	Au secours!

QUESTIONS AND REQUESTS

The simplest way of asking a question is to start with "s'il vous plaît" (please), then name the thing you want in an interrogative tone of voice. For example:

Where is there a bakery?	S'il vous plaît, la boulangerie?
Which way is it to the Eiffel Tower?	S'il vous plaît, pour aller à la Tour Eiffel?
We'd like a room for two	S'il vous plaît, une chambre pour deux
Can I have a kilo of oranges?	S'il vous plaît, un kilo d'oranges
where?	où?
how?	comment?
how many?	combien?
how much is it?	c'est combien?
when?	quand?
why?	pourquoi?
at what time?	à quelle heure?
what is/which is?	quel est?

GETTING AROUND AND DIRECTIONS

metro/subway station	métro
Where is the nearest metro?	Où est le métro le plus proche?
bus	bus
bus (coach)	car
bus station	gare routière
bus stop	arrêt
car	voiture
train/taxi/ferry	train/taxi/ferry
boat	bateau
plane	avion
railway station	gare
platform	quai
What time does it leave/arrive?	Il part/arrive à quelle heure?
a ticket to...	un billet pour...
single ticket	aller simple
return ticket	aller retour
validate your ticket	compostez votre billet
valid for	valable pour

ticket office	vente de billets
how many kilometres?	combien de kilomètres?
how many hours?	combien d'heures?
on foot	à pied
Where are you going?	Vous allez où?
I'm going to...	Je vais à...
I want to get off at...	Je voudrais descendre à...
the road to...	la route pour
near	près/pas loin
far	loin
left	à gauche
right	à droite
straight on	tout droit
on the other side of	de l'autre côté de
on the corner of	à l'angle de
next to	à côté de
behind	derrière
in front of	devant
before	avant
after	après
under	sous
to cross	traverser
bridge	pont
to park the car	garer la voiture
car park	un parking
no parking	défense de stationner/
	stationnement interdit
petrol station	poste d'essence

ACCOMMODATION

a room for one/	une chambre pour une
two people	personne/deux personnes
with a double bed	avec un grand lit
a room with a shower	une chambre avec douche
a room with a bath	une chambre avec baignoire
for one/two/three	pour une/deux/trois nuit(s)
night(s)	
Can I see it?	Je peux la voir?
a room in the courtyard	une chambre sur la cour
a room over the street	une chambre sur la rue
first floor	premier étage
second floor	deuxième étage
with a view	avec vue
key	clé
to iron	repasser
do laundry	faire la lessive
sheets	draps
blankets	couvertures
quiet	calme
noisy	bruyant
hot water	eau chaude
cold water	eau froide
Is breakfast included?	Est-ce que le petit déjeuner
	est compris?

SIGN LANGUAGE

Défense de	It is forbidden to...
Fermé	closed
Ouvert	open
Rez-de-chaussée (RC)	ground floor
Sortie	exit

I would like breakfast	Je voudrais prendre le petit déjeuner
I don't want breakfast	Je ne veux pas le petit déjeuner
campsite	un camping/terrain de camping
youth hostel	auberge de jeunesse

MONTHS, DAYS AND DATES

January	janvier
February	février
March	mars
April	avril
May	mai
June	juin
July	juillet
August	août
September	septembre
October	octobre
November	novembre
December	décembre
Monday	lundi
Tuesday	mardi
Wednesday	mercredi
Thursday	jeudi
Friday	vendredi
Saturday	samedi
Sunday	dimanche
August 1	le premier août
March 2	le deux mars
July 14	le quatorze juillet
November 23, 2010	le vingt-trois novembre, deux mille dix

NUMBERS

1	un
2	deux
3	trois
4	quatre
5	cinq
6	six
7	sept
8	huit
9	neuf
10	dix

11	onze	50	cinquante
12	douze	60	soixante
13	treize	70	soixante-dix
14	quatorze	75	soixante-quinze
15	quinze	80	quatre-vingts
16	seize	90	quatre-vingt-dix
17	dix-sept	95	quatre-vingt-quinze
18	dix-huit	100	cent
19	dix-neuf	101	cent un
20	vingt	200	deux cents
21	vingt-et-un	1000	mille
22	vingt-deux	2000	deux mille
30	trente	1,000,000	un million
40	quarante		

FOOD AND DRINK TERMS

BASICS

déjeuner	lunch
dîner	dinner
menu	set menu
carte	menu
à la carte	individually priced dishes
entrées	starters
les plats	main courses
une carafe d'eau/de vin	a carafe of tap water/wine
eau minérale	mineral water
eau gazeuse	fizzy water
eau plate	still water
carte des vins	wine list
un quart/demi de rouge/blanc	a quarter/half-litre of red/white house wine
un (verre de) rouge/blanc	a glass of red/white wine
Je voudrais réserver une table pour deux personnes, à vingt heures et demie	I'd like to reserve a table for two people, at eight thirty
Je prendrai le menu à quinze euros	I'm having the €15 menu
Monsieur/Madame!	Waiter! (never say "garçon")
l'addition, s'il vous plaît	the bill, please
une pression	a glass of beer
un café	coffee (espresso)
un café americain	black coffee
un crème	white coffee
un café au lait	big bowl of milky breakfast coffee
un cappuccino	cappuccino

COOKING TERMS

Chauffé	Heated
Cuit	Cooked
Cru	Raw
Emballé	Wrapped
À emporter	Takeaway
Fumé	Smoked
Salé	Salted/savoury
Sucré	Sweet

ESSENTIALS

Beurre	Butter
Bio	Organic
Bouteille	Bottle
Couteau	Knife
Cuillère	Spoon
Fourchette	Fork
Huile	Oil
Lait	Milk
Oeufs	Eggs
Pain	Bread
Poivre	Pepper
Sel	Salt
Sucre	Sugar
Verre	Glass
Vinaigre	Vinegar

SNACKS

Crêpe	Pancake (sweet)
au sucre	with sugar
au citron	with lemon
au miel	with honey
à la confiture	with jam
aux œufs	with eggs
Galette	Buckwheat (savoury) pancake
Un sandwich/ une baguette	A sandwich…
jambon	with ham
fromage	with cheese
mixte	with ham and cheese
Croque-Monsieur	Grilled cheese & ham sandwich
Croque-Madame	Croque-Monsieur with an egg on top

Oeufs	Eggs
au plat	fried
à la coque	boiled
durs	hard-boiled
brouillés	scrambled
Omelette	Omelette
nature	plain
aux fines herbes	with herbs
au fromage	with cheese

SOUPS (SOUPES)

Bisque	Shellfish soup
Bouillabaisse	Marseillais fish soup
Bourride	Thick fish soup
Potage	Thick vegetable soup
Velouté	Thick soup, usually with fish or poultry

STARTERS (ENTREES, OR HORS D'OEUVRES)

Assiette de charcuterie	Plate of cold meats
Crudités	Raw vegetables with dressings
Hors d'œuvres variés	Combination of the above

FISH (POISSON), SEAFOOD (FRUITS DE MER) AND SHELLFISH (CRUSTACES OR COQUILLAGES)

Anchois	Anchovies
Anguilles	Eels
Bar	Sea bass
Barbue	Brill
Brème	Bream
Brochet	Pike
Cabillaud	Cod
Calmar	Squid
Carrelet	Plaice
Claire	Type of oyster
Colin	Hake
Coquilles St-Jacques	Scallops
Crabe	Crab
Crevettes grises	Shrimps
Crevettes roses	Prawns
Daurade	Sea bream
Escargots	Snails
Flétan	Halibut
Friture	Whitebait
Gambas	King prawns
Hareng	Herring
Homard	Lobster
Huîtres	Oysters
Langouste	Spiny lobster
Langoustines	Saltwater crayfish (scampi)
Limande	Lemon sole

Lotte de mer	Monkfish
Loup de mer	Sea bass
Louvine, loubine	Similar to sea bass
Maquereau	Mackerel
Merlan	Whiting
Morue	Dried, salted cod
Moules (marinière)	Mussels (with shallots in white-wine sauce)
Raie	Skate
Rouget	Red mullet
Sandre	Pike-perch
Saumon	Salmon
Seiche	Squid
Sole	Sole
Thon	Tuna
Truite	Trout
Turbot	Turbot

FISH: DISHES AND RELATED TERMS

Aïoli	Garlic mayonnaise served with salt cod and other fish
Béarnaise	Sauce made with egg yolks, white wine, shallots & vinegar
Beignets	Fritters
La douzaine	A dozen
Frit	Fried
Fumé	Smoked
Fumet	Fish stock
Gigot de mer	Large fish baked whole
Grillé	Grilled
Hollandaise	Butter & vinegar sauce
A la meunière	In a butter, lemon & parsley sauce
Mousse/mousseline	Mousse
Quenelles	Light dumplings

MEAT (VIANDE) AND POULTRY (VOLAILLE)

Agneau (de pré-salé)	Lamb (grazed on salt marshes)
Andouille, andouillette	Tripe sausage
Bavette	beef flank steak
Boeuf	Beef
Boudin blanc	Sausage of white meats
Boudin noir	Black pudding
Caille	Quail
Canard	Duck
Caneton	Duckling
Contrefilet	Sirloin roast
Coquelet	Cockerel
Dinde	Turkey
Entrecôte	Ribsteak
Faux filet	Sirloin steak

Foie	Liver	**Daube, estouffade,**	All are types of stew
Foie gras	Fattened (duck/goose) liver	**hochepot, navarin and ragoût**	
Gigot (d'agneau)	Leg (of lamb)	**En croûte**	In pastry
Grillade	Grilled meat	**Epaule**	Shoulder
Hachis	Chopped meat or mince hamburger	**Farci**	Stuffed
		Au feu de bois	Cooked over wood fire
Langue	Tongue	**Au four**	Baked
Lapin, lapereau	Rabbit, young rabbit	**Garni**	With vegetables
Lard, lardons	Bacon, diced bacon	**Gésier**	Gizzard
Lièvre	Hare	**Grillé**	Grilled
Merguez	Spicy, red sausage	**Magret de canard**	Duck breast
Mouton	Mutton	**Marmite**	Casserole
Museau de veau	Calf's muzzle	**Médaillon**	Round piece
Oie	Goose	**Mijoté**	Stewed
Onglet	Cut of beef	**Museau**	Muzzle
Os	Bone	**Pavé**	Thick slice
Pièce de boeuf	Steak	**Rôti**	Roast
Porc	Pork	**Sauté**	Lightly cooked in butter
Poulet	Chicken	**Steak au poivre**	Steak in a black (green/red)
Poussin	Baby chicken	**(vert/rouge)**	peppercorn sauce
Ris	Sweetbreads	**Steak tartare**	Raw chopped beef, topped
Rognons	Kidneys		with a raw egg yolk
Rognons blancs	Testicles		
Sanglier	Wild boar	**FOR STEAKS**	
Tête de veau	Calf's head (in jelly)	**Bleu**	Almost raw
Tournedos	Thick slices of fillet	**Saignant**	Rare
Tripes	Tripe	**A point**	Medium
Veau	Veal	**Bien cuit**	Well done
Venaison	Venison	**Très bien cuit**	Very well cooked
		Brochette	Kebab

MEAT AND POULTRY: DISHES AND RELATED TERMS

GARNISHES AND SAUCES

Aile	Wing	**Beurre blanc**	Sauce of white wine and shallots, with butter
Blanquette de veau	Veal in cream & mushroom sauce	**Chasseur**	White wine, mushrooms and shallots
Boeuf bourguignon	Beef stew with red wine, onions & mushrooms	**Diable**	Strong mustard seasoning
Canard à l'orange	Roast duck with an orange-and-wine sauce	**Forestière**	With bacon and mushroom
		Fricassée	Rich, creamy sauce
Carré	Best end of neck, chop or cutlet	**Mornay**	Cheese sauce
		Pays d'Auge	Cream and cider
Cassoulet	A casserole of beans & meat	**Piquante**	Gherkins or capers, vinegar and shallots
Choucroute garnie	Sauerkraut served with sausages or cured ham	**Provençale**	Tomatoes, garlic, olive oil and herbs
Civet	Game stew		
Confit	Meat preserve	**VEGETABLES (LEGUMES), HERBS (HERBES) AND SPICES (EPICES)**	
Coq au vin	Chicken with wine, onions & mushrooms, cooked till it falls off the bone	**Ail**	Garlic
		Algue	Seaweed
Côte	Chop, cutlet or rib	**Anis**	Aniseed
Cou	Neck	**Artichaut**	Artichoke
Cuisse	Thigh or leg	**Asperges**	Asparagus

Avocat	Avocado
Basilic	Basil
Betterave	Beetroot
Carotte	Carrot
Céleri	Celery
Champignons, cèpes, chanterelles	Mushrooms of various kinds
Chou (rouge)	(Red) cabbage
Chou-fleur	Cauliflower
Ciboulette	Chives
Concombre	Cucumber
Cornichon	Gherkin
Echalotes	Shallots
Endive	Chicory
Epinards	Spinach
Estragon	Tarragon
Fenouil	Fennel
Flageolets	White beans
Gingembre	Ginger
Haricots	Beans
verts	string (French)
rouges	kidney
beurres	butter
Laurier	Bay leaf
Lentilles	Lentils
Maïs	Corn
Menthe	Mint
Moutarde	Mustard
Oignon	Onion
Pâtes	Pasta
Persil	Parsley
Petits pois	Peas
Pignons	Pine nuts
Piment	Pimento
Poireau	Leek
Pois chiche	Chickpeas
Pois mange-tout	Snow peas
Poivron (vert, rouge)	Sweet pepper (green, red)
Pommes (de terre)	Potatoes
Primeurs	Spring vegetables
Radis	Radishes
Riz	Rice
Safran	Saffron
Salade verte	Green salad
Sarrasin	Buckwheat
Tomate	Tomato
Truffes	Truffles

VEGETABLES: DISHES AND RELATED TERMS

Beignet	Fritter
Farci	Stuffed
Forestière	With mushrooms
Gratiné/au gratin/ gratin de	Browned with cheese or butter
Jardinière	With mixed diced vegetables
A la parisienne	Sautéed in butter (potatoes); with white wine sauce & shallots
Parmentier	With potatoes
Sauté	Lightly fried in butter
A la vapeur	Steamed

FRUITS (FRUITS) AND NUTS (NOIX)

Abricot	Apricot
Amandes	Almonds
Ananas	Pineapple
Banane	Banana
Brugnon, nectarine	Nectarine
Cacahouète	Peanut
Cassis	Blackcurrants
Cerises	Cherries
Citron	Lemon
Citron vert	Lime
Figues	Figs
Fraises (des bois)	Strawberries (wild)
Framboises	Raspberries
Fruit de la passion	Passion fruit
Groseilles	Redcurrants & gooseberries
Mangue	Mango
Marrons	Chestnuts
Melon	Melon
Myrtilles	Bilberries
Noisette	Hazelnut
Noix	Nuts
Orange	Orange
Pamplemousse	Grapefruit
Pêche (blanche)	(White) peach
Pistache	Pistachio
Poire	Pear
Pomme	Apple
Prune	Plum
Pruneau	Prune
Raisins	Grapes

FRUIT: RELATED TERMS

Beignets	Fritters
Compote de...	Stewed...
Coulis	Sauce
Flambé	Set aflame in alcohol
Frappé	Iced

DESSERTS (DESSERTS) AND PASTRIES (PATISSERIE)

Bavarois	Refers to the mould, could be mousse or custard
Bombe	A moulded ice-cream dessert

Brioche	Sweet, high-yeast breakfast roll
Charlotte	Custard & fruit in lining of almond fingers
Coupe	A serving of ice cream
Crème Chantilly	Vanilla-flavoured and sweetened whipped cream
Crème fraîche	Sour cream
Crème pâtissière	Thick, eggy pastry filling
Crêpe	Pancake
Crêpe suzette	Thin pancake with orange juice and liqueur
Galette	Buckwheat pancake
Glace	Ice cream
Île flottante/oeufs à la neige	Soft meringues floating on custard
Macarons	Macaroons
Madeleine	Small sponge cake
Marrons Mont Blanc	Chestnut purée and cream on a rum-soaked sponge cake
Mousse au chocolat	Chocolate mousse
Palmiers	Caramelized puff pastries
Parfait	Frozen mousse, sometimes ice cream
Petit suisse	A smooth mixture of cream and curds
Petits fours	Bite-sized cakes/pastries
Sablé	Shortbread biscuit
Savarin	A filled, ring-shaped cake
Tarte	Tart
Tartelette	Small tart
Truffes	Truffles, chocolate or liqueur variety
Yaourt, yogourt	Yoghurt

CHEESE (FROMAGE)

There are over 400 types of French cheese, most of them named after their place of origin. *Chèvre* is goat's cheese and *brebis* is cheese made from sheep's milk. *Le plateau de fromages* is the cheeseboard, and bread – but not butter – is served with it.

Small print and Index

390 Small print

392 Index

402 Maps

A ROUGH GUIDE TO ROUGH GUIDES

Published in 1982, the first Rough Guide – to Greece – was a student scheme that became a publishing phenomenon. Mark Ellingham, a recent graduate in English from Bristol University, had been travelling in Greece the previous summer and couldn't find the right guidebook. With a small group of friends he wrote his own guide, combining a highly contemporary, journalistic style with a thoroughly practical approach to travellers' needs.

The immediate success of the book spawned a series that rapidly covered dozens of destinations. And, in addition to impecunious backpackers, Rough Guides soon acquired a much broader readership that relished the guides' wit and inquisitiveness as much as their enthusiastic, critical approach and value-for-money ethos.

These days, Rough Guides include recommendations from budget to luxury and cover more than 200 destinations around the globe, as well as producing an ever-growing range of eBooks and apps.

Visit **roughguides.com** to see our latest publications.

Rough Guide credits

Editors: Lara Kavanagh, Mandy Tomlin
Layout: Ankur Guha
Cartography: Swati Handoo
Picture editor: Rhiannon Furbear
Proofreader: Diane Margolis
Managing editor: Keith Drew
Assistant editor: Jalpreen Kaur Chhatwal
Production: Rebecca Short
Cover design: Nicole Newman, Ankur Guha
Photographers: James McConnachie and Lydia Evans
Editorial assistant: Lorna North

Senior pre-press designer: Dan May
Design director: Scott Stickland
Travel publisher: Joanna Kirby
Digital travel publisher: Peter Buckley
Reference director: Andrew Lockett
Operations coordinator: Becky Doyle
Operations assistant: Johanna Wurm
Publishing director (Travel): Clare Currie
Commercial manager: Gino Magnotta
Managing director: John Duhigg

Publishing information

This thirteenth edition published January 2012 by
Rough Guides Ltd,
80 Strand, London WC2R 0RL
11, Community Centre, Panchsheel Park,
New Delhi 110017, India
Distributed by the Penguin Group
Penguin Books Ltd,
80 Strand, London WC2R 0RL
Penguin Group (USA)
375 Hudson Street, NY 10014, USA
Penguin Group (Australia)
250 Camberwell Road, Camberwell,
Victoria 3124, Australia
Penguin Group (NZ)
67 Apollo Drive, Mairangi Bay, Auckland 1310, New Zealand
Rough Guides is represented in Canada by Tourmaline Editions Inc. 662 King Street West, Suite 304, Toronto, Ontario M5V 1M7
Printed in Singapore
© James McConnachie, Ruth Blackmore 2012

Maps © Rough Guides
No part of this book may be reproduced in any form without permission from the publisher except for the quotation of brief passages in reviews.
416pp includes index
A catalogue record for this book is available from the British Library
ISBN: 978-1-40538-695-1
The publishers and authors have done their best to ensure the accuracy and currency of all the information in **The Rough Guide to Paris**, however, they can accept no responsibility for any loss, injury, or inconvenience sustained by any traveller as a result of information or advice contained in the guide.
1 3 5 7 9 8 6 4 2

MIX
Paper from
responsible sources
FSC
www.fsc.org   FSC™ C018179

Help us update

We've gone to a lot of effort to ensure that the thirteenth edition of **The Rough Guide to Paris** is accurate and up-to-date. However, things change – places get "discovered", opening hours are notoriously fickle, restaurants and rooms raise prices or lower standards. If you feel we've got it wrong or left something out, we'd like to know, and if you can remember the address, the price, the hours, the phone number, so much the better.

Please send your comments with the subject line "**Rough Guide Paris Update**" to ⊕ mail@uk.roughguides.com. We'll credit all contributions and send a copy of the next edition (or any other Rough Guide if you prefer) for the very best emails.

Find more travel information, connect with fellow travellers and book your trip on ⊛ roughguides.com

SMALL PRINT 391

ABOUT THE AUTHORS

Ruth Blackmore is a contributor to the *Rough Guide to France* and the *Rough Guide to Classical Music*, and was also a Senior Editor at Rough Guides. Francophilia set in in her early teens with a trip to Paris, and led on to a degree in French at Durham, followed by a stint at Larousse working on French-English bilingual dictionaries. She grew up in South Wales, and lives in Dorset with her young family.

James McConnachie is based in the UK, but Channel-hops regularly for the Rough Guides to *Paris*, *The Loire* and *France*. His other titles include the controversial *Rough Guide to Conspiracy Theories* and a biography of one of the world's most notorious books: *The Book of Love: In Search of the Kamasutra*.

Acknowledgements

The authors would like to thank Lara Kavanagh for her admirable editing and enthusiasm as an ex-Parisienne; Mandy Tomlin, Keith Drew, Jo Kirby, Swati Handoo, Rhiannon Furbear, Ankur Guha and Dan May at Rough Guides; Tim Salmon and Kate Baillie, the authors of the first eight editions of the Paris guide; and all the Parisian restaurateurs, hoteliers, museum officials and friends who make this book such a pleasure to write and update.

James McConnachie would particularly like to thank Ruth Blackmore, my ever-amiable co-author on the Right Bank;

Claire Williams, for her insider tips and indefatigably enthusiastic researches; Julia Melvin, for her generous hospitality in the Sixième; Melissa Graham, Richard Danbury and their expert assistants, Joseph, Benedict and Eleanor Danbury, for their hard work at Disneyland (and Kate Brackenborough at Disney UK for helping arrange it).

Ruth Blackmore would especially like to thank Dylan and Anna Reisenberger, who helped to make this update possible; Luce Herriou for invaluable insider tips; and, as ever, my co-author James McConnachie.

Readers' letters

Thanks to all the readers who have taken the time to write in with comments and suggestions (and apologies if we've inadvertently omitted or misspelt anyone's name):

Rebecca Ambury, Jacinthe Battaglino, John Benjafield and Ann Farrant, David and Carol Cottrell, David Craven, Martha Graber, Jeff Hyman, Dr Jeannette Littlemore, Clive Probert, Eileen Sanchez, Raewyn Thomas, Victoria Roberts.

Index

Maps are marked in grey.

10ᵉ arrondissement and
    Goutte d'Or 191
13ᵉ arrondissement........... 173
15ᵉ arrondissement.... 170–171
59 Rivoli.. 90
1863 Salon des Refusés..........144
1968, May 122, 373

A

Abbesses.....................................179
Abélard, Peter 45, 363
Académie du Spectacle
    Equestre................................227
Académie Française................133
access..38
accommodation see hotels,
    hostels & apartments and B&Bs
addresses......................................30
AFP...80
Air de Paris 169
airlines 21
airports
    Beauvais 23
    Orly.. 23
    Roissy-Charles de Gaulle................ 22
Albert Kahn, Jardins et Musée
   215
Alexandre-Nevsky, Cathédrale
    66
allée des Cygnes 168
allée Vivaldi..............................112
American Church...... 28, 153, 349
apartments and B&Bs 262
    Air BnB 262
    Alcôve & Agapes 262
    Citadines 262
    Coach House Rentals...........262
    France Lodge 262
    Good Morning Paris.............262
    Lodgis....................................262
    Paris B and B 263
aperitifs......................................267
Arago line..................................165
Arc de Triomphe 61
Arc du Carousel 68
Arènes de Lutèce 130
Armée, Musée de l'................151
arrival
    by air.................................... 22
    by bus and car.................... 23
    by train................................ 21
arrondissements 30
Art Deco...................... 150, 163

Art et d'Histoire de la Ville de
    St-Denis, Musée d'................232
Art et d'Histoire du Judaïsme,
    Musée d'.................................. 98
Art Moderne de la Ville de Paris,
    Musée d'.................................156
Art Moderne, Musée National
    d'....................................... 84–86
Art Nouveau 59, 150, 182, 212
Arts Décoratifs, Musée des 58
Arts et Métiers, Musée des.....103
Arts Forains, Musée des 114
Assistance Publique – Hôpitaux
    de Paris, Musée de l' 122
Atelier Brancusi 87
athletics.....................................347
Auteuil 212–215
Auteuil and Passy 213
avenue Daumesnil 112
avenue Frochot 188
avenue Junot 184
avenue de Wagram....................65
avenue Winston Churchill 64

B

B&Bs see apartments and B&Bs
babies, travelling with 350
Bagnolet 210
Balabus 24
balloon, Air de Paris................169
balloon rides 340
banks.. 35
Banque de France 78
Barbès..188
Barbizon School.................52, 143
bars................................ 295–302
    10, Le 299
    3W-Kafé................................358
    Abracadabar, L'....................300
    Alimentation Générale, L'....301
    Andy Wahloo.......................297
    Autre Café, L' 301
    Babel Café 301
    Bar Costes 296
    Bar Hemingway 296
    Bar du Marché 299
    Bar Ourcq 300
    Bateau Ivre, Le 298
    Belle Hortense, La 297
    Bellevilloise, La....................301
    Belushi's Bar.........................300
    Bistrot des Augustins 299
    Café Charbon........................301
    Café Chéri(e)........................301

Café Cox 359
Café de l'Industrie............. 277, 298
Café Noir, Le 297
Cannibale, La 301
Carmen, Le 299
Champmeslé, La.......................358
Chez Camille 300
Chez Georges...........................299
Chez Jeannette 300
Conserverie, La 297
Curio Parlor 298
Cyrano.......................................300
De La Ville Café 297
Duplex, Le 359
Entrepôt, L'...................... 166, 285
Etages St-Germain, Les 299
Flûte L'Etoile............................296
Folie en Tête, La 299
Folies, Aux......................... 293, 301
Fourmi Café, La 300
Free DJ, Le................................359
Fumoir, Le 297
Jemmapes, Le..........................300
Kitty O'Shea's...........................297
Kong 297
Lèche Vin, Le............................298
Lou Pascalou 301
Lutetia Bar 299
Marcheurs de Planète, Les..........298
Merle Moqueur, Le 299
Mezzanine de l'Alcazar, La 299
Olympic Café 193, 300
Open Café, L' 359
Palette, La 299
Pantalon Bar, Le 298
Perle, La 297
Pershing Lounge 296
Petit Fer a Cheval, Le..............297
Piano Vache, Le 298
Piston Pélican 302
Point Ephémère 300
Pompon, Le 300
Prescription.............................299
Progrès, Le (Montmartre).... 288, 300
Quiet Man................................298
Rendez-Vous des Amis, Au 300
Rosebud, Le 299
Sans Souci, Le 300
SanZSanS 298
Sir Winston 296
Stolly's 298
Tambour, Le 297
Tartine, La 298
Trappiste, Au............................297
Trois Mailletz, Aux..................298
Troisième Lieu, Le 359
Violon Dingue, Le 299
Zèbre à Montmartre, Un 288, 300
Basilique St-Denis....................230
Bassin de la Villette 199
Bastille, place de la 107
Bastille and east 108–109

Bateau-Lavoir.............................181
Batignolles 193
Batignolles 193
Batobus....................................26
Beaubourg 87
Beaubourg and Les Halles
..85
Beaux Arts de la Ville de Paris,
   Musée des 65
Beaux-Arts, Musée des 242
belle époque.........................371
Belleville...................................205
Bercy......................................112
Bercy 113
Bercy Village............................114
Bibliothèque Forney.......105, 341
Bibliothèque Historique de la
   Ville de Paris.....................95, 342
Bibliothèque Mazarine...........133
Bibliothèque Nationale...........78
Bibliothèque Nationale de
   France 176, 342
Bibliothèque Publique...........84
Bibliothèque-Musée de l'Opéra
  74
Bièvre, river......................128, 172
bike rental 26
billiards....................................345
Black Death.............................364
Blanche...................................187
blues.......................................304
boat trips.................................340
boats 26
Bois de Boulogne.....................218
Bois de Boulogne.............. 217
Bois de Vincennes...................115
Bois de Vincennes.............. 115
Bon Marché, Le...............141, 323
books 378–380
boules.....................................346
boulevard de Belleville...........205
boulevard de la Chapelle 193
boulevard des Capucines........71
boulevard Edgar-Quinet market
   ....162, 338
boulevard des Italiens 71
boulevard Richard Lenoir.......199
boulevard St-Germain ...132, 136
boulevards...............................366
Bourdelle, Musée......................162
Bourse.......................................80
Brancusi, Constantin 87
Brook, Peter 192, 313
Bruni, Carla.............................377
Buddhist centre.....................116
Buren, Daniel............77, 86, 156
buses.......................................24
buses from the UK 20
Butte-aux-Cailles 174
Butte Montmartre....................181

C

cabarets................................188
Cabinet des Monnaies, Médailles
   et Antiques 80
café culture..............................273
cafés and wine bars..... 265–294
400 Coups, Les.............................293
A Priori Thé........................78, 272
Angélina...............................94, 271
Armagnac, L'.................................277
As du Falafel, L' 275
Assignat, L'.....................................281
Atmosphère, L'.............................292
Avant Comptoir, L' 281
Bar de l'Entracte, Le 272
Bar du Marché 137, 281
Baron Rouge, Le 111, 278
Berthillon.............................46, 268
Bistrot des Augustins 282
Café des Anges.............................277
Café des Arts.................................279
Café Beaubourg............................274
Café Charlot 102, 276
Café des Deux Moulins................287
Café de l'Industrie........................277
Café des Initiés, Le 274
Café Jacquemart-André, Le...67, 270
Café de la Mairie...............138, 282
Café du Marché 285
Café Martini..................................275
Café de la Mosquée 130, 279
Café de la Nouvelle Mairie.........279
Café de la Paix..............................272
Chez Prosper................................278
Chez Prune.....................198, 292
A la Cloche des Halles...................274
Cochon à l'Oreille, Le 274
Crèmerie, La 282
Dada, Le...270
Dame Tartine.................................274
Dénicheur, Le................................273
Dilan..273
Ebouillanté, L'.......................104, 275
Ecritoire, L'....................................280
Enchotte, L'...................................291
Entrepôt, L' 166, 285
Etages St-Germain, Les.......137, 282
Eté en Pente Douce, L'.......186, 287
Faitout, Le.....................................293
Flore, Le 136, 282
Folies, Aux....................................293
Fouquet's, Le................................270
Fourmi Ailée, La 280
Fourmi Café, La 288
Frenchie..273
Fuxia..292
Gare, La...294
Ladurée...............................272, 282
Legrand Filles et Fils....................272
Loir dans la Théière, Le 275
Mariage Frères 275
Mère Lachaise, La.........................293
Négociants, Aux...........................288
Palette, La......................................282
Pause Café.....................................278

Petit Marcel, Le............................274
Petit Suisse, Au............................282
Pipos, Les 280
Pozzetto...275
Progrès (Marais), Le.............102, 276
Progrès (Montmartre), Le...........288
Reflet, Le.......................................280
Refuge, Le......................................288
Relais de la Butte, Le....................288
Réveil du Dixième, Le..................291
Rubis, Le 271
Ruche à Miel, La..................111, 278
Sancerre, Le..................................288
Select, Le.......................................285
Taverne Henri IV 268
Tea and Tattered Pages................286
Verlet...272
Verre à Pied, Le 126, 280
Vieux Colombier, Au 282
Zèbre à Montmartre, Un 288
café-theatre..............................312
camping....................................264
Canal St-Denis 232
Canal St-Martin 198
Canal St-Martin,
   Ménilmontant and Belleville
   ..196–197
canal trips.........................198, 340
Canauxrama 107, 340
Canopée, La 88
car rental...................................27
Carnavalet, Musée......................94
Carré Rive Gauche..........132, 142
Carreau du Temple....................102
carrefour de la Croix Rouge...140
Carte Musées et Monuments...32
Carte Orange..............................25
Cartier-Bresson, Henri............166
catacombs.................................165
Cathédrale Alexandre-Nevsky
  66
Cathédrale Notre-Dame 44
Centquatre, Le 200
Central Marais 96
Centre International du Vitrail
  242
Cernuschi, Musée 66
Champ de Mars........................147
Champs-Elysées 60–67
Champs-Elysées and around
   ... 62–63
Channel Tunnel 20
chanson 296, 304
Chantal Crousel, Galerie...........100
Chantilly 235–238
Chapelle des Auxiliatrices 181
Chapelle Ste-Ursule.................122
Chapelle St-Louis......................174
Charles de Gaulle airport..........22
Charles V....................................364
Charonne....................................210
Chartres 240–243
Chartres 241

Chasse et de la Nature, Musée de la.................97
Château de Chantilly.............235
Château Fontainebleau..........239
Château de Malmaison...........227
Château de la Reine Blanche 174
Château de Versailles.............223
Château de Vincennes............116
Châtelet, place du...................89
chauffeur-driven tours 346
children, Paris for........ 348–356
children, travelling with.........350
Chinatown..................... 102, 174
Chirac, Jacques.......104, 147, 374
Chopin, Frédéric......189, 208, 218
Cimetière des Batignolles 194
Cimetière des Chiens..............194
Cinaxe.....................................204
Cinéaqua.................................154
cinemas 308–312
Cinémathèque.........................114
circuses...................................352
Cité de l'Architecture et du Patrimoine.........................154
Cité de la Mode et du Design 177
Cité de la Musique 204
Cité Nationale de l'Histoire de l'Immigration 116
Cité des Sciences et de l'Industrie...........................201
Cité Universitaire 167
classical music........................316
climate......................................31
Closerie des Lilas, La...............163
clubs.................................... 302
  Batofar..........................176, 302
  Club 18, Le..........................359
  CUD.....................................359
  Favela Chic.........................302
  Glaz'art...............................302
  Machine du Moulin Rouge, La....302
  Montana, Le.........................302
  Nouveau Casino, Le.............302
  Point Ephémère...................304
  Queen..................................359
  Redlight, Le.........................302
  Rex Club..............................303
  Rive Gauche, Le 359
  Scène Bastille, La 303
  Scopitone............................303
  Showcase.............................303
  Social Club...........................303
  Tango, Le.............................359
  WAGG..................................303
CNIT building...........................222
Cognacq-Jay, Musée...............95
Collège de France....................123
Collège des Quatre-Nations....133
Collégiale de St-André............242
Colonne de Juillet 110
Colonne Vendôme 76

Colonnes, Les............................166
Comédie Française....................77
Comédie Italienne....................162
Commune, the................. 185, 370
Conciergerie..............................43
Condé, Musée...........................235
consulates..................................33
cookery courses........................342
Corbusier, Le... 154, 167, 176, 214
costs..31
Coulée Verte.............................111
Cour Damoye............................110
Cour du Commerce St-André 137
Cour St-Emilion.........................114
Couvent des Récollets..............190
Crazy Horse..............................188
credit cards................................35
crime..32
crypte archéologique 45
cycling 26, 345, 347

D

Da Vinci Code, The 48, 138
da Vinci, Leonardo.........49, 54, 56
dance.......................................314
dance festivals.........................314
Day-trips from Paris 236
de Beauvoir, Simone 118, 132, 136, 164
Défense, La 220
Défense, La........................ 222
Défense, Musée de la...............222
Delacroix, Eugène 52, 55, 136, 138, 209
Delacroix, Musée 136
Delanoë, Mayor Bertrand 377
Depression...............................372
Deyrolle............................. 142, 337
Diana, Princess.........................157
disabilities, travellers with........38
discounts....................................31
Disneyland Paris 244–251
Disneyland Paris 246
Docks en Seine.........................177
doctors......................................33
Domaine Marie-Antoinette ...226
Dôme Imax 222
Dreyfus Affair 98
driving 26

E

Ecole des Beaux-Arts...............133
Ecole de Médecine...................138
Ecole Militaire 147

Ecole Normale Supérieure 125
Edith Piaf, Musée 207
Eglise du Dôme........................152
Eglise de la Madeleine..............74
Eglise St-Roch...........................76
Eglise des Soldats.....................151
Egouts de Paris, Musée des 150
Eiffel Tower..............................146
Eiffel Tower quarter ... 148–149
electricity...................................32
embassies..................................33
emergency numbers..................32
Emmanuel Perrotin, Galerie... 100
Enfants-Rouges, Marché des 102
Erotisme, Musée de l'..............188
Espace Montmartre Salvador Dalí.................184
Esplanade des Invalides..........150
ethnic cuisine................. 267, 290
euro...375
European Health Insurance Card 33
Eurostar............................. 19, 21
Eurotunnel 20
Eventail, Musée de l'................192
exchange...................................35
Explora.....................................203
Exposition d'Automne.............140
Exposition Universelle....... 64, 71, 146, 153, 156, 166

F

Fascism....................................373
faubourgs, the 190
Faubourg-St-Antoine 111
Fauchon 332
Fauré, Gabriel...........................75
ferries 20
Festival de Chopin 218, 319
festivals......................... 318–320
festivals, dance........................314
festivals, film...........................309
film 308–312
flea market, Puces de Vanves 166, 337
flea market, St-Ouen 228
flights
  from Australia, New Zealand and South Africa.....................20
  from the UK and Ireland.......19
  from the US and Canada........19
flower market, place Lépine....43
Folies Bergère 188
Fondation Cartier pour l'Art Contemporain 164
Fondation Cartier-Bresson 166

Fondation Louis Vuitton pour la Création..............218
Fontaine des Innocents...........89
Fontaine de l'Observatoire 140
Fontaine des Quatre-Saisons 141
Fontainebleau...............239
food and drink terms... 384–388
football....................346
Forge, La 205
Forum des Halles 88
Forum des Images......................88
Foucault's Pendulum......103, 125
François I....................48, 365
Franks............................362
French language 381–388
Frigos, Les...........................177
funfairs 126, 138, 351

G

Gainsbourg, house of Serge 136
Gainsbourg, Serge..........136, 164
Gaîté Lyrique.....................103
Galerie des Glaces....................224
Galerie Véro-Dodat 78
Galerie Vivienne......................78
Galeries Lafayette..............74, 323
Galeries Nationales....................64
Galeries du Panthéon Bouddhique................155
galleries, private....................100
Gare de l'Est......................190
Gare du Nord 19, 21, 190
gare routière........................23
gay and lesbian Paris... 357–359
Gehry, Frank 114, 218
Géode, La....................204
Giverny 243
glossary 381–388
Gobelins tapestry workshops 172
gourmet restaurants 271
Goutte d'Or.....................192
Grand Ecurie du Roy..............227
Grand Palais......................64
Grand Pari', Le 376
Grand Plan de Paris.............24
Grande Arche, La 220
Grande Galerie de l'Evolution 129, 355
Grands Boulevards 71–77
Grands Boulevards and passages 72–73
Grands Moulins de Paris 176
Grévin, Musée......................71
Guimard, Hector 182, 212
Guimet, Musée 155

guinguette....................341
gyms........................342

H

Halle St-Pierre 187
Halles, Les........................88
Hameau des Artistes 184
Hammam de la Mosquée......130, 344
hammams 344
Haussmann, Baron......41, 71, 95, 218, 370, 371
Haut Marais....................99–103
health............................33
Hédiard.............................322
Hemingway, Ernest.......118, 126, 138, 163, 273, 296
Henri IV............ 41, 68, 89, 92, 365
Histoire de France, Musée de l' 97
Histoire Naturelle, Muséum National d'....................129
history of Paris 361–377
holidays, public.....................36
Hôpital de la Pitié-Salpêtrière 174
horse racing......................347
hostels 263–264
Auberge Internationale des Jeunes 264
BVJ Louvre 263
BVJ Paris Quartier Latin 263
D'Artagnan 263
Fauconnier, Le 263
Fourcy, Le........................263
Foyer International d'Accueil de Paris Jean Monnet..............263
Foyer Tolbiac.....................263
Hôtel Caulaincourt Square......264
Jules Ferry.....................263
Maubuisson 263
Maurice Ravel....................263
Oops................................264
Peace and Love Hostel................264
St Christopher's Paris...........200, 263
Village Hostel, Le 264
Woodstock Hostel..................264
Young and Happy Hostel..............264
Hôtel d'Albret......................97
Hôtel de Cluny....................123
Hôtel Drouot 81
Hôtel des Invalides...............150
Hôtel Lambert 46
Hôtel Lauzun 46
Hôtel Lutetia......................141
Hôtel du Nord..................198, 310
Hôtel de la Païva 189
Hôtel de Rohan 97
Hôtel de Sens......................105
Hôtel de Soubise 97

Hôtel de Sully......................94
Hôtel Thiers......................189
Hôtel de Ville......................87
hotels 253–262
123, Le.........................254
Appi Hôtel 255
Belle Juliette, La....................258
Bristol, Le.......................254
Caron de Beaumarchais 256
Citizen Hotel, Le 261
Costes.............................254
Ermitage Hôtel......................260
Familia Hôtel......................257
Général Hôtel, Le....................261
Grand Hôtel du Loiret 256
Grand Hôtel Jeanne d'Arc.............256
Hameau de Passy......................262
Henri IV............................253
Hôtel, L'...................... 132, 258
Hôtel de l'Abbaye.....................258
Hôtel Amour.....................260
Hôtel Arioso......................254
Hôtel des Arts....................260
Hôtel de l'Avre....................259
Hôtel Bonséjour Montmartre 260
Hôtel Bourg Tibourg 255
Hôtel de la Bretonnerie 256
Hôtel Brighton 254
Hôtel Central Marais 256
Hôtel du Champ-de-Mars........259
Hôtel Chopin...................81, 255
Hôtel du Commerce 257
Hôtel du Cygne.....................255
Hôtel du Danube 258
Hôtel Degrés de Notre-Dame 257
Hôtel Eldorado......................261
Hôtel Esmeralda....................257
Hôtel des Grandes Ecoles 257
Hôtel des Grands Hommes 258
Hôtel Lancaster......................254
Hôtel Langlois 260
Hôtel Le Lavoisier....................254
Hôtel de Lille......................261
Hôtel de la Loire....................259
Hôtel Lorette.......................260
Hôtel Louis II....................258
Hôtel de Lutèce....................253
Hôtel Mansart 255
Hôtel Marais Bastille 257
Hôtel Marignan......................258
Hôtel Meurice....................254
Hôtel Michelet-Odéon 258
Hôtel Mistral......................259
Hôtel de Nesle....................258
Hôtel de Nevers......................261
Hôtel de Nice......................256
Hôtel du Nord......................261
Hôtel Odéon St-Germain 258
Hôtel du Palais Bourbon 259
Hôtel Particulier Montmartre......260
Hôtel Pavillon de la Reine 256
Hôtel Pergolèse......................254
Hôtel du Petit Moulin 256
Hôtel Picard......................256
Hôtel Port-Royal....................259
Hôtel de la Porte Dorée............257
Hôtel Printemps....................259
Hôtel Résidence Henri IV...........258

Hôtel St-Jacques................................258
Hôtel St-Louis Marais...................257
Hôtel Saint-Merry 255
Hôtel de Sers 254
Hôtel Sévigné..................................256
Hôtel Sezz..262
Hôtel Stanislas................................259
Hôtel Thérèse 255
Hôtel Tiquetonne...........................255
Hôtel Tolbiac...................................260
Hôtel de la Trémoille......................254
Hôtel de Verneuil...........................259
Hôtel Vivienne................................255
Mama Shelter 210, 261
Manufacture, La.............................259
Mercure Paris Terminus Nord 261
Nouvel Hôtel....................................257
Perfect Hotel...................................260
Quartier Bercy Square, Le 257
Relais Christine 258
Relais du Louvre 255
Relais St-Honoré.............................254
Relais Saint-Sulpice 259
Résidence Les Gobelins..................260
Select Hôtel.....................................258
Solar Hôtel.......................................259
Vert-Galant, Le 260
house of Serge Gainsbourg
....136
Hugo, Victor..................61, 92, 110

I

ice rink (Hôtel de Ville)................. 88
ice skating 344
Ile de la Cité 40–45
Ile de la Cité and Ile St-Louis
.... 42–43
Ile St-Louis..................................... 46
Impressionism 143
Impressionnismes, Musée des
....243
Institut de France 133
Institut du Monde Arabe........130
Institut Français de la Mode....177
insurance 34
internet 34
Invalides quarter 150–154
IRCAM 87
ISIC Card.. 31

J

Jacquemart-André, Musée... 66
Jardin d'Acclimatation ...218, 349
Jardin Atlantique 159
Jardin du Luxembourg..............138
Jardin des Plantes 128
Jardin des Poètes.........................215
Jardin du Ranelagh.......................214

Jardin de Reuilly........................112
Jardin de Ste-Périne 212
Jardin des Serres d'Auteuil.....215
Jardin Shakespeare...................218
Jardin des Tuileries.................... 68
Jardins et Musée Albert Kahn
....215
jazz...304
Jean Moulin, Musée....................162
Jeu de Paume 69
Jewish quarter..............................99
Joan of Arc.....................................364
jogging..345
Jussieu campus 130

K

Karsten Greve, Galerie 100
Kilomètre Zéro............................... 45
Knights Templar 102

L

La Canopée....................................88
La Grande Arche 220
La Mouffe 126
La Villette.......................................201
laundry... 34
Le Bourget.....................................233
Le Croissant.................................... 80
Le Plateau......................................207
Left Bank..118
Les Halles.. 88
Les Olympiades............................174
lesbian and gay Paris... 357–359
Lettres et Manuscrits, Musée des
....133
libraries...341
Lido..188
live music *see* music venues
listings magazines.......................... 38
Longchamp racecourse 218
Louis XIV 54, 68, 77, 223, 237,
238, 366
Louis XVI 68, 95, 103, 367
Louis XVII 103, 110, 369
Louvre, The 47–59
Louvre, The 49
Louvre: plan of first floor 51
Louvre, architecture 48, 54
Louvre, Medieval 58
Louvre, Palais du..................48, 58
Luxembourg gardens................138
Luxembourg, Musée du..........140
Lycée Louis-le-Grand 123

M

Mac/Val...233
Madeleine, place de la.............. 75
Magie, Musée de la...................105
mail... 35
Maillol, Musée..............................141
Maison de l'Air 206
Maison de Balzac.........................216
Maison de la Culture du Japon à
Paris...168
Maison Européenne de la
Photographie.............................105
Maison de l'Histoire de France
.... 97
Maison du Jardinage...............114
Maison Picassiette....................242
Maison Rouge..............................107
Maison de Victor Hugo............. 92
maps... 35
Marais 91–105
Marais 93
Marais, Central 96
Marché d'Aligre 111
Marché Bio 140, 338
Marché Dejean 192
Marché des Enfants-Rouges ...102
Marché St-Denis..........................232
Marian Goodman, Galerie......100
Marine, Musée de la 154
markets 337
Marmottan, Musée 214
Matisse, Henri 69, 84, 86, 156
May 1968 ....122, 373
media.. 27
Médiathèque.................................204
Médicis, Catherine de 68, 232,
365
Medieval Paris...............................363
Mémorial de la Déportation.... 45
Mémorial de la Shoah..............104
Ménagerie, Jardin des Plantes
....129
Ménilmontant................................207
métro 23, 182
Ministère des Finances............113
Mitterrand, François 374
MK2..................................200, 309
Mobilis pass................................... 25
Mode, Musée de la....................155
Mode et du Textile,
Musée de la 59
Mona Lisa 49, 54, 56
Monet, Claude ...65, 69, 143, 214,
243
money..35
Montfaucon gallows 199
Montmartre 179–187
Montmartre and the 9ᵉ 180
Montmartre cemetery 187

Montmartre vineyard............186
Montmartre, Musée de 186
Montmartrobus....................179
Montparnasse 158–168
Montparnasse and the 14e
..................................160–161
Montparnasse cafés............163
Montparnasse cemetery........164
Montparnasse, Musée du......162
Moreau, Musée...................190
Morisot, Berthe.................214
Morrison, Jim 208
mosque...........................129
Mouffe, La 126
Mouffetard quarter.................126
Moulin de la Galette.............182
Moulin Rouge 188
Moulin, Jean 162, 242
Moyen Age, Musée National du
................................123
Mur des Fédérés 210
Musée de – look up under
  proper name; eg Musée
  d'Orsay is listed under "O"
museum passes 32
museums for kids 354
music venues 303–306
  Atelier Charonne, L'..........306
  Baiser Salé, Le................306
  Bataclan, Le..................303
  Café de la Danse..............303
  Casino de Paris...............306
  Caveau de la Huchette.........306
  Cigale, La....................304
  Divan du Monde, Le............304
  Duc des Lombards, Au..........306
  Flèche d'Or, La..........210, 304
  Instants Chavirés.............306
  Jazz Club Lionel Hampton......306
  Lapin Agile, Au 186, 306
  Limonaire, Au.................306
  Magique, La...................306
  Maroquinerie..................304
  New Morning 192, 306
  Point Ephémère................304
  Social Club...................304
  Sunset/Le Sunside, Le 306
  Trois Baudets, Les............306
Musique, Musée de la.............205

N

Napoleon................44, 48, 49,
  55, 56, 61, 68, 74, 76, 77, 80,
  81, 95, 102, 110, 137, 147, 151,
  152, 154, 220, 226, 227, 237,
  239, 366, 368, 378
Napoléon III 41, 48, 54, 56, 57,
  68, 71, 151, 185, 198, 367, 369,
  370
National War Museum.............151

Natural History Museum........129
Navigo pass 25
newspapers 28
night buses 24
Nissim de Camondo, Musée....66
Notre-Dame, Cathédrale de 44
Notre-Dame de Lorette.........189
Notre-Dame de la Médaille
  Miraculeuse 141
Notre-Dame du Travail 166
Nouvel, Jean ...130, 147, 163, 375
Nouvelle Athènes.................189

O

Observatoire de Paris.............165
Odéon quarter....................137
Olympiades, Les.................174
opening hours 36
opera..........................317
Opéra Bastille..................107
Opéra Garnier 71
Opéra, Bibliothèque-
  Musée de l'....................74
Orangerie (Jardin du
  Luxembourg) 140
Orangerie (Tuileries)............69
Orsay, Musée d' 142–144
Orwell, George 126, 163, 169

P

packages...........................21
Pagode, La.......................153
Palais de Chaillot..............154
Palais de la Découverte...........65
Palais de Justice 41
Palais du Luxembourg............138
Palais Omnisports de Paris
  Bercy................114, 344, 347
Palais Royal 77
Palais de Tokyo 155
Palais de Tokyo Site de Création
  Contemporaine 156
Palais des Tuileries.............68
Panthéon.........................124
Parc André-Citroën 168
Parc de Bagatelle...............218
Parc de Belleville..............206
Parc de Bercy 114
Parc des Buttes-Chaumont....206
Parc Clichy-Batignolles..........194
Parc Floral......................115
Parc Georges-Brassens 169
Parc Monceau 66
Parc Montsouris 167
Parc de St-Cloud................228

Parc de la Turlure 186
Paris Mosque......................129
Paris Plage...............200, 320
Paris Rive Gauche................176
Paris Visites pass 25
Parisii, the......................361
Paris-Story........................74
parking............................26
parks for kids...................349
passages.......................77–82
passage Brady.....................192
passage du Caire...................81
passage Choiseul...................80
passage du Grand-Cerf 82
passage Jouffroy...................81
passage des Panoramas...........80
passage des Princes...............81
passage Verdeau....................81
Passerelle Debilly...............155
Passerelle Simone de Beauvoir
 176
Passy............................216
Pavillon Amont...................144
Pavillon de l'Arsenal............105
Père-Lachaise cemetery
  207–210
Père-Lachaise cemetery 208
perfumeries......................329
Pernety quarter..................166
pet cemetery......................194
Petit Palais.......................65
pharmacies 34
phones 36
Piaf, Edith..........206, 207, 209
Picasso, Musée...................100
Picasso, Pablo.....69, 84, 100, 118,
  182, 273
picnic food......................277
Pigalle..........................187
Pinacothèque de Paris............75
Piscine Josephine Baker
  ....176, 343
place des 5 Martyrs du Lycée
  Buffon........................166
place des Abbesses...............179
place de l'Alma..................157
place de la Bastille............. 107
place de la Bataille de
  Stalingrad....................199
place du Caire.....................81
place de Catalogne...............166
place du Châtelet 89
place de Clichy 188, 194
place de la Concorde 67
place de la Contrescarpe........126
place Dalida.....................184
place Dauphine 41
place du Dr Félix Lobligeois... 194
place de l'Etoile 61
place Igor Stravinsky.............87
place d'Italie....................172

place Lépine 43
place Lorrain 212
place de la Madeleine 75
place Marcel Aymé 184
place du Marché-Ste-Catherine
.... 94
place Maubert 123
place de la Nation 111
place Pigalle 188
place St-Georges 189
place St-Germain-des-Prés ...136
place St-Michel 118
place de la Sorbonne 122
place des Ternes 65
place du Tertre 184
place Vendôme 76
place des Victoires 78
place des Vosges 92
Plans-Reliefs, Musée des 151
police 32
Pompidou Centre 84–87
Pont Alexandre III 153
Pont de l'Alma 157
Pont de l'Archevêché 122
Pont des Arts 133
Pont de Bir-Hakeim 168, 217
Pont-Neuf 41
Pont des Suicides 206
pool 345
Port de l'Arsenal 107
Porte St-Denis 191
Porte St-Martin 192
post 35
Potager des Princes 237
Potager du Roi 227
Poupée, Musée de la 87
Préfecture de Police, Musée de
la 123
Printemps 74
private galleries 100
Promenade Plantée 111
pronunciation 381
public transport 23–26
Publicité, Musée de la 59
Puces de St-Ouen 228
Puces de Vanves 166, 337
Pyramide, the 48

Q

Quai Branly, Musée du 147
quai de Jemmapes 198
quai de la Mégisserie 90
quai d'Orsay 153
quai de Valmy 198
quartier du Commerce 169
Quartier Latin 117–130
Quartier Latin 120–121

Quartier St-Paul 104
quartier du Temple 102
Quatre Temps shopping centre
.... 222

R

radio 28, 303
Radio-France, Musée de 212
rafle du Vel d'Hiv 168
Raspail organic market ... 140, 338
Renaissance 364
RER 23
Resistance, the 373
restaurants 265–294
404 276
A Mi Chemin 286
Abribus, L' 293
Al Ajami 270
Allard 283
Ambassade d'Auvergne 276
Aquarius 285
Ardoise, L' 271
Arpège, L' 285
Astrance, L' 294
Atelier Maître Albert, L' 280
Atlas, L' 137, 283
Auberge Pyrénées Cévennes, L' ... 292
Avant Goût, L' 287
Babylone, Au 283
Bambou, Le 287
Baratin, Le 293
Biche au Bois, A la 278
Bistrot des Dames, Le 292
Bistrot Paul Bert 279
Bistrot du Peintre, Le 278
Bistrot des Victoires 273
Bofinger 278
Bon Accueil, Au 285
Brasserie Balzar 280
Brasserie Lipp 136, 283
Breizh Café 276
Buisson Ardent, Le 280
Café Burq 288
Café du Commerce, Le ... 169, 286
Café des Musées 276
Cantine Merci, La 292
Casa Olympe 288
Châteaubriand, Le 293
Chez Casimir 291
Chez Imogène 292
Chez Marianne 276
Chez Nénesse 276
Chez Omar 276
Chez Paul 278
Cinq Saveurs d'Anada, Les 280
Clocher du Village, Au 294
Coco de Mer 287
Comptoir du Relais St-Germain, Le
.... 283
Crêperie Josselin 159, 286
Drouant 272
Ecurie, L' 280
Encrier, L' 279

Enoteca, L' 276
Entracte, L' 288
Epi Dupin, L' 283
Epigramme, L' 283
Estaminet, L' 277
Ferrandaise 283
Flo 192, 291
Fontaine de Mars, La 285
Fontaines, Les 280
Gaigne, Le 277
Gallopin 273
Gaya Rive Gauche 283
Gazzetta, La 279
Georges 84, 274
Gladines, Chez 287
Grain de Folie, Au 288
Grand Véfour, Le 78, 273
Gros Minet, Le 274
Hélène Darroze 283
Higuma 273
Ile de Gorée 292
Jacques-Mélac 278
Jardin des Pâtes, Le 280
Jules Verne, Le 285
Julien 192, 291
Lao Lane Xang 2 287
Lao Siam 293
Lasserre 270
Lyonnais, Aux 273
Maison de l'Amerique Latine ... 284
Maison de l'Aubrac, La 270
Maison Blanche, La 270
Mansouria, Le 279
Marchés du Palais, Aux 284
Martel, Le 291
Mer de Chine, La 287
Meurice, Le 272
Mini Palais 272
Mon Vieil Ami 268
Mono, Le 288
Moulin de la Galette, Le 290
Os à Moelle, L' 286
P'tit Troquet, Le 285
Paris-Hanoï 278
Pavillon Montsouris 286
Perraudin 281
Petit Pontoise, Le 281
Petit St-Benoît, Le 284
Pho 67 281
Pied de Cochon, Au 274
Pied de Fouet, Au 285
Pierre Gagnaire 270
Plaza-Athénée 270
Pomponnette, A la 290
Pooja 291
Potager du Marais, Le 276
Pramil 277
Pré Verre, Le 281
Refuge des Fondus 290
Régalade, La 286
Relais de l'Entrecôte, Le 271
Relais Gascon, Le 290
Relais de l'Isle, Le 268
Relais du Parc, Le 294
Reminet, Le 281
Rendez-Vous de la Marine, Au ... 292
Repaire de Cartouche, Le 293
Restaurant, Le 291

Restaurant de Bourgogne 293
Ribouldingue..................................281
Robe et le Palais, La....................274
Rotonde, La 286
Spoon..271
Table Lauriston, La.......................294
Taillevent..271
Tashi Delek....................................281
Temps des Cerises, Le... 174, 287
Timbre, Le 286
Tokyo Eat/Tokyo Self..................284
Tour de Montlhéry
  (Chez Denise), La 275
Tourelle, La 284
Train Bleu, Le 279
Tricotin..287
Vagenende......................................284
Vaudeville, Le 273
Vieux Chêne, Au 279
Waly Fay...278
Wepler 194, 292
Yam'Tcha 275
Ze Kitchen Galerie 284
Zerda Café 291
Restoration 369
Retz, passage de 102
Revolution, the.............................367
Rive Gauche...................................118
riverside quarter 132
rock climbing 346
rock music......................................303
Rodin, Musée 152
rollerblading.........................344, 352
Roman baths...................................123
Roman Paris....................................361
Rond-Point des Champs-
  Elysées 64
Rotonde de la Villette 199
Ruche, La 172
rue de l'Annonciation 216
rue Berton 216
rue Boileau.....................................212
rue Brancion 172
rue de Bretagne 102
rue de Buci 137
rue Charlot 100
rue de Charonne............................110
rue du Commerce..........................169
rue Cler 150
rue Daval 110
rue des Ecoles 122
rue du Faubourg-St-Denis......192
rue de la Fontaine 212
rue des Francs-Bourgeois.........94
rue de la Gaîté 162
rue Jean Pierre Timbaud 207
rue Keller 110
rue de Lappe 110
rue de Lévis....................................194
rue Louise Weiss...........................177
rue Mallet-Stevens........................214
rue de Ménilmontant....................207
rue des Moines..............................194

rue Monsieur le Prince............138
rue de la Montagne-
  Ste-Geneviève 125
rue Montmartre 82
rue Montorgueil........................... 82
rue Mouffetard market...........126
rue Oberkampf..............................207
rue de la Parcheminerie.........119
rue Poncelet street market 65
rue Quincampoix............................ 87
rue de Rivoli.................................. 92
rue de la Roquette 111
rue des Rosiers.............................. 99
rue St-Blaise................................210
rue St-Denis.................................. 82
rue St-Honoré 76
rue St-Jacques.............................119
rue du Télégraphe......................206
rue de la Tour des Dames.......189

S

Sacré-Cœur, church of............185
St Bartholomew's Day 365
St-Denis 230–233
St-Denis 231
St-Etienne-du-Mont 125
St-Eustache................................. 89
St-Germain.................. 131–144
St-Germain 134–135
St-Germain-de-Charonne.......210
St-Germain-des-Prés 136
St-Gervais-St-Protais................104
St-Jean Baptiste de Grenelle,
  church of....................................169
St-Jean de Montmartre, church
  of...181
St-Julien-le-Pauvre....................119
St-Laurent......................................190
St-Médard 126
St-Ouen market............................228
St-Ouen market 229
St-Paul-St-Louis............................ 94
St-Pierre de Montmartre.........184
St-Séverin 119
St-Sulpice.......................................138
Sainte-Chapelle 42
Ste-Marguerite............................110
Ste-Marie-des-Batignolles......194
Ste-Trinité......................................189
sales tax..37
Salon des Refusés, 1863..........144
Salvador Dalí, Espace
  Montmartre 184
Samaritaine...................................90
Sarkozy, Nicolas 97, 220, 376
Sartre, Jean-Paul 118, 132, 164,
  273

School of Fine Art......................133
semaine sanglante....................185
Sentier 81
Service de Santé des Armées,
  Musée du...................................125
Sèvres Cité de la Céramique
 228
sewers museum 150
Shakespeare & Co..........119, 330
Shoah, Mémorial de la............104
shopping in Paris....322, 324, 327
shops
  1 et 1 font 3.................................329
  66, Le 326
  A. Simon.................................82, 336
  Abbey Bookshop........................330
  Abdon 337
  Abeilles, Les................................334
  agnès b...323
  Album 331
  Alice à Paris 356
  Alternatives.................................327
  Amuzilo...356
  Analog Collector 331
  Androuet.......................................333
  Anne Willi......................110, 326
  Annick Goutal 329
  Anthony Peto 328
  Antoine et Lili 198, 326
  APC...323
  Archives de la Presse 337
  Artcurial..331
  Artisanat Monastique, L'..........337
  Astier de Villatte 336
  Attica 332
  Autour du Monde........................328
  Autour du Saumon.....................334
  Ba&sh..323
  Bague de Kenza, La 333
  Baron Rouge, Le 334
  Barthélémy..................................333
  Bazar de l'Hôtel de Ville (BHV)
 322
  Belle de Jour 329
  Boîte à Musique Anna Joliet.......337
  Bon Marché, Le 141, 323
  Bonhomme de Bois, Le.............355
  Bonpoint.......................................356
  Boudoir de Marie, Le 328
  Bovida......................................82, 336
  Cadolle 328
  Cancan 326
  Caves Augé, Les 334
  Caves Michel Renaud 334
  Caves St-Antoine, Les 334
  Caviar Kaspia 334
  Cécile et Jeanne 328
  Chambre Claire, La 331
  Chantelivre...................................355
  Chezel..327
  Chocolaterie Jacques Genin 333
  Ciel Est à Tout le Monde, Le 355
  Ciné-Images.................................330
  Ciné Reflet 331
  Clef des Marques, La..................327
  Colette 76, 326
  Comme des Garçons...................326

Comptoir de la Gastronomie, Le 333
Comptoir des Cotonniers.............323
Comptoir des Ecritures 330
Cousins d'Alice, Les 355
Crèmerie, La 334
Crocodisc 331
Dam Boutons...............................337
De Vinis Illustribus......................334
Debauve et Gallais.......................333
Défilé de Marques 327
Deyrolle 142, 337
Dominique Picquier......................336
Du Pain et Des Idées....................332
Du Pareil au Même.......................356
Dubois..330
Ducs de Gascogne, Aux.................333
E. Dehillerin...............................336
Editions de Parfums Frédéric
    Malle.....................................329
En Attendant Bébé........................329
Entrée des Fournisseurs 328
Et Vous......................................323
Fauchon......................................332
Flo Prestige...............................333
Fnac..330
Free "P" Star..............................327
Freelance...................................328
Fromagerie Alléosse....................333
Galerie Patrick Séguin..................336
Galeries Lafayette.......................323
Galignani....................................330
Gallimard...................................331
Ganachaud..................................332
Gibert Jeune..............................331
Gibert Joseph.............................331
Grande Epicerie, La 332
Harpo...328
Heaven.......................................326
Hédiard......................................332
Hermès......................................329
Hervé Chapelier...........................329
Hune, La 331
Institut Géographique National
    (IGN)......................................332
Isabel Marant.............................323
Jamin-Puech...............................329
Jean-Paul Hévin...........................333
Joséphine Vannier.......................333
Kabuki.......................................323
Kiliwatch...................................327
Labeyrie....................................333
Lanvin.......................................326
Lavinia......................................334
Legrand Filles et Fils...................334
Librairie le Moniteur....................331
Librairie Musicale Paris 331
Librairie Ulysse..........................332
Louvre des Antiquaires.................336
Lulu Berlu..................................336
Maille.......................................333
Maison de l'Escargot, La...............334
Maison Sauvlat............................331
Maison de la Truffe......................333
Maje...323
Marché St-Pierre.........................336
Mariage Frères............................334
Marie-Hélène de Taillac................329

Marie Mercié...............................329
Maroquinerie Saint Honoré 329
Merci..336
MORA 82, 336
Mots à la Bouche, Les...................358
Mouton à Cinq Pattes, Le.............327
Nain Bleu, Au..............................356
Occaserie, L'...............................327
Oeuf, L'......................................329
P'tits Bo'Bo, Les..........................356
Papier Plus.................................330
Pâtisserie Stohrer........................333
Patricia Louisor...........................323
Paul Beuscher.............................331
Paul & Joe..................................323
Petit Bonheur la Chance, Au........336
Petite Maison dans la Villette, La
   356
Pigalle......................................326
Poilâne......................................332
Pot à Tabac, Le...........................337
Princesse Tam Tam.......................328
Printemps...................................323
Puzzles Michèle Wilson.................356
Réciproque.................................327
Red Wheelbarrow.........................330
Rendez-Vous de la Nature 333
Repetto......................................328
Résonances.................................336
Roxan..326
Rûchers du Roy, Les 334
Sabbia Rosa................................328
Sam...336
Samy Chalon...............................324
Sennelier...................................330
Séphora......................................329
Shakespeare & Co........................330
Shinzo 328
Sonia by Sonia Rykiel....................324
Sonia Rykiel................................324
Spree...324
Swildens.....................................326
Tang Frères......................174, 334
Tati...323
Tessa Delpech.............................326
Thé-Troc....................................331
Tout s'arrange.............................356
Trousselier.................................337
Vaissellerie, La............................337
Vanessa Bruno............................324
Verlet..334
Viaduc des Arts, Le......................336
Village Voice...............................330
Vintage Désir..............................328
Violette & Léonie.........................328
Virgin Megastore.........................331
WH Smith...................................330
Y-3..326
YSL...324
Yves Andrieux et Vincent Jalbert
   324
Zadig & Voltaire..........................326
shops for kids............................355
siege, the..................................370
Site de Création Contemporaine,
    Palais de Tokyo.......................156
skateboarding.............................344
smoking 37

soft drinks 267
Soldiers' Church 151
Sorbonne....................................122
spectacles, Versailles 224
sports 342–347
square des Batignolles 194
square Charles Dickens.................217
square d'Orléans..........................189
square René-le-Gall......................172
square du Temple.........................102
square Villemin...........................190
square Viviani.............................119
square Willette............................185
squash 346
Stade de France 232
Stade Roland Garros.....................215
Statue of Liberty 168
Studio Ozenfant...........................167
studying in Paris 30
suburbs, The...................... 221
SUDAC building 176
swimming 343, 352

T

takeaways...................................277
taxis 25
tea dances..................................341
tennis 346, 347
Tenniseum..................................215
Terror, The..................................368
theatre 312–314
Théâtre des Champs-Elysées
    ....64, 314
Théâtre du Châtelet..........89, 313
Théâtre de la Huchette...119, 313
Théâtre National de Chaillot
    ....154, 313
Théâtre de l'Odéon.......................138
Théâtre de la Ville..........89, 314
theatre for kids...........................352
theme parks 351
time 37
tipping.......................................267
toilets 37
tomb of an unknown soldier ...61
Tour Eiffel..................................146
Tour de l'Horloge......................... 43
Tour Jean Sans Peur..................... 81
Tour Montparnasse.......................159
Tour Phare..................................220
Tour St-Jaques............................. 90
tourist information....................... 38
train stations 21
trains from the UK............... 19, 21
trams 25
transvestite cabarets.................188
travel agents............................... 21

travel passes 25
Triangle d'Or 64
Trocadéro 154–157
Tuileries gardens 68
Tuileries, Palais des 68
Tumult of St-Médard 126
Turkish embassy 216
TV 28, 303

U

underground Paris 167
unemployment benefit 30
UNESCO 147
University quarter 122–126
unknown soldier, tomb of 61

V

Val-de-Grâce 125
Vaux-le-Vicomte 238
vegetarian food 268
Vélib' bikes 26
Vendôme, place 76

Versailles 223–227
Versailles town 226
Vert-Galant, square du 41
Viaduc des Arts 112
Vie Romantique, Musée de la
.... 189
Villa La Roche 214
Villa Montmorency 214
Villa Seurat 167
Village St-Paul 105
Village Suisse 169
Villette and around, La 200
Villette, Parc de la 201–205
Villette, Parc de la 202
Vin, Musée du 217
Vincennes 114
visas 33
Vivant du Cheval, Musée 237
Voguéo boat-bus 176
Voûtes, Les 177

W

Wallace fountains 181
Watermen's guild 364
Wilde, Oscar 132, 209

wine 267
wine courses 342
working in Paris 28–30
World Cup 374
world music 303

Y

Yellow Korner, Galerie 100
Yves Saint Laurent Rive Gauche
.... 138
Yvon Lambert, Galerie 100

Z

Zadkine, Musée 164
Zadkine, Ossip 164
Zola, Emile 98, 187
zoos 116, 118, 129, 349

Maps

Index

Ile de la Cité and Ile St-Louis	42–43
The Louvre	49
Louvre: plan of first floor	51
The Champs-Elysées and around	62–63
The Grands Boulevards and *passages*	72–73
Beaubourg and Les Halles	85
The Marais	93
Central Marais	96
Bastille and east	108–109
Bercy	113
Bois de Vincennes	115
Quartier Latin	120–121
St-Germain	134–135
The Eiffel Tower quarter	148–149
Montparnasse and the 14ᵉ	160–161
The 15ᵉ	170–171
The 13ᵉ	173
Montmartre and the 9ᵉ	180
The 10ᵉ and Goutte d'Or	191
Batignolles	193
The Canal St-Martin, Ménilmontant and Belleville	196–197
La Villette and around	200
Parc de la Villette	202
Père-Lachaise cemetery	208
Auteuil and Passy	213
Bois de Boulogne	217
The suburbs	221
La Défense	222
St-Ouen market	229
St-Denis	231
Day-trips from Paris	236
Chartres	241
Disneyland Paris	246

Listings key

● Accommodation
● Café/wine bar/restaurant
● Bar/club/live music venue
● Shop

City plan

The **city plan** on the pages that follow is divided as shown:

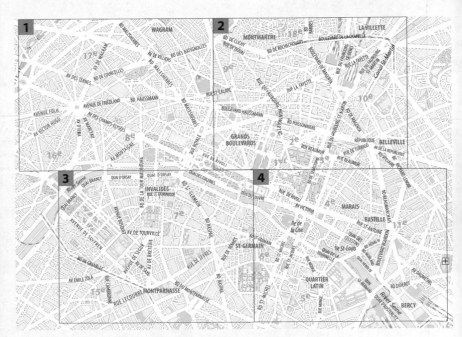

Map symbols

)(	Bridge	**P**	Parking	◆	Place of interest
✈	Airport	✉	Post office		Building
Ⓜ	Métro	(i)	Tourist information		Church
Ⓡ	RER	✚	Hospital		Stadium
Ⓣ	Tram stop	⊙	Statue		Cemetery
	Boat stop		Synagogue		Park

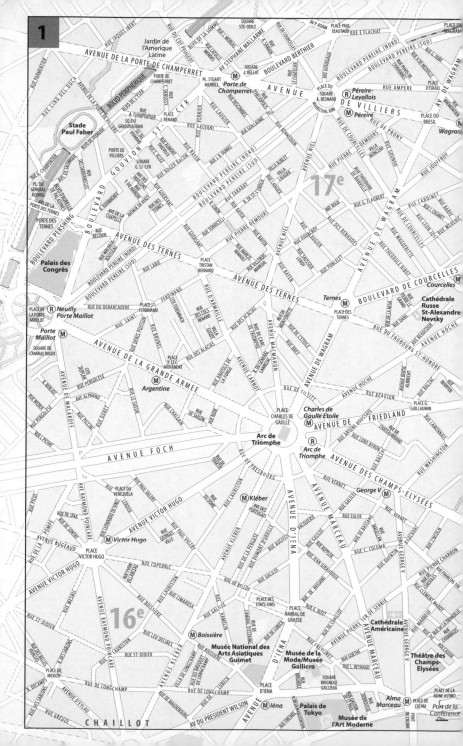

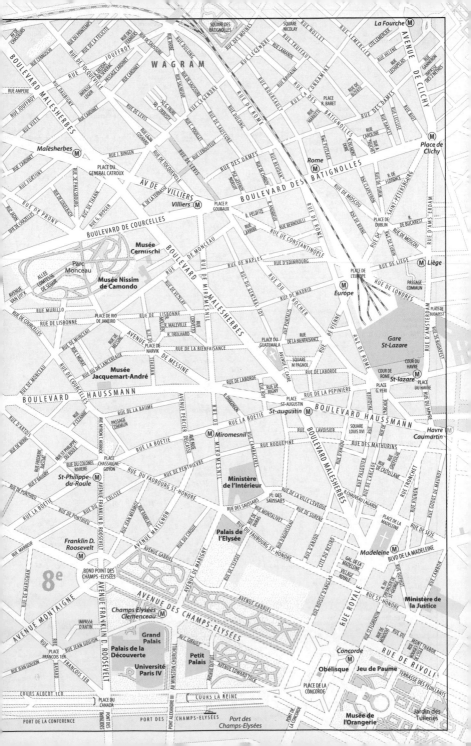

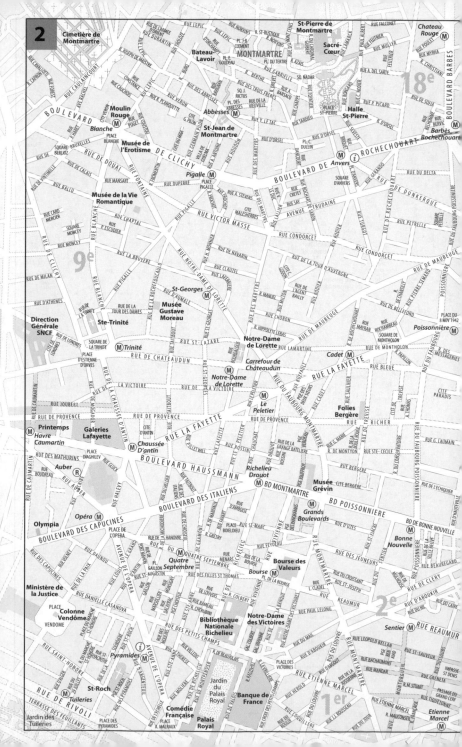

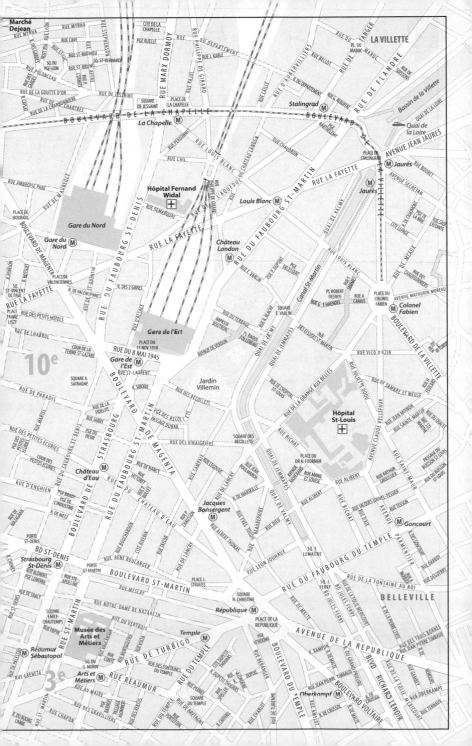

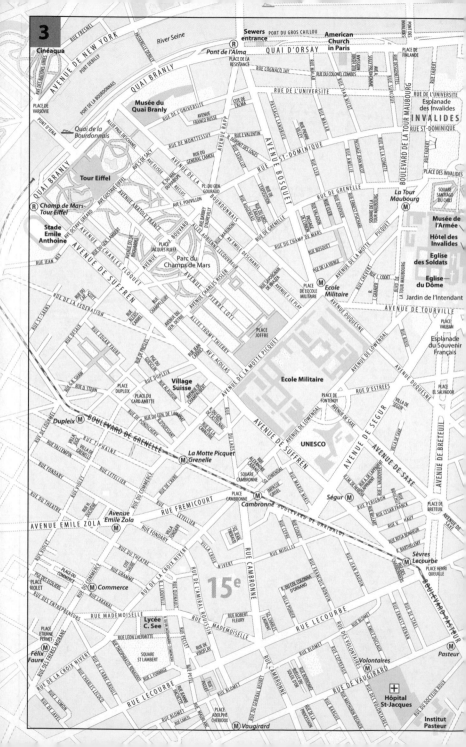

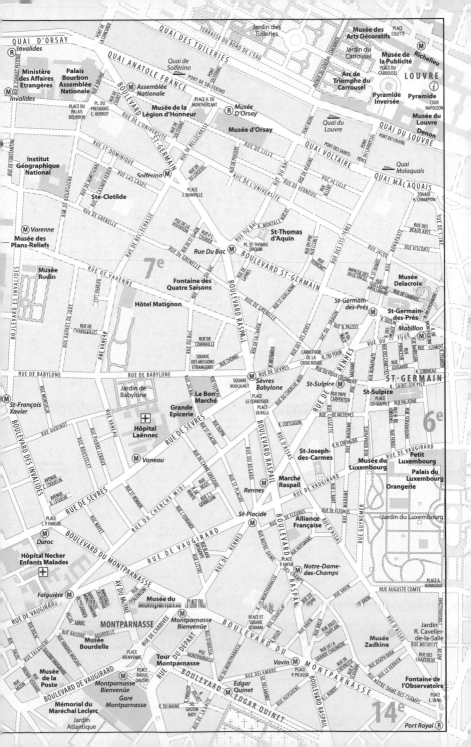

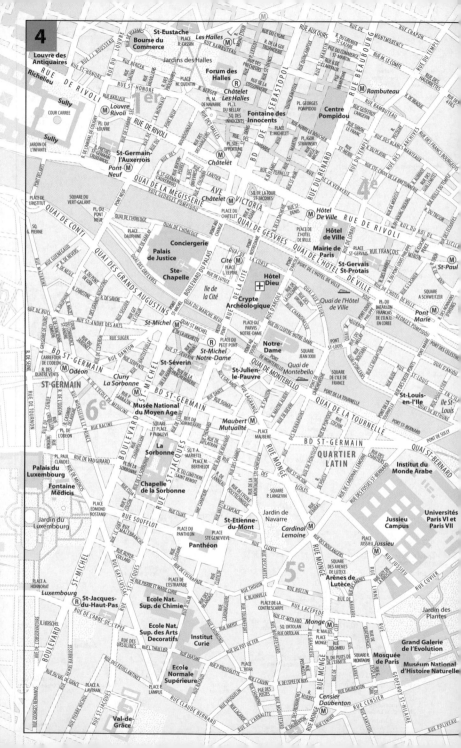

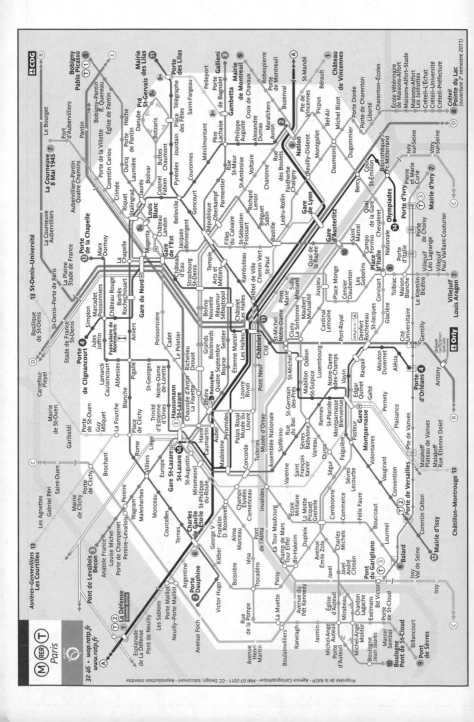